Papers in

QUANTITATIVE ECONOMICS

A selection from papers given at meetings of the Kansas-Missouri Joint Seminar in Theoretical and Applied Economics

edited by

James P. Quirk & Arvid M. Zarley

Sponsored by
Southern Illinois University (Carbondale),
The State University of Iowa,
The University of Missouri,
and The University of Kansas

THE UNIVERSITY PRESS OF KANSAS
Lawrence & London

Library of Congress Card Catalog Number 68-25878
Printed in the United States of America

PREFACE

The papers contained in this volume represent a selection from those presented at meetings of the Kansas-Missouri joint seminar in theoretical and applied economics held during the academic years 1966-67 and 1967-68. The joint seminar was inaugurated in the fall of 1966 with a meeting on the campus of the University of Kansas, followed by three other meetings during 1966-67, two at the University of Missouri and one at the University of Kansas. Meetings during 1967-68 were held at the University of Kansas, the University of Missouri, Southern Illinois University (Carbondale), and the University of Iowa. The seminar meetings have been attended by a substantial number of economists from the "mid-America" region, with participants and guest speakers from such schools as Kansas State University (Manhattan), Kansas State University (Fort Hays), Wichita State University, Ottawa University, University of Missouri (St. Louis), University of Missouri (Kansas City), Washington University (St. Louis), Iowa State University, University of Colorado, Air Force Academy, Purdue University, University of Washington, Wayne State University, Texas A & M University, as well as the sponsoring schools. Present plans envisage an expansion of the seminar in the future to encompass a wider geographical area, and support from the National Science Foundation for the programs during 1968-69 and 1969-70 has already been approved.

Financial support to defray publication costs of this volume was received from the University of Kansas, the University of Missouri, Southern Illinois University, and the University of Iowa. We also wish to thank Mrs. Leigh Riker, Mrs. Lois Clark, Miss Edna Turner, and Mrs. Carole Weeks for a superlative typing job, performed under severe time constraints. Mr. John Dessauer, Director of The University Press of Kansas, has been of major assistance in the planning and execution of this collection. Finally, the editorial board of Professor Trout Rader, Professor Sam Y. Wu, Professor Charles Stalon and Professor James Moore was responsible for the selection and suggested revisions of the papers appearing here.

James Quirk
Arvid Zarley

CONTENTS

I.

TOPICS IN ECONOMIC THEORY

TOWARDS A THEORY OF EFFICIENCY

by

Paul V. Moeseke
University of Louvain and Iowa State University

No hay otra cosa en la tierra más honrada
ni de más provecho que servir a Dios ...
[Por] las armas se alcanzan si no más
riquezas, a lo menos, más honra que por
las letras; ... puesto que han fundado más
mayorazgos las letras que las armas,
todavía llevan un no sé qué los de las armas
a los de las letras.
Miguel de Cervantes Saavedra: Don Quixote
II, 24.

Summary

An abstract definition of efficiency is introduced in terms of a partial order on a linear (decision) space. The definition supersedes several logically equivalent notions occurring in a variety of economic and statistical contexts. Some basic properties of efficient decisions are established (section 1) and applied to (a) the joint-production model (section 2) and (b) portfolio selection (section 3), in order to characterize the set of efficient allocations, respectively portfolios.

Both models allow further choice via the additional criteria of price guided allocation in (a) and maximal caution in (b). Existence theorems for a price guided allocation (maximizing both NNP and factor earnings) and for a maximal-caution portfolio are derived.

Introduction

A broad class of economic (and statistical) problems does not allow the evaluation of feasible decisions by a single (scalar) criterion. Such problems require the simultaneous application of two or more optimality criteria -- like wealth and honor in Quixote's counsel to the penniless page -- and there is no _a priori_ weighting of competing criteria that might indicate an optimal decision, for instance as an extremizer of a real-valued function.

While it _may_ happen that some decision is preferable on _all_ counts -- as the opening line of the Cervantes quotation suggests -- the criteria typically conflict. One can, in general, merely restrict choice to decisions x^* _not dominated_ by any other feasible decision x', where domination has this intuitive meaning: x' dominates x^* if, on every criterion, x' is at least as good as, and on at least one criterion better than, x^*. Decisions x^* are called _efficient_ below.

In the _first section_ of this paper we introduce the abstract notion of efficiency, defined in terms of a partial order on a linear space. We indicate the precise correspondence between maximal points of a set in the space and decisions called efficient in various contexts. We state properties of those decision sets allowing the identification of any efficient decision by an appropriate scalar efficiency measure. It is pointed out that in particular problems, like those considered in the sequel, the very nature of the model may suggest an additional criterion (apart from maximality) for the selection of optimal decisions among the efficient ones.

In the _second section_ results obtained in the first are applied to the general joint-production model where all commodities enter at both the input and output stages. Among the efficient allocations an allocation will be called price guided if there exists a (nonzero) nonnegative price system that sustains the allocation at _both_ stages in the sense of maximizing both net national product and aggregate factor earnings.

Section three applies the results of section 1 to the selection of portfolios that are efficient in terms of the first two moments of their yield distributions. We demonstrate the possibility of determining the entire subset of efficient portfolios (by either homogeneous or quadratic programming) and indicate how the additional criterion of maximal caution permits the choice of an optimal portfolio.

1. Efficient decision sets

Denote by R^m the set of real mtuples, by R^m_+ the set of nonnegative real mtuples. For any pair y, z ε R^m one writes

(1.1) $$\begin{cases} y \geqq z \text{ if } y_i \geq z_i, & (\text{all } i \in I = \{1,\ldots,m\}). \\ y \geq z \text{ if } y \geqq z \text{ and } z \not\geqq y; \end{cases}$$

one further denotes

$$y > z \text{ if } y_i > z_i, \quad (\text{all } i \in I),$$

where the relations $\geq$, $>$ between scalars have the usual meaning.

Clearly, the relation $\geqq$ is reflexive, antisymmetric, and transitive, and hence defines a partial order on R^m. It is immediate that the relation is invariant under translation and under multiplication by nonnegative scalars: for all $y \in R^m$, $a \in R_+$, $x + y \geqq z + y$ and $ax \geqq az$ whenever $x \geqq z$. Hence the relation is a vector order [12, ch. 1.2]. Further, since a cone in R^m is a nonvoid set C such that $P + P \subset P$ and, for all $a \in R_+$, $a P \subset P$, the set $\{y = x - z | x \geqq z;\ x, z \in R^m\}$ is a cone, called the nonnegative cone corresponding to the vector order $\geqq$. In our case that cone is the nonnegative orthant R^m_+ itself.

Definition 1.1: We call the above vector order $\geq$ the efficiency order.

Denote by f: $R^n \to R^m$ a single-valued function. Let $X \subset R^n$ and denote $Y \equiv f(X)$. We call $x^* \in X$ efficient if $y^* \equiv f(x^*)$ is maximal in Y under the efficiency order on R^m (figure 1).

Definition 1.2: Let the efficiency operator $\not{E}$ denote the set

(1.2a) $\not{E}Y \equiv \{y^* \in Y | \bar{y} \in Y,\ \bar{y} \geq y^* \text{ imply } \bar{y} = y^*\}$

of points y^* maximal in Y under the efficiency order. Let

$$\xi X \equiv X \cap f^{-1}\not{E}Y.$$

Then x^* is efficient in X, relative to f, if $x^* \in \xi X$. (When it is necessary to distinguish between decisions efficient relative to alternative mappings f, g, we write $\xi_f X$, $\xi_g X$.)

Since, as explained, the efficiency order is a vector order with the nonnegative orthant as corresponding nonnegative cone, $\not{E}Y$ may alternately be described as

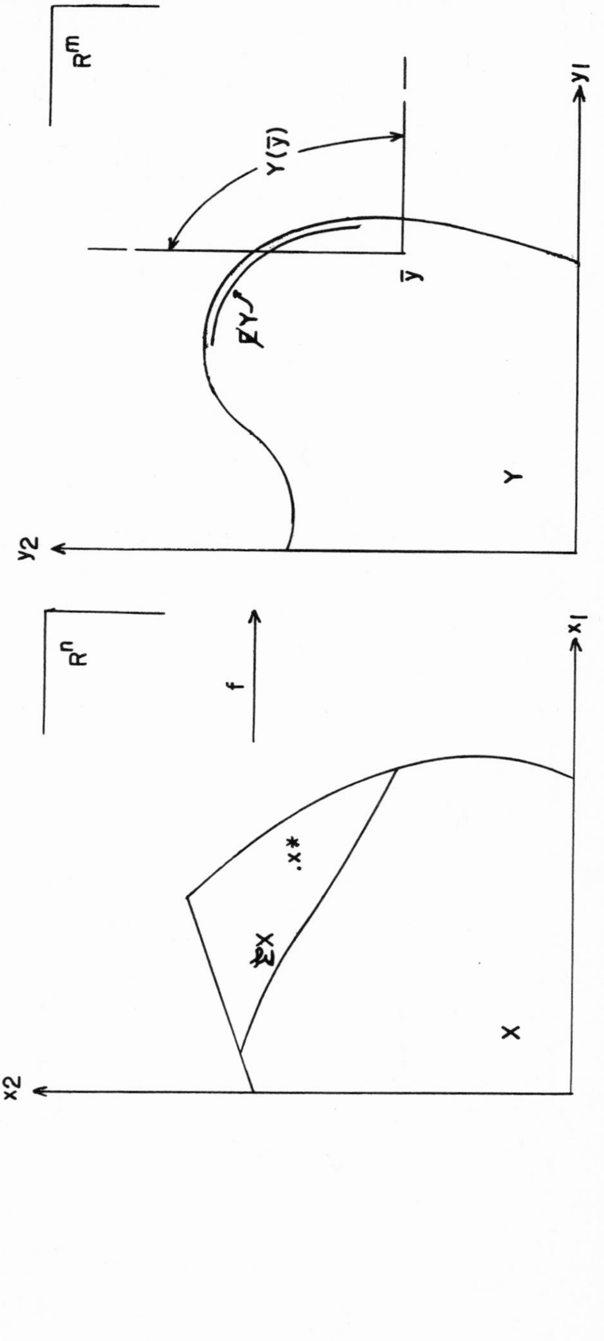

Figure 1

(1.2b) $\not{E}Y \equiv \{y^* \in Y \mid Y(y^*) \cap Y = \{y^*\}\}$,

where $Y(y^*) \equiv \{y \in R^m \mid y \geq y^*\}$. In words: y^* is maximal in Y if the translated nonnegative orthant with y^* as origin has but y^* in common with Y. Formula (1.2b) may, in turn, be restated algebraically:

(1.2c) $\not{E}Y \equiv \{y^* \in Y \mid y' \geq y^* \text{ implies } y' \notin Y\}$.

All three expressions (1.2a, b, c), which are clearly equivalent, will be needed below.[1]

We propose definition 1.2 in order to unify several logically equivalent concepts, obtained in various areas such as (1) welfare economics [22, ch. 6; 6] (2) linear [13, ch. 3] and (3) nonlinear [10] activity analysis, (4) the intertemporal allocation of resources [23, 15], (5) stochastic programming [26, 19] in general and (6) portfolio selection [16; 19, ch. 3.2] in particular, (7) the theory of admissible decision rules in statistics, initiated by [27]. We briefly point out the different guises under which the efficiency notion reappears in each of these areas.

In *welfare economics* X represents the social set of feasible decisions and f the mtuple of utility functions[2] of the m consumers. Efficient points are here called *Pareto optima*. *Linear activity analysis*, as treated in [13, ch. 3], is the special case where X is a polyhedral cone and $f(x) \equiv x$ so that $\xi X = \not{E}X$. In *nonlinear activity analysis* X is functionally specified: $X \equiv \{x \in X' \mid g(x) \geq 0,\ g: R^n \to R^m\}$; in *convex* nonlinear activity analysis X' is convex (usually *identified* with R^n_+) and g concave.[3]

In intertemporal allocation theory one may put $X \equiv \prod_{t=0}^{T} X_t$

where $\prod$ denotes a Cartesian product, T the number of time periods considered, X_t the set of (socially) feasible decisions in period t. An intertemporal path $x^* \in X$ (where $x^* = \{x^{*t} \in X_t;\ t = 0, \ldots, T\}$), called a *chronic* by Malinvaud [15], is *Malinvaud efficient* if, in our notation, $x^* \in \not{E}X$ and *Malinvaud optimal*[4] if $x^* \in \xi X$. Alternatively, one may, as in Dorfman, Samuelson, and Solow [7, ch. 12], and in Radner [24], restrict attention to one future period ($X = X_T$; T finite). Note that Malinvaud efficient, as well as Malinvaud optimal, chronics are special cases of points that are maximal under the efficiency order, hence efficient in our terminology. (The former concept refers to the special case where, for all x, $f(x) = x$.) We shall reserve the adjective 'optimal' for a more specific use, as explained below.

The notion of efficient portfolios and stochastic programs will be explained in detail in section 3.

Regarding the application to *statistical decision*

theory,[5] consider the following general class of statistical problems. Let Q, R denote the spaces of samples and outcomes, respectively. Denote further by Θ the set of m possible joint distributions θ of the elements $q \in Q$ and $r \in R$; and by D the set of n possible decisions d. After observing a q one has to choose a decision rule $x = x(d, q)$ such that $x(d, q) \geq 0$ (all d, q) and $\sum_D x(d, q) = 1$ (all q). Clearly, the set X of possible decision rules is the simplex $\{x \in R^n_+ \mid \sum x_i = 1\}$.

Denote by $h = h(q, r, \theta)$ the density function of the distribution corresponding to θ and by $h = h(q, r)$ the mtuple of density functions (one for each θ). Indicating by $w = w(q, d, r)$ the loss associated with sample q, decision d, and outcome r, the mtuple of expected-loss functions (one for each θ) is[6]

$$-f(x) \equiv \sum_{Q,R,D} w(q, d, r)\, h(q, r)\, x(d, q).$$

According to our general definition, decision rule x^* is efficient if $x^* \in \xi X$, i.e. if $f(\bar{x}) \geq f(x^*)$ for no $\bar{x} \in X$: this coincides with the notion of an admissible rule in statistical terminology.[7]

Typically, the set ξX of efficient decisions is broad. We shall discuss below (theorem 1.7) how, under convexity assumptions, every efficient point may be revealed as the solution to a maximization problem. Although only efficient decisions should be considered, one is still left with a difficult choice problem. (An extreme example: if a \$100,000 inheritance has to be split between two heirs and both prefer more, rather than less, money, every division -- e.g. \$1,000 and \$99,000 -- is readily seen to be Pareto optimal, i.e. efficient.)

The nature of the decision problem may, however, give rise to an additional criterion[8] allowing one to single out an optimal decision from ξX or at least select a subset of optimal decisions, further choice among which is a matter of indifference. International-trade theory affords a well-known illustration. In figure 2 every point of the contract curve -- here the locus of tangencies of trade indifference curves (cf. Meade [17, ch. 1-4] of countries A and B for A- and B- exportables -- is efficient. Among all efficient points the additional requirement of balanced trade indicates as optimal point P where the terms of trade line OP is tangent to indifference curves of both partners.[9]

Such optimal decisions will be sought below in the contexts of the general joint-production model (section 2) and of portfolio selection (section 3).

We shall need the following propositions.

Remark 1.3: Be $g: R^m \to R$ a strictly monotone function:

Figure 2

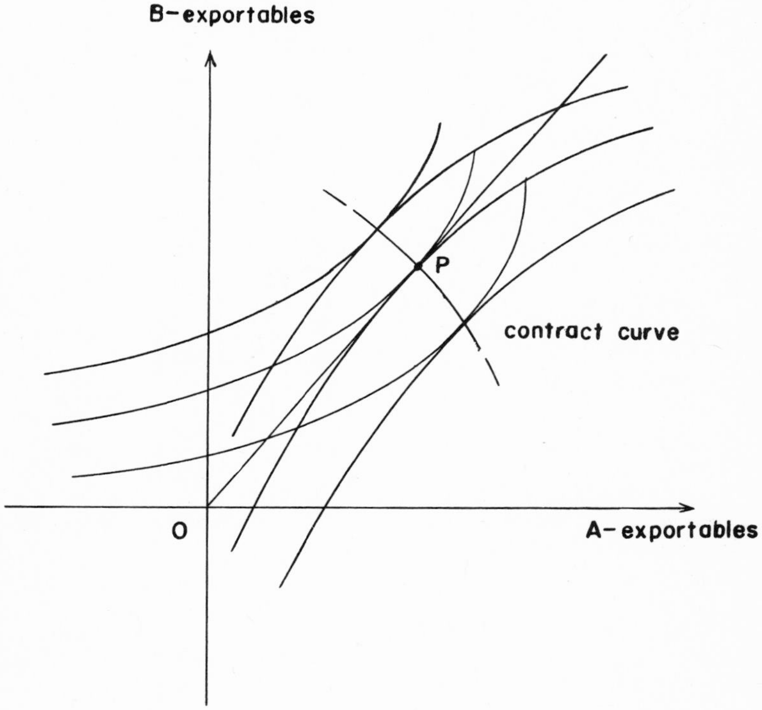

(1.3) $\qquad g(y + \Delta y) > g(y) \quad$ for all $\Delta y \geq 0$.

Then every maximizer y^* of g on Y satisfies $y^* \varepsilon \not{E}Y$.

Proof: For suppose Y owns a $\bar{y} \geq y^*$. Then $\bar{y} - y^* \geq 0$ and, by (1.3), $g(\bar{y}) = g[y^* + (\bar{y} - y^*)] > g(y^*)$ contrary to the assumption that y^* is a maximizer. QED.

Lemma 1.4: For all $\bar{y} \varepsilon Y$, $\not{E}(Y(\bar{y}) \cap Y) \subset \not{E}Y$.

Proof: If $\not{E}(Y(\bar{y}) \cap Y)$ is empty, the proposition is trivially true. Otherwise, for any $y^* \varepsilon \not{E}(Y(\bar{y}) \cap Y)$, by (1.2b)

(1.4) $\qquad Y(y^*) \cap (Y(\bar{y}) \cap Y) = \{y^*\}$.

Since $y^* \varepsilon Y(\bar{y})$, necessarily $Y(y^*) \subset Y(\bar{y})$ and (1.4) becomes

$$Y(y^*) \cap Y = \{y^*\}.$$

By (1.2b), this proves the lemma. QED.

For any $x \varepsilon X$ denote $A(x) \equiv \{y \varepsilon R^m | y \leqq f(x)\}$ and let $A \equiv A(X)$. The set $A(x)$ is the translated nonpositive orthant of R^m with origin $f(x)$. Clearly, $Y \subset A$ (figure 3).

Lemma 1.5: $\not{E}Y = \not{E}A$.

Proof:[10]

(a) $\not{E}Y \subset \not{E}A$. Otherwise, for some $y^* \varepsilon \not{E}Y$ one has $y^* \notin \not{E}A$. Hence, as $y^* \varepsilon A$, A owns a $y' \geq y^*$ and, for some $x' \varepsilon X$, $y' \varepsilon A(x')$. Then $f(x') \geqq y' \geq y^*$ so that $y^* \notin \not{E}Y$, a contradiction.

(b) $\not{E}A \subset \not{E}Y$. First, $\not{E}A \subset Y$. For $y^* \varepsilon \not{E}A$ implies that, for some $x' \varepsilon X$, $y^* \leqq f(x') \varepsilon Y \subset A$. Hence, by (1.2a), $y^* = f(x') \varepsilon Y$.

Further, by (1.2c), $y' \geq y^*$ implies $y' \notin A$ and, as $Y \subset A$, $y' \notin Y$. Hence, since $y^* \varepsilon Y$ and $y' \geq y^*$ implies $y' \notin Y$, by (1.2c) $y^* \varepsilon \not{E}Y$. QED.

Remark 1.6: If X is convex and f concave then A is convex.

Proof: Let $y^1, y^2 \varepsilon A$. Then there are points $x^1, x^2 \varepsilon X$ such that

(1.5) $\qquad y^1 \leqq f(x^1) \quad , \quad y^2 \leqq f(x^2)$.

By the convexity of X one has $x^t \equiv tx^1 + (1\text{-}t)x^2 \varepsilon X$, where $t \varepsilon [0, 1]$. By the concavity of f and (1.5)

$$f(x^t) \geqq tf(x^1) + (1\text{-}t)f(x^2) \geqq ty^1 + (1\text{-}t)y^2 \equiv y^t.$$

Hence $y^t \varepsilon A(x^t) \subset A$. QED.[11]

Let $p \varepsilon R^m_{\neq}$. We denote by py the scalar product $\sum p_i y_i$. If $pf(x^*) \geq pf(x)$ for all $x \varepsilon X$ we shall, somewhat inaccurately, call x^* a maximizer of p.

The next proposition correlates the set of efficient

Figure 3

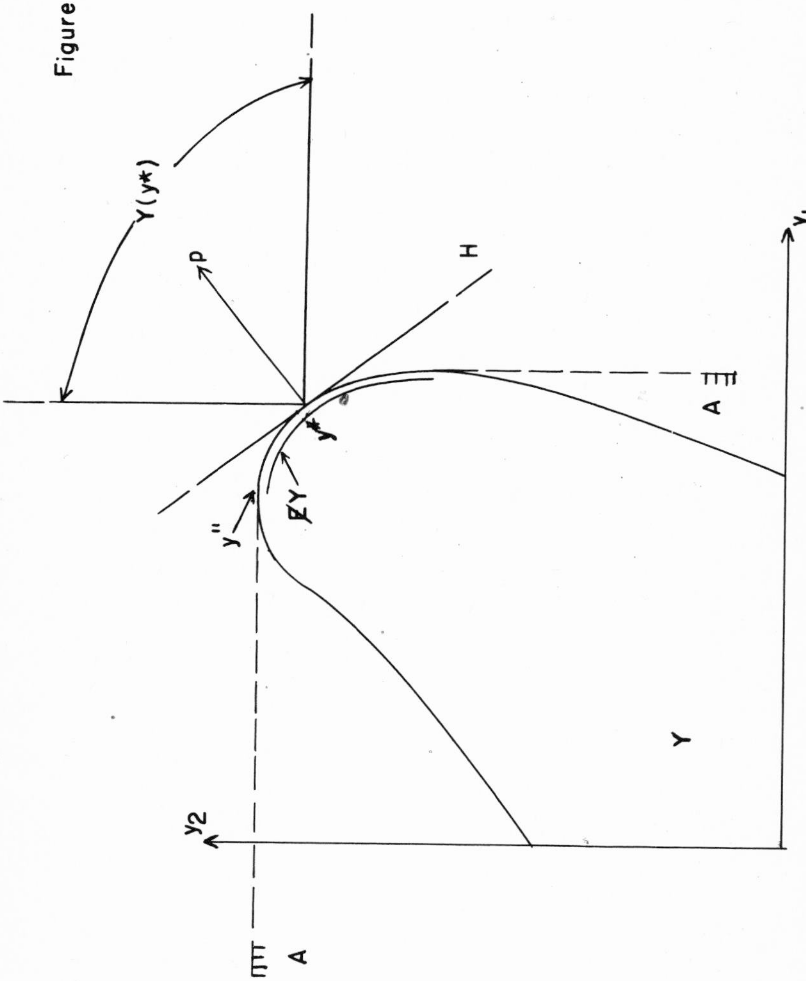

decisions and a set of scalar efficiency measures $pf(x)$.

Theorem 1.7:

(a) if $p > 0$ every maximizer x^* of p is efficient.
(b) if Y is closed, bounded above[12], and nonempty then every $p \geq 0$ possesses an efficient maximizer.
(c) if X is convex and f concave, then every efficient x^* is a maximizer of some $p \geq 0$.

Proof:

(a) The assertion is a special case of remark 1.3.
(b) By the premise of (b) every $p \geq 0$ possesses a maximizer, say $\bar{x}$:

(1.6) $\qquad pf(\bar{x}) \geq pf(x)$, all $x \in X$.

If $\bar{y} \equiv f(\bar{x}) \in \not{E}Y$ the proposition holds. If $\bar{y} \notin \not{E}Y$, take an arbitrary $p^* > 0$ and consider any y^* such that $p^*y^* \geq p^*y$ for all $y \in Y(\bar{y}) \cap Y$. (By the premise of (b) there is such a y^*.) By (a), $y^* \in \not{E}(Y(\bar{y}) \cap Y)$ so that

(1.7) $\qquad y^* \geqq \bar{y}$

and, by lemma 1.4, $y^* \in \not{E}Y$. By (1.6) $p\bar{y} \geq py^*$ and by (1.7) $py^* \geq p\bar{y}$, hence $p\bar{y} = py^*$ and the proposition follows.
(c) The assertion follows from lemma 1.5 and remark 1.6. Indeed, as $\not{E}Y = \not{E}A$, for any $y^* \in \not{E}Y$, by (1.2b),

(1.8) $\qquad A \cap Y(y^*) = \{y^*\}$.

As the nonempty interiors of the convex sets A and $Y(y^*)$ are disjoint, and y^* belongs to the boundaries of both, by a separation theorem of convex sets,[13] there is a hyperplane $H \equiv \{y \in R^m | py = py^*, p \neq 0\}$ separating $Y(y^*)$ from A and hence from Y (figure 3). Choosing $Y(y^*)$ above H, one necessarily obtains $p \geq 0$ as $Y(y^*)$ is a translated nonnegative orthant. QED.

Regarding theorem 1.7(c), note that it is not always possible to associate with an arbitrary $x^* \in \xi X$ an mtuple $p > 0$ that has x^* as a maximizer (example: any $x^* \in f^{-1}y''$, figure 3).

Corollary 1.8:

(a) If $p > 0$ every x^* that maximizes px on X satisfies $x^* \in \not{E}X$.
(b) If X is closed, bounded above, and nonempty then there is, for every $p \geq 0$, an $x^* \in \not{E}X$ that maximizes px on X.
(c) If X is convex every $x^* \in \not{E}X$ maximizes px on X for some $p \geq 0$.

Proof: The corollary is the special case of theorem 1.7 where $f(x) = x$ (all $x \in X$), hence $\xi X = \not{E}X$. QED.

The next two remarks will not be used in the sequel.

However, they provide some information of intrinsic interest for the decentralization of efficient decision sets. One may interpret X_i and $X \equiv \sum X_i$ ($i = 1,\dots,k$; k finite), e.g. in a welfare context, as the sets of socially feasible decisions for, respectively, the ith region and the entire economy.

<u>Remark 1.9</u>: Let $X \equiv \sum X_i$. Then $\not{E}X \subset \sum \not{E}X_i$.

<u>Proof</u>: For suppose $x^* \in \not{E}X$, $x^* \notin \sum \not{E}X_i$. As $x^* = \sum x^{*i}$ ($x^{*i} \in X_i$, all i), there is a j such that, for some $\bar{x}^j \in X_j$, $\bar{x}^j \geq x^{*j}$. Hence, $\bar{x} \equiv \bar{x}^j + \sum_{i \neq j} x^{*i} \geq x^*$. As $\bar{x} \in X$, $x^* \notin \not{E}X$, a contradiction. QED.

<u>Remark 1.10</u>: If f satisfies:[14]

(1.9) $f(\bar{x}) \geq f(x')$ implies $f(\bar{x} + x) \geq f(x' + x)$ (all $x \in X$), then $\xi X \subset \sum \xi X_i$.

<u>Proof</u>: For suppose $x^* \in \xi X$, $x^* \notin \sum \xi X_i$. As $x^* = \sum x^{*i}$ ($x^{*i} \in X_i$, all i), there is a j such that, for some $\bar{x}^j \in X_j$, $f(\bar{x}^j) \geq f(x^{*j})$. Hence, by (1.9), $f(\bar{x}) \equiv f(\bar{x}^j + \sum_{i \neq j} x^{*i})$ $\geq f(x^{*j} + \sum_{i \neq j} x^{*i}) = f(x^*)$. As $\bar{x} \in X$, $x^* \notin \xi X$, a contradiction. QED.

Regarding remark 1.9 note that the converse inclusion, $\sum \not{E}X_i \subset \not{E}X$, does not hold, in general: e.g. in <u>figure</u> 4, $x^{*1} \in \not{E}X_1$, $x^{*2} \in \not{E}X_2$, while clearly $x^{*1} + x^{*2} \notin \not{E}X$. The same observation holds for remark 1.10. (To see this, consider the case where $f(x) = x$, all x; then the figure equally applies to remark 1.10.)

2. Application to the general joint-production model

Consider the joint-production model where further all commodities (finite in number) appear as both inputs and outputs. The model may be represented by <u>figure</u> 5, a special case of the model in <u>figure</u> 1, with $X, Y \subset R^n$. The pair (X, Y), where $Y \equiv f(X)$, represents society's <u>technology</u>, i.e. the set of feasible allocations. An <u>allocation</u> $(x, f(x))$ in turn is defined as a procedure f whereby input bundle x, available at the beginning of the relevant accounting period, is converted into output bundle $y = f(x)$, available at the end.

The model might be given a <u>dynamic formulation</u> by denoting the above pair as (X_o, Y_o) or technology of the base period; introducing subsequent technologies as $(X_t, Y_t \equiv f_t(X_t))$, $t = 1,2,\dots T$; connecting successive

Figure 4

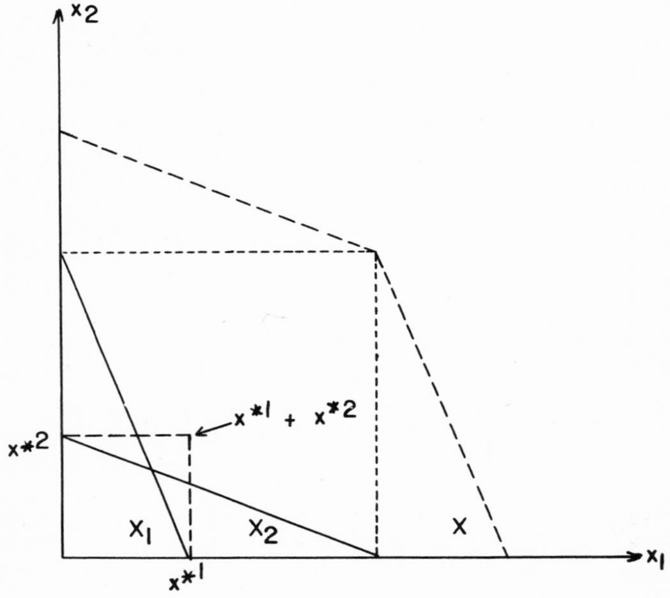

technologies by

(2.1) $X_{t+1} = Y_t$;

and somehow linking f_t to f_{t-1}, e.g. assuming $f_t = f_o$ (all t). These, as well as several other rather restrictive assumptions (proportionality, additivity, etc.) characterize von Neumann's [21] original study of the closed production model.

A flaw of the dynamic formulation is revealed by (2.1): instead of being an end in itself, consumption is merely instrumental to further growth. The static model, to which we here restrict our attention, is not open to this criticism: one may, for instance, interpret $z \equiv f(x) - x$ (assuming $z \geqq 0$) as the achievable set of consumption programs[15] desired for their own sake: z is the flow of commodities available in excess of resource flows x committed to production. Because of this, we do not call ours a closed production model: the latter epithet would fit only the dynamic formulation, which leaves no room for outside deliveries (either way), except for the initial and terminal bundles in X_o and Y_T (T finite), respectively.

The following result is immediate.

Remark 2.1: $\not{E}(X \times Y) = \not{E}Y \times \not{E}Y$ (where $X \subset R^n$, $Y \subset R^m$).

Applying the remark to our present case (where $Y \equiv f(X)$, $n = m$), an allocation $(x^*, f(x^*)) \in X \times Y$ is efficient if both $x^* \in \not{E}X$ and $f(x^*) \in \not{E}Y$, i.e. if $x^* \in \not{E}X \cap \xi X$ (by definition 1.2). Under the premise of theorem 1.7(b) there is, to every $p' \geqq 0$, an $x^* \in \xi X$ such that $p'f(x^*)$ maximizes $p'f(x)$ on X, i.e. maximizes net national product. Further, for f monotone this x^* belongs to $\xi X \cap \not{E}X$, as will be shown below. Finally, for every $x^* \in \not{E}X$, there is, under the premise of corollary 1.8(c), a $p'' \geq 0$ such that $p''x^*$ maximizes $p''x$ on X, i.e. maximizes aggregate factor earnings.

The problem is, Does there exist a price system $p^+ \geq 0$ that simultaneously sustains an efficient allocation on both the input and output sides (i.e., maximizes both net national product and factor earnings)? Such a p^+ fulfils the tasks of both p' and p'' above (figure 5). Accordingly, we shall now, among the efficient allocations $(x^*, f(x^*))$, select an optimal allocation, called price guided allocation,[16] by the following criterion.

Definition 2.2: Denote by S the simplex $\{p \in R^n_{\not+} \mid \sum p_i = 1\}$. The triple (x^+, y^+, p^+) is a price guided allocation if

(a) $x^+ \in \not{E}X$, $y^+ \equiv f(x^+) \in \not{E}Y$, $p^+ \in S$;

Figure 5

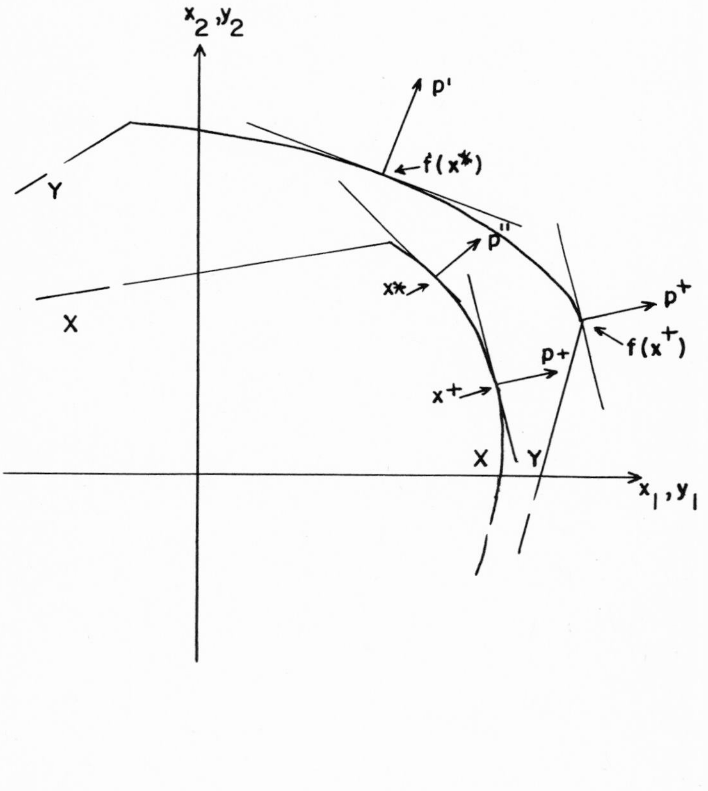

(b) for all $x \in X$, $p^+x^+ \geq p^+x$ and $p^+f(x^+) \geq p^+f(x)$.

The definition states that an efficient allocation is price guided if units of the same commodity can be assigned the <u>same value</u> whether regarded as an input or as an output. The 'guiding' price system p^+ evaluates net national product at $p^+ y^+$ and aggregate factor payments at $p^+ x^+$, while $p^+ (y^+ - x^+)$, the residual,[17] measures aggregate profits.

We now develop the argument leading up to an <u>existence proof</u> for such a price guided allocation.

<u>Remark 2.3</u>: Let f be monotone: $f(x') \geq f(x)$ whenever $x' \geq x$. Then $\xi X \subset \not{Z}X$.

<u>Proof</u>: For let $x^* \in \xi X$, $x^* \notin \not{Z}X$. As $x^* \in X$ there is in X an $\bar{x} \geq x^*$ such that $f(\bar{x}) \geq f(x^*)$, contradicting $x^* \in \xi X$. QED.

Economically, the monotonicity assumption means this: when, besides inputs x, some additional input(s) is (are) available one can at least equal, and for some output(s) surpass, production $f(x)$.

<u>Remark 2.4</u>: Let f be continuous and monotone. If X is bounded above and Y closed, then both X and Y are closed and bounded above.

<u>Proof</u>: By continuity $X = f^{-1}Y$ is closed as the inverse image of a closed set. As there exists a majorant $x' \geqq x$, all $x \in X$, for any $e \in R^n$ such that $e \geq 0$, $x' + e \geq x$, all $x \in X$. By monotonicity $f(x' + e)$ is a majorant to Y. QED.

Define the mappings F_1, F_2: $S \rightarrow X$ as follows:

$$(2.2) \qquad F_1(p) \equiv \{x^* \in X \mid pf(x^*) \geq pf(x), \text{ all } x \in X\},$$

$$(2.3) \qquad F_2(p) \equiv \{x^* \in X \mid px^* \geq px \qquad , \text{ all } x \in X\}.$$

One has, accordingly,

$$F_2^{-1}(x^*) = \{p \in S \mid px^* \geq px, \text{ all } x \in X\}.$$

In what follows we shall need the upper semicontinuity of F_1, F_2^{-1}: this property will be established with the help of theorem 2.5, translated from [4, ch. 6.3], where the reader is referred for the proof. (Symbols adapted to present context.)

<u>Theorem 2.5 (Maximum Theorem)</u>: Be $\phi(x)$ a continuous numerical function on X and H a continuous mapping on S into X such that, for all p, $H(p) \neq \emptyset$. Then $M(p) \equiv \max_{x \in H(p)} \phi(x)$ is a continuous numerical function on S and $F(p) \equiv \{x \in H(p) \mid$

$\phi(x) = M(p)\}$ is an usc (upper semicontinuous) mapping on S into X.

Definition 2.6:[18] The mapping F: $S \to X$ is closed if, whenever $p' \varepsilon S$, $x' \varepsilon X$, $x' \notin F(p')$, there exist neighborhoods $N(p') \subset S$, $N(x') \subset X$ such that, for any $p \varepsilon N(p')$, $F(p) \cap N(x') = \emptyset$.

Lemma 2.7: F_2 is closed.

Proof: By definition F_2 is closed if

$$(2.4) \qquad p'x' < p'x^* \qquad (\text{where } p' \varepsilon S,\ x' \varepsilon X,\ x^* \varepsilon F_2(p'))$$

implies the existence of positive numbers ε, δ such that, for all $p' + e \varepsilon S$, $x' + d \varepsilon X$ satisfying[19] $||e|| < \varepsilon$, $||d|| < \delta$,

$$(2.5) \qquad (p' + e)(x' + d) < (p' + e)x^e ,$$

where x^e is any point in $F_2(p' + e)$.

Indeed, by (2.4) and the continuity of px on S x X, there is a number ε such that

$$(p' + e)x' < (p' + e)x^*$$

and hence a number δ such that

$$(2.6) \qquad (p' + e)(x' + d) < (p' + e)(x^* + d) ,$$

where ε, δ are related to e, d as above. As $x^e \varepsilon F_2(p' + e)$,

$$(2.7) \qquad (p' + e)(x^* + d) \leq (p' + e)x^e$$

and (2.5) follows from (2.6), (2.7). QED.

Lemma 2.8: Let X, Y be closed, bounded above and non-empty. Then

(a) F_2^{-1} is usc. If further f is continuous, then (b) F_1 is usc.

Proof:

(a) The graph $G \equiv \{(p, x) \varepsilon S \times X \mid x \varepsilon F_2(p)\}$ of F_2 is closed, since by lemma 2.7, F_2 is a closed mapping. As F_2^{-1} is a mapping with compact range S, it is usc if, and only if, its graph, which is also G, is closed.

(b) If f(x) is continuous, so is pf(x). In theorem 2.5 substitute: $\phi(x) = pf(x)$; $H(p) = X$ for all $p \varepsilon S$ (mapping H is constant and thus trivially continuous); $F = F_1$. Observe that, as Y is closed and bounded above, M(p) exists (all $p \varepsilon S$). Hence, by theorem 2.5, F_1 is usc. QED.

The existence of a price guided allocation will now be proved with the help of Kakutani's [11] fixed-point theorem.[20]

Proposition 2.9 (Existence): Under the assumptions,

(a1) X is convex[21], bounded above, and nonempty,
(a2) f is

(a21) strictly concave on an open set (say R^n) containing X,
(a22) monotone,

(a3) $Y \equiv f(X)$ is closed,

there exists a price guided allocation (x^+, y^+, p^+).

Proof: By (a21) f is continuous on X so that, by (a22), (a3), and remark 2.4, the premises of lemma 2.8 are satisfied. Hence, F_1, F_2^{-1} are usc and $H \equiv F_1 \cdot F_2^{-1}$ is usc as the product of usc mappings. By (2.2), (2.3) H takes the compact S into itself.

By theorem 1.7(b), for every $p \in S$, the intersection $F_1(p) \cap \xi X$ is nonempty, so that it owns a point x^*; further, by (a1), (a21)

(2.8) $F_1(p) = F_1(p) \cap \xi X = \{x^*\}$,

as pf is strictly concave and hence possesses a unique maximizer on the convex X.

By (2.8), (a22), and remark 2.3, $x^* \in \not\xi X$ so that, by corollary 1.8(c),

(2.9) $F_2^{-1}(x^*)$ is nonempty. Further, it is convex:

indeed, let p^o, $p^1 \in F_2^{-1}(x^*)$, i.e. for all $x \in X$, $p^o x^* \geq p^o x$ and $p^1 x^* \geq p^1 x$; then, for any $t \in (0, 1)$, multiplying both sides of the inequalities by, respectively, t and (1 - t), and adding, yields, for all $x \in X$, $p^t x^* \geq p^t x$ (where $p^t \equiv tp^o + (1 - t)p^1$) so that $p^t \in F_2^{-1}(x^*)$.

Since H is an usc mapping taking the convex compact S into itself and, by (2.8), (2.9) H(p) is nonempty and convex for all p, there is, by Kakutani's theorem, a fixed point $p^+ \in H(p^+)$. Taking $x^+ \in F_1(p^+) \cap F_2(p^+)$, $y^+ = f(x^+)$, we have proved the existence of a price guided allocation. QED.

The strict concavity of f in premise (a21) is needed to insure the uniqueness of x^* in (2.8). (This, in turn, is needed because, unless $F_1(p)$ is a singleton for all p, F_2^{-1} is not, in general, a convex mapping.) Uniqueness may be secured in an alternative way.

Corollary 2.10: Proposition 2.9 remains valid if (a1), (a2) are replaced by:

(a1') X is strictly convex, bounded above, and nonempty,
(a2') f is

(a21') concave on an open set containing X,
(a22') strictly monotone: $f(x^o) > f(x^1)$ whenever $x^o > x^1$.

Proof: The proof of proposition 2.9 carries over, except for the uniqueness of maximizer x^* of pf (for any $p \in S$). If x' were another maximizer, by (a1'), for all $t \in (0, 1)$, $x^t \in \overset{o}{X}$ (where $x^t \equiv tx^* + (1 - t)x'$) and X owns an $x^o > x^t$. By (a22') $f(x^o) > f(x^t)$ and by (a21') $f(x^t) \geqq f(x^*)$ so that $f(x^o) > f(x^*)$ and $pf(x^o) > pf(x^*)$, a contradiction. QED.

3. Efficient and optimal portfolios

Denote the yield of a portfolio by

$$h(x) \equiv cx \ , \quad x \in X \ ;$$

$$(3.1) \qquad X \equiv \{x \mid rx \leq 1 \ , \ x \geqq 0\} \ ; \qquad x, c, r \in R^n \ , r > 0,$$

where x is a portfolio containing x_i units of the ith security; c, the ntuple of yields (dividends plus net capital gains per accounting period); r, the ntuple of security prices. Without loss of generality, we fix the investor's budget at unity.

Markowitz [16, ch. 7] has suggested, for stochastic c with (subjective) distribution D, first moments $\bar{c} \equiv \int c \, dD$, and second moments $V \equiv [\sigma_{ij}] \equiv [\int (c_i - \bar{c}_i)(c_j - \bar{c}_j) \, dD]$, that the investor restrict his attention to portfolios x^* that satisfy

$$(3.2) \qquad \begin{cases} \sigma h(x^*) \leq \sigma h(x) \text{ for all } x \in X \text{ such that } Eh(x) \geq Eh(x^*) \\ Eh(x^*) \geq Eh(x) \text{ for all } x \in X \text{ such that } \sigma h(x) \leq \sigma h(x^*) \end{cases}$$

where $Eh(x) \equiv \bar{c}x, \quad \sigma h(x) \equiv (xVx)^{1/2}$

Letting $f\colon \ R^n \to R^2$, where $f_1(x) \equiv Eh(x)$, $f_2(x) \equiv -\sigma h(x)$, one sees readily that efficiency criterion[22] (3.2) is a special case of our general efficiency criterion (definition 1.2). Before stating some propositions on efficient portfolios, we need several preliminary results.

Remark 3.1: Let $p^o, p^1 \in R^m$. Let $y^o, y^1 \in Y \subset R^m$ satisfy

$$(3.3) \qquad \left.\begin{aligned} p^o y^o &\geq p^o y \\ p^1 y^1 &\geq p^1 y \end{aligned}\right\} \qquad \text{(all } y \in Y)$$

and denote $\Delta p \equiv p^1 - p^o$, $\Delta y \equiv y^1 - y^o$. Then $\Delta p \, \Delta y \geq 0$.

Proof: By (3.3)

$$p^1y^1 \geq p^1y^o \quad \text{or} \quad p^1 \Delta y \geq 0$$

$$p^oy^o \geq p^oy^1 \quad \text{or} \quad -p^o \Delta y \geq 0 \, .$$

Addition of the inequalities on the right yields $\Delta p \, \Delta y \geq 0$. QED.

Note that, in particular, if $\Delta p_i > 0$, $\Delta p_{j \neq i} = 0$, the remark implies $\Delta p_i \, \Delta y_i \geq 0$ so that $\Delta y_i \geq 0$.

Remark 3.2: Let $Y, P \subset R^m_{\neq}$. Let further

$$(3.4) \qquad M(p) \equiv \max_{y \in Y} py$$

and denote by $P' \subset P$ the set such that, for all $p \in P'$, (3.4) exists.
Then M is monotone on P'.

Proof: Let $p^o, p^1 \in P'$ satisfy

$$(3.5) \qquad p^1 \geqq p^o$$

and be y^o, y^1 as in (3.3). Multiplying (3.5) by y^o yields $p^1y^o \geq p^oy^o$ and, since $p^1y^1 \geq p^1y^o$, $p^1y^1 \geq p^oy^o$, or $M(p^1) \geq M(p^o)$. QED.

Remark 3.3: Let $Y, P \subset R^m$ and define M and P' as in the previous remark. If P' is convex then M is convex on P'.

Proof: Be p^o, p^1 as in (3.3), p^t as in proposition 2.9, and let y^t satisfy $p^ty^t \geq p^ty$ (all $y \in Y$). By (3.4),

$$(3.6) \qquad M(p^o) = p^oy^o \geq p^oy^t,$$

$$(3.7) \qquad M(p^1) = p^1y^1 \geq p^1y^t.$$

Multiplying (3.6) by t, (3.7) by $(1-t)$, and adding yields

$$tM(p^o) + (1-t)M(p^1) \geq p^ty^t = M(p^t). \quad \text{QED.}$$

Remark 3.4: ξX is invariant under increasing transformations of f on X.

Proof: An increasing transformation g satisfies, for any pair $x^1, x^2 \in X$ and all $i \in I$: $g_i(x^1) \geq g_i(x^2)$ if, and only if, $f_i(x^1) \geq f_i(x^2)$. The existence, for $x^* \in \xi_f X$, of an $\bar{x} \in X$ such that $g(\bar{x}) \geq g(x^*)$ would thus imply the contradiction $f(\bar{x}) \geq f(x^*)$. Similarly, the existence, for $x^* \in \xi_g X$, of an $\bar{x} \in X$ such that $f(\bar{x}) \geq f(x^*)$ would imply the contradiction $g(\bar{x}) \geq g(x^*)$. QED.

For the portfolio problem let $f(x) \equiv [\bar{c}x, -\sigma(x)]$, $p \equiv [1, m]$, where $m \geq 0$; $\sigma(x)$ abbreviates $\sigma h(x)$ and exists for all $x \in X$. Define

$$\phi(x, m) \equiv Eh(x) - m\sigma\, h(x) = \bar{c}x - m\sigma\,(x) = pf(x) \tag{3.8}$$

and consider the mathematical-programming problem

$$\max_{x \in X} \phi(x|m). \tag{3.9}$$

Since X is convex by (3.1) and f is concave[23] we can, in addition to the remarks of this section, apply theorem 1.7 of section 1 to obtain:

<u>Proposition 3.5</u>:

(1) For all $m > 0$ (≥ 0) every (at least one) solution x^* of (3.9) is an efficient portfolio (theorem 1.7(a) and (b)).
(2) Varying $m \geq 0$ reveals the complete set of efficient portfolios as solutions to (3.9) (theorem 1.7(c)).
(3) $\Delta m \quad \Delta\sigma(x^*) \leq 0$: the standard deviation of a solution to (3.9) is a nonincreasing function of the relative weight m attached to it in (3.8) (remark 3.1).
(4) $\max_{x \in X} \phi(x|m)$ is a <u>nonincreasing convex</u> function of m (remarks 3.2, 3.3).
(5) Results (1) through (4) remain valid if xVx is substituted[24] for $\sigma(x)$ in ϕ (remark 3.4).

We have proposed (3.9) in [18, 19] as the <u>truncated-minimax criterion</u>[25] in the more general context of stochastic programming. It suffices here to indicate the criterion's principal characteristics:
(a) It represents a linear weighting of expectation and standard deviation (considered as a scalar risk measure), i.e., m expresses the investor's risk aversion.
(b) It possesses an interpretation in terms of confidence limits: (3.9) is equivalent to

$$\max_{k \in K} k, \qquad K \equiv \{k \mid \text{prob}\ (cx \leq k) \leq a,\ x \in X\},$$

where, when D is normal for instance, $a = (2\pi)^{-\frac{1}{2}} \int_{-\infty}^{-m} \exp(-t^2/2)\,dt$.
(c) When the distribution of h has the entire real line as domain (if c is normally distributed, for instance), the minimax criterion is generally indeterminate. (For all $x \neq 0$, $\min_{c \in R^n} h(x) = -\infty$). The new criterion obviates the indetermination by truncating the left tail of the distribution of h(x).
(d) The criterion converts a stochastic linear into a linear homogeneous programming problem. Hence the results of homogeneous programming [19, ch. 2, 3] are applicable. Homogeneity of ϕ in x further avoids partial investment of the

available budget: (3.9) has a solution x^* satisfying $rx^* = 1$ --apart from the trivial case where the origin is the sole solution.

Whereas proposition 3.5 allowed us to derive and characterize the entire set of efficient portfolios, property (d) will make it possible to identify a portfolio that is optimal under the following criterion:

$$(3.10) \qquad \max_{x \in X} \phi(x \mid m^+) \; ,$$

where

$$(3.11) \qquad m^+ \equiv \max_{m \in M} m \; ; \quad M \equiv \{m \geq 0 \mid \max_{x \in X} \phi(x|m) \geq i\} \; ;$$

and i is the relevant rate of interest on the capital market.[26] By proposition 3.5(4) criterion (3.10) implies the minimax problem

$$(3.12) \qquad \min_{m \in M} \max_{x \in X} \phi(x, m) \; .$$

(We shall see below that (3.10) - (3.11) and (3.12) are in fact equivalent.)

We motivate this optimality criterion. By the duality theorem of homogeneous programming [19, ch. 2.3], primal problem (3.9) implies the dual problem

$$(3.13) \qquad \min_{\lambda \in L} \lambda \quad , \qquad L \equiv \{\lambda \geq 0 \mid \lambda r \geqq \phi_x ; \; x \in X\},$$

where ϕ_x is the gradient vector $[\partial\phi/\partial x_1, \ldots, \partial\phi/\partial x_n]$. The theorem adds that, for any dual solution λ^* ,

$$(3.14) \qquad \lambda^* = \phi(x^*|m) = \bar{c}x^* - m\sigma(x^*).$$

It is known[27] that the dual variable λ measures the marginal return of the budget dollar in terms of 'utility function' ϕ, i.e. that dollar's marginal value to the investor using criterion ϕ. Hence rule (3.10) has this interpretation:

Among the efficient portfolios (found, according to proposition 3.5(1) (2), by varying m in (3.9))select an optimal portfolio x^+ that allocates the budget with maximal caution (maximal $m = m^+$) under restriction (3.11) that the marginal value of the budget dollar is not exceeded by its marginal cost i.

In practice (3.10) - (3.11) is solved as follows.[28] Trivial cases apart, one can select a value $m_o \geq 0$ (say $m_o = 0$) small enough, and an $m_1 > m_o$ big enough so that

$$(3.15) \qquad \max_{x \in X} \phi(x \mid m_o) > i > \max_{x \in X} \phi(x \mid m_1) \; .$$

If there exists an m^+ such that

(3.16) $$\max_{x \in X} \phi(x \mid m^+) = i$$

then, if x^+ denotes a solution to (3.16), (x^+, m^+) clearly solves (3.10) - (3.11) and x^+ is an optimal portfolio.[29] The proposition below demonstrates the existence and uniqueness of m^+.

Proposition 3.6 (Existence): If there are values m_o, m_1 satisfying (3.15) then there exists a unique m^+ satisfying (3.16).

Proof: By convexity (proposition 3.5(4)) $\max_{x \in X} \phi(x, m)$ is continuous on the open interval (m_o, m_1) so that, by Bolzano's theorem, there is an

(3.17) $$m^+ \in (m_o, m_1)$$

satisfying (3.16).

To show uniqueness, abbreviate $\max_{x \in X} \phi(x, m)$ to $g(m)$. Suppose, contrary to the proposition, that $[m_o, m_1]$ owns an $m' \neq m^+$ such that $g(m') = g(m^+) = i$. Without loss of generality, let $m' > m^+$. Then, by (3.17), for some $t \in (0, 1)$, $m' = tm^+ + (1-t) m_1$; hence, by convexity, $g(m') \leq tg(m^+) + (1-t)g(m_1) < i$, a contradiction. QED.

Corollary 3.7: If there exist values m_o, m_1 satisfying (3.15) problems (3.10) - (3.11) and (3.12) are equivalent.

Proof: The equivalence follows at once from the existence and uniqueness of an m^+ satisfying (3.16). QED.

By (3.8), (3.16) $\overline{c}x^+ - m^+ \sigma(x^+) = i$ so that

(3.18) $$m^+ = (\overline{c}x^+ - i)/ \sigma(x^+).$$

The last formula states that an optimal portfolio will be found when the portfolio problem $\max_{x \in X} \phi(x|m)$ is solved with $m = m^+$ set equal to the inverse of the coefficient of variation of net profits (the expected value of which is $\overline{c}x^+ - i$).

As indicated in figure 6, m^+ is computed by linear interpolation: solving the portfolio problem for m_1, m_o allows to compute m_2 by interpolation between (by convexity, proposition 3.5(4)) m_1 and m_o; m_3 by interpolation between m_2 and m_o;...m_t between m_{t-1} and m_o. As $[m_o, m_1]$ is bounded, convergence of m_t to m^+ is assured by construction.[30]

Figure 6

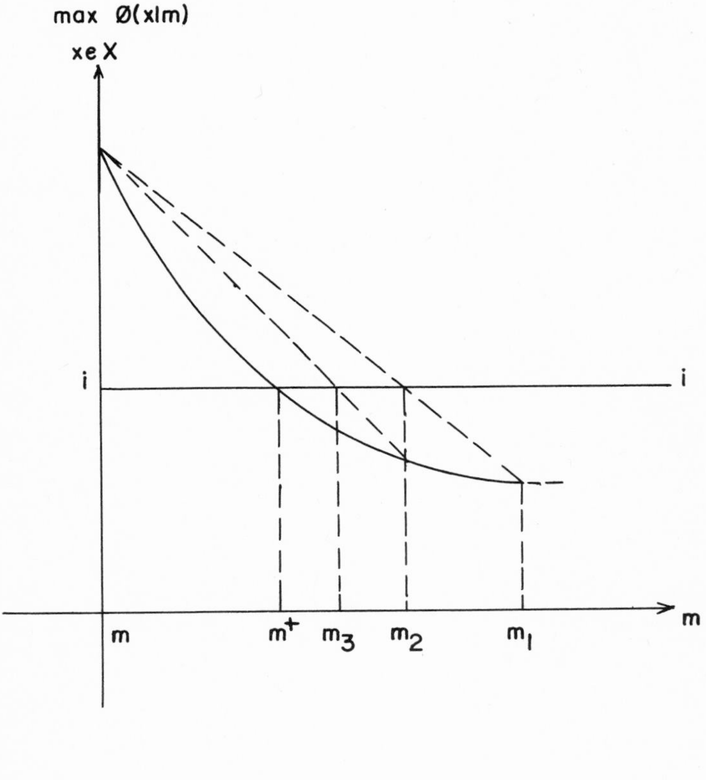

FOOTNOTES

1. One may note at this point that, if Y is open, necessarily $\not{E}Y = \emptyset$, where $\emptyset$ denotes the empty set. Indeed let δY denote the boundary of Y: clearly, $\not{E}Y \subset \delta Y$.

2. Assuming the individual preference preorders to be numerically representable.

3. In the general activity analytic model one may want to distinguish between the sets Z, X, Y of <u>primary</u>, <u>intermediate</u>, and <u>final</u> commodities, respectively, where $Z = \underline{R}^m_+$, $X = X' \cap g^{-1}Z$, $Y = f(X)$ like in [10].

4. Consumers may not fully appreciate the relative urgency of their present and future needs and ignore the preferences of future generations. A weaker concept of Malinvaud optimality, viz. <u>Allais</u> [2, ch. 6] <u>optimality</u>, then obtains by including all future preference patterns (of both present and unborn consumers) among the components of f (rather than just one pattern per present agent). Our formal characterizations of chronics remains unaffected. Intertemporal allocation especially has given rise to a proliferation of terms used to describe the same efficiency concept: different terms merely refer to alternative mappings and time spans considered relevant (in determining what we denote ξX) by the various authors surveyed in e.g., Drèze [8, pp. 36 sqq.] and Rader [23].

5. A link between the theory of statistical decision functions and welfare economics was perceived by Debreu [6, ch. 11, 12] in the 'minimax interpretation of the coefficient of resource utilization'.

6. Substitute integration for summation in the nondiscrete case, when possible.

7. Efficient ('admissible') decision rules are a (not necessarily proper) subset of the Bayesian decision rules [28, ch. 5]. (Precisely: the sets of Bayesian and of efficient decision rules are in the same relation as the sets of maximizers and of efficient maximizers to any $p \geq 0$ in theorem 1.7 below.)

8. For instance, the existence of a law specifying the heirs' relative shares in the above example.

9. Since each country's offer curve is the locus of tangencies between terms of trade lines and indifference curves, point P is found as the intersection of the two offer curves (omitted from the drawing).

10. The proofs of lemma 1.5 and theorem 1.7 owe much to comments by Guy de Ghellinck, Edmond Malinvaud, and James C. Moore.

11. Contrary to what one might expect, the premises of remark 1.6 do <u>not</u> imply convexity of $Y = f(X)$. A simple counterexample is the following: let $X = R^m_{\neq}$, $f(x) = [f_1(x) = x;\ f_2(x) = \log x]$; $f(X)$ is then the graph of $\log x$, which is clearly not a convex set.
Further, because of the role of quasiconcave functions (representing convex preference preorders) in general-equilibrium analysis [1, p. 269], it is of interest to know that remark 1.6 (and hence theorem 1.7(c) below) cannot be extended to <u>quasiconcave</u> f. Counterexample: let $X = R$, $f(x) = [f_1(x) = x;\ f_2(x) = n(x)]$, where $n(x)$ is the (clearly quasiconcave) normal density function; $f(X)$ again coincides with the graph of the density function. One checks readily that this graph does not generate a convex A.

12. I.e., for some $y' \in R^m$, $y' \geqq y$ for all $y \in Y$. (y' is a <u>majorant</u> to Y, cf. Dubreil and Dubreil-Jacotin [9, ch. 5.3].

13. When two convex sets with nonempty interiors have but one point y^* in common there is at least one hyperplane that separates them and owns y^* (cf. Bonnesen and Fenchel [5, p. 5]). The interior $\mathring{X}$ of a set X is defined as $X \sim \delta X$.

14. Assumption (1.9) is not needed below. It postulates that the efficiency order on Y is invariant under translation of X; it is satisfied e.g. for additive f.

15. There is no need, in the present model, to distinguish between coordinates referring to capital goods and those indexing consumption goods. We call z a consumption program since the static equilibrium renders the indefinite accumulation of capital assets pointless.

16. The term appears in Koopmans and Bausch [14, topic 3], where it refers to a specialization of the competitive-equilibrium notion to the context of linear activity analysis.

17. Cf. Samuelson [25, p. 181].

18. Cf. Berge [4, p. 116].

19. Where $||e||$ is the norm of e, say $(\sum e_i^2)^{\frac{1}{2}}$.

20. Let $S \subset R^n$ nonempty, convex, and compact. If $H(p)$: $S \to S$ is usc and, for all p, nonempty and convex, S owns a p^+ such that $p^+ \in H(p^+)$.

21. Economic meaning: nondecreasing rate of resource transformation.

22. The same criterion applies to stochastic programming [19, ch. 2.1] generally, of which portfolio selection is a special case.

23. f_1 is concave because linear; the concavity of f_2 is proved in [19, ch. 2.2].

24. This is the portfolio programming problem studied by Markowitz [16, ch. 8].

25. I first proposed this criterion in a communication to the Econometric Society (Pittsburgh, December 1962. See Moeseke [18]). W. Baumol [3] later has independently proposed the same criterion under the name 'expected gain-confidence limit criterion'.

26. More specifically, the cost, to the security (and mortgage) buying financial intermediary, of the marginal dollar attracted on the capital market to which it has access (via time deposits and the sale of its own shares). For the private investor, that cost may be an opportunity cost, measured by the rate on time deposits. I am indebted to Charles W. Meyer for this comment.

27. For a formal proof see Moeseke [20, p. 164].

28. A finite algorithm for portfolio problem (3.9) was developed and applied to an empirical program in [19, ch. 3].

29. Solution x^+ usually is, but need not be, unique. Further choice among solutions is, at any rate, a matter of indifference.

30. Clearly $m_t \geq m^+$ (all $t \geq 1$) and the sequence $\{m_t\}$ is monotone decreasing. If the sequence is finite then its last member is necessarily m^+. If the sequence is

30. (continued)

infinite, it possesses a limit m_L (by the Bolzano-Weierstrass theorem). Suppose $m_L > m^+$. Then $\max_{x \varepsilon X} \phi(x|m_L) < i$. By construction there is an m_t sufficiently close to m_L so that $m_{t+1} < m_L$, contradicting monotonicity. Hence $\lim_{t\to\infty} m_t = m^+$.

REFERENCES

1. Arrow, K.J. and Debreu, G.: "Existence of an Equilibrium for a Competitive Economy," Econometrica, 22 (July 1954), 265-290.

2. Allais, M.: Economie et Intérêt. Paris: Imprimerie Nationale, 1947.

3. Baumol, W.J.: "An Expected Gain-Confidence Limit Criterion for Portfolio Selection," Management Science, 10 (October 1963), 174-182.

4. Berge, C.: Espaces Topologiques. Paris: Dunod, 1959.

5. Bonnesen, T. and Fenchel, W.: Theorie der Konvexen Körper. New York: Chelsea, 1948.

6. Debreu, G.: "The Coefficient of Resource Utilization," Econometrica, 19 (July 1951), 273-292.

7. Dorfman, R., Samuelson, P.A., and Solow, R.M.: Linear Programming and Economic Analysis. New York: McGraw-Hill, 1958.

8. Drèze, J.H.: "Some Postwar Contributions of French Economists to Theory and Public Policy," American Economic Review, 54 (June 1964), 1-64.

9. Dubreil, P. and Dubreil-Jacotin, M.L.: Lecons d'Algèbre Moderne. Paris: Dunod, 1964.

10. Hurwicz, L.: "Programming in Linear Spaces," in Arrow, K.J., Hurwicz, L., and Uzawa, H., eds.: Studies in Linear and Nonlinear Programming. Stanford: Stanford University Press, 1958.

11. Kakutani, S.: "A Generalization of Brouwer's Fixed-Point Theorem," Duke Mathematical Journal, 8(1941), 457-459.

12. Kelley, J.L., Namioka, I., et al.: Linear Topological Spaces. Princeton: Van Nostrand, 1963.

13. Koopmans, T.C., ed.: Activity Analysis of Production and Allocation. New York: Wiley, 1951.

14. Koopmans, T.C. and Bausch, A.F.: "Selected Topics in Economics Involving Mathematical Reasoning," SIAM Review, 1(July 1959), 79-148.

15. Malinvaud, E.: "Capital Accumulation and Efficient Allocation of Resources," Econometrica, 21(April 1953), 233-268.

16. Markowitz, H.M.: Portfolio Selection. New York: Wiley, 1959.

17. Meade, J.E.: A Geometry of International Trade. London: Allen and Unwin, 1952.

18. Moeseke, P.V.: "Minimax-Maximax Solution to Linear Programming Under Risk," Econometrica, 31(October 1963), 749-750.

19. Moeseke, P.V.: "Stochastic Linear Programming," Yale Economic Essays, 5(Spring 1965), 197-253.

20. Moeseke, P.V.: "A General Duality Theorem of Convex Programming," Metroeconomica, 17(September 1965), 161-170.

21. Neumann, J.V.: "Über ein Ökonomisches Gleichungs - System und eine Verallgemeinerung des Brouwerschen Fixpunktsatzes," in Menger, K., ed.: Ergebnisse eines Mathematischen Kolloquiums, 8(1935-36). Translated: "A Model of General Economic Equilibrium," Review of Economic Studies, 13(1945-6), 1-9.

22. Pareto, V.: Manuel d'Economie Politique (2nd ed.). Paris: Giard, 1927.

23. Rader, J.T.: "On Intertemporal Efficiency," Metroeconomica, 17(September 1965), 152-160.

24. Radner, R.: "Paths of Economic Growth that are Optimal with Regard only to Final States: a Turnpike Theorem," Review of Economic Studies, 28(February 1961), 98-104.

25. Samuelson, P.A.: Economics (6th ed.). New York: McGraw-Hill, 1964.

26. Tintner, G.: "Stochastic Linear Programming with Applications to Agricultural Economics," Second Symposium in Linear Programming. Washington: National Bureau of Standards (Vol. 1, 1955), 197-228.

27. Wald, A.: Statistical Decision Functions. New York: Wiley, 1950.

28. Weiss, L.: Statistical Decision Theory. New York: McGraw-Hill, 1961.

SOME EXTENSIONS OF THE KUHN-TUCKER RESULTS IN CONCAVE PROGRAMMING[1]

by

James C. Moore
University of Missouri

I. INTRODUCTION, NOTATION

In their seminal paper [11], Kuhn and Tucker proved an equivalence between the existence of a saddle point and the maximization of a concave function f subject to $x \geqq 0$, and $g(x) \geqq 0$, where g is a vector of concave functions.[2] Uzawa later provided a somewhat simpler proof of this result [14], as well as extending the basic theorem to the case where the function f and the functions g_i are not necessarily differentiable nor even continuous.[3] In a fundamental article in the same volume, Hurwicz [8] generalized the Kuhn-Tucker results to the case where the functions involved map a (real) linear space into linear topological spaces; as well as providing interesting and important extensions of the saddle point notion to cases involving more general orderings.[4]

The purpose of this paper is two-fold:

1.) We shall provide a fairly systematic treatment of the theory of the constrained maximization of nondifferentiable vector-valued functions defined on a finite-dimensional Euclidean space (Sec. II). In some respects, much of this portion of the paper is not new. In fact, some of the theorems presented are special cases of Professor Hurwicz's results for the non-differentiable case. However, where the results presented here are special cases of Professor Hurwicz's work, we have generally been able to take advantage of the more elementary spaces with which we are concerned here to develop somewhat simpler proofs. Moreover, some of the results presented in Section II are at least mild generalizations of the heretofore published work on the constrained maximization of nondifferentiable vector-valued functions.

2.) In Section III, we undertake a systematic exploration of the nature of the constraint qualifications which have been used in this type of maximization problem. We there examine both the geometric role the constraint qualification plays in the problem, and the relationships among the various constraint qualifications which have been used.

In order to more clearly define the kind of problem with which we shall be dealing, suppose we first introduce the following notation.

Let E_n denote n-dimensional Euclidean space. We shall use x, y, z, etc., to denote points in this space, which we think of (where the distinction is important) as column vectors. If x is the vector with elements $x_1, x_2, \ldots, x_n$, we write

$$x = \langle x_1, x_2, \ldots, x_n \rangle.$$

We shall denote the set of unit (Cartesian) coordinate vectors in E_n by $\{e^1, \ldots, e^n\}$, i.e.,

$$e^i = \langle \delta_{i1}, \delta_{i2}, \ldots, \delta_{in} \rangle \text{ for } i = 1,\ldots,n;$$

where δ_{ij} is the Kronecker delta.

We shall use what seems to be a standard notation for vector inequalities:

$$x \geq y \text{ iff } x_i \geqq y_i \text{ for } i = 1,\ldots,n;$$

$$x > y \text{ iff } x \geq y \text{ and } x \neq y;$$

$$x \gg y \text{ iff } x_i > y_i \text{ for } i = 1,\ldots,n.$$

Using these definitions, we define the non-negative orthant in E_n, E_n^+, by:

$$E_n^+ = \{x \in E_n | x \geq \theta_n\};$$

where θ_n denotes the origin in E_n. In line with this notation, E_1 will denote the real line, and E_1^+ the set of non-negative real numbers.

If x, y $\in E_n$, we shall denote the:

1.) INNER PRODUCT OF x AND y by $x \cdot y$,

$$x \cdot y = \textstyle\sum_{i=1}^n x_i y_i.$$

2.) NORM OF x by $||x||$, i.e.,

$$||x|| = (x \cdot x)^{1/2}$$

3.) DISTANCE BETWEEN x AND y (the metric on E_n) by

$$d(x, y) = ||x - y|| = [\textstyle\sum_{i=1}^n (x_i - y_i)^2]^{1/2}$$

4.) SPHERICAL NEIGHBORHOOD OF x WITH RADIUS $\varepsilon > 0$ by

$$N(x, \varepsilon) = \{y \in E_n | d(x, y) < \varepsilon\}.$$

Where the radius is unimportant, we use $N(x)$ to denote an arbitrary (non-empty) spherical neighborhood of x.

If $X \subseteq E_n$, we denote the closure of X by $\overline{X}$, and the interior of X by $\text{int}(X)$, *i.e.*, $(\exists N(x))$:

$$\text{int}(X) = \{x \in X \mid (N(x))\ N(x) \subseteq X\}.$$

If A and B are subsets of E_m and E_n, respectively, we denote the Cartesian Product of A and B by

$$A \times B = \{\langle a, b\rangle \in E_{m+n} \mid a \in A,\ b \in B\}.$$

Extending the above notation, we shall frequently partition vectors in, say, E_m, writing, *e.g.*, $x = \langle x^1, x^2\rangle$. Where we write

$$\langle x^1, x^2\rangle \in E_{n+p},$$

we shall understand that

$$x^1 \in E_n,\ x^2 \in E_p.$$

We say that a set $X \subseteq E_n$ is:

1.) a CONE if $(x \in X)\quad (\lambda \in E_1^+)$: $\lambda x \in X$.[5]

2.) CONVEX if $(x^1, x^2 \in X \qquad \lambda \in [0, 1])$:

$$\lambda x^1 + (1 - \lambda)x^2 \in X$$

3.) a CONVEX CONE if $(x^1, x^2 \in X) \quad (\lambda_1, \lambda_2 \in E_1^+)$:

$$\lambda_1 x^1 + \lambda_2 x^2 \in X;$$

while if $X \subseteq E_n$, we define:

1.) the CONJUGATE CONE OF X, denoted X^*, by

$$X^* = \{y \in E_n \mid (x \in X): x \cdot y \geq 0\},$$

2.) $X^{\perp} = \{y \in E_n \mid (x \in X): x \cdot y = 0\}$

3.) $-X = \{y \in E_n \mid (-1)y \in X\}$

4.) (for $Y \subseteq E_n$):

$$X + Y = \{z \in E_n \mid (\exists x \in X,\ y \in Y)\ z = x + y\}.$$

Finally, we shall make frequent use of the following definitions.

Definition 1: Let $g: E_m \to E_n$. We shall say that g is AFFINE[6] if g is of the form:

$$g(x) = Gx + b,$$

where G is an n x m matrix of constants, and b is an n x 1 column vector of constants.

Definition 2: Let $D \subseteq E_n$ be convex, let $g: D \to E_m$, and let $Y \subseteq E_m$ be a convex cone. We shall say that g is Y-CONCAVE ON D if for every x^1, $x^2 \in D$ and $\lambda \varepsilon [0, 1]$, we have

$$g[\lambda x^1 + (1 - \lambda)x^2] - [\lambda g(x^1) + (1 - \lambda)g(x^2)] \in Y.$$

This second definition is equivalent (for the case with which we're dealing here) to the definition of concavity introduced by Professor Hurwicz in [8],(p. 68). Note that if $g: D \to E_1$, the usual definition of concavity is equivalent to the statement that g is E_1^+-concave on D; while if g is an m-vector of functions, each of which is concave by the usual definition, then g is E_m^+-concave on D.

We now set out the maximization problem with which we shall deal in this paper as follows:

Definition 3: Let $D \subseteq E_m$, and suppose that:

$$f: D \to E_n, \; g: D \to E_p,$$

and that $X \subseteq D$ is non-empty, $Y \subseteq E_p$ is a non-empty convex cone. We shall then say that $<f, g, X, Y>$ defines a MAXIMIZATION PROBLEM, π, and that $\bar{x}$ is a SOLUTION of π provided that:

(1) $\bar{x} \in X$, $g(\bar{x}) \in Y$,

and

(2) $\not\exists\; \hat{x} \in X \ni g(\hat{x}) \in Y$ and $f(\hat{x}) > f(\bar{x})$.[7]

Notice that if n = 1, so that f is real-valued, we have, as a special case, the maximization (in the usual sense) of a real-valued function subject to the constraints $x \in X$ and $g(x) \in Y$. Moreover, in the very special case where n = 1, $X = E_m^+$, and $Y = E_p^+$; our maximization problem reduces to the much more familiar problem of maximizing f subject to $x \geq \theta_m$, $g(x) \geq \theta_p$. We note also that, since $\{\theta_p\}$ is a convex cone, the general maximization problem formulated in Definition 3 includes as a special case the classical Lagrangian problem of maximizing a real-valued function f subject to the constraint $g(x) = \theta$ (in the case where $n = 1$, $X = D$, and $Y = \{\theta_p\})$[8]. As a final example, suppose we wish to maximize (in the sense of definition 3)[9] some vector-valued function f subject to $x \in X$ and

$$(3)\quad \begin{cases} h_i(x) = b_i \text{ for } i = 1,\ldots,q; \\ h_i(x) \geqq b_i \text{ for } i = q+1, \ldots, r \\ h_i(x) \leqq b_i \text{ for } i = r+1, \ldots, p. \end{cases}$$

Define

$$g^{(1)}(x) = \langle h_1(x) + (-b_1),\ldots, h_q(x) + (-b_q)\rangle$$

$$g^{(2)}(x) = \langle h_{q+1}(x) - b_{q+1}, \ldots, h_p(x) - b_p\rangle$$

$$g(x) = \langle g^{(1)}(x), g^{(2)}(x)\rangle;$$

and

$$Y_1 = \{\theta_q\},$$

$$Y_2 = E^+_{r-q} \times (-E^+_{p-r}),$$

$$Y = Y_1 \times Y_2.$$

Then Y, being the Cartesian Product of convex cones, is itself a convex cone; and the constraints in (3) can equivalently be expressed by the requirement $g(x) \in Y$.[10] Hence this example is also a special case of the type of general maximization problem formulated in Definition 3.

One further aspect of this definition deserves some discussion. The reader will note that in Definition 3, we have not required D, the domain of definition of the functions f and g, to coincide with E_m (and in fact, our definition and the theorems of the next section apply to the case where $D = X$). The extent of the domain of definition is important in this kind of maximization problem for at least two reasons.

First of all, the saddle point theorems of the next section do not require the functions f and g to be continuous. However, the necessity theorems (Theorems 3-5 of Section II) do require f and g to be concave (in the usual applications); and a function which is defined and concave on an open convex set in E_m is continuous on this set (see Berge [6], p. 193). Hence if we assume $D = E_m$, we would implicitly be assuming that f and g were continuous.

A more important consideration stems from the following

reasoning. One might conjecture[11] that if a function is defined and concave on a convex set in E_m, it is always extendible to a function which is defined and concave over all of E_m. However, in spite of the apparent plausibility of this statement, it is incorrect; as we can easily see from the following counterexample: let

$$f(x) = \begin{cases} 0 \text{ if } x = 0 \\ 1 \text{ if } x > 0. \end{cases}$$

It is clear that f is defined and concave on E_1^+, but it is obvious that there is no way of extending it to a function which is defined and concave over all of E_1.[12] Hence if we have, say, a function f which is defined and concave over the non-negative orthant in E_m (e.g., a production function), a saddle point theorem which requires the domain of definition to be E_m (and the functions f and g to be concave on this domain) is not applicable without enough additional specifications on the nature of the function f to guarantee that it is extendible. The formulation of our Definition 3, which is followed in the theorems of the next section, is applicable to this sort of situation without the additional specifications.

Definition 4: Let π be the maximization problem defined by $\langle f, g, X, Y\rangle$. We define the GENERALIZED LAGRANGIAN EXPRESSION ASSOCIATED WITH π, Φ_π, on $D\times E_n\times E_p$ by:

$$\Phi_\pi(x, v, w) = v \cdot f(x) + w \cdot g(x).$$ [13]

In the next section, we shall be concerned with the investigation of the relationship between the existence of the solution of a maximization problem, π, and the existence of a Saddle Point, of one of the following types, for Φ_π.

Definitions:[14] Let $\langle f, g, X, Y\rangle$ define a maximization problem, π, and let Φ_π denote the Generalized Lagrangian Expression associated with π. Then we shall say that:

5. a point $\langle\bar{x}, \bar{v}, \bar{w}\rangle \in E_{m+n+p}$ is a GENERALIZED SADDLE POINT (GSP) for Φ_π, or that Φ_π has a GSP at $\langle\bar{x}, \bar{v}, \bar{w}\rangle$, if:

(4) $\bar{x} \in X$, $\bar{v} \in E_n^+$, $\bar{w} \in Y^*$, $\langle\bar{v}, \bar{w}\rangle \neq \theta_{n+p}$,

and

(5) $\Phi_\pi(x, \bar{v}, \bar{w}) \leqq \Phi_\pi(\bar{x}, \bar{v}, \bar{w}) \leqq \Phi_\pi(\bar{x}, \bar{v}, w)$ for all $x \in X, w \in Y^*$.

Extending this terminology somewhat, we shall sometimes say that Φ_π has a GSP at $\bar{x} \varepsilon X$, or that a GSP exists for Φ_π at $\bar{x}$, if $(\exists <\bar{v}, \bar{w}> \varepsilon E_n^+ \times Y^*)$: $<\bar{x}, \bar{v}, \bar{w}>$ is a Generalized Saddle Point for Φ_π. (Similar conventions will be followed for the types of saddle points defined in the following.)

6. a point $<\bar{x}, \bar{v}, \bar{w}> \varepsilon E_{m+n+p}$ is a GENERALIZED NON-DEGENERATE SADDLE POINT (GNSP) for Φ_π, or that Φ_π has a GNSP at $<\bar{x}, \bar{v}, \bar{w}>$, if:

$$\bar{x} \varepsilon X, \ \bar{v} \varepsilon E_n^+ \setminus \{\theta_n\}^{15}, \ \bar{w} \varepsilon Y^*,$$

and (5) holds. Equivalently, Φ_π has a GNSP at $<\bar{x}, \bar{v}, \bar{w}>$ if Φ_π has a GSP at $<\bar{x}, \bar{v}, \bar{w}>$ and $\bar{v} \neq \theta_n$.

7. a point $<\bar{x}, \bar{v}, \bar{w}> \varepsilon E_{m+n+p}$ is a GENERALIZED PROPER SADDLE POINT (GPSP) for Φ_π if $\bar{x} \varepsilon X$, $\bar{v} >> \theta_n$, $\bar{w} \varepsilon Y^*$, and (5) holds.

8. a point $<\bar{x}, \bar{w}> \varepsilon E_{m+p}$ is a SADDLE POINT for Φ_π (in the special case where n = 1, i.e., f: D $\rightarrow E_1$) if Φ_π has a GNSP at $<\bar{x}, 1, \bar{w}> \varepsilon E_{m+1+p}$, that is, if:

(6) $\bar{x} \varepsilon X, \bar{w} \varepsilon Y^*$,

and

(7) $f(x) + \bar{w} \cdot g(x) \leqq f(\bar{x}) + \bar{w} \cdot g(\bar{x}) \leqq f(\bar{x}) + w \cdot g(\bar{x})$

for all $x \varepsilon X$, $w \varepsilon Y^*$.

Note that for the special case where n = 1 (i.e., where f: D $\rightarrow E_1$), the distinction between a GNSP and a GPSP disappears (the distinction is of some importance when n > 1, however, as we shall see). Moreover, in the case where n = 1, the existence of a GNSP is logically equivalent to the existence of a Saddle Point. To see this, we first note that a Saddle Point in this situation is a special case of a GNSP (having $\bar{v} = 1$). Moreover, if Φ_π has a GNSP at $<\bar{x}, \bar{v}, \bar{w}> \varepsilon E_{m+1+p}$; then, as we can easily verify, Φ_π has a Saddle Point at $<\bar{x}, (1/\bar{v})\bar{w}>$.

II. THE PRINCIPAL THEOREMS

The following theorem is a special case of theorem V.1, p. 86, in Hurwicz [8]. It deals with a sufficient condition for a constrained maximum; and, it should be noted, holds with no restrictive assumptions (e.g., concavity) on f and g whatever. It is also perhaps worth emphasizing that X can be <u>any</u> point set in E_m (even a finite point set), while Y can be <u>any</u> closed convex cone in E_p (and we may have, for instance, $Y \cap E_p^+ = \{\theta_p\}$).

<u>Theorem 1</u> (Hurwicz).

If:

1. $\langle f, g, X, Y \rangle$ defines a maximization problem, π (see Definition 3), where Y is a closed convex cone;

2. $\langle \bar{x}, \bar{v}, \bar{w} \rangle \in E_{m+n+p}$ is a GPSP for Φ_π;

then $\bar{x}$ is a solution of π.

<u>Proof</u> (Hurwicz):

By hypothesis (2), we have

(1) $\bar{x} \in X, \bar{v} \gg \theta_n, \bar{w} \in Y^*$,

and

(2) $\bar{v} \cdot f(x) + \bar{w} \cdot g(x) \leqq \bar{v} \cdot f(\bar{x}) + \bar{w} \cdot g(\bar{x}) \leqq \bar{v} \cdot f(\bar{x}) + w \cdot g(\bar{x})$ for all $x \in X$, $w \in Y^*$.

From the r.h.s. of (2), we have:

(3) $\bar{w} \cdot g(\bar{x}) \leqq w \cdot g(\bar{x})$ for all $w \in Y^*$.

However, since $\bar{w} \in Y^*$, we have $w + \bar{w} \in Y^*$ for all $w \in Y^*$ (since Y^* is a convex cone). Hence, from (3), we have:

$$\bar{w} \cdot g(\bar{x}) \leqq (w + \bar{w}) \cdot g(\bar{x}) \text{ for all } w \in Y^*,$$

or

(4) $w \cdot g(\bar{x}) \geqq 0$ for all $w \in Y^*$.

Therefore $g(\bar{x}) \in Y^{**}$. However, since Y is a closed convex cone, we have (see Karlin [10], p. 403) $Y = Y^{**}$. Hence

(5) $g(\bar{x}) \in Y$.

Moreover, it follows immediately from (1), (3), and (5), that

(6) $\bar{w} \cdot g(\bar{x}) = 0$

Suppose now that $x \in X$ and $g(x) \in Y$. Then by (1), (6), and the l.h.s. of (2), we have:

$$\bar{v} \cdot f(x) \leqq \bar{v} \cdot f(x) + \bar{w} \cdot g(x) \leqq \bar{v} \cdot f(\bar{x}) + \bar{w} \cdot g(\bar{x}) = \bar{v} \cdot f(\bar{x}).$$

Hence

(7) $\bar{v} \cdot f(x) \leqq \bar{v} \cdot f(\bar{x})$ for all $x \in X$ such that $g(x) \in Y$.

Therefore, since $\bar{v} >> \theta_n$, (7) implies that:

$$\nexists\ \hat{x} \in X \text{ with } g(\hat{x}) \in Y \text{ such that } f(\hat{x}) > f(\bar{x}),$$

and it follows from (1) and (5) that $\bar{x}$ is a solution of π. QED.

Our next theorem deals with necessary conditions for a constrained maximum, and is a generalization of a theorem by Berge (cf., Berge [6], p. 227).[16] The theorem stated here is implicit in Hurwicz's treatment in [8], although it is not stated explicitly. It is a fairly natural extension of the approach to the classical Lagrangian problem developed by Bliss in [7].

Theorem 2.

If:

1. $\langle f, g, X, Y\rangle$ defines a maximization problem, π, where:
   a. X is convex,
   b. f is concave (i.e., E_n^+-concave) on X,
   c. g is Y-concave on X,
2. $\bar{x} \in X$ is a solution for π;

then

$$(\exists\ \bar{v} \in E_n^+,\ w \in Y^*):\ \Phi_\pi \text{ has a GSP at } \langle\bar{x}, \bar{v}, \bar{w}\rangle.$$

The method of proof used in the following is an adaptation of that originated by Hurwicz in [8] and Uzawa in [14]. It depends heavily on two convex and disjoint sets, A and B, which are (in our case) subsets of E_{n+p}. In order to define these sets, we first define:

$$(8)\quad \begin{cases} h(x) = \langle f(x), g(x)\rangle \text{ for } x \in X, \\ Z = E_n^+ \times Y. \end{cases}$$

We note that h is Z-concave on X, and that Z is a convex cone (since it is the Cartesian Product of two convex cones).

For each $x \in X$, define:

(9) $A(x) = \{a \in E_{n+p} \mid h(x) - a \in Z\}$.

We then define:

(10) $A = \{a \in E_{n+p} \mid (\exists x \in X): a \in A(x)\} = \bigcup_{x \in X} A(x)$

$= \{a = \langle s, t\rangle \in E_{n+p} | (\exists x \in X): f(x) \geq s,\ g(x) - t \in Y\},$

and

$$(11) \quad \begin{cases} B = \{b = \langle z, y\rangle \in E_{n+p} | z > f(\bar{x}),\ y \in Y\} \\ = \{b = \langle z, y\rangle \in E_{n+p} | \langle z, y\rangle \in [f(\bar{x}) + (E_n^+ \setminus \{\theta\})] \\ \times\ Y\}. \end{cases}$$

Lemma 1: Under the hypotheses of Theorem 2, the sets A and B defined in (10) and (11) are disjoint, convex, and non-empty. Moreover, for every $x \in X$, we have $h(x) = \langle f(x), g(x)\rangle \in A$.

Proof of Lemma 1:

i.) Since $\theta_{n+p} \in Z$, it is clear that

$$(x \in X):\quad h(x) \in A.$$

Since this is the case, it is obvious that if $X \neq \emptyset$, then $A \neq \emptyset$. It is also obvious that if $Y \neq \emptyset$, then $B \neq \emptyset$; and it is clear that B is convex, since it is the Cartesian Product of two convex sets.

ii.) In order to prove that A is convex, suppose that

(12) $\hat{a} = \langle \hat{s}, \hat{t}\rangle,\ \tilde{a} = \langle \tilde{s}, \tilde{t}\rangle \in A.$

Then$(\exists \hat{x}, \tilde{x} \in X)$:

(13) $h(\hat{x}) - \hat{a} \in Z,$

(14) $h(\tilde{x}) - \tilde{a} \in Z.$

Let $\lambda \in [0, 1] \subseteq E_1^+$, and define

(15) $a(\lambda) = \lambda\hat{a} + (1 - \lambda)\tilde{a},$

(16) $x(\lambda) = \lambda\hat{x} + (1 - \lambda)\tilde{x}.$

Since Z is convex, we have by (13) and (14):

(17) $\lambda[h(\hat{x}) - \hat{a}] + (1 - \lambda)\ [h(\tilde{x}) - \tilde{a}]$

$= \lambda h(x) + (1 - \lambda)\ h(\tilde{x}) = -\ a(\lambda) \in Z.$

Moreover, since X is convex, and h is Z-concave on X:

(18) $h[x(\lambda)] - [\lambda h(\hat{x}) + (1 - \lambda)h(\tilde{x})] \in Z.$

Hence, since Z is a convex cone, we have by (17) and (18):

$$\{h[x(\lambda)] - [\lambda h(\hat{x}) + (1 - \lambda)h(\tilde{x})]\} + \{\lambda h(\hat{x}) + (1 - \lambda)\ h(\tilde{x}) - a(\lambda)\} = h[x(\lambda)] - a(\lambda) \in Z.$$

Therefore

$$a(\lambda) \in A[x(\lambda)] \subseteq A;$$

and we conclude that A is convex.

iii.) In order to show that $A \cap B = \emptyset$, suppose b.w.o.c. that $\exists \langle \hat{s}, \hat{t} \rangle \in A \cap B$.

Then, since $\langle \hat{s}, \hat{t} \rangle \in A$,

$$(\exists \hat{x} \in X): h(\hat{x}) - \langle \hat{s}, \hat{t} \rangle \in Z.$$

But then, since $\langle \hat{s}, \hat{t} \rangle \in B$, we have

(19) $f(\hat{x}) \geq \hat{s} > f(\bar{x})$,

$\hat{t} \in Y$, $g(\hat{x}) - \hat{t} \in Y$,

and therefore, since Y is a convex cone:

(20) $(g(\hat{x}) - \hat{t}) + \hat{t} = g(\hat{x}) \in Y$.

However, (19) and (20) together contradict the assumption that $\bar{x}$ is a solution of π. Hence $A \cap B = \emptyset$. QED.

Lemma 2: Under the hypotheses of Theorem 2, and with A and B defined as in (10) and (11),

$$(\exists \langle \bar{v}, \bar{w} \rangle \in E_{n+p}):$$

i.) $\langle \bar{v}, \bar{w} \rangle \neq \theta$;

ii.) $\bar{v} \cdot s + \bar{w} \cdot t \leqq \bar{v} \cdot z + \bar{w} \cdot y$ for all $\langle s, t \rangle \in A$, $\langle z, y \rangle \in B$;

iii.) $\bar{v} \in E_n^+$, $\bar{w} \in Y^*$,

iv.) $\bar{v} \cdot f(x) + \bar{w} \cdot g(x) \leqq \bar{v} \cdot f(\bar{x})$ for all $x \in X$,

v.) $\bar{w} \cdot g(\bar{x}) = 0$.

Proof of Lemma 2:

By lemma 1 and the "separating hyperplane theorem" (Cf., Berge [6], p. 163):

$$\exists \langle \bar{v}, \bar{w} \rangle \in E_{n+p}$$

satisfying (i) and (ii).

By the conclusion of Lemma 1, $\langle f(x), g(x) \rangle \in A$ for every $x \in X$. Hence it follows from (ii) that we must have, in particular:

(21) $\bar{v} \cdot [z - f(\bar{x})] + \bar{w} \cdot [y - g(\bar{x})] \geqq 0$ for all $z > f(\bar{x})$, $y \in Y$;

from which it follows immediately that:

(22) $\bar{v} \varepsilon E_n^+$, $\bar{w} \varepsilon Y^*$,

which verifies (iii).

Since $<f(\bar{x}), \theta_p>$ is on the boundary of B and by Lemma 1,

$$(x \varepsilon X): <f(x), g(x)> \varepsilon A,$$

it also follows from (ii) that we must have:

(23) $\bar{v} \cdot f(x) + \bar{w} \cdot g(x) \leqq \bar{v} \cdot f(\bar{x})$ for all $x \varepsilon X$,

which verifies (iv).

Finally, letting $x = \bar{x}$ on the l.h.s. of (23), and using (22) and the fact that $g(\bar{x}) \varepsilon Y$, we have

$$\bar{w} \cdot g(\bar{x}) = 0,$$

which verifies (v). QED.

We are at last ready to prove Theorem 2.

Proof of Theorem 2:

Combining (iii) - (v) of the conclusion of Lemma 2, we have:

$$\bar{v} \cdot f(x) + \bar{w} \cdot g(x) \leqq \bar{v} \cdot f(\bar{x}) = \bar{v} \cdot f(\bar{x}) + \bar{w} \cdot g(\bar{x})$$
$$\leqq \bar{v} \cdot f(\bar{x}) + w \cdot g(\bar{x}) \text{ for all } x \varepsilon X,\ w \varepsilon Y^*.$$

Combining this result with (iii) of Lemma 2 and the definition of $\bar{x}$, we see that $<\bar{x}, \bar{v}, \bar{w}>$ is a GSP for Φ_π. QED.

Under certain assumptions, one obtains in the classical theory of constrained extrema (with equality constraints, and where all the functions involved are differentiable):

(24) $(\exists <\lambda_0, \lambda> \varepsilon E_{1+p}): \lambda_0 f_x(\bar{x}) + \lambda \cdot g_x(\bar{x}) = 0$,

where $\bar{x}$ maximizes f subject to $g(x) = \theta_p$, f_x represents the gradient vector of f, and g_x the matrix of partial derivatives $[\partial g_i/\partial x_j]$. Theorem 2 is the analogue of this result in the case where our maximand function is vector-valued and nondifferentiable (more specifically, where our maximization problem is of the form specified in Definition 3). If we add the rank condition to the hypotheses implying (24), we can conclude $\lambda_0 \neq 0$, and obtain:

$$f_x(\bar{x}) + \bar{\lambda} \cdot g_x(\bar{x}) = 0,$$

where $\bar{\lambda} = (1/\lambda_0)\lambda$. Similarly, if we add a constraint qualification (together with some assumptions about the dimensions of Y and X) to the hypotheses of Theorem 2, we can conclude that $\bar{v} \neq \theta$ in our GSP, and hence that a GNSP exists at $<\bar{x}, \bar{w}, \bar{v}>$ (and if n = 1 obtain a Saddle Point at $<\bar{x}, (1/\bar{v})\bar{w}>$ as we noted in our earlier discussion).[17] This is essentially the content of Theorem 3, to which we now turn. We shall, however, have need for the following lemmas in our proof. The result in Lemma 3 is quite well known, and a proof is included here only for the sake of providing a convenient reference.[18]

Lemma 3: Let $X \subseteq E_n$, and suppose that $\bar{x} \in int(X)$, $\bar{y} \in E_n$. If $y \cdot \bar{x} \geqq y \cdot x$ [resp., $y \cdot \bar{x} \leqq y \cdot x$] for every $x \in X$, then $y = \theta_n$.

Proof:

If $\bar{x} \in int(X)$, $(\exists\bar{\lambda} > 0): \bar{x} + \bar{\lambda}y \in X$, and we have

$$y \cdot [\bar{x} + \bar{\lambda}y] = y \cdot \bar{x} + \bar{\lambda}y \cdot y.$$

Hence, if $y \neq \theta_n$,

$$y \cdot [\bar{x} + \bar{\lambda}y] > y \cdot \bar{x}.$$

The result with the reversed inequality follows immediately from this. QED.

Lemma 4:

If:

1.) $g: E_m \rightarrow E_n$, where $m \geqq n$,

2. g is affine, i.e., $g(x) = Gx + b$, and rank $(G) = n$,

3. $X \subseteq E_m$, $\bar{x} \in int(X)$;

then there exist open neighborhoods $N_1(\bar{x}) \subseteq X$, $N_2[g(\bar{x})] \subseteq E_n \ni$

$$N_2[g(\bar{x})] \subseteq g[N_1(\bar{x})].$$

Proof:

Partition the matrix G by

$$G = [G_1 \; G_2],$$

where G_1 is n x n, and we assume w.l.o.g. that rank $(G_1) = n$. By assumption, $(\exists N_1(\bar{x}))$: $N_1(\bar{x}) \subseteq X$.

Write

$$\bar{x} = <\bar{x}^1, \bar{x}^2>,$$

where $\overline{x}^1 \varepsilon E_n$, $\overline{x}^2 \varepsilon E_{m-n}$. Then$(\exists N_3(\overline{x}^1))$: $z \varepsilon N_3(\overline{x}^1))$

$\Rightarrow <z, \overline{x}^2> \varepsilon N_1(\overline{x})$.

Define h on E_n by

$$h(z) = G_1 z.$$

It then follows by Theorems 7-3 and 7-4, pp. 141 and 143, respectively, in Apostol [1], that:

$$(\exists N_4[h(\overline{x}^1)]):$$

$$N_4[h(\overline{x}^1)] \subseteq h[N_3(\overline{x}^1)].$$

But, it is clear that

$$\overline{y} \equiv g(\overline{x}) \varepsilon N_4[h(\overline{x}^1)] + G_2\overline{x}^2 + b \subseteq g[N_1(\overline{x})].$$

Hence, noting that if M is an open sphere containing $\overline{y}$, $M + \hat{y}$ is an open sphere containing $\overline{y} + \hat{y}$; we see that if we define:

$$N_2[g(\overline{x})] = N_4[h(\overline{x}^1)] + G_2\overline{x}^2 + b,$$

N_2 is an open sphere containing $g(\overline{x})$ and

$$N_2[g(\overline{x})] \subseteq g[N_1(\overline{x})].$$

QED.

Theorem 3.

If:

1. <f, g, X, Y> defines a maximization problem, π, where:

   a.) X is convex, $int(X) \neq \emptyset$,

   b.) f is concave (i.e., E_n^+-concave) on X,

   c.) Y is of the form $Y = Y_1 \times Y_2$, where

      i.) $Y_1 \subseteq E_q$, $Y_2 \subseteq E_r$ $(q + r = p)$

      ii.) $int(Y_2) \neq \emptyset$ (in E_r)

   d.) g is of the form $g(x) = <g^{(1)}(x), g^{(2)}(x)>$, where

      (i.) $g^{(1)}: D \rightarrow E_q$, $g^{(2)}: D \rightarrow E_r$

ii.) $g^{(1)}$ is affine[19] ($g^{(1)}(x) = Gx + b$), and we assume w.l.o.g. that rank $(G) = q$

iii.) $g^{(2)}$ is Y_2-concave on X,

2.) g satisfies:

<u>CQ_1</u>: i.) $(\exists x^{\dagger} \varepsilon \operatorname{int}(X))$: $g^{(1)}(x^{\dagger}) \varepsilon Y_1$

ii.) $(\exists x^* \varepsilon X)$: $g^{(1)}(x^*) \varepsilon Y_1$,

$g^{(2)}(x^*) \varepsilon \operatorname{int}(Y_2)$)

3.) $\bar{x} \varepsilon X$ is a solution of π;

then

$(\exists \bar{v} \varepsilon [E_n^+ \backslash \{\theta_n\}], \bar{w} \varepsilon Y^*)$: Φ_π has a GNSP at $\langle \bar{x}, \bar{v}, \bar{w} \rangle$.

<u>Proof</u>:

It is clear that g is Y-concave on X. Hence, we can readily verify that the hypotheses of Theorem 2 are satisfied. Therefore, by Theorem 2:

$(\exists \langle \bar{v}, \bar{w} \rangle \varepsilon E_{n+p})$:

(25) $\langle \bar{v}, \bar{w} \rangle \neq \theta$

(26) $\bar{v} \varepsilon E_n^+, \bar{w} \varepsilon Y^*$

and Φ_π has a GSP at $\langle \bar{x}, \bar{v}, \bar{w} \rangle$. Moreover, by Lemma 2:

(27) $\bar{v} \cdot s + \bar{w} \cdot t \leqq \bar{v} \cdot z + \bar{w} \cdot y$ for all $\langle s, t \rangle \varepsilon A$, $\langle z, y \rangle \varepsilon B$;

where A and B are defined in (10) and (11), above.

Writing $\bar{w} = \langle \bar{w}^1, \bar{w}^2 \rangle$, where $\bar{w}^1 \varepsilon E_q$, $\bar{w}^2 \varepsilon E_r$,

we see that we have from (27):

(28) $\bar{v} \cdot f(x) + \bar{w}^1 \cdot g^{(1)}(x) + \bar{w}^2 \cdot g^{(2)}(x) \leqq \bar{v} \cdot z + \bar{w}^1 \cdot y^1 + \bar{w}^2 \cdot y^2$ for all $x \varepsilon X$, $y^1 \varepsilon Y_1$, $y^2 \varepsilon Y_2$.

Suppose now that $\bar{v} = \theta$. Then by (28) and (ii) of CQ_1, we have:

$$\bar{w}^1 \cdot g^{(1)}(x^*) + \bar{w}^2 \cdot g^{(2)}(x^*) \leqq \bar{w}^1 \cdot g^{(1)}(x^*)$$

$$+ \bar{w}^2 \cdot y^2 \text{ for all } y^2 \in Y_2,$$

or

(29) $\bar{w}^2 \cdot g^{(2)}(x^*) \leqq \bar{w}^2 \cdot y^2$ for all $y^2 \in Y_2$.

Hence by Lemma 3:

(30) $\bar{w}^2 = \theta_r$ (if $\bar{v} = \theta_n$)

We then have from (28) (if $\bar{v} = \theta_n$):

(31) $\bar{w}^1 \cdot g^{(1)}(x) \leqq \bar{w}^1 \cdot y^1$ for all $y^1 \in Y_1$, $x \in X$.

By (i) of $CQ_1(\exists x^\dagger \in \text{int}(X))$: $g^{(1)}(x^\dagger) \in Y_1$. Since $x^\dagger \in \text{int}(X)$,

$$\exists N(x^\dagger) \subseteq X.$$

Define

$$y^\dagger = g^{(1)}(x^\dagger).$$

We then have by Lemma 4:

$$(\exists N_1(y^\dagger) \subseteq E_q): N_1(y^\dagger) \subseteq g^{(1)}[N(x^\dagger)].$$

Hence by (31), we have:

$$\bar{w}^1 \cdot y^1 \leqq \bar{w}^1 \cdot y^\dagger \text{ for all } y^1 \in N_1(y^\dagger).$$

It then follows from Lemma 3 that:

(32) $\bar{w}^1 = \theta_q$ (if $\bar{v} = \theta_n$).

Combining (30) and (32), we see that if $\bar{v} = \theta_n$, we have:

$$\langle \bar{v}, \bar{w} \rangle = \theta_{n+p},$$

contradicting (25). Therefore $\bar{v} \neq \theta$, and Φ_π has a GNSP at $\langle \bar{x}, \bar{v}, \bar{w} \rangle$. QED.

The following result is almost a special case of Theorem 3[20]; and is, moreover, essentially a special case of Professor Hurwicz's Theorem V.3.1 in [8] (p. 91). It is included here for the sake of completeness.

Theorem 4 - Corollary (Hurwicz).

If:

1. $<f, g, X, Y>$ defines a maximization problem, π, where:

   a.) X is convex,

   b.) f is concave (i.e., E_n^+-concave) on X,

   c.) $\text{int}(Y) \neq \emptyset$, g is Y-concave on X

2. g satisfies:

   CQ_s: $(\exists x^* \in X): g(x^*) \in \text{int}(Y)$,[21]

3. $\bar{x} \in X$ is a solution of π;

then

$(\exists \bar{v} \in [E_n^+ \setminus \{\theta_n\}], \bar{w} \in Y^*)$: Φ_π has a GNSP at

$<\bar{x}, \bar{v}, \bar{w}>$.

Proof:

Re-examining the proof of Theorem 3, we see that the only steps in the argument which used the assumption $\text{int}(X) \neq \emptyset$ were in the proof that $\bar{v} = \theta_n$ implies $\bar{w}^1 = \theta_q$. Hence Theorem 4 follows as a corollary of the proof of Theorem 3. QED.

The following result is an immediate corollary of the proof of Theorem 3:

Theorem 5 - Corollary.

If:

1. $<f, g, X, Y>$ defines a maximization problem, π, where:

   a.) X is convex, $\text{int}(X) \neq \emptyset$,

   b.) f is concave (i.e., E_n^+- concave) on X,

   c.) g is affine,

2. g satisfies:

   CQ_3: $(\exists x^\dagger \in \text{int}(X)): g(x^\dagger) \in Y$,

3. $\bar{x} \in X$ is a solution of π;

then: $(\exists \bar{v} \in [E_n^+ \setminus \{\theta_n\}], \bar{w} \in Y^*)$: Φ_π has a GNSP at $<\bar{x}, \bar{v}, \bar{w}>$.

Theorem 3 is a generalization and slight correction of Theorem 3 in Uzawa [14], p. 36.[22] An example of a situation wherein Theorem 3, but not Theorem 4, is applicable is given by the last example on p. 5; if the functions h_i appearing there are assumed to be affine for $i = 1, \ldots, q$, concave for $i = q+1, \ldots, r$, and convex for $i = r+1, \ldots, p$ (and we suppose that X is convex, and f is E_n^+-concave on X). To see this, suppose we define

$$Y_1 = \{\theta_q\},\ Y_2 = E^+_{r-q} \times [-E^+_{p-r}], \text{ and } Y = Y_1 \times Y_2.$$

We note that, under the current assumptions, $<f, g, X, Y>$ defines a maximization problem, and g is Y-concave on X. However, it is impossible for g to satisfy CQ_s in this case, since $\text{int}(Y) = \emptyset$.[23] We can, however, apply Theorem 3 if g satisfies CQ_1.

III. CONSTRAINT QUALIFICATIONS AND THE GEOMETRY OF GENERALIZED SADDLE POINTS

We shall begin our discussion by considering some facets of the geometric nature of a GSP. Suppose we have a maximization problem, π, defined by $<f, g, X, Y>$, and suppose Φ_π has a GSP at $<\bar{x}, \bar{v}, \bar{w}> \varepsilon E_{m+n+p}$. Then

(1) $\bar{v} \ \varepsilon \ E_n^+,\ \bar{w} \ \varepsilon \ Y^*$,

and

(2) $\bar{v} \cdot f(x) + \bar{w} \cdot g(x) \leqq \bar{v} \cdot f(\bar{x}) + \bar{w} \cdot g(\bar{x}) \leqq \bar{v} \cdot f(\bar{x}) + w \cdot g(\bar{x})$ for all $x \ \varepsilon \ X$, $w \ \varepsilon \ Y^*$.

It is clear, then, that the existence of a GSP at $<\bar{x}, \bar{v}, \bar{w}>$ implies:

(3) $\bar{w} \cdot g(\bar{x}) = 0$.

Therefore, if $b = <z, y> \varepsilon \ E_{n+p}$ is such that:

(4) $z \geqq f(\bar{x}),\ y \ \varepsilon \ Y$;

we have:

$$\bar{v} \cdot f(\bar{x}) + \bar{w} \cdot g(\bar{x}) \leqq \bar{v} \cdot z + \bar{w} \cdot y.$$

Recalling the definition of the set B used in Section II:

(5) $B(\pi, \bar{x}) = \{b = <z, y> \varepsilon \ E_{n+p} \mid z > f(\bar{x}),\ y \ \varepsilon \ Y\}$,

we see that:

(6) $\bar{v} \cdot f(\bar{x}) + \bar{w} \cdot g(\bar{x}) \leqq \bar{v} \cdot z + \bar{w} \cdot y$ for all $<z, y> \varepsilon B(\pi, \bar{x})$.

Moreover, by (1) and (2), we see that if $\hat{x} \varepsilon X$, $<s, t> \varepsilon E_{n+p}$ are such that:

$$f(\hat{x}) \geq s, \; g(\hat{x}) - t \; \varepsilon \; Y,$$

then

$$\overline{v} \cdot [f(\hat{x}) - s] \geqq 0, \; \overline{w} \cdot [g(\hat{x}) - t] \geqq 0;$$

and therefore

(7) $\overline{v} \cdot s + \overline{w} \cdot t \leqq \overline{v} \cdot f(\hat{x}) + \overline{w} \cdot g(\hat{x}) \leqq \overline{v} \cdot f(\overline{x}) + \overline{w} \cdot g(\overline{x}).$

Recalling our definition of the set A given in Section II:

(8) $A(\pi) = \{a = <s, t> \varepsilon E_{n+p} \mid (\exists x \varepsilon X) f(x) \geq s, \; g(x) - t \varepsilon Y\};$

we see that:

(9) $\overline{v} \cdot s + \overline{w} \cdot t \leqq \overline{v} \cdot f(\overline{x}) + \overline{w} \cdot g(\overline{x})$ for all $<s, t> \varepsilon A(\pi)$.

If as in Section II we write

(10) $h_{\pi}(x) = <f(x), g(x)>$,

and

(11) $\overline{u} = <\overline{v}, \overline{w}> \varepsilon E_n^+ \times Y^*$,

we have by (6) and (9):

(12) $\overline{u} \cdot a \leqq \overline{u} \cdot h_{\pi}(\overline{x}) \leqq \overline{u} \cdot b$ for all $a \varepsilon A(\pi)$, $b \varepsilon B(\pi, \overline{x})$.

From (12) we see, therefore, that a <u>necessary</u> condition for the existence of a GSP for Φ_{π} at $\overline{x}$ is that there exist a vector $\overline{u} = <\overline{v}, \overline{w}> \varepsilon E_n^+ \times Y^*$ such that $\overline{u}$ separates the set $A(\pi)$ and $B(\pi, \overline{x})$ (Clearly this is also a sufficient condition, as we showed in the proof of Theorem 2). The question of whether Φ_{π} also has a GNSP at $\overline{x}$ boils down to whether there exists such a vector $\overline{u}$ which has $\overline{v} \neq \theta_n$. We shall now examine the function of the constraint qualification in guaranteeing that such a $\overline{u}$ does exist.

Suppose we begin by examining an illustrative situation in which no GNSP exists. In his very important 1950 article [13], Slater presents an example to show that the constraint qualification he'd introduced could not be dispensed with if one was concerned with the existence of a GNSP (in our terminology). Slater's example deals with the maximization problem, $\overline{\pi}$, defined by $<f, g, E_1, E_1^+>$, where

$$f(x) = 1 - x$$

$$-(x - 1).^2$$

Clearly, only solution of this problem is at $\overline{x} = 1$. The image of the function $h_{\overline{\pi}}(x)$ and the sets $A(\overline{\pi})$ and $B(\overline{\pi}, 1)$ for this case are graphed in Figure 1, below.

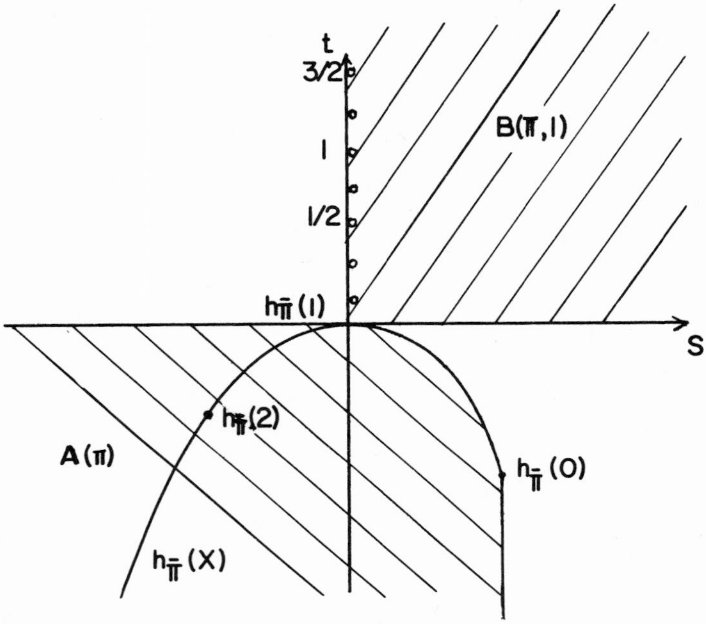

Fig. 1

In this case, it is apparent from Figure 1 that no vector $\overline{u} \in E_1^+ \times E_1^+ = E_2^+$ exists which has a non vanishing first coordinate and which separates the sets $A(\overline{\pi})$ and $B(\overline{\pi}, 1)$. Hence no GNSP exists for Φ_π at $\overline{x} = 1$. Notice, however, that Φ_π does have a GSP at $\overline{x}$ (as we would expect, since all the hypotheses of Theorem 2 are satisfied here); in fact, Φ_π has a GSP at <1, 0, 1>.

In order to examine the workings of the Slater Constraint Qualification (which we shall hereafter refer to as the Slater CQ) in a little greater detail, suppose we consider the class of maximization problems, P, defined by $\langle f, g, X, E_1^+ \rangle$, where:

$$(13) \qquad \begin{cases} X \subseteq D \subseteq E_1, \\ f\colon \; D \to E_1, \\ g\colon \; D \to E_1, \end{cases}$$

and f and g are concave on X. Let $\pi \in P$ and suppose $\bar{x}$ is a solution of π. If the Slater CQ holds, we can distinguish two cases, as follows.[24]

Case 1: $g(\bar{x}) > 0$.

In this case we'll have the sort of situation shown in Figure 2, below. While we don't have enough information to graph the set $A(\pi)$, we know that the set A^1 shown in Fig. 2 will be a subset of $A(\pi)$. Clearly, then, any vector $\bar{u}$ separating $A(\pi)$ and $B(\pi, \bar{x})$ must have $\bar{u}_1 = \bar{v} \neq 0$ (in fact, any separating vector u must be a scalar multiple of $\bar{u} = \langle 1, 0 \rangle$).[25]

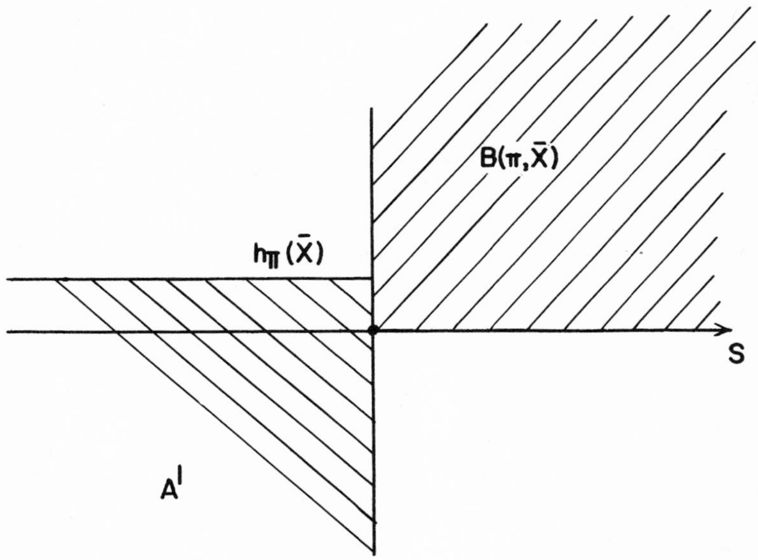

Fig. 2

Case 2: $g(\bar{x}) = 0$.

In this situation, according to the Slater CQ, there exists $x^* \in X \ni g(x^*) > 0$. Hence $h_\pi(x^*)$ must stand in something like the relationship to $h_\pi(\bar{x})$ shown in Figure 3, below. While once again we do not have sufficient information to graph $A(\pi)$, we know that the set A^1 shown in Fig. 3 will be a subset of $A(\pi)$. Hence, it is clear from our diagram that any vector $\overline{u} = \langle \overline{v}, \overline{w} \rangle \in E_2^+$ which separates $A(\pi)$ and $B(\pi, \overline{x})$ must have $\overline{v} \neq 0$.

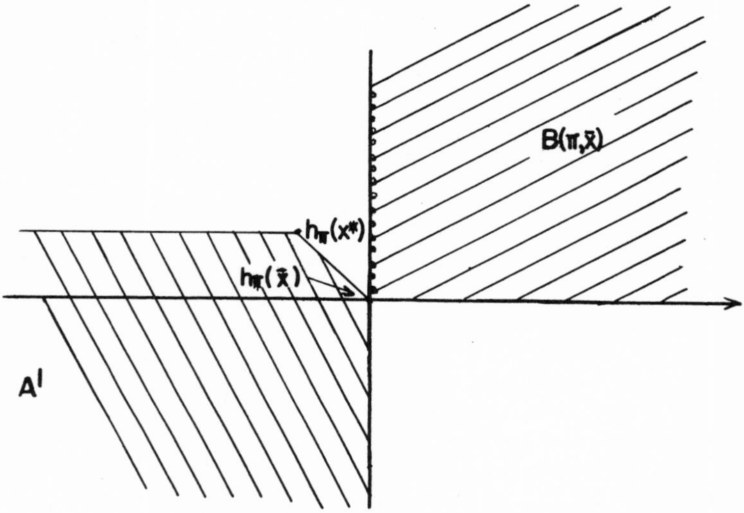

Fig. 3

It is apparent from our discussion of the above two cases (and from a careful reading of the proof of Theorem 3) that if $\pi \in P$, the Slater CQ does more than guarantee the existence of a GNSP for Φ_π at a solution of π. It actually guarantees that if Φ_π has a GSP at $\langle \overline{x}, \overline{v}, \overline{w} \rangle$, it is necessarily a GNSP. Consequently, it might appear that if one wished to concentrate on developing a set of conditions sufficient only to ensure the existence of a GNSP at $\overline{x}$, a solution of π, for some $\overline{u} \in E_n^+ \times Y^*$ (and allowing for the possibility of the existence of other vectors $u = \langle v, w \rangle \ni \langle x, v, w \rangle$ is a GSP for Φ_π, but $v = \theta_n$); one could weaken the Slater CQ for this purpose. However, if the Slater CQ does not hold, the possibility arises of obtaining the sort of tangency solution depicted in Fig. 1; and it is difficult to see how any weaker condition could be developed which would have anything like the "nice" operational properties of the Slater CQ, and which would guarantee that this sort of tangency could not occur.

In the development of a theorem analogous to our Theorem 4, Karlin introduced ([10] p. 201) an interesting constraint qualification of a form different from the Slater CQ. Hurwicz and Uzawa proved in [9] that in very general spaces these two constraint qualifications were actually equivalent. Our next lemma is a special case of the Hurwicz-Uzawa result. It is presented here for both the sake of completeness and because it seems reasonable to take advantage of the more elementary spaces with which we're dealing to present a proof involving more elementary mathematics than that used by Professors Hurwicz and Uzawa.

Lemma 5 (Hurwicz-Uzawa):

If:

1. $X \subseteq D \subset E_m$, $g\colon D \to E_p$,
2. X is convex and non-empty,
3. $Y \subseteq E_p$ is a convex cone, $\text{int}(Y) \neq \emptyset$,
4. g is Y-concave on X;

then the following are equivalent:

CQ_S: $(\exists x^* \in X)$: $g(x^*) \in \text{int}(Y)$,

CQ_K: $(z \in [Y^* \setminus \{\theta_p\}])$ $(\exists x \in X)$: $z \cdot g(x) > 0$.

Proof:

i.) $CQ_S \Rightarrow CQ_K$.

If $\bar{z} \in Y^*$ is such that $\bar{z} \cdot g(x^*) = 0$, we have

$$\bar{z} \cdot g(x^*) \leqq \bar{z} \cdot y \text{ for all } y \in Y.$$

Hence by Lemma 3, $\bar{z} = \theta_p$. Therefore:

$$(z \in [Y^* \setminus \{\theta_p\}]): z \cdot g(x^*) > 0.$$

ii.) $CQ_K \Rightarrow CQ_S$.

Suppose CQ_K holds, but that:

(13) $\nexists x^* \in X$ such that $g(x^*) \in \text{int}(Y)$.

Define

$$A = \{t \in E_p \mid (\exists x \in X): g(x) - t \in Y\}.$$

Clearly A is convex (see the statement and proof of Lemma 1, above), and non-empty. Moreover, if there existed a vector $\bar{t}$ such that $\bar{t} \in A \cap \text{int}(Y)$, then we would have:

$$(\exists \bar{x}): g(\bar{x}) - \bar{t} \in Y.$$

But then, since $\bar{t} \in \text{int}(Y)$, it would follow that:

$$[g(\bar{x}) - \bar{t}] + \bar{t} = g(\bar{x}) \in \text{int}(Y)$$

(since if $y \varepsilon Y$, $\overline{y} \varepsilon \text{int}(Y)$, $y + \overline{y} \varepsilon \text{int}(Y)$; for Y a convex cone), which contradicts (13). Therefore:

(14) $A \cap \text{int}(Y) = \emptyset$.

Hence, since the convexity of int(Y) follows from the convexity of Y; we have by the "Separating Hyperplane Theorem" (see Berge [6], p. 163):

$$(\exists w \varepsilon E_p):$$

(15) $w \neq \theta_p$, and

(16) $w \cdot t \leqq w \cdot y$ for all $t \varepsilon A$, $y \varepsilon \text{int}(Y)$.

However, it is clear from (16) that:

(17) $w \varepsilon Y^*$,

and from (16), and the definition of A that:

(18) $(x \varepsilon X)$: $w \cdot g(x) \leqq 0$.

But (17) and (18) together contradict the assumption that the Karlin CQ (CQ_K) holds. Therefore (13) is false, that is,

$(\exists x^* \varepsilon X)$: $g(x^*)$ int(Y). QED.

In reading the literature on saddle point theorems for the non-differentiable case, one is likely to get the feeling that a constraint qualification is not needed for the existence of a GNSP in the case where the constraint function g is affine.[24] More precisely, one might speculate that Theorem 5 of the previous section would remain correct if hypothesis 2 (CQ_3) were omitted. The constraint qualification cannot be dispensed with in this case, however, as the following example shows. Let the maximization problem $\overline{\pi}$ be defined by $<f, g, E_1^+, E_1^+>$, where $X = D = E_1^+$,

$$f(x) = \begin{cases} 0 \text{ for } x = 0 \\ 1 \text{ for } x > 0 \end{cases}$$

$$g(x) = -x.$$

Clearly $\overline{x} = 0$ is the only solution for $\overline{\pi}$, and all the hypotheses of Theorem 4 are satisfied except hypothesis 2 (CQ_3).[27] The sets $A(\overline{\pi})$ and $B(\overline{\pi}, \overline{x})$, and the image of the function $h_{\overline{\pi}}$ are shown in Figure 4, below. It is apparent that any vector $\overline{u} = <\overline{v}, \overline{w}> \varepsilon E_2$ which separates $A(\overline{\pi})$ and $B(\overline{\pi}, \overline{x})$ must have $\overline{v} = 0$. Hence $\Phi_{\overline{\pi}}$ does not have a GNSP at $\overline{x}$. It should be noted that the need for the constraint qualification is not eliminated by requiring the maximand function, f, to be continuous. The reader can easily verify that the maximization problem defined by $<f, g, X, Y>$, where

$$D = X = [0, 1],$$
$$f(x) = {}^{+}\sqrt{1 - x^2},$$
$$g(x) = x - 1,$$
$$Y = E_1^+ \text{ or } Y = \{0\};$$

does not have a GNSP at its solution, $\bar{x} = 1$.

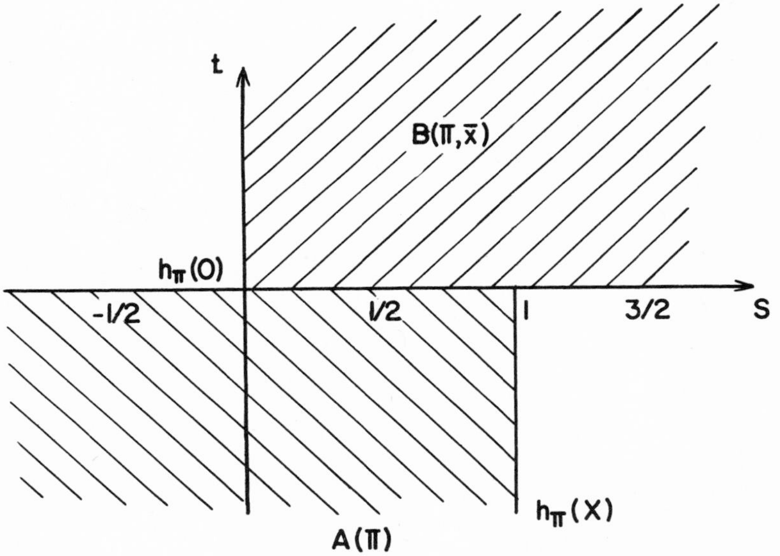

Fig. 4

We have shown in the above examples that the constraint qualifications used in Theorems 3-5 of Section II cannot be dispensed with. Theorem 3 can be proved, however, with any one of several constraint qualifications; which, at least at first glance, appear to be non-equivalent. Hence the following result may be of some interest.

Lemma 6:

If:

1. $X \subseteq D \subsetneq E_m$, $g(x) = \langle g^{(1)}(x), g^{(2)}(x) \rangle$, where $g^{(1)}: D \to E_q$, $g^{(2)}: D \to E_r$,

2. X is convex, $\text{int}(X) \neq \emptyset$,

3. $Y_1 \subseteq E_q$ and $Y_2 \subseteq E_r$ are convex cones,

4. $\text{int}(Y_2) \neq \emptyset$ (in E_r),

5. $g^{(1)}$ is affine,

6. $g^{(2)}$ is Y_2-concave on X;

then the following are all equivalent:

CQ_1: i.) $(\exists x\dagger \in int(X))$: $g^{(1)}(x\dagger) \in Y_1$

ii.) $(\exists x^* \in X)$: $g^{(1)}(x^*) \in Y_1$,
$g^{(2)}(x^*) \in int(Y_2)$,

CQ_4: $(\exists \tilde{x} \in int(X))$: $g^{(1)}(\tilde{x}) \in Y_1$,
$g^{(2)}(\hat{x}) \in int(Y_2)$

CQ_5: i.) $(\exists \hat{x} \in int(X))$: $g^{(1)}(\hat{x}) \in Y_1$, $g^{(2)}(\hat{x}) \in Y_2$

ii.) ($x^{**} \in D$): $g^{(1)}(x^{**}) \in Y_1$,
$g^{(2)}(x^{**}) \in int(Y_2)$.

Proof:

i.) Obviously $CQ_4 \Rightarrow CQ_1$. To prove the converse, define
$$y\dagger = g^{(2)}(x\dagger),\ y^* = g^{(2)}(x^*).$$
Since $y^* \in int(Y_2)$, $(\exists \bar{\lambda} \in (0, 1))$:

(18) $\bar{\lambda} y\dagger + (1 - \bar{\lambda})\, y^* \in int(Y_2)$.

Define
$$\tilde{x} = \bar{\lambda} x\dagger + (1 - \bar{\lambda}) x^*.$$
Then, since $x\dagger \in int(X)$, $\bar{\lambda} > 0$, and X is convex:

(19) $\tilde{x} \in int(X)$.

Moreover, since $g^{(1)}$ is affine, and Y_1 is convex:

(20) $g^{(1)}(\tilde{x}) = \bar{\lambda} g^{(1)}(x\dagger) + (1 - \bar{\lambda}) g^{(1)}(x^*) \in Y_1$;

while, since $g^{(2)}$ is Y_2-concave:

(21) $\{g^{(2)}(\tilde{x}) - [\bar{\lambda} y\dagger + (1 - \bar{\lambda}) y^*]\} \in Y_2$.

By (18) and (21), it follows that:

(22) $\{g^{(2)}(\tilde{x}) - [\bar{\lambda} y\dagger + (1 - \bar{\lambda}) y^*]\} + \{\bar{\lambda} y\dagger + (1 - \bar{\lambda}) y^*\} =$

$$g^{(2)}(\tilde{x}) \; \varepsilon \; \text{int}(Y_2).$$

Therefore, by (19), (20), and (22), we see that x satisfies the requirements of CQ_4. Hence,

$$CQ_4 \Longleftrightarrow CQ_1.$$

ii.) Obviously $CQ_4 \Rightarrow CQ_5$. The proof of the converse proceeds in a fashion very similar to that developed in (i), above. This time we can choose $\bar{\lambda} \; \varepsilon \; (0, 1)$ small enough so that, letting

$$\tilde{x} = \bar{\lambda}x^{**} + (1 - \bar{\lambda})\hat{x},$$

we have:

$$\tilde{x} \; \varepsilon \; \text{int}(X).$$

We then can easily show, in the same way as in (i), that:

$$g^{(1)}(\tilde{x}) \; \varepsilon \; Y_1, \; g^{(2)}(\tilde{x}) \; \varepsilon \; \text{int}(Y_2).$$

Hence $CQ_5 \Longleftrightarrow CQ_4$. QED.

By way of concluding our discussion, suppose we consider a problem tangentially related to the material of this section. In many applications of saddle point theorems to problems in Economics, one may be interested in conditions sufficient to guarantee that $\bar{w}$ does not vanish. For instance, the vector $\bar{w}$ may lend itself to a "shadow price" interpretation; and in these circumstances, it is clearly of some importance to determine whether or not $\bar{w} = \theta$. After our discussion of the function of the constraint qualification in guaranteeing that $\bar{v} \neq \theta$, however, the following result is fairly obvious.

Theorem 6.

If:

1. $\langle f, g, X, Y\rangle$ defines a maximization problem, π,
2. Φ_π has a GSP at $\langle \bar{x}, \bar{v}, \bar{w}\rangle \; \varepsilon \; E_{m+n+p}$,
3. $(\exists \hat{x} \; \varepsilon \; X)$: $f(\hat{x}) >> f(\bar{x})$

then

$$\bar{w} \neq \theta.$$

Proof:

If $\bar{w} = \theta$, then by the existence of a GSP at $\langle \bar{x}, \bar{v}, \bar{w}\rangle$, we have:

$$\bar{v} \cdot f(x) \leqq \bar{v} \cdot f(\bar{x}) \text{ for all } x \in X,$$

where $\bar{v} > \theta_n$. But this would mean

$$\bar{v} \cdot f(\hat{x}) \leqq \bar{v} \cdot f(\bar{x});$$

which is impossible; since

$$\bar{v} \cdot [f(\hat{x}) - f(\bar{x})] > 0.$$

Hence $\bar{w} \neq \theta$.

QED.

Corollary.

If:

1. $\langle f, g, X, Y\rangle$ defines a maximization problem, π, where:
   a.) X is convex,
   b.) f is concave (i.e., E_n^+-concave) on X,
   c.) g is Y-concave on X,
2. $\bar{x} \in X$ is a solution for π,
3. $(\exists \hat{x} \in X)$: $f(\hat{x}) \gg f(\bar{x})$,

then

$$(\exists \bar{v} \in E_n^+, \bar{w} \in [Y^* \setminus \{\theta_p\}]): \pi \text{ has a GSP at } \langle\bar{x}, \bar{v}, \bar{w}\rangle.$$

Proof:

This result follows immediately from Theorems 2 and 6.

Notice that the conditions sufficient for the non-vanishing of $\bar{w}$ stated in the above results require that the constraint $g(x) \in Y$ be effective in the sense that the solution $\bar{x}$ is not a solution of the problem:

$$\text{maximize } f(x) \text{ subject to } x \in X.$$ [28]

Moreover, in the special case where n = 1, (i.e., where $f\colon D \to E_1$), we see that the effectiveness of the constraint $g(x) \in Y$ (in the sense just stated) is sufficient to guarantee the non-vanishing of $\bar{w}$.[29]

APPENDIX

1. In this section, we shall show that if f is defined on E_1^+ by

$$f(x) = {}^{+}\sqrt{x},$$

then $\nexists$h such that

$$h: \; E_1 \to E_1, \; h(x) = f(x) \text{ for } x \in E_1^+,$$

and h is concave on all of E_1.

Proof:

Suppose b.w.o.c. that there exists such a function, h. Then clearly we must have:

$$h(x) < 0 \text{ for } x < 0.$$

Suppose, then, that we are given $\bar{x} < 0$, and

(1) $\bar{y} \equiv h(\bar{x}) < 0.$

Consider the point x defined by

(2) $x = \dfrac{\bar{x}^2}{4\bar{y}^2}$

Clearly $x > 0$, and therefore

(3) $h(x) = +\sqrt{x} = \dfrac{\bar{x}}{2\bar{y}} > 0.$

Define

(4) $\bar{\lambda} = \dfrac{4\bar{y}^2}{4\bar{y}^2 - \bar{x}}$

Then, since $\bar{x} < 0$, we have:

$$0 < \bar{\lambda} < 1.$$

Therefore, if h is concave, it must be the case that

$$h[\bar{\lambda}x + (1 - \bar{\lambda})\bar{x}] \geqq \bar{\lambda}h(x) + (1 - \bar{\lambda})h(\bar{x})$$

(5) $= \left[\dfrac{4\bar{y}^2}{4\bar{y}^2 - \bar{x}}\right] \dfrac{\bar{x}}{2\bar{y}} + \left[1 - \dfrac{4\bar{y}^2}{4\bar{y}^2 - \bar{x}}\right] \bar{y} = \dfrac{\overline{yx}}{4\bar{y}^2 - \bar{x}} > 0.$

However, we have:

$$\bar{\lambda}x + (1 - \bar{\lambda})\bar{x} = 0,$$

and therefore

$$h[\bar{\lambda}x + (1 - \bar{\lambda})\bar{x}] = f(0) = 0,$$

which contradicts (5). Consequently if h: $E_1 \to E_1$ and $h(x) = f(x)$ for $x \in E_1^+$, h is not concave.

2. Professor Uzawa's Theorem 3.

As indicated previously (n. 22), there appear to be some misprints in the statement and proof of Professor Uzawa's Theorem 3, pp. 35-37, in [14]. Because of the importance of the Uzawa article, it would seem that a brief discussion of these apparent misprints would be of some value; especially since the published version of Professor Uzawa's Theorem 3 (with misprints) makes it appear that some of the hypotheses of our Theorem 3 could be weakened in a fashion which would, in fact, make the theorem incorrect.

Using the notation developed in this paper, the necessity portion of Professor Uzawa's Theorem 3 can be stated as follows:

If:

1. $\langle f, g, E_m^+, Y\rangle$ defines a maximization problem, π, where

   a.) $D = E_m$,

      i.) $f: E_m \to E_1$

      ii.) $g = \langle g^{(1)}, g^{(2)}\rangle$, where

      $g^{(1)}: E_m \to E_q$

      $g^{(2)}: E_m \to E_r$, $(q+r=p)$,

   b.) f is concave on E_m,

   c.) Y is of the form $\{\theta_q\} \times E_r^+$

   d.) $g^{(1)}$ is affine, $g^{(1)}(x) = Gx + b$, and we assume w.l.o.g. that rank (G) = q,

   e.) $g^{(2)}$ is concave (i.e., E_r^+-concave) on E_m,

2. g satisfies:

   $\overline{CQ}_u$: for each i, $i = 1,\ldots,m$, $(\exists x^i > \theta_m)$: $x_i^i > 0$, $g^{(1)}(x^i) = \theta_q$, $g^{(2)}(x^i) \geq \theta_r$,

3. $\bar{x} \in X$ is a solution of π;

then

$$(\exists \bar{w} \in Y^*(= E_q \times E_r^+)): \Phi_\pi \text{ has a Saddle Point at } \langle \bar{x}, \bar{w}\rangle.$$

This statement is incorrect, the problem being a misprint in the Constraint Qualification, apparently. We can verify this as follows:

First of all, we note that $\overline{CQ}_u$ is equivalent to:

$$\overline{CQ}: (\exists x^\dagger >> \theta_m): g^{(1)}(x^\dagger) = \theta_q, \; g^{(2)}(x^\dagger) \geq \theta_r.$$

(To show that $\overline{CQ}_u \Rightarrow \overline{CQ}$, let

$$x^\dagger = \sum_{i=1}^m \lambda_i x^i, \text{ where } \lambda_i > 0 \text{ for } i = 1,\dots,m;$$

$$\text{and } \sum_{i=1}^m \lambda_i = 1)$$

The following then provides a counterexample (it was, of course, developed from the counterexample presented by Slater in [13]) to the above statement. Let

$$f(x) = x_1 + 2x_2$$

$$g(x) = \langle g^{(1)}(x), g^{(2)}(x)\rangle$$

$$= \langle x_1 + x_2 - 1, -(2x_1 + x_2 - 3/2)^2\rangle.$$

Let π be defined by $\langle f, g, E_2^+, \{0\} \times E_1^+\rangle$. We can readily verify that π satisfies hypothesis 1, and that $\bar{x} = \langle 1/2, 1/2\rangle$ satisfies $\overline{CQ}$ and is the solution of π. We can readily show, however, that if there existed a $\bar{w} \in E_1 \times E_1^+ \ni \Phi_\pi$ had a Saddle Point at $\langle \bar{x}, \bar{w}\rangle$, it would be necessary that

$$\bar{w}_2 \geq -\frac{x_1 - 1/2}{(x_1 - 1/2)^2} = \frac{1}{1/2 - x_1} \quad \text{for } x_1 \in [0, 1/2),$$

$$x_1 + x_2 = 1.$$

But this is impossible, since the expression on the right approaches $+\infty$ as $x_1 \to 1/2^-$. Hence $\nexists \bar{w} \in E_1 \times E_1^+ \ni \Phi_\pi$ has a Saddle Point at $\langle \bar{x}, \bar{w}\rangle$.

Professor Uzawa's Theorem 3 becomes correct if we substitute:

$$CQ_u: \text{ for each } i, \; i = 1,\dots,m(\exists x^i > \theta_m):$$

$$x_i^i > 0,\ g^{(1)}(x^i) = \theta,\ g^{(2)}(x^i) >> \theta_m;$$

which is apparently the constraint qualification which would have appeared in his Theorem 3 but for the misprint. Equivalently, we could use:

$$CQ_4^+: (\exists\, x^\dagger >> \theta_m);\ g^{(1)}(x^\dagger) = \theta,\ g^{(2)}(x^\dagger) >> \theta.$$

It should also be pointed out, however, that there is a misprint of some significance in Professor Uzawa's proof. The set B used in the proof should be defined by (in Prof. Uzawa's notation):

$$B = \{\langle z_o, z, y\rangle \mid z_o > f(\bar{x}),\ z^I = 0,\ z^{II} > 0,\ y \geqq 0\}.$$

3. The Existence of a GNSP When the Constraint Function Is Affine

This appendix was written after the completion of the text of this paper, as a result of a conversation with Professor Uzawa, in which he pointed out that I had been rather ambiguous in my treatment of the following sort of question. Suppose $\langle f, g, X, Y\rangle$ defines a maximization problem, π, where:

(1) $f: D \to E_n$, where $D \subseteq E_m$,

(2) $g: E_m \to E_p$,

(3) g is affine,

(4) f is concave (i.e., E_n^+-concave) on X;

(5) $X \subseteq D$ is convex;

and suppose that:

(6) $\bar{x} \in X$ is a solution of π.

Given that (1)-(5) hold, it follows from Theorem 2 of Section II that:

(7) $(\exists\langle\bar{v}, \bar{w}\rangle \in E_{n+p}^+)$: Φ_π has a GSP at $\langle\bar{x}, \bar{v}, \bar{w}\rangle$.

The question is, does Φ_π also have a GNSP at $\bar{x}$?

We saw in Section III that Theorem 5 of Section II actually states that, in this sort of situation, if we also have

(8) $\text{int}(X) \neq \emptyset$,

(9) g satisfies:

$$CQ_3:\ (\exists x^* \in \text{int}(X)): g(x^*) \in Y;$$

then Φ_π actually has a GNSP at $\langle\bar{x}, \bar{v}, \bar{w}\rangle$. Our question, then, amounts to asking: Will Φ_π have a GNSP at $\bar{x}$ even in the absence of (8) and (9)? or, alternatively, can we dispense with the constraint qualification in obtaining a GNSP at $\bar{x}$ if the constraint function, g, is affine? We have a partial answer to this question at our disposal:

1) If f is affine, then a GNSP exists at $\bar{x}$, for this is, in effect, a basic result in Linear Programming (Cf., Karlin [10], Theorem 5.3.1, p. 121).

2) If D is a proper subset of E_m, then Φ_π may fail to have a GNSP at $\bar{x}$ (see the example preceding Fig. 4 in Section III).

The portion of our question which remains unanswered is: Does a GNSP necessarily exist for Φ_π at $\bar{x}$ if f is defined and concave on all of E_m (i.e., if $D = E_m$, and f is concave, but not necessarily affine, on E_m)? Karlin's Theorem 7.1.2 (p. 203 of [10]) provides an affirmative answer to this question for the case where $n = 1$, $X = E_m^+$, $Y = E_p^+$. However, Professor Karlin's theorem is stated without proof; and while he presents an outline of the proof, the details of the argument outlined are perhaps not so easy to carry out. In any case, we can obtain a generalization of the Karlin result by a fairly straightforward application of Theorem 5; the trick here being that, in effect, the constraint qualification (9) is automatically satisfied if g is affine, $D = E_m$, and f is concave on D.

Theorem 7.

If:

1. $\langle f, g, X, Y\rangle$ defines a maximization problem, π, where:

   a. X is convex[30],

   b. $f: E_m \to E_n$, $g: E_m \to E_p$,

   c. f is concave on E_m,

   d. g is affine,

2. there exists an affine function, $g^{(2)}$, where $g^{(2)}: E_m \to E_q$, such that:

$$X = \{x \in E_m | g^{(2)}(x) \in E_q^+\},$$ [31]

3. $\bar{x} \in X$ is a solution for π;

then

$$(\exists\langle\bar{v}, \bar{w}\rangle \in E_{n+p}^+): \Phi_\pi \text{ has a GNSP at } \langle\bar{x}, \bar{v}, \bar{w}\rangle.$$

Proof:

Define

$$h(x) = \langle g(x),\ g^{(2)}(x)\rangle \text{ for } x \in E_m, \text{ and}$$

$$Z = Y \times E_q^+;$$

and consider the maximization problem, π^*, defined by $\langle f, h, E_m, Z\rangle$. Noting that

$$(\exists x^\dagger \in \text{int}(E_m)):\ h(x^\dagger) \in Z \quad (\text{let, \underline{e.g.}, } x^\dagger = \bar{x}),$$

and that h is affine, we easily verify the fact that π^* satisfies the hypotheses of theorem 5. Hence, it is clear that:

$$(1)\quad \begin{cases} (\exists \bar{v} \in E_n^+\setminus\{\theta_n\},\ \langle \bar{w}^1, \bar{w}^2\rangle \in Y^* \times E_q^+: \\ \quad \bar{v}\cdot f(x) + \bar{w}^1\cdot g(x) + \bar{w}^2\cdot g^{(2)}(x) \leqq \bar{v}\cdot f(\bar{x}) \\ \quad + \bar{w}^1\cdot g(\bar{x}) + \bar{w}^2\cdot g^{(2)}(\bar{x}) \\ \quad \leqq \bar{v}\cdot f(\bar{x}) + w^1\cdot g(\bar{x}) + w^2\cdot g^{(2)}(\bar{x}) \text{ for all } x\in E_m, \\ \qquad w^1 \in Y^*,\ w^2 \in E_q^+. \end{cases}$$

From the r. h. s. of (1), the fact that $g(\bar{x}) \in Y$, $\theta_p \in Y^*$, we have:

$$(2)\quad \begin{aligned} \bar{v}\cdot f(\bar{x}) + \bar{w}^2\cdot g^{(2)}(\bar{x}) &\leqq \bar{v}\cdot f(\bar{x}) + \bar{w}^1\cdot g(\bar{x}) + \bar{w}^2\cdot g^{(2)}(\bar{x}) \\ &\leqq \bar{v}\cdot f(\bar{x}) + w^2\cdot g^{(2)}(\bar{x}) \quad \text{for all } w^2 \in E_q^+. \end{aligned}$$

But then it follows from (2), the fact that $g^{(2)}(\bar{x}) \in E_q^+$ (since $\bar{x} \in X$), and the fact that $\theta_q \in E_q^+$, that:

$$(3)\quad \bar{w}^2\cdot g^{(2)}(\bar{x}) = 0.$$

Using (3), the fact that $\theta_q \in E_q^+$, and the r.h.s. of (1), we then obtain:

$$(4)\quad \bar{v}\cdot f(\bar{x}) + \bar{w}^1\cdot g(\bar{x}) \leqq \bar{v}\cdot f(\bar{x}) + w^1\cdot g(\bar{x}) \text{ for all } w^1 \in Y^*.$$

Now, from the l.h.s. of (1), (3), and hypothesis 2, we see that:

$$(5)\quad \bar{v}\cdot f(x) + \bar{w}^1\cdot g(x) \leqq \bar{v}\cdot f(\bar{x}) + \bar{w}^1\cdot g(\bar{x}) \text{ for all } x \in X.$$

Combining our results in (1), (4), and (5), we conclude that Φ_π has a GNSP at $\langle \bar{x}, \bar{v}, \bar{w}^1\rangle$. QED.

FOOTNOTES

1. This work was supported by a N.A.S.A. grant to the University of Missouri. The author would like to express his gratitude to NASA, the University of Missouri project director Prof. John C. Murdock, and the director of the School of Business and Public Administration Research Center of the University of Missouri, Prof. Robert W. Paterson, for this support. Many thanks are also due Professors John S. Chipman, Mohamed El-Hodiri, Melvin D. George, and Stanley R. Johnson; all of whom read at least one version of this paper and made many helpful comments and suggestions. Thanks are also due Professors Akira Takayama and Russell Thompson for their helpful comments. Any remaining errors or ambiguities are, of course, solely the responsibility of the author. The major portion of an earlier version of this paper was presented in Lawrence at the October 14, 1966, session of the Kansas-Missouri Seminars in Theoretical and Applied Economics.

2. If $g\colon D \to E_n$, where $D \subseteq E_m$ is convex, we say that g is CONCAVE on D if for all x^1, $x^2 \in D$, and for all scalars $\lambda \in [0, 1]$, we have

$$g(\lambda x^1 + (1 - \lambda)x^2] \geqq \lambda g(x^1) + (1 - \lambda)g(x^2).$$

A function, g, is CONVEX if -g is concave.

3. A line of development first explored by Slater [13].

4. Kuhn and Tucker, in [11], had begun this investigation with their consideration of the "vector maximum problem."

5. We use the following logical quantifier notation. If X is a set, the expression:

$(x \in X)$: x satisfies...,

is read: "for every x in X it is true that x satisfies...," while the expression:

$(\exists x \in X)$: x satisfies...,

is read: "there exists an x in X such that x satisfies..."

6. The terminology used here is not quite consistent with normal mathematical terminology, since the term "affine" is normally used for a mapping of a space into itself. "Affine" seems to be a better term than "linear," however, since "linear" is normally taken to mean (in the Euclidean case) that g is of the form $g(x) = Gx$.

7. Our notation here is an adaptation of that introduced by Hurwicz in [8]. Note that we're using π generically to denote maximization problems of the type defined in Definition 3. It should also be noted that our treatment here is somewhat asymmetric. If $Y \subseteq E_p$ is a convex cone, the ordering defined by $x \geq y$ iff $x-y \in Y$ is what is known as a vector ordering. Moreover, the ordering, $\geq$, of E_n which we've defined in the text, is a special case of a vector ordering. Hence in many ways a more natural approach would be to deal with maximization problems, π, defined (given the situation of Definition 3) by $<f, g, X, \geq_1, \geq_2$, where $\geq_1$ is a vector ordering of E_n and $\geq_2$ is a vector ordering of E_p. We would then say that $\bar{x}$ is a solution of π iff:

(1^1) $\bar{x} \in X$, $g(\bar{x}) \geq_2 \theta_p$,

and

(2^1) $\nexists \hat{x} \in X \ni g(\hat{x}) \geq_2 \theta_p$ and $f(\hat{x}) >_1 f(\bar{x})$.

This is the kind of approach taken by Prof. Hurwicz in [8] (a more symmetric approach is also followed by the present author in [12]). For the purposes of this paper, however, it seemed that the problem under discussion here was sufficiently simpler than this more symmetric treatment, and sufficiently general, to justify our Definition 3.

8. Recall, however, that we intend to treat only the case where the functions f and g are not necessarily differentiable.

9. A case of this sort which is familiar to Economists occurs when f is a vector of utility functions, and we are seeking a Pareto-optimal point.

10. Moreover, if $g^{(1)}$ is affine, h_i is concave for $i = q+1, \ldots, r$, and convex for $r+1, \ldots, p$; g will be Y-concave, so that the necessity results of Section II will apply. Note in particular Theorems 2 and 3.

11. As is apparently the case in the parenthetical remark on p. 780 of the valuable work by Arrow and Enthoven [2]. It may be that Professors Arrow and Enthoven did not mean to imply that a function defined and concave on a convex subset of E_m could be extended to a function defined and concave on all of E_m; but rather that, under these circumstances, it could be extended to a function defined and quasi-concave over the whole space. This latter statement also appears to be incorrect, however, as the following example shows. Let

f be defined on $E_1^+ \setminus \{0\}$ by:

$$f(x) = \log x.$$

Then f is defined and concave on $E_1^+ \setminus \{0\}$, which is a convex set, but it is clear that there is no way of extending f to a real-valued function defined and quasi-concave over the whole space. It should be emphasized, however, that the statement in question is in the nature of an aside, and in no way affects the text of the Arrow and Enthoven article.

12. An example of a function which is concave and continuous on E_1^+, has continuous derivatives of all orders on the interior of E_1^+, but which is nonetheless not extendible is provided by:

$$f(x) = {}^{+}\sqrt{x} \text{ for } x \geqq 0.$$

For a proof that this function is not extendible see Appendix (1).

13. This terminology is an adaptation of that introduced by Hurwicz in [8]. Note that if n = 1 (<u>i.e.</u>, if f: $D \to E_1$), we have

$$\Phi_\pi (x, 1, w) = f(x) + w \cdot g(x);$$

which is the usual form of the Lagrangian expression.

14. The types of saddle points introduced here are given somewhat different definitions by the author in [12]. The concepts developed there reduce to the definitions presented here, however, for the type of maximization problem with which we are concerned in this paper. Once again the notation is an adaptation of that introduced by Hurwicz in [8].

15. We denote the set-theoretic difference of A and B by $A \setminus B$, <u>i.e.</u>,

$$A \setminus B = \{a \in A \mid a \notin B\}.$$

16. The author is grateful to Dr. Mohamed El-Hodiri for bringing both the book and this particular theorem to his attention. The theorem stated by Berge is also implicit in Uzawa's proof of his Theorem 2 in [14].

17. The reader might argue, however, that in view of Theorem 1, the more basic question is whether a GPSP exists. We shall not examine this question in the present paper, but the author has essayed such an investigation in [12]. Note, however, that if π has a GNSP at $\langle \bar{x}, \bar{v}, \bar{w} \rangle$, and we define

$F(x) = \overline{v} \cdot f(x)$, and consider the maximization problem, π^1, defined by $\langle F, g, X, Y\rangle$, π^1 has a Saddle Point at $\langle \overline{x}, \overline{w}\rangle$. Therefore, by Theorem 1, $\overline{x}$ is a solution of π^1. This property is often useful in applications.

18. Lemma 4 is more or less a standard result of Functional Analysis, and in fact is usually proved for spaces of greater generality than those with which we are dealing here. The author has been unable, however, to locate a reference presenting the special case of Lemma 4 (which makes possible a more elementary proof than that usually provided in the texts on Functional Analysis). This is why a proof is included here.

19. Note that we can generalize this theorem by substituting

ii') $g^{(1)}$ is open and Y_1-concave on X, for hypothesis 1-d-ii of the text.

20. It is not quite a special case of Theorem 3, for the reader will note that the assumption

$$\text{int}(X) \neq \emptyset$$

is not included in the hypotheses of Theorem 4.

21. The reader will recognize this as a generalization of the constraint qualification introduced by Slater in [13]. It was first used in this general form by Hurwicz in [8].

22. There is an apparent misprint in the statement of the constraint qualification in Professor Uzawa's theorem. We shall discuss this result in Appendix (2).

23. Defining $g^{(3)} = -g^{(1)}$, and $Y = E_q^+ \times Y_2 \times E_q^+$ does not, of course, solve the problem either; since, defining $g = \langle g^{(1)}, g^{(2)}, g^{(3)}\rangle$, the existence of an $x^* \in X$ satisfying CQ_s would then involve a contradiction.

24. The reader will recall that, for the class of maximization problems with which we are dealing in this paper, the Slater CQ can be stated (Cf., n. 21):

$$CQ_s: \quad (\exists x^* \in X): \quad g(x^*) \in \text{int}(Y).$$

For the sub-class P, of maximization problems defined in the text, the Slater CQ becomes:

$$CQ_s^+: \quad (\exists x^* \in X): \quad g(x^*) > 0.$$

25. Notice that in this case the constraint $g(x) \varepsilon E_1^+$ is not effective in the sense that, if f and g are concave on X, $\bar{x}$ maximizes f subject to $x \varepsilon X$. We can show that this must be the case by supposing b.w.o.c. that $(\exists \hat{x} \varepsilon X): f(\hat{x}) > f(\bar{x})$. Define

$$\bar{\lambda} = \frac{-g(\hat{x})}{[g(\bar{x})-g(\hat{x})]}, \text{ and } \tilde{x} = \bar{\lambda}\bar{x} + (1 - \bar{\lambda})\hat{x}.$$

Then

$$0 < \bar{\lambda} < 1, \text{ so that } \tilde{x} \varepsilon X;$$

but

$$g(\tilde{x}) \geqq \bar{\lambda} g(\bar{x}) + (1 - \bar{\lambda}) g(\hat{x}) = 0, \text{ and}$$

$$f(\tilde{x}) \geqq \bar{\lambda} f(\bar{x}) + (1 - \bar{\lambda}) f(\hat{x}) > f(\bar{x}),$$

which contradicts the assumption that $\bar{x}$ is a solution of π. Alternatively, we can show the same result by the following reasoning. It follows by Theorem 2 that a GSP exists for π at $\bar{x}$; and therefore we have by the parenthetical remark in the text:

$$f(x) \leqq f(\bar{x}) \text{ for all } x \varepsilon X.$$

26. See, e.g., Karlin [10], Theorem 7.1.2, p. 203. Note, however, that the example in the text is not a counterexample to Professor Karlin's theorem, which requires (in the context of our example) f to be defined and concave over all of E_1. In fact, no constraint qualification is needed if the domain is the whole space (see Appendix 3).

27. Note, moreover, that all the hypotheses of Theorem 4 are satisfied except CQ_s. Hence this example also shows that Theorem 4 does not remain correct if the assumption that g is affine is substituted for CQ_s.

28. See p. 24 and n. 25, above.

29. See [12] for applications of these results to Activity Analysis.

30. Note that this assumption is actually superfluous, being implied by hypothesis 2.

31. For instance, if $X = E_m^+$, we can take $g^{(2)}(x) = I_m x$, where I_m denotes the m x m identity matrix.

REFERENCES

[1] Apostol, Tom M.: Mathematical Analysis. Reading, Mass., Addison-Wesley, 1957.

[2] Arrow, Kenneth J., and A. C. Enthoven: "Quasi-Concave Programming," Econometrica, 29, 4: October, 1961, pp. 779-800.

[3] Arrow, K. J., and Leonid Hurwicz: "Reduction of Constrained Maxima to Saddle-Point Problems," from: Neyman, Jerzy, ed. Proceedings of the Third Berkeley Symposium on Mathematical Statistics and Probability, Vol. V. Berkeley and Los Angeles: University of California Press, 1956.

[4] Arrow, K. J., L. Hurwicz and H. Uzawa: "Constraint Qualifications in Maximization Problems," Naval Research Logistics Quarterly, 8, 2: June, 1961, pp. 175-191.

[5] Arrow, K. J., L. Hurwicz and H. Uzawa, eds.: Studies in Linear and Non-Linear Programming. Stanford; Stanford University Press, 1958.

[6] Berge, Claude: Topological Spaces. New York: The Macmillan Co., 1963. (English translation of Espaces Topologiques, Fonctions Multivoques, Paris: Dunod, 1959. Translation by E. M. Patterson).

[7] Bliss, Gilbert A.: Lectures on the Calculus of Variations. Chicago: The University of Chicago Press, 1946.

[8] Hurwicz, Leonid: "Programming in Linear Spaces," Chapter 4, pp. 38-102, in [5], above.

[9] Hurwicz, L., and H. Uzawa: "A Note on the Lagrangian Saddle Points," Chapter 5, pp. 103-13, in [5], above.

[10] Karlin, Samuel: Mathematical Methods and Theory in Games, Programming and Economics, Vol. 1. Reading, Mass.: Addison-Wesley, 1959.

[11] Kuhn, H. W., and A. W. Tucker: "Non-Linear Programming" pp. 481-492 in: Neyman, Jerzy, ed.: Proceedings of the Second Berkeley Symposium on Mathematical Statistics and Probability. Berkeley and Los Angeles: University

of California Press, 1951.

[12] Moore, James C.: On the Theory and Economic Applications of a Generalized Saddle Point Concept. Ph.D. Dissertation (Economics), 1968. University of Minnesota.

[13] Slater, Morton: "LaGrange Multipliers Revisited," Cowles Commission Discussion Paper: Mathematics, 403, November 7, 1950.

[14] Uzawa, Hirofumi: "The Kuhn-Tucker Theorem in Concave Programming," Chapter 3, pp. 32-37, in [4], above.

MAXIMIZATION AND THE QUALITATIVE CALCULUS*

by

James Quirk and Richard Ruppert
University of Kansas

1. Introduction

Recently, Archibald [1] presented a theorem concerning the scope of comparative statics analysis based solely on the hypothesis that equilibrium positions of an economic model represent a regular constrained maximum of some criterion function such as utility or profit. His main result asserts that, in the absence of other information, the constrained maximization hypothesis leads to known comparative statics results if and only if the shift parameter enters only one equation of the system of equilibrium conditions.

This paper extends Archibald's findings by examining the class of cases in which qualitative information is assumed to be available for the entries in the matrix of second partial derivatives characterizing constrained and unconstrained maximum (or minimum) positions. In particular we derive necessary and sufficient conditions on the sign patterns of such matrices so that the sign pattern of the inverse matrix (or one of its columns) may be determined, and the application of these and related results to comparative statics problems is shown. The main results for the unconstrained maximization problem reemphasize the central role played by "Morishima" matrices in qualitative analysis, a role that has been the subject of several recent studies [2, 3, 6]. The results for the constrained case indicate that qualitative information extends the scope of comparative statics analysis beyond that obtained by Archibald only under extremely restrictive conditions.

2. Preliminary formulation of the problems

Consider first the case of unconstrained maximization. Let $f(x_1, x_2, \ldots, x_n, \alpha)$ be a real valued function with continuous second partial derivatives. α is a shift parameter.

Let $f_i = \frac{\partial f}{\partial x_i}$, $f_{ij} = \frac{\partial^2 f}{\partial x_i \partial x_j}$, for $i,j=1,\ldots,n$.

Then f attains a regular maximum at a point $\bar{x} = (\bar{x}_1, \ldots, \bar{x}_n)$, given that $\alpha = \bar{\alpha}$, if and only if

$$f_i = 0, \quad i=1,\ldots,n \text{ and}$$

$$\sum_{i=1}^{n} \sum_{j=1}^{n} f_{ij}\, h_i\, h_j < 0 \text{ for any } h = (h_1,\ldots,h_n)\ h \neq 0, \text{ i.e.}$$

the n x n matrix $[f_{ij}]$ is negative definite (all derivatives evaluated at the point $(\overline{x}, \overline{\alpha})$).

Assume that a change occurs in α. The resulting changes in the maximizing values of the x_i variables are obtained by solving the system $A \frac{d\overline{x}}{d\alpha} = -b$, where $A = [f_{ij}]$, $\frac{d\overline{x}}{d\alpha} = \left[\frac{d\overline{x}_i}{d\alpha}\right]$, and $b = [f_{i\alpha}]$, $\left(f_{i\alpha} = \frac{\partial^2 f}{\partial x_i \partial \alpha}\right)$, $i,j=1,\ldots,n$. The question of interest for comparative statics analysis can now be raised. Given that A is a negative definite matrix and that the sign patterns (+,-,0) of A and b are known,

(I.1) For which sign patterns of A is A^{-1} of known sign pattern independent of the values of the entries in A?

(I.2) For which sign patterns of A and b can the sign pattern of $\frac{d\overline{x}}{d\alpha}$ be known independent of the values of the entries in A and b?

The constrained maximization case is similar. Let $f(x_1,\ldots,x_n, \alpha)$ and $g(x_1,\ldots,x_n, \alpha)$ be real valued functions with continuous second partial derivatives. In the problem of maximizing f subject to g=0, let $L = f + \lambda g$ be the Lagrange expression, with λ the Lagrange multiplier. Let $L_i = \frac{\partial L}{\partial x_i}$, $L_{ij} = \frac{\partial^2 L}{\partial x_i \partial x_j}$, with corresponding notation for the partials of f and g. Then f attains a regular constrained maximum subject to g=0 at $\overline{x} = (\overline{x}_1,\ldots,\overline{x}_n)$ given that $\alpha = \overline{\alpha}$ if and only if

$$L_i = 0 \quad , i=1,\ldots,n.$$

$$L_\lambda = 0 \quad , \text{ and}$$

$$\sum_{i=1}^{n} \sum_{j=1}^{n} L_{ij} h_i h_j < 0$$

for any $h = (h_1,\ldots,h_n)$ $h \neq 0$, such that $\sum_{i=1}^{n} g_i h_i = 0$, i.e., the $(n + 1) \times (n + 1)$ matrix $\left[\begin{array}{c|c} L_{ij} & g_i \\ \hline g_j & 0 \end{array}\right]$ is negative definite under constraint, (all derivatives evaluated at $(\overline{x}, \overline{\alpha})$.

The changes in the equilibrium values of the x_i variables and λ resulting from a change in the shift parameter α are obtained by solving the system

$$A^*y^* = -b^*, \text{ where}$$

$$A^* = \begin{bmatrix} L_{ij} & g_i \\ g_j & 0 \end{bmatrix}, \quad y^* = \begin{bmatrix} \frac{d\bar{x}_i}{d\alpha} \\ \frac{d\lambda}{d\alpha} \end{bmatrix}, \quad b^* = \begin{bmatrix} L_{i\alpha} \\ L_{\lambda\alpha} \end{bmatrix}$$

$\left(L_{i\alpha} = \frac{\partial^2 L}{\partial x_i \partial\alpha}, \; L_{\lambda\alpha} = \frac{\partial^2 L}{\partial\lambda\partial\alpha}\right)$, $i,j=1,\ldots,n$. As in the unconstrained case, there are two questions of interest. Given that A^* is negative definite under constraint and that the sign patterns (+,-,0) of A^* and b^* are known,

(II.1) For which sign patterns of A^* is A^{*-1} of known sign pattern independent of the values of the entries in A^*?

(II.2) For which sign patterns of A^* and b^* can the sign pattern of y^* be known independent of the values of the entries in A^* and b^*?

3. Preliminary results, notation, and reformulation of the problems

The assumption that the relevant functions have continuous second partial derivatives implies that the matrices A and A^* are symmetric. It may further be noted that the existence of inverse matrices A^{-1} and A^{*-1} is not an issue under the assumptions stated. In fact, the following propositions hold (see [9]):

Proposition 1. If A is a symmetric negative definite matrix, then A^{-1} is a symmetric negative definite matrix.

Proposition 2. If $A^* = \begin{bmatrix} L_{ij} & g_i \\ g_j & 0 \end{bmatrix}$, $i,j=1,\ldots,n$, is a symmetric matrix negative definite under constraint, then A^{*-1} is symmetric and in $A^{*-1} = \begin{bmatrix} \hat{L}_{ij} & \hat{g}_i \\ \hat{g}_j & d \end{bmatrix}$, the n x n submatrix $[\hat{L}_{ij}]$ is negative semi-definite of rank n-1.

Proposition 3. If A is a symmetric negative definite matrix, then every i^{th} order principal minor of A has sign

$(-1)^i$, $i=1,\ldots,n$.

<u>Proposition 4</u>. If $A^* = \left[\begin{array}{c|c} L_{ij} & g_i \\ \hline g_j & 0 \end{array}\right]$ is a symmetric matrix negative definite under constraint, then

$$\left|\begin{array}{cccc|c} L_{11} & L_{12} & \cdots & L_{1r} & g_1 \\ L_{21} & L_{22} & \cdots & L_{2r} & g_2 \\ \vdots & & & \vdots & \vdots \\ L_{r1} & L_{r2} & \cdots & L_{rr} & g_r \\ \hline g_1 & g_2 & \cdots & g_r & 0 \end{array}\right| \text{ has sign } (-1)^r \text{ for } r=2,\ldots,n.$$

The terminology and notation used in what follows is borrowed from [3]:

Given a real n x n matrix $A = (a_{ij})$, define sgn A = (sgn a_{ij}) where sgn $a_{ij} = +1$ if $a_{ij} > 0$, sgn $a_{ij} = -1$ if $a_{ij} < 0$ and sgn $a_{ij} = 0$ if $a_{ij} = 0$. Let $Q_A = \{C|\text{sgn } C = \text{sgn } A\}$. Then Q_A is an equivalence class of matrices each of which has the same sign pattern as A. Q_A will be referred to as a <u>qualitative matrix</u>. The subset (perhaps empty) of matrices in Q_A that are symmetric negative definite will be denoted N_A, i.e., $N_A = \{C|C \in Q_A$ and C is symmetric negative definite$\}$. Similarly, the subset of matrices in Q_A that are symmetric and negative definite under constraint will be denoted by N_A^*, i.e., $N_A^* = \{C|C \in Q_A$ and C is symmetric and negative definite under constraint$\}$. Finally, given an n-dimensional real vector $x = (x_1,\ldots,x_n)$, define sgn x = (sgn $x_1,\ldots,$sgn x_n). Let $Q_x = \{y|\text{sgn } y = \text{sgn } x\}$; Q_x is said to be a <u>qualitative vector</u>.

In terms of this notation, questions (I.1), (I.2), (II.1), (II.2) may be restated as follows:

(I.1) determine Q_A such that A has <u>signed inverse under the maximization hypothesis</u>, i.e., $B, C \in N_A \Rightarrow B^{-1} \in Q_{C^{-1}}$;

(I.2) determine Q_A, Q_b such that $Ax = -b$ is <u>sign solvable under the maximization hypothesis</u>, i.e., $By = -c$, $Cz = -d$, $B,C \in N_A$, $c,d \in Q_b \Rightarrow z \in Q_y$.

(II.1) determine Q_A such that A has signed inverse under the constrained maximization hypothesis, i.e., $B,C \in N_A^* \Rightarrow B^{-1} \in Q_{C^{-1}}$;

(II.2) determine Q_A, Q_b such that $Ax = -b$ is sign solvable under the constrained maximization hypothesis, i.e., $By = -c$, $Cz = -d$, $B,C \in N_A^*$, $c,d \in Q_b \Rightarrow z \in Q_y$.

4. Qualitative Calculus and Unconstrained Maximization

We first consider questions (I.1) and (I.2) dealing with the qualitative analysis of unconstrained maximum positions. By Propositions 1 and 3, if A is symmetric and negative definite, then sgn $|A| = (-1)^n$ and in A and A^{-1} all diagonal elements are negative, hence the problem of "signing" A^{-1} under the maximization hypothesis reduces to that of finding conditions on A for which the off diagonal cofactors of A are signed. In the arguments concerned with this, we will use the notion of a dominant diagonal matrix, defined as follows:

Let $A = (a_{ij})$ be an n x n real matrix. Then A is said to be a dominant diagonal matrix if

$$|a_{ii}| > \sum_{j \neq i} |a_{ij}| \qquad i=1,\ldots,n$$

or

$$|a_{ii}| > \sum_{j \neq i} |a_{ji}| \qquad i=1,\ldots,n.$$

Proposition 5. Let $A = (a_{ij})$ be a n x n real symmetric dominant diagonal matrix with all diagonal elements negative. Then A is a negative definite matrix. Proof: McKenzie [7] has shown that any dominant diagonal matrix with all diagonal elements negative is a stable matrix (has real parts of all characteristic roots negative). A symmetric implies all characteristic roots of A are real, hence under the assumptions of the proposition, all characteristic roots of A are negative, which in the symmetric case implies A is negative definite.

The argument used in connection with finding conditions on A for which the off diagonal elements of A^{-1} are signed under the maximization hypothesis is essentially that used in [3]. The argument may be illustrated for the case n = 3:[1] the cofactor A_{31} of the element a_{31} of A is given in this case by $a_{12}a_{23} - a_{22}a_{13}$ where $a_{ii} < 0$, i=1,2,3, and $a_{ij} = a_{ji}$ for all i,j. We will show that if $a_{12} \neq 0$, $a_{23} \neq 0$, $a_{13} \neq 0$ and if sgn $a_{12}a_{23} \neq$ sgn a_{13}, then A does not have a signed inverse under the maximization hypothesis. Let $C \in Q_A$ be chosen so that $|c_{12}| = |c_{23}| = 1$, and $|c_{13}| = \varepsilon$, where $\varepsilon < 1/3$. Choose C symmetric so that $|c_{21}| = |c_{32}| = 1$ and $|c_{31}| = \varepsilon$ as well, and in addition choose $c_{11} = c_{22} = c_{33} = -3$. Then C satisfies the hypothesis of Proposition 5 and thus $C \varepsilon N_A$ with sgn C_{31} = sgn $a_{12}a_{23}$. Similarly, let $B \varepsilon Q_A$ be chosen so that $|b_{12}| = |b_{23}| = \delta$, $|b_{13}| = 1$, where $\delta < 1$. B symmetric implies $|b_{21}| = |b_{32}| = \delta$, $|b_{31}| = 1$. Let $b_{11} = b_{22} = b_{33} = -2$. Then B satisfies the hypothesis of Proposition 5 and thus $B \varepsilon N_A$ with sgn B_{31} = sgn $a_{13} \neq$ sgn C_{31}. Hence $B, C \varepsilon N_A$ but $B^{-1} \notin Q_{C^{-1}}$ so that the inverse of A is not signed under the maximization hypothesis.

$$C = \begin{bmatrix} -3 & \underline{+}1 & \underline{+}\varepsilon \\ \underline{+}1 & -3 & \underline{+}1 \\ \underline{+}\varepsilon & \underline{+}1 & -3 \end{bmatrix} \qquad B = \begin{bmatrix} -2 & \underline{+}\delta & \underline{+}1 \\ \underline{+}\delta & -2 & \underline{+}\delta \\ \underline{+}1 & \underline{+}\delta & -2 \end{bmatrix}$$

$$\text{sgn } c_{12}c_{23} \neq \text{sgn } c_{13} \qquad \text{sgn } b_{12}b_{23} \neq \text{sgn } b_{13}$$

The generalization of this argument to the case where n is arbitrary utilizes the notion of <u>cycles</u> in a matrix:

Let $A = (a_{ij})$ be a matrix. A <u>cycle</u> in A (of length r) is a product of the form $a_{i_1 i_2} a_{i_2 i_3} \cdots a_{i_{r-1} i_r} a_{i_r i_1}$, $i_1, \ldots, i_r$ distinct integers. See [5] for a discussion of the role of cycles in matrix analysis.

<u>Lemma 1</u>. Let $A = (a_{ij})$ be an n x n real matrix with $a_{ii} < 0$ for all i and sgn a_{ij} = sgn a_{ji} for all i,j. Then A has signed inverse under the maximization hypothesis only if every non-zero cycle in A is positive.

(Proofs of this and succeeding lemmas appear in the appendix to this paper).

Maybee [5] was the first to note that an indecomposable matrix with non-negative diagonal elements has all of its cycles non-negative if and only if the matrix is a <u>Morishima matrix</u>, defined as follows:

An n x n real matrix M is a Morishima matrix if by simultaneous row and column interchanges, M can be brought into the form

$$M = \left[\begin{array}{c|c} M_{11} & M_{12} \\ \hline M_{21} & M_{22} \end{array}\right]$$

where M_{11} and M_{22} are square blocks and $M_{11} \geqq 0$, $M_{22} \geqq 0$, $M_{12} \leqq 0$, $M_{21} \leqq 0$. Morishima [8] studied this class of matrices in the case where all entries in M are non-zero and proved a generalized Frobenius theorem concerning the class. This result in turn was generalized to the indecomposable case by Debreu and Herstein [4]. We note several of the propositions that hold for Morishima matrices:

Proposition 6 [4]. Let $M = (m_{ij})$ be a real $n \times n$ indecomposable Morishima matrix. Then there exists a maximal characteristic root λ^* of M with the properties that

(i) λ^* is real, simple and positive

(ii) $\lambda^* \geq |\lambda|$ for every characteristic root λ of M

(iii) $\lambda^* > m_{ii}$ for every $i=1,\ldots,n$

Proposition 7 [4]. Let $A = (a_{ij})$ be a real $n \times n$ matrix such that $A = M - aI$ where M is an indecomposable Morishima matrix and a is a real number. Then A is a stable matrix (every characteristic root of A has negative real part) if and only if $a > \lambda^*$, where λ^* is the maximal characteristic root of M. Further, when $a > \lambda^*$, A^{-1} exists and has all elements non-zero, with sign pattern given by: $\begin{bmatrix} A^{-1}_{11} & A^{-1}_{12} \\ A^{-1}_{21} & A^{-1}_{22} \end{bmatrix}$

the partition corresponding to that of M, with $A^{-1}_{11} < 0$, $A^{-1}_{22} < 0$, $A^{-1}_{12} > 0$, $A^{-1}_{21} > 0$.

Proposition 8 [5]. Let $M = (m_{ij})$ be a real $n \times n$ indecomposable matrix, with $m_{ii} \geq 0$ $i=1,\ldots,n$. Then M has all cycles non-negative if and only if M is a Morishima matrix.

We can now identify the class of qualitative matrices for which the inverse matrix is signed under the maximization hypothesis. Remark: N_A is non-empty if and only if (1) $a_{ii} < 0$ $i=1,\ldots,n$; (2) $\operatorname{sgn} a_{ij} = \operatorname{sgn} a_{ji}$ for all $i,j=1,\ldots,n$.

Theorem 1. Assume N_A is non-empty. Then A has signed inverse under the maximization hypothesis ($B, C \in N_A \Rightarrow B^{-1} \in Q_{C^{-1}}$) if and only if

$$A = \begin{bmatrix} A_1 & & & & 0 \\ & A_2 & & & \\ & & \cdot & & \\ & & & \cdot & \\ 0 & & & & A_r \end{bmatrix}$$

where (1) $a_{ii} < 0$ $i=1,\ldots,n$; (2) $\operatorname{sgn} a_{ij} = \operatorname{sgn} a_{ji}$ for all $i,j=1,\ldots,n$; (3) $A_k = M_k - \alpha_k I$

for $k=1,\ldots,r$, where M_k is an indecomposable Morishima matrix and α_k is larger than every diagonal element in M_k.

Proof: Sufficiency is a straightforward application of Proposition 7. If A satisfies the conditions of the theorem, and $B,C \in N_A$, then B^{-1} and C^{-1} have the form

$$B^{-1} = \begin{bmatrix} B_1^{-1} & & & 0 \\ & B_2^{-1} & & \\ & & \ddots & \\ 0 & & & B_r^{-1} \end{bmatrix} \quad C^{-1} = \begin{bmatrix} C_1^{-1} & & & 0 \\ & C_2^{-1} & & \\ & & \ddots & \\ 0 & & & C_r^{-1} \end{bmatrix}$$

the diagonal blocks having the sign patterns given in Proposition 7. Thus $B^{-1} \in Q_{C^{-1}}$.

To establish necessity, we first note that by the remark, N_A non-empty implies conditions (1) and (2). Consider any indecomposable diagonal block A_k of A of dimension $m_k \times m_k$. By lemma 1, $B,C \in N_{A_k} \Rightarrow B^{-1} \in Q_{C^{-1}}$ only if every non-zero cycle of length two or greater in A_k is positive, hence by Proposition 8, $A_k = M_k - \alpha_k I$ where M_k is Morishima with α_k larger than every diagonal element in M_k.

Theorem 1 provides the answer to question (I.1): A has a signed inverse under the maximization hypothesis if and only if A may be written in the form of a "completely decomposable" matrix symmetric in signs with diagonal blocks having all diagonal elements negative and otherwise obeying the Morishima conditions.

Lemma 2 underlies the answer to question (I.2).

Lemma 2. Let $A = (a_{ij})$ be an $n \times n$ indecomposable matrix with $a_{ii} < 0$ $i=1,\ldots,n$, $\operatorname{sgn} a_{ij} = \operatorname{sgn} a_{ji}$, $i,j=1,\ldots,n$. If there exists a negative cycle of A of length r $(3 \leq r \leq n)$, then no column of A^{-1} is signed under the maximization hypothesis.

Theorem 2. Assume A is an $n \times n$ real indecomposable matrix satisfying $a_{ii} < 0$ $i=1,\ldots,n$ and $\operatorname{sgn} a_{ij} = \operatorname{sgn} a_{ji}$ $i,j=1,\ldots,n$. Let A_{ij} be the cofactor of a_{ij} in A. Then $B,C \in N_A$ implies $\operatorname{sgn} B_{ij} = \operatorname{sgn} C_{ij}$ for some i and for every $j=1,\ldots,n$ (a column of A^{-1} is signed) if and only if $A = M - aI$ where M is a Morishima matrix and $a > m_{ii}$ $i=1,\ldots,n$.

Corollary: In the comparative statics system $Ay = -b$,

where A is an $n \times n$ real indecomposable matrix, $B, C \in N_A$, $c, d \in Q_b$, $Bz = -c$, $Cw = -d$ implies $z \in Q_w$ if and only if $A = M - aI$ where M is a Morishima matrix and $a > m_{ii}$ $i=1, \ldots, n$, and if M is permuted to the form $M = \begin{bmatrix} M_{11} & M_{12} \\ M_{21} & M_{22} \end{bmatrix}$ where

$M_{11} \geq 0$, $M_{22} \geq 0$, $M_{12} \leq 0$, $M_{21} \leq 0$, the vector b is permuted

to the form $b = \begin{bmatrix} b^1 \\ b^2 \end{bmatrix}$, the partitioning corresponding to that

of M, with every element in b^1 weakly of the same sign and every element in b^2 weakly of the same sign, opposite to that of the elements in b^1.[2]

4. Applications.

Consider the traditional comparative statics problem involving the analysis of the operations of a single product profit maximizing competitive firm. Let y denote the number of units of output, p the price per unit of output, x_i the number of units of the ith input hired, and w_i the price per unit of the ith input. We assume the existence of a strictly concave production function $y = f(x_1, \ldots, x_n)$. Then the firm chooses amounts of each input to maximize

$$\pi = py - \sum_{i=1}^{n} w_i x_i .$$

The equilibrium conditions characterizing a regular maximum of profits are given by

$$(1) \quad \frac{\partial \pi}{\partial x_i} = pf_i - w_i = 0 \qquad i=1, \ldots, n$$

$$(2) \quad [pf_{ij}] \text{ is a symmetric negative definite matrix,}$$

where $f_i = \dfrac{\partial f}{\partial x_i}$, $f_{ij} = \dfrac{\partial^2 f}{\partial x_i \partial x_j}$ $\qquad i,j=1, \ldots, n.$

Differentiating (1) totally with respect to $p, w_1, \ldots, w_n$, we obtain

$$(3) \quad [pf_{ij}] \begin{bmatrix} dx_1 \\ \vdots \\ dx_n \end{bmatrix} = \begin{bmatrix} dw_1 - f_1\, dp \\ \vdots \\ dw_n - f_n\, dp \end{bmatrix}$$

Assume now that the signs (+,-,0) of the entries in $[pf_{ij}]$ are specified. For which such sign patterns is it possible to solve for the signs of all $\frac{dx_i}{dp}$ ($dw_i = 0$ for $i=1,\ldots,n$), and for the signs of all $\frac{dx_i}{dw_j}$ ($dp = 0$ and $dw_k = 0$ for $k \neq j$)? Because of the complications noted above, we will restrict ourselves to the case in which $[pf_{ij}]$ is indecomposable. From Theorems 1 and 2 of the previous section, we have the following results:

(1) Only in the case in which $f_{ij} \geq 0$ for all $i \neq j$ is it possible to solve for the signs of all $\frac{dx_i}{dp}$, since it is only in this case that the entire inverse matrix is signed, with all elements in the inverse of the same sign. Because $f_i > 0$ for $i=1,\ldots,n$, every term in the inverse must be weakly of the same sign if complete comparative statics information is to be present. Given these "gross substitute" assumptions, an increase in the price of the product will lead to an increase in the quantity demanded of <u>every</u> input, i.e., $\frac{dx_i}{dp} > 0$ for $i=1,\ldots,n$.

(2) When $dp = 0$ and $dw_k = 0$ for $k \neq j$, complete comparative statics information is available concerning $\frac{dx_i}{dw_j}$ ($i=1,\ldots,n$) only in the case in which $[f_{ij}]$ satisfies the Morishima conditions, i.e.,

$$[f_{ij}] = M - \alpha I \text{ where } M = \left[\begin{array}{c|c} M_{11} & M_{12} \\ \hline M_{21} & M_{22} \end{array}\right], \quad M_{11} \geq 0,\ M_{22} \geq 0,$$

$M_{12} \leq 0$, $M_{21} \leq 0$.

Then an increase in w_j leads to a decrease in the quantity demanded of input i if row i appears in M_{11} or M_{22} ($f_{ij} \geq 0$ $i \neq j$) and to an increase in the quantity demanded of input i if row i appears in M_{12} or M_{21} ($f_{ij} \leq 0$ $i \neq j$). An increase in w_j always leads to a decrease in the quantity demanded of input j, of course.

These rather restrictive results indicate again the limitations to the use of qualitative information in obtaining definite comparative statics conclusions even when the powerful assumption of regular maximization is introduced. Because of the importance of the Morishima conditions in obtaining definite qualitative conclusions in comparative statics analysis, it would be of some interest to determine the class of production functions that satisfy the Morishima conditions. While no such specification has been attempted, we might note that the most widely used functions in empirical and theoretical work, the Cobb-Douglas function and its generalized form, the CES function, both satisfy the Morishima conditions- in fact, both exhibit the "gross substitute" properties.

5. Constrained Maximization

In this section we provide an answer to questions (II.1) and (II.2), covering the case where in $A^* = \begin{bmatrix} A & c \\ c' & 0 \end{bmatrix}$, it is assumed that all diagonal entries in A are negative. The general case in which the diagonal entries in A have arbitrary signs is however covered by the analysis (see section 6 below). In the proofs that follow, we utilize the fact that if A is a negative definite symmetric matrix, then if $A^* = \begin{bmatrix} A & c \\ c' & 0 \end{bmatrix}$, A^* is a matrix negative definite under constraint. This follows, e.g., from the proposition that if f is a strictly concave function, then f is strictly quasi-concave, i.e., $\sum_{i=1}^{n} \sum_{j=1}^{n} f_{ij}h_ih_j < 0$ for every $h = (h_1, \ldots, h_n)$, $h \neq 0$ implies $\sum_{i=1}^{n} \sum_{j=1}^{n} f_{ij}h_ih_j < 0$ subject to $\sum_{i=1}^{n} c_ih_i = 0$, $h \neq 0$.

The class of matrices with signed inverse under the constrained maximization hypothesis is severely restricted, as the lemma and theorem below indicate:

<u>Lemma 3</u>. Let $A^* = \begin{bmatrix} A & c \\ c' & 0 \end{bmatrix}$ where A is an n x n matrix, c is an n x 1 column vector, and c' is the transpose of c. Assume $c_i \neq 0$ for $i=1,\ldots,n$ and $a_{ii} < 0$ for $i=1,\ldots,n$, $\text{sgn } a_{ij} = \text{sgn } a_{ji}$, $i,j=1,\ldots,n$. Then A^* has a signed inverse under the constrained maximization hypothesis only if $a_{ij} = 0$, for $i \neq j$, $i,j=1,\ldots,n$.

<u>Theorem 3</u>. Let $A^* = \begin{bmatrix} A & c \\ c' & 0 \end{bmatrix}$ where A is an n x n matrix and c is an n x 1 column vector, and c' is the transpose of c. Assume $c_i \neq 0$ $i=1,\ldots,n$, $a_{ii} < 0$, $i=1,\ldots,n$. Then A^* has signed

inverse under the constrained maximization hypothesis if and only if $a_{ij} = 0$ for $i \neq j$, $i,j=1,\ldots,n$.

Proof: Necessity follows from lemma 3. Further, if A is a negative diagonal matrix, it is easy to verify that every cofactor in A* has every term in its expansion of the same sign, hence every element in A^{*-1} will be non-zero and of known sign under the constrained maximization hypothesis.

In particular, we might note that if c is a strictly positive vector and A is a diagonal matrix with all diagonal elements negative, then $B^* \in N^*_{A^*}$ implies B^{*-1} has sign pattern

$$\begin{bmatrix} - & + & \ldots & + \\ + & - & + \ldots & + \\ \cdot & + & - & \cdot \\ & & \cdot & \\ & & \ddots & \\ \cdot & & - & \cdot \\ + & \ldots & \ldots & + \end{bmatrix}$$

We consider next the problem of signing a column of A^{*-1}. As the argument of Lemma 3 (given in the appendix) indicates, if there are non-zero off diagonal elements in A (all diagonal elements in A being negative), then the n+1 st column of A^{*-1} is not signed since $|A|$ is of unknown sign. Consider, however, a matrix negative definite under constraint with sign pattern $\begin{bmatrix} - & + & + \\ + & - & + \\ + & + & 0 \end{bmatrix}$. By simple computations, it may be verified that the inverse has sign pattern $\begin{bmatrix} - & + & + \\ + & - & + \\ + & + & ? \end{bmatrix}$, hence columns #1 and #2 of the inverse matrix are signed and complete comparative statics information is available if the shift parameter enters only equation #1 or equation #2 of the comparative statics system. In what follows, we restrict our attention to the case $n > 2$.

<u>Lemma 4</u>. Let $A^* = \left[\begin{array}{c|c} A & c \\ \hline c' & 0 \end{array}\right]$ where A is an n x n matrix ($n > 2$) c is an n x 1 column vector, c' is the transpose of c, $c_i \neq 0$, $i=1,\ldots,n$, $a_{ii} < 0$, $i=1,\ldots,n$, sgn a_{ij} = sgn a_{ji} for all $i,j=1,\ldots,n$. Then $a_{ij} \neq 0$ for any $i \neq j$ implies that every column of A^{*-1} has an unsigned element under the constrained maximization hypothesis.

This leads into the following result:

<u>Theorem 4</u>. Let $A^* = \left[\begin{array}{c|c} A & c \\ \hline c' & 0 \end{array}\right]$ where A is an n x n matrix ($n > 2$), c is an n x 1 column vector and c' a 1 x n row vector

$c_i \neq 0$, $i=1,\ldots,n$, $a_{ii} < 0$, $i=1,\ldots,n$ and sgn a_{ij} = sgn a_{ji} $i,j=1,\ldots,n$. Then A^{*-1} has a column of known sign pattern under the constrained maximization hypothesis if and only if A^{*-1} is signed, i.e., $a_{ij} = 0$ for $i \neq j$, $i,j=1,\ldots,n$.

6. Applications: constrained maximization

That the inverse can be signed for only an extremely limited class of sign patterns in the case of constrained maximization can be explained at least partially by the fact that most of the properties of the inverse matrix are preserved under monotonic increasing transformations of the function being maximized under constraint.

Let $f(x_1,\ldots,x_n)$ be maximized subject to $\sum g_i x_i = c$. At a regular constrained maximum,

$$f_i + \lambda g_i = 0 \qquad i=1,\ldots,n$$

$$\sum g_i x_i = c, \text{ and}$$

$$A^* = \left[\begin{array}{c|c} f_{ij} & g_i \\ \hline g_j & 0 \end{array}\right] \qquad \text{is a matrix negative definite}$$

under constraint. If f is subjected to a monotonic transformation, $u = T(f)$ where $T' > 0$, the corresponding conditions for a constrained maximum of u subject to $\sum g_i x_i = c$ are

$$T' f_i + \mu g_i = 0 \qquad \text{where } \mu = T'\lambda$$

$$\sum g_i x_i = c, \text{ and}$$

$$C^* = \left[\begin{array}{c|c} T' f_{ij} + T'' f_i f_j & g_i \\ \hline g_j & 0 \end{array}\right] \qquad \text{is a matrix}$$

negative definite under constraint.

While A^* negative definite under constraint implies C^* is negative definite under constraint [10, p. 397] we wish to examine the relationship between A^{*-1} and C^{*-1}. Let

$$B^* = \left[\begin{array}{c|c} T'' f_i f_j & 0 \\ \hline 0 & 0 \end{array}\right], \quad D^* = \left[\begin{array}{c|c} T' f_{ij} & g_i \\ \hline g_j & 0 \end{array}\right],$$

so that $C^* = B^* + D^*$. $|C^*|$ may be calculated by computing the sum of all determinants that can be formed by using any r rows from B^* and the complementary n+1-r rows from D^*, where r=0, 1,...,n+1. Clearly all such determinants involving the n+1st row of B* are zero. The remaining determinants have their $n+1^{st}$ row taken from D*. Suppose the ith row is taken from B*. Then the ith row consists of entries $T'' f_i f_1$, $T'' f_i f_2$, $\ldots, T'' f_i f_j, \ldots, T'' f_i f_n$, 0, while the $n+1^{st}$ row consists of the entries $g_1, g_2, \ldots, g_n$, 0. From the first order conditions, $f_j = -\lambda\, g_j$ $(j=1,\ldots,n)$, it is seen that the ith row is a multiple of the $n+1^{st}$ row, so the "mixed" determinants are all zero. Thus $|C^*| = |D^*| = (T')^{n-1}\, |A^*|$.

Consider next any cofactor C^*_{ij} $(i,j=1,\ldots,n)$ of the element c_{ij} in C*. By the argument used above, $C^*_{ij} = D^*_{ij} = (T')^{n-2}\, A^*_{ij}$, $(i,j=1,\ldots,n)$. Similarly, $C^*_{n+1,j} = D^*_{n+1,j} = (T')^{n-1}\, A^*_{n+1,j}$ $(j=1,\ldots,n)$, while $C^*_{n+1,n+1}$ is a bit more complicated. Let $B = [T''\, f_i f_j]$ and $D = [T'\, f_{ij}]$, so that $C^*_{n+1,n+1} = |T'\, f_{ij} + T''\, f_i f_j| = |B + D|$ which may be evaluated by the determinant of sum procedure followed above. Since the ith row of B is f_i/f_j times the jth row, the only non-zero determinants are $|D| = D^*_{n+1,n+1}$ and those involving one row from B. Thus $C^*_{n+1,n+1} = D^*_{n+1,n+1} + \sum_{j=1}^{n} T''\, f_j (T')^{n-1} \Big(\sum_{\substack{i=1\\ i\neq j}}^{n} f_i\, (A^*_{n+1,n+1})i,j\Big)$, where $(A^*_{n+1,n+1})i,j$ is the cofactor of f_{ij} in the cofactor $A^*_{n+1,n+1}$. Since $f_j = -\lambda g_j$, by the first order conditions,

$$C^*_{n+1,n+1} = D^*_{n+1,n+1} + T''(T')^{n-1}\lambda^2 \sum_{j=1}^{n} g_j \Big(\sum_{\substack{i=1\\ i\neq j}}^{n} g_i (A^*_{n+1,j})i,n+1\Big)$$

$$= D^*_{n+1,n+1} + T''(T')^{n-1}\lambda^2 \sum_{j=1}^{n} g_j A^*_{n+1,j}$$

$$= (T')^{n}\, A^*_{n+1,n+1} + T''(T')^{n-1}\lambda^2\, |A^*|$$

The relationship between C^{*-1} and A^{*-1} is, thus,

$$C^{*-1} = \left[\frac{C^*_{ij}}{|C^*|}\right] = \left[\begin{array}{c|c} \dfrac{A^*_{ij}}{T'\,|A^*|} & \dfrac{A^*_{i,n+1}}{|A^*|} \\ \hline \dfrac{A^*_{n+1,j}}{|A^*|} & \dfrac{(T')A^*_{n+1,n+1}}{|A^*|} + T''\lambda^2 \end{array}\right]$$

From the point of view of qualitative analysis, the important thing to note is that while in general the sign pattern of C^* need not correspond to that of A^*, C^{*-1} and A^{*-1} have identical sign patterns except perhaps for the element in the $n+1^{st}$ row and column. In particular, given any sign pattern for the diagonal elements of A in $A^* = \begin{bmatrix} \underline{A} & | & \underline{b} \\ b' & | & 0 \end{bmatrix}$, and assuming A^* is negative definite under constraint and $f_i \neq 0$ $(i=1,..,n)$ a monotonic increasing transformation of the objective function can be chosen (with $T'' < 0$ and large in absolute value) such that in $C^* = \begin{bmatrix} \underline{C} & | & \underline{b} \\ b' & | & 0 \end{bmatrix}$, diagonal elements are negative, and A^{*-1} and C^{*-1} have identical signs everywhere except perhaps for the $(n+1,n+1)$ position. For this reason, the argument in the preceding section which considered only the case where all diagonal elements of A are negative, in fact covers the general case of arbitrary signs for such diagonal elements if $f_i \neq 0$ for all i. In light of this, it perhaps should not be particularly surprising that signed inverses exist under the constrained maximization hypothesis only in the diagonal case.

In production theory, the problem of maximizing output for a given level of cost (or minimizing cost for a given level of output) illustrates theorems 3 and 4 of the preceding section. Let x_i denote the number of units of the ith input, w_i the per unit price of the ith input, and let $y = f(x_1,...,x_n)$ denote output with $f_i > 0$ for every i. The conditions for a regular maximum of output are

$$f_i + \lambda w_i = 0 \qquad i=1,...,n$$

$$\sum w_i x_i = c, \text{ and}$$

$$A^* = \begin{bmatrix} f_{ij} & | & w_i \\ \hline w_j & | & 0 \end{bmatrix} \quad \text{is negative definite under con-}$$

straint, where c is the given level of cost and $-\frac{1}{\lambda}$ is marginal cost.

From the total differentials of the first order conditions,

$$\begin{bmatrix} f_{ij} & w_i \\ w_j & 0 \end{bmatrix} \begin{bmatrix} dx_1 \\ \vdots \\ dx_n \\ d\lambda \end{bmatrix} = - \begin{bmatrix} \lambda dw_1 \\ \vdots \\ \lambda dw_n \\ \sum x_i \, dw_i - dc \end{bmatrix}$$

If $n > 2$ the signs of all $\frac{dx_i}{dc}$ can be obtained only in the case of "complete independence" where $f_{ij} = 0$ for all $i \neq j$. As indicated by theorem 3 and the discussion of Morishima matrices, the inverse matrix in this case has sign pattern

$$\begin{bmatrix} - & + & + & \ldots & + & + \\ + & - & + & \ldots & + & + \\ + & + & - & \ldots & + & + \\ \ldots & \ldots & \ldots & \ldots & \ldots & \ldots \\ + & + & + & \ldots & - & + \\ + & + & + & \ldots & + & + \end{bmatrix}$$

so that $\frac{dx_i}{dc} > 0$ for every i, and $\frac{d\lambda}{dc} > 0$ as well (marginal cost rises). For a wage change, however, even in the case of "complete independence", we have $\frac{dx_i}{dw_j} = - \frac{A^*_{ji}}{|A^*|} (\lambda) - x_j \frac{A^*_{i,n+1}}{|A^*|}$ and $\frac{d\lambda}{dw_j} = - \frac{A^*_{j,n+1}}{|A^*|} (\lambda) - x_j \frac{A^*_{n+1,n+1}}{|A^*|}$ so that for $i \neq j$, the two terms have opposite signs. Hence the only determinate sign is $\frac{dx_i}{dw_i} < 0$. In fact, the following lemma holds:

<u>Lemma 5</u>. Let $A^* = \begin{bmatrix} A & c \\ c' & 0 \end{bmatrix}$, where A is an n x n matrix, c is an n x 1 column vector and c' its transpose, $a_{ii} < 0$ $i=1,\ldots,n$, sgn a_{ij} = sgn a_{ji} for $i,j=1,\ldots,n$, and $c_i > 0$ $i=1,\ldots,n$. If $\frac{A^*_{ij}}{|A|}$ is signed for $i \neq j$ under the constrained maximization hypothesis, then $\frac{A^*_{ij}}{|A|} > 0$.

<u>Theorem 5</u>. Let $A^* = \begin{bmatrix} A & c \\ c' & 0 \end{bmatrix}$, where A is an n x n matrix ($n > 2$), c is an n x 1 column vector and c' its transpose, $a_{ii} < 0$ $i=1,\ldots,n$, sgn a_{ij} = sgn a_{ji} for $i,j=1,\ldots,n$, and

$c_i > 0$ $i=1,\ldots,n$. Then in the comparative statics system $A^*y = b^*$, the solution vector y is signed under the constrained maximization hypothesis (i.e., $B^*w = d^*$, $D^*z = f^*$, $B^*, D^* \varepsilon N_A^*$, $d^*, f^* \varepsilon Q_b{}^* \Rightarrow z \varepsilon Q_w$) if and only if 1) $a_{ij} = 0$ for $i \neq j$, $i,j=1,\ldots,n$ and 2) b^* has at most one non-zero element.

<u>Proof</u>: The necessity of 1) follows from Theorem 4. To show the necessity of 2), suppose b^* has two non-zero elements b_i^* and b_j^*, $i \neq j$, then

$$y_i = \frac{A_{ii}^*}{|A^*|} b_i^* + \frac{A_{ji}^*}{|A^*|} b_j^*,$$

$$y_j = \frac{A_{ij}^*}{|A^*|} b_i^* + \frac{A_{jj}^*}{|A^*|} b_j^*,$$

$$\text{and } y_k = \frac{A_{ik}^*}{|A^*|} b_i^* + \frac{A_{jk}^*}{|A^*|} b_j^*, \text{ where } k \neq i,\ k \neq j.$$

$\frac{A_{ii}^*}{|A^*|}$ and $\frac{A_{jj}^*}{|A^*|}$ are negative while by Lemma 5,

$\frac{A_{ji}^*}{|A^*|}$, $\frac{A_{ik}^*}{|A^*|}$, and $\frac{A_{jk}^*}{|A^*|}$ are positive (if signed). Therefore, if sgn b_i^* = sgn b_j^*, y_i and y_j are unsigned; if sgn $b_i^* \neq b_j^*$, y_k is unsigned. Sufficiency follows immediately: if $a_{ij} = 0$ for $i \neq j$, $i,j=1,\ldots,n$, then A^{*-1} has sign pattern

$$\begin{bmatrix} - & + & \cdots & + \\ + & - & \cdots & + \\ + & + & - \cdots & + \\ \vdots & & & \\ + & + & \cdots - & + \end{bmatrix}$$

If the non-zero element is b_i^*, for $i=1,\ldots,n$, then sgn y_i = -sgn b_i^* and sgn y_j = sgn b_i^* for $j \neq i$, $j=1,\ldots,n+1$, while if $b_{n+1}^* \neq 0$, then sgn y_j = sgn b_{n+1}^* for $j=1,\ldots,n+1$, completing the proof.

The notion of conjugate pairs discussed by Samuelson [9] and Archibald [1] arose from consideration of the qualitative content of maximizing models when no other information is assumed to be available. Theorem 5 above forms a partial counterpart of the conjugate pairs theorem when qualitative information is available to supplement the assumption that the equilibrium values of the variables satisfy a constrained maximum position. In part the highly restrictive conditions of Theorem 5 arise because a <u>complete</u> qualitative solution is sought. Since the conjugate pairs theorem deals with partial qualitative solutions, Theorem 5 is not its exact counterpart. While we have not been concerned here with partial qualitative solutions, we might note in conclusion, some cases in which they can be obtained.

Under the constrained maximization hypothesis, the sign pattern of the inverse of a matrix A* with sign pattern

$$\text{sign } A^* = \begin{bmatrix} - & + & + \\ + & - & + \\ + & + & 0 \end{bmatrix} \quad \text{is sign } A^{*-1} = \begin{bmatrix} - & + & + \\ + & - & + \\ + & + & ? \end{bmatrix},$$

For n = 3, the sign pattern

$$\begin{bmatrix} - & + & 0 & + \\ + & - & 0 & + \\ 0 & 0 & - & + \\ + & + & + & 0 \end{bmatrix} \text{ has inverse } \begin{bmatrix} - & ? & + & ? \\ ? & - & + & ? \\ + & + & - & ? \\ ? & ? & ? & ? \end{bmatrix}, \text{ so that } y_1, y_2$$

and y_3 can be signed if $b_3^* \neq 0$, $b_i^* = 0$ $i \neq 3$.

Precisely what is the generalization of cases like this is not known; clearly the conditions under which qualitative information together with the constrained maximization hypothesis gives partial comparative statics results are less restrictive than those given here for complete comparative statics results.

APPENDIX

Lemma 1. Let $A = (a_{ij})$ be an n x n real matrix with $a_{ii} < 0$ for all i and sgn a_{ij} = sgn a_{ji} for all i,j. Then A has a signed inverse under the maximization hypothesis only if every non-zero cycle in A is positive.

Proof: Since sgn a_{ij} = sgn a_{ji} for all i,j, every cycle of length two in A is non-negative. Assume that some cycle in A of length r ($3 \leq r \leq n$) is negative. By reindexing, if necessary, the cycle may be written as $a_{12}a_{23}\cdots a_{r-1,r}a_{r1} < 0$. Consider the cofactor A_{r1} of the element a_{r1} of A.

$$A_{r1} = (-1)^{r+1} \{(a_{12}a_{23}\cdots a_{r-1,r} + (-1)^r a_{1r}a_{22}\cdots a_{r-1,r-1}) a_{r+1,r+1}\cdots a_{nn} + \text{other terms}\}$$

Because $a_{ii} < 0$ for every i, sgn $(-1)^r a_{1r}a_{22}\cdots a_{r-1,r-1}$ = sgn a_{1r}. Since sgn a_{ij} = sgn a_{ji} for all i,j, the assumption that the r cycle is negative implies sgn $a_{12}a_{23}\cdots a_{r-1,r} \neq$ sgn a_{1r}. Choose $C \in Q_A$ such that $|c_{12}| = |c_{23}| = \cdots = |c_{r-1,r}| = 1$, and $|c_{1r}| = \varepsilon$ where ε is an arbitrarily small positive number. Let C be symmetric so that $|c_{21}| = \cdots = |c_{r,r-1}| = 1$, $|c_{r1}| = \varepsilon$. Choose all other off diagonal elements with absolute value of ε and choose $c_{ii} = -3$ for all i. Then C has negative dominant diagonal, hence by Proposition 5, $C \in N_A$ and sgn $|C| = (-1)^{n+1}$ sgn $a_{12}a_{23}\cdots a_{r-1,r}$. Similarly, choose $B \in Q_A$ symmetric such that $|b_{1r}| = |b_{r1}| = 1$, $|b_{ij}| = \varepsilon$ for every other $i \neq j$, where ε is an arbitrary small positive number, and $b_{ii} = -2$ for all i. Then $B \in N_A$ and sgn $B_{r1} = (-1)^{n+1}$ sgn $a_{1r} \neq$ sgn C_{r1}. Thus, $B, C \in N_A$ and $B^{-1} \notin Q_{C^{-1}}$, so that the lemma is proved.

Lemma 2. Let $A = (a_{ij})$ be an n x n indecomposable matrix with $a_{ii} < 0$ for all i and sgn a_{ij} = sgn a_{ji} for all i,j. If there exists a negative cycle of A of length r ($3 \leq r \leq n$), then no column of A^{-1} is signed under the maximization hypothesis.

Proof: We will show that the existence of a negative

cycle of A of length r ($3 \leq r \leq n$) implies that there is an unsigned cofactor of an element in every row of A under the maximization hypothesis. Specifically, we find two non-zero terms of opposite sign in the expansion of the cofactor. Re-index the hypothesized negative cycle into $a_{12}a_{23}\cdots a_{r-1,r}a_{r1}$ and consider a cofactor A_{i1} of an element a_{i1}, where $i \in \{1, \ldots, r\}$. ($i \in \{r+1,\ldots,n\}$ is considered later).

$$A_{i1} = (-1)^{i+1} \{a_{12}a_{23}\cdots a_{i-1,i}a_{i+1,i+1}\cdots a_{nn} + (-1)^{r} a_{1r}a_{22}\cdots a_{i-1,i-1}\, a_{i+1,i}\cdots a_{r,r-1}\, a_{r+1,r+1}\cdots a_{nn} + \text{other terms}\}$$

Choose $B \in Q_A$ such that B is symmetric with $b_{ii} = -3$ $i=1,\ldots,n$, $|b_{12}| = |b_{23}| = \ldots = |b_{i-1,i}| = 1$, $|b_{21}| = \ldots = |b_{i,i-1}| = 1$, and all other off-diagonal elements in B are arbitrarily small. Then B is dominant (negative) diagonal, hence $B \in N_A$ and sgn $B_{i1} = (-1)^{n+1}$ sgn $(b_{12}b_{23}\cdots b_{i-1,i})$. Choose $D \in Q_A$ such that D is symmetric with $d_{ii} = -3, i=1, \ldots,n$, $|d_{1r}| = |d_{i+1,i}| = \ldots = |d_{r,r-1}| = 1$, $|d_{r1}| = |d_{i,i+1}| = \ldots = |d_{r-1,r}| = 1$, and all other off-diagonal elements in D are arbitrarily small. Then D is dominant (negative) diagonal, hence $D \in N_A$ and sgn $D_{i1} = (-1)^{n+1} (-1)^{2(i-1)}$ sgn $(d_{1r}d_{i+1,i}\cdots d_{r,r-1})$. Thus sgn $D_{i1} \neq$ sgn B_{i1}, so that there is an unsigned element in the ith column of A^{-1} for $i=1,\ldots,r$.

There remains to show that there is an unsigned cofactor for every row i, $i \in \{r+1,\ldots,n\}$. To pinpoint two non-zero terms of opposite sign in one cofactor for each such row is the problem. Since A is indecomposable, there exists at least one row i, $i \in \{r+1,\ldots,n\}$, with a non-zero element in the first r columns. Suppose there are s-r such rows ($s \leq n$). By reindexing if necessary these rows may be placed in the $r+1,\ldots,s$ positions. We will consider each of these s-r rows separately. For $i \in \{r+1,\ldots,s\}$, reindex the first r rows and columns so that $a_{ir} \neq 0$ (this can be done in such a way that the hypothesized negative cycle after reindexing is still $a_{12}a_{23}\cdots a_{r-1,r}a_{r,1}$). Then $a_{ri} \neq 0$. Consider the cofactor A_{i1} of a_{i1}, where $i \in \{r+1,\ldots,s\}$,

$$A_{i1} = (-1)^{i+1}\{a_{12}a_{23}\cdots a_{r-1,r}(-1)^{i-r}\, a_{ri}\, a_{r+1,r+1}\cdots$$

$a_{i-1,i-1}a_{i+1,i+1}\cdots a_{n,n}$

$+ (-1)^r a_{1r}a_{22}\cdots a_{r-1,r-1}(-1)^{i-r} a_{ri}a_{r+1,r+1}\cdots$

$a_{i-1,i-1}$

$a_{i+1,i+1}\cdots a_{nn}$ + other terms}.

Choose $B \varepsilon Q_A$ such that B is symmetric with $b_{ii} = -3$ i=1,..., n $|b_{12}| = |b_{23}| = \ldots = |b_{r-1,r}| = |b_{ri}| = 1$, $|b_{21}| = |b_{32}| = \ldots = |b_{r,r-1}| = |b_{ir}| = 1$, and all other off-diagonal elements in B are arbitrarily small. Then B is dominant (negative) diagonal, hence $B \varepsilon N_A$ and sgn $B_{i1} = (-1)^{n+2(i-1)}$ sgn $(b_{12}b_{23}\cdots b_{r-1,r}b_{ri})$. Choose $D \varepsilon Q_A$ such that D is symmetric with $d_{ii} = -3$ i=1,...,n, $|d_{1r}| = |d_{ri}| = 1$, $|d_{r1}| = |d_{ir}| = 1$, and all other off-diagonal terms in D are arbitrarily small. Then D is dominant (negative) diagonal, hence $D \varepsilon N_A$ and sgn $D_{i1} = (-1)^{n+2(i-1)}$ sgn $(d_{1r}d_{ri})$. Thus sgn $D_{i1} \neq$ sgn B_{i1}, so that there is an unsigned element in the ith column of A^{-1} for i ε {r+1,...,s}.

There remains to show that there is an unsigned cofactor for every row i, i ε {s+1,...,n}. The last r-s rows consist of zero entries in the first r columns. By the indecomposability of A, therefore, there must exist at least one row i, i ε {s+1,...,n}, with a non-zero element in at least one of the columns r+1,...,s. Suppose there are t-s such rows and by reindexing if necessary bring these rows to the s+1,...,t positions. We will consider each row separately. For i ε {s+1,...,t} reindex the rows and columns {r+1,...,s} so that $a_{is} \neq 0$. Then $a_{si} \neq 0$. Now reindex the first r rows and columns so that $a_{rs} \neq 0$ (again, this can be done in such a way that the negative cycle after reindexing is still $a_{12}a_{23}\cdots a_{r-1,r}a_{r1}$). Consider the cofactor A_{i1};

$A_{i1} = (-1)^{i+1} \{a_{12}a_{23}\cdots a_{r-1,r}(-1)^{s-r} a_{rs}a_{r+1,r+1}\cdots a_{i-1,i-1}$

$a_{si}a_{i+1,i+1}\cdots a_{nn}$

$+ (-1)^r a_{r1}a_{22}\cdots a_{r-1,r-1}(-1)^{s-r} a_{rs}a_{r+1,r+1}\cdots a_{i-1,i-1}$

$a_{si}a_{i+1,i+1}\cdots a_{nn}$ + other terms}.

Following a procedure similar to that employed in the preceding paragraph B and D can be found such that $B, D \in N_A$, but $\text{sgn } B_{i1} \neq \text{sgn } D_{i1}$, so that there is an unsigned element in the ith row for $i \in \{s+1, \ldots, t\}$. If $t = n$, the proof is complete; otherwise, the procedure used in this paragraph can be continued until all the rows of A have been considered.

Lemma 3. Let $A^* = \begin{bmatrix} A & c \\ c' & 0 \end{bmatrix}$ where A is an n x n matrix, c is an n x 1 column vector, and c' is the transpose of c. Assume $c_i \neq 0$ for every i and $a_{ii} < 0$ for every i, $\text{sgn } a_{ij} = \text{sgn } a_{ji}$ for every i,j. Then A* has a signed inverse under the constrained maximization hypothesis only if $a_{ij} = 0$ for every $i \neq j$.

Proof: Assume $a_{ij} \neq 0$, $a_{ji} \neq 0$ for some $i \neq j$ and reindex i into 1, j into 2, so that $a_{12} \neq 0$, $a_{21} \neq 0$. Choose $B^* \in Q_{A^*}$, $B^* = \begin{bmatrix} B & b \\ b' & 0 \end{bmatrix}$ with B* symmetric. Choose $b_{ii} = -1$ for all i and let all off diagonal elements in B* be arbitrarily small in absolute value. Then B is a dominant negative diagonal matrix, hence B is negative definite and B* is a matrix negative definite under constraint, i.e., $B^* \in N^*_{A^*}$. The cofactor of the element 0 appearing in the $n+1^{st}$ row and $n+1^{st}$ column of B*, to be denoted by $B^*_{n+1,n+1}$, satisfies $B^*_{n+1,n+1} = |B|$ so that $\text{sgn } B^*_{n+1,n+1} = (-1)^n$.

Similarly, choose $D^* \in Q_{A^*}$, $D^* = \begin{bmatrix} D & d \\ d' & 0 \end{bmatrix}$ with D* symmetric. Choose $d_{ii} = -1$ for all i, $|d_{12}| = |d_{21}| = 2$, $|d_1| = 1$, $|d_2| = 1/4$ and let all other off diagonal elements in D* be arbitrarily small in absolute value. Then D* satisfies the condition that all bordered principal minors involving r rows and columns from D have sign $(-1)^r$, hence $D^* \in N^*_{A^*}$. $D^*_{n+1,n+1} = |D|$ and $\text{sgn } |D| = (-1)^{n+1}$ so that $D^{*-1} \notin Q_{B^{*-1}}$ and A* does not have signed inverse under the constrained maximization hypothesis.

Lemma 4. Let $A^* = \begin{bmatrix} A & c \\ c' & 0 \end{bmatrix}$ where A is an n x n matrix $(n > 2)$ and c is an n x 1 column vector, c' is the transpose of c, with $a_{ii} < 0$ for all i, $c_i \neq 0$ for all i, $\text{sgn } a_{ij} = \text{sgn } a_{ji}$ for all i,j. Then $a_{ij} \neq 0$ for any $i \neq j$ implies that every column of A* has an unsigned element under the constrained maximization hypothesis.

<u>Proof</u>: Assume $a_{ij} \neq 0$, $a_{ji} \neq 0$ for some $i \neq j$. Reindex i into 1 and j into 2, so that $a_{12} \neq 0$, $a_{21} \neq 0$. Consider the cofactors A^*_{12} and A^*_{13} of the elements a_{12}, a_{13} of A^*:

$$A^*_{12} = (-1)^{1+2} \{-a_{21}a_{33}\cdots a_{n-1,n-1}c_n^2 + (-1)\, c_1c_2a_{33}\cdots a_{nn}$$
$$+ \text{ other terms}\};$$

$$A^*_{13} = (-1)^{1+3} \{-a_{21}c_2c_3a_{44}\cdots a_{nn} + c_1c_3a_{22}a_{44}\cdots a_{nn}$$
$$+ \text{ other terms}\}.$$

Assume sgn a_{21} = sgn c_1c_2. Choose $B^* \varepsilon Q^*_A$ such that $B^* = \begin{bmatrix} B & b \\ b & 0 \end{bmatrix}$ and B^* is symmetric. Choose $b_{11} = -2$, $|b_{12}| = |b_{21}| = 1$, $b_{ii} = -1$, $i=2,\ldots,n$, $|c_n| = 1$, and choose all other off diagonal entries in B^* arbitrarily small in absolute value. Then B is dominant negative diagonal and $B^* \varepsilon N^*_{A^*}$, with sgn $B^*_{12} = (-1)^{1+2}(-1)^{n-2}$ sgn b_{12}. Further, choose $D^* \varepsilon Q^*_A$ such that $D^* = \begin{bmatrix} D & d \\ d' & 0 \end{bmatrix}$ and D^* is symmetric. Choose $d_{ii} = -1$ for all i, $|d_1| = |d_2| = 1$ and choose all other off diagonal entries in D^* arbitrarily small in absolute value. Again, D is dominant negative diagonal and $D^* \varepsilon N^*_{A^*}$ with sgn $D^*_{12} = (-1)^{1+2}(-1)^{n-3}$ sgn d_1d_2. Since sgn $D^*_{12} \neq$ sgn B^*_{12}, the first column of A^{*-1} contains an unsigned element.
Assume sgn $a_{21} \neq$ sgn c_1c_2. If in B^* and D^*, bordering elements are chosen arbitrarily small relative to b_1, b_2, b_3 (d_1, d_2, d_3) and the other assignment of values is as above, then sgn $B^*_{13} = (-1)^{1+3}(-1)^{n-2}$ sgn b_3b_2 sgn b_{21} and sgn $D^*_{13} = (-1)^{1+3}(-1)^{n-2}$ sgn b_3 sgn b_1, hence sgn $B^*_{13} \neq$ sgn D^*_{13} and again the first column of A^{*-1} contains an unsigned element.

The argument establishing the existence of an unsigned element in the second column of A^{*-1} is identical to that given for the first column, and, under the condition that $a_{12} \neq 0$, $a_{21} \neq 0$, lemma 3 has already established that the $n+1^{st}$ column of A^{*-1} has an unsigned element since $A^*_{n+1,n+1}$ is unsigned.

Consider next the cofactor $A^*_{j,n+1}$ of the element $a^*_{j,n+1}$

$(=c_j)$, where $j=3,\ldots,n$:

$$A^*_{j,n+1} = (-1)^{j+n+1}\{(-1)^{n-j}c_j a_{j+1,j+1}\cdots a_{nn}(a_{11}a_{22}\cdots a_{j-1,j-1} - a_{12}a_{21}a_{33}\cdots a_{j-1,j-1}) + \text{other terms}\}.$$

Because $\text{sgn } a_{11}a_{22} = \text{sgn } a_{12}a_{21}$, the argument of lemma 3 above can again be applied so that there exist $B^*, D^* \varepsilon N^*_{A^*}$ such that $\text{sgn } B^*_{j,n+1} \neq \text{sgn } D^*_{j,n+1}$ and the $j^{\underline{th}}$ column of A^{*-1} contains an unsigned element for $j=3,\ldots,n$, which completes the proof of the lemma.

<u>Lemma 5</u>. Let $A^* = \begin{bmatrix} A & | & c \\ - & - & - \\ c' & | & 0 \end{bmatrix}$, where A is an n x n matrix, c is an n x 1 column vector and c' is the transpose of c, $a_{ii} < 0$ for all i, $\text{sgn } a_{ij} = \text{sgn } a_{ji}$ for all i,j, and $c_i > 0$ for all i. Then if $\frac{A^*_{ij}}{|A^*|}$ is signed for any $i \neq j$ under the constrained maximization hypothesis, $\frac{A^*_{ij}}{|A^*|} > 0$.

<u>Proof</u>: Given any $i > j$, $i,j=1,\ldots,n$, choose $B^* \varepsilon Q_{A^*}$, $B^* = \begin{bmatrix} B & | & b \\ - & - & - \\ b' & | & 0 \end{bmatrix}$ and B^* symmetric. Choose $c_i = c_j = 1$, $b_{ii} = -1$ for all i and all other off diagonal entries in B^* arbitrarily small in absolute value. Then if $\frac{A^*_{ij}}{|A^*|}$ is signed under the constrained maximization hypothesis, $B^*, C^* \varepsilon N^*_{A^*} \Rightarrow \text{sgn } \frac{C^*_{ij}}{|C^*|} = \text{sgn } \frac{B^*_{ij}}{|B^*|}$,

$$B^*_{ij} = (-1)^{i+j}\{b_{11}\cdots b_{j-1,j-1}(-1)^{n+1-j}c_j b_{j+1,j+1}\cdots b_{i-1,i-1}(-1)^{n+1-i}\,c_i b_{i+1,i+1}\cdots b_{nn} + \text{other terms}\}.$$

Hence $\text{sgn } \frac{B^*_{ij}}{|B^*|} = \frac{(-1)^{3n}}{(-1)^n} > 0$. Because $\frac{B^*_{ij}}{|B^*|} > 0$ in this case, if $\frac{A^*_{ij}}{|A^*|}$ is to be signed, $C^* \varepsilon N^*_{A^*}$ must also satisfy $\frac{C^*_{ij}}{|C^*|} > 0$.

A similar argument applies for i or j = n+1, by choosing the appropriate c_i (or c_j) equal to 1.

FOOTNOTES

* This work was supported in part by grants from the National Science Foundation and the University of Kansas Research Fund.

[1] In what follows, we will assume A satisfies sgn a_{ij} = sgn a_{ji} and $a_{ii} < 0$ for all i so that N_A is not empty.

[2] The generalization of the corollary to the decomposable case is straightforward. For complete comparative statics information, at least one indecomposable diagonal block of A (and the associated portion of the vector b) must satisfy the conditions of the corollary, with the remainder of the b vector being zero, and with arbitrary signs for the remainder of the matrix A.

REFERENCES

[1] Archibald, G. C., "The Qualitative Content of Maximizing Models", Journal of Political Economy, February, 1965, pp. 27-36.

[2] Bassett, L., H. Habibagahi, and J. Quirk, "Qualitative Economics and Morishima Matrices", Econometrica, April, 1967.

[3] Bassett, L., J. Maybee, and J. Quirk, "Qualitative Economics and the Scope of the Correspondence Principle", Econometrica, April, 1968.

[4] Debreu, G. and I. N. Herstein, "Nonnegative Square Matrices", Econometrica (1953), pp. 597-607.

[5] Maybee, J., "Remarks on the Theory of Cycles in Matrices", (mimeographed), Purdue University, 1966.

[6] Maybee, J. and J. Quirk, "Qualitative Problems in Matrix Theory", (mimeographed), Research Paper No. 1, University of Kansas, 1966.

[7] McKenzie, L., "The Matrix with Dominant Diagonal and Economic Theory", Mathematical Methods in the Social Sciences, 1960 (Arrow, Karlin and Scarf, eds.), Stanford: Stanford University Press, 1960.

[8] Morishima, M., "On the Laws of Change of the Price System in an Economy Which Contains Complementary Commodities", Osaka Economic Papers (1952), pp. 101-113.

[9] Samuelson, P., Foundations of Economic Analysis, Cambridge: Harvard University Press, 1955.

[10] Hicks, J. R., Value and Capital, Oxford, 2nd Edition, 1946.

PAIRWISE OPTIMALITY AND NON-COMPETITIVE BEHAVIOR*

by

Trout Rader
Washington University, St. Louis, Missouri

1. Pareto Optimality Implies Pairwise Optimality

A theorem of classical welfare economics commonly provides information about the relationship between competition and Pareto optimality. For example, competitive equilibria are Pareto optimal (Debreu [1954] and Arrow [1951]). A related question is, what kind of market organization is non-optimal. For example, it is often claimed that monopoly and taxes prevent Pareto optimality. (Pigou [1920] and Little [1951]). The main aim here is to provide necessary and sufficient conditions for Pareto optimality which are easily tested in a particular institutional or behavioral framework.

A trade is a vector, x, in E^n, representing disposals (positive components) or acquisitions (negative components) of commodities. For example, for i and j out of the m traders, we define the i-j trade as the vector x^{ij}, where positive components represent transfers from i to j and negative components, transfers from j to i. We assume that each trader j has preferences which compare the summed trades

$$x^i = \sum_{j=1}^{n} x^{ij}$$

deciding which are better or equivalent to each other. These preferences are defined on the set of possible trades, X_i, which is called the trade set of i. Presumably, these preferences are derived from more fundamental relationships vis à vis consumption and production (Rader [1964], pp. 150-155). The preferences are denoted $x^i R_i \bar{x}^i$ to be read, x^i is at least as good as x^i. If $x^i R_i \bar{x}^i$ and $\bar{x}^i R_i x^i$, then x^i and $\bar{x}^i$ are indifferent, which is written $x^i I_i \bar{x}^i$. Similarly, if not $x^i R_i \bar{x}^i$, then $\bar{x}^i P_i x^i$ or $\bar{x}^i$ is preferred to x.

Let

$$R_i(x) = \{\bar{x} | \bar{x} R_i x\},$$

$$R_i^{-1}(x) = \{\bar{x} | x R_i \bar{x}\}$$

$$P_i(x) = \{\overline{x} | \overline{x} P_i x\},$$

$$P_i^{-1}(x) = \{\overline{x} | x P_i \overline{x}\},$$

and

$$I_i(x) = \{\overline{x} | \overline{x} I_i x\}$$

be the "no worse than", "no better than", "better than", "worse than", and "indifferent to" sets, respectively. The <u>community trade set</u> is

$$X = \sum_{i=1}^{n} X_i$$

A trade, $x = (x^1,\ldots,x^n)$ is said to be <u>Pareto optimal</u> if

(i) $\sum_{i=1}^{n} x_i = 0,\ x^i \in X_i,$

(ii) $\sum_{i=1}^{n} \overline{x}^i = 0,\ \overline{x}^i \in X_i,\ \overline{x}^i R_i x^i$, for all i,

implies that $x^j I_j \overline{x}^j$ for all j.

A trade, $x = (x^1,\ldots,x^n)$ is said to be <u>i-j pair wise optimal</u> if

(i) $\sum_{i=1}^{n} x^i = 0,\ x^i \in X_i$

(ii) $\overline{y}^i + \overline{y}^j = 0,\ \overline{y}^i \in X_i,\ \overline{y}^j \in X_j,$

$x^i + \overline{y}^i\ R_i\ x^i,\ x^j + \overline{y}^j R_j x^j$

implies that $x^j + \overline{y}^j\ I_j x^j,\ x^j\ I_j\ x^i.$

A trade, x, is <u>pairwise optimal</u>, if it is i-j pair wise optimal for all ij. Pareto optimal trades are those which cannot be made better for one trader without hurting others. Pair wise optimal trades are those which are Pareto optimal for two traders considered alone, the transactions with the remaining traders being held fixed.

<u>Remark 1.</u>

It is clear from the above that Pareto optimality implies pairwise optimality. Hence, if a system can be shown to be not pairwise optimal, it follows that it is not Pareto optimal. However, this is not always easy. What is needed is a condition insuring pairwise optimality. Evidently,

Remark 2.

a trade x is pairwise optimal for i and j if and only if $P_i(x) \cap (-P_j(x)) = \phi$. For example, a monopolist may refrain from an otherwise mutually advantageous contract for fear of a buyer selling to a third party at a lower price than the monopolist. Similarly, expectation of a tax on the exchange of a good may restrain two parties from trading for material benefit.

A more refined analysis than that of Remark 2 is possible whenever preferences are convex. For this and other applications we must accumulate some intellectual capital.

2. Quasi-transferable Preferences: A Digression

Preferences are quasi-transferable from j at y in X provided that whenever xR_iy for all i and

$$x \, P_j \, y,$$

there exists an $\bar{x}$ in X such that

$$\bar{x} \, P_i \, y \text{ for all } i.$$ [1]

In effect, the extra preferences of j for x over y can be reallocated so that each individual benefits. Clearly this is a property of the whole system, although it also relates to individual preferences. It is tantamount to saying that all individuals have some degree of opposing interests to j at the social position y. Obviously, this may not be true of all y in all social situations.

As we shall see, the notion of quasi-transferability is important in connecting minimization of cost of the budget, given the level of preferences, with optimization of preferences given a budget constraint. Before making applications, it is best to ascertain cases in which quasi-transferability is to be expected.

Preferences R_i are said to be unsaturated at y if there is a trade

$$x \in X$$

such that $x \, P_i \, y$. They are locally unsaturated if for any "neighborhood" of y, x may be taken to be in that "neighborhood", i.e. if x can be chosen (arbitrarily) "close" to y. Preferences, R_i, are regular if the upper contour set, $R_i(x)$, is closed. They are continuous if $R_i^{-1}(x)$ is closed as well. (Alternatively, they are regular if $P_i^{-1}(x)$ is open and continuous if also $P_i(x)$ is open.) Preferences are continuous along line segments if x^n tends to x along a line, and $\bar{x}^n \varepsilon R_i(x^n)$, $\bar{y}^n \varepsilon R_i^{-1}(x^n)$, implies that

$$\lim \bar{x}^n = \bar{x} \varepsilon R_i(x),$$

$$\lim \bar{y}^n = \bar{y} \varepsilon R_i^{-1}(x).$$

Preferences are weakly convex if $R_i(x)$ is convex. They are convex if $y P_i x$ implies $ty + (1-t)x P_i x$ for $0 < t < 1$, and they are strictly convex if $y R_i x$, $x \neq y$, implies $ty + (1-t)x P_i x$ for $0 < t < 1$.

If there is a good which is always preferred by all consumers in larger quantities, we say that it is a Renoir good.

Theorem 1. Let preferences, R_i, depend only upon $x^i \varepsilon X_i$, $i=1,\ldots n$, if preferences for $i \neq j$ are convex and unsaturated and preferences for j are continuous along straight lines, then preferences are quasi-transferable from j on interior points of the community trade set X.

Proof: Consider $x \varepsilon \text{Int } X$, $x P_j z$, $x R_i z$, $i \neq j$. Let $y^i P_i x^i$ for all $i \neq j$. Then consider

$$\bar{x}^i = t(y^i - x^i) + x^i, \ i \neq j,$$

$$\bar{x}^j = x^j - t \sum_{i \neq j} (y^i - x^i).$$

For t sufficiently small, $\bar{x} \varepsilon X$. Also continuity along straight lines gives that

$$\bar{x} P_j z$$

for t sufficiently small. QED.

We continue the analysis of the case of independence of preferences. In many cases there may be a similarity of preferences in that an increase in certain commodities always leads to a higher level of preferences. Preferences have a similarity if

$$S = \bigcap_{i=1}^{n} \bigcap_{x \varepsilon X} (P_i(x^i) - x^i) \neq \phi.$$

An element $y \varepsilon S$ is called a direction of greater preference. They have an essential similarity if preferences have a similarity and if for z^i giving the minimum level of preference in X_i, $x^i \; P_i \; z^i$ if and only if

$$x^i = \bar{x}^i + \bar{\bar{x}}^i,$$

$$\bar{x}^i \; R_i \; z^i,$$

$$\bar{\bar{x}}^i \in S.$$

It is easy to verify the

Theorem 2. Suppose there is a Renoir good. Then there is a similarity. If there is a class of commodities, I, for which

$$\text{(i)} \quad x \; P_i \; y$$

whenever

$$x_j \geq y_j, \; j \in I,$$

$$x_{j_o} > y_{j_o}, \; \underline{\text{some}} \; j_o \in I,$$

$$x_k = y_k, \; k \notin I,$$

and

(ii) x is non-minimal on X_i if and only if there is some coordinate $j \in I$ in which x can be reduced,

then there is an essential similarity. Condition (ii) above is to say that there must be a reducible (possibly positive) amount of at least one "good" in order to have a non-minimal level of preference.

Theorem 3. If preferences are convex, continuous on straight lines, and have essential similarity, then they are quasi-transferable.

Proof: By hypothesis, if

$$x_i \; R_i \; \bar{x}_i,$$

$$x_j \; P_j \; \bar{x}_j,$$

x_j is non-minimal and

$$x_j = y + z, \; z \in X_j$$

for

$$y \in S.$$

Also by convexity

$$ty \varepsilon \bigcap_{i=1}^{n} \bigcap_{x_i} (P_i(x_i) - x_i) = S$$

for all $1 > t > 0$. Therefore

$$\bar{\bar{x}}_i = x_i + \frac{t}{n-1} \; y \; P_i \; \bar{x}_i,$$

while by continuity along line segments

$$\bar{\bar{x}}_j = x_i - t \; y \; P_j \; \bar{x}_j$$

for t sufficiently small. Clearly

$$\sum_{i \neq j} \bar{\bar{x}}_i + \bar{\bar{x}}_j = 0,$$

$$\bar{\bar{x}}_i \; \varepsilon \; X_i$$

for all i. Therefore

$$\bar{\bar{x}} \; \varepsilon \; X. \qquad \text{QED.}$$

One may still question the reasonableness of quasi-transferability. Consider an economy with two commodities, food and labor. The trade set for all consumers, assumed identical, is illustrated in figure 1 below.

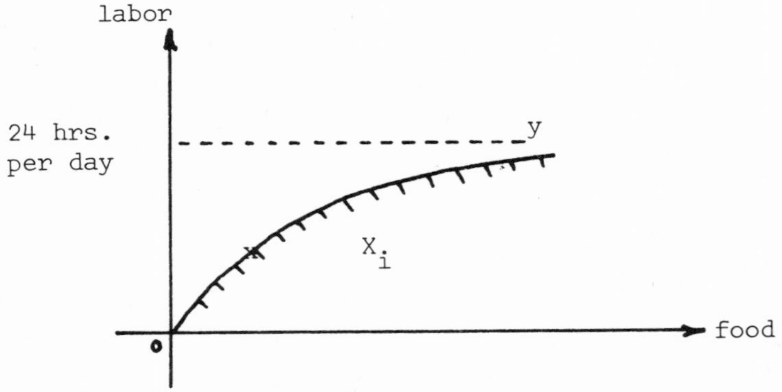

figure 1

It is not possible to produce more than a certain amount of labor, given a certain amount of food. Assuming that food is a Renoir good there is a similarity of preference. Is there an essential similarity? Suppose zero is the point of minimal preference. Then x may very well be preferred, but there is no way to improve zero by transferring from an individual located at x a quantity of food, upon which the similarity is based. Therefore, there is not an essential similarity. Nevertheless, if preferences are convex, there is quasi-transferability by placing both individuals on the line segment between zero and x, say tx and (1-t)x. If a third individual is added with y, say inferior to tx, a further transfer may take place from tx to y. The point here is that the fact that the trade sets are identical allows quasi-transferability as well (as a paraphrase of the proof of theorem 1 will indicate) even if one might quarrel with the assumption that there is an essential similarity of preferences.

3. Pairwise Optimality is Equivalent to Competitive Behavior

We present the result which will be the basis of most of our applications. It states that the mathematical property of bounding a convex upper contour set by a hyperplane is the equivalent of maximizing preferences using the hyperplane as the budget plane.

Lemma. Let $p\bar{x}^i \geq px^i$ for all $\bar{x}^i$ such that $\bar{x}^i \; P_i \; x^i$, $i=1,\ldots,n$, $\sum_{i=1}^{n} x^i = 0$. Suppose

(1) preferences are quasi-transferable for any pair of traders,

(2) preferences are continuous along line segments and locally unsaturated, and

(3) the zero trade is in the interior of the sum of the individual trade sets

$$0 \in \text{Int} \sum_{i=1}^{n} X_i .$$

Then

$$p\bar{x}^i > px^i$$

for all $\bar{x}^i$ preferred to x^i.

Hypothesis (3) is simply a statement that for every new trade sufficiently small, there is some trader or group of traders who can make that trade. An example where hypothesis (3) holds is where initial wealth of the commodity is positive for every good. Then one can increase or decrease in any direction the holdings of commodities by the community, provided the change is small. Thus any nearly zero "trade" is consumable by the community.

A counter example to the conclusion of the lemma appears in figure 2 where the indifference curve is tangent to the vertical axis. Clearly, at x, only $p_2 = 0$ is compatible with cost minimization, but this leads to infinite consumption of good 2 whenever there is preference optimization subject to

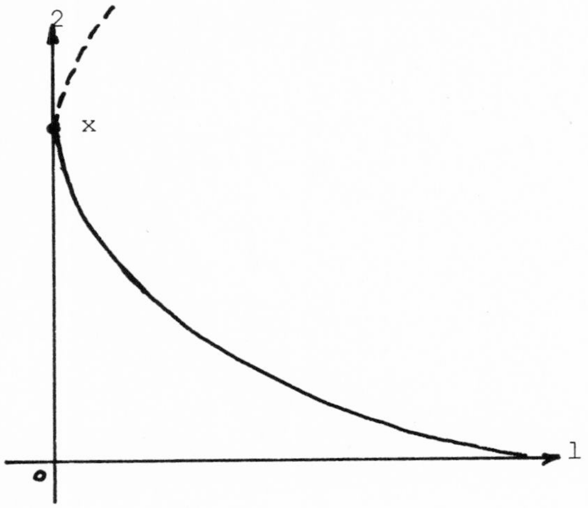

figure 2

the budget constraint. It might seem unlikely that the economy would place the trader at x, but in the general case of many commodities, it might be that optimality required that some person have zero quantities of a good such as 2. If so, one would have to supplement the price system with a rationing of the trader to no less than x of good 2.

The above lemma can be applied to the standard proofs of

(1) the existence of competitive equilibrium (Arrow and Debreu [1954], Gale [1955], McKenzie [1959], Rader [1964] and Scarf [1966]).

(2) Pareto optimality implies a competitive equilibrium with a possible redistribution of income (Arrow [1951] and Debreu [1954]), or

(3) the core tends to the competitive equilibrium as the traders are multiplied indefinitely (Scarf [1962], Debreu and Scarf [1963]).

By doing so one substitutes the hypothesis of the lemma for the assumptions that

(1) $0 \varepsilon \text{ Int } X_i$ for each trader, i, or

(2) $px_i < 0$ for some $x_i \varepsilon X_i$ for each trader, i.

(1) is overly restrictive and (2) is often assumed quite artifically (from an economic viewpoint) whenever the price system is derived. To illustrate the power of the lemma and its extensive implications, the applications to standard

theorems are outlined in the appendices.

Proof of the lemma: We can change the community trade to $\bar{x}^i$, $i=1,\ldots,n$, such that

$$p(\sum_{i=1}^{n} \bar{x}^i) = p\bar{x} < p(\sum_{i=1}^{n} x^i).$$

Consequently, for some i_o,

$$p\bar{x}^{i_o} < px^{i_o}.$$

This gives a consumption with a smaller value than x^{i_o}, and if

$$\bar{\bar{x}}^{i_o} \; P_{i_o} \; x^{i_o}$$

then

$$t\bar{\bar{x}}^{i_o} + (1-t)\bar{x}^{i_o} \; P_{i_o} \; x^{i_o}$$

for t nearly one by virtue of continuity along line segments. Therefore

$$px^{i_o} \leq p(t\bar{\bar{x}}^{i_o} + (1-t)\bar{x}^{i_o})$$

$$= tp\bar{\bar{x}}^{i_o} + (1-t)p\bar{x}^{i_o}$$

$$< tp\bar{\bar{x}}^{i_o} + (1-t)px^{i_o}$$

Therefore

$$px^{i_o} < p\bar{\bar{x}}^{i_o}$$

for all

$$\bar{\bar{x}}^{i_o} \in P_{i_o}(x^{i_o})$$

We extend the result to all i. Suppose $\bar{\bar{x}}^i \; P_i \; x^i$. Then by quasi-transferability, there is a change, δ, in $\bar{\bar{x}}^i$ which can be transferred to i_o to give i_o a level of preference greater than x^{i_o} but which does not reduce i's preference level to that of x^i. Therefore

$$p(x^{i_o} + \delta) > px^{i_o}$$

or

$$p\delta > 0.$$

But also

$$\bar{\bar{x}}^i - \delta t \; P_i x^i$$

so that

$$p(\bar{\bar{x}}^i - t\delta) \geq px^i,$$

or

$$p\bar{\bar{x}}^i \geq px^i + tp\delta > px^i$$

for all

$$\bar{\bar{x}}^i \in P_i(x^i),$$

which is the conclusion of the lemma. QED.

Trader j is said to follow a non-competitive policy (or behavior) at x with respect to the price system, p, if there exists an $\bar{x}^j \; P_j \; x^j$ for which $p\bar{x}^j \leq px^j$. Otherwise, j follows a competitive policy (or behavior). (A competitive policy does not necessarily lead to a competitive equilibrium since it is not required that $px^j = 0$). For example, a monopolist follows a non-competitive policy since he would sell more at the going price, were he not fearful of driving the price down. Similarly, a taxed producer would produce and sell more of a good were he not fearful that he would have to pay more of his income to the state.

Theorem 4. If preferences are weakly convex, locally unsaturated, quasi-transferable between i and j, continuous along line segment and $0 \in \text{Int } X_i + X_j$ then i and j pairwise optimize with respect to each other if and only if they follow a competitive policy with respect to a price system, p.

Proof: Evidently, if i and j follow competitive policies with respect to p, $p(P_i(x_i) + P_j(x_j)) > p(x_i + x_j)$ so that

$$0 = x_i + x_j \notin P_i(x_i) + R_j(x_j),$$

i.e. the trade is pairwise optimal for i and j.

On the other hand, if i and j are pairwise optimal, apply Minkowski's theorem to obtain p for which

$$p(R_k(x_k)) \geq px_k, \; k=i, \; j.$$

Apply the lemma to obtain theorem 4. QED.

Incidentally, a competitive policy might not involve the competitive income, as would be the case in bilateral bargaining whenever one party got the best of the other. Normally, the parties would move to the "contract curve" but would not necessarily move to the competitive equilibrium.

4. Pareto Optimality is Equivalent to Pairwise Optimality

Up to this point, the analysis is not entirely satisfactory. For example, in theorem 4, it was required that $0 \varepsilon \text{Int } X_i + X_j$, which is still quite strong in a many person economy. Also, no method has been given to ascertain when a system other than the competitive equilibrium is Pareto optimal. To present such results, we need one more concept.

Preferences are directionally dense at x^i, if there exists a set, S, dense in E^n, such that for every y in S,

$$x^i + ty \, P_i \, x^i$$

for some $t \neq 0$. Directional density is simply another way of saying that $P_i(x^i)$ has but one separating hyperplane at x^i. In effect, it is a differentiability or smoothness assumption. In particular, it implies that preferences are locally unsaturated, since some change in a direction near zero, $y \varepsilon S$, will improve preferences. In the case of a consumer as in figure 2, directional density requires that the trade be in the interior of the trade set. In a geographical setting, where goods are distinguished according to location, the directionally dense trader must deal in all goods in all places, at least in small quantities.

Theorem 5. Let preferences be quasi-transferable, continuous along line segments, regular, weakly convex and locally unsaturated at the trade x^i for all i. Let preferences for j be directionally dense at x^i, for some i. Then x is Pareto optimal if and only if it is i-j pairwise optimal for all j. In particular, x is pairwise optimal if and only if it is Pareto optimal.

The theorem gives a simple criterion for testing Pareto optimality. Simply find an i with directionally dense preferences and make sure that it is pairwise optimizing with the others. In traditional terms, if all pairs of traders are on the contact curve vis a vis i, then there is Pareto optimality. In particular, the case of bilateral monopoly, where one or more pairs of individuals face each other and pair wise optimize, is a case of Pareto optimality. Contrary to the opinion of Pigou [1920], objections to bilateral monopoly must be based upon distributional considerations, not upon the lack of efficiency of trade.

The conclusion of theorem 1 depends in an essential way upon the assumption of directional density. In effect, the trader with directionally dense preferences acts as an instrument of overall economic efficiency. To see this, consider three traders whose preference to no trade is given by

(i) x^i for each trader i,

(ii) any non-positive, non-zero trade,

(iii) any sum of x^i and a non-positive trade, or

(iv) any convex combination of the above.

In effect, the trader i likes proportions of x^i, and also, he likes to obtain positive additional quantities of the goods. It is assumed that

$$\sum_{i=1}^{n} x^i = 0,$$

so that the community can obtain a position better for each trader than that of no trade at all. On the other hand, for i, a position $\overline{y}^i$ is superior or equivalent to zero if and only if

$$y^i = t^i x^i - w^i,$$

$$t^i \geq 0,\ w^i \geq 0.$$

Therefore, if i and j can obtain trades superior to zero for one and not inferior for the other,

$$y^i + y^j = 0,$$

then

$$t^i x^i + t^j x^j - w^i - w^j = 0,$$

or

$$t^i x^i + t^j x^j = w^i + w^j = w \geq 0.$$

In order to make one trader better off, at least one t must be greater than zero, since otherwise

$$-w^i - w^j = 0,$$

$$w^i + w^j = 0,$$

$$w^i \geq 0$$

$$w^j \geq 0$$

implies that

$$w^i = 0$$

$$w^j = 0.$$

Therefore,

$$x^i + \frac{t^j}{t^i} x^j \geq 0.$$

If there are three goods, we need only choose x^i, $i=1, 2, 3$, in a plane containing zero which otherwise has no points in common with the non-negative orthant and for which $x^i + tx_j \geq 0$, $t > 0$ for all i,j. No pair of traders could do better than zero by trading. This is illustrated in figure 3.

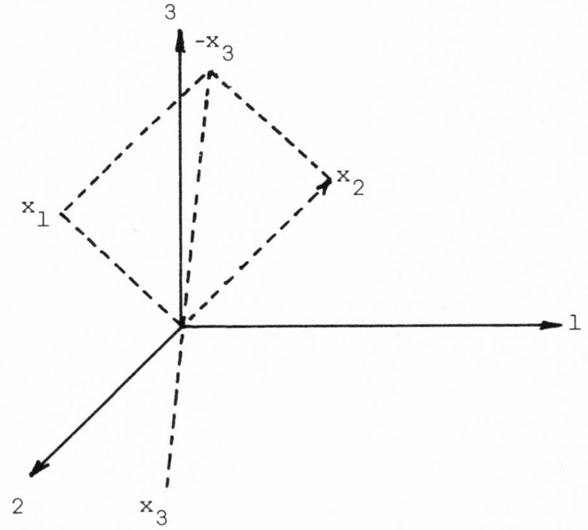

figure 3

So long as there are at least three goods and at least three consumers, this example can be constructed. Only in the case of two goods would it necessarily follow that three co-planar vectors could not be arranged without $x^i + tx^j \geq 0$ for some t, i, j.

<u>Proof of Theorem 5</u>: If x is Pareto optimal, apply remark 1.

On the other hand, after the i-j pairwise optimal trade x, apply Minkowski's theorem. Then there is a non-zero price vector, p, such that

$$p\bar{x}^i - px^i \geq 0,$$

$$p\bar{x}^j - px^j \geq 0,$$

for $\bar{x}^i \; R_i \; x^i$, $\bar{x}^j \; R_i \; x^j$. Since R_i is directionally dense, p is uniquely determined, so that for all j,

$$p\bar{x}^j \geq px^j$$

whenever

$$\bar{x}^j \; R_j \; x^j.$$

Applying the lemma,

$$p\bar{\bar{x}}^j > px^j$$

whenever

$$\bar{\bar{x}}^j \; P_j \; x^j$$

Since

$$\Sigma p\bar{x}^j = p(\Sigma\bar{x}^j) = 0 \; (= p(\Sigma x^j)),$$

whenever

$$\Sigma\bar{x}^j = 0, \; p\bar{x}^j = px^j,$$

whenever

$$\bar{x}^j \; R_j \; x^j.$$

Therefore, if $\bar{\bar{x}}^j \; R_j \; x^j$ for all j, then

$$x^j \; R_j \; \bar{x}^j$$

for all j. QED.

The second paragraph of the proof of theorem 5 is worth listing separately.

Theorem 6. Let preferences be weakly convex, quasi-transferable, and locally unsaturated, and let i have preferences directionally dense at x. Then x is i-j pair-wise optimal, if and only if, there is a vector p unique up to a positive multiplicative constant, such that

$$p\bar{x}^i - px^i > 0$$

$$\bar{p}^j\bar{x}^j - px^j > 0$$

(for all $x^i \; P_i \; x^i$ and all $\bar{x}^j \; P_j \; x^j$).

Theorem 6 says simply that a Pareto optimal trade is obtainable by a competitive equilibrium for the two person economy. However, it is not a competitive equilibrium from a no trade position but only from the initial position, x. QED.

Proof: It remains to verify the necessity which follows immediately from the lemma. QED.

Theorem 6 implies that the price system associated with individual i is the key one. This price system is the unique separating price system for i at x^i, for which

$$p\bar{x}^i > px^i$$

whenever

$$\bar{x}^i \; P_i \; x^i.$$

Corollary. Let preferences be weakly convex, locally unsaturated, and quasi-transferable. Let preferences for i be directionally dense at x^i. If j follows a non-competitive policy at x with respect to the separating price system for i at x^i, then x is not Pareto optimal. Conversely, if each j follows a competitive policy with respect to the separating price system for i at x^i, then x is Pareto optimal.

As an example, suppose that traders follow a competitive policy vis a vis the price system. If a tax is imposed which falls upon all individuals and which is such that it is paid when goods are purchased, but if the tax loss from purchases can be recouped by sales, then the market equilibrium is Pareto optimal. Such a tax would be one on a fixed asset, such as upon the value of unimproved land, a la Henry George. A land tax has no inefficiency associated with it. On the other hand, a tax on commodities traded is such that resale after purchase at best entails no further taxes and does not recoup the tax paid. Therefore, sellers and buyers follow competitive policies with respect to different price systems. This leads to non Pareto optimal trade; whereupon the tax places a burden on the economy above and beyond the amount of its collection.

In general, one can check the Pareto optimality of government or business practices by simply checking each individual in comparison with the one with directionally dense preferences. If pair wise optimization always occurs or what amounts to the same thing, policies are competitive with respect to i's separating price systems, then the community trade is necessarily not Pareto optimal.

5. Irreducible Sets of Traders and Bans on Trading

Under certain conditions there may be bans on trades between i and j, due perhaps to a taboo or to the fact that i and j are located in different times or places. To analyze this case, we consider that trades (i,j) are allowed for (i,j) in the set of possible consumer pairs, T. T is irreducible if all trades are allowed, either directly or indirectly, i.e. for every i-j, there is a "chain" of elements in T beginning in i and ending in j, (i,k), (k,l),...,(m,j). A subset of traders, I, is called universal if for any i,

$$(i,j) \in T$$

for some j in I, and if all trades (i,j), $i \in I$, $j \in I$, are allowed, either directly or indirectly. For example, if there are no bans on trade, T is the set of all trades and any consumer j is universal.

Theorem 7. Let preferences be quasi-transferable, continuous on line segments, weakly convex, and locally unsaturated at the trade x^i, for all i. Let

$$\sum_i x_i \in \text{Int}\, \Sigma X_i.$$

Let preferences be directionally dense at x^i for all i in S. Let T be irreducible, I universal. Then x is Pareto optimal if and only if for all i in I, it is i-j pairwise optimal for all $(i,j) \in T$. Alternatively, x is Pareto optimal if and only if there is a (unique) p such that $p\bar{x}_i > px_i$ for all $\bar{x}_i\, P_i\, x_i$, for all i.

Proof: Simply use the proof of Theorems 5 and 6, observing that the same p must be used for all i in I. To see this, consider (i,j), $i \in I$, $j \in I$. Then there is a chain, I, which leads from i to j. All along the chain each pair of traders must have the same (unique) separating hyperplane. QED.

An application of Theorem 7 is the case of an economy over time where consumers in the same time period trade and intergenerational transfers take place between certain later generations and earlier ones. If there is one family all of whose members, including descendants, are directionally dense, then there is Pareto optimality if and only if there is pairwise optimality.

Samuelson [1958] and Cass and Yaari [1966] give examples of trades which are not Pareto optimal although they are pairwise optimal. Their examples depend upon the assumption that to generation t, goods at time t+2 and thereafter are of no use. Therefore, Pareto optimality requires that they hold zero quantities of such goods. On the other hand, should a person at time t hold claim on goods in time t+3, there would be no way to negotiate with those who would find them useful since they would have nothing to give in return of use to the generation at time t_o.Only intermediation by an intervening generation could transfer the benefits. Preferences are not directional dense since individuals of generation t are unaffected by different (non-negative) prices of later goods. (Alternatively, from

$$x_{t+2} = 0,$$

consider vectors

$$x = (\bar{x}_t, \bar{x}_{t+1}, -\bar{x}_{t+2})$$

$$x_{t+1} > 0, i=0, 1, 2.$$

Addition of ax is impossible for

$$a > 0,$$

whereas for

$$a < 0,$$

addition of ax leads to a lower level of preference).
As seen in the example in figure 3, the failure of Pareto optimality is due to the failure of the property of directional density, <u>not</u> to the ban on trades between individuals of different generations, since under certain circumstances, as Cass and Yaari point out, different generations would have nothing to trade with each other, even if they could. In such cases, pairwise optimality is insufficient and instead the competitive system is a method of obtaining a Pareto optimal trade.

APPENDICES

A. Pareto Optima Are Competitive Equilibria

Arrow [1951] and Debreu [1954] have sought to establish the equivalence of the set of Pareto optimal trades and the set of competitive equilibrium trades for all possible wealth distributions. The part that a competitive equilibrium is Pareto optimal has been established on a rather broad level of generality (in addition to Arrow and Debreu, see Koopmans and Bausch [1959]. On the other hand, the proposition that a Pareto optimum is a competitive equilibrium was studied by Arrow and Debreu and a theorem derived (theorem A-1 below). which did not resolve the question but which did reduce it to the verification of a relatively simple mathematical proposition. This section may be regarded as putting the finishing touches on their theorem so as to establish a definite relationship. An earlier version, announced in Rader [1964], was proved in Rader [1963].

Theorem A-1. A Pareto optimal trade, x, is a competitive equilibrium for some price system p and the initial position, x, provided that

(a) preferences are weakly convex, regular, locally unsaturated, and continuous along line segments, and

(b) px^i is not the minimum expenditure for the ith consumers, $i=1,\ldots,n$.

If px^i is the minimum expenditure, then

$$p\bar{x}^i \geq px^i$$

for all $\bar{x}^i \in P_i(x^i)$.

(This theorem is put together from the proof of Debreu [1954] as modified in Rader [1963], [1964] and it differs slightly from Debreu's theorem in that he has the stronger assumption that preferences are continuous, which is not required. The finiteness of the types of commodities is not required but rather only their divisibility into arbitrarily small units.)

The problem with theorem 4 is that (b) is a purely artificial condition, since we have no information in the theorem about the derived price system p or about the final position, x. Hence, it cannot be concluded that (b) will be satisfied. It is stated by Debreu [1960, p. 96], that a violation of (b) would be "exceptional". Unfortunately, what may be "exceptional", say of measure zero or perhaps nowhere dense, in the price space may not be exceptional in the space of Pareto optima, since there is no necessary reason why Pareto optima should ever map onto sets of positive measure in the price space. A particular case would be that which awards each consumer a positive amount of each good. It would be easy to verify (b) in Theorem A-1. However, if two consumers differed on whether or not a good was desirable, it might well be that every Pareto optimal allocation required that the consumer not liking the good have no positive holding of that good. However suggestive Theorem 4 is, it is short of the program of proving that Pareto optima are competitive equilibria.

The fundamental lemma allows us to use the last sentence of Theorem A-1 in order to immediately deduce that

Theorem A-2. A Pareto optimal trade, x, is a competitive equilibrium for some price system p and some initial position x, provided that preferences are continuous along straight lines, locally unsaturated, quasi-transferable, weakly convex, and regular.

With the aid of the Koopmans-Bausch theorem and Theorem A-2, and Rader [1964], we have

Theorem A-3. If preferences are similar, weakly convex, regular, locally unsaturated, continuous along line segments, quasi-transferable, and if X is bounded as well as closed, then the set of Pareto optima is non-empty and is equivalent to the set of competitive equilibria from all possible initial positions.

Theorem A-3 accomplishes the Arrow-Debreu program. Incidentally the definition of competitive equilibrium here employed allows the disposal of waste products by negative prices.

B. The Core and the Competitive Equilibrium

A trade, x, is in the core provided that for no coalition of individuals,

$$C \subset \bigcup_{i=1}^{m} \{i\}$$

is it possible that there is an

$$(\bar{x}^i, i \in C) \subset \underset{i \in C}{\times} X$$

such that

$$\text{(a)} \quad \bar{x}^i \; R_i \; x^i \text{ for all } i \in C,$$

$\bar{x}^j \; P_j \; x^j$ for some $j \in C$, and

(b) $\sum_{i \in C} \bar{x}^i = 0.$

If the definition fails for some $(\bar{x}^i, \; i \in C)$, it is said that C blocks x and $(\bar{x}^i, \; i \in C)$ dominates x via C.

Although the concept of the core arose in the game theoretic context, the idea that no coalition should (or would) be made worse off than it could be by going it alone is due to Edgeworth [1881]. Therefore, elements of the core are called Edgeworth optimal.

If for x in the core,

$$\underbrace{(x, \ldots, x)}_{k \text{ times}}$$

is in the core as we multiply the economy by a factor of k (so that there are k individuals with each type of preference on trade), then x is an Edgeworth optimal trade which is invariant to the multiplication of the economy. In effect, with x, no individual benefits from his "oneness" or from a monopoly position. As in the case of Edgeworth optimality, this invariance would seem an elementary welfare requirement.

Shapley has shown that the competitive equilibrium is Edgeworth optimal, and it is obviously invariant under multiplication of the economy since the number of consumers does not affect choice with regard to a price system nor the fact that these choices sum to zero over the community. A still stronger result is that of Debreu and Scarf [1963];

Theorem B-1. If preferences are strictly convex, unsaturated, continuous on line segments and $0 \in \text{Int } X_i$, $i=1,\ldots,n$, then x is Edgeworth optimal and invariant to multiplication of the economy if and only if x is a competitive equilibrium for some price system, p, and from the initial position 0. If there is not $0 \in \text{Int } X_i$, then still,

$$p\bar{x}^i \geq px^i = 0$$

for all $\bar{x}^i \in P_i(x^i)$.

(Debreu and Scarf actually do not state the last sentence, but they prove it, nor do they list continuity along straight lines, which is the property they actually use, but instead, they have the stronger condition of full continuity.)

The only problem with this theorem is that the requirements that $0 \in \text{Int } X_i$ may be an important restriction on the applicability of the theorem, especially when a large number of commodities are involved. In effect, it is required that each individual be able to obtain from production and/or wealth a positive amount of each good (which in fact is the way Debreu and Scarf state it).

Again, the fundamental lemma applies.

Theorem B-2. If preferences are regular, strictly convex, unsaturated, continuous on line segments, and quasi-transferable, then x is Edgeworth optimal and invariant to muliplication of the economy if and only if x is a competitive equilibrium for some price system, p, for which 0 is the initial position.

Incidently, this theorem narrows the possible ambiguities of welfare economics due to distributional questions. If the present distribution is regarded as inviolable *vis à vis* individuals and coalitions, then only the competitive equilibrium is "fair" in the sense of not depending upon the monopolization of talents or demands or property by a single individual. Possible applications are

(1) whenever the inviolable and correct initial position is ascertained, upon whatever principle of distribution, the final method of economic organization should be the competitive equilibrium, or

(2) if all present wealth has been honestly accumulated from past labor of individuals and their ancestors, no transfers should be made except those dictated by competitive equilibrium.

C. The Existence of the Competitive Equilibrium, I.

Theorem A-3 insures that competitive equilibrium trade (and associated price system) exists from at least one initial position. On the other hand, the question arises as to how general the theory is from the viewpoint of organizing markets. Is it true that from any initial position, at least in $\chi_{i=1}^{n} X_i$, you can always find a price system which will take you to an equilibrium? Only then would it be regarded as a system of economic organization, independent of some other kind of transfers.

Let

$$\eta(x) = \{\bar{x} \mid \text{there exists } p \text{ such that } p x^i = p\bar{x}^i \text{ and } p\bar{\bar{x}}^i > p x^i \text{ for } \bar{\bar{x}}^i \, P_i \, x^i,\ i=1,\ldots,n\}.$$

Clearly $\eta(x)$, if non-empty, is a cone with origin x. Under certain conditions, it is known that

$$\eta(X) \supset \text{Int} \mathop{\chi}_{i=1}^{n} X_i$$

This is the Arrow-Debreu existence theorem (Arrow and Debreu [1954], Gale [1955], McKenzie [1959], or Rader [1964]). We use the version from Rader [1964, p. 169] which is very similar to that of McKenzie [1959].

Theorem C-1. Suppose preferences are regular, continuous on line segments, continuous in the interior of the trade set, and weakly convex. Suppose the community trade possibility set, X, is bounded and closed. Then a competitive equilibrium exists from and initial point x in $\mathop{\chi}_{i=1}^{n} X_i$, i.e. $\eta(X) \supset \mathop{\chi}_{i=1}^{n}$ Int X_i. (It happens that the use of the particular definition of equilibrium here employed allows the inclusion of waste products, whose prices are negative. This was not the case of the Arrow-Debreu existence theorem nor of that of Gale, although it appears to have been the case for their theorem that Pareto optima were competitive equilibria.) The restriction of initial positions to the interior of $\mathop{\chi}_{i=1}^{n} X_i$ is fairly serious for the case of a large number of commodities, all of which, even in a production economy, no consumer can expect to obtain on his own.

It is possible to use the fundamental lemma to verify that

Theorem C-2. Suppose preferences are similar, regular, continuous on line segments, weakly convex, locally unsaturated, and quasi-transferable. Suppose that X is closed and bounded. Then the competitive equilibrium exists for all x in $\mathop{\chi}_{i=1}^{n} X_i$, i.e.

$$\eta(X) \supset \mathop{\chi}_{i=1}^{m} X_i$$

Consequently, there exists at least one Edgeworth optimal trade which is invariant under multiplication of the economy, whether or not

$$0 \in \text{Int} \mathop{\chi}_{i=1}^{n} X_i$$

Theorem C-2 is more or less that of McKenzie [1959]. It removes a serious restriction to the proof of the existence of a competitive equilibrium. We present a different proof from McKenzie so as to derive C-2 from C-1.

Proof: Possibly by taking subsequences, for any $\bar{x} \in \chi_{i=1}^{n} X_i$ we can find

$$\bar{x}(n) \to \bar{x}, \quad \frac{p(n)}{|p(n)|} \to p,$$

$p(n)/|p(n)|$ a competitive price system for initial position $\bar{x}(n)$ which gives $x(n)(\to x)$ as an equilibrium. We show that p is a competitive price system giving the equilibrium $\bar{x}$. Choose p so that $py > 0$, for some $y \in S$. Suppose $\bar{\bar{x}}^i \; P_i \; x^i$. By the regularity of R_i, $P_i^{-1}(\bar{\bar{x}}^i)$ is open and contains $x^i(n)$ for large n, so that $\bar{\bar{x}}^i \; P_i \; x^i(n)$ for n sufficiently large. Therefore, the remark in section 4 applies to show that $p\bar{\bar{x}}^i > px^i(n)$. Therefore

$$p\bar{\bar{x}}^i \geq px^i = \lim px^i(n)$$

Applying the lemma,

$$p\bar{\bar{x}}^i > px^i,$$

so that x is the competitive choice. That it is an equilibrium is verified by the fact that

$$\sum_{i=1}^{n} x^i = \lim \sum_{i=1}^{n} x^i(n) = 0.$$

QED.

D. The Existence of the Competitive Equilibrium, II.

Scarf [1962] has recently suggested an alternative approach to the existence of the competitive equilibrium whereby one first proves the existence of the core and then uses Theorem B-2 to show that the set of competitive equilibria is non-empty since it is equal to the limit of the core as multiplication of the economy takes place. Since Scarf proves the existence of the core constructively, this gives a constructive proof of the existence of the competitive equilibrium. That the core is decreasing under multiplication is a result of Debreu and Scarf [1963]. That the core is a decreasing set of compact sets which therefore has a non-empty intersection is easy to verify when you have full continuity of preferences. However, full continuity of induced preferences is not a reasonable condition to impose on an economy with production (Rader [1964, p. 180]). Therefore, we need an alternative proposition.

Theorem D-1. If preferences are regular, and quasi-transferable for each coalition

$$C \subset \bigcup_{i=1}^{n} \{i\},$$

the core (equals the set of Edgeworth optimal trades) is bounded and closed.

This theorem and Scarf's proof of the existence of the core allows a constructive proof of Theorem C-2. (It is the only result in these appendices not dependent upon the fundamental lemma.)

Proof: If the core were not closed, then for some x^n in the core, $x^n \to x$, x is blocked by some coalition C. In that case, there would exist $\bar{x}$ such that $\bar{x}^i \; R_i \; x^i$, $i \in C$, $\bar{x}^j \; P_j \; x^j$ for some $j \in C$,

$$\sum_{i \in C} \bar{x}^i = 0.$$

By virtue of quasi-transferability, there would be an $\bar{\bar{x}}$ for which

$$\sum_{i \in C} \bar{\bar{x}}^i = 0,$$

$\bar{\bar{x}}^i \; P_i \; \bar{x}^i$ for all $i \in C$. (In effect, C "strictly" blocks x whenever C blocks x.) Since $P_i^{-1}(\bar{\bar{x}})$ is open, $x^n \to x (\in P_i^{-1}(\bar{\bar{x}}))$ would be eventually in $P_i^{-1}(\bar{\bar{x}})$ for all i and therefore would be blocked by C. This is contrary to the assumption that x^n is in the core. Therefore the core is closed. It is clearly bounded whenever X is since it is contained in X. QED.

FOOTNOTES

* The research for this paper was financed by the National Science Foundation (GS-1024).

1 The notion of quasi-transferable preferences was first introduced by McKenzie [1959] under the name "indecomposability".

REFERENCES

Arrow, [1951] "An Extension of the Basic Theorems of Classical Welfare Economics," Proceedings of the Second Berkeley Symposium on Mathematical Statistics and Probability, J. Neyman, ed., University of California Press, pp. 507-32.

Arrow and Debreu, [1954] "Existence of an Equilibrium for a Competitive Economy," Econometrica, 22, pp. 265-90.

Cass and Yaari, [1966] "A Re-examination of the Pure Consumption Loans Model," Journal of Political Economy, 74, pp. 353-67.

Debreu, [1954] "Valuation Equilibrium and Pareto Optimum," Proceedings of the National Academy of Sciences of the U.S.A., 40, pp. 588-92.

________, [1960] Theory of Value, Wiley, New York.

Debreu and Scarf, [1963] "A Limit Theorem on the Core of an Economy," International Economic Review, vol. 4, pp. 235-46.

Edgeworth. [1881] Mathematical Physics, Kegan Paul, London.

Gale, [1955] "On the Laws of Supply and Demand," Mathematica Scandinavica, 3, pp. 155-69.

Koopmans. [1957] Three Essays on the State of Economic Science, McGraw-Hill, New York.

Koopmans and Bausch, [1959] "Selected Topics in Economics Involving Mathematical Reasoning," SIAM Review, 1.

Little, [1951] "Direct versus Indirect Taxes," Economic Journal 61.

McKenzie, [1959] "On the Existence of General Equilibrium for a Competitive Market," Econometrica, 27.

Pigou. [1920] The Economics of Welfare, Macmillan, London

Rader, [1963] "Edgeworth Exchange and General Economic Equilibrium," Unpublished doctoral dissertation, Yale University.

________, [1964] "Edgeworth Exchange and General Economic

Equilibrium," Yale Economic Essays, 4, pp. 132-80.

Samuelson, [1958] "An Exact Consumption Loan Model of Interest with or without the Contrivance of Money," Journal of Political Economy, 66, pp. 467-82.

Scarf, [1966] "The Core of an N Person Game," Cowles Foundation Discussion Paper, No. 182, Revised.

A NOTE ON POINT-SET MAPPINGS[1]

by

James C. Moore
University of Missouri

From the standpoint of Economic applications, some of the more important results of modern mathematics are Kakutani's Fixed Point Theorem and its various generalizations.[2] The reader will recall that the statement of the Kakutani Theorem is as follows:[3]

Theorem (Kakutani).[4] Let C be a non-empty compact convex set in R^n. If Γ is an upper semi-continuous mapping of C into the power set of C, and if for each $x \in C$, Γx is convex and non-empty, then

$$(\exists x^o \in C): x^o \in \Gamma x^o.$$

An Economist attempting to apply this result to an Economic problem is likely, however, to encounter a bewildering variety of definitions of what is meant by an "upper semi-continuous point-set mapping." As a matter of fact, all of the following have been given as definitions of upper semi-continuity for point-set mappings.[5]

Definitions: Let X and Y be topological spaces, and let Γ be a point-set mapping of X into Y, i.e.,

$$\Gamma: \quad X \rightarrow 2^Y.$$

We say that Γ is:

1. CLOSED if whenever $x^o \in X$, $y^o \in Y$, $y^o \notin \Gamma x^o$, $\exists$(open) neighborhoods $U(x^o)$, $V(y^o)$ such that

$$(x \in U(x^o)): \quad \Gamma x \cap V(y^o) = \emptyset.$$

2. CLOSED* if whenever $x^o \in X$ and $\langle x^n \rangle$, $\langle y^n \rangle$ are sequences such that

$$\lim_{n\to\infty} x^n = x^o, \ \lim_{n\to\infty} y^n = y^o, \text{ and}$$

$$y^n \in \Gamma x^n \text{ for } n = 1, 2, \ldots,$$

we have

$$y^o \in \Gamma x^o.$$

3. QUASI UPPER SEMI-CONTINUOUS (abbreviated q.u.s.c.) if whenever $x^o \varepsilon X$ and 0 is an open subset of Y $\ni \Gamma x^o \subseteq 0$,

$$(\exists U(x^o))\ (x \ \varepsilon\ U(x^o));\ \Gamma x \subseteq 0.$$

4. UPPER SEMI-CONTINUOUS$_F$ (abbreviated u.s.c.$_F$) if Γ is q.u.s.c. and $(x \ \varepsilon\ X)$: Γx is closed in Y.

5. UPPER SEMI-CONTINUOUS (abbreviated u.s.c.) if Γ is q.u.s.c. and $(x \ \varepsilon\ X)$: Γx is a compact set.

A part of the variety in the above definitions is more apparent than real. As Professor Berge points out ([1], p. 111), Definitions 1 and 2 are equivalent. Moreover, as we show below, in the situation where the range of Γ is the power set of a compact space (as is required by the hypotheses of the Kakutani Theorem), Definitions 1, 2, 4, and 5 are all equivalent. On the other hand, there is a considerable degree of independence in Definitions 1, 3, 4, and 5 when the range space is a topological space which is not necessarily compact. This independence is also of some significance, because these four types of mappings differ considerably with respect to the behavior of the composition product of two mappings of the same type, where we define the composition product of two point-set mappings as follows.

<u>Definition 6</u>. Let X, Y, and Z be topological spaces, and suppose that:

$$\Gamma_1: \ X \to 2^Y,\ \Gamma_2: \ Y \to 2^Z.$$

We define the COMPOSITION PRODUCT of Γ_1 and Γ_2, $\Gamma_2 \cdot \Gamma_1$, by:

$$\Gamma_2 \cdot \Gamma_1\ x = \bigcup_{y \varepsilon \Gamma_1 x} \Gamma_2 y = \Gamma_2(\Gamma_1 x).$$

Our principal concern in this paper will be to investigate the question of which of the above properties of point-set mappings is invariant under the composition product of two mappings of the respective type. For the sake of completeness, however, we shall begin by examining the relationships among the above definitions; first for the case where the range is not necessarily the subsets of a compact space, and then for the case where compactness is assumed. Since in Economic applications, one is usually dealing with metric spaces, we shall examine the relationships among these concepts in the situation where Y is a Regular Topological Space.

<u>Lemma 1</u>. Let X be a Topological Space and Y be a Regular Space. Define

$$C = \{\Gamma | \Gamma: \ X \to 2^Y\},$$

and

$C_1 = \{\Gamma \in C | \ \Gamma \text{ is u.s.c.}\}$

$C_2 = \{\Gamma \in C | \ \Gamma \text{ is u.s.c.}_F\}$

$C_3 = \{\Gamma \in C | \ \Gamma \text{ is q.u.s.c.}\}$

$C_4 = \{\Gamma \in C | \ \Gamma \text{ is closed}\}.$

Then we have:

a.) $C_1 \subseteq C_2$

Proof: Since Y is a Regular Space, it is a Hausdorff Space. Hence if $\Gamma \in C_1$, we have

$(x \in X)$: Γx is closed in Y.

b.) it is not necessarily the case that $C_2 \subseteq C_1$.

Proof: Let $X = R$, $Y = R^2$, and let Γ be defined on X by

$$\Gamma x = \{y \in R^2 | y_1 = 0\} \quad \forall x \in X.$$

It is immediately apparent that Γ is u.s.c.$_F$, but not u.s.c.

c.) $C_1 \subseteq C_2 \subseteq C_3$.

Proof: Given part (a), this follows trivially from our definitions.

d.) $C_1 \subseteq C_2 \subseteq C_4$.

Proof:[6] Let $\Gamma \in C_2$, $x^o \in X$, $y^o \in Y$, and suppose that

$$y^o \notin \Gamma x^o.$$

Then since Γx^o is closed, and Y is a Regular Space, $\exists$ open sets $V(y^o)$, 0 in Y $\ni$ $y^o \in V(y^o)$, $\Gamma x^o \subseteq 0$, $V(y^o) \cap 0 = \emptyset$. Since Γ is u.s.c.$_F$, ($\exists$ open $U(x^o) \subseteq X$) $(x \in U(x^o))$: $\Gamma x \subseteq 0$, and therefore

$$(x \in U(x^o)): \Gamma x \cap V(y^o) = \emptyset.$$

Hence Γ is closed.

e.) it is not necessarily the case that $C_3 \subseteq C_4$[7] (and hence not necessarily $C_3 \subseteq C_2$, or $C_3 \subseteq C_1$).

Proof: Let $X = R$, $Y = [0, 1]$ (with the subspace topology), and let Γ be defined by

$$\Gamma x = (0, 1) \ \forall x \in R.$$

It is then immediately apparent that Γ is q.u.s.c., but not closed.

f.) it is not necessarily the case that $C_4 \subseteq C_3$[8] (and hence not necessarily $C_4 \subseteq C_2$, or $C_4 \subseteq C_1$)

Proof: Let $X = [-\pi/2, \pi/2] \subseteq R$ (with the subspace topology) and $Y = R^2$.

Define Γ on X by

$$\Gamma x = \begin{cases} \{y = \langle\rho \cos\theta, \rho \sin\theta\rangle \in R^2 \mid \pi/2 \leqq \theta \leqq \pi/2 - x, \rho \geqq 0\} \\ \quad \text{if } x \leqq 0 \\ \{y = \langle\rho \cos\theta, \rho \sin\theta\rangle \in R^2 \mid \pi/2 - x \leqq \theta \leqq \pi/2, \rho \geqq 0\} \\ \quad \text{if } x > 0. \end{cases}$$

Clearly Γ is a closed mapping. On the other hand, let U be defined by:

$$U = \{y \in R^2 \mid -1 < y_1 < 1\}.$$

Then

$$\Gamma 0 = \{\langle\rho \cos\theta, \rho \sin\theta\rangle \in R^2 \mid \theta = \pi/2, \rho \geqq 0\} =$$

$$\{y \in R^2 \mid y_1 = 0, y_2 \geqq 0\} \subseteq U;$$

but it is clear that every open neighborhood of 0 contains a point $x \ni \Gamma x \not\subseteq U$. Therefore Γ is not q.u.s.c.

It is apparent from the above results that there is a considerable degree of independence among the concepts defined in Definitions 1-5, even if the space Y is a metric space. However, as we mentioned above, if we require that Y also be compact, the situation is changed considerably, as the following result shows.

Lemma 2. Let X be a topological space, and Y be a compact Regular Space.[9] Define C and C_i for i = 1, ..., 4, as in Lemma 1. Then we have:

a.) (Berge) $C_1 = C_2 = C_4$.

Proof: We see by Lemma 1-d that it suffices to prove that $C_4 \subseteq C_1$. For a proof of this result, see Berge [1], Corollary to Theorem 7, p. 112.

b.) it is not necessarily the case that $C_3 \subseteq C_4$.

Proof: The reader will note that the example presented in the proof of Lemma 1-e, above, proves this result also (since the space Y involved there is compact).

c.) $C_i \subseteq C_3$ for i = 1, 2, 4.

Proof: This result follows immediately from Lemma 1-c and part (a), above.

The reader may wonder at this point what all the fuss has been about. After all, the Kakutani Fixed Point Theorem requires that the space on which our "upper semi-continuous" mapping Γ is defined (and whose subspaces constitute the range of Γ) be compact. We have shown that in this context we can get into trouble by using the q.u.s.c. definition, but it appears that it makes no difference whether Γ is u.s.c., u.s.c.$_F$ or closed. The difficulty arises from the fact that in applications of the Kakutani Theorem the natural procedure may be to begin with a mapping whose range is not the subsets of a compact space; and to consider the composition product of that mapping with a point-set mapping whose range is the subsets of a compact metric space. Thus in his ingenious article [6], Negishi considers a mapping Γ_1 defined on

$$X = Z \times T^{n-1},$$

where $Z \subseteq R^m$ is compact, and T^{n-1} denotes the (n-1) dimensional simplex:

$$T^{n-1} = \{p \in R^n_+ | \Sigma^n_{i=1} p_i = 1\};$$

and mapping into the power set of

$$Y = Z \times [R^n_+ \setminus \{\theta\}].$$ [10]

He then considers the (single-valued) mapping Γ_2 defined on Y by

$$\Gamma_2(<z, p>) = <z, (1/\Sigma_i p_i)p>,$$

where $z \in Z$, $p \in [R^n_+ \setminus \{\theta\}]$. The composition product,

$$\Gamma = \Gamma_2 \cdot \Gamma_1,$$

then maps X into the power set of X. Hence, if one could show that the mapping Γ is closed (and for each $x \in X$, Γx is convex and non-empty), the hypotheses of Kakutani's Fixed Point Theorem apply.

One is tempted, given the situation outlined in the preceding paragraph, to argue that the composition product of two closed mappings is necessarily closed, and therefore the mapping Γ is closed. However, in spite of the apparent plausibility of this statement, the composition product of two closed mappings is not necessarily closed. In fact, even if we add the stronger hypotheses[11] of the following conjecture, the composition product is not necessarily closed.

<u>(False) Conjecture</u>: Let $X \subseteq R^n$, $Y \subseteq R^m$, and suppose that:

i.) X is compact

ii.) Φ is a closed point-set mapping of X into 2^Y;

iii.) ϕ is a continuous, open, single-valued mapping of Y into X.

Then

$$\Gamma = \phi \cdot \Phi$$

is closed.

The following provides a counterexample[12] to this conjecture. Let $X = [-\pi/2, \pi/2] \subseteq R$ (with the subspace topology), and let

$$Y = R^2,$$

$$W = \{y \in R^2 \mid -1 \leq y_1 \leq 1\}.$$

Define Φ on X by

$$\Phi x = \begin{cases} \{y = \langle \rho\cos\theta, \rho\sin\theta \rangle \in R^2 \mid \pi/2 \leq \theta \leq \pi/2 - x,\ \rho \geq 0\} \cap W & \text{if } x \leq 0 \\ \{y = \langle \rho\cos\theta, \rho\sin\theta \rangle \in R^2 \mid \pi/2 - x \leq \theta \leq \pi/2,\ \rho \geq 0\} \cap W & \text{if } x > 0; \end{cases}$$

and ϕ on Y by

$$\phi(y) = y_1.$$

Clearly Φ is closed, and ϕ is continuous and open. Moreover,

$$\Gamma = \phi \cdot \Phi$$

maps X into the power set of X. However, let

$$V = (-1/2, 1/2) \subseteq X.$$

Then

$$\Gamma 0 = \{0\} \subseteq V;$$

but we see that for any $x > 0$, Φx intersects the line

$$L = \{y \in R^2 \mid y_1 = 1\},$$

and therefore for any $x > 0$, $1 \in \Gamma x$. Hence

$$(\nexists U(0))\ (x \in U(0)):\ \Gamma x \subseteq V;$$

and consequently Γ is not q.u.s.c. Therefore, by Lemma 2-c, Γ is not closed.

A principal difficulty, then, in dealing with closed

point-set mappings is that the composition product of two closed point-set mappings is not necessarily closed. The same difficulty arises in dealing with u.s.c.$_F$ mappings, as the following (rather familiar) example shows. Let

$$X = [0, 1] \subseteq R \text{ (with the subspace topology)}$$

$$Y = (0, 1) \subseteq R \text{ (with the subspace topology),}$$

and let Γ_1 be defined on X into 2^Y by

$$\Gamma_1 x = Y \quad \forall \ x \in R;$$

and Γ_2 be defined on Y into 2^X by:

$$\Gamma_2 y = [y, 1].$$

It is apparent that Γ_1 and Γ_2 are u.s.c.$_F$ mappings. Consider, however, the composition product, $\Gamma = \Gamma_2 \cdot \Gamma_1$, mapping X into 2^X. We have, for instance, $\Gamma(1/2) = (0, 1]$, which is not closed in X. Therefore, Γ is not u.s.c.$_F$.

The situation is somewhat different with regard to u.s.c. and q.u.s.c. mappings, however, as the following results show. Moreover, if we reverse the situation holding in the conjecture on p. 7, the composition product is closed, as we show in Lemma 4.

Lemma 3. Let X, Y, and Z be topological spaces, and suppose that Γ_1 and Γ_2 are q.u.s.c., where

$$\Gamma_1: \ X \to 2^Y, \ \Gamma_2: \ Y \to 2^Z.$$

Then the composition product

$$\Gamma = \Gamma_2 \cdot \Gamma_1$$

is q.u.s.c.

Proof: Let $x^o \in X$ and let $W \subseteq Z$ be $\ni$ W is open, and $\Gamma x^o \subseteq W$. Consider

$$V \equiv \Gamma_2^+(W) = \{y \in Y | \ \Gamma_2 y \subseteq W\}.$$

Since, by hypotheses, Γ_2 is q.u.s.c., it is clear that V is open. But, since Γ_1 is q.u.s.c.,

$$(\exists U(x^o)) \ (x \in U(x^o)): \ \Gamma_1 x \subseteq V$$

(note that, since $\Gamma x^o \subseteq W$, it follows that $\Gamma_1 x^o \subseteq V$), and hence

$$x \in U(x^o) \quad \Gamma x \subseteq W.$$

Therefore Γ is q.u.s.c.

Lemma 4. Let X, Y, and Z be topological spaces, and suppose that Γ_1 is u.s.c. and Γ_2 is closed, where:

$$\Gamma_1: \ X \to 2^Y, \ \Gamma_2: \ Y \to 2^Z.$$

Then the composition product, $\Gamma = \Gamma_2 \cdot \Gamma_1$, is closed.

Proof:

Let $x^o \in X$, and $z^o \in Z$ be such that

$$z^o \notin \Gamma x^o.$$

If $y \in Y$ is $\ni y \in \Gamma_1 x^o$, it then follows that $z^o \notin \Gamma_2$. Hence, since Γ_2 is closed $\exists$ open sets $V_y(y)$, $W_y(z^o)$

$$(\bar{y} \in V_y(y)): \Gamma_2 \bar{y} \cap W_y(z^o) = \emptyset$$

Since Γ_1 is u.s.c., $\Gamma_1 x^o$ is compact, and therefore $\exists V_{y_1}, \ldots, V_{y_n}$ such that

$$\Gamma_1 x^o \subseteq V \equiv \bigcap_{i=1}^{n} V_{y_i}.$$

Moreover, again by the fact that Γ_1 is u.s.c., it then follows that:

$$(1) (\exists U(x^o)) \ (x \in U(x^o)): \Gamma_1 x \subseteq V.$$

Define

$$W(z^o) = \bigcap_{i=1}^{n} W_{y_i}(z^o).$$

We note that $W(z^o)$ is open and non-empty. Moreover, it follows by (1) and the definitions of W_{y_i} and V_{y_i} that:

$$(x \in U(x^o)): \Gamma x \cap W(z^o) = \emptyset$$

Therefore Γ is closed. QED.

We conclude by stating, for the sake of reference, the following theorem. A proof may be found in Berge [1], p. 113.

Theorem (Berge). Let X, Y, and Z be topological spaces, and suppose that Γ_1 and Γ_2 are u.s.c., where

$$\Gamma_1: \; X \to 2^Y, \; \Gamma_2: \; Y \to 2^Z.$$

Then the composition product

$$\Gamma = \Gamma_2 \cdot \Gamma_1$$

is u.s.c.

FOOTNOTES

1. The author gratefully acknowledges his indebtedness to Professors Charles E. Clark and Melvin D. George for many helpful conversations on subjects related to the topic with which this paper is concerned.

2. See, for instance, Fan [2] and Glicksberg [3].

3. See Kakutani [4], pp. 457-8. The wording of the statement used here is more or less from Berge [1], p. 174.

4. We shall denote n-dimensional Euclidean space by R^n. The non-negative orthant in R^n will be denoted by R^n_+; that is

$$R^n_+ = \{x \in R^n | x_i \geqq 0 \text{ for } i = 1,\ldots,n\}.$$

We shall denote the origin in R^n by θ.

5. Definition 2 is identical to the definition of upper semi-continuity used by Kakutani. Professor Karlin in [5], p. 409, appears to state that Definition 3 is equivalent to upper semi-continuity (for Euclidean spaces), which he defines à la Kakutani. Definition 4 is the definition of upper semi-continuity used by Fan in [2] (see p. 122). Definition 5 is due to Professor Berge (see eg., [1], p. 109). Definitions 1 and 2 are equivalent. The formulation of Definition 1 and the term "closed" are due to Berge (see [1], p. 111). The reader will note that all these definitions are equivalent to continuity for the special case where Γ is a single-valued mapping.

6. This proof is an adaptation of a similar proof by Berge. See Berge [1], p. 112.

7. This is in apparent contradiction to a statement made by Professor Karlin ([5], p. 409), which seems to imply that if X and Y are Euclidean spaces, then (in our terminology) $C_3 = C_4$.

8. Again this is in apparent contradiction to the statement by Professor Karlin cited above. It is also in apparent contradiction to a statement by Professor Fan (see [2], p. 121) to the effect that if X and Y are metric spaces, then (in our terminology) $C_4 = C_2$. Since his principal theorem deals with the situation in which Y is compact, however, Professor Fan may have meant to imply only that the equality held in the situation wherein Y is a compact metric space

(the equality does, in fact, hold in this case, as we show below). The counterexample used here is developed from a counterexample presented orally to the author by Professor Melvin D. George in connection with a related conjecture.

9. We could, of course, equivalently require that Y be a compact Hausdorff Space.

10. The mapping in question is the mapping of

$$\alpha \varepsilon S^{n-1} \rightarrow (x_i^o, y_K^o, p_j^o)$$

of α into the saddle points of $\phi(x_i, y_K, P_j, \mu_K) = \Sigma_i \alpha_i U_i(x_i) - \Sigma_j P_j(\Sigma_i x_{ij} - \Sigma_K y_{Kj} - \Sigma_i \overline{x}_{ij}) + \Sigma_K \mu_K F_K(y_K)$ defined by Professor Negishi on pages 95-6 of [6].

11. Recall that closedness is equivalent to continuity for single-valued mappings.

12. This counterexample may have some relevance to Prof. Negishi's proof that his mapping Γ (used as an example in the text) is closed. It should be noted, however, that the counterexample is only an objection to Negishi's method of proof of his Theorem 5 (see p. 96 of [6]) and not a counter-example to the theorem itself. As a matter of fact, Professor Negishi has indicated in private correspondence that his objection can be removed in, roughly, the following fashion. The functions U_i and F_k, to which the mapping Γ_1 (see n. 10, above) is related are concave and have compact domains. Hence one should be able to prove the existence of some compact set $\overline{P} \subseteq R_+^n \setminus \{\theta\}$ such that the mapping Γ_1 used in his proof can be replaced by $\overline{\Gamma}_1$ defined by $\overline{\Gamma}_1 x = \Gamma_1 x \cap Z \times \overline{P}$. Since the range of $\overline{\Gamma}_1$ is compact, $\overline{\Gamma}_1$ would be u.s.c., and consequently one could apply the Berge Theorem stated on the last page of the text to prove that Γ is u.s.c.

REFERENCES

[1] Berge, Claude, Topological Spaces. New York: The Macmillan Co., 1963 (English translation of Espaces Topologiques, Fonctions Multivoques. Paris: Dunod, 1959. Translation by E. M. Patterson)

[2] Fan, Ky, "Fixed-Point and Minimax Theorems in Locally Convex Topological Linear Spaces," Proc. N.A.S.; 38, 2; Feb. 15, 1952; 121-126

[3] Glicksberg, I. L. "A Further Generalization of the Kakutani Fixed Point Theorem, With Application to Nash Equilibrium Points," Proc. Amer. Math. Soc.; 3, 1, Feb., 1952; 170-4

[4] Kakutani, Shizuo, "A Generalization of Brouwer's Fixed Point Theorem," Duke Math. Jnl.; 8, 3; Sept., 1941; 457-9

[5] Karlin, Samuel, Mathematical Methods and Theory in Games, Programming, and Economics, Vol. I. Reading, Mass.: Addison-Wesley, 1959

[6] Negishi, Takashi, "Welfare Economics and Existence of an Equilibrium for a Competitive Economy," Metroeconomica 12, 1960; 92-97

II.

ECONOMIC THEORY AND EMPIRICAL STUDIES

HYPOTHESIS FORMULATION IN QUANTITATIVE ECONOMICS: A CONTRIBUTION TO DEMAND ANALYSIS

by

R. L. Basmann*
Purdue University

1. Introduction

In several recent articles I have discussed some aspects of the formulation and statistical testing of econometric hypotheses (Basmann, 1963, 1965a, 1965b, 1965c, 1965d, 1966). The type of econometric hypothesis considered in those articles is characterized by its form of expression, namely, a set of restrictions--functional dependences and inequalities--on the parameters of a family of statistical joint distribution functions of endogenous economic variables, all of the statistical distribution functions having the same definite form, *e.g.*, multivariate normal. For instance, in a recent paper on the distribution of the identifiability test statistic and its application the structural hypothesis is the statement that the *marginal propensity to consume*, β_1^*, belongs to the interval $\{\beta_1 | 5/6 < \beta_1 < 17/20\}$, *i.e.*,

(1.1) $$\beta_1^* \in \{\beta_1 | 5/6 < \beta_1 < 17/20\}$$

(*cf.* Basmann, 1965d, p. 398).[1] Actually, the hypothetical restriction (1.1) is deduced from the following structural hypothesis: $(\beta_1^*, \beta_6^*, \beta_3^*)$ *belongs to the set of all parameter points* $(\beta_1, \beta_6, \beta_3)$ *that satisfy the restrictions*

(1.2.a-d)
$$3/4 < \beta_1 < 17/20,$$
$$1 < \beta_1 + \beta_6 < 61/60,$$
$$0 < 3\beta_6 < \beta_3,$$
$$\beta_3 < 1/2.$$

β_6^* and β_3^* are coefficients of gross national product in the structural investment function and demand for money function respectively. The restrictions (1.2a-d) conjoined with other parameter restrictions of the same type express a statistical null hypothesis to be tested against a class of alternative hypotheses.

Some readers--especially graduate students--have raised questions (chiefly of a practical sort) about the origins of such hypotheses. For several reasons my comments about hypothesis formulation in those earlier papers do not go far in answering such questions. In the articles referred to, attention is focused on the process of statistical testing of econometric hypotheses and, especially, on the derivation of the sampling distributions of test statistics (cf. Basmann, 1966, especially). The econometric statistical hypotheses, i.e., the hypothetical parameter restrictions, which are used chiefly as illustrations in those papers, were simply put forward and described briefly with little or no discussion of how they were formulated, and--of course--without any attempt to make them plausible or convincing to the reader either before or after the outcomes of the statistical tests. Because there are so many details to be examined it is convenient to treat the problems of hypothesis formulation and hypothesis testing in separate articles; moreover, the logical structure of the general problem of hypothesis formulation and testing permits this. Discussion of hypothesis testing takes the hypotheses (whose tests are to be discussed) as given members of its universe of discourse.

In the present article some aspects of econometric hypothesis formulation are examined in considerable detail. The purpose of the present article is to suggest answers only to the first of the two distinct questions listed below, which readers of my previous papers frequently ask:

(1) How do you find, or invent, hypothetical structural parameter restrictions in the first place?

(2) What a priori knowledge do you possess that tells you that these hypothetical parameter restrictions are plausibly true?

In giving some answers to question (1) I shall make use of an illustration drawn from my dissertation research in consumer demand analysis conducted some years ago (Basmann, 1953, 1954, 1956). One question with which that investigation had to do was concerned with the specific mathematical forms that functions adjusted to price, income, and quantity data can take when those functions are required to possess all the mathematical properties deduced for demand functions in theory of consumer demand.[2] (In this discussion a system of functions is said to be a system of demand functions if, and only if, it possesses all of the foregoing properties.) The objective sought was a collection of specific mathematical forms of demand functions with help of which hypotheses about the structure of consumer preferences can be expressed and--ultimately--tested against empirical data. Discussion of this illustration will focus on its hypothesis formulation aspects primarily.

For sake of effective discussion of hypothesis formulation I shall try to clarify the distinction between question (1) and question (2). Although the question (1) is by no means susceptible of brief answer--that is to say, there is no general rule of "hypothesis discovery" that is applicable to all cases--the meaning of question (1) is clear. To put it another way, question (1) indicates the specific class of statements that serve as its answers. In particular, question (1) allows for the fact (about logic and semantics) that an empirical hypothesis has to be expressed before it can be tested and justified empirically. A brief and quite correct answer to question (2) can be given, namely, "none whatsoever!" But that answer may at best seem cryptic, at worst snobbish, and always unsatisfactory, to those who ask question (2). Question (2) is itself cryptic, however. In many cases that I have encountered, the interpretations of question (2) offered by those who ask it involve some special presuppositions about logic in general and its application in science, once fashionable among logicians, but no longer so. To put it briefly, those presuppositions that appear most frequently to underlie question (2) amount to the notion that logic is a branch of psychology--that the rules of deductive logic (truth-functional logic)[3].and the decision criteria of inductive logic (logic of confirmation)[4] are "laws of thinking" to which our mental processes somehow conform--at least when our "minds" are healthy. A semantic presupposition underlying question (2) seems to be that the set of circumstances that cause us to express a proposition is identical with, or at least a proper subset of, the set of circumstances that makes that proposition true (or makes its negation true).[5] On the basis of such psychological presuppositions it might seem crucial to ascertain first whether or not an hypothesis proposed for discussion and subsequent test is a product of healthy mental processes, especially if the hypothesis in question is unfamiliar or appears to contradict another hypothesis already judged to be the product of right thinking; furthermore, it might seem crucial to fathom the origins of the hypothesis in order to assess the evidence in its support. Question (2) cannot be answered (nor can the persistence with which satisfying answers are demanded be ignored).[6] I mention question (2) here only to emphasize the essentially practical and objective character of question (1) and, before attempting to give some practical answers to that question, to draw a clear distinction between question (1) and question (2).

It is taken for granted that the reader is well-acquainted with the theory of consumer demand. Reference to the presentation by Hicks (1946, esp. pp. 305-314) will suffice for present needs. The pure, or abstract, theory of consumer demand can usefully (for present purposes, at least) be regarded as an axiom system capable of several different but logically equivalent presentations (Blanché, 1962, esp. 25-27). In each presentation there is (i) a definite collection of primitive, or undefined symbols; (ii) a set of definitions (some symbols in the given presentation being defined in terms of undefined symbols); (iii) a set of undemonstrated propositions; and (iv) a set of demonstrated propositions. Logic and arithmetic are presupposed by the abstract theory of consumer demand.

In the usual presentation of the theory of consumer demand the undemonstrated propositions ascribe some definite mathematical properties to a _utility function_

$$u(x_1, \ldots, x_n)$$

defined on the subset $\{x \mid x_i \geqq 0, i = 1, 2, \ldots, n\}$ of R^n, where R^n is the set of all ordered _n-tuples_ $(x_1, \ldots, x_n)$ of real numbers. The undemonstrated propositions prescribe that for every positive real number c, the equation

$$u(x_1, \ldots, x_n) = c$$

determines an (n-1)-_dimensional_ surface in R^n that is everywhere convex towards the origin (0, ..., 0), and which is called an _indifference surface in_ R^n.

The system of demand functions

$$x_i = x_i(p_1, p_2, \ldots, p_n, M) \qquad i = 1, 2, \ldots, n, \tag{1.3}$$

where the ordered n-tuple $(p_1, p_2, \ldots, p_n)$ is a variable over a set of n-tuples of prices and M is a variable over a set of consumer incomes, is _defined_ by the solution of the constrained maximum problem indicated by

$$G = u(x_1, \ldots, x_n) - \mu\left[\sum_{i=1}^{n} p_i x_i - M\right], \tag{1.4}$$

where μ is a Lagrangean multiplier, _viz_., the system of demand functions (1.3) is the solution of the following system of first-order equations of consumer equilibrium

$$\begin{cases} -\mu p_i + u_i = 0, \quad i = 1, 2, \ldots, n \\ \displaystyle\sum_{i=1}^{n} p_i x_i - M = 0 \end{cases} \tag{1.5}$$

where u_i designates the partial derivative of $u(x_1, \ldots, x_n)$

with respect to x_i.

The so-called "laws" of consumer demand, i.e., the mathematical sentences that express restrictions on Slutsky-Hicks substitution terms (cf. Hicks, 1946, p. 311, p. 314) are, in the usual presentation, demonstrated propositions. [These "laws" are stated in Section 3 in connection with checking their fulfillment by the definite form of demand functions introduced there.]

Another presentation of the abstract theory of consumer demand, which is employed in Section 3, takes the system of demand functions (1.3) as primitive, and the so-called "laws" of consumer demand as undemonstrated propositions. The remaining propositions about indifference surfaces in R^n and the utility function are demonstrated in this presentation.[7] To the reader accustomed only to the usual textbook presentation of the theory of consumer demand it may seem that we are "doing things backwards" in Section 3. The two presentations are logically equivalent, however, and the second has some definite advantages in the kind of investigation that is to be discussed in this article.

It is also taken for granted that the reader is acquainted with modern general predicate logic, semantics, and the logic of confirmation of hypotheses--in a general way at least.[8] However, no specialized manipulative knowledge of those subjects will be required of the reader. What is essential is that the reader bear in mind some basic concepts of logic and decision theory and the distinctions between them. I shall keep the discussion of these concepts and distinctions brief, partly because econometricians often resent discussions of concepts with which they claim to be well acquainted; yet, because it is precisely the failure to maintain essential distinctions that is the bane of discussion of hypothesis formulation and testing in econometrics, I shall not entirely omit mention of required concepts and distinctions.

The concept of general predicate logic as a system of deduction rules (as distinct from the older notion of logic as a psychological theory of right thinking) is essential. The same is to be said for the distinction between object languages, in which propositions are asserted, and metalanguages in which object languages or lower level metalanguages are talked about. In the present article no proposition in the object language of economics, i.e., no empirical economic proposition, is asserted. The truth-value concept of truth-functional logic (deductive logic) is to be kept distinct from the confirmation concept of inductive logic (logic of confirmation). In the present article no economic proposition is ascribed a degree of confirmation, or logical probability. [Notice that some empirical data are employed in Section 4 in reaching a decision in respect of the use of a suggested interpretation of some parameters in the demand functions we are studying. The decision reached is not an empirical economic proposition, however.]

The reader should be aware of the distinction between sentences that express propositions, whether in the object language of economics, or in one of the metalanguages, on the one hand, and egocentric, or belief expressing, sentences, *viz.*, sentences which express the emotional states (attitude of belief) of the user towards given propositions. A few examples suffice to make the distinction clear: Let Q designate the proposition expressed by (1.1), *viz.*, for the United States economy and the period 1922-1940, the marginal propensity to consume, β_1^*, belongs to the interval $\{\beta_1 | 5/6 < \beta_1 < 17/20\}$. Let us take for granted that Q is concretely interpreted, *i.e.*, that a specified circumstance or state of the world makes Q false. Now consider the following sentences: (a) 'I (we) believe Q;' (b) 'Certainly Q;' (c) 'It is self-evident that Q;' (d) 'The probability (subjective) of Q is greater than 2/3;' (e) 'Necessarily Q.'[9] Each of these sentences expresses the emotional state of the person who asserts it, *i.e.*, his attitude of belief towards the proposition Q. For instance, (b) and (e) express the proposition that the user feels an irresistible impulse to assert Q. Although it is a traditional practice to admit such egocentric propositions in discourse on economics and econometrics, we cannot do so in the present discussion without obliterating the distinction we intend to maintain between question (1), which we propose to answer, and question (2), which we do not.

In the present article the discussion focuses on the employment of decision rules in the conduct of economic research. The term 'decision rule' is to be interpreted broadly. The notion of 'decision rule' includes such rules as are encountered in the formal theory of decision in which explicit formulation of decision functions, loss functions and risk functions is an essential feature (*cf.* Wald, 1950, Chapter 1; also Birnbaum, 1962, Chapter 17). However, the notion (as we shall use it) also includes general maxims that are not so precisely expressed, and it is with the latter that most of our discussion has to do. Some preliminary remarks about decision rules in general will help to keep the discussion focused on question (1).

In doing research one decides which hypotheses are to be tested, *e.g.*, one decides to test the hypothetical parameter restrictions (1.2a-d) against a definite class of alternative hypotheses. To say that one decides which hypothetical parameter restrictions one is going to test does not answer question (1), but it does indicate one essential aspect of appropriate answers; namely, that the considerations on which the decision to test hypothetical parameter restrictions is based might not all be such as influence our attitudes of belief. Indeed, neither belief nor disbelief in an hypothesis is essential to the decision to explore and test it. For instance, it is the convenience of the hypothetical restrictions on demand function parameters expressed by (3.39), the greater simplicity of explanation of consumer behavior which those restrictions allow, that motivates the decision to test them empirically.[10] Decision sentences, i.e., sentences that express one's decision to take or eschew taking some specified action, are not belief sentences, viz., decision sentences do not express the decision maker's emotional attitude towards any statement of hypothesis. To say in the metalanguage (for talking about the language in which decisions are expressed) that decision sentences do not express emotional states of belief or conviction, is not tantamount to saying (in the object language of scientific psychology) that such emotions do not influence decisions.

The distinction between decision rules on the one hand, and the deduction rules of general predicate logic is essential. In applications of formal decision theory the distinction is easily recognized. The cogency of rules for minimization of the loss function (Wald, 1950, esp. pp. 8-14; Birnbaum, 1962, pp. 288-289) is rooted in the empirical character of the latter, more precisely in the supposition that the loss function represents (with a specified degree of approximation) an empirical relation between actual states of the world and actions, on the one hand, and real losses, on the other. For instance, what actual loss do we sustain in case the decision we take in respect of the hypothesis expressed by the parameter restrictions (3.40) is "wrong?" See the discussion at the end of Section 4. On the other hand, the cogency of the deduction rules does not presuppose any empirical proposition.

The plan of this article is as follows: The introduction of a specific hypothetical form of a system of demand functions in Section 3 is preceded in Section 2 by a general discussion of the problem of making an empirical, or extensional, interpretation of the mathematical theory of consumer demand. The discussion in Section 2 is intended to assist the reader in understanding why the problem of hypothesis formulation is approached in the particular way it is, i.e., with help of the Requirements I-V put forward in Section 3.

In Section 4, pursuant to a general requirement, a theory of the consumption and savings functions is derived from the special theory of consumer demand, and with help of numerical data on "real consumption" and "real income" a set of parameter restrictions that apply to all demand functions--

an hypothesis suggested by a verbal interpretation (naming of parameters) by Samuelson and Frisch--is tested empirically.

Section 5 affords a general critique of the Requirements I-V put forward at the beginning of Section 3.

At appropriate places in the text of this article due credit is given to Klein and Rubin (1947), Samuelson (1947), and Frisch (1954) for their earlier contributions. To Klein and Rubin belongs credit for having first introduced the special demand functions (3.12a-c), which I generalized eight years later. In making this generalization I was aided by an exercise that appears in the book by Wold (1953, p. 140, Ex. 5).

2. The Nonintuitive Character of Hypothesis Formulation

It will be found that each of the requirements to be put forward in Section 3 to guide the formulation of definite hypotheses in theory of consumer demand is of a practical sort, and none of them is a knowledge claim. Those requirements express personal decisions to proceed with research in a given way, but they are objective in this sense, that anyone who is aware of the distinction between the object language of (say) theory of consumer demand and the technical method language (for talking about research) is not likely to mistake those requirements for expressions of proffered laws, hypotheses, and facts belonging to economic science proper; furthermore, all persons who understand those requirements can, by following them, arrive at the same formulation of hypothesis.[11]

From the foregoing remarks it follows that the requirements are not intuitive, viz., that they are not immediate inferences from descriptions of direct personal experiences with economic objects and events; nor are the hypotheses that are formulated with their help intuitive in that sense. Indeed, the motivation for employing only practical requirements is the consideration that personal intuition of economic objects and events is likely to be a very poor guide in the formulation of hypotheses on the very high level of theoretical abstraction that is typified by the theory of consumer demand. However, because such personal intuition of objects and events can be a reliable and very useful guide in the formulation of hypotheses at lower levels of abstraction, some special remarks are called for.

We begin by considering the system of operations on economic objects and events, and definitions that provide an empirical, or extensional, interpretation of the mathematical symbols that appear in the abstract theory of consumer demand.[12]

A brief description of the logical structure of concrete, empirical interpretations will be helpful to many readers. The following sketch emphasizes only the main features and leaves out fine details. Let S be a given set of commodity bundles, which are designated by α, β, γ, ... and let v, w designate variables over S. For sake of simplicity let us assume that S is noncountable. Our present discussion presupposes some physical operations and explicit definitions by means of which it can be decided, for any entity a, which of ($a \in S$) and ($a \notin S$) is the case. S is called the commodity space. Let P and I designate empirical two-term relations on S, called respectively "preference" and "indifference." The extensions of P and I are subsets of the cartesian product S^2, i.e., the extensions of P and I are sets of ordered pairs of commodity bundles. The basic theory of choice is adequately described as a set of premises--called axioms of preference--from which it can be deduced that the pair (P, I) is a quasi-serial, or weak, order relation on S.[13] Let us call (P, I) a preference-indifference ordering. According to the theory of choice, the indifference relation I partitions the set S of commodity bundles into a collection {J} of equivalence classes J, which are called indifference classes.[14]

As no member of the set S of commodity bundles is either a real number or n-tuple of real numbers, the representation of the foregoing collection of indifference classes {J} by a system of indifference surfaces in Rn, as is called for by the theory of consumer demand, requires the introduction of a one-to-one mapping M of S into R^n. Under such a mapping, for every $v \in S$, the image M(v) is a definite ordered n-tuple $x = (x_1, \ldots, x_n)$ of real numbers. Let M(S) designate the image of S under M; usually M is chosen so that $M(S) \subset \{x \mid x_i \geq 0, i = 1, 2, \ldots, n\}$. Let $a = (a_1, \ldots, a_n)$ be a definite n-tuple of real numbers belonging to M(S); then $(a_1, \ldots, a_n)$ represents a definite commodity bundle (say) $\alpha = M^{-1}(a)$ that belongs to S, and that commodity bundle is said to be the extension of the ordered n-tuple of real numbers $(a_1, \ldots, a_n)$. Let J be a definite indifference class of S; then the image M(J) of J is a definite subset of ordered n-tuples of real numbers. M(J) is said to represent on R^n the indifference class J of commodity bundles, and J is said to be the extension of the set M(J) of ordered n-tuples of real numbers.

Up to now no special restriction on the choice of mapping M has been mentioned, apart from its one-to-one character. Were it the case that our only concern was to represent commodity bundles by n-tuples of positive real numbers, and indifference classes of commodity bundles by definite sets of n-tuples of positive real numbers, then any one-to-one mapping of S into the set $\{x \mid x_i \geq 0, i = 1, 2, \ldots, n\}$ would suit our purpose. Without specification of additional restrictions on the choice of mapping M, however, no logical connection between the statements of theory of choice, on the one hand, and theory of consumer demand, on the other, is established. At this stage of the discussion it would be logically premature to assert that M(J) is an (n-1)-dimensional indifference surface in R^n; such a statement cannot be deduced from the premises of _theory of choice_ alone. The premises of that theory do not entail any restrictions on the mapping M. Under those premises alone the choice of mapping M is arbitrary. The failure of the image M(J) of the indifference class J to have the geometrical properties specified by the _theory of consumer demand_, _viz._, the failure of M(J) to be an (n-1)-dimensional surface everywhere convex towards the origin (0, ..., 0) in R^n, is of no empirical significance for the premises of _theory of choice_. Nor would it be significant if M(J) turned out to have each of the geometrical properties specified for indifference surfaces in R^n by _theory of consumer demand_.

The theory of consumer demand does not rest on the premises of theory of choice alone. In addition to the premises that imply that the preference-indifference relation (P, I) is a quasi-serial order relation there underlies the theory of consumer demand a system of empirically testable statements that are logically independent of the axioms of preference. The logical structure of that system of statements is provided by the _theory of quantity and magnitude_.[15] The empirically testable statements presupposed by the theory of consumer demand are extensionally interpreted statements of the theory of quantity and magnitude. For sake of brevity, I shall remark only that the presupposed empirical statements provide the basis for characterizing each commodity bundle by a set of _n_ different additive measurements. (Do not assume, however, that each commodity bundle contains _n_ different commodities.)[16] Each of these _n_ measurements represents, by a real number, the magnitude of a definite quantitative property. Furthermore, the theory of consumer demand presupposes that the position of each commodity bundle in the preference-indifference ordering (P, I) depends on its magnitudes of the _n_ quantitative properties, and on nothing else.[17] Thus, with each commodity bundle in S there is associated a definite _n_-tuple of numerical measurements, _e.g._, with the commodity bundle α there is associated a definite _n-tuple_ of numerical measurements $(x_1^{(\alpha)}, \ldots, x_n^{(\alpha)})$. The mapping M is now restricted in the following way: for every commodity bundle $v \in S$, the image M(v) is the _n_-tuple $(x_1^{(v)}, \ldots, x_n^{(v)})$ of numerical measurements on _v_. Let M(J) be the image of the indifference class J under the one-to-one mapping M thus restricted. The failure of M(J) to be an (n-1)-dimensional surface everywhere convex towards (0, ..., 0) in R^n, _i.e._, the failure of M(J) to possess the properties of an indifference surface in R^n, is empirically significant for the theory of consumer demand.

The foregoing sketch of the logical structure of connections between the symbols appearing in the theory of consumer demand, on the one hand, and factual descriptions of economic objects and events, on the other, omits most of the details. Nonetheless that sketch may help the reader grasp the intended meaning of the remark, namely, that the formulation of hypotheses about the mathematical forms of systems of demand functions is quite remote from those objects and events that are more or less directly experienced by human beings.

Even the more fundamental task of formulating an adequate system of basic operations and explicit definitions for an empirical interpretation of the concepts and symbols in abstract theory of consumer demand is a very formidable one. For instance, the notion of 'consumer'--as that term is used in theory of consumer demand--is by no means easy to explicate. A crude sketch of the logical structure of the concept of 'consumer' is afforded by the remark that a "consumer" is a set A, the members of which are live human beings, and that on the set A there are several definite _many-place relations_ R_1, R_2, ... (the extensions of which are subsets of the cartesian products A^2, A^3, ..., A^q) that have some definite properties, _e.g._, symmetry, transitivity, etc.[18] The notion of 'consumer choice' is equally as complicated and difficult to explicate. To determine which specific quantitative properties alone determine the position of each commodity bundle in the preference-indifference ordering of the consumer is another difficult task for empirical research, as, indeed, is the task of explicating the notion of 'commodity bundle' itself.

Even in those cases of hypothesis formulation for which, by reason of the simplicity of the system of operational and explicit definitions required to achieve adequate empirical interpretation, intuition can be regarded as a reliable guide in selecting mathematical forms, purely practical considerations may nonetheless play an equally important role. In this connection it may be helpful to compare hypothesis formulation in the theory of consumer demand with the formulation of Newton's _laws of motion_ in respect of the relative complexity of their empirical interpretations, and to indicate the role of practical requirements therein. The basic notions of displacement, velocity, acceleration and mass are readily explicated by simple physical operations with straight rods, uniform periodic processes (oscillation of pendulums and diurnal rotation of the Earth), with pendulum balances, and by some very simple definitional equations.[19] The basic notions of terrestrial mechanics and the explications of those notions by operations and formal definitions are intuitive in the sense indicated at the head of this section. Because of its likeness to the problem in our illustration in Section 3, the formulation of the "law of acceleration," or, more precisely, the choice of a mathematical function to express an hypothetical relation between velocity, v, and time of motion, t, is of chief interest here. Galileo selected, from a set of alternative functional forms, the form

$$v = at, \tag{2.1}$$

where a is a constant, chiefly on grounds of its simplicity, deduced therefrom the consequence

$$s = \frac{at^2}{2}, \tag{2.2}$$

which--with help of an auxiliary hypothesis--he proceeded to test by means of his famous experiments with heavy balls rolling down smooth inclined planes. Galileo's motive for collecting numerical data on the motion of balls constrained to roll down inclined planes was chiefly practical, having to do with technological limitations on the precision with which short time intervals could be measured in his day.[20]

The foregoing considerations indicate why the attempt to use intuition as a guide in the formulation of definite hypotheses in theory of consumer demand has been eschewed in the present investigation. That personal research decision is based on the consideration that any adequate extensional interpretation of the theory of consumer demand (when such adequacy is achieved) will turn out to be much too complex to be grasped in its entirety, and in its detail, in a single mental act, or intuition. Furthermore, in the absence of an adequate system of operations and explicit definitions that afford a more or less precise extensional interpretation of the theory of consumer demand, there is no scope for the operation of intuition at all.[21]

3. A Class of Systems of Demand Functions

The search for specific mathematical forms of demand functions is influenced by several practical considerations that are derived (so to speak) from the purpose for which the search is undertaken. In this section five requirements, to be met by the specific mathematical forms of demand functions, are set forth. Discussion of the considerations that underlie the adoption of these requirements is postponed to Section 5, the solution--the class of systems of demand functions--being presented first. While this order of presentation does not reflect the succession of steps taken in the investigation, it does have the merit of rendering the discussion of the requirements more concrete and specific than would be the case if the natural order were followed. Without further ado, we list the requirements:

I. The income variable M and each of the price variables $p_1, p_2, \ldots, p_n$ shall appear in each of the demand functions

$$x_i = x_i(p_1, \ldots, p_n, M) \qquad i = 1, 2, \ldots, n \tag{3.1}$$

II. All of the demand functions (3.1) shall have the same form in $p_1, p_2, \ldots, p_n, M$. That is to say, for every pair (i, j), the demand function

$$x_j(p_1, \ldots, p_n, M)$$

shall be obtainable from the demand function

$$x_i(p_1, \ldots, p_n, M)$$

by interchange of the commodity names i and j only.

Special remark: Trout Rader, referring to the fact that 'form of function' and 'parameter' are terms not formally defined in this paper, has averred that Requirement II is cryptic. The following brief remark may be helpful: Looking ahead, consider the expression (3.38a). Let i and j be names of definite commodities; then (3.38a) is the demand function for i. To obtain the demand function for j, replace x_i by x_j, interchange p_j and p_i, interchange the parameters β_j and β_i, interchange the parameters γ_j and γ_i. For a system of demand functions that does not fulfill Requirement II consult the book by Wold (1953, p. 106). That I have not introduced explicit definitions of 'form of function' and 'parameter' reflects only the consideration that the meanings of those terms in the present discussion will be sufficiently clear to all readers that detailed explications may safely be dispensed with. I agree that in some other discussion such explications might well be essential.

III. The system of demand functions shall be obtained from a broader class of functions solely by imposition of parameter restrictions.

IV. The total number of functionally dependent structural parameters in the set of demand functions

$$x_i = x_i(p_1, \ldots, p_n, M) \qquad i = 1, 2, \ldots, n$$

shall be rendered as small as possible as a consequence solely of

(a) _the common form of the proffered demand functions_;

(b) _the requirement that the selected common form of demand function satisfies the "laws" of consumer demand_.

The next requirement narrowly restricts the form of demand functions. It also very clearly suggests a class of suitable forms. Before introducing an explicit statement of _Requirement V_, I make a few preliminary remarks. It is taken for granted that the reader is acquainted with the Leontief-Hicks theorem on composite commodities in theory of consumer demand (_cf_. Leontief, 1936; Hicks, 1946, pp. 312-313; Wold, 1953, pp. 108-110). For the time being, it suffices as a reminder merely to state that theorem loosely, in words, as follows: _If the prices_ $p_1, \ldots, p_m$, $m < n$ _of each commodity in a group of commodities_ $\{1, 2, \ldots, m\}$ _change in the same proportion then that group of commodities behaves exactly as a single commodity_ (Hicks, 1946, p. 313). Requirement V refers to a special application of the foregoing theorem.

The _consumption function_ and _savings function_ of Keynesian theory,

$$(3.2a\text{-}b)\qquad \begin{aligned} c &= \beta y + \gamma, \\ s &= (1 - \beta)y - \gamma, \end{aligned}$$

where c denotes "real consumption," s denotes "real savings" and y denotes "real income," can be formally interpreted as demand functions derived from a utility function u(c, s) subject to the budget constraint

$$(3.3)\qquad p_c c + p_s s = M$$

under the special initial, or background conditions, described by

$$(3.4)\qquad p_s = p_c,$$

(_cf_. Basmann, 1960, p. 44; also 1963, p. 946).[22] Notice that the domain of u(c, s) is the set of all (c, s) such that $c > \gamma$, $s > -\gamma$, where $\gamma > 0$.

V. _Let us partition the set of commodities into two classes (1) consumption goods_ $N_c = \{1, 2, \ldots, m\}$ _and (2) savings goods_ $N_s = \{m + 1, \ldots, n\}$. _The common form of demand functions_

$$x_i = x_i(p_1, \ldots, p_n, M)$$

$$i = 1, 2, \ldots, n$$

shall be such that in case all prices $p_1, \ldots, p_n$ change in the same proportion, i.e.,

$$(3.5) \qquad p_i = \pi_i p, \qquad i = 1, 2, \ldots, m$$

$$(3.6) \qquad p_j = \pi_j p, \qquad j = m + 1, \ldots, n,$$

where the π_i and π_j are historical constants, the composite demand functions for consumption goods and savings goods are of Keynesian form, i.e.,

$$(3.7a\text{-}b) \qquad \begin{aligned} c &= \beta\left(\frac{M}{p}\right) + \gamma \\ s &= (1 - \beta)\left(\frac{M}{p}\right) - \gamma \end{aligned}$$

where

$$(3.8) \qquad c = \frac{1}{p} \sum_{i=1}^{m} p_i x_i$$

$$(3.9) \qquad s = \frac{1}{p} \sum_{j=m+1}^{n} p_j x_j .$$

In discussing the practical motivations for the requirements I-V later on, we shall make reference to the stochastic demand functions

$$(3.10a) \qquad x_i = x_i(p_1, \ldots, p_n, M) + \xi_i$$

$$i = 1, 2, \ldots, n,$$

where $\xi = (\xi_1, \ldots, \xi_n)$ is a continuous random disturbance vector with marginal distribution function

$$(3.10b) \qquad G(\xi_1, \ldots, \xi_n; \omega),$$

completely specified in respect of form, where ω designates a q-tuple $(\omega_1, \ldots, \omega_q)$ of real valued parameters (let Ω designate the parameter space), and the mean vector is $(0, \ldots, 0)$. From (3.10a) and

$$\sum_{i=1}^{n} p_i x_i(p_1, \ldots, p_n, M) = M,$$

$$(3.11) \qquad \sum_{i=1}^{n} p_i \xi_i = 0$$

can be deduced, hence that the distribution of ξ is singular.

In order to meet Requirement V the system of demand functions must be derivable from a family of indifference surfaces on $\{x | x_i \geqq 0,\ i = 1, 2, \ldots, n\}$ for which every income expansion line is linear. Hence Requirement V determines the form of systems of demand functions. Determination of specific form is straightforward and requires no extended comment. [The actual steps in obtaining the system (3.38a-c) below were taken in this sequence: (i) writing down the system defined by (4.18) as a leading special case; (ii) finding of the special system (3.12a-c) in Frisch's paper; (iii) derivation of the functions (4.10a-b) for n = 2 from d'Alembert's differential equation (in the marginal rate of substitution); (iv) generalizing the number of prices in (4.10a-b) without change of functional form to obtain (3.38a-c).][23]

Ragnar Frisch, in his expository article "Linear Expenditure Functions" (1954), mentions a system of demand functions of the following form

$$(3.12a\text{-}c) \qquad x_i = \frac{\nu_i}{p_i}\left[M - \sum_{k=1}^{n} \gamma_k p_k\right] + \gamma_i$$

$$i = 1, 2, \ldots, n$$

$$\sum_{i=1}^{n} \nu_i = 1$$

$$\nu_i > 0 \qquad \nu_i = 1, 2, \ldots, n,$$

which he called Samuelson demand functions (cf. Frisch, 1954, p. 510). [Until very recently I was under the impression that Samuelson invented the special demand functions (3.12a-c); however, these special demand functions were first published by L. R. Klein and H. Rubin in their article "A Constant Utility Index of the Cost of Living" (1947, p. 86).] The domain of the foregoing set of demand functions is the set of all (n + 1)-tuples $(p_1, \ldots, p_n, M)$ such that

$$(3.13) \qquad M - \sum_{k=1}^{n} \gamma_k p_k > 0.$$

The set of demand functions (3.12a-c)-(3.13) satisfies the "laws" of consumer demand as required, and meets the practical criteria laid down in Requirements I, II, III and V.

The systems of demand functions defined by (3.12a-c) belong to a class of more general systems of functions (not necessarily demand functions) of the form

$$(3.14a\text{-}d) \quad x_i = \Phi_i \left[M - \sum_{k=1}^{n} \gamma_k p_k \right] + \gamma_i$$

where

$$\Phi_i = \Phi_i(p_1, \ldots, p_n)$$

$$\Phi_i > 0$$

$$\sum_{i=1}^{n} p_i \Phi_i = 1,$$

and (3.13) is retained in the specification of the domain. A subclass of systems of functions (3.14a-d) is determined by

$$(3.15a\text{-}b) \quad \Phi_i = \frac{\beta_i p_i^{\sigma_i - 1}}{\sum_{k=1}^{n} \beta_k p_k^{\sigma_k}}$$

$$i = 1, 2, \ldots, n$$

where

$$\beta_k > 0, \quad k = 1, 2, \ldots, n.$$

Fulfillment of the conditions (3.14c-d) by the definition (3.15a-b) is readily checked. Let us designate by C the class of systems of functions defined by (3.14a-d)-(3.15a-b). Notice that not every member of C is a system of demand functions. The system of demand functions (3.12a-c) introduced by Klein and Rubin belongs to C. The system (3.12a-c) can be obtained from (3.14a-d) and (3.15a-b) by means of the parameter restriction

$$(3.16) \quad \sigma_k = 0, \quad k = 1, 2, \ldots, n,$$

in which case the constants ν_i in (3.12a-c) are defined by

$$(3.17) \qquad \nu_i = \frac{\beta_i}{\beta_1 + \beta_2 + \ldots + \beta_n}$$

$$i = 1, 2, \ldots, n.$$

Systems of demand functions specified by (3.12a-c) do not, however, meet the condition laid down in Requirement IV. The weaker restrictions

$$(3.18) \qquad \sigma_k = \sigma, \qquad k = 1, 2, \ldots, n$$

where

$$\sigma < 1$$

suffice to make demand functions of (3.14a-d), viz., (3.14 a-d) and (3.18) define a subclass C_d of C such that each member of C_d is a system of demand functions, as I shall demonstrate shortly. In this respect the strong parameter restrictions (3.16) define a class C_f of systems of demand functions that is an arbitrary structural hypothesis eminently worthwhile testing empirically against alternative structural hypotheses belonging to the class C_d.[24]

Let us check whether the proffered system of demand functions expressed by (3.14a-d) and (3.15a-b) fulfills the "laws" of consumer demand. Let s_{ij}, $i,j = 1, 2, \ldots, n$ be defined as follows:

$$(3.19) \qquad s_{ij} = \frac{\partial x_i}{\partial p_j} + x_j \frac{\partial x_i}{\partial M}.$$

We require

$$(3.20) \qquad s_{ij} = s_{ji} \text{ for all } i,j \text{ such that } j \neq i$$

$$(3.21) \qquad s_{ii} < 0$$

$$(3.22) \qquad \sum_{i=1}^{n} p_i s_{ij} = 0$$

$$(3.23) \qquad \sum_{i=1}^{n} \sum_{j=1}^{n} s_{ij} z_i z_j \text{ is negative semi-definite}$$

where the z_i $i = 1, 2, \ldots, n$ are any real numbers; (cf.

Hicks, 1946, p. 311). From (3.14a) we obtain

(3.24) $$\frac{\partial x_i}{\partial p_j} = \frac{\partial \Phi_i}{\partial p_j}\left[M - \sum_{k=1}^{n} \gamma_k p_k\right] - \Phi_i \gamma_j$$

and

(3.25) $$\frac{\partial x_i}{\partial M} = \Phi_i,$$

hence--from (3.19)--that

(3.26) $$s_{ij} = \left(\frac{\partial \Phi_i}{\partial p_j} + \Phi_i \Phi_j\right)\left[M - \sum_{k=1}^{n} \gamma_k p_k\right]$$

Now, for $j \neq i$

(3.27) $$\frac{\partial \Phi_i}{\partial p_j} = -\frac{\sigma \beta_i \beta_j (p_i p_j)^{\sigma-1}}{K^2}$$

where

(3.28) $$K = \sum_{k=1}^{n} \beta_k p_k^{\sigma}$$

Also

(3.29) $$\frac{\partial \Phi_i}{\partial p_i} = \frac{(\sigma - 1)\beta_i p_i^{\sigma-2}}{K} - \frac{\sigma \beta_i^2 (p_i^2)^{\sigma-1}}{K^2}$$

Hence, for $j \neq i$,

(3.30) $$\frac{\partial \Phi_i}{\partial p_j} + \Phi_j \Phi_i = -\frac{(\sigma - 1)\beta_i \beta_j (p_i p_j)^{\sigma-1}}{K^2}$$

Interchanging i and j in (3.30) we verify

$$s_{ij} = s_{ji}$$

with help of (3.26).

$$(3.31)\qquad \frac{\partial \Phi_i}{\partial p_i} + \Phi_i^2 = \frac{(\sigma-1)\beta_i p_i^{\sigma-2}}{K} - \frac{(\sigma-1)\beta_i^2 (p_i^2)^{\sigma-1}}{K^2}$$

$$= \frac{(\sigma-1)\beta_i p_i^{\sigma-2}(K-\beta_i p_i^{\sigma})}{K^2}$$

Since $\sigma < 1$, and $K-\beta_i p_i^{\sigma} > 0$, the foregoing expression is negative; hence from (3.31) and (3.26) we deduce

$$s_{ii} < 0$$

as required.

The following expression for s_{ij} will be found useful in checking (3.23) later on:

$$(3.32)\qquad s_{ij} = (1-\sigma)\left[\frac{\beta_i p_i^{\sigma-1}}{K} - \delta_{ij} p_i^{-1}\right]\frac{\beta_j p_j^{\sigma-1}}{K} \times \left[M - \sum_{k=1}^{n} \gamma_k p_k \right]$$

where

$$\delta_{ij} = \begin{cases} 1, & j = i \\ 0, & j \neq i. \end{cases}$$

From (3.22) and (3.26) we deduce the requirement

$$(3.33)\qquad \sum_{i=1}^{n} p_i \left(\frac{\partial \Phi_i}{\partial p_j} + \Phi_j \Phi_i \right) = 0.$$

Making the substitutions called for in (3.33) we obtain

$$(3.34)\qquad \sum_{i=1}^{n} p_i \left(\frac{\partial \Phi_i}{\partial p_j} + \Phi_j \Phi_i \right)$$

$$= \frac{-\sigma\beta_j p_j^{\sigma-1}}{K} + \frac{(\sigma-1)\beta_j p_j^{\sigma-1}}{K} + \frac{\beta_j p_j^{\sigma-1}}{K} = 0$$

as required.

Finally we check fulfillment of (3.23). Let Δ_m designate any m^{th} order principal minor of the matrix

$$[s_{ij}]$$

such that $m < n$. Without loss of generality let

$$\Delta_m = |s_{ij}| \qquad i,j = 1, 2, \ldots, m. \tag{3.35}$$

We have

$$\Delta_m = (1-\sigma)^m \left[M - \sum_{k=1}^{n} \gamma_k p_k \right]^m \tag{3.36}$$

$$\times \left| \left(\frac{\beta_i p_i^{\sigma-1}}{K} - \delta_{ij} p_i^{-1} \right) \frac{\beta_j p_j^{\sigma-1}}{K} \right|$$

With help of elementary column and row operations we obtain

$$\Delta_m = \frac{(-1)^m (\beta_1 \beta_2 \ldots \beta_m)}{K^m} \left[M - \sum_{k=1}^{n} \gamma_k p_k \right]^m (p_1 p_2 \cdots p_m)^{\sigma-2} \tag{3.37}$$

$$\times (1-\sigma)^m \left[1 - K^{-1} \sum_{k=1}^{m} \beta_k p_k^\sigma \right].$$

Except for $(-1)^m$ each of the terms on the right of (3.37) is a positive number. Δ_m is negative (positive) according as $\underline{m}$ is odd (even). Hence, for all real numbers z_i, $i = 1, 2, \ldots, n$, the quadratic form in (3.23) is negative semi-definite, account being taken of the linear dependence (3.34).

Hence, the class C_d, the members of which are systems of functions having the form

$$x_i = \frac{\beta_i p_i^{\sigma-1}}{\sum_{k=1}^{n} \beta_k p_k^\sigma} \left[M - \sum_{k=1}^{n} \gamma_k p_k \right] + \gamma_i \tag{3.38a-c}$$

$$i = 1, 2, \ldots, n$$

$$\beta_k > 0 \quad k = 1, 2, \ldots, n$$

$$\sigma < 1$$

on the domain (3.13), is a class of systems of demand functions. Furthermore, C_d is a proper subclass of the class C defined by (3.14a-d) - (3.15a-b), and fulfills the _Requirements I-IV_. The class C_d also fulfills _Requirement V_; that it does so is demonstrated in Section 4.

So far we have specified no hypothetical restrictions on the parameters γ_k, k = 1, 2, ..., n. A convenient set of hypothetical restrictions on those parameters is expressed by

$$(3.39) \quad \gamma_k < 0, \quad k = 1, 2, \ldots, n.$$

The convenience is that, under those restrictions, the system of _(n-1)-dimensional_ indifference surfaces that implicitly underlies the system of demand functions (3.38a-c) covers the entire set $\{x | x_i \geqq 0, \ i = 1, 2, \ldots, n\}$, so that we may drop (3.13) as an explicit specification of the price-income domain and replace it by the specification of the range of (3.38) as the positive orthant of R^n. In view of _Requirement IV_, however, we shall not augment the restrictions already laid down, _i.e._, (3.18), by the restrictions (3.39). It should be emphasized that it is not the case that the motive for eschewing the restrictions is either of the following: (i) the failure of (3.39) to be in good agreement with observational evidence, (ii) the "implausibility" of the restrictions (3.39).

Samuelson (1947, pp. 88-89) and Frisch (1956, p. 510), referring to the special system of demand functions (3.12a-c), introduce a _verbal interpretation_ of the parameters γ_k, k = 1, 2, ..., n, that suggests the hypothetical parameter restrictions[25]

$$(3.40) \quad \gamma_k > 0, \quad k = 1, 2, \ldots, n.$$

Samuelson refers to $(\gamma_1, \ldots, \gamma_n)$ as a _necessary set of goods_, and Frisch calls $\gamma_1, \ldots, \gamma_n$ _minimum quantities of goods_ i = 1, 2, ..., n, which the consumer is committed to use. This verbal interpretation cannot do in place of an extensional interpretation of $\gamma_1, \ldots, \gamma_n$ in scientific economics (recall Section 2); nonetheless it can play an important role in the initial stages of empirical research by serving as a preliminary sketch for construction of an important part of the required extensional interpretation of the class C_d of demand function systems (3.38a-c). The imagery that is excited by the Samuelson-Frisch verbal interpretation is that of definite events and objects that human beings are capable of experiencing more or less directly,[26] and it is that concreteness of reference that confers on the purely verbal interpretation its potential fruitfulness.

A decision to follow the lead given by such a verbal interpretation, by trying to construct an extensional interpretation along the lines it suggests, commits us to an intricate and difficult task that may turn out to be expensive and, in the end, fruitless. Consequently, it is desirable to perform an inexpensive empirical test of the hypothetical restrictions (3.40), which are suggested by the Samuelson-Frisch verbal interpretation of $\gamma_1, \ldots, \gamma_n$. The objective of such a preliminary test is solely to provide information that can aid us to make a decision in respect of undertaking a suggested line of research. From the hypothetical parameter restrictions (3.40) definite empirically testable statements about the parameters of the consumption and savings functions can be deduced with help of statements of special initial conditions. Those deductions, and the results of the preliminary empirical test, are described in Section 4. Some other relevant criteria are discussed in Section 5.

4. Derivation of the Consumption Function

Requirement V, mentioned in Section 3, calls for the proffered system demand functions to have such a form that under the special initial conditions described there, the Keynesian linear consumption function and savings function can be deduced. The statement of special initial conditions is that all prices $p_1, \ldots, p_n$ change in the same proportion. Whether it is the case that the actual commodity prices that interpret $p_1, \ldots, p_n$ in a given application actually do change in approximately the same proportion during some historical period is a question to be decided by empirical research. What is required by V is that the proffered system of demand functions be capable of explaining--in conjunction with statements of special initial conditions--the close adjustment of the Keynesian linear consumption function and savings function to numerical "real consumption" and "real income" data, whenever such a close fit is obtained. Consider the following least squares approximation of the Keynesian linear consumption and savings functions by Haavelmo (1947, p. 89) for the United States and the succession of years 1922-1941:[27]

$$\begin{aligned} c &= \underset{(24.5)}{0.732y} + \underset{(5.77)}{84.0} + u \\ s &= \underset{(24.5)}{0.268y} - \underset{(5.77)}{84.0} - u \end{aligned} \qquad (4.1a\text{-}b)^{28}$$

$$Av(u^2) = 58.2$$

(4.2a-b)

$$R = 0.984.$$

Because the least squares formulas here impose two linear restrictions on the residuals $u_1, \ldots, u_{20}$, the average squared residual (4.2a) and the multiple correlation coefficient (4.2b) are calculated using eighteen degrees of freedom. In the present discussion we shall consider (4.1a-b) and (4.2a) as approximations, not as statistical estimates; thus, for example, $Av(u^2)$ is not interpreted here as an estimate of the variance of a random disturbance in the consumption function.[29]

Table 4.1

Year	u	$(\frac{u}{c}) \times 100$
1922	- 7.03	-1.8
1923	-14.6	-3.5
1924	2.29	0.52
1925	- 5.83	-1.3
1926	1.31	0.29
1927	- 1.62	-0.36
1928	7.86	1.7
1929	- 0.976	-0.21
1930	5.02	1.1
1931	- 7.15	-1.8
1932	- 6.37	-1.8
1933	1.04	0.28
1934	1.22	0.31
1935	3.26	0.78
1936	4.86	1.1
1937	4.27	0.91
1938	10.8	2.4
1939	8.47	1.8
1940	8.77	1.8
1941	-15.5	-2.9

The residuals $u_1, \ldots, u_{20}$ are shown in Table 4.1. The rightmost column of Table 4.1 shows the percentage of "real consumption" c_t accounted for by the residual u_t, $t = 1$ (1922), ..., $t = 20$ (1941). The linear approximations (4.1 a-b), (4.2a-b) and Table 4.1 afford a partial description of the sample of "real consumption" and "real income" data for the period 1922-1941 in the United States (see Haavelmo, 1947, p. 88). It is this description, the set of factual statements expressed in part by (4.1a-b), (4.2a-b) and Table 4.1, that the proffered system of demand functions is required by V to explain with help of appropriate initial conditions statements: For every collection of time periods (say) years, if the prices of all commodities change in approximately the same proportion (all price ratios approximately constant for the time periods in question), then the numerical relation between "real consumption" and "real income" is approximately linear. In other words, the precision with which the numerical relation between "real consumption" and "real income" (for a given collection of time periods) can be approximated by a linear function is to be deductively explained in terms of the approximate constancy of all price ratios, with help of the mathematical form of the proffered system of demand functions--the less the price ratios vary from period to period, the better the fit of the linear approximation. For instance, the closeness of fit of (4.1a-b) to the consumption and income data for the succession of years 1922-1941 in the United States is to be explained by the form (and parameter values) of the proffered demand functions in terms of the variations of individual commodity price ratios for the years 1922-1941. Some indication of the variation of individual price ratios of consumption goods from year to year (1922-1941) is afforded by Table 4.2. The numbers shown in Table 4.2 are ratios of price indexes for several different commodity groups, (i) food, (ii) rent, (iii) apparel, (iv) fuel and electricity, (v) household furnishings, (vi) all other commodities; the denominator in each ratio is the B.L.S. cost of living index (1935-1939 base). Under Requirement V a part of the residual variation of "real consumption" exhibited in (4.1a-b), (4.2a-b) and Table 4.1 is to be attributed to deviation of price ratios from exact constancy as exhibited in Table 4.2.[30]

Table 4.2*

Ratios of Commodity Group Price Indexes to General Price Index

Year	Food	Rent	Apparel	Fuel & Elec.	House Furn.	Misc.
1922	1.00	1.19	1.04	.94	.98	.84
1923	1.01	1.20	1.03	.94	1.03	.82
1924	1.00	1.24	1.02	.93	1.01	.82
1925	1.05	1.21	.97	.92	.96	.81
1926	1.08	1.19	.95	.92	.93	.81
1927	1.06	1.19	.95	.93	.93	.83
1928	1.06	1.18	.95	.92	.92	.84
1929	1.08	1.15	.94	.91	.91	.85
1930	1.05	1.15	.94	.93	.91	.88
1931	.95	1.19	.94	1.00	.90	.95
1932	.88	1.19	.93	1.05	.87	1.04
1933	.91	1.08	.95	1.08	.91	1.06
1934	.97	.98	1.00	1.05	.96	1.02
1935	1.02	.96	.98	1.02	.96	1.00
1936	1.02	.97	.98	1.01	.97	.99
1937	1.02	.98	1.00	.97	1.01	.98
1938	.97	1.03	1.01	.99	1.02	1.00
1939	.95	1.04	1.01	.99	1.01	1.01
1940	.96	1.04	1.01	.99	1.00	1.00
1941	1.00	1.01	1.01	.97	1.01	.98

*Source: Monthly Labor Review, Vol. 76, No. 2, February, 1953; p. 223. Table D-1. Consumers' Price Index for Moderate Income Families in Large Cities, by Group of Commodities (1935-1939 base).

Let us consider the formal derivation of the consumption and savings functions from the system of demand functions (3.38a-c).

Let the class $N = \{1, 2, \ldots, n\}$ of n commodities be partitioned into two subclasses $N_c = \{1, 2, \ldots, m\}$, called 'consumption goods' and $N_s = \{m + 1, \ldots, n\}$, called 'savings goods.' How this partition is accomplished in any given empirical application influences the conclusions reached in that application, but has no implication for the present discussion, which is confined to the mathematical properties of the proffered system of demand functions (3.38a-c). Suppose that

(4.3a-b)
$$p_i = \pi_i \bar{p}_1, \quad i = 1, 2, \ldots, m$$
$$p_j = \pi_j \bar{p}_2, \quad j = m+1, \ldots, n$$

where π_i, π_j $i = 1, 2, \ldots, m$, $j = m+1, \ldots, n$ are positive empirical constants (fixed for definite time periods) and $\bar{p}_1 > 0$, $\bar{p}_2 > 0$. For the class N_c of "consumption goods," the price ratios are fixed, <u>i.e.</u>,

(4.4)
$$\frac{p_h}{p_i} = \frac{\pi_h}{\pi_i}, \quad h, i = 1, 2, \ldots, m.$$

Similarly, for the class N_s of "savings goods," the price-ratios are fixed,

(4.5)
$$\frac{p_j}{p_k} = \frac{\pi_j}{\pi_k}, \quad j, k = m+1, \ldots, n.$$

However, $\bar{p}_1$ and $\bar{p}_2$ vary independently, so the price ratios

(4.6)
$$\frac{p_i}{p_j} = \frac{\pi_i}{\pi_j}\left(\frac{\bar{p}_1}{\bar{p}_2}\right),$$

where

$$i = 1, 2, \ldots, m$$
$$j = m+1, \ldots, n,$$

are not constant.

The preceding paragraph exhibits the logical structure of a <u>statement of initial conditions</u> for empirical application of the theory of consumer demand to aggregate consumption and savings. In such applications the variables $\bar{p}_1$ and $\bar{p}_2$ designate <u>indexes</u> (weighted averages) of prices of consumption goods and savings goods respectively. No statement has been made that the price ratios (4.4) and (4.5) are constants for all periods, and no such statement can be deduced from any statement that appears in the present discussion. Whether or not the actual prices designated by $p_1, \ldots, p_n$ in any given empirical application vary in accordance with (4.3a-b)-(4.5) for some collection of time periods (not necessarily a temporal succession of such periods) is a question for direct empirical research, and--being logically independent of theory of consumer demand--is a separate question.

The symbols $\bar{x}_1$ and $\bar{x}_2$, which we use to designate "real consumption" and "real savings" respectively, are defined as follows:

$$\bar{x}_1 = \frac{1}{\bar{p}_1} \sum_{i=1}^{m} p_i x_i$$

(4.7a-b)

$$= \sum_{i=1}^{m} \pi_i x_i$$

$$\bar{x}_2 = \frac{1}{\bar{p}_2} \sum_{j=m+1}^{n} p_j x_j$$

(4.8a-b)

$$= \sum_{j=m+1}^{n} \pi_j x_j .$$

Notice that

(4.9) $\bar{p}_1 \bar{x}_1 + \bar{p}_2 \bar{x}_2 = M.$

From the demand functions (3.38), (4.3a-b), (4.7a-b)-(4.8a-b) we deduce

$$\bar{x}_1 = \frac{\bar{p}_1^{\,\sigma-1}}{\bar{p}_1^{\,\sigma} + \sqrt{\lambda}\,\bar{p}_2^{\,\sigma}} \left[M - \bar{\gamma}_1 \bar{p}_1 - \bar{\gamma}_2 \bar{p}_2 \right] + \bar{\gamma}_1$$

(4.10a-b)

$$\bar{x}_2 = \frac{\sqrt{\lambda}\,\bar{p}_2^{\,\sigma-1}}{\bar{p}_1^{\,\sigma} + \sqrt{\lambda}\,\bar{p}_2^{\,\sigma}} \left[M - \bar{\gamma}_1 \bar{p}_1 - \bar{\gamma}_2 \bar{p}_2 \right] + \bar{\gamma}_2$$

where $\bar{\gamma}_1$, $\bar{\gamma}_2$ and $\sqrt{\lambda}$ are defined by

$$\bar{\gamma}_1 = \sum_{k=1}^{m} \gamma_k \pi_k ,$$

(4.11a-b)

$$\bar{\gamma}_2 = \sum_{k=m+1}^{n} \gamma_k \pi_k ,$$

(4.12) $$\sqrt{\lambda} = \frac{\sum_{k=m+1}^{n} \beta_k \pi_k^{\sigma}}{\sum_{k=1}^{m} \beta_k \pi_k^{\sigma}}$$

[Notice, for later reference, that under the arbitrary parameter restrictions (3.16), which are implicit in the system of demand functions (3.12a-c) introduced by Klein and Rubin, the consumption function parameter $\sqrt{\lambda}$ is independent of the historical parameters π_k, $k = 1, 2, \ldots, n$. Thus under the Klein-Rubin parameter restrictions, the coefficients of $\frac{M}{\overline{p}_1}$ in (4.10a-b) are functionally dependent structural constants.]

The system (4.10a-b) is a system of demand functions having the form of (3.38a-c) specialized in dimension $\underline{n}$ to $n = 2$. (4.10a) is the consumption function and (4.10b) is the savings function relative to the initial conditions specified by (4.3a-b). Formulas (4.11a-b) and (4.12) indicate how the parameters of the consumption function and savings function depend on the fixed parameters of the underlying system of demand functions and on the specific initial conditions expressed by (4.3a-b). The logical structure of the study of the variations in the parameter of the consumption and savings functions (4.10a-b) is afforded by the theory of consumer demand with variable preferences; (cf. Basmann, 1956).

The statement of initial conditions under which the consumption and savings functions (4.10a-b) are deduced allows the ratio

$$\frac{\overline{p}_2}{\overline{p}_1}$$

to vary. Consequently, the conjunction of that statement of initial conditions and the system of demand functions (3.38) does not imply that the consumption function and savings function (4.10a-b) can be closely approximated by a linear equation in "real consumption" $\overline{x}_1$ and "real income," $\frac{M}{\overline{p}_1}$, and a linear equation in "real savings" $\overline{x}_2$ and "real income." The advantage this feature confers is not merely one of practical convenience in the empirical testing of the theory; the details are postponed to Section 5.

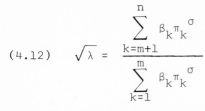

A more restrictive set of initial conditions is afforded by the statement that--in addition to the price ratios (4.4) and (4.5) being constant--the price ratios (4.6) are constant, for some set of time periods (not necessarily temporally successive).

In case all prices $p_1, p_2, \ldots, p_m, p_{m+1}, \ldots, p_n$ increase and decrease in the same proportion, we may set

$$\bar{p}_2 = \bar{p}_1 \qquad (4.13)$$

Let us use $\bar{p}$ to denote the common value of $\bar{p}_1$ and $\bar{p}_2$ in this case. From (4.10a-b) and (4.13) we deduce

$$\text{(4.14a-b)} \begin{cases} \bar{x}_1 = \dfrac{1}{1+\sqrt{\lambda}}\left(\dfrac{M}{\bar{p}}\right) + \dfrac{\sqrt{\lambda}\,\bar{\gamma}_1 - \bar{\gamma}_2}{1+\sqrt{\lambda}} \\[2ex] \bar{x}_2 = \dfrac{\sqrt{\lambda}}{1+\sqrt{\lambda}}\left(\dfrac{M}{\bar{p}}\right) + \dfrac{\bar{\gamma}_2 - \sqrt{\lambda}\,\bar{\gamma}_1}{1+\sqrt{\lambda}} \end{cases}$$

Letting

$$\beta = \frac{1}{1+\sqrt{\lambda}} \qquad (4.15)$$

and

$$\gamma = \frac{\sqrt{\lambda}\,\bar{\gamma}_1 - \bar{\gamma}_2}{1+\sqrt{\lambda}}, \qquad (4.16)$$

one readily verifies that the corresponding coefficients in (4.14b) are $(1-\beta)$ and $-\gamma$. Thus it turns out that the system of demand functions (3.38a-c) satisfies <u>Requirement V</u>.

In case we regard the numerical coefficients $\tilde{\beta} = 0.732$ and $\tilde{\gamma} = 84.0$, and $\text{Av}(u^2) = 58.2$, as statistical estimates of (4.15), (4.16) and the variance of u, respectively, the <u>historical parameters</u> π_k, $k = 1, 2, \ldots, n$, as well as the <u>structural parameters</u>, σ, β_k, γ_k, have to be regarded as parameters of the joint and marginal distribution functions of the estimators in question, namely, $\tilde{\beta}, \tilde{\gamma}$ and Var(u). Since $\tilde{\beta}$ is interpreted as an estimator of (4.15), and $\tilde{\gamma}$ as an estimator of (4.16), due account of the dependence of the sampling distributions of $\tilde{\beta}$, $\tilde{\gamma}$ and Var(u) on the historical π_k's has to be taken when we interpret the statistical estimates of (4.15) and (4.16), as well as of Var(u), obtained from another sample of consumption and income data, e.g., from a collection of data for the postwar years (1946-1967). For instance, in case postwar estimates of (4.15) and (4.16) differ significantly from the estimates shown in (4.1a-b), and (on that basis) we accept the statement that the parameters (4.15) and (4.16) have different values for the postwar years, we cannot deduce, however, that structural parameters σ, β_k, γ_k, $k = 1, 2, \ldots, n$, have changed. Without ruling out structural change as an hypothesis to explain significant differences in the estimates, the concept of consumption and savings functions that is laid down in Requirement V directs attention to alternative explanations that are already more precisely formulated and can be more directly studied and checked empirically than hypotheses about structural change.[31] In this respect the concept of consumption and savings functions in the present article differs from most other concepts with which the reader is likely to be familiar. In one respect, the contrast is most strikingly exhibited by comparison with Friedman's concept of consumption function with which it is taken for granted the reader is acquainted (Friedman, 1957, esp. Chapter 2). Friedman's concept is that of a linear consumption function that is a fundamental, invariant structural relation, its linear form (3.2a), and the parameters β and γ that fix that form, being fundamental structural constants; in addition to which the intercept parameter γ is $= 0$. Maintenance of the parameter restriction '$\gamma = 0$,' together with Friedman's adherence to the methodological convention that attaches great significance to large values of sample multiple correlation coefficients, poses the old problem of "saving the appearances"--see (4.1a-b)-(4.2a-b) and Table 4.1--which Friedman attempts to solve by introducing a new empirical notion 'permanent income.' Having thus decided to disregard the maxim of Occam's razor, Friedman faces the problem of specifying an adequate extension of 'permanent income.'[32] However, it is another aspect of Friedman's concept with which we are now concerned.

Inspection of (4.10a-b) reveals that a pair of consumption and savings functions that conform to Friedman's concept can be derived from the system of demand functions (3.38a-c) under the arbitrary hypothetical parameter restrictions

$$(4.17\text{a-b})\quad \begin{cases} \sigma = 0 \\ \gamma_k = 0, \quad k = 1, 2, \ldots, n. \end{cases}$$

Let C_F be the subclass of systems of demand functions (3.38a-c) under restrictions (4.17a-b). Each system of demand functions that belongs to C_F has the exceptionally simple form

$$(4.18) \qquad x_i = \nu_i \left(\frac{M}{p_i} \right), \qquad i = 1, 2, \ldots, n,$$

where the constants ν_i, $i = 1, 2, \ldots, n$, are defined by (3.17).

Friedman's concept of consumption function possesses the highly desirable feature of affording a sharp null hypothesis for test against the alternative hypothesis $(C_d - C_F)$, a remark we shall clarify in Section 5. Within the class C_d every system of demand functions that is consistent with Friedman's concept of consumption function is defined by (4.18). Interpreting the variable M by suitable "permanent income" data we should encounter little difficulty in determining how closely the system of demand functions (4.18) adjust to price and quantity data for individual commodities.[33]

Friedman was not the only economist to conceive of the linear consumption function as an invariant structural economic relation. The special attention given to Friedman's linear consumption function here arises from the fact that it is derivable from a special subclass C_F of systems of demand functions that belong to the class C_d, whereas no system of demand functions that belongs to $(C_d - C_F)$ yields a consumption function that is linear under all variations of price ratios.

In contrast with Friedman's concept, the price theory concept of consumption and savings functions involves no basic theoretical issues concerning the parameters β and γ, (4.15) and (4.16). For instance, if some very special initial conditions just happen to be fulfilled for a definite collection of time periods--it is important that those conditions can be specified in terms of the system of demand functions (3.38a-c) and the empirical historical parameters π_k, $k = 1, 2, \ldots, n$,--then the intercepts in (4.14a-b) are = 0, *viz.*,

$$\frac{\sqrt{\lambda}\,\bar{\gamma}_1 - \bar{\gamma}_2}{1 + \sqrt{\lambda}} = 0,$$

and the coefficient of income in (4.14a) is large (say)

$$\frac{1}{1 + \sqrt{\lambda}} > 0.9.$$

Employing the present concept of consumption and savings functions, which may appropriately be termed a price theory concept (because it allows scope for varying price ratios to affect the form and parameters of the consumption and savings functions as Friedman's does not),[34] we regard empirical approximations that happen to agree well with the foregoing equation and inequality, as descriptive of historical accidents, important, perhaps, but historical nonetheless.

Let us return to the consideration of the Samuelson-Frisch verbal interpretation of the parameters $\gamma_1, \ldots, \gamma_n$, which (as was mentioned in Section 3) provides a lead for empirical research aimed towards the construction of an extensional interpretation of the class C_d of systems of demand functions (3.38a-c). On the basis of a preliminary empirical test of the hypothetical parameter restrictions (3.40) we shall decide whether or not to follow up that lead. In one respect it is misleading to call the following empirical investigation a test of the hypothetical parameter restrictions (3.40), as the objective is not tentative assertion or denial of (3.40). Verbal interpretations of mathematical symbols, especially when expressed in concrete words, as the Samuelson-Frisch interpretation of the symbols $\gamma_1, \ldots, \gamma_n$ is, exhibit a tendency to become permanent features of expositions of pure, or abstract theories. The tendency is strong in case the verbal interpretation strikes us as plausible.[35] In such cases an inexpensive preliminary empirical investigation serves a useful purpose; in the present circumstance by its indecisiveness, in case (3.40) agrees well with available data, or by its foreshadowing the result of a more stringent test, in case (3.40) does not agree well with the available data. The decision sought is whether to follow the Samuelson-Frisch verbal lead. The decision now reached is not to be regarded as irrevocable, however.

The preliminary empirical investigation of the hypothetical parameter restrictions (3.40) involves two auxiliary hypotheses:

(4.19) $\sigma > 0$;

and, for the United States economy (1922-1941),

(4.20) $\bar{p}_2 = \bar{p}_1(1 + z)^{-1}$

where $\bar{p}_1$ is the consumer price index used in Haavelmo's study (Haavelmo, 1947, p. 88) and z is a rate of interest on high grade corporate bonds (Source: Economic Report of the President 1961, Table C43, p. 177).

The parameter restriction (4.19) serves as a special maintained hypothesis; its role in simplifying the test of the parameter restrictions (3.40) is made clear in formula (4.23a).

The auxiliary hypothesis expressed by (4.20)--intended to apply solely to the United States economy and succession of years 1922 through 1941--also serves to simplify the preliminary test of the hypothetical parameter restrictions (3.40). According to (4.20) the variation in the ratio of the general price level of "savings goods" to the general price level of "consumption goods" is accounted for (but not explained by) variations in the long-term rate of interest. This auxiliary hypothesis arose in connection with another minor investigation. The reader is to understand that I do not have much empirical evidence that would tend either to support or refute the hypothesis. To gather and analyze highly reliable evidence concerning the year-to-year variations in the price ratio $\frac{\overline{p}_2}{\overline{p}_1}$ would be expensive. We are not at present seeking definitive results.[36]

Making the substitution (4.20) in the consumption function (4.10a) we obtain

$$(4.21)\qquad \overline{x}_1 = \frac{1}{1+\sqrt{\lambda}\,(1+z)^{-\sigma}}\left[\left(\frac{M}{\overline{p}_1}\right)-\overline{\gamma}_1 - \overline{\gamma}_2(1+z)^{-1}\right] + \overline{\gamma}_1$$

From (3.40), (4.3a-b), (4.11a-b) and (4.19) we deduce that

$$(4.22\text{a-b})\qquad \frac{\partial \overline{x}_1}{\partial y} = \frac{1}{1+\sqrt{\lambda}\,(1+z)^{-\sigma}} > 0$$

where

$$y = \frac{M}{\overline{p}_1};$$

and

$$(4.23\text{a-b})\qquad \frac{\partial \overline{x}_1}{\partial z} = \frac{\sigma\sqrt{\lambda}(1+z)^{-(\sigma+1)}}{\left[1+\sqrt{\lambda}(1+z)^{-\sigma}\right]^2}\left[\left(\frac{M}{\overline{p}_1}\right)-\overline{\gamma}_1 - \overline{\gamma}_2(1+z)^{-1}\right]$$

$$+\frac{1}{1+\sqrt{\lambda}(1+z)^{-\sigma}}\left[\frac{\overline{\gamma}_2}{(1+z)^2}\right]$$

$$> 0.$$

We shall adjust the linear approximation

$$(4.24)\qquad \overline{x}_1 - m_{\overline{x}_1} = \frac{\partial \overline{x}_1}{\partial y}(y - m_y) + \frac{\partial \overline{x}_1}{\partial z}(z - m_z),$$

to the available consumption, income and interest rate data by the method of least squares. In (4.24) $m_{\overline{x}_1}$, m_y, and m_z are sample arithmetic means. In view of the deduced inequality (4.23b) the sign of the coefficient of $\underline{z}$ in the linear least squares adjustment is of central interest.

We shall also adjust (4.21) to the given numerical data by the method of nonlinear least squares under the special restriction[37]

(4.25) $$\sigma = 0.5.$$

This procedure yields "estimates" of $\bar{\gamma}_1$ and $\bar{\gamma}_2$ more or less directly.

In adjusting (4.24) to the numerical data and judging the extent of disagreement between (4.23b) and the numerical coefficient of z in (4.26) below we shall be making a test of the conjunction of the hypothetical parameter restrictions (3.40) and the auxiliary hypotheses expressed by (4.19) and (4.20). In case the extent of disagreement leads us to regard that conjunction as disconfirmed, we may continue to maintain (3.40) in case we wish to do so, a point of elementary logic that requires no clarification here.

The linear least squares approximation to (4.21) is

(4.26) $$\bar{x}_1 = \underset{(21.6)}{0.694}\left(\frac{M}{\bar{p}_1}\right) - \underset{(2.23)}{504z} + \underset{(5.59)}{124} + v$$

(4.27a-b) $$\mathrm{Av}(v^2) = 47.7$$ $$R = 0.987$$

Each of the residuals $\underline{v}$ in (4.26) is shown in Table 4.3, Column 1.

The nonlinear least squares approximation to (4.21) is

(4.28) $$\bar{x}_1 = \frac{\bar{p}_1^{-0.5}}{\bar{p}_1^{\,0.5} + \sqrt{0.2}\,\bar{p}_2^{\,0.5}}\left[M + 3164\bar{p}_1 + 1596\bar{p}_2\right] - 3164 + w$$

(4.29) $$\mathrm{Av}(w^2) = 47.3$$

The minimization of sum of squares of residuals with respect to λ, $\bar{\gamma}_1$ and $\bar{\gamma}_2$ is restricted by '$\sigma = 0.5$.' Each of the residuals $\underline{w}$ in (4.28) is shown in Table 4.3, Column 2.,

The nonlinear "estimates" of λ, $\bar{\gamma}_1$, and $\bar{\gamma}_2$ for the period 1922-1941 are:

$$\hat{\lambda} = 0.20,$$

$$\hat{\bar{\gamma}}_1 = -3164,$$

$$\hat{\bar{\gamma}}_2 = -1596.$$

Table 4.3

Year	(1) Eqn. (4.26) v	(2) Eqn. (4.28) w
1922	-4.21	-4.20
1923	-9.80	-9.91
1924	6.37	6.29
1925	-2.09	-2.17
1926	4.60	4.53
1927	1.02	0.962
1928	10.9	10.8
1929	3.86	3.69
1930	6.80	6.78
1931	-6.69	-6.64
1932	-6.35	-6.17
1933	-1.22	-1.04
1934	-2.05	-1.94
1935	-0.877	-0.807
1936	1.30	1.31
1937	1.16	1.17
1938	5.63	5.67
1939	3.98	3.99
1940	4.61	4.61
1941	-16.9	-16.9

Recall (4.11a-b) and (4.12). The linear approximation (4.26) and the nonlinear approximation (4.28) are very close approximations of each other, as comparison of residuals *v* and *w* in *Table 4.3* indicates.

I judge that the conjunction of the hypothetical restrictions (3.40) and the auxiliary hypotheses (4.19)-(4.20) is in poor agreement with the sample data. Accordingly, I consider the adoption of the Samuelson-Frisch verbal interpretation of $\gamma_1, \ldots, \gamma_n$ as a guide for the construction of an extensional interpretation of $\gamma_1, \ldots, \gamma_n$ in the demand function systems (3.38a-c) as premature now.[38]

5. Discussion of the Requirements

Of the five practical requirements listed in Section 3, only *Requirement V* will be discussed in much detail. Moreover, we shall discuss _Requirement V_ first.

A. _Discussion of Requirement V_

Several important considerations underlie the decision to require that the form of the demand functions allow derivation of the Keynesian linear consumption and savings functions under the special initial conditions mentioned in _Requirement V_:

(a) Recall the discussion of 'domain of empirical interpretation' in Section 2. Most economists have viewed the Keynesian consumption and savings functions as intended to apply (somehow) to the same empirical phenomena as the theory of consumer demand. This notion is partially explicated by the remark that in any adequate empirical interpretation the _extensions_ of symbols that appear in the Keynesian consumption and savings functions are composed of directly observable objects and events that belong to the fundamental domain of interpretation of the theory of consumer demand. In the terminology of logic, discourses in the theory of consumer demand and the Keynesian theory of the consumption function are said to have the same _domain of individuals_.

When it is agreed further that discourse within the theory of consumer demand and the Keynesian theory of the consumption and savings function shall be structured in accordance with the rules of general predicate logic, it becomes the first item of the economists' business to ensure by deductive exploration, that the conjunction of the two theories is consistent, _i.e._, not a contradiction. However, this practical task of ensuring consistency of the theory of consumer demand and Keynesian theory of the consumption and savings functions does not arise as a practical problem until definite forms are prescribed for demand functions and definite forms are prescribed for the Keynesian consumption and savings functions.

The specification of linear consumption functions in econometric statistical work, exemplified by (4.1a-b) above, had become quite common by the middle Fifties. From a practical point of view, the closeness of adjustment of linear consumption functions to the available annual consumption and income data for the period between the two preceding great wars did not warrant a claim that the hypothesis expressed by the Keynesian consumption function was thereby disconfirmed. On the other hand--quite apart from appropriate questions about the reliability of the available consumption and income data--this failure to disconfirm the hypothesis expressed by the linear Keynesian consumption function never warranted acceptance of the conclusion that the parameters of the linear Keynesian consumption and savings functions are fixed, _i.e._, structural economic constants. What had been tested empirically was not the linear Keynesian hypothesis alone, but the conjunction of that hypothesis and an implicit statement of initial conditions, which--if made explicit--would describe a set of circumstances that held during that historical period, namely, 1922-1941.

The requirement that the linear consumption and savings functions be derivable from the system of demand functions and linear only under special conditions is fruitful in this respect, namely, that--as is mentioned in Section 3--it requires that at least one important hypothetical restriction be imposed on the form of demand functions: All income expansion paths on the preference field $\{x | x_i \geq 0, \; i = 1, 2, \ldots, n\}$ must be linear and intersect in a common point.

(b) Requirement V is motivated in part by other considerations of a practical sort that nonetheless have their basis in pure logic, being suggested by the fact that explanatory hypotheses take the form of universal conditional statements in which the antecedent statement function expresses initial conditions.[39] In scientific work explanatory hypotheses are tested by the agreement of their logical consequences with independent factual descriptions of objects and events belonging to the appropriate domain of interpretation. The statement function that describes initial conditions has as its domain a class of distinct circumstances, not merely a single circumstance. In some circumstances that fulfill the statement of initial conditions, a test of derived consequences against factual descriptions of objects and events may be easier to perform and less expensive than in other circumstances, and the test may be more reliable. In this connection notice that Requirement V indicates an initial condition under which we may use linear statistical and approximation techniques in making a test of the hypothesis that the demand functions belong to the class C_d, *i.e.*, are of the form (3.38a-c). That is to say, the linear expressions (4.14a-b) being deductive consequences of (3.38a-c) and the statement that all prices change in the same proportion (for the sample period in question) the failure of good agreement of (4.14a-b) with descriptions of objects and events, would tend to disconfirm the hypothesis expressed by C_d.

Under the initial conditions for the nonlinear consumption and savings functions (4.10a-b) we are not entitled to the use of simple linear statistical techniques, except as approximations. However, under these initial conditions the complexity and magnitude of the practical problem of testing the hypothesis expressed by C_d are much less than in case the individual commodity prices vary independently.

In case empirical tests of C_d under initial conditions for the linear consumption and savings functions (4.14a-b) and empirical tests of C_d under the initial conditions specified for (4.10a-b) do not disconfirm the hypothesis C_d (under the specific decision rules that we happen to use), we proceed to test the hypothesis in more detail, and under more complicated initial conditions. For instance, we might be able to partition the set of individual commodities into three or more groups (say) in accordance with the headings of Table 4.2. In case the prices of individual commodities within each group of commodities change in the same proportion, we can derive a complete system of composite demand functions, one demand function for each group; recall the Leontief-Hicks theorem mentioned in Section 3. Under such conditions empirical test of the hypothesis expressed by C_d is more difficult and expensive to perform than under initial conditions for (4.10a-b), but less difficult and expensive than under initial conditions that require a larger number of composite commodities. We need not commit ourselves to making difficult and very expensive empirical tests of C_d until that hypothesis has successfully passed relatively simple and inexpensive empirical tests. The practical advantage secured by formulating general hypotheses, some deductive consequences of which are relatively easy and inexpensive to test, calls for no special comment; the advantage sought is minimization of the cost of securing a disconfirmation of the hypothesis in question.[40] In this connection notice that the special initial conditions mentioned in Requirement V, and those for (4.10a-b), are specified in quantitative terms. Numerical description of initial conditions renders easier the practical task of specifying those circumstances in which the initial conditions are approximately fulfilled--easier, at least, than would be the case otherwise. Several alternative numerical measures of the degree of approximation of actual circumstances to ideal initial conditions can be tried out in practice. Notice that the problem of specifying definite circumstances that fulfill initial conditions approximately cannot be studied independently of empirical applications of the hypothesis C_d, and, in practice, is never definitively solved.[41]

The aim of hypothesis formulation in scientific economics being to organize economic facts in accordance with the rules of general predicate logic, it is desirable at the outset of an investigation to require of any hypothesis that it be capable of explaining--with help of precisely specified initial conditions--some given factual statements that belong to the prescribed domain of application, and that are regarded (tentatively) as established. It is essential, however, that the set of factual statements initially accepted not be allowed to define implicitly the domain of the hypothesis that ultimately is formulated; there must be other factual statements that, with help of other statements of initial conditions, the hypothesis can explain deductively. The hypothesis must be capable of predicting new facts (as is commonly said). In other words, the hypothesis formulated must be more than an equivalent expression of the initially accepted set of factual statements. The consumption and income for 1922-1941 (Haavelmo, 1947, p. 88) and the linear approximations (4.1a-b), (4.2a-b) and Table 4.1 have been taken as expressing factual statements the proffered system of demand functions is required to explain deductively with help of the statement of initial conditions mentioned in Requirement V. Notice, however, that the hypothesis C_d, defined by (3.38a-c), cannot be deduced from the factual statements expressed by (4.1a-b), (4.2a-b), and Table 4.1, and that the hypothesis C_d is capable of predicting new factual statements from different initial conditions, *e.g.*, as under the initial conditions for (4.10a-b).

The cautionary remarks about referring to the empirical investigations in Section 4 as *tests* requires no special comment.

B. *Discussion of Requirements I-IV.*

In the discussion of Requirements I-IV and especially in the discussion of IV, which refers to hypothetical restrictions on structural parameters, great care is required to keep clear the distinction between question (1) and question (2) mentioned in Section 1. Economists and econometricians are wont to say that hypothetical parameter restrictions are "a priori knowledge," "a priori information," or "intuitive knowledge," to be "realistic," etc. As mentioned in Section 1 such verbal expressions are left too vague by those who use them to be at all useful in the present discussion. There is, however, another verbal distinction that is commonly made, between "a priori parameter restrictions," *i.e.*, restrictions that are said "to come from theory," and "ad hoc," or "arbitrary," parameter restrictions. Of hypothetical parameter restrictions it is common for economists and econometricians to call "a priori" those that, like (3.18), secure for a system of definite functions the properties that define a special class of functions in abstract economic theory; and, on the other hand, to call "ad hoc," or "arbitrary," those parameter restrictions, like the restrictions (3.16) that are implicit in the Klein-Rubin demand functions (3.12a-c), which go further than is required to make (3.38a-c) a system of demand functions. The distinction between hypothetical parameter restrictions that "come from theory" and those that are "ad hoc," when appropriately clarified by the logical relations in which the former stand to the latter, can be useful in discussions like the present. Such a clarification occurs naturally in this discussion. It is not expected that all readers will find that clarification satisfactory. Many economists and econometricians object to the formulation, deductive exploration, and <u>subsequent</u> statistical testing of hypothetical parameter restrictions that do not "come from theory." [Referring to the Klein-Rubin system of special demand functions and, hence, to the parameter restrictions (3.16), Samuelson (1947, p. 88) writes of the empirical implications of that hypothesis as "implied strait-jackets on the facts." Although Samuelson's remark very likely was not intended to express an objection to the empirical testing of the Klein-Rubin "ad hoc" parameter restrictions which would involve comparison of their deductive consequences with relevant factual statements independently confirmed, Samuelson's metaphor is unfortunate nonetheless, it being devoid of an explication in the language of modern logic, and productive of muddles.] Many economists and econometricians consider the distinction between hypothetical restrictions that "come from theory" and "ad hoc" hypothetical restrictions as something more than a logical relation. A few of these, willing to discuss the question, express the view that hypothetical parameter restrictions that "come from theory" are "better known" than "ad hoc" hypothetical parameter restrictions. Furthermore, that part of <u>Requirement IV</u> that expresses the resolve to employ a minimum of hypothetical parameter restrictions, just sufficient in number to give the proffered system of functions the properties of a system of demand functions, can easily be misconstrued as a methodological injunction against the introduction, deductive exploration and empirical testing of "ad hoc" parameter restrictions on the grounds that such hypothetical parameter restrictions do not "come from theory." Such an injunction, however, would be inconsonant with what I called in an earlier paper my <u>anti-limitationist bias</u>, <u>i.e.</u>, the constructive policy of encouraging free creation of empirically testable hypotheses in economics (Basmann, 1965a, pp. 164-165, also p. 181). That <u>Requirement IV</u> is not the kind of methodological encumbrance that I have criticized elsewhere is made clear in the course of the subsequent discussion.

On the other hand, <u>Requirement II</u>, which expresses the decision to restrict the present investigation to systems of functions such that the latter have the same form can be construed as "ad hoc," <u>i.e.</u>, as a restriction that does not "come from theory." Indeed, any specification of a definite form of functions to be adjusted to quantity, price and income data is "ad hoc" in the sense that it does not "come from theory." In following the discussion it is important to bear in mind how the <u>Requirements I-IV</u>, and economic hypotheses like those expressed (in part) by the parameter restrictions (3.18) and (3.16) are actually used in empirical investigations.

For sake of brevity in the discussion of <u>Requirements I-IV</u> many special details are omitted, general indications sufficing for present purposes.

Let us begin with Requirement III in a given investigation, the general class (call it H for now) of systems of stochastic functions to be adjusted to quantity, price and income data is intended to serve as a maintained statistical hypothesis. Refer to formulas (3.10a-b). The maintained hypothesis H is specified by a set of propositions that restrict the form of the functions

$$x_i(p_1, \ldots, p_n, M) \quad i = 1, 2, \ldots, n$$

and the form of the distribution function $G(\xi_1, \ldots, \xi_n; \omega)$. In formulating the system of functions (3.14a-d)-(3.15a-c) we specified a part of the maintained hypothesis in the present investigation. Recall that any proper subclass H_1 of H affords a statistical hypothesis that may be tested against alternative hypotheses, *viz.*, H_1 may be tested against H_1', where H_1' is a non-empty subclass of the class-difference $(H-H_1)$. The decision to confine an investigation to a given class H of systems of stochastic functions is logically arbitrary, and may be the result of practical, noncognitive, considerations only. Requirement III expresses the resolution that the maintained hypothesis H shall contain a proper subclass of systems of stochastic functions that are not systems of demand functions, or--to put it another way--H shall contain a proper subclass H_d of systems of stochastic demand functions. This formulation of H makes it feasible to test H_d against any alternative hypothesis H_d' where $H_d' \subset (H-H_d)$, *i.e.*, to test systems of stochastic demand functions against alternative systems of stochastic functions that are not demand functions. Our aim is to determine whether the so-called "laws" of consumer demand, as expressed in abstract theory of consumer demand, serve well to organize factual statements about consumer behavior; recall Section 2. The testing of H_d against $(H-H_d)$ provides information that is relevant to that determination.[42]

That part of Requirement III that calls for the class of systems of demand functions to be obtained from a more general class of systems of functions by means of parameter restrictions alone is intended to secure the following practical objective: Under a given principle of parameter estimation, (say) maximum likelihood, a single method of computation shall be applicable to every system of functions in H, so that the systems of functions belonging to $(H-H_d)$, *i.e.*, those that are not systems of demand functions necessarily adjust to given samples of quantity, price and income data at least as closely--in respect of the principle of estimation--as any system of demand functions that come in question, *i.e.*, members of H_d. Since the subclass H_d is specified by parameter restrictions alone, every system of functions that belongs to H has the same form as every other. Consequently, a single form of transformation of sample data into a set of parameter estimators and auxiliary statistics[43] is applicable to every system of functions that belongs to the maintained hypothesis H. Test statistics for H_d, the most general subclass of systems of demand functions that belong to H, are obtained by imposing the parameter restrictions that define H_d as side conditions on the parameter estimators.

Under Requirement II each demand function in a given system of demand functions has the same form. The chief aim of this requirement is to facilitate joint estimation of structural parameters and construction of test statistics. To begin with, notice that each structural parameter in a system of demand functions (regardless of the form of the system) is a structural parameter of the corresponding system of indifference surfaces in R^n; recall Section 2. Furthermore, notice that each system of demand functions (regardless of form) defines a one-to-one mapping of the preference field $\{x \mid x_i \geqq 0,\ i = 1, 2, ..n\}$ into a definite n-dimensional subspace of R^{n+1} that is a subset of all (n+1)-tuples

$$\left(\frac{M}{p_1}, \ldots, \frac{M}{p_n}, 1\right).$$

In other words the structural parameters in a definite system of demand functions can be expressed in terms of quantity data--samples of $(x_1, \ldots, x_n)$--alone with help of the so-called "laws" of consumer demand. In consequence of Requirement I, the structural parameters, thus expressed, are functions of samples of all quantities $x_1, x_2, \ldots, x_n$. The foregoing remarks account for our practical interest in working out joint estimation methods for systems of demand functions.

An attempt to explain in detail how Requirement II might facilitate the development of a joint estimation method and its associated statistical distribution theory that are simpler and more convenient than would be the case otherwise is beyond the scope of this paper, and probably would not achieve much success with many readers. In giving answers to question (1) mentioned in Section 1, the chief points of interest are what practical steps are taken in order to find hypothetical parameter restrictions and, in general, what practical advantages are sought.

Requirement I seems to call for no special comment.

Requirement IV is intended to keep the number of parameters in the general class of functions as small as possible given that the other requirements are met. It takes account of the fact that in practice--in order to meet the general requirement that the general class actually contains a proper subclass of systems of demand functions--we proceed to the general class by generalizing our first invention of a system of demand functions, which is likely to be a highly restricted form. Recall the systems of demand functions belonging to C_F defined by formula (4.18); see also the remarks in Section 3 just preceding (3.12a-c). [In this connection it should be mentioned, for the benefit of students, at least, that familiarity with the details of the Rule of Universal Quantifier Introduction[44] encountered in general predicate logic can be very helpful in recognizing those special cases (of a deduction) which are also representative; *cf*. Polyà (1954, Vol. I, pp. 12-34; *esp*. pp. 15-17). The relevance of the foregoing rule is not always appreciated by econometricians; *cf*. Basmann (1966, pp. 234-236, *esp*. 236n). I have made use of universal quantifier introduction in this way to generalize the class C_d of systems of demand functions (3.38a-c) to include systems of demand functions for which income expansion paths are nonlinear.[45]]

In view of the scarcity of reliable quantity, price and income data there are practical advantages to be gained by making do with as few independent structural parameters as possible. It is taken for granted that the reader is well acquainted with the problem encountered in linear regression when the number of coefficients to be adjusted to numerical data exceeds the sample size. In such circumstances we have to reduce the number of independent coefficients in order to compute unique coefficient estimates, or to obtain a specified level of precision in estimates. Reference to this familiar case serves well enough to indicate the practical consideration that underlies *Requirement IV*.

C. *Some Concluding Remarks*

Question (1), "How do you find, or invent, hypothetical structural parameter restrictions in the first place?", presupposes a system of structural economic functions having definite forms and definite parameters. Structural parameters do not "exist" apart from definite forms of structural functions. In attempting to give answers to question (1), I have stressed the foregoing presupposition more or less covertly by choosing as an illustration an application of the abstract theory of consumer demand.

The abstract theory of consumer demand defines the concept of system of demand functions, *viz*., it specifies definite mathematical properties that any system of functions is required to possess if that system is to be considered as a system of demand functions. The abstract theory of demand does not contain any statement that prescribes definite mathematical forms of systems of demand functions, however, and--consequently--contains no symbols that designate any parameters. It is transparent (as a point in elementary logic) that no parameter restriction can be deduced from the so-called "laws" of consumer demand alone. Definite structural parameters first come into consideration with the decision to confine attention (in a given investigation) to a definite form of systems of functions to be adjusted to quantity, price and income data. In case the functions are to be stochastic, the set of statements that prescribe the forms of systems of functions is a proper subset of the set of statements that is the maintained hypothesis H for the investigation in question. The statements that prescribe the maintained hypothesis H are treated as premises, i.e., undischarged assumptions, for subsequent deductions. Those premises, which are essential to the application of abstract theory of consumer demand, do not "come from theory."

Every null hypothesis H_1 (with respect to H) is formulated by augmenting the undischarged assumptions that prescribe H by one or more additional assumptions that are consistent with the former. This augmentation of the initial set of premises is logically arbitrary. From the augmented set of undischarged assumptions we may deduce some definite parameter restrictions in accordance with the deduction rules of general predicate logic.

In the present illustration we chose to augment the statements that compose the maintained hypothesis H by the explicit definitions and "laws" of consumer demand. The structural parameter restrictions (3.18) are deduced from the augmented set of undischarged assumptions. For example, in Section 3 the abstract Slutsky-Hicks substitution symbols s_{ij}, i, j = 1, 2, ..., n are interpreted by the functions (3.14a-d)-(3.15a-c) and their partial derivatives in accordance with (3.19). Those partial derivatives contain the structural parameters σ_k, β_k, γ_k, k = 1, 2, ..., n. The <u>n-1</u> parameter restrictions

$$\sigma_i = \sigma_j \text{ for all } i,j = 1, 2, \ldots, n$$

are deduced from (3.14a-d)-(3.15a-b), (3.13) and the abstract "law" of consumer demand expressed by (3.20). As (3.14a-d)-(3.15a-b) and (3.13) do not belong to abstract economic theory, the parameter restrictions (3.18) do not "come from theory" alone.

Having introduced the explicit definitions and "laws" of consumer demand as logically arbitrary assumptions (the deductive consequences of which we wish to test empirically) we may go further in specifying parameter restrictions directly as, in effect, did Klein and Rubin in formulating the special demand functions (3.12a-c). We may do this simply because we wish to test some of the special consequences of the so-called "ad hoc" hypothesis expressed by the special parameter restrictions (3.16).

Returning to the hypothetical parameter restrictions (1.2a-d) mentioned in Section 1, we remark that logical status of those restrictions is precisely the same as that of the Klein-Rubin "ad hoc" restrictions (3.16). The form of the system of functions in which the parameters designated by β_1, β_6 and β_3 appear is specified by a logically arbitrary maintained hypothesis. Unlike the abstract theory of consumer demand, however, Keynesian theory contains no set of restrictions on partial derivatives of the consumption, investment, liquidity preference and money supply functions. It is usual, says Samuelson (1948, p. 277), to make some assumptions about the signs of partial derivatives "on a basis of a priori, intuitive, empirical experience." In the case of the hypothetical parameter restrictions (1.2a-d), as well as the rest of the hypothetical parameter restrictions tested empirically in my earlier papers (1965d, 1966), only curiosity and practical considerations influenced the formulation. I mention just one of the latter: for linear equation systems choose parameter restrictions such that the image (under the mapping afforded by identifiability relations) of the structural null hypothesis is a convex set in the reduced form space (Basmann, 1965c; also 1965d, esp. 404-410). This facilitates the test of the structural hypothesis with help of ellipsoidal confidence regions.

The terminological distinction between hypothetical parameter restrictions that "come from theory" and "ad hoc" hypothetical parameter restrictions is of very limited usefulness in the formulation and testing of economic hypotheses.

To students and younger economists I suggest that the first and perhaps most crucial step in formulating and testing hypotheses is to understand the distinction between question (1) and question (2).

FOOTNOTES

*I am indebted to my students, Lee Brown, James Ciecka, James Kenkel, James McDonald, Marvin Margolis, James Marsden, Gregory Schoepfle and Eugene Warren for helpful comments in connection with the preparation of this paper, and for performing the computations in Section 4. Responsibility for errors is mine alone.

Section 3 and part of Section 4 constitute a revision of an earlier draft prepared at the University of Oslo, where I was a Fulbright Scholar (1955-1956).

The numerical computations in Section 4 were done in connection with a research project supported by the National Science Foundation and the Krannert grant.

[1]The representation in that paper is composed of four structural equations: (i) consumption function, (ii) investment functions, (iii) demand for money function, (iv) supply of money function and linkages among them. The representation is "Keynesian" in form; however, as consumption, savings, income and quantity of money are represented in undeflated terms, the economic hypothesis is not Keynesian.

[2]Another interesting class of systems of demand functions, called <u>additive logarithmic demand functions</u>, has been studied by Houthakker (1960), Arrow (1961) and Gorman (1963). The class of systems of additive logarithmic demand functions and the class C_d of systems of demand functions developed in Section 3 have a single system in common, namely, the system of demand functions defined by (4.18) in Section 4.

[3]Here I am considering as truth-functional the logic of universal and existential propositions for finite domains of individuals.

It is taken for granted that the reader is well-acquainted with truth-functional logic. For a concise review, especially adopted to the needs of the present discussion, consult the book by Carnap (1958, pp. 4-38).

In this paper I use "statement" and "proposition" interchangeably.

[4]For a brief statement of the logical problem of confirmation see the book by Carnap (1962, <u>esp</u>. pp. 19-23).

[5]A weaker version of this presupposition is that the set of circumstances that cause us to <u>assert</u> a given proposition is identical with, or at least a proper subset of, the set

of circumstances that makes that proposition true.

[6]That students actually intending to ask question (1) often phrase their queries in the language of question (2), should not be overlooked.

[7]We shall not have occasion to make use of the utility function that is derived from the system of demand functions (3.38a-c).

[8]For an account that stresses deduction rules see the book by Anderson and Johnstone (1962, Chapters 2, 5 and 6). The concepts of discharged and undischarged assumptions will be needed in Section 5. Consult Anderson and Johnstone (1962, *esp*. pp. 22-23). The book by Ogden and Richards (1923, *esp*. Chapter 1) provides an excellent general background for the discussion in Section 2. For technical semantic concepts we shall refer to the book by Carnap (1956).

[9]For a brief analysis of belief expressing sentences consult the book by Carnap (1956, *esp*. pp. 53-55).

Not every sentence that contains personal pronouns is egocentric as "egocentric" is used in this discussion. For instance

> "*I* take (4.1a-b)-(4.2a-b) and *Table 4.1* as factual statements to be explained by *my* hypothesis"

is not egocentric (it does not express a belief but, rather, a *decision*), whereas

> "Certainly the underlying structure of the American economy changed during 1941-1945"

is egocentric in the sense that it expresses strong belief (experienced by one who speaks or writes it) in the subsentence "the underlying structure ..."

Notice (e); the contingent character of Q is essential to the classification of (e) as egocentric. For instance

> "Necessarily $A \supset (B \supset A)$"

would not be considered egocentric in the present discussion since the subsentence is a tautology of truth-functional logic. In modal logic '$A \supset (B \supset A)$' is said to be a *strict implication*, and 'necessarily' in the foregoing sentence is used to express that '$A \supset (B \supset A)$' is a strict implication alternatively the connective '$-\!\!<$', called 'necessity' is employed:

$$A -\!\!< (B \supset A).$$

[10]As a matter of fact it is not the set of restrictions (3.39) that are tested in this article, but the set of restrictions (3.40), which imply the negation of (3.39). See Section 4.

[11]The "objectivity" of the practical requirements *I-V* mentioned in Section 3 should not be confused with the "objectivity" sought for in laying down rules of inductive inference, *e.g.*, the *expectation criterion of objectivity*, *cf.* Ackermann (1966, *esp.* pp. 8-9). A nondeductive rule of inference (from given factual statements) is said to meet the foregoing criterion of objectivity only if any two scientists using that rule choose the same hypothesis on the basis of the given factual statements. As *Requirements I-V* are not rules of inductive inference, the expectation *criterion of objectivity* does not apply to them.

In this connection it may assist the reader in following the present discussion to point out that I do not regard the achievement of consensus or conformity of choice of, or belief in, hypotheses as of much practical importance in scientific economic research. This is not tantamount to saying that serious efforts to solve technical logical and semantical problems of nondeductive inference are misplaced.

[12]In case the reader wishes to review the concept of *extension*, the book by Carnap (1958, pp. 38-42) is suggested. For more detail consult the book by Carnap (1956, *esp.* Chapter 1).

[13]One formulation of theory of choice is the following: u, v, w are variables over S (mentioned in the text).

—— P.1 $(u)(v)[\sim Iuv \;.\supset.\; Puv \vee Pvu]$
—— P.2 $(u)(v)[Puv \;.\supset.\; \sim Iuv]$
—— P.3 $(u)(v)(w)[Puv \,\&\, Pvw \;.\supset.\; Puw]$
—— P.4 $(u)(\exists v)Puv$
—— P.5 $(u)(v)[Puv \supset Pvu]$
—— P.6 $(u)(v)(w)[Puv \,\&\, Ivw \;.\supset.\; Puw]$
—— P.7 $(u)(\exists v)[Iuv \,\&\, \sim(v = u)]$
—— P.8 $(u)(v)[(v = u) \supset Iuv]$

The horizontal bar placed to the left of each of the foregoing expressions indicates that *P.1* - *P.8* are assumptions for all deductions within the theory of choice, *viz.* all deductions are within the scope of *P.1* - *P.8*. The presence of the nonfalsifiable assumptions *P.4* and *P.7* serves to remind us that it is the theory of choice *as a whole* that is tested against a system of factual statements; *cf.* Quine (1953, pp. 42-46).

None of the expressions *P.1* - *P.8* contains a sign that

designates a real number or any n-tuple of real numbers n = 2, 3, ... Consequently, no statement about any real number or any n-tuple of real numbers can be deduced from the theory of choice alone.

[14]The statement (u)Iuu and

$$(u)(v)(w)[(Iuv \,\&\, Ivw \,.\supset.\, Iuw]$$

are deduced from P.1 - P.8 in Note 13 above.

[15]This view remains controversial in econometrics; see the papers by Basmann (1967a), Fromm and Klein (1967) and Basmann (1967b). The views expressed by Fromm and Klein deserve very close scrutiny. Recently one academic economist has expressed the view that the mapping M of the commodity bundle space S into R^n is not relevant to the problem of interpreting the purely mathematical theory of consumer demand in precise empirical terms. That the one-to-one mapping M of S into R^n is not relevant to the empirical application of the mathematical theory of consumer demand may have been "inferred" from the fact that the mapping is not mentioned in articles and treatises on the abstract theory. While it is the case that writers of textbook chapters on pure theory of consumer demand (quite understandably) do not go into much detail about the logical structure of empirical interpretations of that theory--typical are the presentations by Allen (1956, pp. 658 ff), Hicks (1946), Lloyd (1967, p. 6 ff), Samuelson (1948, pp. 92 ff) and Wold (1953, p. 81 ff)--it does not follow that those writers consider the logical structure of extensional interpretations as irrelevant to empirical applications of pure, or abstract, theory of consumer demand.

[16]For instance a given commodity-object in a commodity bundle may have two or more quantitative properties on the magnitudes of which the position of the commodity bundle in the preference ordering depends.

[17]Recall the assumption of nonsatiety, assumption of continuity, and assumption of differentiability, cf. Wold (1953, pp. 82-83) and Lloyd (1967, pp. 9-15). These assumptions mention n additive quantitative properties commodity bundles are assumed to possess, which are not mentioned by P.1 - P.8.

[18]For a review of logic of relations consult the book by Anderson and Johnstone (1962, pp. 198-210; also pp. 225-227).

[19]Consult the book by Carnap (1966, Chapters 6, 7, 8, 9, 10).

[20]For brief accounts consult the books by Ripley (1964, _esp_. pp. 93-109) and Cohen (1960, _esp_. pp. 95-129).

[21]Of course, my conjecture that a definite extensional interpretation of theory of consumer demand will turn out to be very complicated remains open to refutation.

[22]The basic utility function was

$$u(c,s) = \frac{(c - \gamma_1)(s - \gamma_2)}{\rho_1(c - \gamma_1) + \rho_2(s - \gamma_2)}$$

$$\rho_1 > 0, \quad \rho_2 > 0$$

$$\text{on } c > \gamma_1, \; s > \gamma_2$$

The utility function

$$v(c,s) = \rho_2 u(c,s)$$

is equivalent to $u(c,s)$; _cf_. Hicks (1946, pp. 306-307). In (3.2a-b)

$$\beta = \frac{1}{1 + \sqrt{\frac{\rho_1}{\rho_2}}}$$

$$\gamma_1 = \gamma, \quad \gamma_2 = -\gamma.$$

[23]More precisely, the system of functions (3.14a-c) - (3.15a-b) was derived as an intermediate step and (3.38a-c) obtained by the specialization (3.18).

[24]I am indebted to Jan Kmenta and James Ramsey for bringing to my attention recently the interesting unpublished paper by Goldberger and Gamaletsos (1967). Goldberger and Gamaletsos have computed some new statistical estimates of systems of demand functions having the special form (3.12a-c). The earliest use of the system (3.12a-c) in statistical demand analysis appears to be that by Stone (1954).

[25]The verbal interpretation does not strictly imply the hypothetical parameter restrictions (3.40), however.

[26]Goldberger and Gamaletsos (1967, pp. 22 _ff_) adopt the Samuelson-Frisch interpretation of $\gamma_1, \ldots, \gamma_n$ for the

special system of demand functions (3.12a-c).

[27]Recomputed by <u>7094 ECOMP Program</u>.

[28]Numbers shown in parenthesis are calculated in accordance with formulas for "t-ratios" in general linear hypothesis with independently and identically normally distributed disturbances; <u>cf</u>. Mood and Graybill (1963, pp. 333-335). However, in the present discussion no assumption has been made to the effect that disturbances are independently and identically normally distributed. Here the "t-ratios" are used solely to indicate how closely the functions (4.1a-b) fit the numerical data.

[29]The concept of <u>estimator</u> used in this discussion is as follows: Let θ^* designate a definite real-valued parameter, $\hat{\theta}$ a real-valued function of T observations, and let $H_T(\hat{\theta})$ designate the marginal distribution function of $\hat{\theta}$. Finally let m_T be defined by

$$\int_{-\infty}^{m_T} d\, H_T(\hat{\theta}) = 0.5.$$

$\hat{\theta}$ is said to be an estimator of θ^* if, and only if, the sequence $\{m_T\}$ converges to θ^* as $T \to \infty$.

A definite value of $\hat{\theta}$ (computed from a given sample) is said to be an estimate of θ^* if, and only if, $\hat{\theta}$ is an estimator of θ^*.

In statistical inference the use of parameter estimators is not essential.

[30]<u>Requirement V</u> does not specify how this is to be done. See <u>Note 42</u> below.

[31]By an hypothesis about structural change (say) of σ, β_k, γ_k, $k = 1, 2, \ldots, n$, I mean a system of definite functions involving σ, β_k, γ_k and the partial derivatives (or differences) of σ, β_k, γ_k with respect to time <u>t</u>, the system of differential or difference equations being hypothetically restricted in specified ways. In case the structural change hypothesis specifies a definite form of system of differential or difference equations, there will be introduced some new parameters to be considered (tentatively) as invariant structural parameters.

Since the theory of the consumption and savings function put forward in this section is capable of explaining the difference between prewar and postwar "estimates" of (4.15) and (4.16) in terms of changes in price ratios of individual commodities, an appropriate first step would be to investigate prewar and postwar price ratios directly, postponing meanwhile the formulation of a structural change hypothesis as premature.

[32]Consult the book by Friedman (1957, esp. Chapter 2). In research conducted by Friedman and others, "permanent income" is defined (with help of a difference equation the parameters of which have to be estimated) in terms of current and past magnitudes of "real income" (Friedman, 1957, pp. 144-149).

[33]Some of my students are conducting this investigation at the present time.

[34]While a graduate student I considered (and still consider) that a concept of consumption function that is affected by variations in commodity price ratios in a specified definite way as a more suitable fiscal policy concept than the notion of consumption function with invariant or arbitrarily varying parameters. This consideration was one of several that underlay the introduction of Requirement V. That consideration needs no special comment here.

Recalling (4.17a-b) - (4.18), notice that

$$\frac{\partial x_i}{\partial p_j} = 0 \quad \text{for all } i, j \text{ such that } j \neq i$$

and

$$\frac{p_i}{x_i}\left(\frac{\partial x_i}{\partial p_i}\right) = -1$$

$$\frac{M}{x_i}\left(\frac{\partial x_i}{\partial M}\right) = 1,$$

for every $i = 1, 2, \ldots, n$. From a methodological point of view, the class C_F of systems of demand functions lends itself well to partial equilibrium analysis.

[35]Another verbal interpretation that becomes of some importance in connection with the class C_d of systems of demand functions (3.38a-c) has to do with 'substitutability' and 'complementarity' of commodities. Substitutability and complementarity are two-place relations on the set $N = \{1, 2, \ldots, n\}$ of definite commodities, and are explicitly defined within the abstract theory of consumer de-

mand as follows:

(1) Sub (i, j) $\equiv_{df}$ [($s_{ij} \geqq 0$) & ($j \neq i$)]

(2) Comp (i, j) $\equiv_{df}$ [($s_{ij} < 0$) & ($j \neq i$)]

where s_{ij} is the Slutsky-Hicks substitution term abstractly defined by (3.19); cf. Hicks (1946, p. 311). For 'Sub (i, j)' read 'i is a substitute for j'; for 'Comp (i, j)' read 'i is a complement of j.' In other words Sub and Comp designate properties of ordered pairs (i, j) of commodities. Furthermore, Sub and Comp are completely explicated by purely mathematical properties of systems of demand functions. For every system of demand functions, and for at least one ordered pair (i, j) such that j ≠ i, Sub (i, j).

For every system of demand functions that belongs to the class C_d and every (i, j) such that j ≠ i, Sub (i, j); for every ordered pair (i, j), ~Comp (i, j); recall (3.26)-(3.28), (3.13) and (3.18). It might be supposed that the exclusion of complementarity by (3.38a-c) is a severe empirical limitation.

The existence of an ordered pair of real commodities that are complements is problematical. It is indeed the case that textbook writers sometimes attempt to assist their readers' understanding of Sub and Comp by introducing empirical examples, e.g.,

(3) Sub (butter, margarine),
(4) Comp (butter, bread);

cf. Lloyd (1967, pp. 74-75). Such examples are, however, empirical hypotheses that presuppose the definitions (1) and (2)--to understand the empirical hypotheses (3) and (4) you must first understand the definitions (1) and (2). Furthermore, empirical tests of (3) and (4) involve specification of a system of demand functions and its adjustment to quantity, price and income data. The explicit definitions of substitutability and complementarity (1)-(2) make it clear that Sub and Comp are not fundamental empirical relations that exist independently of abstract theory of consumer demand.

[36] In particular the results shown in (4.28) are not offered as an argument in support of the hypothetical restrictions (3.39).

[37] Since the writing of Section 4 my students have adjusted (4.21) to the numerical data free of the restriction (4.25), finding the minimum sum of squares of residuals at $\sigma = 0.85$. For $0.5 < \sigma < 1$, the value of sum of squares of

residuals is relatively insensitive to variations in σ.

38 On the other hand, the statistical results obtained by Goldberger and Gamaletsos (1967, Table 4.1, p. 35) for composite demand functions having the form (3.12a-c)-(3.13) are more favorable to the hypothetical restrictions (3.40).

39 For a brief account consult my earlier paper (Basmann, 1967a, Section 2).

40 This practical consideration rests on the logic of strictly universal statements. A brief remark serves to indicate the connection: under the definitions (of quantifiers) and the rules of logic we are entitled in every finite set of relevant circumstances to assign truth-value f to any strictly universal statement; moreover, in some specified circumstances we are required (by the rules of logic) to assign truth-value f. Maxim: Proceed on the assumption that the latter circumstance has already occurred, making the least expensive test first, and so on.

41 Notice that the foregoing discussion omits mention of hypotheses about the form of the distribution function $G(\xi_1, \ldots, \xi_n; \omega)$ and hypothetical restrictions on its parameter $(\omega_1, \ldots, \omega_q)$; recall (3.10a-b). Such hypotheses have to be taken into account in specifying definite circumstances in which the initial conditions for a given explanatory deduction are fulfilled. Consider Table 4.2. The ratios of commodity group indexes do not exhibit the constancy that is mentioned in the specification of exact initial conditions for the linear consumption and savings functions (4.14a-b). However, the results shown (4.1a-b) - (4.2a-b) and Table 4.1 are relevant to measuring of the degree to which the ratios in Table 4.2 approximate exact initial conditions for (4.14a-b).

42 It does not provide all relevant information, of course, as $(H-H_d)$ does not contain all possible systems of functions that can be adjusted to quantity, price and income data. The immediate objective of the test of H_d against $(H-H_d)$ is the decision whether to formulate a new class of systems of demand functions, etc.

43 Viz., the transformation of the sample data into a minimally sufficient statistic (vector) some components of which may be parameter estimators, the remaining auxiliary statistics being available for testing special restrictions.

[44] For a detailed account consult the book by Anderson and Johnstone (1962, *esp*. pp. 162-170). In classical logic the rule is called the *rule of universal generalization*.

[45] This generalization will be presented in a subsequent paper.

REFERENCES

[1] Ackermann, R. (1966): _Nondeductive Inference_, London: Routledge and Kegan Paul.

[2] Allen, R. G. D. (1956): _Mathematical Economics_, New York: St. Martin's Press.

[3] Anderson, J. M. and H. W. Johnstone, Jr. (1962): _Natural Deduction_, Belmont, Cal., Wadsworth Publishing Company, Inc.

[4] Arrow, K. J. (1961): "Additive Logarithmic Demand Functions and the Slutsky Relations," _Review of Economic Studies_, Vol. XXVIII, pp. 176-181.

[5] Basmann, R. L. (1953): "A Note on an Invariant Property of Shifts in Demand," _Metroeconomica_, Vol. VI, pp. 69-71.

[6] Basmann, R. L. (1954): "A Note on Mr. Ichimura's Definition of Related Goods," _Review of Economic Studies_, Vol. XXII, pp. 67-69.

[7] Basmann, R. L. (1956): "A Theory of Demand with Variable Consumer Preferences," _Econometrica_, Vol. 24, pp. 47-58.

[8] Basmann, R. L. (1960): _On the Exact Finite Sample Distribution of Generalized Classical Linear Structural Estimators_, Santa Barbara, Cal., General Electric Company, TEMPO, SP-91.

[9] Basmann, R. L.(1963): "Remarks Concerning the Application of Exact Finite Sample Distribution Functions of GCL Estimators in Econometric Statistical Inference," _Journal of the American Statistical Association_, Vol. 58, pp. 943-976.

[10] Basmann, R. L. (1965a): "The Role of the Economic Historian in the Predictive Testing of Proffered 'Economic Laws'," _Explorations in Entrepreneurial History/Second Series_, Vol. 2, pp. 159-186.

[11] Basmann, R. L. (1965b): "A Note on the Statistical Testability of 'Explicit Causal Chains' against the Class of 'Interdependent' Models," _Journal of the American Statistical Association_, Vol. 60, pp. 1080-1093.

[12] Basmann, R. L. (1965c): "A Tchebychev Inequality for the Convergence of a Generalized Classical Linear Estimator, Sample Size Being Fixed," Econometrica, Vol. 33, pp. 608-618.

[13] Basmann, R. L. (1965d): "On the Application of the Identifiability Test Statistic in Predictive Testing of Explanatory Economic Models," Econometric Annual of the Indian Economic Journal, Vol. XIII, pp. 387-423.

[14] Basmann, R. L. (1966): "On the Application of the Identifiability Test Statistic in Predictive Testing of Explanatory Economic Models--Part II," Econometric Annual of the Indian Economic Journal, Vol. XIV, pp. 233-252.

[15] Basmann, R. L. (1967a): "The Brookings Quarterly Economic Model: Science or Number Mysticism?" Ohio State University Conference on the Current State of Econometrics (mimeo).

[16] Basmann, R. L. (1967b): "Argument and Evidence in the Brookings--S.S.R.C. Philosophy of Econometrics," Ohio State University Conference on the Current State of Econometrics (mimeo).

[17] Birnbaum, Z. W. (1962): An Introduction to Probability and Mathematical Statistics, New York: Harper and Brothers, Publishers.

[18] Blanché, Robert (1962): Axiomatics, New York: Dover Publications, Inc. (Translated by G. B. Keene).

[19] Carnap, Rudolf (1956): Meaning and Necessity, Enlarged Edition, Chicago: University of Chicago Press.

[20] Carnap, Rudolf (1958): Introduction to Symbolic Logic and Its Applications, New York: Dover Publication, Inc.

[21] Carnap, Rudolf (1962): Logical Foundations of Probability, Second Edition, Chicago: University of Chicago Press.

[22] Carnap, Rudolf (1966): Philosophical Foundations of Physics, New York: Basic Books, Inc.

[23] Cohen, I. Bernard (1960): The Birth of a New Physics, Garden City, New York: Doubleday Anchor Books.

[24] Friedman, Milton (1957): A Theory of the Consumption Function, Princeton, New Jersey: Princeton University Press.

[25] Frisch, Ragnar (1954): "Linear Expenditure Functions," Econometrica, Vol. 22, pp. 505-510.

[26] Fromm, Gary and L. R. Klein (1967): "The Brookings Econometric Model: A Rational Perspective," Ohio State University Conference on Current State of Econometrics (mimeo).

[27] Goldberger, A. S. and T. Gamaletsos, "A Cross-country Comparison of Consumer Expenditure Patterns," Social Systems Research Institute (University of Wisconsin), Workshop Paper 6706.

[28] Gorman, W. M (1963): "Additive Logarithmic Preferences: A Further Note," Review of Economic Studies, Vol. XXX, pp. 56-62.

[29] Haavelmo, T. (1947): "Measuring the Marginal Propensity to Consume ," Journal of the American Statistical Association, Vol. 42, pp. 105-122. Reprinted in Hood, W. C. and T. C. Koopmans (1953) Studies in Econometric Method, New York: John Wiley and Sons, pp. 75-91.

[30] Hicks, J. R. (1946): Value and Capital, Second Edition, Oxford: Oxford University Press.

[31] Houthakker, H. S. (1960): "Additive Preferences," Econometrica, Vol. 28, pp. 244-257.

[32] Klein, L. R. and H. Rubin (1947): "A Constant Utility Index of the Cost of Living," Review of Economic Studies, Vol. XV, pp. 84-87.

[33] Leontief, W. (1936): "Composite Commodities and the Problem of Index Numbers," Econometrica, Vol. 4, pp. 39-59.

[34] Lloyd, Cliff (1967): Microeconomic Analysis, Homewood, Illinois: Richard D. Irwin, Inc.

[35] Mood, A. M. and F. A. Graybill (1963): Introduction to the Theory of Statistics, Second Edition. New York: McGraw-Hill Book Co., Inc.

[36] Ogden, C. K. and I. A. Richards (1923): The Meaning of Meaning, New York: Harcourt, Brace and World, Inc.

[37] Polyà, G. (1954): Mathematics and Plausible Reasoning, Vol. I, Princeton, New Jersey: Princeton University Press.

[38] Quine, Willard Van Orman (1963): From a Logical Point of View, Second Edition. New York: Harper and Row.

[39] Ripley, Julien A. (1964): The Elements and Structure of the Physical Sciences, New York: John Wiley and Sons, Inc.

[40] Samuelson, P. A. (1947): "Some Implications of Linearity," Review of Economic Studies, Vol. XV, pp. 88-90.

[41] Samuelson, P. A. (1948): Foundations of Economic Analysis, Cambridge: Harvard University Press.

[42] Stone, Richard (1954): "Linear Expenditure Systems and Demand Analysis," Economic Journal, Vol. 64, pp. 511-527.

[43] Wald, A. (1950): Statistical Decision Functions, New York: John Wiley and Sons.

[44] Wold, Herman (1953): Demand Analysis, New York: John Wiley and Sons.

ON THE DISTRIBUTION OF THE
IDENTIFIABILITY TEST STATISTIC

by

David H. Richardson*
University of Kansas

1. Introduction

In estimating the parameters of a system of simultaneous stochastic equations one often imposes overidentifying restrictions on the parameters of the model. When these restrictions take the form of excluding exogeneous variables from a given structural equation, appropriate test statistics and their large sample distributions have been determined [2, 3, 7]. In the case in which the structural equation includes two endogenous variables and excludes two exogenous variables, Basmann has derived the exact distribution of the GCL[1] identifiability test statistic [5]. In this paper we consider the exact distribution for the case in which any number of exogenous variables are excluded from the structural equation.

In this section we define the test statistic and in section 2 we derive the exact density function of the test statistic. The density function is expressed as a rather complicated infinite series in four parameters, one of which is the sample size. Since the asymptotic (large sample) distribution is known [2], we are interested in finding an approximation that is valid when the sample size is fixed. In section 3 we show that for any values taken by the sample size parameter and the other two parameters, as the fourth parameter increases indefinitely the moments of the distribution converge to the moments of the central F (variance ratio) distribution. This result forms the basis for the finite sample approximation discussed in section 4.

The structural equation is

$$(1.1)\quad y_1 = y_2\beta_1^* + Z_1\gamma_1^* + Z_2\gamma_2^* + e_1$$

where y_1 and y_2 are column vectors of N independent observations on the endogenous variables; Z_1 is an $N\text{x}K_1$ matrix of independent observations on the K_1 exogenous variables appearing in the equation and Z_2 is an $N\text{x}K_2$ matrix of observations on exogenous variables hypothetically excluded from the structural equation but appearing elsewhere in the model.

The structural equation (1.1) may appear in a system of structural equations containing $G > 2$ equations. The identifiability hypothesis for equation (1.1) is that the K_2 components of the vector γ_2^* are identically equal to zero. Finally, e_1 denotes a column vector of N independently and identically distributed random disturbance terms. We assume that the components of e_1 are normally distributed with mean zero and variance ω^*.

The reduced form equations for y_1 and y_2 are

$$(1.2)\quad \begin{aligned} y_1 &= Z_1\Pi_{11} + Z_2\Pi_{12} + \eta_1 \\ y_2 &= Z_1\Pi_{21} + Z_2\Pi_{22} + \eta_2 \end{aligned}$$

where the $t^{\underline{th}}$ components of η_1 and η_2 are distributed independently of the other components according to the bivariate normal distribution with means zero and positive definite covariance matrix

$$(1.3)\quad \Sigma = \begin{pmatrix} \sigma_{11}^* & \sigma_{12}^* \\ \sigma_{12}^* & \sigma_{22}^* \end{pmatrix}$$

In terms of the reduced form coefficients, the identifiability hypothesis is that the rank of the $K_2 x 2$ matrix

$$(1.4)\quad \begin{pmatrix} \Pi_{12}' \\ \Pi_{22}' \end{pmatrix}$$

is one.

Under the identifiability hypothesis the structural coefficients are related to the reduced form coefficients by the vanishing of the K <u>identifiability functions</u> [4, 6]

$$(1.5)\quad \Phi = \begin{bmatrix} \phi_1 \\ \vdots \\ \phi_k \end{bmatrix} = \begin{bmatrix} \Pi_{11} - \Pi_{21}\beta_1^* - \gamma_1^* \\ \\ \Pi_{12} - \Pi_{22}\beta_1^* \end{bmatrix}$$

the two stage least squares estimators of β_1^* and γ_1^* are obtained by minimizing the quadratic form

$$(1.6)\quad Q(\beta_1^*, \gamma_1^*) = \hat{\Phi}' (Z'Z) \hat{\Phi}$$

where $Z = (Z_1 : Z_2)$ and $\hat{\Phi}$ is the Φ vector with the reduced form coefficients replaced by their maximum likelihood estimators.

The estimator of β_1^* is usually defined as the value of β_1^* which minimizes the variance-difference quadratic form

$$(1.7) \quad G_1(\beta_1^*) - G_2(\beta_1^*)$$

where

$$G_2(\beta_1^*) = (y_1 - y_2\beta_1^*)'[I - Z(Z'Z)^{-1}Z'](y_1 - y_2\beta_1^*)$$

$$G_1(\beta_1^*) = (y_1 - y_2\beta_1^*)'[I - Z_1(Z_1'Z_1)^{-1}Z_1'](y_1 - y_2\beta_1^*)$$

[2, p. 101]. The identifiability test statistic is defined as

$$(1.8) \quad F = \frac{N-K}{\nu} \; \frac{G_1(\beta_1^*) - G_2(\beta_1^*)}{G_2(\beta_1^*)}$$

where β_1^* is the estimate of β_1^* and $\nu = K_2 - G_\Delta + 1 = K_2 - 1$ (in this case).

Since

$$Q(\beta_1^*, \hat{\gamma}_1^*) = G_1(\beta_1^*) - G_2(\beta_1^*)$$

where $\hat{\gamma}_1^*$ is the solution of $\frac{\partial Q}{\partial \gamma_1^*} = 0$, we have

$$(1.9) \quad F = \frac{N-K}{\nu} \; \frac{Q(\hat{\beta}_1^*, \hat{\gamma}_1^*)}{G_2(\hat{\beta}_1^*)}$$

for our definition of the identifiability test statistic.

In deriving the probability density of F our task is simplified considerably if we transform the original variables and parameters so that

$$Z'Z = I_K$$

and

$$\sum = I_2.$$

The identifiability test statistic (1.9) is invariant with respect to these transformations so there is no loss of generality in proceeding with the standardized form [5: pp. 234-236].

2. The Exact Distribution of F

Denote the standardized values of $\hat{\beta}_1^*$, $Q(\hat{\beta}_1^*, \hat{\gamma}_1^*)$ and $G_2(\hat{\beta}_1^*)$ by the random variables v_1, v_2^2 and v_3 respectively. The joint density of v_1 and v_2^2 is [10]

$$(2.1)\quad f_1(v_1, v_2^2) = \frac{e^{-\frac{\mu^2}{2}(1+\beta^2)}\,(v_2^2)^{\frac{\nu-2}{2}}\,e^{-\frac{v_2^2}{2}}}{2^{\frac{\nu}{2}}\,\Gamma(\frac{1}{2})\quad(\frac{\nu}{2})}$$

$$\sum_{s=0}^{\infty}\ \sum_{j=0}^{\infty} \frac{\Gamma(j+\frac{\nu+2}{2})\,(\beta^2 v_2^2)^s\,(1+\beta v_1)^{2j}\left(\frac{\mu^2}{2}\right)^{s+j}}{2^s\,\Gamma(s+j+\frac{\nu+1}{2})\,j!\quad s!\quad (1+v_1^2)^{\frac{\nu+2}{2}+j}}$$

$$-\infty < v_1 < \infty$$

$$0 < v_2^2 < \infty$$

where

$$\beta = \frac{\sigma_{22}^*\beta_1^* - \sigma_{12}^*}{(\sigma_{11}^*\sigma_{22}^* - \sigma_{12}^{*2})^{1/2}}$$

$$\mu^2 = \frac{\Pi_{22}'\ S\ \Pi_{22}}{\sigma_{22}^*}$$

$$S = Z_2'Z_2 - Z_2'Z_1(Z_1'Z_1)^{-1}\,Z_1'Z_2.$$

The conditional density function of v_3 given v_1 is [9, p. 47]

$$(2.2)\quad f_2(v_3|v_1) = \frac{e^{\frac{-v_3}{2(1+v_1^2)}}\left(\frac{v_3}{2}\right)^{\frac{m}{2}-1}}{2\,\Gamma(\frac{m}{2})\quad(1+v_1^2)^{\frac{m}{2}}}$$

$$0 < v_5 < \infty$$

where $m = N - K$.

We seek the joint density

$$(2.3) \quad f_3(v_2^2, v_3) = \int_{-\infty}^{\infty} f_1(v_1, v_2^2)\, f_2(v_3 | v_1)\, dv_1$$

$$= \frac{e^{-\frac{\mu^2}{2}(1+\beta^2)} \, (v_2^2)^{\frac{\nu-2}{2}} \, e^{-\frac{v_2^2}{2}} \left(\frac{v_3}{2}\right)^{\frac{m}{2}-1}}{2^{\frac{\nu}{2}} \, \Gamma(1/2)\, \Gamma(\frac{\nu}{2}) \quad 2 \quad \Gamma(\frac{m}{2})}$$

$$\sum_{s=0}^{\infty} \sum_{j=0}^{\infty} \frac{\Gamma(j + \frac{\nu+2}{2})\, (\beta^2 v_2^2)^s \, (\frac{\mu^2}{2})^{s+j}}{2^s \, \Gamma(s + j + \frac{\nu+1}{2})\, s! \; j!}$$

$$\sum_{k=0}^{\infty} \frac{\left(-\frac{v_3}{2}\right)^k}{k!} \int_{-\infty}^{\infty} \frac{(\beta\, v_1 + 1)^{2j}\, dv_1}{(1 + v_1^2)^{\frac{\nu+m+2}{2} + j + k}}$$

For the j, k term in the series the integral is

$$(2.4) \quad \sum_{\ell=0}^{j} \binom{2j}{2\ell} \beta^{2\ell} \frac{\Gamma(\ell + 1/2)\, \Gamma(\frac{\nu+m+1}{2} + j + k - \ell)}{\Gamma(\frac{\nu+m+2}{2} + j + k)}$$

$$= \sum_{\ell=0}^{j} \binom{2j}{2\ell} \beta^{2\ell} \frac{\Gamma(\ell + 1/2)\, \Gamma(\frac{\nu+m+1}{2} + j - \ell)\, (\frac{\nu+m+1}{2} + j - \ell)_k}{\Gamma(\frac{\nu+m+2}{2} + j) \, (\frac{\nu+m+2}{2} + j)_k} .$$

The joint density $f_3(v_2^2, v_3)$ now contains a confluent hypergeometric series in $-\frac{v_3}{2}$. Applying Kummer's first formula[2] to this series yields

$$(2.5) \quad f_3(v_2^2, v_3) = \frac{e^{-\frac{\mu^2}{2}(1+\beta^2)} \, (v_2^2)^{\frac{\nu-2}{2}} \, e^{-\frac{v_2^2}{2}} \, (\frac{v_3}{2})^{\frac{m}{2}-1} \, e^{-\frac{v_3}{2}}}{2^{\frac{\nu}{2}} \, \Gamma(1/2)\, \Gamma(\frac{\nu}{2}) \qquad 2\, \Gamma(\frac{m}{2})}$$

$$\sum_{s=0}^{\infty} \sum_{j=0}^{\infty} \frac{\Gamma(j + \frac{\nu+2}{2}) \quad (\beta^2 v_2^2)^s \; (\frac{\mu^2}{2})^{s+j}}{2^s \; \Gamma(s + j + \frac{\nu+1}{2}) \quad s! \quad j!}$$

$$\sum_{\ell=0}^{j} \binom{2j}{2\ell} \beta^{2\ell} \frac{\Gamma(\ell + {}^1/2) \quad \Gamma(\frac{\nu+m+1}{2} + j - \ell)}{\Gamma(\frac{\nu+m+2}{2} + j)} {}_1F_1 \left(\ell + {}^1/2; \frac{\nu+m+2}{2} + j; \frac{v_3}{2}\right).$$

Since

$$F = \frac{m}{\nu} \frac{v_2^2}{v_3}$$

we let

$$v_2^2 = \frac{\nu}{m} \; v_3 F$$

$$dv_2^2 = \frac{\nu}{m} \; v_3 dF$$

to obtain the joint density of v_3 and F. The marginal density function of F is then easily obtained by integrating out v_3. After evaluating the gamma integrals we have

$$\text{(2.6)} \quad g(F) = \frac{\nu}{m} \; \frac{e^{-\frac{\mu^2}{2}(1+\beta^2)} \left(\frac{\nu}{m} F\right)^{\frac{\nu-2}{2}}}{\Gamma({}^1/2) \; \Gamma(\frac{\nu}{2}) \quad \Gamma(\frac{m}{2})}$$

$$\sum_{s=0}^{\infty} \sum_{j=0}^{\infty} \frac{\Gamma(j + \frac{\nu+2}{2}) \; \Gamma(s + \frac{\nu+m}{2}) \; \beta^{2s} \left(\frac{\mu^2}{2}\right)^{s+j}}{\Gamma(s + j + \frac{\nu+1}{2}) \quad s! \quad j! \; (1 + \frac{\nu}{m} F)^{\frac{\nu+m}{2} + s}}$$

$$\sum_{\ell=0}^{j} \binom{2j}{2\ell} \frac{\beta^{2\ell} \; \Gamma(\ell + {}^1/2) \; \Gamma(\frac{\nu+m+1}{2} + j - \ell)}{\Gamma(\frac{\nu+m+2}{2} + j)}$$

$${}_2F_1 \left(\ell + {}^1/2, \; \frac{m+\nu}{2} + s; \; \frac{m+\nu+2}{2} + j; \frac{1}{1+\frac{\nu}{m} F}\right).$$

To obtain the final form of the density function we replace j by j + ℓ, let

$$\frac{(2j + 2\ell)!}{(2j)!\,(2\ell)!} = \frac{\Gamma(j + \ell + {}^{1}/2)\,(j + \ell)!\,\Gamma({}^{1}/2)}{\Gamma(j + {}^{1}/2)\,j!\,\Gamma(\ell + {}^{1}/2)\,\ell!}$$

and

$$2z = \frac{\beta^2\mu^2}{2}.$$

$$(2.7)\quad g(F) = \frac{\nu}{m}\,\frac{e^{-\frac{\mu^2}{2}(1+\beta^2)}}{\Gamma(\frac{\nu}{2})\,\Gamma(\frac{m}{2})}$$

$$\sum_{j=0}^{\infty}\sum_{s=0}^{\infty}\sum_{\ell=0}^{\infty}\frac{\Gamma(j+\ell+\frac{\nu+2}{2})\,\Gamma(j+\ell+{}^{1}/2)\,\Gamma(j+\frac{m+\nu+1}{2})\,\Gamma(s+\frac{m+\nu}{2})}{\Gamma(s+j+\ell+\frac{\nu+1}{2})\,\Gamma(j+{}^{1}/2)\,\Gamma(j+\ell+\frac{m+\nu+2}{2})}$$

$$\frac{(2z)^{s+\ell}\left(\frac{\mu^2}{2}\right)^{j}\,(\frac{\nu}{m}F)^{s+\frac{\nu}{2}-1}}{s!\;\ell!\;\;j!\;(1+\frac{\nu}{m}F)^{\frac{s+m+\nu}{2}}}$$

$${}_2F_1\left(\ell + {}^{1}/2;\ s + \frac{m+\nu}{2};\ j + \ell + \frac{m+\nu+2}{2};\ \frac{1}{1+\frac{\nu}{m}F}\right)$$

$$0 < F < \infty$$

3. The Moments of F

In this section we evaluate the $h^{\underline{th}}$ moment of F

$$E(F^h) = \int_0^{\infty} F^h\,g(F)\,dF$$

and show that it converges to the $h^{\underline{th}}$ moment of the central F distribution as the parameter μ^2 approaches infinity.

The basic integral in computing the $h^{\underline{th}}$ moment is

$$(3.1)\quad \int_0^{\infty}\frac{(\frac{\nu}{m}F)^{h+s+\frac{\nu}{2}-1}}{(1+\frac{\nu}{m}F)^{s+k+\frac{m+\nu}{2}}}\,dF$$

$$= \frac{\Gamma(h+s+\frac{\nu}{2})\,\Gamma(\frac{m}{2}+k-h)}{\Gamma(s+k+\frac{m+2}{2})},\quad h < \frac{m}{2}.$$

Consequently

(3.2) $$E(F^h) = \left(\frac{m}{\nu}\right)^h \frac{\Gamma\left(\frac{m}{2} - h\right) e^{-\frac{\mu^2}{2}(1+\beta^2)}}{\Gamma\left(\frac{\nu}{2}\right)\Gamma\left(\frac{m}{2}\right)}$$

$$\sum_{j=0}^{\infty}\sum_{s=0}^{\infty}\sum_{\ell=0}^{\infty} \frac{\Gamma\left(j+\ell+\frac{\nu+2}{2}\right)\Gamma\left(j+\ell+{}^1/2\right)\Gamma\left(j+\frac{m+\nu+1}{2}\right)}{\Gamma\left(j+s+\ell+\frac{\nu+1}{2}\right)\Gamma\left(j+{}^1/2\right)\Gamma\left(j+\ell+\frac{m+\nu+2}{2}\right)}$$

$$\frac{\Gamma\left(s+h+\frac{\nu}{2}\right)(2z)^{s+\ell}\left(\frac{\mu^2}{2}\right)^j}{s!\ \ell!\ j!} \; {}_2F_1\left(\ell+{}^1/2;\ \frac{m}{2}-h;\right.$$

$$\left. j+\ell+\frac{m+\nu+2}{2};\ 1\right).$$

The hypergeometric function with unit argument can be written in closed form[3], reducing (3.2) to

(3.3) $$E(F^h) = \frac{\left(\frac{m}{\nu}\right)^h \Gamma\left(\frac{m}{2} - h\right)}{\Gamma\left(\frac{\nu}{2}\right)\Gamma\left(\frac{m}{2}\right)} e^{-\frac{\mu^2}{2}(1+\beta^2)}$$

$$\sum_{j=0}^{\infty}\sum_{s=0}^{\infty}\sum_{\ell=0}^{\infty} \frac{\Gamma\left(j+\ell+\frac{\nu+2}{2}\right)\Gamma\left(j+\ell+{}^1/2\right)\Gamma\left(s+h+\frac{\nu}{2}\right)}{\Gamma\left(j+s+\ell+\frac{\nu+1}{2}\right)\Gamma\left(j+{}^1/2\right)\Gamma\left(j+\ell+h+\frac{\nu+2}{2}\right)}$$

$$\frac{\Gamma\left(j+h+\frac{\nu+1}{2}\right)(2z)^{s+\ell}\left(\frac{\mu^2}{2}\right)^j}{s!\ \ell!\ j!}$$

If we set $h = 0$ in (3.3) we can check to make sure that

$$\int_0^{\infty} g(F)\,dF = 1.$$

We get

(3.4) $$\frac{e^{-\frac{\mu^2}{2}(1+\beta^2)}}{\Gamma\left(\frac{\nu}{2}\right)} \sum_{j=0}^{\infty} \frac{\Gamma\left(j+\frac{\nu+1}{2}\right)}{\Gamma\left(j+{}^1/2\right)} \frac{\left(\frac{\mu^2}{2}\right)^j}{j!}$$

$$\sum_{s=0}^{\infty}\sum_{\ell=0}^{\infty} \frac{\Gamma\left(s+\frac{\nu}{2}\right)\Gamma\left(\ell+j+{}^1/2\right)(2z)^{s+\ell}}{\Gamma\left(s+\ell+j+\frac{\nu+1}{2}\right) s!\ \ell!}$$

The double series in 2z equals

$$e^{2z}\,\frac{\Gamma(\frac{\nu}{2})\,\Gamma(j+{}^{1}/2)}{\Gamma(j+\frac{\nu+1}{2})}$$

by summing by diagonals. Hence

$$\int_0^\infty g(F)\,dF = e^{-\frac{\mu^2}{2}}\sum_{j=0}^{\infty}\frac{(\frac{\mu^2}{2})^j}{j!} = 1.$$

In order to apply a known asymptotic expansion to the expression (3.3) we rewrite it as

$$(3.5)\quad (\tfrac{m}{\nu})^h\,\frac{\Gamma(\frac{m}{2}-h)\,\Gamma(h+\frac{\nu}{2})}{\Gamma(\frac{\nu}{2})\,\Gamma(\frac{m}{2})}\,e^{-\frac{\mu^2}{2}}$$

$$\sum_{s=0}^{\infty}\sum_{\ell=0}^{\infty}\Big\{\sum_{j=0}^{\infty}\frac{\Gamma(j+\ell+\frac{\nu+2}{2})\,\Gamma(j+\ell+{}^{1}/2)\,\Gamma(j+h+\frac{\nu+1}{2})}{\Gamma(j+{}^{1}/2)\,\Gamma(j+\ell+h+\frac{\nu+2}{2})\Gamma(j+s+\ell+\frac{\nu+1}{2})}$$

$$\frac{\Gamma(j+s+\ell+{}^{1}/2-h)}{\Gamma(j+\ell+{}^{1}/2-h)}\,\frac{(\frac{\mu^2}{2})^j}{j!}\Big\}\quad\frac{(-)^s}{s!}\,\frac{(2z)^{\ell+s}}{\ell!}$$

(3.5) is obtained from (3.3) by writing the series in s as a confluent hypergeometric series and then applying Kummer's first formula.

We can now apply Stokes' asymptotic expansion[4] to the series in curled braces in (3.5) and obtain

$$(3.6)\quad E(F^h) = (\tfrac{m}{\nu})^h\,\frac{\Gamma(\frac{m}{2}-h)\,\Gamma(h+\frac{\nu}{2})}{\Gamma(\frac{\nu}{2})\,\Gamma(\frac{m}{2})}$$

as $\mu^2 \to \infty$. This expression is the $h^{\underline{th}}$ moment of the central F distribution with ν and m degrees of freedom.

4. Concluding Remarks

In the preceding section we have demonstrated that the moments of the distribution of the identifiability test statistic F converge to the moments of the central F distribution with ν and m degrees of freedom as the concentration parameter μ^2 increases indefinitely. Although this in itself is not sufficient to guarantee that the distribution function of F converges to the central F distribution function[5], we can use this result in support of the conjecture that the distribution of F can be closely approximated by the distribution of the central F for large values of μ^2. This conjecture was originally proposed by Basmann and was strongly supported by the results of a sampling experiment.[3].

Although the sampling distributions in this paper are not valid if lagged values of the endogenous variables are included in the model, there is some empirical evidence that the resulting approximation may be valid for these models. Two sampling experiments have been designed to test conjectures about sampling distributions in these dynamic models.[6] In each of these experiments there is a structural equation of the form (1.1); for the equation in the first experiment two predetermined variables are excluded and for the equation in the second experiment three predetermined variables are excluded. For each of the experiments one thousand samples of size twenty each were generated and values of the identifiability test statistic were computed for each sample and arrayed by order of magnitude. The hypothesis that this empirical distribution was generated by a central F distribution with ν and m degrees of freedom was tested using the Kolmogorov-Smirnov test statistic D_N. For the equation in the first experiment we computed

$$D_N = .022$$

and for the equation in the second experiment

$$D_N = .019.$$

Since

$$\Pr\{D_N \geq .022\} = .72$$

$$\Pr\{D_N \geq .019\} = .86$$

under the null hypothesis, we conclude that the central F approximation is valid in these cases and does not seem to be seriously affected by the addition of lagged endogenous variables.

We might also mention in this connection that the magnitude of μ^2 does not have to be extremely large for the approximation to be a good one. In the above sampling experiments μ^2 is a function of the lagged values of the endogenous variables and is, therefore, a random variable. Its mathematical expectation was 39 in the first experiment and 642 in the second.

Finally we would like to draw the reader's attention to the importance of the distribution of the identifiability test statistic and its approximation in the predictive testing of economic hypotheses represented by simultaneous equations models. In these representations it is desirable to map the economic hypothesis in the structural parameter space into the reduced form parameter space. _If the identifiability test statistic fails to reject the identifiability hypotheses_, the econometrician can proceed to test the economic hypotheses with the jointly sufficient and tabulated reduced form statistics. An application of this procedure is given in a recent paper by Basmann [5].

FOOTNOTES

* This work was financed in part by the National Science Foundation, GS-983. The author is indebted to R. L. Basmann for his comments. Any errors that remain are the sole responsibility of the author.

1. Two stage least squares in this case.

2. ${}_1F_1(a,b;x) = e^{-x}\,{}_1F_1(b-a;b;x)$ for b neither zero nor a negative integer [8, p. 125].

3. ${}_2F_1(a;b;c;1) = \dfrac{(c)\ (c-a-b)}{(c-a)\ (c-b)}$ for $c-a-b > 0$ and c neither zero nor a negative integer [8, p. 49].

4. $$\sum_{n=0}^{\infty} \frac{\prod_{i=1}^{k} \Gamma(n + \alpha_i)\ x^n}{\prod_{i=1}^{k} \Gamma(n + \beta_i)\ n!} = x^{\lambda} e^{x}\{1 + O(x^{-1})\}$$

as $x \to \infty$ where $\lambda = \sum_{i=1}^{k} \alpha_i - \sum_{i=1}^{k} \beta_i$ and no β_i is either zero or a negative integer [1; p. 62].

5. Since not all of the moments of the distribution exist, the distribution could converge to a distribution function with first $\frac{m}{2}$ moments equal to the moments of the central F but with <u>finite</u> moments of higher order.

6. For a more complete discussion of the design of the experiments and the testing procedure see [10, 11].

REFERENCES

[1] Barnes, E. W., "The Asymptotic Expansion of Integral Functions Defined by Generalized Hypergeometric Series," Proceedings of the London Mathematical Society (2), Vol. 5, (1907), pp. 59-116.

[2] Basmann, R. L., "On the Asymptotic Distribution of Generalized Linear Estimators," Econometrica, Vol. 28 (1960), pp. 97-106.

[3] Basmann, R. L., "On Finite Sample Distributions of Generalized Classical Linear Identifiability Test Statistics," Journal of the American Statistical Association, Vol. 55 (1960), pp. 650-659.

[4] Basmann, R. L., "On Predictive Testing of a Simultaneous Equations Model: The Retail Market for Food in the U.S.," Institute for Quantitative Research in Economics and Management, No. 78, Purdue University, 1964.

[5] Basmann, R. L., "On the Application of the Identifiability Test Statistic in Predictive Testing of Explanatory Economic Models," Econometric Annual of the Indian Economic Journal, Vol. 13 (1965), pp. 387-423 and Vol. 14 (1966), pp. 233-252.

[6] Ginsberg, P. M. and Richardson, D. H., "Some Economic Applications of the GCL Principle of Estimation" Institute for Quantitative Research in Economics and Management, No. 130, Purdue University, 1966.

[7] Hood, W. C. and T. C. Koopmans, eds., Studies in Econometric Method, New York: John Wiley, 1953.

[8] Rainville, E. D., Special Functions, New York: Macmillan, 1960.

[9] Richardson, D. H., An Investigation of the Sampling Distributions of Estimators and Test Statistics Associated with a Simultaneous Equations Model (unpublished Ph.D. Thesis) Purdue University, 1966.

[10] Richardson, D. H., "The Exact Distribution of a Structural Coefficient Estimator", Journal of the American Statistical Association (forthcoming).

[11] Rohr, R. J., An Investigation of the Stability Properties

and the Sampling Distributions of Estimators and Test Statistics Associated with a Dynamic Simultaneous Equations Model (unpublished Ph.D. Thesis) Purdue University, 1967.

ON SUPPLY CONDITIONS IN CONSUMER CREDIT MARKETS

by

David I. Fand
Wayne State University

and

Ronald W. Forbes
State University of New York at Buffalo

Consumer credit is defined to include "all short and intermediate-term credit that is extended through regular channels to finance the purchase of commodities and services for personal consumption, or to refinance debts incurred for such purposes".[1] With the removal of regulation W in 1952 consumer credit has grown rapidly from $27.5 billion to $94.8 billion at the end of 1966. The total volume of consumer debt is made up of two broad categories: instalment debt and non-instalment debt. Instalment debt is the sum of (1) automobile loans, (2) loans for other consumer goods, (3) home repair and modernization loans and (4) personal loans. Non-instalment debt consists of single payment loans, charge accounts and service credit. These loans are made by many lenders, including commercial banks, sales finance and consumer finance companies, credit unions, thrift institutions, pawn brokers and other financial intermediaries, and by department stores and other retail establishments that supply vendor credit.

Consumer credit outstanding in 1964 is shown in Table 1. Instalment debt accounted for $60.5 billion or approximately 77% of the total.[2] The four categories of instalment loans and the three categories of non-instalment loans are also shown. For each of these categories we show the loans supplied by different lenders where the data are readily available.[3]

The institutions that supply these various types of consumer loans operate under legal regulations that are determined by the state legislature, and differ in several other respects. Commercial banks make instalment loans <u>directly</u> to consumers in a particular retail market, and <u>indirectly</u> through the purchase of dealer paper. And, they may also supply funds <u>indirectly</u> to consumers in many other markets by granting loans or lines of credit to the finance companies. Department stores, retail establishments and small loan companies may limit themselves to a local market; sales finance, consumer finance companies and other financial institutions

Table I

CONSUMER CREDIT OUTSTANDING BY TYPE AND LENDER, DECEMBER 1964 -- ($ MILLION)

Consumer Credit
$78,442

Instalment Loans $60,548				Noninstalment Credit $17,894		
Automobile Loans	Other Consumer Goods Credit	Repair and Modern Credit	Personal Loans	Single-Payment Loans	Charge Accounts	Service Credit
$25,195	$15,593	$3,532	$16,228	$6,954	$6,300	$4,640
Commercial Banks Direct	Commercial Banks	Commercial Banks	Commercial Banks	Commercial Banks	Department Stores	
$4,734	$3,670	$2,457	$5,542	$5,950	$909	
Purchased						
$8,691						
Sales Finance Cos.	Sales Finance Cos.	Sales Finance Cos.	Sales Finance Cos.		Other Retail Outlets	
$8,691	$3,889	$142	$2,030		$4,756	
Other Fin. Institutions	Other Fin. Institutions	Other Fin. Institutions	Other Fin. Institutions	Other Fin. Institutions	Credit Cards	
$13,285	$997	$933	$8,656	$1,004	$635	
Auto Dealers	Dept. Stores					
$370	$3,922					
	Other Retail Outlets					
	$3,915					

Source: Federal Reserve Bulletin, Sept. 1967, pp. 1628-29.

including commercial banks may function in state-wide markets; and the largest consumer and sales finance companies and large chain store retailers operate at a national level.

Some lenders are primarily concerned with cash loans; others, with retail instalment financing; and the commercial banks, who play a dominant role in consumer credit markets, supply both kinds of loans. Since each of the lenders in this market typically has some unique feature, and since all lenders are subject to regulations that vary from state to state, it is natural to ask whether there are significant differences in supply conditions among the various markets in different states. We shall attempt to analyze this question in this paper.

1. Fragmented Laws and Segmented Markets

The demand for consumer loans reflects a wide variety of needs: in recent times we tend to think of an individual who may be reasonably affluent, but who seeks a cash loan or retail instalment financing so that he may purchase an automobile or some other luxury good; in the past we would probably think of a "distressed" borrower who was seeking a small cash loan; and between these hypothetical extremes many individuals, when they buy appliances and other consumer durables, when they modernize their homes, or when they take a vacation, may finance these activities with instalment contracts or cash loans. These loans are supplied by a variety of lenders, as indicated in Table 1, operating under a patched-up ad hoc legal framework of specialized laws governing cash loans under usury statutes, and interest ceilings and retail instalment financing under the time-price doctrine.

Historically, these two systems of financing evolved under different legal bases. But legal segmentation of the markets for cash loans and credit (retail instalment) sales, though it may have been justified in the past, no longer corresponds to economic realities; and though the legal structure is updated periodically it continues to remain specialized to particular institutions, transactions, and classes of consumers. Curran, in her authoritative study, summarizes the gap between these laws and market developments as follows:

> Various pieces of legislation were initially restricted in their application to particular institutions (e.g., industrial loan laws), to specific arrangements offered by particular institutions (e.g., instalment loans by banks), or by the characteristics of the consumer serviced (e.g., small loan laws). Although such legislation was amended from time to time for the purpose of updating, it nevertheless continued to remain specialized to a particular institution,

> arrangement, or class of consumer. In the same period, consumer credit expanded, the type of arrangements offered began to overlap in purpose and function, and the once sharp divisions among types of consumers serviced by particular institutions became blurred.[4]

Aside from the fragmentation implicit in the legal structure, the proliferation of laws and the multiplicity of regulations in each state tends further to segment markets. Lenders competing for the same class of borrowers must function under different rules, and while powerful economic forces are operating to unify and integrate consumer credit markets, the laws and regulations have tended to remain specialized and fragmented. Competition among lenders in the legislature is a poor substitute for competition in the market, and to the extent that the legal fragmentation is effective, the market for consumer loans is segmented and the supply of loans in a particular area dependent on local conditions.

This expectation of segmented markets and localized supplies of funds is borne out in several empirical studies that have presented evidence of considerable variation in the terms (finance charge, maturity and availability) for a given instalment loan among similar lenders in the same market, among different lenders in a given market and among different markets. To cite some examples:

Jung reports dealer rates on new car loans that vary as much as 80% within the same city; Fredrikson reports that a given borrower could pay between 12.68% and 30.96% for a $600 personal loan in the Philadelphia-Pittsburgh area; and Kohn reports automobile rates for New York State banks that vary from 9.28% in New York City banks to 11.72% in major branch banks in upstate communities.[5]

In addition to these market surveys there is also some indirect evidence which, while far from conclusive, nevertheless does point to the possibility of substantial differences in supply conditions. In Table 2, we summarize data for 25 states on per capita instalment loans and personal loans. Per capita personal loans from commercial banks and credit unions, and finance company loans granted under small-loan statutes ranged from $48 (in Iowa) to $119 (in Nevada) in these 25 states; and the average for the eight highest ranking states, $103, is more than 50% greater than the average for the eight lowest ranking states, $68. If we broaden this debt concept and include all instalment loans from commercial banks and credit unions, per capita instalment credit varies from $130 in Maryland to $295 in Nevada, and again outstandings in the top eight states are approximately 50% higher than in the bottom eight states.[6]

Differences in per capita instalment debt do not necessarily imply differences in supply conditions, but they are suggestive. This hypothesis is reinforced when we consider the fragmented legal framework, the ceilings and other regulations on consumer credit in these states, the associated differences in banking structure, and the differences in financial intermediation. These considerations, together with the survey studies, all tend to give added weight to the hypothesis that the market for consumer loans is not integrated. Fragmented laws and segmented markets imply substantial variations in supply conditions.

Table 2

PER CAPITA INSTALMENT CREDIT OUTSTANDING, 1964 -- FOR 25 STATES*

States Ranked by Per Capita Loans Outstanding	Instalment Loans Outstanding Per Capita		Personal Loans Outstanding Per Capita	
	Average	Range	Average	Range
High 8 states	$233	$202-$295	$103	$91-$119
Medium 9 states	$189	$183-$199	$ 86	$82-$92
Low 8 states	$155	$130-$177	$ 68	$48-$79

* Source: See Appendix A.

In this paper we attempt to study some of the factors affecting supply conditions in different states.[7] In principal we would like to analyze the factors that determine the cost (finance charge), the terms and the availability of these loans, but statewide data on cost and terms are not readily available. Similarly we do not have the data to study differences among markets in a state; we therefore concentrate on statewide variations in the quantity outstanding, and seek to determine the extent to which differences in outstandings can be traced to supply conditions.

In our first approximation we start with the recent studies by Goudzwaard (1965), Johnson (1967) and Shay (1967), and consider rate ceilings as a key factor accounting for differences in supply conditions in different states. In our second approximation we go on to consider other factors that may affect supply, including lender attitudes towards risk and the degree of commercial bank participation in the consumer credit market. In our third approximation we consider these supply factors together with the demand factors.

2. The Influence of Rate Ceilings

One way to rationalize variations in the per capita instalment debt outstanding among the 25 states in our sample is to point out the connection between level of rate ceilings and the quantity of consumer credit supplied. According to this hypothesis, lenders prefer to avoid risk and must be compensated if they are to extend risky loans. They will therefore adjust the volume of loans, and the risk inherent in their portfolio, to accord with prevailing rate ceilings. Thus if rate ceilings rise lenders may be willing to extend more risky loans, and the volume of loans supplied should rise. Higher ceilings in a state may also attract additional funds and additional lenders, to the extent that its markets become more attractive relative to markets in states with lower ceilings. This would be an additional factor increasing the volume of loans.[8] Robert Johnson has summarized this position in the following fashion:

> . . . other things being equal, ceilings on rates determine which consumers can be served by legitimate credit granters and which must forego the use of credit or turn to illegal lenders. If ceilings were lowered, consumers who were only marginally credit-worthy and costly to serve would be driven from the legal market. . . What would be out of line if rates are too low is the level of service provided consumers by legal lenders.[9]

To test empirically the effect of rate ceilings on the quantity of loans supplied, we are faced with a multiplicity of rate structures,[10] varying not only by state but also by the transaction and by lender as well. To deal with this problem we take the schedule of rate ceilings under small-loan statutes as a measure of differences in ceilings among states. Since ceiling rates on credit unions are more nearly uniform, and since there is less dispersion in the ceiling rates on commercial bank loans, it would appear that small-loan ceilings may be a sensitive index for distinguishing ceiling structures among states. But this assumption leads us to the next question of how to convert the vector of small loan ceiling rates in a state into a single variable. In general, the average ceiling rate declines with loan size but the marginal changes in rate for additional increments in loan size differ among states. For this reason we use three representations of the ceiling rates.

The first two are based on the maximum finance charge allowed on a typical small loan in the 25 states. Although the average small loan in 1964 was approximately $400, we can calculate ceiling rates only on $300 and $500 loans. As a third measure of ceiling rates, we follow other investigators and take gross yield per dollar of small loans as given in state reports on licensed lender activity.[11] We view these three variables as indicators of the ceiling structures in the

25 states, summarizing the opportunities open to lenders, and not necessarily as measures of the actual rates paid by borrowers. It is for this reason that we treat these indices as parameters determining supply, and not as endogenous rate variables determined by supply and demand.

The hypothesis that ceiling rates are a parameter in the supply function and that higher ceilings lead to a greater quantity of credit would imply that these rates should be associated with per capita instalment credit. But when we rank the 25 states by per capita loans outstanding and the ceiling rates in Table 3, we do not find any clear association between ceilings and amounts outstanding. Gross yield (r_1) is inversely related to credit outstanding, reflecting perhaps most significantly the impact of average loan size. Average loan size varies from $286 in Iowa to $588 in Ohio, and the gross yield variable may be measuring this variation rather than the differences in rate ceilings on small loans.[12] Our other estimates of rate ceilings do not appear to be consistently related to average per capita loans outstanding, although (r_2) the $300 loan ceiling does appear positively related to personal loans per capita. And when we set up simple regressions using these three variables to predict either per capita instalment loans or per capita personal loans the R^2 are all quite low, and none of the regression coefficients are significant. This would suggest that the explanatory power of ceiling rates alone may be somewhat limited and we therefore consider other factors which may influence supply.

3. Additional Influences: Risk and Commercial Bank Participation

The effect of ceiling rates on supply conditions and on the quantity of loans outstanding may possibly appear more clearly if we consider them in conjunction with other factors. Lenders may differ in their willingness to bear risk and this could lead to differences in supply. There is some evidence that suppliers of consumer credit differ in their attitudes towards losses, and these attitudes may be conditioned by the structure of their liabilities, by the rate ceilings and other regulations, and by any other factors which may affect the incentive to bear risk.[13] In any event if, for whatever reason, the lenders in a given state are more willing to incur risk, this should increase supply. The hypothesis that lender attitudes towards risk affects supply and outstandings in a state rests upon the assumption that instalment loan markets are segmented; otherwise, lenders would shift among states until the return for risk would tend to be equalized. To measure risk we follow other investigators and use L_s -- the loss ratio on small loans.

Table 3

RELATIONSHIP BETWEEN INSTALMENT LOANS PER CAPITA AND RATE CEILINGS -- 25 STATES*

States Ranked by Loans Per Capita	Amount Outstanding	$300 Small Loan Rate ($r_2$)	$500 Small Loan Rate ($r_3$)	Gross Yield on Small Loans (r_1)
Top 8 states				
Instalment Loans	$233	36.42%	32.84%	24.18%
Personal Loans	$103	38.73%	31.38%	23.30%
Medium 9 states				
Instalment Loans	$189	37.57%	33.03%	24.55%
Personal Loans	$ 86	38.07%	34.43%	24.40%
Low 8 states				
Instalment Loans	$155	35.12%	32.43%	24.80%
Personal Loans	$ 68	35.25%	32.32%	25.96%

*The dollar amounts outstanding and the finance rates are averages for the three groups of states. See Appendix A.

Other factors--structural or behavioral--may also affect availability in particular markets. Such factors include licensing procedures, convenience and advantage provisions, supervision, regulations on loan size, collateral and maturity and, perhaps most important, the structure of the banking system and the kinds of financial intermediaries that operate in a particular state. These factors may affect supply and presumably may therefore be reflected in instalment credit outstanding.

Of these, the type of banking structure in a state may be a crucial influence on the availability of consumer credit. Thus branch banks apparently invest a greater proportion of their funds in consumer loans. Schweiger and McGee, after allowing for the influence of population growth, type of community, size of bank, and deposit mix, conclude that

> In general, unit banks do not lend as much in the form of consumer instalment credit as do branch banks. At the end of 1959, branch banks of every size and in every type of community had a larger percentage of assets in consumer instalment credit than unit banks.[14]

A study of New York State banks indicates that unit banks are generally more restrictive in loan terms on direct, new car loans; in 1962, for banks outside New York City, 11% of the unit banks reported maximum maturities of less than 36 months compared with less than 2% of the branch banks; 73% of the unit banks reported loan-value ratios of 67% or less, compared with only 26% of the major branch banks and less than half of the remaining branch banks.[15]

Further, it is sometimes held that limited-area branching and home office protection insulate bank markets and thereby limit competition and the supply of consumer credit. Thus as a result of the 1960 Omnibus Banking Act, New York City banks opened 29 de novo branches in Nassau County in the period 1960-1964, half of all new banking offices approved in that period. A study by Motter and Carson noted that the number of commercial banks increased in 14 of the 16 submarkets in Nassau County. Further, replies for eight banks indicated that direct auto loan rates were lower for 6 banks, unchanged for two; for personal instalment loans, rates were lower in four cases, unchanged in four; and for six banks, rates on dealer paper for new car loans were lower in three cases and unchanged in three. In commenting on this episode, the authors conclude:

> The evidence. . .indicates that the increase in banking competition, stemming in part from the advent of New York City banks, lowered instalment loan rates. . .(This result) may be attributed to the significant increase in number of offices and

number of banks per submarket.[16]

It has been noted[17] that New York City banks have typically held a small proportion of their loan portfolio in instalment credit. The rapid move to expand into suburban areas during 1960-1964 suggests that the large New York City banks, prior to 1960, were somehow not able to reach their preferred portfolio position. It also suggests that banking laws helped maintain an area of excess supply, in New York City, and an adjacent area of excess demand in Nassau County.

At the other end of the spectrum, small banks have been found to exhibit less willingness to grant instalment loans. Schweiger and McGee have noted that:

> Refusal to extend this type of unsecured personal loan ($500/18 mos.) was found to be most frequent among small banks. In St. Louis, for example, three of seven sample banks with deposits less than $50 million would not extend such loans while all seven of the larger banks would do so. In Cleveland, two of the three banks in the under $50 million category would not make such loans while all five of the larger banks would do so.[18]

Kohn's study of New York State banks has much the same implication with regard to the restrictiveness of loan terms in that unit banks, the smallest in size as a group, and small New York City banks were less likely to offer 36-month maturities and to lend more than two-thirds of the value of a new car.[19]

As may be expected, competition also plays a role in the availability of instalment credit. Thus, in Kohn's study, it was noted that:

> . . .unit banks in multi-office communities usually offered more liberal loan terms than did unit banks in one-office communities, although there were exceptions to this generalization. . .Similarly, small branch banks headquartered where other lending institutions were also located offered somewhat more liberal loan terms than did small branch banks headquartered where they were the only lender in the community.[20]

To summarize, several factors, not mutually exclusive, appear to be associated with the availability of consumer credit from commercial banks. Guttentag and Herman, in discussing commercial bank asset allocation, treat the ratio of bank instalment loans to total bank loans as a characteristic of bank portfolio behavior, and in turn relate this ratio to bank structure, bank size and size of metropolitan area. They also consider the possibility that this ratio is demand determined--that banks supply more instalment credit when demand is high--but argue that this view is not supported by the empirical evidence. We will follow these and other investigators and include B_{il}, the ratio of bank instalment to total loans or, B_{pl}, the ratio of bank personal/total loans, aggregated by state, as approximations for the level of bank participation in instalment loan markets. As such, this variable is viewed as reflecting bank portfolio policy, given the regulations in that state, and as a parameter determining supply although it may also be viewed, at least formally, as a ratio that is determined by demand conditions.[21]

We will test the proposition that the degree of bank participation influences the supply of instalment credit by including these variables as independent variables. Our hypothesis is that this variable is associated with differences in supply conditions; more precisely, we assume that the greater the degree to which banks participate in consumer credit markets, the greater is the supply.

In Table 4, we present regression results using instalment loans per capita and personal loans per capita as dependent variables, with rate ceilings r_2, r_3, risk, L_s and bank participation B_{il} and B_{pl} as independent variables. Although R^2 terms are low and not statistically significant, some of our results can be mentioned. Whether included separately or with the risk variable, the regression coefficients for the ceiling variable are uniformly of the wrong sign. Although the risk variable is not significant, its coefficient is consistently positive. None of the partial regression coefficients for ceiling or risk variables are significant. On the other hand, since our measures of ceiling rates and risk are correlated it may also suggest that L_s, the loss ratio, is not a good measure of risk and that it may be the vehicle through which the ceiling effect operates.

The coefficients for the bank participation variable are significant and suggest that commercial banks may play an important role in the consumer credit market. The 't' values for the instalment loan equations range from 1.703 to 2.297, and from 1.642 to 1.766 for the personal loan equations. However, before concluding that bank participation is an important supply determining variable, we should deal with four distinct possibilities.

Formally, the bank participation ratio may be (1) a parameter determining supply, (2) a parameter determining demand, or a ratio reflecting movements in either (3) demand or (4) supply. In principle, we cannot distinguish between supply and demand determining parameters on the basis of quantity data alone, but there is a theoretical basis for treating the bank participation variable as a determinant of supply; no such case has been advanced for treating it as a determinant of demand. Thus if we are faced with choosing

Table 4

SUMMARY OF REGRESSION RESULTS USING CEILING RATES, RISK, BANK PARTICIPATION AS SUPPLY VARIABLES -- 25 STATES*

Dependent Variable	Independent Variables					R^2
	r_2	r_3	L_s	B_{il}	B_{pl}	
IL/P		-2.104 (.748)		4.115 (2.046)		.160
IL/P	-.172 (-.065)			3.578 (1.828)		.139
IL/P			8.940 (.873)	3.217 (1.703)		.167
IL/P	-3.164 (-.891)		17.379 (1.243)	3.545 (1.833)		.198
IL/P		-6.321 (-1.811)	23.866 (1.870)	4.392 (2.297)		.280
PL/P		-.254 (-.230)			3.810 (1.759)	.126
PL/P	.170 (.159)				3.831 (1.766)	.124
PL/P			2.617 (.615)		3.733 (1.733)	.138
PL/P	-.554 (-.367)		4.162 (.688)		3.635 (1.642)	.144
PL/P		-1.248 (-.849)	5.824 (1.020)		3.604 (1.658)	.167

*The figures in parentheses are the "t" values for each coefficient.

between alternatives (1) and (2) there is a basis for selecting (2). Let us now consider the fourth alternative and think of the bank participation ratio as responding to some other parameter that is affecting supply. This introduces some unknown parameter that complicates the analysis but does not detract from the use of bank participation as a predictor of supply. In effect, what we are saying is that the implications following alternative (4) are not basically different from those in alternative (2). It is, however, important to consider the case (2) where the bank participation ratio is reflecting demand, and we will proceed to analyze the role of demand on the amount of credit outstanding.

4. A Further Influence: The Effect of Demand

Studies on the demand for consumer credit indicate that differences in outstandings are attributable at least in part to differences in demand conditions among the 25 states. This would suggest that we may be able to get a better view of the supply variables if we can adjust the influence of demand.

In considering the empirical studies of demand, it is useful to think of the amount of credit outstanding within a state in terms of the numbers of borrowers and the distribution of amounts borrowed. Studies by Lansing, et. al., by Miner, and by Katona[22] suggest that the number of spending units within an income class in debt tends to rise as disposable income rises to $7500; but as income goes above $7500, the proportion of debtors declines. The probability of having instalment debt is also higher for young families with children, and is negatively related to liquid asset holdings and to the stability of income.

Several of the cross section studies use different variables for predicting the amount of debt owed by a spending unit. Miner finds that disposable income is the only significant factor associated with the amount of debt outstanding. Tobin finds that additions to debt are positively related to current income (for all but the lowest--less than $1000--income levels) and negatively related to the level of debt outstanding.[23] Lansing, et. al. report that the amount of debt repayment increases with income (although at a slower rate than income), decreases with stage in life cycle, and decreases with the level of liquid asset holdings.

Similar variables have also been used in time series studies. Hunter finds that both consumer credit outstanding and extensions of instalment credit are positively related to the number of income-receiving units and to income, and negatively related to liquid assets; Enthoven uses a life cycle model to study the debt/income ratio; and Kisselgoff and Evans have noted that the amount of credit extended depends on consumer purchases and repayments, and the volume of auto instalment debt may depend on the contract maturity.[24]

It is clear that to account for differences in demand among the states we would have to include variables on disposable income, family life cycle, liquid asset holdings, and previous debt holdings, to mention the more prominent. Unfortunately, such data are not available. We therefore use state per capita personal income, and we use it as an independent variable to adjust for the influence of demand.

Before discussing our regression results it may be desirable to outline the model that we have in mind. We assume that the per capita demand for instalment debt is a function of the finance charge, per capita income, liquid assets or wealth, and possibly other variables such as repayments. If we let $\left(\frac{IL}{P}\right)^d$ be the demand for instalment debt we may write

(1) $\left(\frac{IL}{P}\right)^d$ = f(finance charge, per capita income, per capita liquid assets plus other variables, etc.)

We also assume that the supply of instalment debt is a function of the finance charge, ceiling rates, risk, bank participation and possibly other variables. If we let $\left(\frac{IL}{P}\right)^s$ be the supply of instalment debt we may write

(2) $\left(\frac{IL}{P}\right)^s$ = f(finance charge, ceiling rates, risk, bank participation, plus other variables, etc.)

The only variable common to both equations is the finance charge, so that the variables (or parameters) that affect supply are different from those that affect demand. With this assumption the least squares equation would, at least in principle, enable us to separate out demand effects from supply effects. And similar considerations apply to the personal loans equations. Since we do not have data on finance charges we necessarily have to leave this variable out. This omission would not be serious if both demand and supply were relatively inelastic with respect to changes in the finance charge. But to the extent that there is significant variation among the states in the actual finance rate charged, and to the extent that demand or supply is elastic with respect to such variations, our results will be biased.

From the regression results reported in Table 5, it is evident that the inclusion of Y/P, a variable to account for demand substantially improves our estimating equation. The R^2 have doubled in almost each instance; those equations which include rate ceilings but not risk give coefficients of the correct sign, but they are not significant and seem to suggest that ceilings are not particularly important in

Table 5

SUMMARY OF REGRESSION RESULTS USING CEILING RATES, RISK, AND BANK PARTICIPATION AS SUPPLY VARIABLES AND INCOME PER CAPITA AS A DEMAND VARIABLE -- 25 STATES*

Dependent Variables	Independent Variables						R^2
	r_2	r_3	L_s	B_{il}	B_{pl}	Y/P	
IL/P	1.099 (.511)			5.125 (3.148)		.063 (3.624)	.470
IL/P		2.018 (.794)		4.951 (3.023)		.069 (3.588)	.479
IL/P			13.859 (1.742)	4.924 (3.258)		.066 (4.038)	.531
IL/P	-2.286 (-.833)		19.872 (1.842)	5.131 (3.326)		.065 (3.927)	.547
IL/P		-1.276 (-.392)	16.613 (1.547)	5.071 (3.194)		.063 (3.312)	.535
PL/P	.756 (.757)				4.753 (2.371)	.008 (2.397)	.313
PL/P		1.305 (1.128)			4.889 (2.469)	.023 (2.564)	.334
PL/P			4.524 (1.163)		4.556 (2.321)	.020 (2.505)	.336
PL/P	-.044 (-.032)		4.644 (.850)		4.546 (2.237)	.020 (2.410)	.337
PL/P		.735 (.463)	2.864 (.535)		4.731 (2.324)	.022 (2.320)	.344

*The figures in parentheses are the "t" values for each coefficient.

explaining the supply of credit. When we include both ceiling rates and risk none of the regression coefficients are significant, suggesting the possibility that ceilings may work through incentives to bear risk. The bank participation variable is more consistently significant, with 't' values ranging from 3.023 to 3.326 in the instalment loan equations, and from 2.237 to 2.469 in the personal loan equations. Further, per capita income is significant in all cases, with 't' values ranging from 2.320 to 4.038. The fact that B_{il} and B_{pl}, the bank variables, are strengthened when we introduce income tends to support our view that they are supply determining parameters. We also find that the simple correlations between the bank variables and income, and between bank variables and liquid assets, are all relatively low.[25] These findings are not consistent with the view that B_{il} or B_{pl} are merely ratios reflecting movements in demand.

Conclusions

Assuming that our approximations are reasonably correct, our results suggest that the influence of rate ceilings on the supply of credit has been exaggerated relative to other factors, especially those that influence bank participation. They also suggest that there may be impediments to the flow of resources among instalment loan markets in different states. This, if confirmed, would argue for either more national lenders that can easily move across state lines, or for more lenders within those states where supply seems low. It may also be desirable to consider other alternatives for improving the allocational efficiency of instalment loan markets.

In stating our conclusions, we wish to reiterate the numerous assumptions that we have incorporated into our analysis.

1. The use of rate ceilings on small loans as an index of the ceiling structure in different states assumes that the other ceilings are either relatively constant, or that they vary with small loan ceilings.

2. Even if the overall supply of credit were sensitive to such an index of ceiling rates, it may be that the choice of $300 or $500 loans is inappropriate.

3. We have also assumed that the inclusion of non-instalment loans--for which data are not available--would not significantly change our results.

4. There is the possibility that we have a statistical illusion, inasmuch as we do not have data on some important sources of instalment credit. Two possibilities can be noted: (1) that variations in the instalment credit

included in our data are greater than variations in the total instalment credit outstanding, and that the non-included lenders may be behaving in a manner quite different from the included lenders. Although this is a possibility it does not seem likely: (2) that the omission of some lenders overemphasizes the relative importance of commercial banks in the instalment markets since our data include a higher proportion of bank credit and this may bias our estimates. As pointed out in the appendix, in our data over 2/3 of average per capita instalment loans are supplied by banks, compared with 41.5% of the aggregate indicated in Table 1. To counter this argument, we can point to our results for personal loans. Our data cover almost 100% of these loans, and banks account for only 1/3 of the outstandings; the bank variables are nevertheless significant in every regression.

5. We have also assumed that personal income per capita can be used to adjust for the influence of demand. Future work should consider the use of disposable income per capita and other demographic variables that may become available.

6. Also, we have implicitly assumed that the amount of credit outstanding from the institutions within a state is to be allocated to the population of that state. Although it may not be possible or practical to modify this assumption, people in one state may be able to borrow in other states.

7. A related issue deals with the definition of the relevant market. We have focussed on individual states because the legal framework, in some sense, considers this to be a homogenous market. Yet, conditions may vary considerably among cities within a state, between metropolitan areas (especially if they cross state boundaries), or within a given community.

8. The data we use reflect conditions as of 1964. It may be desirable to use time series analysis or data for other selected years to get a more representative picture of supply conditions. Such additional studies may also be helpful in determining whether there are significant cyclical or secular forces affecting supply.

9. The demand and supply functions that we postulate enable us to identify the parameters of these functions. But since we do not have data on finance charges, our results may be biased if the demand or supply elasticities are not low.

10. It may be objected that the ceiling variables do not

appear significant because they are typically associated with states where the outstanding would be even lower without high ceilings. This may be true, but it still suggests that the ceiling effect is small relative to other effects.

Finally, and subject to all these considerable qualifications, our results seem to suggest that for the 25 states in our sample ceiling rates are not a significant influence on supply. This does not mean that raising all the ceilings in a particular state will not tend to raise outstandings. It is not the direction of the effect that we question, but rather the magnitude; and we also question whether the raising of ceilings for some lenders affects the supply of loans from all lenders.

APPENDIX A

Sources and Description of Consumer Loan and Finance Rate Data

A. Consumer Loan Data

Data on consumer finance company loans outstanding by state are taken from Chapman and Shay (1967). This data includes loans made by licensed lenders under small-loan statutes in the 25 states, but does not include finance company loans granted under other legislation.

Per capita loans, in the Shay study, are expressed as the ratio of the average (of beginning- and end-of-year) loans outstanding divided by the 1964 population of the state. Our other series have been constructed in the same manner.

Data on bank loans is taken from the call reports for insured commercial banks, as published by the FDIC (1963, 1964). Personal loans are defined as "other loans for personal expenditures"; instalment loans include, in addition, automobile, other consumer goods, and home repair and modernization loans.

Credit Union Yearbooks (1963, 1964) give data on loans to members, which include instalment loans and real estate loans. To obtain instalment loans we subtract real estate loans from total loans; to obtain personal loans we subtract automobile loans from instalment loans.

B. Ceiling Rate Data

Goudzwaard (1965) presents data for the maximum dollar charge on small loans. These data are derived by cumulating the maximum charge allowed for each increment of loan as given by the ceiling rate schedule for each state. Finance rate ceilings were calculated by dividing the dollar charge by 1/2 the loan principal, for $300 and $500 loans, to approximate the annual simple interest rate. Goudzwaard's data are available for only 25 of the 30 states included in Chapman and Shay, and we restricted our analysis to these states.

C. Coverage of the Data

Some features of the instalment loan data that we have, of the states covered, and of the relative importance of different lenders may be summarized.

First, with respect to the relative importance of the states in our sample. The 25 states account for $10.04 billion, or 66% of total personal loans outstanding, and $22.71 billion or 40% of total instalment credit outstanding.

The difference in these proportions is explained by the fact that we have included all important sources of personal loans in our sample states, but we cannot obtain such complete coverage for the three other types of instalment loans.

Second, the omission of some types of instalment loans opens up the possibility of a systematic bias between the loan aggregates that we are able to measure and the actual loan aggregates. It is therefore possible that the dispersion in our measured data overstates the dispersion in the actual data. However, for this to occur it would be necessary that the lenders that we have not included offset the actions of the lenders that we have included. While this is possible, it does not appear to be very probable since there are some reasons to believe that these supply components often move together.

Third, the omission of some types of instalment loans may introduce another bias in that the relative importance of bank participation may be overstated. For the data that we have the commercial banks account for 33% of the personal loans and 66% of the instalment loans, compared to 33% and 42% for the actual totals as shown in Table 1. Thus if the omission of data produces a bias it would affect the instalment loan equations. It should not, however, affect the personal loan equations.

GLOSSARY

1. r_1 gross operating income/average loans outstanding, for all licensees operating under small loan statutes, by state. See Shay (1967), pp. 89, 100-101.

2. r_2 calculated finance rate on \$300 small loan. See Appendix A.

3. r_3 calculated finance rate on \$500 small loan. See Appendix A.

4. B_{il} ratio of bank instalment loans to total bank loans, for insured commercial banks by state. See Appendix A.

5. B_{pl} ratio of bank personal loans to total bank loans, for insured commercial banks by state. See Appendix A.

6. L_s bad debts/average loans outstanding, for all licensees operating under small loan statutes, by state. See Shay (1967), pp. 90, 100-101.

7. Y/P personal income per capita, by state, 1964.

8. IL/P per capita instalment credit outstanding by state. See Appendix A.

9. PL/P per capita personal loans outstanding, by state. See Appendix A.

FOOTNOTES

1. See: Board of Governors of The Federal Reserve System (1965), p. 2.

2. Op. cit., p. 3. The volume of instalment debt outstanding includes finance charges, and in this sense it is overstated relative to non-instalment debt. Data needed to separate out the finance charges from the principal are not regularly published. In his recent testimony Paul Douglas estimated that of $93.5 billion in consumer credit outstanding in January 1967, finance charges "amounted to at least $12 billion and probably much more." See: Senate Committee on Banking and Currency (1967), p. 58.

3. This table is presented for 1964 since some of the state data that we will use in our empirical work is only available for this year. See Appendix A.

4. Barbara Curran (1965), p. 3.

5. Allen Jung (1962), pp. 387-88, and (1965), pp. 397-401; E. Bruce Fredrikson (1967), pp. 2-14; Ernest Kohn (1964), pp. 124, 150, 152. These studies indicate a considerable dispersion in finance rates even though the characteristics of the loan (e.g., purpose, down-payment, maturity, etc.) and the status of the borrower (income, home ownership status, etc.) are held constant.

6. The data on personal loans in Chapman and Shay (1967) are available only for 1964, while the data on ceilings in Goudzwaard (1965) are available only for 25 of the 30 states covered in Chapman and Shay. We are unable to obtain the other loans made by finance companies in these 25 states. This affects the level of outstandings, but it should not presumably affect the relative ranking of the states. A description of the data is given in Appendix A.

7. Non-instalment credit would appear to be a more heterogenous total since it includes such diverse items as service credit (e.g., medical and utility bills), charge accounts in department stores and retail outlets and credit extended by means of credit cards (national or local). In any event, statewide data for these components are not available.

8. This assumes either that the ceiling rate is an effective rate which may be a fair assumption for consumer finance companies, or that actual rates move with ceiling rates.

9. John Chapman and Robert Shay (1967), p. 143.

10. The National Conference of Commissioners on Uniform State Laws, in their report (1965), pp. 28-29, illustrate this as follows:

> States that have gone the furthest in regulation of consumer credit fix different maximum rates for each recognized form of instalment credit: instalment sales of new automobiles, two or more classes of used automobiles, other goods and services, insurance premiums, and services for which a tariff is filed; revolving retail credit; revolving cash credit offered by banks; instalment loans by banks up to a certain size; small loans by consumer finance companies; home improvement loans; loans by credit unions; loans by savings and loan associations; and loans by pawnbrokers. These many regulations fix widely different maximum ceilings on finance charges for some credit transactions that may involve the same dollar amounts and maturities and serve the same economic function.

Thus, in New York State there are nine different statutes regulating, among others, instalment loans by commercial and industrial banks; bank check credit plans; retail revolving charge accounts; motor vehicle instalment sales financing; instalment sales financing of other goods and services; loans by consumer finance companies; and credit unions. Collectively, these statutes specify 14 different finance rate ceilings, loan maxima and other criteria.

11. Ceiling finance rates were estimated by dividing the maximum dollar charge permitted by the law for loans of $300 and $500. The schedule of dollar charges is shown in Maurice Goudzwaard (1965), Appendix A. Data on gross yield for the states in our sample are given in Chapman and Shay (1967), pp. 100-101.

12. Shay (op. cit., p. 92) does point out that gross yield depends on both rate ceilings and average loan size, and that average loan size is positively correlated with gross yield.

13. Risk is usually defined by the variance-covariance matrix of expected returns. For diversified lenders, this would require the measurement of covariances for the entire loan portfolio. Since we do not have such data, and since Goudzwaard (1965) and Shay (1967) use the loss ratio on small loans as a measure of risk, we have used this variable in our own work. However, it is not clear whether the loss ratio is a characteristic of the loans or of the lenders, and our

results would seem to suggest that the small loan loss ratio is not a good measure of risk.

14. Irving Schweiger and John McGee (1961), p. 226.

15. Ernest Kohn (1964), pp. 100-101.

16. David Motter and Deane Carson (1964), p. 512.

17. Horace J. DePodwin and Howard N. Ross (1965), pp. 16-18.

18. Op. cit., p. 267.

19. Op. cit., p. 100-101.

20. Op. cit., p. 116.

21. For a summary of the discussion in Guttentag and Herman, see their study (1967), pp. 128-129. The same or similar ratios have been used also by DePodwin and Ross (1965), Kreps (1964), and Edwards (1965). Further, there is evidence from Morrison and Selden (1965) that some banks establish various percentage quotas for instalment loans in the total loan portfolio.

22. John B. Lansing, E. Scott Maynes, and Mordechai Kreinin (1957); Jerry Miner (1960); George Katona, Charles Lininger, and Eva Mueller (1965).

23. James Tobin (1957).

24. Helen Hunter (1966); Alain Enthoven (1956); Avram Kisselgoff and Michael Evans (1966). For some evidence on the elasticity of demand, see Juster and Shay (1964).

25. We have experimented with equations that include an approximation for liquid assets (total bank and thrift institutions assets per capita). This term was not significant in any instance. Of equal interest, the correlation between liquid assets and B_{il} or B_{pl} was small and negative, again arguing that bank participation is not a demand-determined variable.

REFERENCES

[1] Board of Governors of the Federal Reserve System, Federal Reserve Bulletin, September 1967.

[2] ______________, Supplement to Banking & Monetary Statistics, Section 16 (New), Consumer Credit, Washington, D.C., 1965.

[3] Chapman, John M. and Shay, Robert P. (eds.). The Consumer Finance Industry: Its Costs and Regulation, New York: Columbia University Press, 1967.

[4] Credit Union National Association, Inc. International Credit Union Yearbook, 1964, Madison Wisconsin, 1965.

[5] ______________, International Credit Union Yearbook, 1963, Madison, Wisconsin, 1964.

[6] Curran, Barbara. Trends in Consumer Credit Legislation, Chicago, Illinois: University of Chicago Press, 1965.

[7] DePodwin, Horace J. and Ross, Howard N. The Supply and Demand for Personal Credit in New York State, 1950-1970, New York: Savings Bank Association of New York State, 1965.

[8] Edwards, Franklin, "The Banking Competition Controversy," The National Banking Review, Vol. 3, No. 1, September 1965, pp. 1-34.

[9] Enthoven, Alain, "Installment Credit and Prosperity," American Economic Review, December 1957, pp. 919-929.

[10] Fand, David I., "Competition and Regulation in the Consumer Credit Markets," Personal Finance Law, Quarterly Report, Vol. 20, Winter 1965, pp. 18-24.

[11] ______________, "Financial Regulation and the Allocative Efficiency of our Capital Markets," National Banking Review, Vol. 3, Sept. 1965, pp. 55-64.

[12] Federal Deposit Insurance Corporation, Assets, Liabilities, and Capital Accounts - Commercial and Mututal Savings Banks, Report of Call No. 66, December 20, 1963, Washington, D.C.

[13] ______________, Report of Call No. 70, December 31,

1964, Washington, D.C.

[14] Fredrikson, E. Bruce, "Consumer-Credit Charges in Philadelphia and Pittsburgh," The Appalachian Financial Review, Spring 1967, pp. 2-14.

[15] Goudzwaard, Maurice. The Effect of Rate Structure Upon the Availability of Credit at Consumer Finance Companies, unpublished Ph.D. dissertation, Michigan State University, 1965.

[16] Guttentag, Jack M. and Herman, Edward S. Banking Structure and Performance, New York: The Institute of Finance of the Schools of Business of New York University, February 1967.

[17] Harper, James B. A Summary of Consumer Installment Credit Laws and Rules in the United States and Canada, privately published by the Beneficial Finance Company, 1966.

[18] Hunter, Helen Manning, "A Behavioral Model of the Long-run Growth of Aggregate Consumer Credit in the United States," Review of Economics and Statistics, May 1966, pp. 124-140.

[19] Johnson, Robert W., "Conclusions for Regulation," Chapter 6 in Chapman and Shay (1967).

[20] ______________, "The Credit Market," unpublished ms., 1965.

[21] ______________, "Regulation of Finance Charges on Consumer Instalment Credit," forthcoming in Michigan Law Review.

[22] Jung, Allen, "Charges for Appliance and Automobile Instalment Credit in Major Cities," The Journal of Business, vol. 35, October 1962, pp. 387-388.

[23] ______________, "Commercial Bank Charges in New York and Ontario," The National Banking Review, vol. 2, March 1965, pp. 397-401.

[24] Juster, F.T. and Shay, R.P. Consumer Sensitivity of Finance Rates: An Empirical and Analytical Investigation, National Bureau of Economic Research, Inc., 1964.

[25] Katona, George, Lininger, Charles A., and Mueller, Eva.

1964 Survey of Consumer Finances, Ann Arbor, Michigan: University of Michigan, 1965, Monograph No. 39, Survey Research Center, Institute for Social Research.

[26] Kisselgoff, Avram, and Evans, Michael K., "Demand for Consumer Instalment Credit and Its Effects on Consumption," unpublished ms., July 1966.

[27] Kohn, Ernest. Branch Banking, Bank Mergers, and the Public Interest, New York State Banking Department, 1964.

[28] Kreps, Clifton H., Jr., Character and Competitiveness of Local Banking (A Summary), Federal Reserve Bank of Richmond, October 1964.

[29] Lansing, John B., Maynes, E. Scott, and Kreinin, Mordechai, "Factors Associated with the Use of Consumer Credit," Board of Governors of the Federal Reserve System, Consumer Instalment Credit, 1957, vol. I, part II, pp. 487-520.

[30] McCracken, Paul W. Mao, James, C.T., and Fricke, Cedric V. Consumer Instalment Credit and Public Policy, Ann Arbor, Michigan: University of Michigan, Bureau of Business Research, 1965.

[31] Miner, Jerry, "Consumer Personal Debt - An Intertemporal Cross-Section Analysis," in Friend, I. and Jones, R. (eds.), Consumption and Savings, University of Pennsylvania, 1960, vol. II, pp. 400-461.

[32] Morrison, George R., and Selden, Richard T. Time Deposit Growth and the Employment of Bank Funds, Chicago, Illinois: Association of Reserve City Bankers, 1965.

[33] Motter, David C. and Carson, Deane, "Bank Entry and the Public Interest: A Case Study," The National Banking Review, vol. 1, June 1964, pp. 469-512.

[34] National Conference of Commissioners on Uniform State Laws, Report of Special Committee on Retail Installment Sales, Consumer Credit, Small Loans and Usury, Chicago, Illinois: August 1965.

[35] National Consumer Finance Association, The Consumer Finance Industry, Englewood Cliffs, New Jersey: Prentice-Hall, Inc., 1962.

[36] Schweiger, Irving, and McGee, John S., "Chicago Banking," The Journal of Business, vol. 34, #3, July 1961, pp. 203-367.

[37] Senate Committee on Banking and Currency, Truth in Lending - 1967, Washington, D.C.: U.S. Government Printing Office, 1967.

[38] Shay, Robert P., "State Regulation and the Provision of Small Loans," Chapter 4 in Chapman and Shay (1967).

[39] ____________, New Automobile Finance Rates, 1924-1962, National Bureau of Economic Research, Inc., 1963.

[40] Smith, Paul F. Consumer Credit Costs, 1949-59, National Bureau of Economic Research, Princeton, New Jersey: Princeton University Press, 1964.

[41] Tobin, James, "Consumer Debt and Spending: Some Evidence from Analysis of a Survey," Board of Governors of the Federal Reserve System, Consumer Instalment Credit, 1957, vol. I, part II, pp. 521-545.

AN ESTIMATE OF THE INCOME OF THE VERY RICH

by

James D. Smith

Office of Economic Opportunity

Introduction

In this essay the income of the very rich in 1958 is estimated and compared to the income of all persons. The rich are defined as persons with gross assets in excess of $60,000.[1] Three broad types of incomes are separately estimated and summed. The three types are: (1) direct returns to property (interest, rent, dividends, and business incomes); (2) capital gains (realized and unrealized) and (3) wage and salary income. Income from personal trusts and estates are not included in the estimates.

The first and second types of income are directly related to the holdings of specific assets. Interest, rent, dividends, and business incomes therefore are estimated by imputing yields to assets owned by the rich and capital gains and losses are estimated by applying the relative change in a price index for each asset against the estimated value of that asset.

The estimate of wage income is made by using a set of ratios of wages to asset holdings of persons with gross assets over $60,000. The ratios were obtained from a study of high income individuals done by the Board of Governors of the Federal Reserve System.

Because the estimates of the income of the rich are to a very large extent based upon estimates of their asset holdings, it is well to pause momentarily to examine the source of the wealth estimates themselves.

The wealth estimates used in this study were made by a technique known as the estate multiplier method. Simply stated, the procedure is to multiply the value of assets held at death by the reciprocal of the age-sex-specific mortality rate associated with the decedent. Thus, if the mortality rate for men age 50 were 5 per 1000 living persons, the value of their assets would be multiplied by $\frac{1000}{5}$, or 200, to obtain an estimate of the wealth of the living.

The value of assets in estates is known only for a small proportion of all U.S. decedents, and it is only for the living population represented by these decedents that wealth estimates can be made. A federal estate tax return must be filed for decedents with gross assets in excess of $60,000. From these tax returns estimates of the number and wealth of living persons with gross assets over $60,000 were made for 1958. Table I shows the estimates of these assets and compares them to the total wealth of all U.S. citizens reported in Goldsmith's national balance sheets.[2]

Dividends, Rent and Interest.

The estimate of dividend income is produced by multiplying the total holdings of corporate stock by the average yield of common stock in 1958. The yield factor is for Standard and Poor's 500 stock index. Use of the common stock yield factor slightly understates dividend income of the rich because the corporate stock classification used in the wealth estimates includes preferred issues, which in 1958, had an average yield 12 percent higher than common stock.

Although the wealth data do not permit a determination of the relative amounts of common and preferred issues held by the rich, the fact that preferred issues held by all individuals and trusts in mid-1958 had a market value of only $9.6 billion and the estimate of this study that the rich owned $195.4 billion of corporate stock, argues strongly against any large understatement.[3]

Table I shows that in 1958, the very rich owned 75.9 percent of the value of all stock directly held by individuals. Reducing dividend income of "persons" in the national income accounts for 1958, by the ratio of stock held in personal trusts and nonprofit institutions to the total value of stock held by "households," yields the dividend flow to individuals.[4] Adjusting national income account dividends for 1958 by the above procedure, results in a $10.7 billion flow to individuals. This study's estimate of dividend income of the rich is $8.0 billion, or about 75 percent of the total dividend income received by individuals.[5] (See Table 2)

Rental income of top wealth-holders was estimated by applying against the values of their real estate an arbitrary 5.5% rate of interest. Using this procedure brings us close to the concept of rental income of the national income accounts. It is estimated that rental income of $6.4 billion was received by the rich in 1958. This was 52.5 percent of rental incomes of persons ($12.2 billion) in the national income accounts.

Total interest income of the rich was estimated as the sum of $0.6 billion on Federal bonds, $0.4 billion on state and local bonds, $0.2 billion on "other bonds", $0.8 billion on time deposits and $1.1 billion from notes and mortgages, or a total of $3.1 billion.

Interest income was estimated by applying the average 1958 rate of yield on each of the three classes of bonds--Federal, state and local, and "other" (essentially corporate)--against the estimated value of such bonds held; applying an

TABLE 1

SHARE OF THE VERY RICH IN NATIONAL WEALTH, 1958

	Wealth of the Rich	National balance sheet wealth	Share of the Rich in total wealth
	(1)	(2)	(3)
	(Billions of dollars)		(Percent)
Real estate	$115.7	$ 599.3	19.3
Federal bonds	16.3	60.2	27.1
State and local bonds	12.2	15.7	77.7
Other bonds	3.7	4.9	75.5
Corporate stock	195.4	257.3	75.9
Cash	39.5	209.4	18.9
Notes and mortgages	17.9	43.9	40.8
Life insurance equity	13.3	103.0	12.9
Miscellaneous assets[a]	57.9	268.6	21.6
Gross assets	$472.0	$1,562.3	30.2
Debt	$ 42.9	$ 222.8	19.3
Net assets	$429.0	$1,339.5	32.0

Sources: Column 1, Smith and Calvert, op. cit., p. 251; column 2, ibid. p. 254. The national balance sheet values, column 2, were derived by modifying Goldsmith's household sector to exclude non-profit corporations, corporate farms and trust funds. After this adjustment, his values for end-of-year 1957 and end-of-year 1958 were averaged to obtain an estimate for mid-year 1958, the point in time to which the estimates of top wealth-holder's wealth is most appropriately related.

[a]Includes annuities.

arbitrary rate of 6 percent against notes and mortgages and a 3 percent rate against a portion of cash holding.

For state and local bonds, Moody's Investors Service average yield, 3.4 percent, for all such bonds was used. For "other bonds," Moody's 4.75 percent for all corporates was used.[6] The yield used for Federal bonds was that for instruments callable in ten years or more.

An arbitrary 6 percent rate was applied against notes and mortgages based upon its common statutory use for tax debts and what appears to be an institutionalized rate on contractual debt among persons.

A 3 percent rate was applied against a portion of cash holdings. This was the maximum rate payable on time deposits by member banks of the Federal Reserve System in 1958. Assuming that the cash of the rich was allocated among time deposits, demand deposits, and currency in the same proportions as for all individuals (see national balance sheet in Appendix), only 65.2 percent would have been earning a yield. On this basis the estimate of interest income on cash holdings of top wealth-holders would amount to (0.03) X ($39.5) X (0.652) = $0.8 billion. But this estimate probably understates the interest received by the rich on their cash holdings. It seems unlikely that the very wealthiest strata of the population would hold as great a portion of their cash in currency and demand deposits as the average for all individuals.

The interest income of the wealthy can be compared to that of all persons by adjusting personal interest in the national income accounts.[7] One necessary adjustment is the removal of imputed interest income from "personal interest income". In 1958 personal interest amounted to $21.0 billion, of which net imputed interest was $9.0 billion. Personal monetary interest was therefore $12.0 billion.

Because non-profit institutions and trust funds are included in the personal sector of the national income accounts, the total monetary interest income of "persons," $12.0 billion, needs further adjustment to correspond with the population of individuals. In mid-1958 interest earning assets of non-profit institutions and trust funds amounted to $25.7 billion, or 7.8 percent of the $330.8 billion interest bearing assets of household and private farms. Reducing interest income in the national income accounts by this percentage achieves the desired correspondence with the population of individuals. Interest income so adjusted totals $11.1 billion, of which the share of the rich, $3.1 billion, accounted for 27.9 percent.

Business income of top wealth-holders was estimated by applying a 6 percent rate of return against one-half the value of property included in miscellaneous assets.[8] The estimate of business income based on the above procedure is $1.6 billion. This is about 3.5 percent of the $46.1 billion pro-

TABLE 2

ESTIMATES OF PROPERTY INCOME OF THE VERY RICH, 1958

Asset	Value of asset	Rate of return	Value of yield
	(1)	(2)	(3)
	(Billions of dollars)	(Percent)	(Billions of dollars)
Real estate	$115.7	5.5	$ 6.4
Federal bonds	16.3	3.4	0.6
State and local bonds	12.2	3.6	0.4
Other bonds	3.7	4.2	0.2
Corporations stock	195.4	4.1	8.0
Cash[a]	25.8	3.0	0.8
Notes and mortgages	17.9	6.0	1.1
Miscellaneous[b]	28.3	6.0	1.6
Gross amounts	$415.3		$19.2
Debt	$ 43.0	6.0	$ 2.6
Net amounts	$372.3		$16.6

Source: Column 1 is from Table 1; column 2, rates are as follows: real estate, average rate of interest on FHA insured loans in 1958; federal bonds, average yield on federal bond callable in ten years or more; state and local bonds, Moody's average yield on all state and local bonds; other bonds, Moody's average yield on all corporate bonds; corporate stock, yield on stock in Standard and Poor's 500 stock index; cash, maximum rate payable on savings deposits in 1958 by member banks of the Federal Reserve System; notes and mortgages, miscellaneous, and debt, are arbitrary selections. Column 4 and 5 are from Table 3.

[a]Cash has been reduced to 65.2 percent of the amount shown in Table 1.

[b]One-half the value miscellaneous assets remaining after excluding $1.5 billion in annuities.

prietor's income in the national income accounts for 1958. A summary of property incomes, interest, rent, dividend and business incomes is presented in Table 2.

Capital Gains and Losses.

It is estimated that the rich had a net capital gain of $57.1 billion in 1958. The estimate of capital gains and losses was made by applying against certain assets the relative change in market value for that type asset during 1958. The estimated wealth of the rich is an average of their wealth over the year because the sample (estate tax decedents) is drawn not at a point, but rather evenly throughout the year. The estimate is as of June 30, 1958. Since the rate of change of each price index and the mid-year value for each asset is known, it is possible to compute the capital gain on asset A_1 $(G_A)_1$ accruing to top wealth-holders during the year.

$$\frac{2M_A(I_A - 1)}{I_A + 1} = G_A$$ where M is the estimated value of asset

A held by top wealth-holders and I_A is a price index for the class of wealth of which A is a member. The value I_A is equal to $\frac{(\text{Price } A_{t+1})}{(\text{Price } A_t)}$. In our estimate t = end-of-year 1957 and t+1, end-of-year 1958. Implicit in this procedure are two assumptions: (1) all exchanges of assets held at the beginning of the year by the rich were made within the group and (2) the change in price level of the asset was linear over the year.

Movements of asset prices in 1958, resulted in capital gains on real estate, corporate stock, and "miscellaneous assets"; and capital losses on Federal, state and local, and other bonds. It should be noted that the estimated capital loss on bonds of all types more than offset the estimated interest on all bonds. By far the most significant source of capital gain, one that swamped not only the total net capital gain on all other assets, but also the total income from all sources, was corporate stock.

The very rapid climb in stock market prices from the end of 1957 to the end of 1958 resulted in significant increases in the wealth of the wealthy. The market moved dramatically upward posting a nearly 34% increase in the price of an average share. The resultant capital gain to the rich was $56.8 billion. A moderate gain was also obtained on real estate holdings; but the upward movement of interest rates in 1958 brought moderate capital losses to bond-holders.

Our estimate of the net capital gain to the rich from all asset holdings is $57.1 billion. This estimate, it should be kept in mind, includes both realized and non realized capital

TABLE 3

ESTIMATES OF CAPITAL GAINS OF THE RICH IN 1958 BY TYPE OF PROPERTY

Type of Property	Value of asset mid 1958	Actual price index value End-of-year 1958	1957	Percentage Change	Capital gain
	(1)	(2)	(3)	(4)	(5)
	(Billions of dollars)				(Billions of dollars)
Real estate	$115.7	278.0	272.9	+ 1.87	+$2.1
Federal bonds	16.3	88.9	95.6	- 7.01	- 1.1
State and local bonds	12.2	102.3	107.5	- 4.84	- 0.6
Other bonds	3.7	98.7	102.7	- 3.89	- 0.1
Corporate stock	195.4	201.1	150.1	+33.98	+56.8
Total	$415.3				$57.1

Detail may not add to totals due to rounding.

Source: Column 1 is from Table 1; columns 2 and 3 are from Goldsmith, Studies in the National Balance Sheet, pp. 170-3; column 5 was computed by the method described on page of this text.

gains. The capital gains estimates are summarized in Table 3.

Salary and Wage Incomes of The Very Rich.

An estimate of the wages of the rich is made by use of ratios of wages to assets obtained from a survey of 1,042 high-income recipients done by the Board of Governors of the Federal Reserve Systems.

In October, 1960, a pilot study, preparatory to the full-scale Survey of Financial Characteristics of Consumers was conducted in four major U.S. cities.[9] The pilot study had two purposes: to obtain detailed information about the financial position of families who had substantial amounts of savings and investment, and to test procedures to be used in a subsequent national survey.[10]

Three census tracts expected to have a high proportion of high-income recipients were selected in each city. One-half of the sample in each city was restricted to families who reported incomes of $15,000 and over in the 1960 decennial census. Eighteen percent of those selected had a net worth of $200,000 or more.

For purposes of this study, ratios of wages to gross assets were computed for heads of families interviewed in the FRB study. These ratios were then applied to the estate multiplier wealth estimates for the rich to make estimates of their wage income. The ratios and the estimated wages are shown in Table 4. Comparing wage of the rich to total wages in the national income accounts shows that the 1.5 percent of the population who are rich received 10.8 percent of all wages. (See Table 5).

Summary and Conclusions.

In Table 5 the estimated income of the rich is summarized and compared to the income going to all individuals. In making the estimate we have allocated all transfer incomes in the national income accounts to the lower 98.5 percent of wealth-holders. On the basis of our concepts of income and wealth, and our allocation of transfer payments we come to the conclusion that the same set of persons who held 30.2 percent of the gross wealth of all individuals received 24 percent of all individuals' income. This finding is surprisingly high for several reasons.

First, the rich are defined as the top 1.5 percent of wealth-holders (based on gross assets), but they almost certainly are not the top 1.5 percent of income recipients. (There is a set of individuals which constitutes the top 1.5 percent of the income distribution. Only in the special case where there was perfect positive correlation among gross wealth and income would the set of wealth-holders and income recipients be identical. Arraying individuals by any charac-

TABLE 4

ESTIMATE OF WAGES RECEIVED BY THE RICH, 1958

	Total assets	Ratios of wages to gross assets	Estimates
	(1)	(2)	(3)
	(Billions of dollars)		(Billions of dollars)
$60,000 under $70,000	$ 12.8	.18	$2.3
$70,000 under $80,000	16.1	.17	2.7
$80,000 under $90,000	14.7	.13	1.9
$90,000 under $120,000	41.9	.12	4.9
$120,000 under $150,000	34.2	.10	3.4
$150,000 under $200,000	38.9	.09	3.5
$200,000 under $500,000	91.5	.05	4.6
$500,000 and over	131.6	.02	2.6
Total	$381.7		$25.9

TABLE 5

THE SHARE OF THE RICH IN TOTAL INCOME, 1958

	All Persons	The Very Rich	Share going to The Very Rich
	(1)	(2)	(3)
	(Billions of dollars)		(Percent)
Wages and salaries	$239.8	$ 25.9	10.8
Dividend[a]	10.7	8.0	74.8
Interest	11.1	3.1	27.9
Rent	12.2	6.4	52.5
Proprietors income	46.1	1.6	3.5
Capital gains	80.7	57.6	71.4
Social insurance	8.5	-	-
Unemployment benefits	3.9	-	-
Veterans benefits	4.6	-	-
Other transfers	9.4	-	-
Total	$427.0	$102.6	24.0

Source: Column 1, all values except capital gains are based on the personal income entries in the national income accounts for 1958. Capital gains are derived by applying to the value assets in the national balance sheet the same procedure that was applied to the corresponding asset values in the hands of top wealth-holders.

[a]Excludes $1.7 billion dividends paid to trust funds and non-profit institutions.

teristic other than income can only err on the side of understating the concentration of income.)

Second, we have assumed only average yields on the assets of the rich. This seems a conservative approach. It can reasonably be argued that the holding of large amounts of wealth permits the use of more specialized investment counselors who, presumably, make investment decisions with a higher expected return.

Third, all transfers have been allocated to the lower 98.5 percent of wealth-holders. This certainly understates the social security income of the very rich, who tend to be an older population.

TABLE 6

DERIVATION OF NATIONAL BALANCE SHEET FOR INDIVIDUALS BY TYPE OF PROPERTY FOR MID-YEAR 1958

Type of Property	Nonfarm households	Farm households	Nonfarm noncorporate businesses	Trust funds	Nonprofit institu-ions	Individuals	
						Total wealth	Prime wealth1/
	(Billions of dollars)						
	(1)	(2)	(3)	(4)	(5)	(6)	(7)
Real estate, total	452.8	113.5	63.4		30.4	599.3	599.3
Residential structures	338.6	18.1	16.1				
Nonresidential structures	25.3	15.8	24.8		25.3		
Land	88.9	79.6	22.5		5.1		
Federal bonds, total	59.7	4.9		2.7	1.7	62.9	60.2
Short-term	3.9						
Savings bonds	43.5	4.9					
Other Federal bonds	12.3						
State and local bonds	24.1			7.8	0.6	23.5	15.7
Other bonds	11.0			2.9	3.2	7.8	4.9
Corporate stock, total	299.6			33.3	9.0	290.6	257.3
Preferred	10.4			1.5	0.8		
Common	289.2			31.8	8.2		
Cash, total	193.6	8.6	12.9	0.4	5.3	209.8	209.4
Currency and demand deposits	59.9	5.8	12.9	0.4	5.3		
Other deposits	133.7	2.8					
Notes and mortgages, total	28.9		16.1	0.7	0.4	44.6	43.9
Nonfarm mortgages:							
Residential	12.4						
Nonresidential	9.4						
Farm mortgages	4.4						
Consumer credit			4.8				
Trade credit			11.3				
Other loans	2.7						
Life insurance reserves	96.8	6.2				103.0	103.0
Pension and retirement funds:							
Private	25.0					25.0	
Government	65.0	0.4				65.5	
Miscellaneous assets, total	172.5	56.4	43.5	1.9	1.9	270.5	268.6
Equity in mutual financial institutions	7.7						
Producer durables	2.0	17.4	26.7		1.9		
Consumer durables	162.2	13.3					
Inventories		22.2	16.8				
Other intangible assets	0.6	3.5		0.6			
Other tangible assets				1.3			
Gross assets	1,429.1	190.0	135.9	49.7	52.5	1,702.5	1,562.3
Debt	170.2	19.0	39.1		5.5	222.8	222.8
Economic Estate	1,258.9	171.0	96.8	49.7	47.0	1,479.7	1,339.5

1/ Prime wealth is total wealth less trust fund assets.

See notes on following pages

NOTES TO TABLE 6

Column 1, Nonfarm households, is the average of end-of-year asset values for 1957 and 1958 from Goldsmith, Studies in the National Balance Sheet, Vol. II, pp. 118f. Nonfarm noncorporate business assets of individuals are not included in column 1, but shown as a separate sector, Nonfarm Noncorporate Businesses, in column 3.

Column 2, Farm households, was derived by averaging Goldsmith's 1957 and 1958 year-end values for his agriculture sector, Studies in the National Balance Sheet, Vol. II, pp. 132f. The values obtained were then reduced by five percent to eliminate corporate farms. The basis for this adjustment is Mary M. B. Harmon, A Statistical Summary of Farm Tenure. Agriculture Research Service, U.S.D.A., 1958, p. 2, which shows five percent of the farm acreage was owned by corporations in 1954. Discussions with personnel of the Department of Agriculture and the Bureau of the Census who deal with agricultural data cast doubt upon the assumption that only five percent of the value of farm assets is owned by corporations. It is suspected that the five percent of farm acreage owned by corporations is above average in value and that corporate farms are more capital intensive than the average. However, for lack of hard data to support a further reduction in Goldsmith's agriculture sector, assets were reduced by only five percent.

Column 3, Nonfarm noncorporate businesses, is an average of Goldsmith's end-of-year asset values for such businesses from Studies in the National Balance Sheet, Vol. II, pp. 126f.

Column 4, The assets and liabilities of trust funds, all of which are included in the nonfarm household sector, are listed separately here as the trust sector. Trust funds, for 1958 is an average of common trust funds for 1957 and 1958 from Goldsmith, Studies in the National Balance Sheet, Vol. II, pp. 122f, plus the values for personal trust funds from the "Report of National Survey of Personal Trust Accounts," (ABA mimeo., 1959) p. 4.

Column 5, Nonprofit Institutions, was derived by applying to the mid-year asset values of nonfarm households (column 1) the percent that each asset held by nonprofit institutions in 1949 was of that asset held by households in 1949. See Goldsmith, A Study of Savings in the United

States, Vol. III, p. 72. This ratio estimating procedure was made necessary because 1949 is the last year for which Goldsmith estimated a nonprofit sector. Goldsmith points out in the preface page to his 1949 nonprofit sector balance sheet, the estimates are rough approximations: "Whoever reads the notes to the tables--or has worked in the field--will be aware of how precarious the estimates are..." (Ibid., p. 449). In spite of the roughness of the 1949 estimate, it is appropriate to use the estimate of the outstanding authority in the field as a basis to adjust downward the assets of the nonfarm household sector, which are known to be too high.

Column 6, To arrive at the total wealth concept for the individual sector, the assets and liabilities of farm households and unincorporated business were added to, and those of nonprofit institutions were subtracted from, the nonfarm household sector. (The assets and liabilities of trust funds are already included in the nonfarm household sector) Thus individuals total wealth is the sum of columns 1, 2, and 3, minus column 5.

Column 7, To obtain a prime wealth individual sector, assets of trust funds and pension reserves were subtracted from total wealth. Thus Individuals prime wealth is the sum of columns 1, 2, and 3, minus columns 4 and 5 and minus private and government pension and retirement funds.

FOOTNOTES

1. The number of such persons and their wealth have been estimated by a technique known as the estate multiplier method. In 1958, there were 2.5 million such persons, and they accounted for 1.5% of the U.S. population. See James D. Smith and Staunton Calvert "Estimating the Wealth of Top Wealth-Holders from Estate Tax Returns," Proceedings of the Business and Economics Statistics Section, American Statistical Association, Philadelphia, 1965.

2. See Raymond W. Goldsmith, Studies in the National Balance Sheet. NBER 1962. Goldsmith's figures were adjusted to mid-year 1958, and an "individual's sector" was derived from his household sector. See Appendix A for the details of this derivation.

3. It should be noted, however, that Atkinson found that for Wisconsin individuals in 1949, yields on stock decreased with higher income, except for his highest income group, $50,000 and over. Atkinson's data for Wisconsin individuals shows the highest income group realized a 7.31 percent yield on traded securities and 5.12 percent on untraded securities. These yields are 7 and 10 percent above the respective average yields for all Wisconsin shareholders. If one assumes Wisconsin shareholders are representative of the national population of shareholders with respect to their propensity for high yield, and income and wealth are closely associated, our estimates understate the dividend income of the rich. See Thomas R. Atkinson, The Pattern of Financial Asset Ownership, Wisconsin Individuals, 1949, The National Bureau of Economic Research (Princeton, New Jersey: Princeton University Press, 1956), p. 131.

4. The personal sector of the national income accounts includes trust funds and non-profit institutions.

5. This is consistent with the estimate that top wealth-holders owned 75.9% of the corporate stock of individuals.

6. The difference in yield is considerable between high and low grade bonds. In the case of State and local bonds, the average yield was 2.92 percent for Aaa bonds and 3.95 percent for Baa bonds, a 35 percent higher return on Baa bonds. The estimated yield is based on Moody's average for all State and local bonds, 3.4 percent. Aaa corporates had an average yield of 3.79 percent and Baa corporates an average of 4.75 percent,

a 25 percent premium for the lower grades. The yield used was the average for all corporate bonds, 4.2 percent.

7. Conceptually, interest, as used in this estimate, is quite close to the Federal income tax definition. However, it is necessary to broaden the tax concept to include interest from tax exempt bonds to achieve complete correspondence. Statistics of Income, 1958, shows that $3.7 billion interest was reported on income tax returns. It is possible to estimate rather closely the additional amount which would have been reportable on individual tax returns were interest from State and local bonds not exempt.

In 1958 State and local governments paid interest of $1.5 billion to holders of their debt. Goldsmith (Studies in the National Balance Sheet, Vol. II, p. 67f.) has estimated total par values of outstanding State and local bonds at the end of 1957 and the end of 1958 were $55.1 billion and $61.1 billion respectively. It is estimated that the mid-1958 value would have been $58.1 billion, the arithmetic mean of the end-of-year values. Since individuals directly held $15.7 billion of State and local bonds in mid-1958 (see column 7 of Appendix of this study), it may be assumed they received 28.1 percent (15.7/58.1) of the total interest paid by State and local governments, or $0.4 billion. In spite of the conceptual similarity of IRS interest to that of this study, the apparent extensive under-reporting of interest by taxpayers makes it preferable to compare our estimates to personal interest income in the national income accounts.

8. As noted above, the estimates of income in this paper are based upon an estate multiplier estimate of the wealth of the rich. The definition of each asset classified in the wealth estimate, is, of course, that used by the Internal Revenue Service. The IRS includes in its "miscellaneous" classification the value of unincorporated businesses and farms, but also the value of interests in trusts, personal property and "transfers contemplation of death." Because of the wide scope of the miscellaneous classification, only one-half of its value was assumed to represent business assets. This assumption is based on an examination of about 100 returns filed in one District Director's Office. The examined returns were not selected on any sampling basis and the 50% role of business assets is impressionistic.

9. Data obtained in the survey was made available through the cooperation of Dorothy Projector of the Board of Governors of the Federal Reserve System and Herman Miller of the Bureau of the Census.

10. See Dorothy Projector, "Survey of Financial Characteristics of Consumers," Federal Reserve Bulletin, March, 1964, p. 285.

A TEST OF A MACRO MODEL WITH TWO INTEREST RATES*

by

Samuel Williamson
University of Iowa

1. Introduction

The purpose of this study is to construct an explanative economic model of the markets for financial assets, with special reference to the consumer sector's saving part of these markets and to test the agreement of the model with a set of annual observations for the years 1947 to 1965. There is no contention that this model explains behavior of any earlier period of time or can be extended after 1965 to explain present or future behavior. This is because one of the underlying premises of the model is that background conditions remain constant. In other words, such things as changes in income distribution, the Korean War, etc., which are factors not explicitly in the model, are maintained not to have changed the parameters of the model during the 19-year period.

The model is similar to a financial IS-LM model, with saving and investment measured in flow terms and the money market in stock terms. For purposes of analysis, however, the model was disaggregated in the following ways: One was by partitioning the saving by the consumer sector from the saving by all the other sectors of the economy, so that the behavior of the consumer sector can be investigated separately. The second disaggregation was to partition saving into two transaction categories: primary saving and secondary saving. The effect of this disjunction is to create three markets instead of the usual two, making it possible not only to analyze the interaction between the securities (i.e., saving and investment) market and the money market, but the interactions within the markets for the two types of savings as well.[1]

As used in this study, saving is defined as the net purchase or acquisition of financial or saving "shares," i.e., any claims that savers receive in exchange for their money. Examples of the two types of saving shares are stock and bond certificates and mortgage paper, and savings passbooks.[2]

1.1 The Types of Saving

Primary saving is the purchase of credit market instruments, such as government securities, corporate bonds and stocks, mortgages, and other loans. The purchase of a primary share is a direct investment.

Secondary saving is the addition to time deposits and savings accounts. This is saving other than the contractual variety,[3] channeled through intermediaries. A characteristic of these shares acquired through secondary saving is that while the principal is constant, the rate of return varies. Thus, although the future value of such shares cannot be determined exactly, they can always be exchanged for at least the value of the principal. Because of this, the secondary share is generally less risky than the primary share.

1.2 The Markets and Their Participants

The model partitions the primary market into the consumer sector's purchase of primary shares, the net of sales minus purchases by the government, the purchase of shares by all other sectors, and the suppliers of shares. The government's activity in this market is regarded as externally determined and is therefore an exogenous variable (see the Appendix). The other sectors purchasing shares in the primary market are predominantly the bank and nonbank financial intermediaries. The suppliers of shares are mainly the corporate and noncorporate business sectors along with the consumer sector.

The consumer sector's participation in the primary market as a supplier is a separate action from its saving or purchase of shares. For example, when a consumer takes out a mortgage loan he is selling a primary share and this is counted as part of the total supply of these shares. If he should make a mortgage loan, this is part of the consumer sector's primary saving.

The secondary market has a division similar to the primary market but without the separate government category. The government's transactions in this market are by the state and local branches and are quite sensitive to market conditions and therefore not exogenous. Their activity, along with the purchases of the corporate and noncorporate business sectors, make up the purchases by all other sectors.

The suppliers of shares in this market are the banks and the savings and loan associations.

In the money market the suppliers are the commercial banks and the demanders are the consumer sector and all other sectors except the Federal government, whose deposits are excluded from the money supply as defined in this study.

1.3 The Plan of the Article

The plan of this paper is as follows: In Section 2 the model is formally presented in three parts; in 2.1 the structural equations are listed along with a discussion of the postulated ranges on the parameters; the simultaneous equations model is presented in 2.2; and in 2.3 the stability conditions are discussed. In Section 3 the maintained hypothesis, the reduced form, the identifiability conditions, and the "weaker hypothesis on the λ space" are presented. This weaker hypothesis in 3.4 is a rectangular set that "just" contains the transformation of the structural hypothesis into the reduced form. The model is tested against a set of data in Section 4. Both the identifiability conditions and the weaker hypothesis are tested.

2. The Model

2.1 The Underlying Economic Premises

For each sector's participation in each market there is a structural representation. Each representation is composed of a mathematical function, or structural equation, and a set of economic premises that restrict the parameters of the function in some definite way. Sometimes there are two or more theories about a particular sector's behavior. If these alternative theories are to be tested, then alternative equations must be specified.

Each structural equation is a distinct mechanism by itself. It can be described in isolation or in its "autonomous state." The structural equation does not change when it is combined with a set of structural equations to form a model. Even if it is used with a different set of equations to form a different model, it still retains its identity.

The variables used in the model are listed in Table 2.1, together with their generic and statistical symbols. The Appendix presents a precise definition of each variable, along with a discussion

Table 2.1.1
List of Symbols Used to Represent Variables

Generic Symbol	Name of Variable	Statistical Symbol
Endogenous		
S_P	Annual consumer saving in the primary market	$Z_{t,3}$
O_P	Annual saving of others in the primary market (excluding government)	$Z_{t,4}$
I_P	Annual supply of claims in the primary market (excluding government)	$Z_{t,5}$
S_s	Annual consumer saving in the secondary market	$Z_{t,6}$
O_s	Annual saving of others in the secondary market	$Z_{t,7}$
I_s	Annual supply of claims in the secondary market	$Z_{t,8}$
L_c	Year-end liquidity preference of consumers	$Z_{t,9}$
L_o	Year-end liquidity preference of others	$Z_{t,10}$
M	Year-end supply of money	$Z_{t,11}$
P	Year-end price level	$Z_{t,12}$
i_P	Annual primary rate of interest	$Z_{t,13}$
i_s	Annual secondary rate of interest	$Z_{t,14}$
Exogenous		
A	Financial assets held by consumers at beginning of year	$X_{t,4}$
G_P	Annual (net) government supply of claims in the primary market	$X_{t,6}$

Table 2.1.1 (continued)

y	Annual national income	$X_{t,8}$
R	Year-end effective reserves	$X_{t,9}$
A_s	Financial assets held by suppliers of secondary claims at beginning of year	$X_{t,12}$

Table 2.1.2

A Listing of Economic Premises

Proposition 2.1.1 (Consumer Primary-Saving Function)

(2.1.1a) $S_p(y,A,i_p,i_s,a) = \alpha_{10}+\alpha_{11}y+ \alpha_{12}A+\beta_3 i_p+ \beta_4 i_s+a$

where a denotes a random disturbance with mean and finite variance.

(2.1.1b) $E(a) = 0$ and

(2.1.1c) $E(a^2) = \omega_a 2$,

with

(2.1.1d-i) $-5 > \alpha_{10} > -10$,

$.05 > \alpha_{11} > .01$,

$.03 > \alpha_{12} > .01$,

$5 > \beta_3 > 3$,

$-2 > \beta_4 > -3$,

$4 > \omega_a 2 > 2$.

Proposition 2.1.2 (Primary-Saving-Of-Others Function)

(2.1.2a) $O_p(y,i_p,i_s,b) = \alpha_{13}+\alpha_{14}y+\beta_5 i_p+\beta_6 i_s+b$

where b denotes a random disturbance with mean and finite variance.

(2.1.2b) $E(b) = 0$ and

(2.1.2c) $E(b^2) = \omega_b 2$,

with

(2.1.2d-h) $-5 > \alpha_{13} > -10$,

$.05 > \alpha_{14} > .01$,

$5 > \beta_5 > 3$,

$-2 > \beta_6 > -3$,

$4 > \omega_b 2 > 2$.

<u>Proposition 2.1.3</u> (Supply of Primary Claims Function)

(2.1.3a) $I_p(y, i_p, c) = \alpha_{15} + \alpha_{16}y + \beta_7 i_p + c$

<u>where</u> c <u>denotes a random disturbance with mean and finite variance</u>,

(2.1.3b) $E(c) = 0$ <u>and</u>

$E(c^2) = \omega_c 2$,

<u>with</u>

(2.1.3d-g) $15 > \alpha_{15} > 10$,

$.3 > \alpha_{16} > .1$,

$-5 > \beta_7 > -13$,

$4 > \omega_c 2 > 2$.

<u>Proposition 2.1.4</u> (Consumer Secondary-Saving Function)

(2.1.4a) $S_s(y, A, i_p, i_s, d) = \alpha_{17} + \alpha_{18}y + \alpha_{19}A + \beta_8 i_p + \beta_9 i_s + d$

<u>where</u> d <u>denotes a random disturbance with mean and finite variance</u>.

(2.1.4b) $E(d) = 0$ <u>and</u>

(2.1.4c) $E(d^2) = \omega_d 2$,

<u>with</u>

(2.1.4d-i) $0 > \alpha_{17} > -5$,

$.06 > \alpha_{18} > .015$,

$-.01 > \alpha_{19} > -.03$,

$-2 > \beta_8 > -5$,

$6 > \beta_9 > 2$,

$4 > \omega_d 2 > 2$.

Proposition 2.1.5 (Secondary-Saving-Of-Others Function)

(2.1.5a) $O_s(y,i_p,i_s,e) = \alpha_{20}+\alpha_{21}y+\beta_{10}i_p+\beta_{11}i_s+e$

where e denotes a random disturbance with mean and finite variance.

(2.1.5b) $E(e) = 0$ and

(2.1.5c) $E(e^2) = \omega_e 2$,

with

(2.1.5d-h) $0 > \alpha_{20} > -5$,

$.02 > \alpha_{21} > .005$,

$-2 > \beta_{10} > -6$,

$7 > \beta_{11} > 3$,

$4 > \omega_e 2 > 2$.

Proposition 2.1.6 (Supply of Secondary Claims Function)

(2.1.6a) $I_s(A_s,i_p,i_s,f) = \alpha_{22}+\alpha_5 A_s+\beta_{12}i_p+\beta_{13}i_s+f$

where f denotes a random disturbance with mean and finite variance.

(2.1.6b) $E(f) = 0$ and

(2.1.6c) $E(f^2) = \omega_f 2$,

with

(2.1.6d-h) $10 > \alpha_{22} > 5$,

$.2 > \alpha_5 > .075$,

$4 > \beta_{12} > 2$,

$-5 > \beta_{13} > -8$,

$4 > \omega_f 2 > 2$.

<u>Proposition 2.1.7</u> (Liquidity-Preference-Of-Consumer Function)

(2.1.7a) $L_c(y,A,i_p,i_s,P,g) = \alpha_{24}+\alpha_{25}y+\alpha_{26}A+\beta_{14}i_p+\beta_{15}i_s+\beta_{16}P+g$

<u>where</u> g <u>denotes a random disturbance with mean and finite variance</u>.

(2.1.7b) $E(g) = 0$ <u>and</u>

(2.1.7c) $E(g^2) = \omega_g 2$,

<u>with</u>

(2.1.7d-j)

$30 > \alpha_{24} > 25$,

$.25 > \alpha_{25} > .20$,

$.005 > \alpha_{26} > .001$,

$-2 > \beta_{14} > -3$,

$-2 > \beta_{15} > -3$,

$1.0 > \beta_{16} > .5$,

$4 > \omega_g 2 > 2$.

<u>Proposition 2.1.8</u> (Liquidity-Preference-Of-Others Function)

(2.1.8a) $L_o(y,i_p,i_s,P,h) = \alpha_{29}+\alpha_{30}y+\beta_{17}i_p+\beta_{18}i_s+\beta_{19}P+h$

<u>where</u> h <u>denotes a random disturbance with mean and finite variance</u>.

(2.1.8b) $E(h) = 0$ <u>and</u>

(2.1.8c) $E(h^2) = \omega_h 2$,

<u>with</u>

(2.1.8d-i)

$30 > \alpha_{29} > 25$,

$.25 > \alpha_{30} > .05$,

$-2 > \beta_{17} > -3$,

$-2 > \beta_{18} > -3$,

$1.0 > \beta_{19} > .5$,

$4 > \omega_h 2 > 2$.

Proposition 2.1.9 (Supply of Money Function)

(2.1.9a) $M(R,i_p,i_s,j) = \alpha_{33}+\alpha_{37}R+\beta_{20}i_p+\beta_{21}i_s+j$

where j denotes a random disturbance with mean and finite variance.

(2.1.9b) $E(j) = 0$ and

(2.1.9c) $E(j^2) = \omega_j 2$,

with

(2.1.9d-h)
$$15 > \alpha_{33} > 10,$$
$$5 > \alpha_{37} > 3.5,$$
$$3 > \beta_{20} > .3,$$
$$-.4 > \beta_{21} > -4,$$
$$4 > \omega_j 2 > 2.$$

Proposition 2.1.10 (Stochastic Premise)

The random vectors

(2.1.10a) $n_t = (a_t,b_t,c_t,d_t,e_t,f_t,g_t,h_t,j_t)$

are independently and identically normally distributed with zero mean vector and non-singular covariance matrix of the form

(2.1.10b)
$$\Omega = \begin{bmatrix} \omega_a 2 & \omega_{ab} & \omega_{ac} & 0 & 0 & 0 & 0 & 0 & 0 \\ & \omega_b 2 & \omega_{bc} & 0 & 0 & 0 & 0 & 0 & 0 \\ & & \omega_c 2 & 0 & 0 & 0 & 0 & 0 & 0 \\ & & & \omega_d 2 & \omega_{de} & \omega_{df} & 0 & 0 & 0 \\ & & & & \omega_e 2 & \omega_{ef} & 0 & 0 & 0 \\ & & & & & \omega_f 2 & 0 & 0 & 0 \\ & & & & & & \omega_g 2 & \omega_{gh} & \omega_{gj} \\ & & & & & & & \omega_h 2 & \omega_{hj} \\ & & & & & & & & \omega_j 2 \end{bmatrix}$$

and

(2.1.10c-m) $5 > (\omega_c 2 + \omega_b 2 + \omega_a 2 - 2\omega_{cb} - 2\omega_{ca} + 2\omega_{ba}) > 2$

$5 > (\omega_f 2 + \omega_e 2 + \omega_d 2 - 2\omega_{fe} - 2\omega_{fd} + 2\omega_{ed}) > 2$

$5 > (\omega_g 2 + \omega_h 2 + \omega_j 2 + 2\omega_{gh} - 2\omega_{gj} - 2\omega_{hj}) > 2$

$0 > (\omega_{ac} - \omega_{ab} - \omega_a 2) > -2$

$0 > (\omega_{bc} - \omega_b 2 - \omega_{ab}) > -2$

$2 > (\omega_c 2 - \omega_{bc} - \omega_{ac}) > 0$

$0 > (\omega_{fd} - \omega_{ed} - \omega_d 2) > -2$

$0 > (\omega_{fe} - \omega_e 2 - \omega_{ed}) > -2$

$2 > (\omega_f 2 - \omega_{fe} - \omega_{fg}) > 0$

$2 > (\omega_g 2 + \omega_{gh} - \omega_{gj}) > 0$

$2 > (\omega_{gh} + \omega_h 2 - \omega_{hj}) > 0$

Proposition 2.1.11 (Domain Premise)

The preceding structural equations explain behavior only on the domain

(2.1.11a) t=1,...,19 or the years 1947 to 1965.

(2.1.11b-i) $A > 400$,

$750 > y > 200$,

$R > 5$,

$25 > G_p > -25$,

$A_s > 100$,

$8 > i_p > .5$,

$8 > i_s > .5$,

$200 > P > 50$.

of the procedure of collecting and constructing it.

Propositions 2.1.1 and 2.1.4 describe the behavior of the consumer sector in planning its primary and secondary saving flows, respectively. Since the sum of the two can be regarded as total consumer financial saving, it will be convenient to discuss them together.

Both intercepts, α_{10} (in 2.1.1) and α_{17} (in 2.1.4) are postulated to be negative. The respective coefficients of income, α_{11} and α_{18}, are hypothesized to be positive. This combination is suggested by the theory that the marginal propensity to save is greater than the average propensity to save.[4]

The range on the sum of α_{11} and α_{18} is $.11 > \alpha_{11} + \alpha_{18} > .025$. That is, the total marginal propensity to save with respect to national income is postulated to be between 2.5 percent and 11 percent for the consumer sector.

There is no definite hypothesis in this model that total consumer saving is a positive or a negative function of the stock assets they hold--i.e., $.02 > \alpha_{12} + \alpha_{19} > -.02$.[5] It does postulate that as the stock of their assets becomes larger, consumers will add increasing amounts to their primary asset holdings and decreasing amounts to their secondary asset holdings. With the negative coefficient of A in the demand for secondary shares function (2.1.4f), it is possible that if assets became large enough, secondary saving would become negative--in other words, consumers would be moving funds from secondary holdings into primary holdings. There are two reasons for this assumption: as assets grow larger: (1) the precautionary motive declines, and (2) consumers become more sophisticated in their portfolio management and look for ways to increase their financial earnings.

The model also does not postulate that total consumer saving is a positive or negative function of either market rate of interest. That is, the range on the sum of the interest coefficients varies from plus to minus: $3 > \beta_3 + \beta_8 > -2$, $4 > \beta_4 + \beta_9 > -1$. It does hypothesize how the allocation between the two types of saving will change, for example, when the primary rate, i_p, increases, primary saving increases, and secondary saving declines. Similarly, when the secondary rate, i_s, increases, secondary saving increases and primary saving declines.

Because of their different composition, it is not meaningful to discuss the behavior of O_p plus O_s as an aggregate behavioral function.

Proposition 2.1.2, primary saving of others, hypothesizes the same ranges both for the coefficients of y, i_p and i_s and for the constant term as those in proposition 2.1.1.[6] The assumption is that "others" respond to these variables in approximately the same manner as consumers.

Proposition 2.1.5, secondary saving of others, has similar ranges for the coefficients of i_p and i_s and the constant term as those in proposition 2.1.4. However, the upper and lower limits on the income coefficient, α_{21}, in 2.1.5 are lower than those on α_{18} in 2.1.4 (.02 to .005 in contrast to .06 to .015). The theory is that state and local governments and businesses hold secondary shares more as an alternative to demand deposits than as an earning asset.

Proposition 2.1.7 describes the behavior of the consumer sector in planning its liquidity preference, L_c.[7] The proposed positive ranges on the intercept, α_{24}, and the coefficient of income, α_{25}, are based on the theory that a given percentage increase in income causes a smaller percentage increase in liquidity preference. α_{25} is the hypothesized "Marshallian k," which is placed in the range of 1/4 to 1/5.

Since y is deflated and L_c is not, the price level must be taken into account. Given the range of β_{16}, if P (100 times the ratio of prices to the prices of 1958) increases by one, then the model hypothesizes consumer demand for liquidity will increase from 500 million to one billion.

The coefficient of assets in the L_c function is specified as positive and small: $.005 > \alpha_{26} > .001$. The hypothesis is that it takes from 1 to 5 million dollars worth of money to maintain a billion dollars worth of assets.

The model postulates that consumer liquidity preference is a negative function of each of the interest rates, i.e., $-2 > \beta_{14} > -3$ and $-2 > \beta_{15} > -3$.

The theory is that the interest rates are opportunity costs of holding money.

Proposition 2.1.8 describes the behavior of the other sectors in planning their liquidity preference. The ranges both on the coefficients of i_p, i_s, and P and on the intercept term are the same in Proposition 2.1.8, as those in Proposition 2.1.7. The lower bound on the coefficient of income in the former, α_{30}, is smaller than that of the latter's, α_{25}, reflecting the possibility that the other sectors (businesses, nonbank financial institutions, and state and local governments) may be more efficient in their use of money, i.e., an increase in income requires only a small increase in their money balances.

Proposition 2.1.3 describes the behavior of the suppliers of primary shares. This function is usually referred to in economic literature as the investment demand equation. 2.1.3 is similar to the usual textbook statement of this equation.[9]

Proposition 2.1.6 describes the behavior of the suppliers of secondary shares. Their motive in selling secondary shares, or borrowing, is to obtain funds to loan at the primary rate. Therefore, the model postulates that I_s is a positive function of i_p and a negative of i_s (the cost of the borrowing). Income is not included in this equation since, in isolation, a change in income has no effect on the suppliers' profits. The other variable in this structural equation is financial assets held by the suppliers of secondary shares at the beginning of each period, A_s. The positive range on its coefficient, α_5, postulates that there are economies of scale within these institutions.

With the exception of the currency component, the supply of money is set by the commercial banks.[11] The banks create money by making loans. In Proposition 2.1.9 the money supply is postulated to be a positive function of effective reserves, R, and the primary rate of interest, i_p, and a negative function of the secondary rate of interest, i_s. The banks make loans at the primary rate, so if it increases they could make loans that previously had not been profitable. Since secondary savings (time deposits in this case) are a source of funds to loan, the stated coefficient of the secondary rate,

β_{21}, has a negative range. The range on the intercept ($15 > \alpha_{33} > 10$) is hypothesized partially to account for the fact that in creating money the banks add to the money (currency) already in existence.

2.2 The Simultaneous Equations Model

The structural equations presented in Section 2.2 describe economic behavior in isolation. In order to simulate a part of the American economy, these separate structural relationships are combined by an additional proposition about market mechanisms. This additional proposition is called the simultaneous equation model.

Proposition 2.2.1 (Simultaneous Equation Model)

For every annual period t, given that the background conditions remain constant, $z_{t,i}$ (i=3,...,14) are jointly determined by $X_{t,j}$ (j=4,6,8,9,12) according to the following system of equations.

$$[S_p(A,y,i_p,i_s,a)+O_p(y,i_p,i_s,b)-I_p(y,i_p,c) - G_p] = 0 \quad (2.2.1a)$$

$$[S_p(A,y,i_p,i_s,a) - S_p] = 0 \quad (2.2.1b)$$

$$[O_p(y,i_p,i_s,b) - O_p] = 0 \quad (2.2.1c)$$

$$[I_p(y,i_p,c) - I_p] = 0 \quad (2.2.1d)$$

$$[S_s(A,y,i_p,i_s,d)+O_s(y,i_p,i_s,e) - I_s(A_s,i_p,i_s,f)] = 0 \quad (2.2.1e)$$

$$[S_s(A,y,i_p,i_s,d) - S_s] = 0 \quad (2.2.1f)$$

$$[O_s(y,i_p,i_s,e) - O_s] = 0 \quad (2.2.1g)$$

$$[I_s(A_s,i_p,i_s,f) - I_s] = 0 \quad (2.2.1h)$$

$$[L_c(A,y,i_p,i_s,P,g]+L_o(y,i_p,i_s,P,h) - M(R,i_p,i_s,j)] = 0 \quad (2.2.1i)$$

$$[L_c(A,y,i_p,i_s,P,g) - L_c] = 0 \quad (2.2.1j)$$

(2.2.1k) $[L_o(y,i_p,i_s,P,h) - L_o] = 0$

(2.2.1l) $[M(R,i_p,i_s,j) - M] = 0$

where

$S_p = Z_{t,3}$ $A = X_{t,4}$ $a = a_t$

$O_p = Z_{t,4}$ $G_p = X_{t,6}$ $b = b_t$

$I_p = Z_{t,5}$ $y = X_{t,8}$ $c = c_t$

$S_s = Z_{t,6}$ $R = X_{t,9}$ $d = d_t$

$O_s = Z_{t,7}$ $A_s = X_{t,12}$ $e = e_t$

$I_s = Z_{t,8}$ $f = f_t$

$L_c = Z_{t,9}$ $g = g_t$

$L_o = Z_{t,10}$ $h = h_t$

$M = Z_{t,11}$ $j = j_t$

$P = Z_{t,12}$

$i_p = Z_{t,13}$

$i_s = Z_{t,14}$

Equation (2.2.1a) asserts that for every annual period under study (1947 to 1965) the excess demand for primary shares is equal to zero. In other words, given the net supply by the government (G_p), the purchasers (consumers and others) interact with the private suppliers to cause the market to clear. Equation (2.2.1e) asserts that for every annual period the excess demand for secondary shares equals zero, and equation (2.2.1i) asserts that at the <u>end</u> of every annual period the excess demand for money is zero. i_p, i_s, and P are the hypothesized clearing "prices" in each of these markets and determine the equilibrium point. Equations (2.2.1b-d, f-h, j-l) assert that for every annual period the respective functions, evaluated at the observations of their arguments, are equal to their observed values.[12]

2.3 The Stability Conditions

To aid in the present discussion as well as to reduce the unwieldiness of the reduced form solution in section 3.2, the following notations are introduced:

(2.3.1a) $\Theta = (\beta_3 + \beta_5 - \beta_7)$

(2.3.1b) $\Omega = (\beta_4 + \beta_6)$

(2.3.1c) $\Psi = (\beta_8 + \beta_{10} - \beta_{12})$

(2.3.1d) $\phi = (\beta_9 + \beta_{11} - \beta_{13})$

(2.3.1e) $F = (\beta_{20} - \beta_{17} - \beta_{14})$

(2.3.1f) $G = (\beta_{21} - \beta_{18} - \beta_{15})$

Equations 2.2.1a, 2.2.1e, and 2.2.1i are now rewritten in the following form:

(2.3.2a) $\Theta i_p + \Omega i_s + k_1 = 0,$

(2.3.2e) $\Psi i_p + \phi i_s + k_2 = 0,$

(2.3.2i) $-Fi_p - Gi_s + (\beta_{16} + \beta_{19})P + k_3 = 0$

where k_1, k_2, and k_3 represent all of the exogenous variables and the disturbance terms of the respective equations. The advantage of this form is that it facilitates discussion of the stability conditions.

It is easily seen that the interaction of the two saving markets determines the equilibrium values of the two interest rates independent of the money market and the price level.[13] The levels of the interest rates are exogenous to the money market where the price level is determined.

The stability of the model, therefore, depends on the values of the coefficients of the interest rates in the saving markets.

Rewriting 2.3.2a and 2.3.2e as

(2.3.3a) $i_p = -\frac{\Omega}{\theta} i_s - \frac{k_1}{\theta}$, and

(2.3.3e) $i_p = -\frac{\Phi}{\Psi} i_s - \frac{k_2}{\Psi}$,

gives the equations of the lines in Figure 2.3.1.

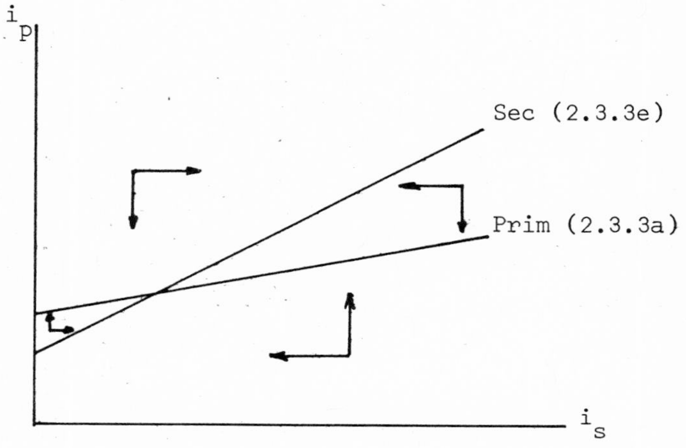

Figure 2.3.1

Where Sec is the schedule of equilibrium points of the two interest rates that equates the demand for the supply of secondary saving shares. And where Prim is the schedule of equilibrium points that equate the demand for and the supply of primary saving shares.

With the help of the economic premises listed in Table 2.1.2 the following proposition is deduced.

Proposition 2.3.1 *The slope of* Sec *is greater than the slope of* Prim; *more precisely*:

(2.3.4) $\frac{7}{2} > -\frac{\Phi}{\Psi} > \frac{2}{3} > \frac{6}{11} > \frac{\Omega}{\theta} > \frac{4}{23}$.

2.3.4 is a necessary condition for stability of the model. This is because points above the Sec schedule move to the right to return to equilibrium, and those below move to the left; however, points above the Prim schedule move down to return to equilibrium and those below move up. If the slopes were reversed the system would be unstable as the path would be away from the intersection of the two curves.

3. Mathematical Analysis of the Model

The structural equations presented in Section 2 postulate planned behavior in isolation. No propositions have been presented predicting how the endogenous variables are determined for a given set of exogenous variables. This is done with a maintained hypothesis.

3.1 The Maintained Hypothesis

Proposition 3.1.1 For every annual period $t=1,\ldots,19$ if the background conditions remain constant, then the mechanism that determines $Z_{t,3},\ldots,Z_{t,14}$ can be represented by the following invariant system of regression equations.[14]

$$Z_{t,3} = \bar{\lambda}_{31}X_{t,4} + \bar{\lambda}_{32}X_{t,6} + \bar{\lambda}_{33}X_{t,8} + \bar{\lambda}_{35}X_{t,12} + \bar{\lambda}_{36} + \bar{\eta}_{t,3} \tag{3.1.1a}$$

$$Z_{t,4} = \bar{\lambda}_{41}X_{t,4} + \bar{\lambda}_{42}X_{t,6} + \bar{\lambda}_{43}X_{t,8} + \bar{\lambda}_{45}X_{t,12} + \bar{\lambda}_{46} + \bar{\eta}_{t,4} \tag{3.1.1b}$$

$$Z_{t,5} = \bar{\lambda}_{51}X_{t,4} + \bar{\lambda}_{52}X_{t,6} + \bar{\lambda}_{53}X_{t,8} + \bar{\lambda}_{55}X_{t,12} + \bar{\lambda}_{56} + \bar{\eta}_{t,5} \tag{3.1.1c}$$

$$Z_{t,6} = \bar{\lambda}_{61}X_{t,4} + \bar{\lambda}_{62}X_{t,6} + \bar{\lambda}_{63}X_{t,8} + \bar{\lambda}_{65}X_{t,12} + \bar{\lambda}_{66} + \bar{\eta}_{t,6} \tag{3.1.1d}$$

$$Z_{t,7} = \bar{\lambda}_{71}X_{t,4} + \bar{\lambda}_{72}X_{t,6} + \bar{\lambda}_{73}X_{t,8} + \bar{\lambda}_{75}X_{t,12} + \bar{\lambda}_{76} + \bar{\eta}_{t,7} \tag{3.1.1e}$$

$$Z_{t,8} = \bar{\lambda}_{81}X_{t,4} + \bar{\lambda}_{82}X_{t,6} + \bar{\lambda}_{83}X_{t,8} + \bar{\lambda}_{85}X_{t,12} + \bar{\lambda}_{86} + \bar{\eta}_{t.8} \tag{3.1.1f}$$

$$Z_{t,9} = \bar{\lambda}_{91}X_{t,4} + \bar{\lambda}_{92}X_{t,6} + \bar{\lambda}_{93}X_{t,8} + \bar{\lambda}_{94}X_{t,9} + \bar{\lambda}_{95}X_{t,12} + \bar{\lambda}_{96} + \bar{\eta}_{t,9} \tag{3.1.1g}$$

$$Z_{t,10} = \bar{\lambda}_{101}X_{t,4} + \bar{\lambda}_{102}X_{t,6} + \bar{\lambda}_{103}X_{t,8} + \bar{\lambda}_{104}X_{t,9} + \bar{\lambda}_{105}X_{t,12} + \bar{\lambda}_{106} + \bar{\eta}_{t,10} \tag{3.1.1h}$$

$$Z_{t,11} = \bar{\lambda}_{111}X_{t,4} + \bar{\lambda}_{112}X_{t,6} + \bar{\lambda}_{113}X_{t,8} + \bar{\lambda}_{114}X_{t,9} + \bar{\lambda}_{115}X_{t,12} + \bar{\lambda}_{116} + \bar{\eta}_{t,11} \tag{3.1.1i}$$

$$Z_{t,12} = \bar{\lambda}_{121}X_{t,4} + \bar{\lambda}_{122}X_{t,6} + \bar{\lambda}_{123}X_{t,8} + \bar{\lambda}_{124}X_{t,9} + \bar{\lambda}_{125}X_{t,12} + \bar{\lambda}_{126} + \bar{\eta}_{t,12} \tag{3.1.1j}$$

$$Z_{t,13} = \bar{\lambda}_{131}X_{t,4} + \bar{\lambda}_{132}X_{t,6} + \bar{\lambda}_{133}X_{t,8} + \bar{\lambda}_{135}X_{t,12} + \bar{\lambda}_{136} + \bar{\eta}_{t,13} \tag{3.1.1k}$$

$$Z_{t,14} = \bar{\lambda}_{141}X_{t,4} + \bar{\lambda}_{142}X_{t,6} + \bar{\lambda}_{143}X_{t,8} + \bar{\lambda}_{145}X_{t,12} + \bar{\lambda}_{146} + \bar{\eta}_{t,14} \tag{3.1.1ℓ}$$

and where the vectors

$$\bar{\eta}_{t\cdot} = (\bar{\eta}_{t,3},\ldots,\bar{\eta}_{t,14})$$

are identically normally distributed with

(3.1.2) $E(\bar{\eta}_{t\cdot}) = 0$

and covariance matrix

(3.1.3) $\sum = [\bar{\sigma}_{h,i}] \qquad h,i=3,\ldots,14$

also

(3.1.4a) $Z_{t,5} = Z_{t,4} + Z_{t,3} - X_{t,6}$

(3.1.4b) $Z_{t,8} = Z_{t,7} + Z_{t,6}$

(3.1.4c) $Z_{t,11} = Z_{t,10} + Z_{t,9}$

The addition of (3.1.4a-*c*) produces 16 dependencies among the λ's, e.g., $\bar{\lambda}_{51} = \bar{\lambda}_{41} + \bar{\lambda}_{31}$ and $\bar{\lambda}_{52} = \bar{\lambda}_{42} + \bar{\lambda}_{32} - 1$, and 33 dependencies among the σ's, e.g., $\bar{\sigma}_{5,5} = \bar{\sigma}_{3,3} + \bar{\sigma}_{4,4} + 2\bar{\sigma}_{3,4}$ and $\bar{\sigma}_{5,3} = \bar{\sigma}_{3,3} + \bar{\sigma}_{4,3}$. The reason for the redundancy is explained in section 3.4.

An additional part of the maintained hypothesis is that: *the vectors*

$$\bar{\eta}^{*}_{t\cdot} = (\bar{\eta}_{t,3}, \bar{\eta}_{t,4}, \bar{\eta}_{t,6}, \bar{\eta}_{t,7}, \bar{\eta}_{t,9}, \bar{\eta}_{t,10}, \bar{\eta}_{t,12}, \bar{\eta}_{t,13}, \bar{\eta}_{t,14})$$

are independently distributed, *and the covariance matrix*

$$\sum^{*} = [\bar{\sigma}_{h,i}] \qquad h,i = 3,4,6,7,9,10,12,13,14$$

is non-singular.

The maintained hypothesis has 142 parameters: 64 regression coefficients and 78 variances and covariances. To define a test space, these parameters are regarded as the coordinates of a definite but unknown point ($\bar{\lambda}$) in a 142 dimensional Euclidean space which will be called the λ space. The axes of this space are labeled $\lambda_{31},\ldots,\lambda_{146}$, $\sigma_{3,3},\ldots,$ $\sigma_{13,14}$. The point $\overline{\lambda}$ falls into a 93 dimensional subspace of λ because of the 49 dependencies produced by (3.1.4a-c).

The point estimate of $\overline{\lambda}$ is the unconstrained maximum likelihood estimate of the 142 parameters. This estimate will be called $\hat{\lambda}$. It is a useful estimate if it can test a meaningful prediction about what its value should be. One meaningful prediction (and the one germane to this paper) is derived from the set of structural propositions presented in Section 2.

3.2 The Reduced Form

To derive this prediction it is necessary to solve for the reduced form, which is a set of functions defining a point in the space, given the values of the β's, α's, and ω's. This is solving for the Z's in terms of X's in (2.2.1a-l)

The reduced form will not be given here to conserve space.[16] It should be realized that most of the terms are quite complicated. For example:

$$(3.2.1)\quad \lambda_{31} = \alpha_{12} + \frac{\beta_3[(\beta_9+\beta_{11}-\beta_{13})\alpha_{12}-(\beta_4+\beta_6)\alpha_{19}] + \beta_4[(\beta_3+\beta_5-\beta_7)\alpha_{19}-(\beta_8+\beta_{10}-\beta_{12})\alpha_{12}]}{\Delta},$$

where

$$(3.2.2)\quad \Delta = (\Psi\Omega-\Phi\Theta)$$

The reduced form gives the coordinates of an unknown point in the λ space. This point is defined in terms of 58 parameters (β's, α's, and ω's). From this it follows that a 58 dimensional subspace, which will be called the λ^{β} space, can be defined that includes this unknown point. Since (2.2.1a), (2.2.1e), and (2.2.1i) place the same restrictions on the structural equations as (3.1.4a-c) place on the regression equations, the subspace λ^{β} is inside the 93 dimensional subspace referred to above. Because of its 58 dimensional property, the λ^{β} space satisfies an additional 35 dependencies within the λ space. Therefore, part of the test of the structural propositions is whether or not the estimate $\hat{\lambda}$ satisfies these 35 dependencies--i.e., is in the λ^{β} space.[17]

3.3 The Identifiability Conditions

Of the 35 dependencies satisfied by λ^{β} space, 27 deal with the σ's, and the other 8 with the λ's. These latter 8 are the only ones to be tested this paper in the form stated in the following proposition.[18]

__Proposition 3.3.1__ __The regression coefficients $\lambda_{i,j}$ in equations 3.1.1a-1 satisfy the following equations__[19]

(3.3.1a)

$$\begin{vmatrix} \bar{\lambda}_{41} & \bar{\lambda}_{131} & \bar{\lambda}_{141} \\ \bar{\lambda}_{42} & \bar{\lambda}_{132} & \bar{\lambda}_{142} \\ \bar{\lambda}_{45} & \bar{\lambda}_{135} & \bar{\lambda}_{145} \end{vmatrix} = 0$$

(3.3.1b)

$$\text{rank} \begin{bmatrix} \bar{\lambda}_{51} & \bar{\lambda}_{131} \\ \bar{\lambda}_{52} & \bar{\lambda}_{132} \\ \bar{\lambda}_{55} & \bar{\lambda}_{135} \end{bmatrix} = 1$$

(3.3.1c)

$$\begin{vmatrix} \bar{\lambda}_{71} & \bar{\lambda}_{131} & \bar{\lambda}_{141} \\ \bar{\lambda}_{72} & \bar{\lambda}_{132} & \bar{\lambda}_{142} \\ \bar{\lambda}_{74} & \bar{\lambda}_{135} & \bar{\lambda}_{145} \end{vmatrix} = 0$$

(3.3.1d)
$$\begin{vmatrix} \bar\lambda_{81} & \bar\lambda_{131} & \bar\lambda_{141} \\ \bar\lambda_{82} & \bar\lambda_{132} & \bar\lambda_{142} \\ \bar\lambda_{83} & \bar\lambda_{133} & \bar\lambda_{143} \end{vmatrix} = 0$$

(3.3.1e)
$$\begin{vmatrix} \bar\lambda_{101} & \bar\lambda_{121} & \bar\lambda_{131} & \bar\lambda_{141} \\ \bar\lambda_{102} & \bar\lambda_{122} & \bar\lambda_{132} & \bar\lambda_{142} \\ \bar\lambda_{104} & \bar\lambda_{124} & 0 & 0 \\ \bar\lambda_{105} & \bar\lambda_{125} & \bar\lambda_{135} & \bar\lambda_{145} \end{vmatrix} = 0$$

(3.3.1f)
$$\text{rank} \begin{bmatrix} \bar\lambda_{111} & \bar\lambda_{131} & \bar\lambda_{141} \\ \bar\lambda_{112} & \bar\lambda_{132} & \bar\lambda_{142} \\ \bar\lambda_{113} & \bar\lambda_{133} & \bar\lambda_{143} \\ \bar\lambda_{115} & \bar\lambda_{135} & \bar\lambda_{145} \end{bmatrix} = 2$$

3.4 A Weaker Hypothesis on the λ Space

So far it has been shown that the structural propositions predict that $\bar\lambda$ is in a 58 dimensional subspace of the λ space. Additional predictions can be derived, however, from the ranges postulated on the β's, α's, and ω's. Under the condition of the following proposition, those ranges will map into a bounded subset of the λ space by substitution in the reduced form equations. This subset will be called λ^{β^*}.

Proposition 3.4.1. The term $(\beta_{16} + \beta_{19})\Delta$ (the common denominator in the reduced form) does not vanish if the parameters in it are in the ranges predicted in the structural premises: more precisely,

(3.4.1) $-20 > (\beta_{16} + \beta_{19})\Delta > -918.$[20]

The $\lambda^{\beta*}$ space specifies the exact subspace of the λ space that the structural propositions predict $\bar{\lambda}$ to be in. Thus $\lambda^{\beta*}$ is called the strict hypothesis that is to be tested against the unrestricted alternative hypothesis $(\lambda - \lambda^{\beta*})$.

The shape of $\lambda^{\beta*}$ is an extremely complicated figure and without computer techniques (yet to be created) it is impossible to define. Therefore, to test the model at this stage a weaker hypothesis $\lambda^{\beta\prime}$ is defined as the 58 dimensional rectangular set such that $\lambda^{\beta*} \subset \lambda^{\beta\prime}$ and $\lambda^{\beta\prime}$ "just" contains $\lambda^{\beta*}$ in the sense that the sides of $\lambda^{\beta\prime}$ contain the infima and suprema of the $\lambda^{\beta*}$ in each coordinate direction. If the weaker hypothesis is rejected, then the strict hypothesis is likewise rejected. The ranges of the 64 regression coefficients and the 12 variances listed in Table 3.4.1 were constructed with a desk calculator by trial and error method.

By inspection of Table 3.4.1 it becomes clear why all the endogenous variables are listed in proposition 3.1.1. It can be seen that even though some λ's are linear combinations of two others (via 3.1.4a-c), the infima and suprema of these λ's may not be. For example, $\bar{\lambda}_{114} = \bar{\lambda}_{94} + \bar{\lambda}_{104}$ and in the reduced form,[21]

$$\alpha_{37} = \frac{\beta_{16}\alpha_{37}}{(\beta_{16} + \beta_{19})} + \frac{\beta_{19}\alpha_{37}}{(\beta_{16} + \beta_{19})},$$

but the suprema of λ_{104}, 3.33, plus the suprema of λ_{94}, 3.33, do not add up to the suprema of λ_{114}, 5.0. The reason for this is that the values of the parameters which set λ_{94} at its suprema will constrain λ_{104} so that it is less than its suprema. That is, λ_{94} is at the value 3.33 when $\alpha_{37} = 5$, $\beta_{16} = 1$, and $\beta_{19} = .5$, but for these values $\lambda_{104} = 1.67$.

By listing all three ranges it is possible to find a rejection of the weaker hypothesis that might not have been found by checking for agreement or disagreement with only two of the ranges. For

Table 3.4.1

The Weaker Hypothesis $\lambda^{\beta'}$

(Infima and Suprema of Regression Parameters Admissible Under Structural Premises)

	$.045 >$	λ_{31}	$> -.005$
	$.383 >$	λ_{32}	$> -.750$
(3.4.1a-e)	$.110 >$	λ_{33}	$> -.185$
	$-.000309 >$	λ_{35}	$> -.150$
	$7.363 >$	λ_{36}	> -51.250
	$.015 >$	λ_{41}	$> -.015$
	$.383 >$	λ_{42}	$> -.750$
(3.4.2a-e)	$.110 >$	λ_{43}	$> -.185$
	$-.000309 >$	λ_{45}	$> -.150$
	$7.363 >$	λ_{46}	> -51.250
	$.060 >$	λ_{51}	$> -.020$
	$-.361 >$	λ_{52}	> -2.500
(3.4.3a-e)	$.420 >$	λ_{53}	$> -.370$
	$-.00515 >$	λ_{55}	$> -.300$
	$2.440 >$	λ_{56}	> -102.500
	$.016 >$	λ_{61}	$> -.032$
	$.537 >$	λ_{62}	> -1.000
(3.4.4a-e)	$.092 >$	λ_{63}	$> -.257$
	$.132 >$	λ_{65}	$> -.080$
	$28.650 >$	λ_{66}	> -48.000

Table 3.4.1 (Continued)

$$.017 > \lambda_{71} > -.015$$
$$.557 > \lambda_{72} > -.750$$
(3.4.5a-e) $$.008 > \lambda_{73} > -.401$$
$$.738 > \lambda_{75} > -.030$$
$$29.290 > \lambda_{76} > -34.250$$

$$.037 > \lambda_{81} > -.029$$
$$.213 > \lambda_{82} > -1.750$$
(3.4.6a-e) $$.124 > \lambda_{83} > -.459$$
$$.150 > \lambda_{85} > -.110$$
$$5.904 > \lambda_{86} > -82.250$$

$$.025 > \lambda_{91} > -.058$$
$$2.467 > \lambda_{92} > -2.616$$
$$.709 > \lambda_{93} > -.225$$
(3.4.7a-f) $$3.333 > \lambda_{94} > 1.167$$
$$.317 > \lambda_{95} > -.367$$
$$121.667 > \lambda_{96} > -98.608$$

$$.023 > \lambda_{101} > -.058$$
$$2.467 > \lambda_{102} > -2.616$$
(3.4.8a-f) $$.609 > \lambda_{103} > -.275$$
$$3.333 > \lambda_{104} > 1.167$$
$$.317 > \lambda_{105} > -.367$$
$$121.667 > \lambda_{106} > -98.608$$

Table 3.4.1 (Continued)

(3.4.9a-f)	.064 >	λ_{111} >	-.029
	1.200 >	λ_{112} >	-2.850
	.756 >	λ_{113} >	-.322
	5.000 >	λ_{114} >	3.500
	.135 >	λ_{115} >	-.422
	70.600 >	λ_{116} >	-131.950
(3.4.10a-f)	.084 >	λ_{121} >	-.209
	8.700 >	λ_{122} >	.098
	2.070 >	λ_{123} >	-.962
	5.000 >	λ_{124} >	1.750
	1.156 >	λ_{125} >	.0014
	385.660 >	λ_{126} >	-45.878
(3.4.11a-e)	.004 >	λ_{131} >	-.012
	.500 >	λ_{132} >	.046
	.134 >	λ_{133} >	-.024
	.060 >	λ_{135} >	.000654
	23.500 >	λ_{136} >	.959
(3.4.12a-e)	.009 >	λ_{141} >	-.017
	.750 >	λ_{142} >	-.013
	.199 >	λ_{143} >	-.044
	.110 >	λ_{145} >	.004
	37.250 >	λ_{146} >	.512

Table 3.4.1 (Continued)

(3.4.13a-1)

$$12.625 > \sigma_{3,3} > 1.278$$

$$12.625 > \sigma_{4,4} > 1.278$$

$$46.500 > \sigma_{5,5} > .354$$

$$11.400 > \sigma_{6,6} > 1.028$$

$$20.150 > \sigma_{7,7} > .889$$

$$31.325 > \sigma_{8,8} > .760$$

$$345.060 > \sigma_{9,9} > .287$$

$$345.060 > \sigma_{10,10} > .287$$

$$23.700 > \sigma_{11,11} > 2.003$$

$$549.790 > \sigma_{12,12} > .520$$

$$1.700 > \sigma_{13,13} > .00434$$

$$4.325 > \sigma_{14,14} > .00536$$

example (only) an estimate $\hat{\lambda}_{94} = 3.7$, $\hat{\lambda}_{104} = 1.2$, and $\hat{\lambda}_{114} = 4.9$ is outside the admissible range on λ_{94}; $\hat{\lambda}_{94} = 1.2$, $\hat{\lambda}_{104} = 3.7$, and $\hat{\lambda}_{114} = 4.9$ is outside the admissible range on λ_{104}; and $\hat{\lambda}_{94} = 3.0$, $\hat{\lambda}_{104} = 3.0$, and $\lambda_{114} = 6.0$ is outside the admissible range on λ_{114}.

4. Empirical Test and Results

This section focuses on the estimate ($\hat{\lambda}$) as it is used to test the identifiability conditions (3.3.1a-f) and the weaker hypothesis exhibited in Table 3.4.1. The actual computation of the estimate was done on the Purdue IBM 7094 computer, using a program written by Clee L. Childress entitled _7094 Econometric Model Program--Version 2_.[22] This program also provided the identifiability test statistics and the GCL estimates of the structural coefficients.

Because of the size limitation of the program, the estimations necessitated two separate runs. The first run estimated equations (2.1.1a) through (2.1.6a) and the second (2.1.7a) through (2.1.9a). For this reason the estimates of the relevant covariances are missing. The data used are found in Table A.1.1 and Table A.1.2.

In equations (4.1.1a-1) the number shown in parentheses below each coefficient is its estimated finite sample standard deviation. The numbers to the right of equations (4.1.1a-1) are the corresponding square roots of multiple correlation coefficients, corrected for degrees of freedom.

4.1 The Estimate of $\overline{\lambda}$

Table 4.1.1

$$(4.1.1a)\quad Z_{t,3} = \underset{(.0210)}{.03083}X_{t,4} - \underset{(.0986)}{.0945}X_{t,6} + \underset{(.0438)}{.0778}X_{t,8} - \underset{(.0383)}{.08650}X_{t,12} - \underset{(9.95)}{18.66} + \hat{\eta}_{t,3} \qquad R = .372$$

$$(4.1.1b)\quad Z_{t,4} = -\underset{(.0525)}{.03099}X_{t,4} + \underset{(.2462)}{.5628}X_{t,6} + \underset{(.1093)}{.0989}X_{t,8} + \underset{(.0956)}{.09170}X_{t,12} - \underset{(24.85)}{11.51} + \hat{\eta}_{t,4} \qquad R = .930$$

$$(4.1.1c)\quad Z_{t,5} = -\underset{(.0528)}{.00015}X_{t,4} - \underset{(.2480)}{.5316}X_{t,6} + \underset{(.1100)}{.1767}X_{t,8} + \underset{(.0961)}{.00517}X_{t,12} - \underset{(24.99)}{30.17} + \hat{\eta}_{t,5} \qquad R = .889$$

$$(4.1.1d)\quad Z_{t,6} = -\underset{(.0174)}{.00753}X_{t,4} + \underset{(.0816)}{.1119}X_{t,6} + \underset{(.0362)}{.0100}X_{t,8} + \underset{(.0317)}{.05161}X_{t,12} - \underset{(8.24)}{4.39} + \hat{\eta}_{t,6} \qquad R = .961$$

$$(4.1.1e)\quad Z_{t,7} = -\underset{(.0117)}{.02958}X_{t,4} - \underset{(.0548)}{.0182}X_{t,6} - \underset{(.0244)}{.0354}X_{t,8} + \underset{(.0213)}{.07768}X_{t,12} + \underset{(5.53)}{9.93} + \hat{\eta}_{t,7} \qquad R = .855$$

$$(4.1.1f)\quad Z_{t,8} = -\underset{(.0261)}{.03710}X_{t,4} + \underset{(.1224)}{.0937}X_{t,6} - \underset{(.0544)}{.0254}X_{t,8} + \underset{(.0475)}{.12929}X_{t,12} + \underset{(12.35)}{5.54} + \hat{\eta}_{t,8} \qquad R = .949$$

$$(4.1.1g)\quad Z_{t,9} = -\underset{(.0215)}{.03704}X_{t,4} - \underset{(.1100)}{.2230}X_{t,6} + \underset{(.0625)}{.1642}X_{t,8} - \underset{(1.196)}{.832}X_{t,9} + \underset{(.0393)}{.05486}X_{t,12} + \underset{(12.89)}{29.07} + \hat{\eta}_{t,9} \qquad R = .962$$

$$(4.1.1h)\quad Z_{t,10} = \underset{(.0138)}{.00682}X_{t,4} + \underset{(.0707)}{.1397}X_{t,6} - \underset{(.0402)}{.0395}X_{t,8} + \underset{(.769)}{4.462}X_{t,9} + \underset{(.0252)}{.00368}X_{t,12} - \underset{(8.29)}{3.54} + \hat{\eta}_{t,10} \qquad R = .988$$

$$(4.1.1i)\quad Z_{t,11} = -\underset{(.0201)}{.03023}X_{t,4} - \underset{(.1028)}{.0833}X_{t,6} + \underset{(.0584)}{.1246}X_{t,8} + \underset{(1.118)}{3.630}X_{t,9} + \underset{(.0367)}{.05854}X_{t,12} + \underset{(12.04)}{25.53} + \hat{\eta}_{t,11} \qquad R = .992$$

$$(4.1.1j)\quad Z_{t,12} = \underset{(.0205)}{.02587}X_{t,4} + \underset{(.1048)}{.0988}X_{t,6} - \underset{(.0595)}{.0405}X_{t,8} + \underset{(1.140)}{3.176}X_{t,9} + \underset{(.0374)}{.00645}X_{t,12} + \underset{(12.28)}{28.26} + \hat{\eta}_{t,12} \qquad R = .980$$

$$(4.1.1k)\quad Z_{t,13} = \underset{(.0021)}{.00078}X_{t,4} + \underset{(.0098)}{.0057}X_{t,6} + \underset{(.0044)}{.0001}X_{t,8} - \underset{(.0038)}{.00112}X_{t,12} + \underset{(.99)}{3.62} + \hat{\eta}_{t,13} \qquad R = -0.23$$

$$(4.1.1\ell)\quad Z_{t,14} = \underset{(.0011)}{.00129}X_{t,4} + \underset{(.0052)}{.0101}X_{t,6} - \underset{(.003)}{.0032}X_{t,8} + \underset{(.0020)}{.00523}X_{t,12} + \underset{(.52)}{.95} + \hat{\eta}_{t,14} \qquad R = .990$$

$$\underset{(h,i=1,\ldots,14)}{\left[\hat{\sigma}_{h,i}\right]} = \begin{bmatrix} 5.05 & -2.35 & 2.70 & -1.20 & -2.05 & -3.25 & & & & & -.066 & -.075 \\ & 31.53 & 29.17 & 1.20 & 1.12 & 2.32 & & & & & -.187 & -.246 \\ & & 31.88 & .0017 & -.93 & -.93 & & & & & -.253 & -.321 \\ & & & 3.46 & 1.38 & 4.85 & & & & & -.179 & .046 \\ & & & & 1.56 & 2.95 & & & & & -.018 & .012 \\ & & & & & 7.79 & & & & & -.161 & .058 \\ & & & & & & 5.27 & -1.43 & 3.85 & -2.82 & & \\ & & & & & & & 2.18 & .75 & 1.97 & & \\ & & & & & & & & 4.60 & -.86 & & \\ & & & & & & & & & 4.79 & & \\ & & & & & & & & & & .050 & .003 \\ & & & & & & & & & & & .014 \end{bmatrix} \qquad (4.1.2)$$

4.2 Test of the Identifiability Relations

The six identifiability conditions (3.3.1a-f) are the result of various exclusions and inclusions of variables from the six structural equations (2.1.2a), (2.1.3a), (2.1.5a), (2.1.6a), (2.1.8a), and (2.1.9a). More specifically, in each of these equations $K_2 - G_\Delta + 1$ is greater than zero, where K_2 is the number of exogenous variables excluded from the equation and G_Δ is the number of endogenous variables included in the equation. The test statistic (for 3.3.1a-f) is called the identifiability test statistic or $\overline{F}$ statistic.

The distribution of the $\overline{F}$ statistic can be approximated by the Snedecor's F. How close this approximation is depends on the value of the concentration parameter.[23]

The concentration parameters for the six $\overline{F}$ statistics from this model have not been derived because of their complexity. Therefore in testing this model Snedecor's F is used with the knowledge that until further analysis is carried out it is not known how close the distribution of the test statistic is approximated.

In testing the identifiability conditions, a 5 percent critical region is used: i.e., $\overline{F}$ > Snedecor's $F_{.95}$ (m,n), where m, the numerator's degrees of freedom, is equal to $(K_2 + G_\Delta + 1)$ and n, the denominator's degree of freedom, is equal to (N-K), with N equal to the number of observations and K equal to the total number of exogenous variables used in the estimation.[24] The $\overline{F}$ statistics calculated by the computer are presented in Table 4.2.1 along with corresponding value of Snedecor's F.

The results presented in Table 4.2.1 show that under this test it cannot be claimed that restrictions (3.3.2a-f) are not in good agreement with the observations.

4.3 Direct Analysis of Regression Estimates

By comparing the estimates exhibited in Table 4.1.1 with the weaker hypothesis $\lambda^{\beta\prime}$ in Table 3.4.1, it is observed that 11 of the 64 λ's and one of the 12 variances have estimates that fall outside of their predicted range. The next step is to compute the probability of observing these 12 estimates, given that the true values are in the

Table 4.2.1

Identifiability Test Statistics

	Test Statistic (F)	Condition	Snedecor's F
(4.2.1a)	.49	(3.3.1a)	F.95(1,14)=4.60
(4.2.1b)	1.12	(3.3.1b)	F.95(2,14)=3.74
(4.2.1c)	.41	(3.3.1c)	F.95(1,14)=4.60
(4.2.1d)	3.54	(3.3.1d)	F.95(1,14)=4.60
(4.2.1e)	4.17	(3.3.1e)	F.95(1,13)=4.67
(4.2.1f)	.58	(3.3.1f)	F.95(2,13)=3.81

ranges shown in Table 3.4.1.

4.3.1 The Analysis of the 11 $\hat{\lambda}_{ij}$'s

Table 4.3.1 contains the probabilities of observing the 11 λ estimates, given that the boundary points closest to the estimates are the true values of the λ's.

The suprema probabilities presented in Table 4.3.1 are computed by dividing the difference between the estimate $(\hat{\lambda}_{ij})$ and the closer boundary point of $(\lambda^{\beta'}_{ij})$ by the suprema of the standard deviation of $(\hat{\lambda}_{ij})$. The resulting quotient is distributed as a standardized normal, and the supremum probability is found by consulting a cumulative normal distribution table. The infima probabilities are computed by the same procedures, but here the difference $(\hat{\lambda}_{ij} - \lambda^{\beta'}_{ij})$ is divided by the infimum of the standard deviation of $(\hat{\lambda}_{ij})$. The standard deviations of the $\hat{\lambda}$'s in repeated sampling are the square roots of the elements of the Kronecker product of the Σ matrix and the matrix $[X'X]^{-1}$.[25] Therefore, in order to compute the range on a standard deviation of $(\hat{\lambda}_{ij})$ at its boundary point, it is necessary to determine the "constrained range" on the variance σ_{ii}. This constrained range may be

Table 4.3.1

Analysis of the 12 $\hat{\lambda}_{ij}$'s

	Estimate ($\hat{\lambda}_{ij}$)	Boundary ($\lambda^{\beta'}_{ij}$)	Difference ($\hat{\lambda}_{ij}-\lambda^{\beta}_{ij}$)	Standard Deviation of($\hat{\lambda}_{ij}$) at boundary: Supremum	Standard Deviation of($\hat{\lambda}_{ij}$) at boundary: Infimum	Probability of Observing ($\hat{\lambda}_{ij}$) given that the boundary point is the true value: Supremum	Probability of Observing ($\hat{\lambda}_{ij}$) given that the boundary point is the true value: Infimum
λ_{41}	- .031	> - .015	.016		.0193		.203
λ_{42}	.563	< .383	.180	.0906		.023	
λ_{45}	.0917	< - .000309	.092	.0352		.0044	
λ_{55}	.00517	< - .00515	.0103		.0158		.256
λ_{71}	- .0296	> - .015	.0146		.0167		.190
λ_{81}	- .0371	> - .029	.0081		.0243		.360
λ_{94}	- .832	> 1.17	2.0	5.90	.502	.339	0
λ_{104}	4.46	< 3.33	1.13	9.68	.279	.454	0
λ_{111}	- .0302	> - .0292	.0010		.0375		.496
λ_{132}	.0057	> .0458	.0401	.00457		0	
λ_{135}	- .00112	> .000654	.00177	.00177	.00113	.158	.058

smaller than the range on the σ_{ii} in Table 3.4.1, because when this original range was constructed, the β's were allowed to vary throughout the ranges hypothesized for them in the structural model. When constructing the constrained range, however, the β's are assigned the values used when the boundary point was found (i.e., the values of the β's substituted in the particular reduced form coefficient which maximized or minimized it).

By employing a 5 percent critical region, the coefficient estimates $\hat{\lambda}_{42}$, $\hat{\lambda}_{45}$, and $\hat{\lambda}_{132}$ seem to disconfirm the weaker hypothesis. It should be noted that λ_{94} and λ_{104} do not reject the hypothesis only because $\sigma_{9,9}$ and $\sigma_{10,10}$ have such large possible maximums (see 3.4.13g-h). A different structural hypothesis, for example fewer non zero entries in the matrix 2.1.10b, would change this.

So far in the discussion only the boundary point has been hypothesized to be the true point ($\overline{\lambda}_{ij}$). However, the estimate ($\hat{\lambda}_{ij}$) might reject this hypothesis while <u>not</u> rejecting the hypothesis that a point within the range (and thus farther away from the estimate) is the true point. This is because this interior point allows the estimate ($\hat{\lambda}_{ij}$) to have a larger supremum variance. This possibility is investigated for the coefficients which reject the weaker hypothesis.

Further analysis of coefficients $\hat{\lambda}_{42}$ and $\hat{\lambda}_{132}$ shows that the suprema probabilities exhibited in Table 4.3.1 remain the suprema for all the values in their respective predicted ranges. Given that the true value $\overline{\lambda}_{45}$ is -.05625 (the largest value in the range on λ_{45} where $\sigma_{4,4}$ is at its maximum), then the supremum probability of observing $\hat{\lambda}_{45}$ is .0072 which is greater than .0044; however, this is still less than 5 percent and therefore $\hat{\lambda}_{45}$ disconfirms the weaker hypothesis. Therefore, the three estimates reject the hypothesis over the entire $\lambda\beta$' space.

4.3.2 Analysis of $\hat{\sigma}_{4,4}$

The estimated variance, $\hat{\sigma}_{4,4}$, is equal to 31.53, which is outside the predicted range 12.6 >

$\sigma_{4,4} > 1.28$. Since $\frac{N\hat{\sigma}_{i,i}}{\bar{\sigma}_{i,i}}$ is marginally distributed as a χ^2 with N-K degrees of freedom, a 5 percent critical region can be employed to test this hypothesis.[26] By using a one tail test, the critical region becomes $\frac{N\sigma_{4,4}}{\bar{\sigma}_{4,4}} > \chi^2_{.95}$ (with 15 d.f.) or 25.0. With $\bar{\sigma}_{4,4}$ at its maximum value of 12.6, $\frac{N\hat{\sigma}_{4,4}}{\bar{\sigma}_{4,4}}$ is at its minimum value, $\frac{19 \times 31.53}{12.6}$ or 47.45. This falls within the critical region, and thus $\hat{\sigma}_{4,4}$ also disconfirms the weaker hypothesis.

4.4 Conclusions

The previous section showed that the four estimates $\hat{\lambda}_{42}$, $\hat{\lambda}_{45}$, $\hat{\lambda}_{132}$, and $\hat{\sigma}_{4,4}$ reject the weaker hypothesis. Therefore, either one or more of the propositions of the model are incorrect, or the data (i.e., the initial conditions) are incorrectly measured, or the background conditions have not remained constant. It is also possible that two or all three of these are at fault. To check the latter two would take independent study beyond the scope of the paper. However, if these two studies were undertaken and the results showed that both conditions are acceptable, then part of the structural model would be at fault. A next possible step could be to formulate a new set of economic premises. Even then, there would be a problem in deciding which new premises to put forth.

In this model there is a large number of different sets of changes that would cause the weaker hypothesis to no longer be rejected. For example, (4.4.1a-f) is an expansion of the structural space such that $\lambda^{\beta\prime}$ now includes the 4 estimates $\hat{\lambda}_{42}$, $\hat{\lambda}_{45}$, $\hat{\lambda}_{132}$ and $\hat{\sigma}_{4,4}$.[27]

$$15 > \omega_b 2 > 2,$$

$$-2 > \beta_4 > -4,$$

(4.4.1a-f)
$$-.5 > \beta_6 > -3,$$

$$.4 > \alpha_5 > .075,$$

$$15 > \beta_5 > 3,$$

and the suprema of $\theta = 65$.

But, the choice of (4.4.1a-f) is arbitrary. There is no additional theory that implies that of all the possible changes, the ranges on these coefficients are the ones that are incorrect. There is also the additional problem that when the weaker hypothesis is no longer rejected, it is still not known whether the "strict" hypothesis $\lambda^{\beta'}$ is rejected or not.

Therefore, rather than making several attempts at reformulating the model "to bring it into agreement with the data" the analysis is terminated at this point.

What are the results of this study then? In the strict sense the only conclusion is that this model is rejected. More generally, however, the study adds to the knowledge of economics and the mechanics of model building.

The fact that none of the identifiability conditions were rejected indicates that the general form of the model is feasible for studying macro problems. This is important because it supports the further development of theories dealing with two securities markets in a macro model. It was shown that only four of the 76 estimates of the reduced form parameters rejected the hypothesized outcome space. This indicates that though the structural space is probably incorrectly specified, the errors may be minor.

More specifically there seems to be no evidence to reject the premises that the rates of interest are important factors in determining saving flows. In fact there are indications (e.g., 4.4.1a-f) that the proposed ranges for interest elasticity were too low.

In terms of the mechanics of building and testing of explanatory economic models, this is probably one of the largest models built in which the reduced form was solved for, and the ranges of its coefficients found. The study has demonstrated that this process is possible; however, it also exposed some problems.

Without computer techniques to handle it, the computation of the ranges was very time consuming and prone to mistakes. Even though each range was checked at least twice, it is impossible to be sure that a global maximum and minimum was achieved for the coefficients that had as many as seventy or eighty terms in them. Even after these computations are finished the model still has the drawback that in its largeness it becomes impossible to visualize how the different sectors interact within the markets.

4.5 The Structural Estimates

The structural estimates are presented here only to illustrate what little use they are in models as large as this one. Since the distributions of the structural parameters are not known, no test can be constructed to determine if these estimates would reject the structural hypothesis. However, 33 of the 40 estimates of the α's and β's are outside their predicted ranges and 12 of the estimates (those underlined in Table 4.5.1) have signs opposite of those predicted for them.

It can be shown that if the structural parameters were changed as in (4.4.1a-f), 32 of the estimates would still be outside the predicted range. This means that a reduced form model which is not rejected can produce a set of structural estimates that might lead us to doubt the validity of the model.

Table 4.5.1

The Structural Estimates

(est. 2.1.1a) $$\hat{S}_p = \underset{(86.5)}{-38.2} + \underset{(.052)}{.033y} + \underset{(.031)}{.043A} + \underset{(23.3)}{9.19i_p} - \underset{(8.3)}{14.6i_s} + \hat{a}$$

(est. 2.1.2a) $$\hat{O}_p = \underset{(408.2)}{-260.2} + \underset{(.239)}{.147y} + \underset{(110.0)}{61.5i_p} + \underset{(19.0)}{3.28i_s} + \hat{b}$$

(est. 2.1.3a) $$\hat{I}_p = \underset{(400.7)}{247.0} + \underset{(.070)}{.193y} - \underset{(110.0)}{74.8i_p} + \hat{c}$$

(est. 2.1.4a) $$\hat{S}_s = \underset{(58.2)}{-19.7} + \underset{(.035)}{.042y} - \underset{(.021)}{.022A} + \underset{(15.7)}{1.56i_p} + \underset{(5.58)}{10.2i_s} + \hat{d}$$

(est. 2.1.5a) $$\hat{O}_s = \underset{(111.4)}{66.3} - \underset{(.065)}{.016y} - \underset{(30.0)}{18.2i_p} + \underset{(5.20)}{4.10i_s} + \hat{e}$$

(est. 2.1.6a) $$\hat{I}_s = \underset{(116.0)}{13.7} + \underset{(.107)}{.031A_s} - \underset{(33.1)}{6.19i_p} + \underset{(1.87)}{4.96i_s} + \hat{f}$$

(est. 2.1.7a) $$\hat{L}_c = \underset{(254.1)}{175.0} + \underset{(.201)}{.158y} - \underset{(.086)}{.0033A} - \underset{(76.7)}{39.0i_p} + \underset{(24.3)}{2.49i_s} - \underset{(1.47)}{.264P} + \hat{g}$$

(est. 2.1.8a) $$\hat{L}_o = \underset{(82.2)}{-58.8} - \underset{(.064)}{.00085y} + \underset{(24.9)}{3.93i_p} - \underset{(4.20)}{7.84i_s} + \underset{(.478)}{1.44P} + \hat{h}$$

(est. 2.1.9a) $$\hat{M} = \underset{(204.8)}{144.1} + \underset{(2.49)}{5.85R} - \underset{(57.2)}{35.6i_p} + \underset{(6.001)}{6.84i_s} + \hat{j}$$

Table 4.5.1 (Continued)

(est.2.1.10a) $\hat{\Omega}$ =

10.5	24.5	-33.7	.86	-10.9	-4.28			
	239.2	-185.9	21.2	-52.0	-1.83			
		244.1	-16.6	57.0	5.85			
			4.74	3.46	3.12			
				17.8	6.00			
					8.54			
						80.4	-17.7	42.3
							85.3	-9.20
								23.9

The numbers shown in parentheses under the estimates of the coefficients are estimates of standard deviations of large-sample normal approximations to the marginal distributions function of the corresponding estimates of coefficients.

FOOTNOTES

* The author is Assistant Professor of Economics, The University of Iowa. This paper is a condensation of the author's Ph.D. dissertation submitted to Purdue University in January, 1968. A full length version of this study is available as a Working Paper 68-1, Bureau of Business and Economic Research, University of Iowa. The author wishes to express his appreciation to George Horwich, R.L. Basmann, William Breen, David H. Richardson, and H. Albert Margolis for assistance in all aspects of the study; he also thanks the members of Econometric Workshop at Iowa for their helpful comments. The author accepts sole responsibility for any errors.

1. In an earlier draft of this paper there was a third transaction category, contractual saving. The contractual market was excluded from discussion in this paper since in the final construction of the model it did not affect the other three markets, and since it is not of primary interest in itself, would be an unnecessary complication.

2. A bank is a supplier of saving share when it gives a person a passbook with a number in it crediting that individual with a deposit. This individual is a demander of this saving share because he has bought this credit from the bank with his money.

3. Additions to life insurance and pension funds are considered contractual saving and are therefore not part of this study.

4. The precise condition for this to be true for total consumer saving is:

$$[(\alpha_{10}+\alpha_{17})+(\alpha_{12}+\alpha_{19})A+(\beta_3+\beta_8)i_p+(\beta_4+\beta_9)i_s] < 0$$

5. Several theories have been put forth in the literature, but they will not be tested in this study. Cassel (1957), Clower and Johnson (1968).

6. The stock of financial assets held by the consumer, A, is of course not a determinant of O_p, O_s

or L_o and therefore is not in propositions 2.1.2, 2.1.5, or 2.1.8.

7. Some theories would suggest that liquidity preference is a negative function of the rate of change in prices because in an inflation, consumers will try to use their money more efficiently. In the domain of this model this effect is assumed to be constant and can be ignored. From 1947 to 1965 a small, fairly constant inflation was an accepted fact.

8. See Dernberg and McDougall, (1968), page 127; Ackley, (1960, page 360.

9. An alternative specification of this market would be to separate the money supply into two components, with currency as an exogenous variable.

10. For example, $S_p(A,y,i_p,i_s,a)$ evaluated at $A = X_{t,4}$, $y = X_{t,6}$, $i_p = Z_{t,13}$, $i_s = Z_{t,14}$, and $a = a_t$, equals $Z_{t,3}$ for every $t=1,\ldots,19$.

11. In algebraic terms this is a system of three equations and three unknowns which reduces to two equations with two unknowns with the solution of those two substituted in the third.

12. $X_{t,9}$ is only in the four equations explaining stock variables. This is because $X_{t,9}$ is a stock variable measured at the end of each year t, and therefore cannot be a variable determining flows during that year (see Appendix A).

13. For a complete listing of derived reduced-form, see Williamson (1968), pp. 27-37.

14. All estimates of $\bar{\lambda}$ automatically satisfy the 49 dependencies produced by 3.1.4a-c, because 3 variables are defined via the same linear combinations. See Williamson (1968). The Appendix, pp. 63-73.

15. For the derivations of (3.3.2a-f) see Williamson (1968) pp. 38-41.

16. Note that 3.3.2b and 3.3.2f define 2 dependencies.

17. It follows from this that Δ does not vanish; more precisely, $-20 > \Delta > -459$.

18. See Williamson (1968), p. 31.

19. This is a modification of the General Electric Document RM 61 TMP--12 Vol. 4.

20. See Basmann (1965b) (1966); Richardson (1968).

21. K is equal to 5 in the first four conditions and 6 in the last two. This is because $X_{t,9}$ is excluded from the estimation of the regression equations (3.1.1a-f, k-1) and the structural equations (2.1.1a-2.1.6a). (See note 14)

22. See Anderson (1958), pp. 182-183; and Basmann (1965), pp. 392-393.

23. See Mood and Graybill (1963), pp. 307, 333; and Basmann (1965b), p. 393.

24. A smaller enlargement could be found that would make $\lambda^{\beta'}$ large enough so that, though the four estimates are still outside it, they no longer reject it.

BIBLIOGRAPHY

[1] Ackley, G. Macroeconomic Theory. New York: The Macmillan Company, 1961.

[2] Anderson, T.W. An Introduction to Multivariate Analysis. New York: John Wiley & Sons, Inc., 1958.

[3] Basmann, R.L., "On Finite Sample Distributions of Generalized Classical Linear Identifiability Test Statistics," Journal of the American Statistical Association, Vol. 55 (1960), pp. 650-59.

[4] Basmann, R.L., "Remarks Concerning the Application of Exact Finite Sample Distribution Functions of GCL Estimators in Econometric Statistical Inference," Journal of American Statistical Association, Vol. 58 (1963), pp. 943-76.

[5] Basmann, R.L., "On Predictive Testing of a Simultaneous Equation Model: The Retail Market for Food in the U.S.," Institute for Quantitative Research in Economics and Management, Institute Paper No. 78: Purdue University (1964).

[6] Basmann, R.L., "The Role of the Economic Historian in Predictive Testing of Proffered Economic Laws," Explorations in Entrepreneurial History, (1965a).

[7] Basmann, R.L., "On the Application of the Identifiability Test Statistic in Predictive Testing of Explanatory Economic Models," (Part I) The Indian Economic Journal, Vol. 13, No. 3 (1965b), pp. 387-423; (Part II) The Indian Economic Journal, Vol. 14, No. 2 (1966), pp. 333-52.

[8] Bear, D.V.T., "The Relationship of Saving to the Rate of Interest, Real Income and Expected Future Prices," The Review of Economics and Statistics, Vol. XLIII, No. 1 (Feb., 1961)

[9] Birnbaum, Z.W. Introduction to Probability and Mathematical Statistics. New York: Harper, 1962.

[10] Board of Governors of the Federal Reserve System, "A Quarterly Presentation of Flow of Funds, Saving and Investment," Federal Reserve Bulletin (August, 1959), pp. 828-59.

[11] Board of Governors of the Federal Reserve System. Flow of Funds Accounts, 1945-62 (1963 Supplement). Washington, D.C.: Board of Governors of the Federal Reserve System, 1963.

[12] Cassel, G. The Nature and Necessity of Interest. New York: Kelley and Millman, Inc., 1957.

[13] Cassel, G. The Theory of Social Economy. London: T. Fisher Unwin, Ltd., 1923.

[14] Clower, R. and B. Johnson, "Income, Wealth and the Theory of Consumption," Capital Value and Growth, Essays in Honor of J.R. Hicks (forthcoming), 1968.

[15] Dernburg, T.F. and D.M. McDougall. Macro-Economics. 3rd Ed. New York: McGraw Hill Book Co., Inc., 1968.

[16] Horwich,G., "Member Bank Effective Reserves and Earning Assets in the Thirties," Econometrica, Vol. XXVI (1958), pp. 602-3.

[17] Horwich, G., "Effective Reserves, Credit and Causality in the Banking System of the Thirties," Banking and Monetary Studies, ed. D. Carson, Washington, D.C.: Richard D. Irwin, Inc.,1963.

[18] Horwich, G. Money, Capital and Prices. Homewood, Illinois: Richard D. Irwin, Inc., 1964a.

[19] Horwich, G., "An Integrated Analysis of Aggregate Supply and Demand," Institute for Quantitative Research in Economics and Management, Institute Paper No. 82: Purdue University (1964b).

[20] Ginsberg, P.M. and D.H. Richardson, "Some Economic Applications of the GCL Principle of Estimation," Institute for Quantitative Research in Economics and Management, Institute Paper No. 130: Purdue University, 1966.

[21] Mood, A.M. and F.A. Graybill. Introduction to the Theory of Statistics. 2d ed. New York: McGraw Hill Book Co., Inc., 1963.

[22] Richardson, David H., "On the Distribution of the Identifiability Test Statistic," this volume.

[23] Williamson, Samuel A., "A Test of a Macro Model with Two Interest Rates," Bureau of Business and Economic Research, Working Paper Series 68-1: The University of Iowa, 1968.

DIFFERENTIAL GROWTH AMONG LARGE U. S. CITIES*

by

Richard F. Muth
Washington University

1. Introduction

Understanding why cities or other sub-national areas grow at different rates over time is one of the most practically important problems in urban and regional economics. The prediction of future population and/or employment is of great importance for city and regional planning, and much effort is expended by planning agencies in making projections of the future size of their city or region. The prediction of growth in earnings, employment, and aggregate income is also important for the determination of so-called "secondary benefits" of public investment. Such effects have played an increasingly important role in evaluating potential water resource investment projects in recent years. While no systematic evaluation of past attempts at such forecasts has, to my knowledge, been made, it is probably fair to say that past forecasts have been largely based upon naive extrapolations of past behavior and have not been singularly successful. The major difficulty in making such forecasts is the lack of an empirically verified theory of sub-national area growth.

The most popular, and, indeed, about the only clearly articulated theory of regional growth, is the so-called export-base theory. It, and most other analyses of why regions grow at differential rates, attributes differential growth in employment to differential shifts in the demand for labor. The export-base theory argues, in essence, that employment in a city or region consists of two kinds, basic or export employment, which is exogenously determined, and service employment, which is a function of total employment. (In my own analysis I will preserve the two-sector distinction, but I prefer the terms exportable and domestic sectors.) With an exogenous increase in basic employment demand, an induced increase in the demand for labor in the production of local goods and services takes place. The total demand for labor in a city thus increases by some multiple of the initial increase in labor demand in the city's export sector.[1]

Most firms, in fact, sell part of their output either directly or indirectly both as exports and to residents of the same region. It is thus quite difficult in practice to determine the relative amounts of so-called basic and service employment. The difficulty just noted is primarily responsible, I suspect, for the lack of extensive empirical testing of the export-base hypothesis. Conceptually, it shares the defect of many early Keynesian models that demand, both for commodities and for labor, is perfectly inelastic with respect to price, while labor supply is infinitely elastic.

Several recent empirical studies of migration are similar to the export-base hypothesis in that the change in employment in a region is assumed to be exogenously determined. Blanco [1] refers to her principal explanatory variable of inter-state migration as the change in unemployment. Her measure of it, however, is essentially the difference between the change in employment and the natural increase of the population of working age (p. 79, n. 4). Mazek [9], in studying migration into Standard Metropolitan Statistical Areas (SMSA's), stresses what he calls potential unemployment--the unemployment rate that would have existed had no migration occurred, which is labor force in the absence of migration less actual employment. Mazek includes potential unemployment for a particular labor force group along with an average regional unemployment rate and median family income in his regression analysis of migration rates for the particular group. Most recently Lowry [8] has used the change in employment and natural increase as separate variables in analyzing migration into SMSA's. These three studies demonstrate that migration can largely be explained by the change in employment taken as exogenous. None makes any effort, however, to determine whether employment change is indeed exogenously determined. Mazek [9; pp. 23-24] and Lowry [8; pp. 42-44] consider the question only briefly.

In their seminal study of regional economic growth, Borts and Stein [2] suggest a quite different explanation for differential regional growth rates. They examine data on changes in employment and earnings by state as well as national changes in the prices of manufactured products for periods from 1919 to 1953. Except for the period 1948-53, they conclude there is little evidence that differential regional growth rates resulted from differential changes in demand for output [2; pp. 55-64]. Rather, Borts and Stein suggest, differential changes in manufacturing employment have resulted from differential shifts in the supply of labor to a region's manufacturing sector. They associate such shifts with migration and the fraction of a region's employment which is in manufacturing.[2] Empirically, they find strong tendencies for manufacturing employment to grow at above-average rates in states where the fraction of employment in manufacturing is below-average and where in-migration is above-average. They make no attempt, however, to test their hypothesis that migration into a region is exogenously determined [2; pp. 67-77].

Later (Chap. 7) Borts and Stein present a detailed general equilibrium analysis of regional growth with two sectors, export and domestic. They suggest the very fruitful hypothesis, also in contrast with the export-base hypothesis, that the demand for a region's exports and its supply of capital are infinitely elastic. As will be argued more fully later, the latter hypothesis implies that a region's demand for labor is infinitely elastic.

This study is concerned primarily with differential growth in population, employment, and earnings among large U.S. cities in the period 1950 to 1960. Methodologically, it differs from the works previously discussed in that it treats the growth in employment and migration as simultaneously determined. Based upon my empirical findings so far, which I regard as highly tentative, it would appear that employment growth and migration both significantly affect and are significantly affected by each other. Differential changes in wage rates--here I feel much more confident in stating my conclusion--influence changes in employment and migration to a small degree but are not affected by them.

Of the two opposing theories already discussed it would appear that the Borts-Stein theory is much closer to the mark than the export-base theory. A city's demand for labor appears to be highly elastic, while its labor supply elasticity is probably rather small. While an interesting multiplier effect upon employment growth may exist, it has little to do with the so-called base-service ratio or the induced increase in demand for a city's domestic output. The latter serves primarily to determine the allocation of the city's labor supply between its domestic and exportable sectors. The total employment multiplier, rather, depends primarily upon the extent to which an increase in employment in excess of natural increase in the labor force induces in-migration.

In the following section I will present a brief description of the model underlying the empirical work described in subsequent sections. The latter, in turn, describe data used, estimates of the determinants of migration and employment change, and estimates of the model's other equations. In the final section I will describe the quantitative implications of the results obtained earlier for the determinants of differential growth in employment among cities and the allocation of the city's labor supply between its exportable and domestic sectors.

2. The model

In this section I shall give a brief, wholly verbal outline of the model used. Appendix A contains a mathematical statement of the model; unless otherwise noted to the contrary, numbers in parentheses refer to equations in Appendix A.

Here I first consider the mutual determination of change in employment and migration. Next I discuss the determinants of differential changes in wage rates. The section closes with a brief discussion of the effects of change in exportable sector demand and in labor supply upon a city's total employment and the latter's allocation between the city's exportable and domestic sectors.

One of the strongest bits of the folklore of regional economics is the belief that location of firms is influenced by the availability of labor. Equally strong in the folklore of labor economics is the belief that migration is influenced by the availability of job opportunities. As was discussed in the introduction, previous studies have treated either employment change or migration as exogenously determined and as determining the other and found a strong empirical relation between them. None of these, however, has treated the two as simultaneously determined. In the following paragraphs I will consider some of the reasons why migration and employment change influence each other and some of the consequences of their interaction.

First, consider the effects of migration upon the change in employment. In-migration, like natural increase of the labor force, tends to increase the aggregate supply of labor to the city. Apart from differences in composition by age and sex and perhaps race, which may in fact be large, one would expect an increase in population from either source to have the same effect upon the city's labor supply schedule. Neglecting unemployment and holding wage rates constant, either in-migration or natural increase of population would produce numerically equal increases in labor force and employment. Furthermore, as will be argued subsequently, there are both a priori and empirical reasons for believing that the aggregate demand for labor in a city is highly elastic. For most primary workers,[3] at least, the effect of wage rate changes on labor force participation is probably small. Thus, neglecting unemployment, even after the effects of wage rate changes are accounted for, employment should increase about proportionally with the labor force, whether the latter increases because of in-migration or because of natural increase in population.

As suggested by the introductory section, the most common reason given for the dependence of migration upon the change in employment is the existence of unemployment. Of the three studies cited, only Mazek [9; pp. 1-6] devotes much attention to analyzing the relationship of unemployment to migration. He assumes that money wage rates are rigid or insensitive to excess demand or supply of labor. With rigid wages, differential shifts in labor demand and supply in different labor markets lead to differential unemployment rates. Since workers' incomes vary inversely with unemployment rates, workers would be expected to migrate from areas where unemployment rates are high to where they are low. Mazek [9; pp. 19-34] argues, further, that the relevant unemployment variable is that which would have existed at the end of the period in the absence of migration. The latter is the initial labor force plus its natural increase during the period less the sum of initial employment and employment change during the period. If so, migration would vary directly with employment change and inversely with the natural increase in the labor force and initial unemployment.

Because of the empirical results described below, especially the finding that employment increases about proportionally with migration, I very much doubt the unemployment explanation of differential rates of migration into cities over periods as long as a decade. Rather, the effect of a change in employment upon migration is probably due to one of two causes. First, if firms wish to expand employment in a particular city they may transfer workers from or recruit them in other places. Secondly, and possibly more important, migrants may be attracted to cities where employment is growing relative to the labor force. In such cities, a migrant is likely to find a job, especially a job of a particular kind, more quickly, so that the costs of migrating are lower to him. Furthermore, where employment is growing relative to the labor force, a migrant could anticipate future periods of cyclical unemployment to be of shorter duration. If so, _ceteris paribus_, his expected future income would be greater than in cities where employment is growing more slowly. Finally, in a city where employment is growing relative to the labor force, a migrant is more likely to find other persons of similar background to his and to learn of job opportunities.

If employment change and migration are simultaneously determined, then an exogenous change in either will lead to multiple increases in both. When the variables are expressed in percentage terms relative to initial employment, as shown by (15) and (16) the denominator of the multiplier is one minus the product of the elasticity of migration with respect to employment and the elasticity of employment with respect to migration. The analysis two paragraphs above suggests the latter elasticity should be about unity. If in-migrants were unable to find jobs in the same proportion as previous workers, however, this elasticity would be less than unity. For stability of equilibrium, of course, the elasticity of migration with respect to employment must be smaller than that of employment with respect to migration. As shown by (15) and (16), the numerator of the multiplier for an exogenous increase in migration is unity for migration and the elasticity of employment with respect to migration for employment, and similarly for an exogenous shift in the employment equation.

Under conditions of full employment, an exogenous increase in employment alone can take place only if labor force participation increases. Since labor force participation is not likely to change much over time, exogenous increases in employment alone are likely to take place only under conditions of less than full employment. One can, of course, readily imagine exogenous increases in employment and migration simultaneously, as when a firm establishes a new plant and transfers managers and other workers to it from elsewhere. Many possible factors could be cited, however, which produce differential in-migration but do not shift the employment change equation. If workers migrate to, say, Chicago from the rural South because they have friends there or to southern California because they prefer a warm climate, the increase in employment is wholly induced by migration. Finally, the joint determination of migration and employment change also implies that the total effect of some factor such as natural increase in the labor force on, say, migration, including the induced effects on employment change and further migration, may be quite different from the initial effect upon migration with employment change held constant.

I turn now to a consideration of differential changes in wage rates. Following Borts and Stein [2], assume first that a single exportable commodity is produced in the city using labor and capital under conditions of constant returns to scale. Such a commodity might be manufacturing value-added, whose price per unit is the f.o.b. value per unit of product shipped less the delivered price of material inputs used per unit. More importantly, suppose that the f.o.b. price per unit of output is given exogenously by the national market in which the output is sold less transport costs and that the rental value of capital per unit time used in the city is likewise fixed exogenously by nationally determined interest rates and capital asset prices. Because the production function is homogeneous of degree one, the fixed price of value added and capital rental value uniquely determine the capital/labor ratio in the exportable sector. The latter, in turn, uniquely determines the exportable sector's real wage and, since the price of value added is given, its money wage rate. The money wage paid will vary directly with the f.o.b. price per unit of product and Hicks-neutral technological changes (4), and inversely with capital rental values and the delivered price of raw material inputs. However, the wage rate is functionally independent of the output of and labor input used by the city's exportable sector.

Because the money wage in the exportable sector is given, the city's aggregate demand for labor is, in effect, infinitely elastic. Since it is assumed here that exportable and domestic firms purchase labor inputs in the same labor market, they must pay the same wage rate.[4] The money wage rate determined in the export sector plus nationally determined capital rental values determine money prices of domestic output within the city if domestic production is also carried on under conditions of constant returns to scale (8'). The local money wage rate is also perhaps the most important determinant of per capita or per worker income.

At different money wage rates, of course, substitution in production and consumption and changes in the city's aggregate income would, in general, lead to different quantities of labor demanded for domestic production (17). The horizontal addition of the domestic sector's labor demand schedule to the export sector's infinitely elastic labor demand schedule, however, results in an infinitely elastic aggregate labor demand schedule for all quantities in excess of the domestic sector's quantity demanded at the exogenously determined export sector money wage. Stated less abstractly, with an exogenous increase in the aggregate supply of labor to the city, enough labor flows into the domestic sector to enable it exactly to maintain the previous money wage, and the exportable sector employs the balance.

Of course, the Borts-Stein hypothesis is not meant as a literal description of a city's export sector. In actual fact, many products are produced by a city's exportable sector, some of which make up a significant fraction of the output coming onto a regional market and even in some cases, a nation- or world-wide market. An excellent example of the latter is the Boeing Company in Seattle, which clearly does not face an infinitely elastic demand for its commercial jet aircraft. However, let Boeing hire labor in the Seattle labor market along with other firms, say producers of wood products, for whom prices other than wage rates are fixed by national markets. Then the wage Boeing pays is, in effect, exogenously determined by national market conditions facing Seattle wood product firms. With an exogenous increase in the demand for Boeing aircraft, as in the federal government's award of the SST contract to it, and the consequent increase in its derived demand for labor, to the extent Boeing hires more labor locally from a given labor force it merely withdraws labor from other Seattle firms. To the extent, of course, that Boeing hires labor outside the Seattle area it causes both the employment change and migration equations to shift upward.

Conditions are similar for the many kinds of producers within a city who as a group sell a substantial part of the output coming into some regional market surrounding a city--producers of bakery and dairy products, inter-city transit, wholesale services, newspapers, etc. So long as the city also includes firms selling products and buying inputs nationally in significant numbers, the local wage is determined by the national markets relevant to the latter firms. Any exogenous shift in regional demand for the city's products ultimately leads to an opposite change in the fraction of its labor force employed in the production of exportable products for the national market. Precisely the same result holds for changes in the local demand for the products of its exportable sector.

Finally, it makes little difference in the analysis if the city possesses firms selling a variety of different products in national markets. For such to be the case, a single money wage must equate total receipts and factor payments for all. If prices of some of these products rise nationally the local money wage rises. Producers of products whose prices have remained unchanged or fallen would then contract production as fixed capital assets wear out. Eventually, production of the commodities whose prices had not risen might cease entirely in the particular city. Or, some firms selling their outputs nationally and buying material inputs from a surrounding regional supply area would reduce the prices they pay for these regionally obtained materials. While their outputs would fall along with the reduced quantity of materials purchased, these firms might continue to produce indefinitely in the particular city. The situation is precisely analogous for firms who sell their output in a regional market but buy non-labor inputs in national markets.

If the Borts-Stein export sector hypothesis is correct, then the role of shifts in export demand, apart from correlated shifts in the migration and/or employment change relations, is quite different than in the export-base hypothesis. With an infinitely elastic exportable demand, the city's aggregate demand for labor will increase only with forces such as increases in the prices of final products sold nationally or reductions in the prices of inputs purchased on national markets. Such increases in demand by (4) increase the local money wage rate. The rise in the latter, in turn, leads to increased total employment only if a greater labor force participation is induced from a given population, to increased in-migration, or both.

Given the labor force, the rise in money wages which results from an increase in export demand merely affects the allocation of labor between the domestic and exportable sectors. The increase in money wages, of course, increases income per family, and the latter by itself leads to an upward shift in the city's demand for domestic output and the derived demand for domestic employment. But the rise in money wages has two effects which reduce the demand for domestic labor. First, by (8') money wage rates must rise relative to the money price of domestic output, so other factors on balance tend to be substituted for labor in domestic production. And second, the rise in money prices of domestically produced goods reduces their quantity demanded, hence reduces the quantity of labor demanded for domestic production.[5] On balance, then, with the rise in money wage rates, the fraction of the city's labor force employed in the domestic sector may either rise or fall (17).

Finally, consider the effects of exogenous shifts in the city's labor force. While increasing total employment directly, of course, such shifts may also affect the fraction of the city's labor force employed in domestic production. Whether or not it does so depends upon the elasticity of the city's aggregate income with respect to increased employment and the elasticity of domestic demand with respect to income. If the product of these two elasticities is unity, then the fraction of the city's labor force employed in domestic production remains unchanged (17). However, if the new members of the labor force, whether in-migrants or part of its natural increase, are less skilled and/or own less non-human capital, the elasticity of aggregate income with respect to total employment will be less than unity. Under these conditions, if the demand for the city's domestic output with respect to its income is no more than unity, the fraction of its labor force employed in the domestic sector would decline.

3. Data used in the empirical analysis

The model described verbally in the preceding section is formulated as a system of eight simultaneous structural equations in eight endogenous variables in Appendix A. One of these, (12), is an identity which states that the sum of the relative changes in exportable and domestic sector employment, when weighted by their initial fractions of total employment, must equal the relative change in total employment; as such it need not be estimated. In addition to the employment change (13), migration (14), and wage rate change (4) equations already discussed at some length, the model contains exportable (5) and domestic sector (9) output equations, the domestic sector demand equation (10'), and the city's aggregate income determination equation (11).

The major purpose of this section is to describe rather generally the nature of the data used as empirical measures of the variables described in Appendix A, the time period and areal units for which these measures were obtained, and especially to discuss my selection of predetermined variables to be included in the analysis. Appendix B contains a precise description of all the variables actually included in estimated equations shown later, together with the data sources and certain subsidiary information about them. In Appendix B and throughout the remainder of the text these variables are identified by code names of not more than six characters.

As the discussion of Section 2 suggests, the determinants of the change in total employment (TLEMPT), migration (MIGRTN), and the change in money wages (DWAGE) are the most important relationships in the model. Since none of the model's other endogenous variables appear in these three equations, they constitute a subsystem which can be considered separately. MIGRTN and natural population increase (NATINC) were estimated from census population data using the well-known forward cohort survival method. (See Isard [6; pp. 59-62]). However, the actual minus expected[6] and expected 1960 populations relative to actual 1950 population for each age-sex cohort were weighted by the fraction of the 1950 labor force contributed by that age-sex cohort before summing over all cohorts. Hence, MIGRTN and NATINC are estimates of the increase in the labor force from the two sources under the assumption of constant 1950 labor force participation rates for the particular SMSA. For reasons already described, NATINC was included as a predetermined variable in both TLEMPT and MIGRTN equations.

Following Blanco [1] and Lowry [8], the change in armed forces personnel relative to the 1950 civilian labor force (DARMFC) was also included in the system. Such changes, of course, obviously affect migration directly. However, the employment measure used is one of civilian employment. In-migration resulting from increases in armed forces personnel would not affect the number counted as in the civilian labor force and employed civilians. For this reason, DARMFC was initially included in the employment change equation in the expectation that its coefficient would have a negative sign.

Also, following Borts and Stein [2], the fraction of the city's 1950 employment accounted for by manufacturing (PRPMFG) was included in the equation system. One recalls that apart from its possible effects upon natural increase, which are already included, Borts and Stein argued that earnings in the manufacturing sector are higher relative to other sectors where the proportion of manufacturing employment is low. Such an earnings differential would be expected to produce a shift of labor out of a region's domestic and into its exportable sector. I initially included PRPMFG as a predetermined variable in the wage equation for reasons to be described below. This variable, however, was strongly negative in the estimated reduced-form equations both for TLEMPT and MIGRTN, so I experimented with it in both of their structural equations. I will comment further upon it when the structural equation estimates are discussed.

Other predetermined variables initially included in the TLEMPT or MIGRTN equations are an index of 1947 manufacturing wage rates (WAGE47), an unemployment rate for 1949 (UNEMPT), and 1950 city population (SIZE). One might expect that migrants would be attracted to areas where incomes are greater than average. The three studies of migration cited in the introduction all included income variables, though with largely negative results. Except for possible differences among cities in governmental transfer payments, however, differences in wage rates would seem a better variable.

Migrants, in effect, take their property income with them when migrating. Partly, at least, to allow for differences in worker skill, WAGE47 is a weighted average of wage rates in a city relative to the national average in the same two-digit manufacturing industry, the weights being the fraction of a city's reported manufacturing employment found in the particular industry.[7]

Like Blanco [1] I also included a measure of initial unemployment, in this case the fraction of males working less than 27 weeks in 1949. Such a measure makes some allowance for the duration of unemployment. The fraction unemployed during the census week, the unemployment measure more commonly used, reflects only the extent of unemployment; as such, it is more subject to error. The 27 week cut-off is, admittedly, somewhat arbitrary, though it does correspond to the usual definition of long-term unemployment. A fuller analysis might, of course, introduce the proportions working 0, 1-13, 14-26, and 27-39 weeks, respectively, as separate variables. One might anticipate that, in cities with above-average initial unemployment, either in-migration would be discouraged or that existing members might withdraw from the labor force.

Finally, SIZE was included because, in earlier estimates not explicitly discussed here, there seemed to be a small though distinct tendency for total employment to increase more rapidly, given population change, in the larger cities. Such an effect might possibly be attributed to increased labor force participation due to the lower transportation costs for workers, especially secondary workers,[8] which resulted from express-highway building in the larger cities. Since on statistical grounds I needed variables in the employment equation to identify the migration equation, I included SIZE in the former with fewer misgivings than I might normally experience over a specification adopted after examining the data.

As a measure of the change in money wage rates (DWAGE) I also used a two-digit manufacturing industry specific index weighted by the fraction of reported manufacturing employment for the city accounted for by the particular industry in 1947. In this case, however, the item so averaged was the average annual wage per production worker in the two-digit industry in the particular city in 1958 relative to that in 1947.[9] As with WAGE47, an industry specific index was used partly to eliminate the effects of differential changes in worker skill associated with changes in industrial composition. Preliminary calculations suggested that it performed better than an index based solely upon the relative change in the average money wage paid in manufacturing regardless of industrial composition. It would have been desirable to use a variable measuring the average change in wages for all industries within a city. From the data which are available, however, it is quite difficult to construct a measure of the change in wage rates for non-manufacturing industries.

As was stressed in the preceding section, the change in money wage rates in the city depends upon the change in the f.o.b. money prices of the products of the city's exportable sector. The latter, in turn, would depend both upon changes in these prices nationally and changes in transport costs. To measure the former I used a weighted average of two-digit manufacturing industry price changes nationally, with weights which are the fraction of a city's reported value added by manufacture accounted for by the particular industry. The national price changes used are the 1957 relative to 1947 current dollar value added divided by the relative values of the Federal Reserve index of industrial production for the same two-digit industry.[10] The resulting measure (PRICE) is an average national price change for the city's manufactured products.

As suggested by Appendix A, a Hicks-neutral technological change in the export sector will have the same effect upon the money wage as an equal percentage price change.[11] In an attempt to capture such effects I included a second variable (PRODTY) in the wage change equation, a weighted average of national changes in output per production worker man-hour. Neutral technological changes, of course, would produce changes in output per man hour, but the latter could be affected by many other forces as well. As for PRICE, the weights are fractions of reported two-digit manufacturing value added accounted for by the particular industry in the city. The national change in productivity was measured by the Federal Reserve index divided by production worker man-hours, both 1957 relative to 1947.[12]

The two other predetermined variables included in the wage change equation, PRPMFG and UNEMPT, have already been described. As noted earlier, changes in the f.o.b. price of the city's exportable sector output depend also upon changes in transport cost. Now it might be argued that the improvements in highway transportation in recent decades have lowered transport costs in the South and West as compared with the Northeast and in smaller as compared with the larger cities. (See Chinitz [4; pp. 114-24].) In preliminary comparisons, therefore, I included SIZE and a regional dummy variable in the wage change equation. Neither performed very well. PRPMFG, whose simple correlation with the regional dummy is about +.85, when included had a fairly strong negative effect. This last, I suspect, may reflect the effects of regional differences in changes in transport costs. Alternatively, PRPMFG might reflect forces associated with other variables such as the relative importance of durable goods manufacturing or the strength of unionization. UNEMPT was included in the wage change equation because it probably resulted from downward rigidities in money wage rates. Over a period of generally rising money prices and wage rates, certainly, one would expect money wages to rise less where unemployment was initially high.

As implied by discussion of the last several paragraphs, I have identified the exportable sector empirically with manufacturing. Of course, some types of manufacture, notably bakery and dairy products, would more properly be considered to be domestic. At the same time, activities other than manufacturing such as inter-city transport, wholesaling, and various kinds of services produce exportable commodities, though not necessarily for national markets. But many manufacturing firms produce products sold in significant amounts outside a city's borders, however broadly defined, and certainly for most cities much of its output sold on national markets is manufactured.

Likewise, I identify the domestic sector empirically with retail and service business as defined by the Census of Business. Again, I recognize that part of the output of such firms is exported, if only through sales to tourists and other visitors. At the same time, other activities such as primary and secondary education and much of local government are certainly part of a city's domestic sector. I would have included them if it were not for the problem of measuring their output. Here too, however, it seemed that the correspondence is close enough for what I regard as merely an initial test of the city growth model discussed in Section 2. Further work might well attempt to improve on the sectoral definitions used here.

Changes in manufacturing value added (MFGOTP) and employment (MFGWKR) were measured using data for 1947 and 1957. The latter year rather than 1958 was used because the comparison of a recession year with a year of essentially full employment would have confounded the effects of unemployment due to national fluctuations in aggregate demand with those of secular change to a greater degree. Retail and service output (DOMOTP) and employment (DOMWKR) were measured for the period 1948-58, the dates being determined by the availability of Census of Business data. Retail and service output and employment, however, are likely to be much less sensitive to national fluctuations in aggregate demand than those of the manufacturing sector. All other data were obtained from the 1950 and 1960 population censuses.

In all cases data for SMSA's were used. While the urbanized area might have been a better approximation to the notion of city, manufacturing and business census data were not tabulated for urbanized areas. The sample of SMSA's used was limited to those 25 for which all the necessary data were available. The primary limiting factor was the availability of comparable SMSA manufacturing data. The SMSA's used are listed in Appendix B.

Except for dummy variables, all variables were converted to natural logarithms. With one exception, all variables which I have referred to earlier as "change in" are logs of final relative to initial values. One was added to estimated in-migration and to the change in armed forces personnel relative to the initial civilian labor force before taking logs. The latter two frequently took negative values, and, except for a few very large positive values, the log of one plus the original value is not much different from the original value. The use of logs was suggested partly by the mathematical relations in Appendix A and partly by scatter diagrams. The latter suggested the log form yielded relationships more nearly linear and with constant variance for the large relative changes which took place in cities such as Houston, San Diego, and Los Angeles.

4. Estimates of the employment change and migration equations

I now wish to discuss my estimates of the model using the data just described. All the estimates were obtained by two-stage least-squares regression, except for equation (3.2). (Throughout the remainder of the paper the notation (m.n) means the equation in Table m, column n.) The latter, which contains only one endogenously determined variable, was estimated by single-equation or conventional least-squares. In this section I concentrate my attention on the employment change and migration equations, while in the following section the other equations of the model are discussed. In these two sections I will be primarily concerned with the statistical features of the estimates. Consideration of some of their economic implications will be delayed until the final section.

Estimates of the employment change equation are presented in Table 1. In equation (1.1) the sign of the coefficient of DARMFC is incorrect. Since members of the armed forces are not counted among the civilian employed, given the rate of migration the greater the increase in armed forces personnel the smaller should be the increase in civilian employment. Similarly, when the unemployment variable is included in (1.2) its coefficient is quite small relative to its standard error. Furthermore, its sign is positive, which may reflect the transitory nature of some unemployment in 1949. A negative sign would be expected if unemployment was eliminated in part by permanent withdrawals from the labor force.

In all four equations in which it was included, the coefficient of DWAGE is actually negative, while one would expect a positive coefficient. While a rise in money wages relative to money prices increases a worker's real income and may cause him to reduce the number of hours he works on

Table 1

ESTIMATES OF TOTAL EMPLOYMENT EQUATION

Endogenous Variables	(1)	(2)	(3)	(4)	(5)	(6)[a]
TLEMPT	-1	-1	-1	-1	-1	-1
MIGRTN	.938 (.0982)	.991 (.0519)	.989 (.0512)	.978 (.0518)	.984 (.0556)	1.12 (.192)
DWAGE	-.0895 (.0713)	-.0878 (.0693)	-.0989 (.0634)	-	-.0862 (.0692)	-.148 (.111)
Predetermined Variables						
NATINC	.598 (.173)	.615 (.156)	.631 (.150)	.532 (.139)	.610 (.141)	.889 (.353)
SIZE	.00561 (.00376)	.00467 (.00342)	.00499 (.00320)	.00541 (.00336)	.00443 (.00307)	.00543 (.00415)
PRPMFG	-.0400 (.0147)	-.0338 (.0131)	-.0359 (.0120)	-.0362 (.0122)	-.0242 (.0122)	-.0128 (.0186)
DARMFC	.0915 (.146)	-	-	-	-	-
UNEMPT	-	.0123 (.0295)	-	-	-	-
SW, W	-	-	-	-	.0172 (.0140)	-
Std. Error of Estimate	.0157	.0144	.0143	.0146	.0133	.0155

[a] Twenty SMSA's only - see text.

this account, no income effect results for a worker not in the labor force. Hence, insofar as the choice between some and no work is concerned, a rise in money wages can only have a substitution effect of some work for none. However, the measure of employment used here is that during the census week. As has been demonstrated by Finegan [5], a rise in wages tends to reduce hours worked, and part of the reduction may take the form of temporary withdrawal from the labor force. Thus, I suspect the negative coefficient for DWAGE reflects shortcomings in the data used rather than a fault of the equation on theoretical grounds. When DWAGE is deleted in (1.4) it makes little difference in the other coefficients.

The other main difficulty with the equations (1.1)-(1.4) is in the relative magnitude of two coefficients. The coefficients of MIGRTN imply that the employment change which results from in-migration is equal to the labor force change in-migration brings about. The coefficient of NATINC, however, suggests the employment change is only about three-fifths as large as the labor force increase produced by natural increase. Now one might argue that new entrants into the labor force in many cases could not find jobs, but the essentially unit coefficient for MIGRTN would seem effectively to demolish this argument. Another possible explanation is that new entrants to the population of labor force age were disproportionately composed of younger persons, whose labor force participation rates are smaller, during the 1950's. However, population increases in each age-sex cohort were weighted by 1950 labor force participation rates, so that the effect suggested in the previous sentence has already been eliminated from that data.

Partly for the above-noted inconsistency, though more for reasons to be described below in connection with the migration equation, equations (1.5) and (1.6) were also estimated. In (1.5) a regional dummy variable, taking the value 1 for Houston, the three California cities, and Portland, Oregon--those in the part of the country where employment has on the average grown most rapidly in recent years, was included. One sees from (1.5) that doing so has relatively little effect upon the coefficients of interest. However, when the five cities just noted are deleted from the sample, leaving only cities in the Northeast plus New Orleans, the coefficient of NATINC jumps to just under +.9 and is now not significantly different from one statistically. The only other important change in the coefficients when the 5 cities in the Southwest and Pacific coast are eliminated is that of PRPMFG, which falls to one-third its numerical value in equations (1.3) and (1.4). The latter finding suggests that the variable describing the relative importance of manufacturing as a source of employment may largely reflect regional forces in these first three.

Let us now consider the estimates of the migration equation in Table 2, since the full significance of either one depends upon both together. Equation (2.1) is not very appealing in that three of the coefficients have incorrect signs--those of DARMFC, WAGE47, and PRPMFG, the last being rather large when compared to its standard error. If a below-average value for PRPMFG were associated with greater than average in-migration from a surrounding underdeveloped agricultural area, along the lines argued by Borts and Stein [2], one would expect its coefficient to be negative. In addition, the coefficient of UNEMPT, while of correct sign, is numerically much smaller than its standard error. When PRPMFG alone was deleted, the coefficient of DARMFC became positive and that of UNEMPT numerically larger, but that of WAGE47, though numerically smaller, remained negative. (The equation just described is not shown.)

Part of the reason for the essentially negative results obtained from WAGE47 is probably a lack of substantial variation in it. For only one SMSA, New Orleans, was the index much more than 10 percent below the national average. In only two, San Francisco and Portland, was it markedly more than 10 percent above. It is also possible that, following the heavy migration during the 1940's, the small differences among SMSA's in manufacturing wages were largely compensated for by factors such as money price differences, costs of migration, or others. If so, there would have been, on balance, no net advantages in terms of real earnings among the included SMSA's to be obtained through in-migration to one of them rather than to others. This is not to claim, of course, that advantages to migrating from rural areas or smaller urban places to some one of these SMSA's did not exist.

Because of the poor showing of WAGE47 it was deleted as well, with the results shown in equation (2.2).[13] The coefficients of DARMFC and UNEMPT are now somewhat larger numerically than their standard errors and of correct sign. Also, the standard errors of the coefficients of TLEMPT and DARMFC drop markedly, as do the coefficients of TLEMPT and DWAGE. Because the latter is now smaller than its standard error, DWAGE was also dropped in (2.3). As in the case of the employment change equation, doing so has no noticeable effect upon the other coefficients.

Equation (2.2), as was (1.2), is also somewhat suspicious because of the relatively small coefficient of NATINC. One might anticipate that a growth in employment relative to natural increase in the labor force would attract migrants. Equation (2.2) implies this may be the case, however, even if employment is growing more slowly than the internal growth of the labor force. More importantly, the elasticity of migration with respect to employment seems implausibly high. Tentatively accepting the elasticity of employment with respect to migration

Table 2

ESTIMATES OF MIGRATION EQUATION

Endogenous Variables	(1)	(2)	(3)	(4)	(5)[a]
MIGRTN	-1	-1	-1	-1	-1
TLEMPT	1.01 (.108)	.851 (.0570)	.860 (.0550)	.782 (.180)	.685 (.173)
DWAGE	.0960 (.0686)	.0674 (.0754)	-	.0951 (.102)	.150 (.0929)
Predetermined Variables					
NATINC	-.600 (.180)	-.507 (.168)	-.434 (.144)	-.513 (.199)	-.694 (.232)
DARMFC	-.0130 (.154)	.166 (.118)	.159 (.116)	.248 (.238)	.648 (.749)
UNEMPT	-.0108 (.335)	-.0459 (.0296)	-.0556 (.0270)	-.0579 (.0485)	-.0527 (.0446)
PRPMFG	.0385 (.0210)	-	-	-	-
WAGE47	-.0461 (.0572)	-	-	-	-
SW, W	-	-	-	.0148 (.0391)	-
Std. Error of Estimate	.0155	.0159	.0156	.0188	.0166

[a]Twenty SMSA's only - see text.

of unity suggested by the estimates shown in Table 1, the coefficient of TLEMPT in (2.2) implies an employment multiplier of about 6.7. It was primarily because the latter seemed implausibly high to me that the additional equations shown in the last two columns of Table 1 and 2 were estimated.

As in (1.5), the inclusion of the regional dummy variable has little effect upon the coefficient of NATINC in (2.4). Unlike the former, it leads to a decline in the coefficient of TLEMPT of considerable practical importance (see below). When the migration equation is estimated using data only for the Northeastern cities plus New Orleans, (2.5), the coefficient of NATINC becomes noticeably larger numerically, that of TLEMPT smaller, and the two are now essentially equal numerically. The only other coefficient change of consequence is that of DARMFC. Since its standard error also rises greatly, the likely explanation is that differences among the remaining SMSA's are so small that the coefficient can no longer be reliably estimated. While the differences among the coefficients of TLEMPT in columns (2), (4), and (5) of Table 2 may not seem particularly crucial at first glance, together with an elasticity of employment with respect to migration of unity they imply multipliers of 6.7, 4.6, and 3.2 respectively. Such differences, of course, are of substantial practical importance.

From the estimates presented in Tables 1 and 2 it would seem that employment change and migration each strongly affect and are in turn strongly affected by the other. Regardless of the other variables included or whether the citi-s in the rapidly growing Southwest and Pacific coast regions are included or not, the estimated elasticity of employment with respect to migration is very close to one. The finding that in-migrants readily find jobs is to be expected if the aggregate demand for labor in a city is highly elastic (see the following section) and if differential changes in unemployment rates are of negligible importance over moderately long periods of time in accounting for differential changes in employment. Furthermore, the unit elasticity is quite inconsistent with the belief that employment is exogenously determined.

The estimated elasticity of migration with respect to employment, however, is rather sensitive to other variables included in the equation and whether or not the Southwest and Pacific coast cities are included. The marked change when these 5 cities are excluded as in (2.5) suggests to me that the omission of some unknown factors affecting migration has biased the coefficient of TLEMPT upward in equations (2.1)-(2.3). Further study of the employment change and migration equations using a larger sample of cities, with separate estimates of the coefficients for various regional groupings of cities and, perhaps, additional predetermined variables included, would be desirable for a firmer understanding of these relationships.[14]

The coefficients of NATINC agree better with those of MIGRTN and TLEMPT in (1.6) and (2.5), respectively. The employment multiplier implied by the coefficients obtained when the 5 Southwest and Pacific cities are deleted also seems more plausible to me. For these reasons, until further evidence is available I am inclined to place more confidence in the estimates obtained in equations (1.6) and (2.5). I must confess, however, to a certain residual uneasiness over explaining employment change and migration largely in terms of each other. For especially when the Northeastern cities plus New Orleans only are used in (1.6) and (2.5), the predetermined variables in one equation which identify the other have coefficients with rather small "t" ratios.

5. Estimates of the model's other equations

I now wish to consider the estimates of the model's other equations. These were all obtained using data for all twenty-five cities. The findings of the preceding section suggest to me that some important predetermined variable has been omitted from the migration equation. Such an omission, while it implies some loss in asymptotic efficiency, does not affect the consistency of the two-stage least-square estimators of the model's other equations. By far the most important of these other equations is the wage change equation. The latter is of critical importance both for interpreting the results of the preceding section and for appraising the empirical relevance of the export-base theory.

Estimates of the wage change equation are shown in columns (1) and (2) of Table 3. In (3.1) TLEMPT was included to test the hypothesis that a city's money wage rate is exogenously determined by conditions of product demand and supply of non-labor inputs of its exportable sector. One sees that, while smaller than its standard error, the coefficient of TLEMPT in (3.1) is actually positive. Hence it was deleted from the equation, and (3.2) was estimated by single-equation least-squares.

In the latter, the coefficients of three of the four predetermined variables are quite large relative to their standard errors, while the coefficient of PRODTY is of the correct sign. I have little to add to my previous remarks on the expected coefficients of PRPMFG and UNEMPT. Appendix A suggests, however, that the coefficients of PRICE and PRODTY should be the same and equal to the inverse of labor's share. Since the latter averages around .4 for the SMSA's included in the sample, even PRICE's coefficient is much too small. These difficulties may be due to the possible measurement errors noted earlier. While further refinement

Table 3

ESTIMATES OF MANUFACTURING SECTOR EQUATIONS

Engogenous Variables	(1)	(2)	(3)	(4)	(5)	(6)
DWAGE	-1	-1	.0648 (.662)	-	-.397 (.568)	-.370 (.492)
MFGOTP	-	-	-1	-1	-	-
MFGWKR	-	-	.930 (.123)	.913 (.0778)	-1	-1
TLEMPT	.145 (.186)	-	-	-	2.55 (.438)	2.34 (.257)
Predetermined Variables						
PRICE	1.04 (.250)	1.05 (.244)	.610 (.726)	.673 (.419)	-	-
PRODTY	.227 (.335)	.348 (.291)	1.03 (.640)	1.08 (.509)	-	-
SIZE	-	-	-	-	-.00269 (.0299)	-
PRPMFG	-.0698 (.0568)	-.104 (.0355)	.0203 (.0896)	-	.0775 (.129)	-
UNEMPT	-.288 (.112)	-.282 (.109)	-	-	-	-
Std. Error of Estimate	.0561	.0548	.103	.0981	.141	.128

of the PRICE and PRODTY variables might yield coefficients more nearly in accord with a priori expectation, their coefficients in (3.2) do provide some support for the hypothesis that a city's money wage rate is exogenously determined. Empirical support for the latter, however, rests primarily upon the finding that, when TLEMPT is introduced into the wage change equation, its coefficient has the wrong sign.

Columns (3) and (4) of Table 3 contain estimates of the determinants of the change in manufacturing value added. In (3.3), the coefficient of PRPMFG has the wrong sign, for I have interpreted it as reflecting greater f.o.b. price increases because of relative declines in transport costs in cities where manufacturing employment is relatively less important, and is very small in relation to its standard error. While the coefficient of DWAGE has the proper sign, it too is small as compared with its standard error. Eliminating these two variables, as in (3.4), results in a considerable reduction in the standard errors of the remaining coefficients but in little change in the values of the coefficients themselves.

The coefficients of PRICE and PRODTY are not very different from each other in (3.3) and (3.4) judging crudely from the size of their standard errors, in accord with equations (5) and (5') in Appendix A. However, these plus the coefficient of DWAGE in (3.3) would make sense only if the elasticity of substitution of labor for other productive factors in the exportable sector were zero, a value I don't find very plausible. Note, too, that while differential changes in value added were associated principally with those in production worker employment, the elasticity is somewhat smaller than unity. MFGWKR's coefficient in (3.3) and (3.4) may reflect the fact that new members of the labor force were less skilled on the whole.

The last two equations in Table 3 give the relation of the change in manufacturing employment to the change in total employment and the change in wage rates. As explained in Appendix A, such an equation is a partial reduced-form derived from the three relationships estimates of which are shown in Table 4 plus the identity which relates relative changes in exportable and domestic sector employment to total employment change. As such it can be interpreted as a supply of labor equation to the manufacturing sector. In (3.5), SIZE and PRPMFG were included to test for inter-sectoral labor supply shifts. Borts and Stein [2] have argued that in regions where the fraction of labor employed in manufacturing is low, labor has shifted out of other activities, especially agriculture. Shifts of labor out of agriculture are not likely to be very important insofar as SMSA's are concerned, of course. One sees that in (3.5) the coefficients of both these variables are small relative to their standard errors and that of PRPMFG has the wrong sign.[15] Deleting them, though, has relatively little effect upon the other coefficients, as (3.6) indicates.

The coefficient of DWAGE is smaller numerically than its standard error, and also, one is at first tempted to claim, of incorrect sign. As was pointed out earlier, however, with a rise in the city's money wage rate aggregate incomes in the city increase, increasing the derived demand for labor in the domestic sector and reducing the labor supply to the exportable sector. In the following section I will demonstrate that the coefficients of DWAGE are quite plausible in sign and magnitude.

It was also argued earlier that, with an increase in the labor supply schedule to the city, the proportion employed in the domestic sector may either increase or decrease depending upon whether the product of the income elasticity of demand for domestic output and the elasticity of aggregate income with respect to the labor force is greater than or less than unity. As will also be explained in the following section, the coefficient of TLEMPT in (3.5) and (3.6) is much too large to account for on the basis of the considerations just described. The best explanation I can offer for the size of the TLEMPT coefficient in (3.5) and (3.6) is the following: In addition to manufacturing, the city's exportable sector contains firms such as public utilities whose demand curve is downward sloping. A growth of the labor force may cause the demand curve for these firms to shift upward somewhat but less than proportionally to the increase in the labor supply to the exportable sector as a whole. Thus, the labor supply schedule to manufacturing firms shifts upward more than proportionally, and firms selling on a national market can always fully employ the additional labor at the exogenously determined wage rate.

Estimates of the other equations of the model are shown in Table 4. Equation (4.1) is the output equation for the trade and service sector. The coefficient of DWAGE strongly suggests that in cities where the money wage rises at above average rates the value of output grows more rapidly than employment as capital is substituted for labor and the money price of domestic goods rises. This coefficient is smaller than would be expected, however. As indicated by (9) in Appendix A, it should be at least equal to labor's share in the total value of trade and service output, which was about .6 in 1948 according to the national income accounts. One sees, too, from (4.1) the tendency for output to rise relatively less than employment in the trade and service sector, as was also seen to be the case for the manufacturing sector in Table 3. This result, too, suggests that new workers were on the whole less skilled.

Table 4

ESTIMATES OF DOMESTIC SECTOR EQUATIONS

Endogenous Variables	(1)	(2)	(3)	(4)	(5)
DOMOTP	-1	-1	-1	-	-
DOMWKR	.842 (.0655)	-	-	-	-
DWAGE	.421 (.131)	.505 (.264)	.458 (.251)	.0476 (.191)	-
INCOME	-	1.31 (.221)	1.35 (.212)	-1	-1
TLEMPT	-	-	-	.650 (.147)	.611 (.0828)
Predetermined Variables					
SIZE	-	.00820 (.0136)	-	-.00004 (.0101)	-
PRPMFG	-	-	-	.0198 (.0435)	-
Std. Error of Estimate	.0335	.0645	.0641	.0474	.0462

Equations (4.2) and (4.3) are estimates of the city's demand equation for domestic output. SIZE was included to test for the possibilities of so-called import substitution. It is frequently argued that as cities grow to moderately large size they are able to sustain domestic production of previously imported commodities. If so, one might expect a negative sign for a sample which includes the largest cities, as is the case here. In (4.2), however, the coeffi cient of SIZE has the wrong sign and is considerably smaller than its standard error. In the demand equation, the coefficient of DWAGE reflects the effect of the increased money price on the demand for domestic output as money wages rise. Equation (10') in Appendix A indicates that the coefficient is equal to labor's share in domestic sector receipts multiplied by one plus the price elasticity of demand for domestic output. Since labor's share is about six-tenths, the coefficient of DWAGE in (4.3) implies a price elasticity of demand for domestic sector output of about -.25. Though small numerically, this value is reasonable in view of the fact there are probably few substitutes for such a broad aggregate of commodities. The aggregate money income elasticity of domestic sector demand appears to be about 1.3.[16]

Equations (4.4) and (4.5) are estimates of the determinants of the city's aggregate money income. SIZE and PRPMFG were originally included as proxies for property in relation to total income. In a period of generally rising interest rates one might expect incomes to rise relatively where property incomes are relatively more important. The coefficients of both of these variables are small relative to their standard errors in (4.4), and that of SIZE has the wrong sign. While positive as would be expected, the coefficient of DWAGE is far too small. Since earnings account for as much as eight-tenths of income, one would expect a much larger elasticity of aggregate money income with respect to money wage rates than shown in Table 4. Finally, the coefficient of TLEMPT is also somewhat small. Even if new members of the labor force had no property income whatsoever, the coefficients in columns (4) and (5) of Table 4 suggest that new members of the labor force had earnings only about eight-tenths as large as those of others.

6. Some implications of the empirical results

Appraising the results of the preceding two sections, one of their major defects is that the numerical values found for several of the coefficients are too small to agree with the model outlined in Appendix A. These included the coefficients of PRICE and PRODTY in the money wage change equation and the coefficients of DWAGE in the two output equations and the aggregate money income change equation. Perhaps a better identification of the groupings of firms in the exportable and domestic sectors and a breakdown of the former into two parts--say firms selling on national markets with exogenously given prices on the one hand and firms facing finitely elastic demand schedules on the other--might produce coefficients more in accord with *a priori* expectation. However, the empirical findings in Tables 3 and 4 do accord with the model in that, in cities where money wages rose at above-average rates during the fifties, the value of output produced by both exportable and domestic sectors rose more rapidly than employment.

The other major defect in the empirical results is the uncertainty over the quantitative effects of employment change on migration and the weakness of the various predetermined variables used in explaining employment change and migration. Regardless of the combination of variables employed and cities included, the estimated elasticity of employment with respect to migration in Table 1 is quite close to unity. In Table 2, however, the estimated elasticity of migration with respect to employment is rather sensitive to variables included and cities used in estimating the migration relation, especially when this elasticity is translated into implied values of the employment multiplier. The latter difficulty may well stem from the omission of some important variable from the migration relationship and from the lack of a really strong predetermined variable in the employment change equation to identify the migration equation. Hopefully, further study using a larger number of cities will result in better estimates of the determinants of migration.

Despite the above-noted problems, the empirical results are of considerable interest. They support the Borts-Stein hypothesis that money wage rates are exogenously determined by firms selling their outputs and buying non-labor inputs in national markets. The fact that money wage changes do not appear to be affected by changes in employment coupled with the relatively low elasticity of the labor supply implied by the results (see below), suggest that the effects of changes in the demand for a city's exportable sector output is quite different than implied by the export-base hypothesis. The findings here, in fact, suggest that the major effect of increases in exportable demand is to raise money wage rates and that such increases have relatively little effect upon changes in total employment. Rather, they merely shift the sectoral composition of employment.

On the basis of the findings in Table 1 it is hard to sustain the hypothesis that employment change is exogenously determined. Likewise, these results plus the coefficient of UNEMPT in Table 3 cast doubt on the hypothesis that wage rigidities or other labor market imperfections limit the availability of jobs and, as a result, some migrants into cities would be unable to find employment. For, over a decade, in-migration of population into an SMSA apparently leads to as great a proportionate increase in employment as it does in the civilian labor force. It is equally clear from Table 2, moreover, that an increase in employment in excess of the labor force growth that natural increase in population brings about is an important stimulus to migration into an SMSA. It therefore appears that a quantitatively important multiplier mechanism affects city growth. The value of the employment change multiplier, however, depends primarily upon the elasticity of migration with respect to employment, given a unit elasticity of employment with respect to migration. The so-called base-service ratio, upon which stress is laid by the export-base theory, would appear to be of little or no importance in influencing differential total employment changes.

Now, if apart from cyclical fluctuations migrants find jobs in the same proportion as other workers, one might ask why workers migrate at all. For, presumably, a worker could equally well have found a job in the city from which he migrated. One possible answer, of course, is that wages or living conditions are better in the city to which he migrated. The estimates in Table 2, though, did not suggest that differences in migration rates are positively related to wage differences among SMSA's. More important, however, is the fact that the conclusions stated above apply to relatively large cities, those of a quarter of a million or more in population. It is well known that the returns to labor in many rural and smaller urban areas are below those in the larger urban centers. During the fifties there was substantial out-migration from rural and some smaller urban areas.

While there are fairly clear advantages to migration to the larger areas, it may well be true that there are no differential economic advantages to migrating to any particular one of the larger urban centers. Thus, the factors which cause the migration equation to shift as among large cities may be varied, largely non-economic, and, perhaps, difficult to quantify. In any event, the estimates in Table 2 suggest that shifts in the migration equation are small, their standard deviation being only about 15 percent of that of migration itself (Table B.1). In addition, the residuals from equations (1.6) and (2.5) are rather strongly negatively correlated ($r \cong -0.8$). It would not appear, then, that migration is importantly affected by firms transferring or hiring workers in other places.

In the remainder of this paper I would like to spell out some of the quantitative implications of the equation system estimated earlier for the growth of a city's total employment and the allocation of this total among its exportable and domestic sectors. To do so I will assume the following:

Elasticity of	With Respect to	Value
Employment	Migration	1
Employment	Natural Increase	1
Employment	Money Wage	.1
Migration	Employment	2/3
Migration	Natural Increase	-2/3
Migration	Money Wage	.1

These values are based primarily upon the estimates in equations (1.6) and (2.5). As I noted in Section 4, these values seem more reasonable to me than those in (1.3) and (2.2), partly because the coefficients of NATINC agree more closely with those of MIGRTN and TLEMPT, respectively, but more importantly because the implied multiplier value seems more plausible. Especially, in view of the uncertainty of the elasticity of migration with respect to employment change, however, the quantitative implications I am about to suggest should be viewed as highly tentative.

The various values of the elasticity of migration with respect to changes in the money wage obtained in Table 2 tended to cluster about +.1, but those of employment change in Table 1 around -.1. As was suggested earlier, the latter is probably the case because employment was measured in relation to the number employed at a given moment. A measure of those employed at some time within a year's time is probably more relevant for my purposes here. The recent work by Bown and Finegan [3] on labor force participation seems to suggest elasticities for primary workers about equal to +.1. These, too, may be algebraically too small because their data also referred to labor force participation during the census week.

Given the above elasticities, the following values for the partial reduced form equations of employment change and migration, equations (15) and (16) in Appendix A, are implied:

	------------Equation---------	
Coefficient of	Employment Change	Migration
Natural Increase	1	0
Money Wage	.6	.5
Exogenous Increase in Employment	3	2
Migration	3	3

That the total effect of natural labor force increase, including the induced effect operating through the migration variable, is to increase employment proportionally and to leave migration unaffected is to be expected. For, those who enter the labor force find jobs in the same proportions as other workers and migration is stimulated only by relative increases in employment which are in excess of that of the labor force. The total effects of money wage changes are larger than those upon either employment or migration with the other held constant. Even despite the rather large induced effects of one upon the other, though, it would appear that the city's aggregate labor supply is not very responsive to differential money wage rate increases.

The above coefficients for the empolyment change and migration partial reduced-form equations imply the following approximate total effects on them for a change of one standard deviation in certain of the predetermined variables (the magnitude of which is indicated in parenthesis after the variable name):

Variable	Equation: Employment Change	Equation: Migration
UNEMPT (±.12)	∓.040	.036
PRPMFG (±.36)	∓.057	.043
SIZE (±1.0)	±.015	.010
Std. deviation 25 cities	.13	.11
Northeastern plus New Orleans only	.054	.052

The above effects of UNEMPT were calculated as follows: In Table 2 the estimated elasticity of migration with respect to UNEMPT was about -.05; since the exogenous migration shift multiplier is 3, the direct effect of a unit change in UNEMPT on both employment and migration is -.15. However, from Table 3 one sees that the effect of a unit change in UNEMPT upon DWAGE is about -.3. The indirect effect operating through the wage change is thus -.18 for TLEMPT and -.15 for MIGRTN, yielding total effects of -.33 and -.30, respectively. Multiplying by ±.12 one obtains the entries shown.

The effects shown for the other variables were obtained in similar fashion, except that in the case of SIZE there is no indirect effect operating through the change in wages. For purposes of comparison the standard deviations of TLEMPT and MIGRTN are also shown. From these calculations one readily sees that the total effects of differences in UNEMPT and PRPMFG are indeed substantial, especially for the cities outside the Southwest and Pacific Coast. From Table 1, however, the direct effect of differences in PRPMFG on TLEMPT and MIGRTN, apart from correlated regional effects, may be only one-third as large for the Northeastern cities and New Orleans as for all 25 combined. Hence, the total effect may be only about half as large as shown above. It appears, moreover, that variations in city size had little effect upon differences in employment change and in migration.

I would now like to consider the effects of money wage changes and labor supply shifts upon the allocation of a city's labor force between its domestic and exportable sectors. To evaluate these effects, I will use the following parameters, upon which equations (17) and (18) of Appendix A show the result depends:

Elasticity of	With Respect to	Value
Domestic Sector Demand	Own Money Price	-.25
Demestic Sector Demand	Aggregate Money Income	1.3
Aggregate Money Income	Total Employment	.6
Aggregate Money Income	Money Wage Rate	.8

The first three of these are based upon coefficients in Table 4, the rationale for the first having already been described. In Table 4 the effect of a differential increase in money wage rates, while positive, was negligible. I find this quite implausible and prefer to use the larger value shown above, which is the approximate fraction of earnings in total income. In addition to the above one needs to know the approximate relative size of a city's domestic and exportable sectors. From a summary of the various estimates given by Leven [7; p. 179] it appears that the export-base multiplier calculated from estimated base-service ratios is about 1.8 for moderately large cities. The latter, in turn, implies that exportable employment is about four-sevenths of total employment.

The parameter values just discussed imply the following relative changes in sector employment for unit relative changes in total employment and in money wages:

Relative Change in Sector Employment	Resulting from Unit Relative Increase in Total Employment	Resulting from Unit Relative Increase in Money Wage
Exportable	1.15	-.4 to -.5
Domestic	.8	.5 to .7

Given the effect of total employment increases on aggregate money income for the city experienced during the fifties, as cities grow in size their exportable sector employment would tend to grow somewhat more rapidly. Retail trade and service demand, however, would grow less than proportionately with total employment due to the fact that aggregate city income grew only six-tenths as rapidly. If income were to grow eight-tenths as rapidly as total employment, however, domestic and exportable sector employment would both grow at about the same rate as total employment.

As seen from (17) and (18), the effects of money wage rate changes upon sector employment depends upon the domestic sector's elasticity of substitution of labor for other factors in production, in addition to those parameters already discussed. The empirical results of this study provide no very good evidence about this last parameter, so I have assumed, alternatively, values of 1 and .5, the larger corresponding to the numerically smaller values shown above. These values suggest that, as money wages rise, their tendency to increase aggregate money income in the city outweights the substitution in production and consumption associated with the rise in money wages. As a result, the fraction of the city's labor force employed in the domestic sector rises. Note especially that the calculated effects shown for the export sector agree quite closely with the coefficients of DWAGE in (3.5) and (3.6).

APPENDIX A

Mathematical Formulation of the Model

NOTATION - Let

X = Output of exportable commodities (when used as a subscript means in the production of exportables);

Z = Local output of commodities consumed locally (as a subscript means in the production of domestic goods and services);

L = Labor-input (without a subscript refers to total for the city, with a subscript refers only to the designated industry);

K = Capital-input into the industry designated by the subscript;

p = Local price of output of the industry designated by subscript;

w = Price per unit of labor input, assumed the same for exportable and domestic industries;

D_X = A Hicks neutral technological change in the exportable industry;

Y = Total income accruing to residents of the city;

M = Shift of labor supply function resulting from in-migration, relative to initial L;

N = Shift of labor supply function resulting from internal population growth, relative to initial L;

μ = An exogenous shift in rate of migration, given employment increase;

ε = An exogenous shift in employment increase, given rate of migration;

ρ = Ratio of total payments to the factor designated by the first subscript by the industry designated by the second;

σ = The elasticity of substitution of labor for capital in the industry designated by the subscript;

E = Partial elasticity of the variable designated by the first subscript with respect to the variable designated by the second;

f = Fraction of the city's total labor input used by the industry designated by the subscript; and

$*$ as a superscript means the logarithmic differential of the variable so designated.

EXPORTABLE SECTOR - Treating the local price per unit of exportable output as exogenously determined and neglecting possible changes in the rent per unit of capital or in other predetermined variables not explicitly noted, the following are readily obtained from an earlier paper of mine:[17]

$$(1)\quad X^* - \rho_{LX} L_X^* - \rho_{KX} K_X^* = D_X$$

$$(2)\quad \rho_{KX} L_X^* - \rho_{KX} K_X^* + \sigma_X w^* = \sigma_X(p_X^* + D_X)$$

$$(3)\quad - \rho_{LX} L_X^* + \rho_{LX} K_X^* = \sigma_X(p_X^* + D_X).$$

Since (3) is equal to $-\rho_{LX}/\rho_{KX}$ times (2) in L_X^* and K_X^*, for consistency,

$$p_X^* + D_X = -(\rho_{LX}/\rho_{KX})(p_X^* + D_X - w^*), \text{ or}$$

$$(4)\quad w^* = \frac{1}{\rho_{LX}}(p_X^* + D_X).$$

Subtracting (2) from (1) and adding p_X^* to each side of the remainder,

$$(5)\quad (p_X X)^* - L_X^* - \sigma_X w^* = (1 - \sigma_X)(p_X^* + D_X),$$

while eliminating w^* by substituting (4) into (5) yields,

$$(5')\quad (p_X X)^* - L_X^* = (1 + \frac{\rho_{KX}}{\rho_{LX}} \sigma_X)(p_X^* + D_X).$$

DOMESTIC SECTOR, PRODUCTION SUBSET - In like manner, for domestic production:

$$(6)\quad Z^* - \rho_{LZ} L_Z^* - \rho_{KZ} K_Z^* = 0$$

$$(7)\quad \rho_{KZ} L_Z^* - \rho_{KZ} K_Z^* + \sigma_Z w^* - \sigma_Z p_Z^* = 0$$

$$(8)\quad -\rho_{LZ} L_Z^* + \rho_{KZ} K_Z^* - \sigma_Z p_Z^* = 0.$$

Here, again, consistency requires that

$$(8')\quad p_Z^* = \rho_{LZ} w^*,$$

which, when substituted into (7), yields

$$\rho_{KZ} L_Z^* - \rho_{KZ} K_Z^* + \rho_{KZ} \sigma_Z d w^* = 0.$$

Subtracting the last equation from (6) and adding

$p_Z^* - \rho_{LZ} w^*$ then yields

$$(9) \quad (p_Z Z)^* - L_Z^* - (\rho_{LZ} + \rho_{KZ} \sigma_Z) w^* = 0.$$

DOMESTIC SECTOR, DEMAND SUBSET - Assuming that the quantity of domestic output demanded is a function only of its price and local income, one readily obtains

$$(10) \quad (p_Z Z)^* - (1 + E_{Z,p_Z}) p_Z^* - E_{ZY} Y^* = 0,$$

or, substituting $\rho_{LZ} w^*$ for p_Z^* in (10),

$$(10') \quad (p_Z Z)^* - \rho_{LZ}(1 + E_{Z,p_Z}) w^* - E_{ZY} Y^* = 0.$$

Neglecting changes in local income received from property or from transfer payments, the relative change in income, in turn, is

$$(11) \quad Y^* - E_{Yw} w^* - E_{YL} L^* = 0.$$

In (11) the elasticity of local income with respect to the wage rate is, of course, the fraction of total income received in the form of earnings. If new members of the labor force owned the same amounts of human and non-human capital, on the average, as previous members, E_{YL} would be equal to unity. However, if previous non-working members or in-migrants have less skill or own less property, E_{YL} would tend to be less than unity.

LABOR SUPPLY SUBSET -

$$(12) \quad f_X L_X^* + f_Z L_Z^* = 0$$

$$(13) \quad L^* - E_{L,M} M - E_{M,w} w^* = E_{L,N} N + \varepsilon$$

$$(14) \quad M - E_{M,L} L^* - E_{M,w} w^* = E_{M,N} N + \mu.$$

Equation (12), of course, is purely definitional. Equation (13) relates the rate of growth in total employment in the city to in-migration of population, the rate of growth of wages, natural increase of the labor force, and other unspecified variables denoted by ε. (14), on the other hand, makes the rate of in-migration dependent upon the rate of growth in employment as well as other factors. Solving (13) and (14) for L^* and M one finds:

$$(15)\quad L^* - \left(\frac{E_{L,w} + E_{L,M}\,E_{M,w}}{1 - E_{L,M}\,E_{M,L}}\right) w^* =$$

$$\left(\frac{E_{L,N} + E_{L,M}\,E_{M,N}}{1 - E_{L,M}\,E_{M,L}}\right) N + \left(\frac{E_{L,M}\,\mu + \varepsilon}{1 - E_{L,M}\,E_{M,L}}\right), \text{ and}$$

$$(16)\quad M - \left(\frac{E_{M,w} + E_{M,L}\,E_{L,w}}{1 - E_{L,M}\,E_{M,L}}\right) w^* =$$

$$\left(\frac{E_{M,N} + E_{M,L}\,E_{L,N}}{1 - E_{L,M}\,E_{M,L}}\right) N + \left(\frac{\mu + E_{M,L}\,\varepsilon}{1 - E_{L,M}\,E_{M,L}}\right).$$

Equation (15) might be interpreted as the aggregate labor supply function to the city as a whole. (15) and (16) could be reduced further, of course, by substituting equation (4) for w^*.

THE ALLOCATION OF LABOR BETWEEN THE DOMESTIC AND EXPORTABLE SECTORS - Equations (4), (5), (9), (10'), (11) and (12) form a system of six simultaneous equations in seven endogenously determined variables, which breaks up into several simpler systems since not all the endogenous variables appear in every equation. For simplicity, the above-noted plus equations (13) and (14) are referred to as the system of structural equations elsewhere in this paper, but their development here clearly shows that they are already partial reduced-form equations obtained by eliminating certain non-observable variables. If one is interested primarily in the exportable sector, one can solve equations (9) through (12) for L^*, L_X^* and w^*. The equation so obtained is a further reduced-form which, also for convenience, one can call the labor supply schedule to the exportable sector.

To do so, first subtract (9) from (10') and then substitute (11) for Y^* in the remainder, yielding

$$(17)\quad L_Z^* + (\rho_{KZ}\sigma_Z - \rho_{LZ}\,E_{Z,p_Z} - E_{ZY}\,E_{Yw})w^* - E_{ZY}\,E_{YL}L^* = 0.$$

Equation (17) indicates that, with a rise in wage rates, the quantity of labor demanded in the city's domestic production declines partly through the substitution of capital for labor in production and partly because of the smaller quantity of domestic output demanded at its now higher price. On the other hand, the increase in wage rates raises local income received and thus the demand for local output, the latter leading to an increase in the quantity of labor demanded in the production of domestic goods. These forces affect the quantity of labor supplied to the exportable sector in the opposite direction, the first two increasing it and the increase in local income reducing it, as seen by substituting (12) for L_Z^* into (17)

$$(18)\quad L_X^* - \frac{f_Z}{f_X}(\rho_{KZ}\sigma_Z - \rho_{LZ}E_{Z,p_Z} - E_{ZY}\,E_{Yw})w^* -$$

$$- \frac{1}{f_X}(1 - f_Z\,E_{ZY}\,E_{YL})L^* = 0.$$

An increase in the total supply of labor to the city's economy, of course, increases the supply to both the domestic and exportable sectors.

APPENDIX B

Definition of Variables and Sources of Data

Unless otherwise noted, all data refer to SMSA's.

DARMFC - Change in populaiion 14 years or over in the armed forces, 1950 to 1960, relative to civilian labor force 14 to 64 years old, 1950, plus one in natural logs. From U.S. Bureau of the Census, 1950 Census of Population, Vol. II, (Washington, D.C.: U.S. Government Printing Office, 1952), State Parts, Table 35 and 1960 Census of Population, Vol. I, (Washington, D.C.: U.S. Government Printing Office, 1963), State Parts, Table 73.

DOMOTP - Retail sales plus service industry receipts, both in dollars, 1958/1948, in natural logs. (For 1948 service industry receipts are the sum of the following categories:

1) Personal, business, and repair services
2) Amusements
3) Hotels
4) Tourists courts.)

From U.S. Bureau of the Census, 1948 Census of Business, Vol. III, (Washington, D.C.: U.S. Government Printing Office, 1951), Table 102; Vol. VII, (Washington, D.C.: U.S. Government Printing Office, 1951), Table 102A; 1958 Census of Business, Vol. II, (Washington, D.C.: U.S. Government Printing Office, 1961), Table 103; and Vol. VI, (Washington, D.C.: U.S. Government Printing Office, 1961), Table 103.

DOMWKR - Employment in retail and service industries, 1958/1948, in natural logs. (For 1948 service industry employment is the sum of employment in the categories described under DOMOTP.) Same source as for DOMOTP.

DWAGE - Weighted average of production worker wages in dollars divided by number of manufacturing production workers, 1958/1947, by two-digit industry; weights are 1947 manufacturing production workers; in natural logs. From U.S. Bureau of the Census, 1947 Census of Manufactures, Vol. II, (Washington, D.C.: U.S. Government Printing Office, 1950), Table 5, and 1958 Census of Manufactures, Vol. III (Washington, D.C.: U.S. Government Printing Office, 1961), Table 5.

INCOME - Natural log of median income of families and unrelated individuals in dollars, 1959/1949, plus natural log of number of families and unrelated individuals, 1960/1950. From 1950 Census of Population, Vol. II, *op. cit.*, State Parts, Tables 37 and 34, respectively; and 1960 Census of Population, Vol. I, *op. cit.*, State Parts, Tables 76 and 72, respectively.

MFGOTP - Value added by manufacture, in dollars, 1957/1947, in natural logs. From U.S. Bureau of the Census, 1958 Census of Manufactures, Vol. III, (Washington, D.C.: U.S. Government Printing Office, 1961), Table 2.

MFGWKR - Number of manufacturing production workers, 1957/1947, in natural logs. Same source as for MFGOTP.

MIGRTN - Weighted average of 1960 actual less expected population divided by 1950 actual population, by age (14-19, 20-24,...,60-64) and sex; expected population is ratio of actual U.S. total population, 1960, to U.S. total population which was 10 years younger in 1950, multiplied by 1950 actual SMSA population;[18] weights are 1950 civilian labor force; plus one in natural logs. U.S. population data from 1950 Census of Population, Vol. II, op. cit., U.S. Summary, Table 37, and 1960 Census of Population, Vol. I, op. cit., U.S. Summary, Tables 157-8; SMSA population data from same volumes, State Parts, Table 33 for 1950, State Parts, Table 20 for 1960. SMSA labor force data from same 1950 volume, State Parts, Table 66.

NATINC - Weighted average of 1960 expected population divided by 1950 actual population, by age (14-19, 20-24,..., 60-64), and sex; expected population as described under MIGRTN; weights are 1950 civilian labor force; in natural logs. Same source as MIGRTN.

PRICE - Weighted average of U.S. value added by manufacture in dollars divided by Federal Reserve Index of Industrial Production, 1957/1947, by two-digit industry; weights are SMSA value added, in dollars, 1947; in natural logs. SMSA value added data from same source as DWAGE; U.S. value added data from U.S. Bureau of the Census, Annual Survey of Manufactures: 1951, (Washington, D.C.: U.S. Government Printing Office, 1953), Table 2, and Annual Survey of Manufactures: 1957, (Washington, D.C.: U.S. Government Printing Office, 1959), Table 2; Federal Reserve Index from U.S. Office of Business Economics, Business Statistics, 1955 Edition, (Washington, D.C.: U.S. Government Printing Office, 1955), pp. 7-9 for 1947 and Federal Reserve Bulletin, 44 (June, 1958), p. 695, for 1957.

PRODTY - Weighted average of Federal Reserve Index of Industrial Production divided by U.S. number of manufacturing production workers, 1957/1947, by two-digit industry; weights are SMSA value added, in dollars, 1947; in natural logs. Same source as for PRICE (Production worker data from same source as value added data for PRICE).

PRPMFG - Proportion of employment in manufacturing, 1950, in natural logs. From 1950 Census of Population, Vol. II, op. cit., State Parts, Table 79.

SIZE - Natural log of 1950 SMSA total population, from 1950 Census of Population, Vol. II, op. cit., U.S. Summary, Table 86.

SW, W - A dummy variable taking the value 1 for the following cities: Houston, Texas; Los Angeles, San Diego, and San Francisco, Calif.; and Portland, Oregon. For other cities it is equal to zero.

TLEMPT - Civilian employment, 1960/1950, in natural logs. Same source as for DARMFC.

UNEMPT - Proportion of males in experienced civilian labor force reporting weeks worked in 1949 who worked 26 weeks or less, in natural logs. From 1950 Census of Population, Vol. II, op. cit., State Parts, Table 85.

WAGE47 - Weighted average of production worker wages in dollars divided by number of manufacturing production workers, SMSA relative to U.S., 1947, by two-digit industry; weights are 1947 SMSA manufacturing production workers; in natural logs. SMSA data from same source as DWAGE, U.S. data from same source as value-added data for PRICE.

The following are the SMSA's for which data were used in the analysis. Their inclusion was determined by the availability of data.

Akron, Ohio
Allentown-Bethlehem-Easton, Pa.
Buffalo, N.Y.
Canton, Ohio
Cincinnati, Ohio

Columbus, Ohio
Detroit, Mich.
Erie, Pa.
Grand Rapids, Mich.
Houston, Texas

Indianapolis, Ind.
Kansas City, Mo.
Los Angeles, Calif.
New Orleans, La.
New York, N.Y.

Peoria, Ill.
Philadelphia, Pa.
Pittsburgh, Pa.
Portland, Oregon
Reading, Pa.

Rochester, N.Y.
San Diego, Calif.
San Francisco, Calif.
Toledo, Ohio
Utica-Rome, N.Y.

Table B.1

MEANS AND STANDARD DEVIATIONS OF DEPENDENT VARIABLES

Variable	Mean	Std. Dev.	Std. Error of Estimate, Reduced Forms[a]
DOMOTP	.451	.141	.0948
DOMWKR	.114	.146	.101
DWAGE	.549	.0765	.0570
INCOME	.764	.102	.0882
MFGOTP	.753	.292	.168
MFGWKR	.0694	.294	.157
MIGRTN	.0681	.113	.0738
TLEMPT	.168	.131	.0778

[a] With the following variables as independent: PRICE, PRODTY, SIZE, PRPMFG, UNEMPT, NATINC and DARMFC.

FOOTNOTES

* This work carried out under contract with U.S. Corps of Army Engineers.

1 For a more complete account of the export-base theory, some of its conceptual and practical difficulties, and citations of the literature on it, see Isard [6; pp. 189-205].

2 The latter is important, it is argued, because, where manufacturing is a smaller proportion of total employment, earnings in manufacturing are higher relative to those in other sectors and labor shifts out of these other sectors into manufacturing. Natural increase in the labor force is also greater where manufacturing is less important because of higher birth rates.

3 By primary worker one means a household's principal wage earner.

4 I abstract, here, from one feature of the Borts-Stein model, namely inter-sectoral shifts in labor supply and differential earnings rates in the several sectors. This feature is admittedly quite important when dealing with broad geographical regions with under-developed agricultural sectors, but it is probably much less important when dealing with cities. Of course, exogenous shifts of labor out of surrounding agricultural areas would be treated as exogenous increases in migration in my analysis.

5 The city's demand for domestic output may also depend upon the prices of its exportable commodities and the commodities it imports. The rise in the price of its exportables could either increase or reduce the demand for the output of and labor in its domestic sector. I doubt, though, that such effects are quantitatively very important. There is, of course, no reason to expect the prices of imported commodities to vary systematically with the demand for the city's exports.

6 Expected 1960 population in a particular age-sex cohort is the 1950 actual population ten years younger for the

same city multiplied by the ratio of 1960 to 1950 actual population in the same age-sex cohort for the nation as a whole. Actual minus expected 1960 relative to actual 1950 population provides an estimate of population increase in the given cohort which occurred because of migration.

7 By reported I mean those two-digit industries for which the necessary 1947 data were given by the Census of Manufacturers.

8 Secondary workers are those who are not principal wage earners of households--most working wives, for example. Their labor force participation rates are typically more responsive to earnings changes than those of principal wage earners.

9 While 1957 might have been more desirable than 1958 as the terminal year for the index to hold the effects of unemployment more nearly constant, the impact of the decline in aggregate demand nationally is likely to be primarily upon employment and output rather than upon money wage rates. If not, why does unemployment increase? 1958 was used because of the considerably greater two-digit industry detail for SMSA's in the 1958 Census of Manufacturers as compared with the 1957 Annual Survey of Manufacturers.

10 As an alternative here, and for the productivity change variable described below, I followed the same procedure but used unpublished Department of Commerce estimates of constant dollar value added instead of the Federal Reserve index of industrial production as a quantity measure. The two sets of series gave rather different values, both for two-digit industries nationally and for the various SMSA aggregates. The measures described in the text gave somewhat better results.

11 The city's export sector is in a position similar to that of a single competitive firm under the assumption of an infinitely elastic exportable demand. At the national level, of course, a neutral technological change will increase the industry's output and bring about a decrease in relative price. Its total effect upon the demand for labor then depends upon the elasticity of demand for the industry's output. The effects of such national price changes, hopefully, are captured by the PRICE variable just described.

12 Appendix A suggests that both PRICE and PRODTY should have the same coefficient in the wage change equation, namely the reciprocal of labor's share, the latter being production worker wages divided by value added. Labor's share, of course, varies from city to city. However, better fits for the wage change equation were obtained using the two separately and not weighted by the inverse of labor's share. This may be the case because of measurement errors in these variables which arise partly from differences in intra two-digit composition of output and partly because some of the city's manufacturing industries do not face infinitely leastic demand schedules.

13 Two-stage least-squares estimates depend not only upon the variables included in the equation in question but also upon the predetermined variables included in other equations of the model. Since WAGE47 is included in none of the others, it was also dropped from all other equations. Except for (2.1), (1.5) and (2.4) the predetermined variables included only PRICE, PRODTY, SIZE, PRPMFG, UNEMPT, NATINC, and DARMFC. In (1.5) and (2.4), the regional dummy variable was included in addition to the above-noted ones.

14 The manufacturing value added and production worker data are not needed for this purpose, and equations (1.4) and (2.3) suggest DWAGE could be omitted without noticeably affecting the other coefficients. Thus, the limitations imposed by data availability in the manufacturing censuses would not prevent more detailed study of employment change and migration for a larger number of cities.

15 In earlier comparisons I included the 1950 ratio of median income for males employed in manufacturing to that for retail trade to test for intra-city labor supply shifts. The coefficient of this variable, however, had the wrong sign in the manufacturing worker reduced-form equation, and I omitted it in subsequent runs.

16 Because there was little variation in the change in median income of families and unrelated individuals among cities, I did not attempt to estimate separately the effects of increased size and per family income. Cf. my remarks below on the effects of differential money wage changes in (4.4).

17 [10; pp. 222-5]. In deriving these results it was assumed that the industry consists of a large number of actual or potential producers of a single homogeneous product having identical production functions, there are no factors which are specialized to any firm, and that no external technological effects are present. These assumptions imply that the industry output depends only upon the aggregate quantities of each factor used by the industry (in addition, of course, to "technology") and, in fact, is a function which is homogeneous of degree one in the quantities of these factors.

18 Since SMSA data for 1950 population 4 years old were not given, expected 1960 population 14-19 years old was obtained by taking the ratio of 1960 actual U.S. population 14-19 years to 1950 actual U.S. population 5-9 years multipled by 1950 actual SMSA population 5-9 years.

REFERENCES

[1] Blanco, Cicely, "The Determinants of Interstate Population Movements," *Journal of Regional Science*, 5 (Summer, 1963), 77-84.

[2] Borts, George H. and Stein, Jerome L., *Economic Growth in a Free Market*, New York: Columbia University Press, 1964.

[3] Bowen, William G. and Finegan, T. A., "Labor Force Participation and Unemployment," ed. Arthur M. Ross, *Employment Policy and the Labor Market*, Berkeley, Calif.: University of California Press, 1965, 115-161.

[4] Chinitz, Benjamin, *Freight and the Metropolis*, Cambridge, Mass.: Harvard University Press, 1960.

[5] Finegan, T. Aldrich, "Hours of Work in the United States: A Cross-Sectional Analysis," *Journal of Political Economy*, LXX (October, 1962), 452-470.

[6] Isard, Walter, *Methods of Regional Analysis: An Introduction to Regional Science*, New York: John Wiley & Sons, Inc., 1960.

[7] Leven, Charles L., "Regional Income and Product Accounts: Construction and Applications," ed. Werner Hochwald, *Design of Regional Accounts*, Baltimore: Johns Hopkins Press for Resources for the Future, 1961, 148-195.

[8] Lowry, Ira S., *Migration and Metropolitan Growth: Two Analytical Models*, San Francisco, Calif.: Chandler Publishing Company, 1966.

[9] Mazek, Warren, "The Efficacy of Labor Migration with Special Emphasis on Depressed Areas," Working Paper CUR 2, Institute for Urban and Regional Studies, Washington University (Processed, June, 1966).

[10] Muth, Richard F., "The Derived Demand Curve for a Productive Factor and the Industry Supply Curve," *Oxford Economic Papers*, New Series 16 (July 1964), 221-234.

III.

MACROECONOMICS, GROWTH THEORY AND INTERNATIONAL TRADE

DISEQUILIBRIUM IN A MACRO ECONOMIC MODEL*

by

Peter Frevert
University of Kansas

In a recent paper Clower [1] argues that "what Keynes really meant" when he wrote the General Theory was to construct a model which described an economy that was out of price equilibrium in the sense of Walras, and more importantly one in which the behavior of transactors differed markedly from that of the Walrasian model precisely because it was out of price equilibrium. This paper is devoted to the examination of two particulars which Clower leads up to but does not consider explicitly: (1) a formal description of behavior in a macro-economic model in which Walras' Law does not hold in Clower's interpretation, and (2) the stability properties of such a model.

Notation. Following for the most part Clower's notation, let

$\overline{X}^i_j$ = the planned or notional excess demand for commodity j by transactor i; and let $\overline{X}^i_j = \overline{d}^i_j$ for $\overline{X}^i_j \geq 0$, and $\overline{X}^i_j = - s^j_i$ for $\overline{X}^i_j < 0$.

X^i_j = the realized values of the amount of commodity j obtained in trade by transactor i. Also $X^i_j = d^i_j$ for $X^i_j \geq 0$; $X^i_j = - s^i_j$ for $X^i_j < 0$.

p_j = the price of the jth commodity

The Market Clearing Mechanism If realized income is not less than notional income, i.e.,

$$\sum_j^n p_j s^i_j \geq \sum_j^n p_j \overline{s}^i_j$$

"We may suppose that the functions $\overline{d}^i_j$ and $\overline{s}^i_j$ constitute the relevant market signaling devices."[1] If on the other hand

*I would like to thank James Quirk and Richard Ruppert for the great amount of help they gave me in the preparation of this paper.

realized income turns out to be less than notional income,[2]

$$\text{i.e.,} \quad \sum_j^n p_j s_j < \sum_j^n p_j \bar{s}_j^i,$$

this imposes a constraint on the $\bar{d}_j^i$, under what Clower calls the "dual decision hypothesis". What is important for our purposes is the implicit market clearing mechanism, which is as follows: for positive notional excess supply, the market is cleared along the demand curve, and for negative notional excess supply the market is cleared along the supply curve. This amounts to a formidable technical complication in the study of stability since it means that, in general, partial derivatives of realized excess supply either do not exist at equilibrium or are discontinuous at equilibrium (see figure 0).

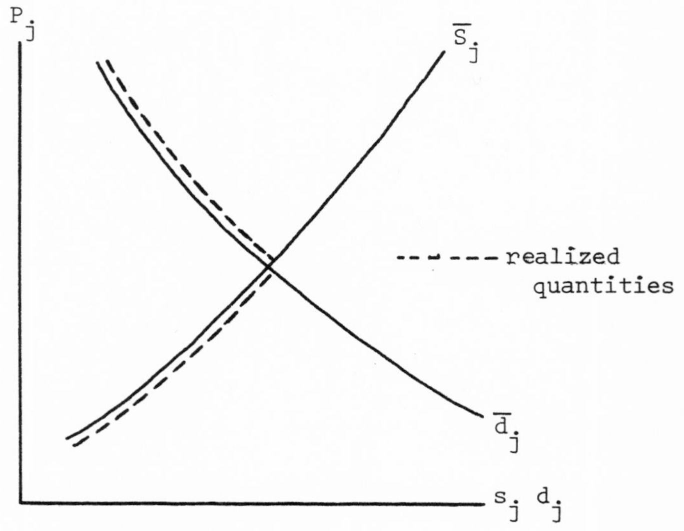

Fig. 0

While this complication may cause insurmountable difficulties in the general case, it turns out that some useful information can be obtained about the effect of this "non-Walrasian" part of behavior in a three-good, aggregative model.

THE THREE GOOD WORLD. Let: L, G, and M index quantities of labor, goods, and money, respectively. Money (M) may be (in addition to a medium of exchange) easily generalized to a composite financial asset; inside and/or outside money, with or without a rate of return. Also let:

p = goods price, w = wage of labor, and let the money price = 1 so that it also serves as numeraire.[3] Conventionally one market excess demand equation, say the money market equation, may be eliminated by Walras' Law and the equilibrium of the model is given by

$$\text{I} \quad \begin{cases} X_G\ (w,p) = 0; \\ X_L\ (w,p) = 0. \end{cases}$$

The X (w,p) represent the aggregate excess demands here in the notional sense; the aggregative property of the model amounts to assuming that no problems arise from aggregation over individual transactors.

For comparison consider the case of an excess supply of labor that affects the suppliers of labor in accordance with Clower's dual decision hypothesis. For these transactors (indexed by i = (1)) we have new excess demand functions

$$X_G^{(1)}\ (p, w\ X_L^{(2)});$$

$$X_L^{(1)}\ (w,p),$$

$wX_L^{(2)}$, labor income realized, appearing as an argument of goods demand. The transactor index (2) in $X_L^{(2)}$ denotes these transactors who are demanders of labor. $X_L^{(1)}$ may have the same form as in the conventional case, i.e., the "classical" supply function for labor. The market excess demand functions become

$$\text{II} \quad \begin{cases} X_G = X_G^{(2)}\ (w,p) + X_G^{(1)}\ (p,w\ X_L^{(2)}), \\ X_L = X_L^{(2)}\ (w,p) + X_L^{(1)}\ (w,p). \end{cases}$$

Stability. Assume that

$$\dot{p} = \alpha_G X_G$$

$$\dot{w} = \alpha_L X_L$$

Under the dual decision hypothesis

$$X_G = \begin{cases} X_G(w,p) & \text{for } X_L > 0; \\ X_G^{(2)}(w,p) + X_G^{(1)}(p, w\, X_L^{(2)}) & \text{for } X_L \leq 0. \end{cases}$$

This means that the partial derivatives of X_G with respect to w, p, are not defined at $X_L = 0$. We may reasonably assume that the function X_G is itself continuous, however. In particular it is <u>assumed</u> that X_G is continuous for $X_L > 0$ and $X_L < 0$, and in addition

$$X_G^{(2)} + X_G^{(1)} \to X_G\ (w,p) \text{ as } X_L \to 0.$$

This is because for $X_L = 0$ (labor market equilibrium) the realized current income term $w\, X_L^{(2)}$ in $X_G^{(1)}$ represents no <u>effective</u> constraint on consumer-laborer behavior.

In examining the stability properties of II, any theorems which depend on the functions being everywhere differentiable cannot be used. Some useful information can be obtained, however, from the phase diagrams constructed for the several cases.

Either System I or II can be approximated in a neighborhood of a point A by

$$X_G \cong b_{GG}(p - p_A) + b_{GL}(w - w_A) + X_G(A)$$

$$X_L \cong b_{LG}(p - p_A) + b_{LL}(w - w_A) + X_L(A)$$

where $b_{GG} = \dfrac{\partial X_G}{\partial p}$

$b_{GL} = \dfrac{\partial X_G}{\partial w}$

$b_{LG} = \dfrac{\partial X_L}{\partial p}$

$b_{LL} = \dfrac{\partial X_L}{\partial w}$

Of course in II, A cannot be a point on $X_L = 0$ since X_G is not generally differentiable there. The existence or nonexistence of derivatives is irrelevant to the main question of convergence, but it will become apparent later that the partial derivatives, where defined, have inherent economic importance. In a recent paper Quirk and Ruppert [3] have explored some applications of a theorem by Olech to the (global) stability problems in economic theory that may be represented by phase diagrams. The theory itself provides a set of sufficient conditions for global stability of a two equation system requiring that certain restrictions on the partial derivatives (above) hold everywhere. While in the present problem difficulties arise in Model II in connection with these restrictions, it is nonetheless helpful to analyze the cases with Quirk and Ruppert's technique.

First, assume that model I has $b_{GG} < 0$; $b_{GL} > 0$; $b_{LG} > 0$; $b_{LL} < 0$ everywhere. Thus the Jacobian has the sign pattern

$$\begin{bmatrix} - & + \\ + & - \end{bmatrix}$$

We assume that model I is stable, and then attempt to determine whether this stability is affected by the changes (the addition of the dual decision hypothesis) necessary to convert the model to II. The additional requirement for stability in I is that $b_{GG}b_{LL} > b_{GL}b_{LG}$ everywhere. The phase diagram for this stable case is presented in Figure 1.

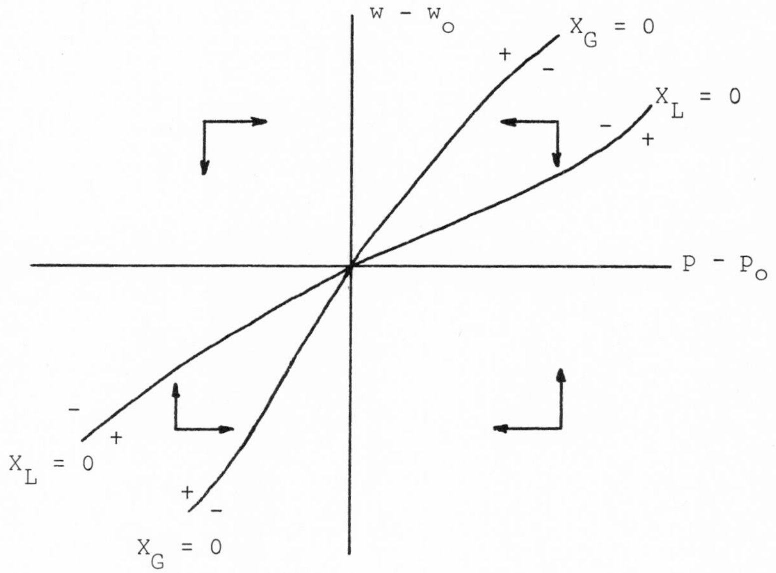

Fig. 1

II is identical to I for $X_L > 0$, but for $X_L \leq 0$, X_G becomes

$$X_G = X_G^{(2)}(w,p) + X_G^{(1)}(p, w X_L^{(2)}).$$

In the linear approximation, for $X_L < 0$

$$b^*_{GG} = \overset{(-)}{\frac{\partial X_G^{(2)}}{\partial p}} + \overset{(-)}{\frac{\partial X_G^{(1)}}{\partial p}} + \overset{(+)}{\frac{\partial X_G^{(1)}}{\partial (w X_L^{(2)})}} \cdot \overset{(+)}{w} \cdot \overset{(+)}{\frac{\partial X_L^{(2)}}{\partial p}}$$

$$b^*_{GL} = \overset{(+)}{\frac{\partial X_G^{(2)}}{\partial w}} + \overset{(+)}{\frac{\partial X_G^{(1)}}{\partial (w X_L^{(2)})}} \; w \left[\overset{(-)}{\frac{\partial X_L^{(2)}}{\partial w}} + \overset{(+)}{X_L^{(2)}} \right]$$

(b_{GG} and b_{GL} are not defined for $X_L = 0$). Here the signs of b_{GG} and b_{GL} are ambiguous, giving rise to several possible cases:

IIa. The sign pattern remains $\begin{bmatrix} - & + \\ + & - \end{bmatrix}$ for $X_L < 0$. This may not be stable for the initial condition $X_L < 0$ since $b^*_{GG} b_{LL} - b^*_{GL} b_{LG}$ may change sign.

IIb. The sign pattern becomes $\begin{bmatrix} + & + \\ + & - \end{bmatrix}$ for $X_L < 0$.

Figure 2 is the phase diagram for case IIb.

While X_G is not differentiable for $X_L = 0$, it is easy to see what happens at these points. Since

$$\left.\begin{array}{l} X_G > 0 \text{ for } X_L < 0 \\ X_G < 0 \text{ for } X_L > 0 \end{array}\right\} \quad p - p_o > 0$$

$$\left.\begin{array}{l} X_G < 0 \text{ for } X_L < 0 \\ X_G > 0 \text{ for } X_L > 0 \end{array}\right\} \quad p - p_o < 0$$

and since X_G is continuous at $X_L = 0$, then $X_G = 0$ at $X_L = 0$. (The locus of points $X_G = 0$ is hence augmented by the points

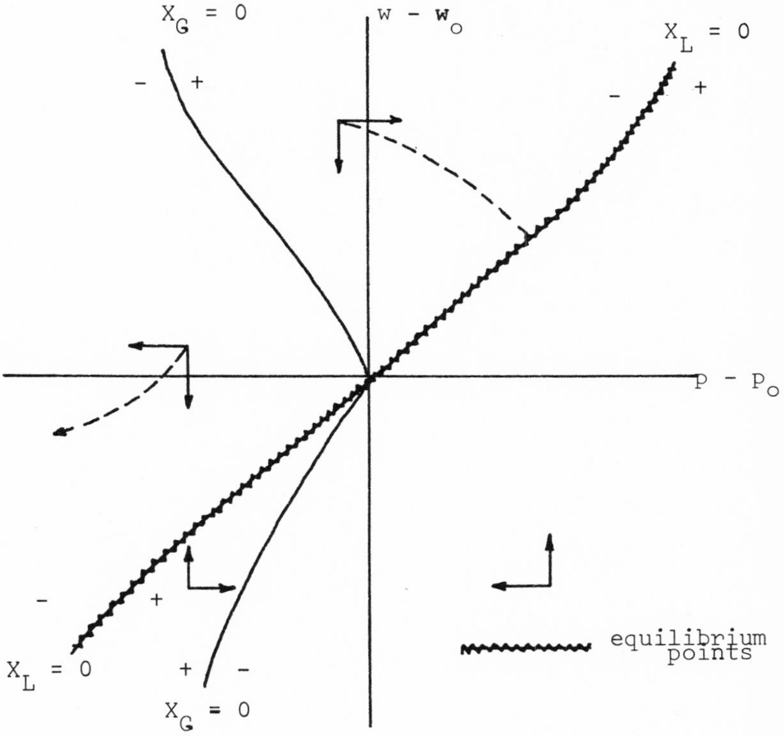

Fig. 2

$X_L = 0$). This implies that whenever the time path arrives at a point $X_L = 0$, it remains there because

$$\dot{p} = \alpha_G X_G = 0,$$

$$\dot{w} = \alpha_L X_L = 0.$$

As the graph indicates all points $X_L = 0$ are equilibrium points. Convergence to an equilibrium point is guaranteed for any initial conditions for which either $X_G > 0$ or $X_L > 0$ or both. For the initial condition $X_G < 0$, $X_L < 0$ the time path may be explosive, depending on the value of

$$\frac{dw}{dp} = \frac{\alpha_L X_L}{\alpha_G X_G}$$

It has been demonstrated that this is probably a vacuous case because, for $X_L > 0$, X_G is identical to that of Case I. But continuity implies $X_G \to 0$ as $X_L \to 0$ from either side of $X_L = 0$ in Case II, so it must imply the same thing for Case I. But the stability assumed in Case I makes this impossible.[4]

IIc. The sign pattern becomes $\begin{bmatrix} + & - \\ + & - \end{bmatrix}$ for all $X_L < 0$.

The phase diagram for this case is presented in Figure 3.

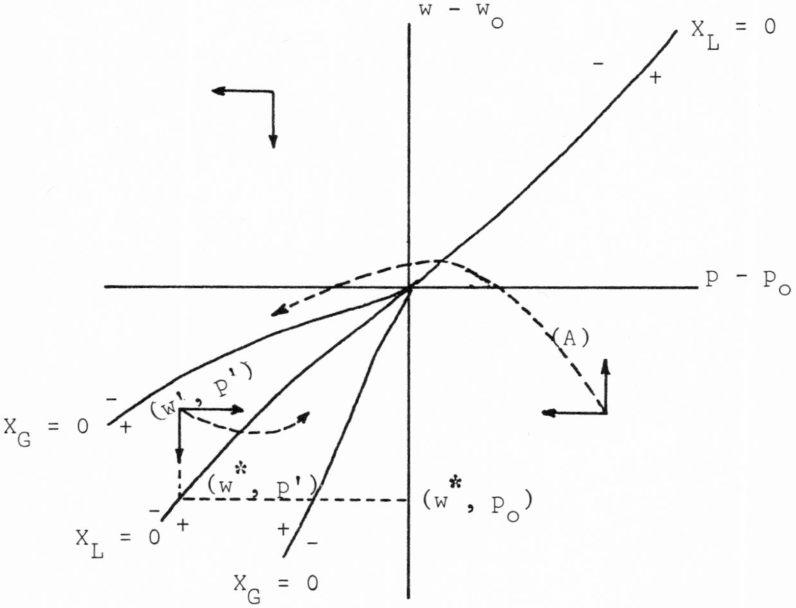

Fig. 3

In this case $X_G \neq 0$ along $X_L = 0$ so it does not possess the multiplicity of unstable equilibrium points as does IIb. For the initial condition $X_G < 0$ the system may be explosive as indicated by the (admissible) time path A. That the time path approaches p_o, w_o from any initial condition $X_G > 0$ requires proof (p_o, w_o is still not a stable equilibrium because of the existence of points $X_G < 0$ in the neighborhood of p_o, w_o).

<u>Proof</u>: Beginning at point (w', p'), choose $w^* | X_L(w^*, p') = 0$ and consider the point (w^*, p_o). Define the distance

function

$$D = (w - w^*)^2 + (p - p_o)^2$$

differentiating:

$$\frac{1}{2}\frac{dD}{dt} = (w - w^*)\,\dot{w} + (p - p_o)\,\dot{p}$$

$$= (w - w^*)\,\alpha_L X_L + (p - p_o)\,\alpha_G X_G < 0$$

so long as $X_L \leq 0$. Since X_L is a continuous function of w and p, and since w and p are continuous functions of time we may choose an $X_L > 0$ sufficiently small so that $\frac{1}{2}\frac{dD}{dt} < 0$, proving that the time path "crosses" $X_L = 0$. Now from a point $X_G > 0$, $X_L > 0$ redefine D such that

$$D' = (w - w_o)^2 + (p - p_o)^2$$

$$\frac{1}{2}\frac{dD'}{dt} = (w - w_o)\,\alpha_L X_L + (p - p_o)\,\alpha_G X_G < 0,$$

since X_G remains non-negative by the hypothesis $\dot{p} = \alpha_G X_G$. That is, along the time path $\frac{dp}{dw} = \frac{\dot{p}}{\dot{w}} = \frac{\alpha_G X_G}{\alpha_L X_L} = 0$ at $X_G = 0$, but the slope of $X_G = 0$: $\frac{dp}{dw}(|X_G = 0) > 0$ (also $\dot{w} = \alpha_L X_L > 0$) so that the time path cannot "cross" $X_G = 0$.

IId. The sign pattern becomes $\begin{bmatrix} - & - \\ + & - \end{bmatrix}$ for $X_L < 0$.

Figure 4 is the phase diagram for this case.

Here the equilibrium is globally stable since w,p converge to w_o, p_o from any initial point. That is, from a starting point $X_G > 0$ the convergence is analogous to Case IIc. Starting at a point $X_G < 0$ (say w', p' where $X_L > 0$) and defining

$$D = (w - w^*)^2 + (p - p_o)^2$$

where $w^* = w|X_L(w,p') = 0$, we have

$$\frac{1}{2}\frac{dD}{dt} = (w - w^*)\,\alpha_L X_L + (p - p_o)\,\alpha_G X_G < 0$$

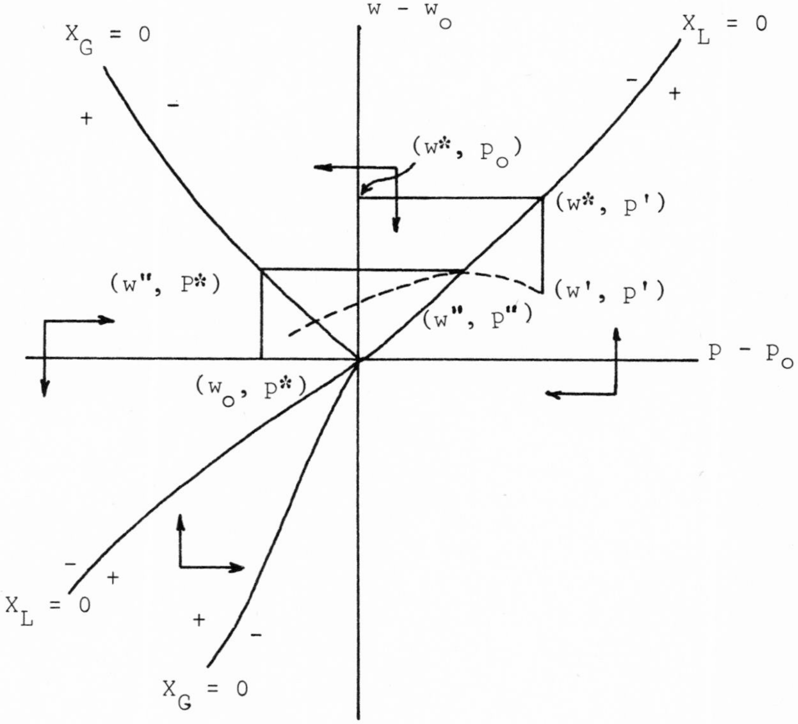

Fig. 4

until $X_L = 0$. Suppose this occurs at w", p". Redefine the distance function

$$D' = (w - w_o^o)^2 + (p - p^*)^2$$

where $p^* = p|X_G(w'',p) = 0$, so that

$$\frac{1}{2}\frac{dD'}{dt} = (w - w_o)\,\alpha_L X_L + (p - p^*)\,\alpha_G X_G < 0$$

until such time as $X_G > 0$ which is the situation mentioned above as covered under IIc.

CONCLUSION. While the cases examined above do not constitute a "theory" capable of any meaningful results in themselves, they indicate the way in which the "dual decision hypothesis", which is Clower's interpretation of Keynes' implicit assumption on transactor behavior, affect the stability - indeed the determinacy - of price equilibrium. The ambiguity of the sign pattern of the Jacobian of the system under model II arises in each case from the presence of the term $\frac{\partial X_G^{(1)}}{\partial (wX_L^{(2)})}$, which can be interpreted as a Keynesian "propensity" of the sort which does not appear in orthodox price theory. Indeed it is the "marginal propensity to consume out of labor income" and its size relative to the several price elasticities determine the signs of the terms in the Jacobian, the sign of its determinant, and hence the stability properties of the system.

FOOTNOTES

1. Clower [1], p.119.

2. Clower [1], p.119.

3. This is, in the Patinkin [2] sense, the "money price" of money. It is alright so long as the "accounting price" of money is greater than zero. Should the accounting price of money equal zero then it is not altogether clear that the money price of money would still be equal to one (1). But this problem is "beyond the scope of the present paper".

4. This was pointed out by Trout Rader and James G. Moore.

REFERENCES

1. Clower, Robert, "The Keynesian Counterrevolution: A Theoretical Appraisal" in The Theory of Interest Rates, Hahn and Brechling, ed., St. Martin's Press, 1965.

2. Patinkin, Don. Money, Interest and Prices, Second Edition, Harper & Row, 1965.

3. Quirk, James P. and Richard W. Ruppert, "Phase Diagrams and Global Stability" Research Papers in Theoretical and Applied Economics, Paper #11, Department of Economics, University of Kansas.

ON BALANCED CONSUMPTION IN A LINEAR PRODUCTION MODEL

by

Rubin Saposnik
University of Kansas

1. Introduction

Models with an explicit time structure in which the variables are assumed to be related in a linear fashion have been studied by Goodwin [3], Chipman [1], Metzler [4], Dorfman, Samuelson and Solow [2] and Nikaido [5]. More specifically, these models are of the form $y(t') = Ay(t'') + c(t''')$, where time is treated as a discrete variable and exactly two of t', t'', t''' are distinct. Depending on the context, y has been interpreted variously as output or income, A as a characterization of production coefficients or propensities to spend, and c as autonomous consumption or investment.

This paper follows these studies in that it is concerned with a relationship of the form:

(1) $y(t) - c(t) = Ay(t + 1)$ or, more generally,

(2) $y(t) - c(t) \geqq Ay(t + 1)$

If y(t) is interpreted as the goods available in period t, and c(t) is interpreted as consumption in period t, then (1) (resp. (2)) asserts that the goods available as inputs to production in period t + 1 must be equal to (resp. no greater than) what is left, net of consumption, from period t.

If it be assumed that there are a finite number of goods, say n, in the economy, then y(t) and c(t) are represented as elements of Euclidean n-space, R_n, and A is an n x n matrix. There does, however, seem to be some justification for positing an infinite number of goods in this model. For one might want to distinguish between goods that are identical except for geographic location. Furthermore even though time enters the model explicitly, in that all "accounting" is done at discrete points in time, there remains the possibility that goods might become available and be drawn off for consumption or production at discrete points (or even continuously) within each time period. Consequently, we assume that there are a (countably) infinite number of goods in the economy so that y(t) and c(t) are represented as infinite dimensional vectors. Also, at least initially, we postulate only that A is a linear operator without imputing any particular representation to A.[1]

Given this, the problem we want to study is the following:

For a given initial stock of goods (capital stock), size of population and autonomous rate of growth of population, under what conditions can we solve for a consumption path such that per-capita consumption of each good is positive, constant and as large as possible in perpetuity?

II. Digression on Normed Spaces

This section is a brief digression dealing with some simple notions involving normed linear spaces and operators that will be used subsequently. A norm, $||\cdot||$, on a linear space X is a non-negative real-valued function satisfying:

(i) $||x + x'|| \leq ||x|| + ||x'||$

(ii) $||\alpha x|| = |\alpha| \; ||x||$

(iii) $||x|| = 0 \Rightarrow x = 0$ [2]

If we consider the linear space composed of all infinite bounded sequences of real numbers ($x = (x_1, x_2, \ldots)$, $|x_i| < \infty$ for all i), then this space may be normed by defining $||x|| = \sup_i |x_i|$ and the resulting normed linear space, denoted ℓ^∞, is complete in this norm.[3]

If A is a linear operator mapping the normed linear space X into the normed linear space Y, then the norm of A, $||A||$, may be defined by $||A|| = \sup_{||x|| = 1} ||Ax||$. In particular, the application made subsequently assumes that $X = Y = \ell^\infty$, so that A is a linear operator from ℓ^∞ into itself.

III. Assumptions and Notation

We now characterize production in this model. Let (w,y) denote an input-output pair. We assume:

(A.1) $w, y \in \ell^\infty$

(A.2) $y \geq 0 \Rightarrow w \geq 0$

(A.3) $w = Ay$

(A.1) asserts that input and output vectors must consist of finite quantities of each good. (A.2) asserts that there is no "free production"; while (A.3) asserts that the input associated with a given output is a linear transform of the output vector. (A.2) and (A.3) together of course imply that A is a non-negative linear operator.

We shall use the following notation:

Let:

(D.1) $y(t)$ = output in period $t = 1, 2, \ldots$

(D.2) $c(t)$ = consumption in period $t = 0, 1, \ldots$

(D.3) $L(t)$ = population in period $t = 0, 1, \ldots$ with $L(0) = Lo$

(D.4) $y(0) = y^o$, stock of goods available in period 0.

(D.5) b = growth factor of population ($b = 1 + n$, where n = % growth rate)

For any $x \in \ell^\infty$ and $z \in \ell^\infty$, $z > 0$, define

$$\text{(D.6)}\quad A_z(x) = \left(\frac{v_1}{z_1}, \frac{v_2}{z_2}, \ldots\right), \text{ where } (v_1, v_2, \ldots) = A(z_1x_1, z_2x_2, \ldots)$$

We note that A_z is obviously a linear operator.

IV. A Theorem on Optimum Balanced Consumption

We wish to discover conditions under which there exists a consumption path such that per-capita consumption of each good is positive and constant in perpetuity and is at least as large as any per-capita consumption attainable in the given environment. Obviously, formulation of the problem in this way contains an implicit value judgment, namely, that an optimum plan for the economy is one that allots the same "standard of living", interpreted as per-capita consumption of all goods, to each generation. Then the time path of total consumption is a "balanced" path in that total consumption of each good grows at the same constant rate throughout. The theorem to be proved is as follows:

Let $\frac{y^o}{L_o} > 0$. Then, for given b, there exists a consumption path $\hat{c}(t)$, $t = 0, 1, \ldots$ with associated per capita consumption $\hat{\gamma}(t)$ such that:

(i) $\hat{\gamma}(t) = \hat{\gamma} > 0$, $t = 0, 1, \ldots$

(ii) $\hat{\gamma} > \gamma'$ for all attainable γ',

if, and only if, $||A_{y^o}|| < \frac{1}{b}$.

Proof: We first prove sufficiency.

We have from (2),

$$(3)\quad Y(t) - c(t) \geqq Ay(t + 1),\ t = 0, 1, \ldots$$

Using (A.3), we get

$$(4)\quad y^o \geqq c(0) + Ac(1) + A^2c(2) + \ldots$$

Letting $\tilde{c}(t) = \left(\frac{c_1(t)}{y_1^o}, \frac{c_2(t)}{y_2^o}, \ldots \right)$, we have from (D.6), (with $z = y^o$, $x = \tilde{c}$ and $zx = c$)

$$(5) \quad u \geqq \tilde{c}(0) + Ay^o \tilde{c}(1) + A^2 y_o \tilde{c}(2) + \ldots, \text{ where}$$

$u = (1, 1, \ldots)$

Dividing through by L_o yields:

$$(6) \quad \frac{u}{L_o} \geqq \tilde{\gamma}(0) + A_{y^o} [b\, \tilde{\gamma}(1)] + A^2_{y^o} [b^2\, \tilde{\gamma}(2)] +$$

$\ldots$, where $\tilde{\gamma}(t) = \frac{\tilde{c}(t)}{L(t)}$

Setting $\tilde{\gamma}(t) = \hat{\gamma}$ for all t, writing $bA_{y^o} = B$, and viewing (6) as an equation, we have

$$(7) \quad \frac{u}{L_o} = [I + B + B^2 + \ldots]\hat{\gamma}$$

It follows from a well-known theorem on linear operators that:[4]

$$(8) \quad \frac{u}{L_o} = [I - B]^{-1}\, \hat{\gamma}, \text{ so that}$$

$$(9) \quad \hat{\gamma} = [I - B]\, \frac{u}{L_o}$$

Clearly $\hat{\gamma} \geqq \gamma'$ for all $\gamma' \leqq [I - B]\,\frac{u}{L_o}$[5]. Moreover, $\hat{\gamma} = (\hat{\gamma}_1, \hat{\gamma}_2, \ldots) > 0$. To see this, suppose $\hat{\gamma}_k \leqq 0$ for some k. This implies that the kth component of Bu is no less than the kth component of u, which is 1 by definition. Then $||B|| \geqq ||Bu|| \geqq 1$, which is a contradiction.

To show necessity we note that it follows from (A.2), (A.3) and the definition of B that $y \geqq y'$ implies $By \geqq By'$. Consequently, since $u \geqq z$ for all z such that $||z|| = 1$, $Bu \geqq Bz$ and $||Bu|| \geqq ||Bz||$, yielding $||B|| = ||Bu||$. Therefore $||B|| \geqq 1$ would mean that not $\hat{\gamma} > 0$.

Translation of γ back into total consumption vectors is of course immediate. In terms of the "normalized" consumption vectors, $\tilde{c}$, total consumption in period t is obviously given by:

$$(10) \quad \tilde{c}(t) = L_o b^t \hat{\gamma}\,. \quad t = 0, 1, \ldots$$

In terms of units as initially defined in the capital stock, we have:

$$(11) \quad c(t) = (c_1(t), c_2(t), \ldots) = (y_1^o \tilde{c}_1(t), y_2^o \tilde{c}_2(t), \ldots) \quad t=0, 1, \ldots$$

Finally, if we take A to be an infinite matrix, then $A_{y^o} = \left(a_{ij} \frac{y_j^o}{y_i^o} \right)$ and the condition of the theorem is equivalent to $\sum_{j=1} a_{ij} \frac{y_j^o}{y_i^o} < \frac{1}{b}$ for $i = 1, 2, \ldots$[6] In this case, $a_{ij} \frac{y_j^o}{y_i^o}$ denotes the quantity of the jth good required to produce one unit of the ith good, where units in which commodities are measured are such that the vector y^o represents one unit of each commodity.

V. Summary and Conclusions

Under the assumption of a linear technology, in an economy having an infinite number of goods, we have derived a condition on the relationship among the stock of capital available to society, the rate of growth of population and the "growth potential" inherent in the technology, necessary and sufficient to guarantee the existence of a highest possible standard of living. We have defined "standard of living" in terms of per-capita consumption over an infinite time span. In essence, the condition is that the "productivity" of the economy (units of goods being chosen so that the stock of capital at the outset consists of one unit of each good) is greater than the growth rate of the population.

The choice of units in which goods are measured turns out to be crucial, for, whereas the issue of what capital stock is adequate to sustain an autonomously specified permanent standard of living may be resolved in terms of the relation between the population growth rate and the growth rate of the economy, irrespective of the units in which goods are measured, the issue of what permanent standard of living can be sustained by a given capital stock does depend on the relative amounts of goods in the capital stock. In particular, units of measurement are defined in terms of the existing stock of capital.

REFERENCES

[1] Chipman, J. S., "The Multi-Sector Multiplier", Econometrica, Vol. 18, October, 1950, pp. 355-374.

[2] Dorfman, R., P.A. Samuelson, and R.M. Solow, Linear Programming and Economic Analysis, McGraw-Hill, 1958.

[3] Goodwin, R. M., "The Multiplier as Matrix", The Economic Journal, Vol. 59, December, 1949, pp. 537-555.

[4] Metzler, L. A., "A Multiple-Region Theory of Income and Trade", Econometrica, Vol. 18, October, 1950, pp. 329-354.

[5] Nikaido, H., "Leontief Model of Reversely Lagged Type", The Review of Economic Studies, Vol. 29, October, 1962, pp. 313-324.

[6] Taylor, A. E., Introduction to Functional Analysis, John Wiley, 1958.

FOOTNOTES

[1] A mapping $A: X \to Y$ where X, Y are linear (vector) spaces is said to be linear if:

$$(1) \quad A(x + x') = Ax + Ax'$$

$$(2) \quad A(\alpha x) = \alpha Ax \qquad \text{for all } x, x' \in X \text{ and all}$$

α in the associated scalar field.

[2] Probably the most familiar norm is that associated with Euclidean space:

$$\text{for } x \in R_n, \ ||x|| = \left[\sum_{i=1}^{n} x_i^2\right]^{1/2}$$

[3] A normed linear space is complete if every Cauchy sequence converges to an element of the space, where the distance between two points x, x' is given by $||x - x'||$.

A normed linear space that is also complete is called a Banach space.

[4] See [6], Theorem 4.1 - c, p. 164 for a statement and proof of this result.

[5] For, suppose $\gamma'' \geq \hat{\gamma}$. Then $[I + B + B^2 + \ldots]\,\gamma'' = [I - B]^{-1}\gamma'' \geq [I - B]^{-1}\hat{\gamma} = \frac{u}{L_o}$.

[6] It is well-known that not all linear operators from ℓ^∞ into ℓ^∞ are representable as infinite matrices. See [6] pp. 215-220.

TECHNICAL PROGRESS AND THE PRODUCTION FUNCTION, A SYNTHESIS

by

Frank S. T. Hsiao*

University of Colorado (Boulder)

1. Introduction

Some of the "stylized" facts about economic growth are the long-run constancy of income distribution between wages and profits, and the incessant changes of technology in the economy. Technological change affects factor shares through its factor-using or -saving character along with its effect on factor prices; when it leaves factor-shares unchanged on some condition, it is then called neutral. For Harrod [7, p. 23] the condition of neutrality is that the rate of profit remains unchanged, and for Hicks [8, pp. 121-122], it is that the capital-labor ratio is unchanged. These are working definitions. Of course, as Hicks puts it in his recent book [9, p. 180], we may also "define a neutral invention as one that leaves factor shares unchanged, if the rate of real wage remains unchanged". The reason for adding this definition is, as he rightly conjectures, that "it might indeed be quite useful to include it as a possibility, if we were attempting a complete discussion of the subject". Nevertheless, he himself does not pursue this point any further, because "it has (obviously) not been a popular notion".

This paper presents a "complete discussion" from the point of view of the relation between the notion of neutral technical progress and the form of the production function. The topic itself is not new in any sense. A pathbreaking work in this direction has been done by Uzawa and Watanabe [17] where they have derived the theorem (for an n-input case) that technical progress represented by a production function $Y = F(K,N;t)$[1] is Hicks neutral if and only if it can be written as $A(t)\ F(K,N)$; later Uzawa [18] proved that it is Harrod neutral if and only if $Y = F(K,A(t)N)$, and is both Harrod and Hicks neutral if and only if it is of the form $Y = A(t) \cdot K^a N^{1-a}$. Furthermore, the "unpopular" alternative definition which Hicks suggests as a possibility has been claimed by analogy in Hahn and Matthews [6, p. 830] to lead to a production function of the type $Y = F(A(t)K,N)$. They attribute this type of neutral technical progress to Solow [16, p. 59]. Later Fei and Ranis [5] also suggest this type of factor neutrality (and bias) of innovation in connection with their discussion of developing economies. In particular, they call it U-neutrality.[2]

Nevertheless, the methods of proof used in Watanabe and Uzawa, and Uzawa are rather cumbersome and unrelated; the proof for the last definition of neutral technical progress, i.e., U-neutrality, is not indicated in Hahn and Matthews nor in Fei and Ranis.

In general, there still seems wanting a kind of synthesis in the method of proof, which will show clearly and analytically in what essential way these definitions of neutrality can lead to certain particular types of production functions and how, at least formally, they are related.

This paper suggests a proof which may lead to a unified view of the relationship between these three definitions and the forms of production function. In all cases, symmetricity in the method of proof is preserved. This is achieved, under certain fundamental assumptions, by using the simplest solution technique of partial differential equations, which I have explained in the Appendix. One remarkable achievement is that the technique used here enabled me to start out from each definition directly and to arrive at the desired form of function as a general solution. The calculation is simple and straightforward. In the third section, this method of approach also enables me to establish, by means of very simple arguments, a general theorem[3] that technical progress is both Hicks and Harrod neutral, or Harrod and U-neutral, or U and Hicks neutral, if and only if the production function is of the Cobb-Douglas type. Then Section 4 shows that the Phelps' recent results on neutrality and the factor augmenting production function can be dealt with by exactly the same methods as were used in Section 2. In Section 5, in view of ever-increasing work in this field, I have sorted out some results which are scattered in the recent literature in connection with the proof. It is then shown that our approach not only gives us a systematic appraisal of the existing results, but also easily yields some more new necessary and sufficient conditions for neutrality, the choice of which naturally depends on its convenience to the model-builder. The last section is devoted briefly to a systematic presentation of various definitions of biased technical progress. It is shown clearly what is held constant and what is not, so as to point up a closer relation between verbal definitions and their analytical formulations. Several possible formulations are also suggested.

2. The Proof

The production function $Y = F(K,N;t)$ is assumed to have constant returns to scale with respect to two factors, labor N and capital K; and there is technical change which is incorporated into the production function through the time factor t, which operates so as to continuously raise the output Y over time, even without the help of capital and labor. Suppose the owners of factors are paid wages (w) per unit of labor employed and profits (r) per unit of capital used according to the (positive) marginal productivity of the factors; then $r = \frac{\partial F}{\partial K}$ and $w = \frac{\partial F}{\partial N}$. Since constant returns to scale prevails, we have $F_K K/Y + F_N N/Y = 1$. Hence, if one factor share is constant, the other must be constant also. Therefore, by way of formal definition, technical progress is neutral in the sense of Harrod [7] if the output-capital ratio remains unchanged when the rate of profit is unchanged; and it is U-neutral[4] if per capita output remains unchanged when the rate of real wages is unchanged. On the other hand, it is neutral in the sense of Hicks [8] if the ratio of two marginal productivities remains unchanged when the capital-labor ratio is unchanged. Rewriting the production function into per capita magnitudes, $y = f(k,t)$, where $y \equiv Y/N$, $k \equiv K/N$, $f(k,t) \equiv F(K/N,1;t)$, we have the relation $r = f_k(k,t)$, $w = f(k,t)-kf_k(k,t)$, where r, as well as w. is a function of k and t. Suppose the law of diminishing returns prevails, then $f_{kk}(k,t) < 0$, and so factor prices and capital-labor ratios have a unique relation. Hence, according to the definitions above, Harrod neutrality implies[5]

$$y/k = f(k(r,t),t)/k(r,t) = G^1(r)$$

i.e., the output-capital ratio is independent of the time factor t. Similarly, U-neutrality implies

$$y = f(k(w,t),t) = G^2(w)$$

i.e., the per capita output is independent of the time factor. Lastly, Hicks neutrality implies

$$w/r = w(k,t)/r(k,t) = G^3(k)$$

i.e., the factor-price ratio is independent of t.

Now we make a fundamental assumption. Suppose, by some way or the other, we have actually observed from an empirical study that neutral technical progress exists, and it takes one of the above three forms. Therefore the G^i's are certain observed known functions. In fact, such an assumption is not unfamiliar in economics, as it has been used to derive the constant-elasticity-of-substitution production function, when f depends only on k, and G^2 is linear logarithmic [Arrow, et al., 3]. With this fundamental assumption, we then write G^i's respectively in the form

(1) $\frac{y}{k} = G^1(\frac{\partial y}{\partial k})$

(2) $y = G^2(y - k\frac{\partial y}{\partial k})$

(3) $(y - k\frac{\partial y}{\partial k})/\frac{\partial y}{\partial k} = G^3(k)$

where G^i does not involve a time factor explicitly, and the superscript i corresponds to each definition mentioned above: 1 for Harrod's, 2 for U- and 3 for Hicks'.

Solving the above equations for the marginal productivity of capital (assuming this can be done), we have

(1)' $\frac{\partial y}{\partial k} = H^1(\frac{y}{k})$; (2)' $\frac{\partial y}{\partial k} = \frac{H^2(y)}{k}$; (3)' $\frac{\partial y}{\partial k} = \frac{y}{H^3(k)}$

These three equations are nothing but a special case of Lagrange's equation, which I have explained in the Appendix, when the coefficient of $\frac{\partial y}{\partial t}$ is zero. Since dt = 0, and hence $t = c_2$, where c_2 is a constant of integration, we know that the time factor must appear separately in the solution of the above three equations. Furthermore, the auxiliary equation in this appendix shows simply:

(1)'' $\frac{dy}{dk} = H^1(\frac{y}{k})$; (2)'' $\frac{dy}{dk} = \frac{H^2(y)}{k}$; (3)'' $\frac{dy}{dk} = \frac{y}{H^3(k)}$

Now, to solve (1)'', we first substitute $z \equiv y/k$ in

(1)'', and obtain $dk/k = dz/(H^1(z)-z)$. Integrating both sides, we finally get $c_1 = k/J^1(z)$, where c_1 is a constant of integration and J^1 is some known function of z resulting from integrating the right-hand side of the above equation. Hence, the general solution of (1) is given by $J^1(z) = k/A(t)$, where A is any arbitrary function. Since average productivity of capital in general increases with respect to capital-efficiency-labor ratio, J^1 can be taken to be monotonic. Hence, solving for z, we have:

$$(1)''' \quad z = \phi^1\left(\frac{k}{A(t)}\right)$$

i.e., $Y/K = \phi^1(K/A(t)N)$; therefore we may write $Y = F(K, A(t)N)$, where F is linearly homogenous in K and A(t)N.

Equations (2)'' and (3)'' can be solved readily: (2)'' gives the solution $c_1 = k/J^2(y)$, where J^2 represents some known function of y resulting from integration. Remembering that A(t) is any arbitrary function, the general solution of (2) can be expressed as $J^2(y) = kA(t)$. Since again J^2 can be expected to be a monotonic function, we may solve for y, and have

$$(2)''' \quad y = \phi^2(kA(t))$$

i.e., $Y/N = \phi^2(KA(t)/N)$. Therefore we may write $Y = F(A(t)K, N)$, where F is linearly homogenous in A(t)K and N.

Similarly, (3)'' gives solution $c_1 = y/J^3(k)$, where J^3 is some known function as before. Hence the general solution of (3) is, rewriting J^3 as ϕ^3,

$$(3)''' \quad y = A(t)\,\phi^3(k)$$

i.e., $Y = A(t)\,F(K,N)$.

On the other hand, since all we have obtained is the solution to a corresponding partial differential equation (see the statement of the theorem in the Appendix), it satisfies the original equation which corresponds to it. This can be checked by a straightforward substitution. Hence, each special form of the production function thus obtained above is a necessary and sufficient condition for Harrod, U- and Hicks neutrality, respectively.

3. Neutrality and the Cobb-Douglas Type Production Function

It has been known for some time that technical progress, represented by a production function $Y = F(K,N;t)$, is both Harrod neutral and Hicks neutral if and only if the production function is of the Cobb-Douglas type; i.e., $Y = A(t)K^{a}N^{1-a}$ where $0 < a < 1$, $A(t) > 0$[6]. What will be the case when technical progress is both U-neutral and Hicks neutral, or both U-neutral and Harrod neutral? The answer is straightforward from the very definitions of neutrality as formulated in the previous section. In the previous section each of three definitions is represented by (1)', (2)' and (3)'. A combination of any two of the definitions is compatible if and only if the left-hand side of the equations considered are constant multiples of y/k. But, again by consulting the theorem in the Appendix, an equation of the form $\frac{\partial y}{\partial k} = \frac{ay}{k}$ has a general solution of the form $y = A(t)k^{a}$. Hence we have proved the following general theorem: Technical progress represented by a production function $Y = F(K,N;t)$ is both U- and Hicks neutral, or both Hicks and Harrod neutral, or both Harrod and U-neutral, if and only if the production function is of the Cobb-Douglas type.

4. Factor-Augmenting Production Function

In this section we extend the Harrod definition and also U-definition to obtain a production function which is factor augmenting: $Y = F(BK,AN)$. This extension has been done recently by Phelps [12]. We will show that our method introduced in Section 2 is also applicable to this general case. As in previous cases, technical progress is neutral in the sense of Phelps if there exists a positive function B(t), where B(t) is a function only of time t, such that the average productivity of capital increases proportionately to B(t) when the rate of profit increases proportionately to B(t). Hence according to this definition, we have

$$\frac{y}{B(t)k} = G^{4}\left(\frac{r}{B(t)}\right)$$

or (4)
$$\frac{y}{B(t)k} = G^{4}\left(\frac{1}{B(t)} \cdot \frac{\partial y}{\partial k}\right).$$

Since at each time point, B(t) is a constant B, we

may write $\frac{1}{B}\frac{\partial y}{\partial k} = \frac{1}{B}\frac{dy}{dk}\Big|_{t\ \text{const}} = \frac{\partial y}{\partial Bk}$. Now let $Bk = k^*$, then equation (4) can be written as

$$(5)\quad \frac{y}{k^*} = G^4\left(\frac{\partial y}{\partial k^*}\right)$$

which is the same form as (1). Therefore we will have $\frac{y}{k} = \phi^4\left(\frac{k^*}{A(t)}\right)$ or $Y = F(BK,AN)$.

Exactly the same kind of extension holds for U-neutrality. We shall say that technical progress is neutral if there exists a positive function B(t), where B(t) is a function only of time t, such that the average productivity of labor increases proportionately to B(t) when the rate of real wages increases proportionately to B(t). Hence according to this definition, we have

$$\frac{y}{B(t)} = G^5\left(\frac{w}{B(t)}\right)$$

$$\text{or } (6)\quad \frac{y}{B(t)} = G^5\left(\frac{y}{B(t)} - \frac{k}{B(t)}\frac{\partial y}{\partial k}\right)$$

Since at each time point, B(t) is again constant, $\frac{\partial y}{\partial k} = \frac{\partial(\frac{y}{B})}{\partial(\frac{k}{B})}$. Now let $y^* = \frac{y}{B}$ and $k^* = \frac{k}{B}$. Then we have

$$(7)\quad y^* = G^5\left(y^* - k^*\frac{\partial y}{\partial k}\right)$$

which is the same form as (2), and hence we obtain $y^* = \phi^5(k^*A(t))$ or $Y = F(AK,BN)$.

In general, let the factor-augmenting production function be $Y = F(BK,AN)$. Then technical progress expressed by the production function F is Harrod neutral if and only if $B = 1$ and $A \neq 1$, U-neutral if and only if $B \neq 1$, $A = 1$, and Hicks neutral if and only if $A = B \neq 1$.

5. Other Formulae for Neutrality Conditions

(A) For the sake of simplicity, rewrite equations (1), (2) and (3) as follows:

$$(8)\quad z = G^1(r);\qquad (9)\quad y = G^2(w);\quad (10)\quad \frac{w}{r} = G^3(k).$$

Since $z \equiv y/k$ and y, r, w are functions of k and t, partially differentiating both sides of each equation with respect to the time factor, and making some re-arrangements, we have

$$(11) \quad \frac{1}{y}\frac{\partial y}{\partial t} = \frac{r}{z}\frac{dz}{dr}\frac{1}{r}\frac{\partial r}{\partial t}$$

$$(12) \quad \frac{1}{y}\frac{\partial y}{\partial t} = \frac{w}{y}\frac{dy}{dw}\frac{1}{w}\frac{\partial w}{\partial t}$$

$$(13) \quad \frac{1}{w}\frac{\partial w}{\partial t} = \frac{1}{r}\frac{\partial r}{\partial t}$$

Since $f_{kk} < 0$, and

$$dz = \frac{kdy - ydk}{k^2},$$

$$dr = \frac{\partial^2 y}{\partial k^2}\, dk ,$$

we have

$$\frac{dz}{dr} = -\left(k^2 \frac{\partial^2 y}{\partial k^2}\right)^{-1}\left(y - k\frac{\partial y}{\partial k}\right)$$

and so

$$\frac{r}{z}\ \frac{dz}{dr} = -\left(y - k\frac{\partial y}{\partial k}\right)\frac{\partial y}{\partial k}\Big/ky\frac{\partial^2 y}{\partial k^2} ;$$

which is exactly the definition of the elasticity of substitution, σ, between the two factors. Similarly, since

$$dw = -k\frac{\partial^2 y}{\partial k^2}\, dk$$

and thus

$$\frac{dy}{dw} = -\left(k\frac{\partial^2 y}{\partial k^2}\right)^{-1}\frac{\partial y}{\partial k}$$

we again have $(w/y)(dy/dw) = \sigma$. Hence (11) and (12) can be written as

$$(14) \quad \frac{1}{y}\frac{\partial y}{\partial t} = \sigma\frac{1}{r}\frac{\partial r}{\partial t}$$

$$(15) \quad \frac{1}{y}\frac{\partial y}{\partial t} = \sigma\frac{1}{w}\frac{\partial w}{\partial t}$$

Conditions (14) and (15) are obtained in Amano [2].

(B) Since the production function $Y = F(K,N;t)$ or $y = f(y/z,t)$, has positive marginal productivities, we may write it as $y = h(z,t)$. Then, since $\frac{\partial y}{\partial k} = (\frac{\partial h}{\partial z} \cdot z^2)(z\frac{\partial h}{\partial z} - h)^{-1}$ by a direct calculation, substituting in (1)', (2)' and (3)', the definitions of neutrality can be expressed, respectively, as:

$$(16)\ \frac{\partial h}{\partial z} = \frac{h}{P^1(z)}\ ;\quad (17)\ \frac{\partial h}{\partial z} = \frac{P^2(h)}{z}\ ;\quad (18)\ \frac{\partial h}{\partial z} = P^3(\frac{h}{z})$$

where P^i's are properly defined known functions. Noticing that the form of (16) corresponds to that of (3)', and (18) to (1)', we can solve these equations by the previous method exactly and obtain equivalent conditions that a production function $Y = F(K,N;t)$. Hence, $y = h(z,t)$ is Harrod neutral, U-neutral, or Hicks neutral, respectively, if and only if it has the form

$$(19)\quad y = A(t)\ \psi^1(z);\quad (20)\quad y = \psi^2(\frac{z}{A(t)});$$

$$(21)\quad y = z\ \psi^3(\frac{z}{A(t)})$$

respectively.

Condition (19) has been derived by Diamond [4] by solving the second order partial differential equation (14)[7].

(C) Another necessary and sufficient condition for Harrod neutrality and Hicks neutrality can be derived from equations (16) and (3)' respectively. Dividing both sides of equation (16) by y and then partially differentiating with respect to the time factor, we have, for Harrod neutrality,

$$(22)\quad \frac{\partial}{\partial t}\ \frac{\partial}{\partial z} \log y(z,t) = 0$$

or

$$(23)\quad \frac{1}{y}\ \frac{\partial y(z,t)}{\partial t} = b^1(t)$$

Similarly, from (3)' we have, for Hicks neutrality,

$$(24)\quad \frac{\partial}{\partial t}\ \frac{\partial}{\partial k} \log y(k,t) = 0$$

or

$$(25)\quad \frac{1}{y}\frac{\partial y(k,t)}{\partial t} = b^3(t)$$

where b^1 and b^3 are arbitrary functions depending at most on t only, and hence may be taken as positive functions.

For the sake of symmetry, we have from (2)' for U-neutrality

$$(26)\quad \frac{\partial \log y(w,t)}{\partial t} = 0 \text{ or } \frac{1}{y}\frac{\partial y(w,t)}{\partial t} = 0$$

where $y \neq 0$ in (23), (25) and (26).

Condition (22) is shown in Uzawa [18] in the course of proving (1)''' and (24) is a lemma in Uzawa and Watanabe [17].

Equations similar to (23), (25) and (26) are described as special cases of neutral technical progress in the sense of Phelps [12], where they are expressed in terms of z: The technical progress is Harrod neutral, U-neutral or Hicks neutral, according as:

$$(27)\ \frac{1}{z}\frac{\partial z(r,t)}{\partial t} = 0,\quad (28)\ \frac{1}{z}\frac{\partial z(y,t)}{\partial t} = b^2(t), \text{ or}$$

$$(29)\ \frac{1}{z}\frac{\partial z(k,t)}{\partial t} = b^3(t),$$

respectively. Equation (27) is equivalent to (8), while (28) can be obtained from (20) and (29) from (3)'''.

(D) To derive one more necessary and sufficient condition for neutrality, let us substitute y = f(k,t) in equations (19) and (20), and differentiate with respect to the time factor t. Then

$$\left(1 - \frac{A}{k}\frac{\partial \psi^1}{\partial z}\right)\frac{1}{y}\frac{\partial y}{\partial t} = \frac{A'(t)}{A(t)}, \text{ and}$$

$$\left(1 - \frac{kA}{\dfrac{\partial \psi^2}{\partial (z/A)}}\right)\frac{1}{y}\frac{\partial y}{\partial t} = \frac{A'(t)}{A(t)},$$

where A'(t) denotes the derivative of A with respect to t. Now, differentiating (19) and (20) with respect to the capital-labor ratio k, solving for $\frac{\partial \psi^1}{\partial z}$ and $\frac{\partial \psi^2}{\partial (z/A)}$, and then substituting into the above two equations respectively, we finally have:

$$(30) \quad \frac{1}{y}\frac{\partial y}{\partial t} = \frac{A'(t)}{A(t)}\left(1 - \frac{k}{y}\frac{\partial y}{\partial k}\right) \text{ for Harrod}$$

neutrality

and $$(31) \quad \frac{1}{y}\frac{\partial y}{\partial t} = \frac{A'(t)}{A(t)}\frac{k}{y}\frac{\partial y}{\partial k} \quad \text{for U-neutrality}.$$

Similarly, differentiation of (21) with respect to time yields

$$(32) \quad \frac{1}{y}\frac{\partial y}{\partial t} = \frac{A'(t)}{A(t)} \quad \text{for Hicks neutrality,}$$

which is the same as (25). Condition (30) has been shown in Diamond [4] in relation to a balanced growth model.

6. Biased Technical Progress

The analytical formulations of various definitions of biased technical progress and their relations have been given by Amano [2] and Fei and Ranis [5]. Their models are all based on the total differential change of the variables, and hence the relation between verbal definitions and analytical formulations are rather obscure. In this section, I have tried to proceed without using differential models, showing clearly what is held constant and what is not, and hence derive their conditions directly from the definitions. Different kinds of formulations of the definitions in accordance with the spirit of Hicks' purpose have been suggested in this section.

As usual, we shall say that technical progress is Harrod (U- or Hicks, respectively) capital saving, neutral, or labor saving if and only if the output-capital ratio (labor-output ratio, or wage-profit ratio, respectively) increases, remains unchanged, or decreases at the constant rate of profit (wage rate, or capital-labor ratio, respectively).

Under the same assumptions as in Section 2, Harrod's definition implies

$$(33) \quad \left.\frac{\partial z}{\partial t}\right|_r \gtreqless 0 \text{ or } \frac{1}{y}\left.\frac{\partial y}{\partial t}\right|_r - \frac{1}{k}\left.\frac{\partial k}{\partial t}\right|_r \gtreqless 0,$$

the U definition implies

$$(34)\quad \frac{\partial}{\partial t}\left(\frac{N}{Y}\right)\Big|_{w} \gtreqless 0 \text{ or } \frac{\partial y}{\partial t}\Big|_{w} \lesseqgtr 0,$$

while Hicks' definition implies

$$(35)\quad \frac{\partial}{\partial t}\frac{w}{r}\Big|_{k} \gtreqless 0 \text{ or } \frac{1}{w}\frac{\partial w}{\partial t}\Big|_{k} - \frac{1}{r}\frac{\partial r}{\partial t}\Big|_{k} \gtreqless 0,$$

where $|_x$ indicates that the differentiation is carried out by holding x constant.

From equations (33) - (35), we may, for a two-factor, one-commodity neoclassical model, redefine our terms in a more general fashion by saying progress is capital saving, neutral, or labor saving according as the relative share of labor increases, remains unchanged, or decreases over time (and similarly for capital share). This latter general definition seems in accordance with the spirit of Hicks' original purpose and motivates further definitions: we may as well define (33) as

$$(36)\quad \frac{\partial r}{\partial t}\Big|_{z} \lesseqgtr 0.$$

Similarly, we may define (34) as

$$\frac{\partial w}{\partial t}\Big|_{y} \gtreqless 0;$$

and (35) as

$$\frac{\partial k}{\partial t}\Big|_{w/r} \lesseqgtr 0.$$

The definition (36) has been used in Ozga [11][8].

Again (under constant returns to scale), increases in the share of one factor necessarily reduces the other, and we may say, from (33), that technical progress is capital saving, neutral, or capital using if and only if capital productivity (y/k) increases, remains constant, or decreases at a constant rate of profit. A similar definition holds for (34), where we are concerned with the labor using, neutral, labor saving in connection with changes in labor productivity (y) over time.

In equations (33) to (35), when there is neutral technical progress the equality holds in each definition, and hence we obtain the functions G^1, G^2 and G^3 of Section 2. On the other hand, when technical progress is biased and the inequalities hold, then we may want to formulate the equivalent conditions for (33) and (34) when k is held constant.

Since $y = f(k(r,t), t)$, $r = f_k(k(r,t), t)$, hence

$$\frac{1}{y}\frac{\partial y}{\partial t}\Big|_r = \frac{kf_k}{y}\,\frac{1}{k}\frac{\partial k}{\partial t}\Big|_r + \frac{1}{y}\frac{\partial y}{\partial t}\Big|_k$$

and

$$\frac{1}{k}\frac{\partial k}{\partial t}\Big|_r = -\frac{f_k}{kf_{kk}}\,\frac{f_{kt}}{f_k} = \frac{f}{f - kf_k}\cdot\sigma\,\frac{1}{r}\frac{\partial r}{\partial t}\Big|_k$$

Substituting into (33), we obtain the equivalent condition that the Harrod definition implies

$$(36)\quad \frac{1}{y}\frac{\partial y}{\partial t}\Big|_k \gtreqless \sigma\frac{1}{r}\frac{\partial r}{\partial t}\Big|_k .$$

Similarly, since $y = f(k(w,t),t)$; $w = f(k(w,t), t) - k(w,t)f_k\,(k(w,t), t)$ for this case, we have:

$$\frac{\partial y}{\partial t}\Big|_w = f_k\frac{\partial k}{\partial t}\Big|_w + \frac{\partial y}{\partial t}\Big|_k ,$$

and

$$\frac{\partial k}{\partial t}\Big|_w = \frac{1}{kf_{kk}}\frac{\partial w}{\partial t}\Big|_k .$$

Substituting into (34) and dividing by y, we have the equivalent condition for the U-definition:

$$(37)\quad \frac{1}{y}\frac{\partial y}{\partial t}\Big|_k \lesseqgtr \sigma\frac{1}{w}\frac{\partial w}{\partial t}\Big|_k .$$

When equality holds in (36) and (37), the condition reduces to the equations (14) and (15)[9].

APPENDIX

ON LAGRANGE'S EQUATION

One simple and much neglected problem of partial differential equations in economics arises in the converse theorem of the well-known Euler's equation[10]: If $x \frac{\partial z}{\partial x} + y \frac{\partial z}{\partial y} = z$ at all (x,y), then z is some linear and homogeneous function of x and y. Without employing "tricks" as Allen [1, p. 433] does, we may prove this theorem directly by using Lagrange's method of solving first order partial differential equations, as I have done on many occasions in the text.

A partial differential equation of the form

$$(38)\quad P(x,y,z) \frac{\partial z}{\partial x} + Q(x,y,z) \frac{\partial z}{\partial y} = R(x,y,z)$$

where P, Q, R are given functions of x, y, z, is called Lagrange's equation or the first order quasi-linear differential equation.

The system of differential equations

$$(39)\quad \frac{dx}{P} = \frac{dy}{Q} = \frac{dz}{R}$$

is called the auxiliary equations of (38).

Let $u(x,y,z) = c_1$ and $v(x,y,z) = c_2$ be the two independent solutions of the auxiliary equations (39), with c_1 and c_2 being constant. Then

Theorem[11]: For an arbitrary function F, the relation

$$F(u,v) = 0$$

is a general solution of the Lagrange's equation (38).

The above relation arises from a relation $F(c_1,c_2) = 0$. Hence we may solve for $c_1 = A(c_2)$, where A is an arbitrary function. Notice that, if $P = 0$, we put $dx = 0$ and so $x = c_2$. Using this theorem, the first converse theorem can be proved at once.

FOOTNOTES

* The main result of this paper is obtained in a chapter in [10]. The author is indebted to Professors Hugh Rose and Lionel W. McKenzie for their valuable comments in an early stage of development. All errors, of course, remain mine.

1 Here K is capital, N labor, t time factor. F has constant returns to scale with K and N, positive marginal productivity and "diminishing returns" prevail. See explanation in the second section.

2 In his new book, Phelps [12] calls it Fei-Ranis neutrality. In fact, it might be called Solow-Fei-Ranis neutrality. In this paper we briefly call it U-neutrality.

3 This theorem is not quite unknown either, but so far, to my knowledge, explicit proof does not exist in the literature.

4 See Fei and Ranis [5].

5 This formulation of Harrod neutrality is the same as that used by Uzawa [18]. Also see Section 6 below.

6 See, e.g., Uzawa [18].

7 In fact, condition (14) yields, after substituting the expression of σ and r in (14) and rearranging both sides:

$$(y - k \frac{\partial y}{\partial k}) \frac{\partial^2 y}{\partial t \partial k} + k \frac{\partial^2 y}{\partial k^2} = 0$$

which is a non-linear second order partial differential equation of Menge-Ampere type, and has

$$y = k\ \phi^1(\frac{k}{A(t)})$$

as its general solution, where ϕ^1 and A are some arbitrary functions. Similarly, the condition of Hicks neutrality (13) yields, after substituting the expression of r and w in (13) and rearranging the both sides,

$$y \frac{\partial^2 y}{\partial t \partial k} - \frac{\partial y}{\partial t} \frac{\partial y}{\partial k} = 0$$

Dividing both sides by $y \cdot \frac{\partial y}{\partial t}$, we have

$$\frac{\partial}{\partial t} (\log \frac{1}{y} \frac{\partial y}{\partial k}) = 0,$$

which obviously has a general integral of the form $y = A(t) \cdot \phi^3(k)$ for some arbitrary function A and ϕ^3 (See equation (3)''').

[8] Since it can be shown that $\frac{wN}{rK} = - \frac{y}{z} \frac{\partial z}{\partial y}$ and also= $- \frac{w}{r} \frac{\partial r}{\partial w}$ (cf. [14], p. 202), using the latter definition, we may define labor saving, neutral or capital saving technical progress as

$$\frac{1}{z} \frac{\partial z}{\partial t}\bigg|_{\frac{\partial z}{\partial y}} - \frac{1}{y} \frac{\partial y}{\partial t}\bigg|_{\frac{\partial z}{\partial y}} \lesseqgtr 0,$$

or

$$\frac{1}{r} \frac{\partial r}{\partial t}\bigg|_{\frac{\partial r}{\partial w}} - \frac{1}{w} \frac{\partial w}{\partial t}\bigg|_{\frac{\partial r}{\partial w}} \lesseqgtr 0.$$

[9] In the above discussion, we have specified the production function as $Y = F(K,N;t)$. But in the original Hicks or Harrod definitions, there is no such specification. We might as well specify the production function as $Y = F(K,N,\alpha)$ where α is a function of time governing the changes of output due to technical progress. In this case all the t's in the above discussion must be substituted by α. Professor Hugh Rose [13] is now working on this type of interpretation.

[10] See Wicksell [19], p. 128 and Allen [1], p. 434.

[11] See Sneddon [15], p. 50.

REFERENCES

[1] Allen, R.G.D. Mathematical Analysis for Economists, New York: Macmillan Company, 1938.

[2] Amano, A., "Biased Technical Progress and A Neo-Classical Theory of Economic Growth", Quarterly Journal of Economics, Vol. 78 No. 1, (February 1964), pp. 129-138.

[3] Arrow, K.J., H.B. Chenery, B. Minhas, and R.M. Solow, "Capital Labor Substitution and Economic Efficiency", Review of Economics and Statistics, Vol. 18 (August 1961), pp. 225-250.

[4] Diamond, P., "Disembodied Technical Change in a One Sector Model", unpublished Working Paper No. 37, Institute of Business and Economic Research, University of California, Berkeley.

[5] Fei, C.H.J. and G. Ranis, "Innovational Intensity and Factor Bias in the Theory of Growth," International Economic Review, Vol. 6, (May 1965), pp. 182-198.

[6] Hahn, F.H. and R.C.D. Matthews, "The Theory of Economic Growth: A Survey", Economic Journal, Vol. 74, (December 1964), pp. 779-902.

[7] Harrod, R.F. Towards a Dynamic Economics, New York: Macmillan Company, 1948.

[8] Hicks, J.R. Theory of Wages, Second Edition, London: Macmillan Company, 1963.

[9] Hicks, J.R. Capital and Growth, Oxford University Press, 1965.

[10] Hsiao, S.T. Technical Progress, Balanced Growth and Asymptote Criterion in Neo-Classical Economic Models, Ph.D. dissertation, Department of Economics, University of Rochester, June 1967.

[11] Ozga, S.A., "The Propensity to Save, the Capital Output Ratio, and the Equilibrium Rate of Growth", Economica, Vol. 31, (November 1964), pp. 363-371.

[12] Phelps, E.S. Golden Rules of Economic Growth--Studies of Efficient and Optimal Investment. New York: Norton, 1966.

[13] Rose, H., "Technical Progress and the General Form of the Production Function", Mimeographed paper, University of Rochester, July 1967.

[14] Samuelson, P.A., "Parable and Realism in Capital Theory: The Surrogate Production Function", Review of Economic Studies, Vol. 29 (3), No. 80 (June 1962).

[15] Sneddon, I.N. Elements of Partial Differential Equations, New York: McGraw-Hill Company, 1957.

[16] Solow, R.M. Capital Theory and the Rate of Return, Amsterdam: North Holland Publishing Company, 1963.

[17] Uzawa, H. and T. Watanabe, "A Note on the Classification of Technical Invention", Technical Report No. 85, Applied Mathematics and Statistics Laboratories, Stanford University, 1960 (Later published in Economic Studies Quarterly, Japan, 1961)

[18] Uzawa, H., "Neutral Invention and the Stability of Growth Equilibrium", Review of Economic Studies, Vol. 28 (February 1961), pp. 117-124.

[19] Wicksell, K. Lectures on Political Economy, Vol. 1, English translation ed. with introduction by Lionel Robbins, London, 1934.

INTERNATIONAL TRADE AND DEVELOPMENT IN A SMALL COUNTRY*

by

Trout Rader
Washington University
St. Louis, Missouri

1. Introduction

We consider a country which produces n goods from m factors. The n goods are subject to the international price system

$$p = (p_1, \ldots, p_n)$$

and a home wage system,

$$w = (w_1, \ldots, w_m).$$

Normally, w is determined by home conditions, namely, the demand and supply for factors. These factors are denoted x,

$$x = (x_1, \ldots, x_m)$$

whose supply is assumed to be invariant to changes in prices or wages.

Production is assumed to proceed according to the laws stated in the production possibility set, Z, whose elements are input-output vectors (x, y) where

$$y = (y_1, \ldots, y_n)$$

gives quantities of goods producible from the factors

$$x = (x_1, \ldots, x_m).$$

Therefore, Z is representable in Euclidean n + m space. Incidentally, if each industry is independent, then each industry has a production possibility set Z_i, in Euclidean m + n space. Presumably, for (x_i, y_i) in Z_i, the output of i is positive, $y_i > 0$; whereas, the other goods are at most used as intermediate products, $y_j^i \leq 0$. The community production possibility set is then

$$Z = \sum_{i=1}^{n} Z_i.$$

The industry takes the price of goods and of factors as given;

*The research for this paper was financed by the National Science Foundation (GS-1024).

whereas from the social viewpoint, the price of goods and the quantity of factors are given.

It is assumed that each industry, and therefore the community, maximizes profits, which are computed to be the value of output minus the cost of factors:

$$py - wx = \sum_{i=1}^{n} p_i y_i - \sum_{i=1}^{n} w_j x_j^i .$$

The relationship between the profits of sub-parts and the whole system is that the whole system maximizes profits if and only if each sub-part does. This is the additivity theorem (Koopmans [3]) and applies whenever the sub-parts operate independently of each other. In summary:

1. p is determined in the international market.
2. Given w and p, (x, y) is chosen from Z in order to maximize the profits.
3. Consequently, w must be such that an x is chosen which is equal to the actual factor supplies.
4. Modification in this structure may be made by the state by adopting tariff or tax policies thereby changing the effective home price system, p. However, internal changes are assumed to affect in no way the international market beyond the country's boundaries. Therefore, the international price at which the country can sell remains fixed.

2. Production and Value

Although indirect, it is convenient to analyze the relationship between the input-output vector, (x, y) and the wage-price vector, (w, p). This is the economy as the productive unit sees it, with given prices and derived production quantities. Many of the points made here may be familiar to the reader so that he is invited to read the theorems first.

Z is closed if $(x^n, y^n) \in Z$, $(x^n, y^n) \to (x, y)$ implies that $(x, y) \in Z$. Z is convex if

$$t(x, y) + (1-t)(\bar{x}, \bar{y}) = (tx + (1-t)\bar{x}, ty + (1-t)\bar{y})$$

is in Z, whenever (x, y) and $(\bar{x}, \bar{y})$ are in Z. Convexity implies non-increasing returns to holding some factors constant while allowing others to vary. There is some degree of free disposal at $z \in Z$, if $z + w \in Z$ for $w \leq 0$, $w \neq 0$, w sufficiently small. Normally, free disposal is allowable whenever y is positive in every component, since a relatively inefficient method of production can be chosen. Factors are not unproductive, if for $x \geq \bar{x}$, $(\bar{x}, \bar{y}) \in Z$, there exists $y \geq \bar{y}$, such that $(x, y) \in Z$.

Theorem 1. Let Z be closed and convex. Suppose (x, y) is in the boundary of Z. Then there exists a pair, (-w, p), such that (x, y) maximizes (py - wx). The set of all such price-wage pairs is a convex cone. Under constant returns, profits are zero. If there is some degree of free disposal, $p \geq 0$. And if also factors are not unproductive, then $w > 0$.

Proof: By virtue of Minkowski's theorem, there exists (-w, p) such that

$$(-w, p)(x, y) \geq (-w, p)(\bar{x}, \bar{y})$$

for all

$$(\bar{x}, \bar{y}) \in Z.$$

Whenever

$$py - wx \geq p\tilde{y} - w\tilde{x}$$

and

$$\bar{p}y - \bar{w}x \geq \bar{p}\tilde{y} - \bar{w}\tilde{x}$$

then

$$(ap + b\bar{p})y - (aw + b\bar{w})x \geq (ap + b\bar{p})\tilde{y} - (aw + b\bar{w})\tilde{x}$$

for

$$a > 0,$$

$$b > 0.$$

Under constant returns, k(py - wx) is a possible profit, $k > 0$. Therefore, $py - wx \leq 0$ for profit maximizing (y, x). In fact, profits are zero since $(0,0) \in Z$. q.e.d.

Z is strongly convex if $tz + (1-t)\bar{z}$, $0 < t < 1$, is an internal point of Z whenever z is not proportional to $\bar{z}$.[1]

Remark 1. If Z is strongly convex, then the set of (x, y) maximizing profits, py - wx, is unique up to a multiplicative constant. If Z is convex, then the set of (x, y) maximizing profits is a convex cone.

Proof: If z and $\bar{z}$ are not proportional, but have the same profit, then so does their convex combination $tz + (1-t)\bar{z}$ $1 > t > 0$. Change $tz + (1-t)\bar{z}$ in a profit improving direction. This gives a greater profit than z and $\bar{z}$. QED.

Z is generated by industries i, i=1,...,k, provided i has an input-output possibility set Z and

$$Z = \sum_{i=1}^{k} Z_i .$$[2]

Under certain circumstances p and w may be unique. In this case, we say that Z is directionally dense at (x, y) for the simple reason the (w, p) is unique up to a multiplicative constant if and only if there is a set of vectors dense in E^{n+m}, whose every vector (δ, ε) has the properties that $(x, y) + t(\delta,\varepsilon)$ is in Z for some $t \neq 0$ (possibly negative).

A particular case of some interest is where the production set Z is generated by (independent) industries whose efficient output is given by functions of the form $y^i = f^i(x^i)$, i=1, k. By this we mean that $(x, y) = (\Sigma x_i, \Sigma y_i)$ and also that any convex combination of the (x, y)'s is in Z. In effect, we have k industries who themselves can produce any output on the production function or any convex combination of outputs on the production function (by utilizing convex combinations of the inputs).

Remark 2. Suppose that f^i displays constant returns to scale and at least $f^i(x^i)$, $f^j(x^j)$ are linearly independent. Then Z is not strongly convex for k > 1.

Proof:

$$(\xi_i x^i + \xi_j x^j, \ \xi_i y^i + \xi_j y^j)$$

is in Z.

$$y^i = f^i(x^i)$$

$$y^j = f^j(x^j),$$

for all

$$\xi_i, \ \xi_j \geq 0.$$

If y^i and y^j are independent, the ξ_i's and ξ_j's, $\xi_i + \xi_j = 1$, form a line segment between non-proportional input-output vectors. No greater output can be obtained so that such points are not internal to Z. QED.

Define

$$F^i = \frac{\partial f^i}{\partial x^i} .$$

It is said that the output ratios or output mix is fixed in industry i, whenever y^i is variable only in proportional multiples. The technology is Leontief, if there are n industries all with linearly independent y^i. In this case, the normalized matrix of outputs is denoted,

$$Y \equiv (\bar{y}^1|\bar{y}^2|\ldots|\bar{y}^k),$$

where

$$|\bar{y}^i| = 1, \ i=1,\ldots,k.$$

The factors producing Y are denoted

$$X = (x^1|x^2|\dots|x^k).$$

Remark 3. If

$$y^i_i > 0,$$

$$y^i_j \leq 0,\ j \neq i,$$

and if it is possible for some input to produce positive amounts of every commodity, then Y^{-1} exists and is non-negative. That is to say, if the country is productive under autarky, then the y^i are in fact linearly independent.

Proof: Y has non-positive off diagonals and there exists $\xi_i > 0$ for which $y^i = \xi_i \bar{y}^i$, $Y\xi = y \gg 0$.[3] Apply the theory of dominant diagonal matrices (McKenzie [9]). QED.

Theorem 2. Let f^i be continuously differentiable and let there be constant returns for all industries, i=1,...,k. Then all industry input-output combinations are equally profitable for all (p, w) leading to profit maximization at (x, y). If x is strongly positive, w is uniquely determined by (x, y) and p.

If the technology is Leontief and if all industries are profitable, p is uniquely determined by w.

Proof: Different ways of producing y from x are equally profitable:

$$y = \Sigma\xi_i y^i$$

$$x = \Sigma\xi_i x^i,$$

$$py - wx = 0$$

$$py^i - wx^i \leqq 0$$

implies that

$$py^i - wx^i = 0$$

whenever

$$\xi_i > 0.$$

Therefore, (x^i, y^i) is profit maximizing, $\xi_i > 0$ whenever (x, y) is profit maximizing. If $x \gg 0$, all factors are used so that the first order condition of maximization is that for some industry f^i

$$\frac{\partial p f^i}{\partial x_j^i} = w_j.$$

If there is a different $\bar{w}$ possible, all ways of producing (x, y) are profitable at $(\bar{w}, p)$ as well and hence $\bar{w}$ is still determined by the preceding equation. Therefore, given p, w is determined.

Also

$$\bar{p}F^i(x^i) = \bar{w}$$

for $(\bar{w}, \bar{p})$ with respect to which (x, y) is profit maximizing. Therefore, <u>the dimension of variation of (p, w) is at most equal to</u> m + n minus the number of linearly independent $(F^i|-I)$ which equals <u>m + n minus the number of linearly independent F^i.</u>

If the technology is Leontief and if all industries are profitable

$$pY = wX$$

and

$$p = wXY^{-1}. \quad \text{QED.}$$

3. Independent and Derived Variables

From the viewpoint of the theory of international trade, the important dichotomy is not (x, y) on the one hand and (w, p) on the other. Rather it is that between the given (x, p) and the derived quantities (w, y). Therefore, we explore the wage-output correspondence, $\eta(x, p)$, and its inverse, the input-price correspondence,

$$\eta^{-1}(w, y) = \{(x, p) \mid (w, y) \in \eta(x, p)\}.$$

We consider the domain and range of η. If we can verify that its range covers virtually all international price systems and factor endowments, then we can be assured that our assumption that the country does not influence the international price system is not nonsense.

<u>Theorem 3.</u>

(i) If Z_i does not allow arbitrarily large output from given input, x^i

(ii) Z is closed and convex, and

(iii) Z_i allows some degree of free disposal on its upper boundary, so that it has a non-empty interior, then for every non-negative, non-zero p and x, x variable in any direction, $\eta(p, x)$ is non-empty, $w \neq 0$. If factors are not unproductive, then $w > 0$. If factors are productive and if also p_i is positive for every good, then w_j is positive for every factor, j.

This theorem gives the set of outputs and factor prices observable in a small country.

Proof: Consider the set

$$\hat{Z} = \{(x, py) \mid (x, y) \text{ is in } Z\}.$$

It is possible to choose (x, py) in the boundary of $\hat{Z}$ if py has an upper bound, and if Z is closed so that the least upper bound is taken. The closedness of $\hat{Z}$ and boundedness of py follows whenever Z is closed and the set of y's producible from x are bounded from above.

If Z is convex then so is $\hat{Z}$, and therefore there exists (-w, k) such that

$$(-\overline{w}, k)(x, py) = -\overline{w} + kpy \geq -\overline{wx} + kp\overline{y}$$

for all other $(\overline{x}, p\overline{y})$ in $\hat{Z}$. This is simply the Minkowski Theorem which says that every point on the boundary of a convex set can be (weakly) separated from the convex set by a bounding hyperplane.

If k = 0, then a small change in x will give $\overline{x}$ for which $\overline{wx}$ is larger. This gives a higher profit which is impossible. Therefore, $k \neq 0$. Also, if $k < 0$ and if there is the slightest degree of free disposal so that py can be reduced to $p\overline{y}$ with changing x, $py > p\overline{y}$. then $-wx + kpy < -wx + kp\overline{y}$, which cannot be. Therefore $k > 0$, and also

$$-\frac{\overline{w}}{k}x + py \geq -\frac{\overline{w}}{k}\overline{x} + p\overline{y}$$

for all $(\overline{x}, \overline{y})$ in Z. Let

$$w = \frac{\overline{w}}{k}$$

be the wage vector.

Incidentally, w is non-negative whenever all factors are not unproductive and p is non-negative since otherwise an increase in x_j for which $w_j > 0$ would not decrease py and therefore would increase profits. If p is positive in every component, an increase in x_j for $w_j = 0$ would actually increase py whenever x is productive and not decrease wx, whereupon profits would increase. Therefore if p is positive in every component, so is w. QED.

Next, consider the range of η.

Theorem 4. Let Z be convex and closed, and let every non-negative output be producible. If no factors are unproductive, then for every non-negative, non-zero (w, y), y an internal point among those outputs producible according to Z, there is a pair, (x, p) for which (w, y) is in $\eta(x, p)$. If there is some degree of free disposal so that a decrease in y can be obtained with no change in x, then p must be non-negative. If Z allows some degree of free disposal at (x, y), $p_i > 0$ for whatever good the free disposal is allowed.

The theorem says that the observable (w, y), for different (x, p), are so broad as to include all of the non-negative vectors.

Proof: If $y \geq 0$, then there is an $x \geq 0$ such that (x, y) is in Z. Consider

$$\underset{\vee}{Z} = \{(-wx, y) | (x, y) \in Z\}.$$

Let x be chosen so as to minimize wx, given that (x, y) is in Z. This is possible if Z is closed and if for every output, the set of inputs giving this output is bounded from below, i.e., if a minimum input (zero) is needed to obtain a given output. Clearly, (-wx, y) is in the boundary of $\underset{\vee}{Z}$. Therefore, we apply Minkowski's Theorem again. There is a vector $(k, \overline{p})$ such that

$$(k, \overline{p})\ (-wx, \overline{p}y) = -kwx + \overline{p}y \geq -kw\overline{x} + \overline{py}$$

for all other $(w\overline{x}, \overline{y})$ in Z or alternatively for all other $(\overline{x}, \overline{y})$ in Z.

As before, k cannot be zero, since otherwise a larger profit could be obtained by changing wx without reducing revenues. Also if there is some degree of free disposal, k cannot be negative since then an increase in x would not decrease output and revenue but would decrease costs. Therefore, as before

$$\frac{\overline{p}}{k} y - wx > \frac{\overline{p}}{k} y - w\overline{x}$$

for all $(\overline{x}, \overline{y})$ in Z.

We conclude that if Z is convex and closed, if every non-negative output is producible and if no factors are unproductive, then for every non-negative, non-zero (w, y) there is a pair (x, p) for which (w, y) is in $\eta(x, p)$.

If there is some degree of free disposal in the ith component, then p must be non-negative in that component. QED.

A correspondence or multi-valued function, $\phi(x)$, is upper semi-continuous if

$$x^n \to x \cdot$$

$$y^n \to y$$

$$y^n \in \phi(x^n)$$

implies

$$y \in \phi(x).$$

We list some properties of η and η^{-1}.

Theorem 5.

(i) Both $\eta^{-1}(w, y)$ and $\eta(x, p)$ are convex sets whenever Z is convex.

(ii) If there are constant returns to scale, multiplication of either x or p leads to a multiplication of y or w, respectively.

(iii) wx is constant in $\eta^{-1}(w, y)$ and py is constant in $\eta(x, p)$. If there are constant returns to scale, wx and py are constant in both $\eta(x, p)$ and $\eta^{-1}(w, y)$.

(iv)

$$\eta(x, p) = (\eta_1(x, p), \eta_2(x, p)),$$

$$(\eta_1 : E^{n+m} \to E^m, \eta_2 : E^{n+m} \to E^n)$$

and

$$\eta^{-1}(w, y) = (\eta^{-1}{}_1(w, y), \eta^{-1}{}_2(w, y)),$$

$$(\eta^{-1}{}_1 : E^{n+m} \to E^m, \eta^{-1}{}_2 : E^{n+m} \to E^n).$$

The dimension of variation in each $\eta_i(\eta^{-1}{}_i)$ is equal to one less than the number of linearly independent vectors in $\eta_i(\eta^{-1}{}_i)$.

(v) η and η^{-1} are upper semi-continuous whenever Z is closed.

Parts (iv) and (v) are particularly noteworthy. In effect, there is no functional interaction between w and y or between x and p. For example, observation of w and y can be used to derive the factor endowments, independently of the international price system. A computation of cost minimizing industry inputs follows from w and the number of (profitable) industries needed to produce y. Also, sequential and convergent changes in independent variables lead to dependent variables which in the limit equilibrate the factor markets vis a vis the limiting values of the dependent variables.

Proof:

(iii) For (w, y), $(\bar{w}, \bar{y})$ in $\eta(x, p)$,

$$py - wx \geq p\bar{y} - wx,$$
$$p\bar{y} - \bar{w}x \geq py - \bar{w}x,$$

or

$$py \geq p\bar{y}$$
$$p\bar{y} \geq py,$$

whereupon

$$py = p\bar{y}.$$

For (x, p), $(\bar{x}, \bar{p})$ in $\eta^{-1}(w, y)$,

$$py - wx \geq py - w\bar{x}$$
$$\bar{p}y - w\bar{x} \geq \bar{p}y - wx$$

or

$$\bar{w}x \geq wx$$
$$w\bar{x} \geq \bar{w}x$$

whereupon

$$\bar{w}x = wx.$$

(iv) Since $py = p\bar{y}$, y and $\bar{y}$ producible from x may be permitted to obtain the same profit. Since $wx = w\bar{x}$, w may be permitted with $\bar{w}$ to obtain the same profit. Also, the dimension of a convex set which is nowhere dense is equal to one less than the number of its linearly independent vectors.

(v)

$$x^n \to x,$$
$$p^n \to p,$$
$$w^n \to w,$$
$$y^n \to y,$$
$$p^n y^n - w^n x^n \geq p^n \tilde{y} - w^n \tilde{x}$$

for all $(\tilde{x}, \tilde{y})$ in Z implies that

$$py - wx \geq p\tilde{y} - w\tilde{x}$$

for all $(\tilde{x}, \tilde{y})$ in Z. QED.

Remark 4. If f^i satisfies the strict concavity assumption,

$$f^i(tx^i + (1-t)\overline{x}^i) = s(tf^i(x^i) + (1-t)f^i(\overline{x}^i),$$

$$s > 1,$$

whenever x^i and $\overline{x}^i$ are not proportional, then given p and w, x^i is uniquely determined.

Proof: If $(x^i, f^i(x^i))$, $(\overline{x}^i, f^i(\overline{x}^i))$ gives a zero profit, then $(tx^i + (1-t)\overline{x}^i, s(tf^i(x^i) + (1-t)f^i(x^i)))$ gives a positive profit whenever $wx \neq 0$. QED.

An important consequence of theorems 2 and 5 is that the wage rate is uniquely determined by p and x alone.[4]

Theorem 6.

(i) If f^i is continuously differentiable, and satisfies constant returns to scale, for all industries, $i=1,\ldots,k$ and if x_j is strictly positive for all factors, $j=1,\ldots,m$, then $\eta_1(x, p)$ is single valued. If outputs are bounded for a given input, then $\eta_1(x, p)$ is a continuous function.

(ii) If also there is a Leontief technology, f^i satisfying a strict concavity assumption and if X^{-1} exists (so that $m = n$), then η_2 is a continuous function also.

According to the second sentence of (i) in theorem 6, small changes in international prices and factor endowments lead to small changes in factor wages.

Proof:

(i) Given (w, y), $(w, \overline{y})$ in $\eta(x, p)$, $(\overline{w}, y)$ is in $\eta(x, p)$ (theorem 5). Therefore, $w = \overline{w}$ (theorem 2).

An upper semi-continuous correspondence is a continuous function whenever it is single valued and it takes bounded sets into bounded sets. Clearly, y is bounded, given x, and therefore

$$wx = yp$$

forces w to be bounded, given p and a strictly positive x.

(ii) Since

$$x = X\xi,$$

and

$$y = Y\xi,$$

$$X^{-1}x = \xi,$$

and

$$y = Y\xi,$$

or

$$y = YX^{-1}x.$$

Also, X is continuous in w whenever f^i is continuously differentiable, and y is a continuous function of x. QED.

Theorem 7.

(i) If technology is Leontief, η_1^{-1} is a continuous function.

(ii) Let there be n profitable industries with linearly independent y^i, constant returns to scale and continuously differentiable as is the case in the Leontief technology. For all y except those in an n-1 dimensional manifold, η_2^{-1} is a continuous function of w alone.

According to (i) changes in x are uniquely related to changes in w. According to (ii) for almost all outputs, price is dependent upon factor wages alone. Given wages, one can immediately compute prices. This gives an alternative proof of wage uniqueness theorem, since given two prices and the same wage (theorem 3), there must be only one price implied by the wage -- a contradiction.

Proof:

(i) $y = Y\xi,$

or

$$\xi = Y^{-1}y,$$

so that

$$x = X\xi$$

$$\xi = XY^{-1}y.$$

X is continuous in w.

(ii) Apply theorem 2, part (ii):

$$p = wXY^{-1},$$

X continuous in w. QED.

Theorems 6 and 7 give conditions under which w and p are uniquely determined by each other, given y and x respectively. Nevertheless, Z might not be directionally dense at (x, y) since there may exist $\overline{w}$ and $\overline{p}$ mutually determining each other and still having (x, y) as a profit maximizing input-output vector. This turns out to be impossible.

Theorem 8.

(i) Let Z_i be convex, i=1,...,k,

(ii) Let technology be Leontief with only one positive

output for each industry

(iii) Let f^i be continuously differentiable, satisfy constant returns to scale and a concavity assumption. Then at strictly positive x and y, Z is directionally dense.

<u>Proof</u>: Since

$$y >> 0,$$

$$y = Y\xi,$$

$$Y^{-1} \geq 0,$$

we must have

$$\xi = Y^{-1}y >> 0.$$

$$Y\xi = y$$

so that

$$\xi = Y^{-1}y.$$

Therefore, industries are always operated at the intensities ξ. Now combining x and $\overline{x}$ convexly, each of which produces y, with industry intensities, ξ, the scale of output increases in each industry. Therefore, ξ is multiplied by a diagonal matrix, D, where

$$d_{ii} > 1$$

is the scale of operation of the ith industry. Combine $d_{ii}y^i$ with the inefficient production y^i (convexity) to reduce scale in all industries except where d_{ii} is minimal. Then $\min(d_{ii})y\xi$ is the new output, which yields a positive profit whether (w, p) or $(\overline{w}, \overline{p})$ is the price system. QED.

4. Comparative Statics

In the k-industry case we have already obtained some information about changes in η and η^{-1} in response to changes of the independent variables (theorems 5, 6, and 7). This is the subject of comparative statics, and we wish to develop it more extensively. We emphasize the k-industry case, which is of special interest in international trade and development theory.

<u>Theorem 9</u>. Let there be constant returns to scale,

(i) For $(w, y) \in \eta(x, p)$, $(\overline{w}, \overline{y}) \in \eta(\overline{x}, p)$,

$$0 \geq \Delta w \Delta x.$$ [5]

If x_i alone increases, w_i must not increase. Strict inequality holds, under the hypothesis of theorem 6, part (i).

(ii) For $(x, p) \in \eta^{-1}(w, y)$, $(\bar{x}, \bar{p}) \in \eta^{-1}(w, \bar{y})$

$$0 \leq \Delta p \Delta y.$$

If y_i alone increases, p_i must not decrease. Strict inequality holds under the hypothesis of theorem 7, part (ii).

(iii) For $(w, y) \in \eta(x, p)$, $(\bar{w}, \bar{y}) \in \eta(x, \bar{p})$,

$$0 \leq \Delta p \Delta y.$$

If p_i alone increases y_i must not decrease. Strict inequality holds under the hypothesis of theorem 6, part (ii).

(iv) For $(x, p) \in \eta^{-1}(w, y)$, $(\bar{x}, \bar{p}) \in \eta^{-1}(\bar{w}, y)$,

$$0 \geq \Delta w \Delta x.$$

If w_i increases, x_i must not increase. Strict inequality holds under the hypothesis of theorem 7, part (i).

The theorem gives some simple rules of change in values.

Proof: (i) Let x change, p fixed. Then,

$$0 = \bar{p}\bar{y} - \bar{w}\bar{x} \geq py - \bar{w}x,$$

and

$$0 = py - wx \geq p\bar{y} - wx,$$

or

$$w\bar{x} \geq \bar{w}\bar{x}$$

and

$$\bar{w}x \geq wx$$

or

$$0 \geq -(\bar{w} - w)\bar{x} + (\bar{w} - w)x = (\bar{w} - w)(\bar{x} - x).$$

Strict inequality holds whenever w is determined by x and p, since then

$$\bar{w}x = wx,$$

given p, implies

$$py - \bar{w}x = py - wx = 0.$$

This condition is insured by theorem 6, part (i). If w changes at all, then strict inequality holds above and w_i actually decreases.

(ii) Let y change, w fixed. Then

$$0 = \bar{p}\bar{y} - w\bar{x} \geq \bar{p}y - wx,$$

and

$$0 = py - wx \geq \overline{py} - \overline{wx},$$

or

$$\overline{py} \geq p\overline{y}$$

and

$$py \geq \overline{p}y,$$

or

$$0 < (\overline{p} - p)\overline{y} - (\overline{p} - p)y = (\overline{p} - p)(\overline{y} - y).$$

Strict inequality holds whenever $\overline{p}$ is uniquely determined by w and x (theorem 7, part (ii)).

(iii) Let p change, x fixed. Then

$$\overline{py} \geq \overline{p}y,$$

and

$$py \geq p\overline{y},$$

so that

$$0 \leq \overline{p}(\overline{y} - y) - p(\overline{y} - y) = (\overline{p} - p)(\overline{y} - y).$$

Strict inequality holds whenever y is uniquely determined by $\overline{p}$ and x (theorem 6, part (ii)). Since w is uniquely determined by y and $\overline{y}$ in the k-industry case, strict inequality holds for that initial price system maximizing the number of profitable industries. Therefore, an increase in p_i increases y_i.

(iv) Similarly, if w changes, y fixed, then

$$\overline{wx} \leq \overline{w}x,$$

and

$$wx \leq w\overline{x},$$

or

$$0 \geq \overline{w}(\overline{x} - x) - w(\overline{x} - x) = (\overline{w} - w)(\overline{x} - x)$$

Strict inequality holds whenever x is uniquely determined by w and y (theorem 7, part (ii)).

Theorem 10. If the technology is Leontief with only one positive output from each industry, then an increase in w increases the p allowing all industries to operate.

Proof:

$$pY = wX,$$

or

$$p = wXY^{-1},$$

$$X \geq 0, \; Y^{-1} \geq 0,$$

so that

$$\Delta p = \Delta w\overline{XY}^{-1} + w\Delta XY^{-1}$$

and since

$$w\Delta X = wX(\overline{w}) - wX \leq 0,$$

$$\Delta p \geq wXY^{-1}$$

Therefore,

$$\Delta p \geq 0$$

whenever

$$\Delta w \geq 0.$$

Normally, wXY^{-1} is positive and Δp is strictly positive. QED. It might be added that an increase in w need not lead to an increase in p since XY^{-1} need not be non-negative.

A final result is due to Stolper and Samuelson [14].

Theorem 11. Suppose m = 2, n = 2, both industries are profitable. Then as p_i increases, w increases in that component which is less intensively used in industry i.

As Chipman [1] has pointed, the theorem does not readily generalize to the m factor case, m > 2, if for no other reason than the fact that there is no 1-1 relationship between industries and intensity of use of each factor.

In order to avoid differentiability assumptions, we adopt a longer proof than that of Samuelson and Stolper.

Proof: Let there be only two factors of production and suppose that a change in p does increase the profitability of industry i but does not increase profits of j. Then the costs of industry i must increase and those of j must not increase:

$$\overline{wx}^i > wx^i$$

$$\overline{wx}^j \leq wx^j$$

or

$$(\overline{w} - w)\overline{x}^i + w(\overline{x}^i - x^i) \geq 0,$$

$$(\overline{w} - w)x^j + w(\overline{x}^j - x^j) < 0.$$

Since profits are a maximum at $(\overline{x}^i, y^i)$ and (x^i, y^i), respectively,

$$w(\overline{x}^i - x^i) < 0,$$

$$\bar{w}(\bar{x}^j - \dot{x}^j) \leq 0.$$

Therefore,

$$(\bar{w} - w)\bar{x}^i \geq 0.$$

$$(\bar{w} - w)x^j < 0.$$

We write this as

$$\Delta w_1 x_1^i + \Delta w_2 x_2^i \geq 0,$$

$$\Delta w_1 x_1^i + \Delta w_2 x_2^j < 0.$$

Suppose

$$\Delta w_1 > 0.$$

Then

$$\frac{x_1^i}{x_2^i} \geq - \frac{\Delta w_2}{\Delta w_1}$$

and

$$\frac{x_1^j}{x_2^j} < - \frac{\Delta w_2}{\Delta w_1}$$

so that

$$\frac{x_1^i}{x_2^i} > \frac{x_1^j}{x_2^j}$$

Similarly, if

$$\Delta w_2 > 0,$$

$$\frac{x_2^i}{x_1^i} > \frac{x_2^j}{x_1^j}$$

Therefore w increases in that component which is less intensively used in the industry with no revenue gain. QED.

5. Factor Price Equalization

The modern theory of international trade is concerned with the influence of changes in x and p on w. It is presumed that there are two or more countries trading at the same prices. If there are a sufficient number of profitable industries, it will be seen that small changes in factor endowment do not change factor prices. When such a factor endowment exists, we say that there is factor price equalization. Nations which have these factor endowments have equal factor prices.

Remark 5. Let there be k-production functions with f^i continuously differentiable, satisfying a strict concavity production, and satisfying constant returns to scale. Then the set of strictly positive factor endowments, small changes in which lead to no change in factor prices, is open and disjoint from any other such set.

Proof:

Clearly, the sets in question are open. They are disjoint, since factor prices are the same on a closure of a set of factor endowments with factor price equalization and different factor endowments lead to different factor prices (theorem 6, (i)). Therefore, the closures of sets of factor price equalization for a given factor price are disjoint. QED.

Samuelson [12] originally showed that in the two industry two factor case, with constant returns to scale, there is factor price equalization provided that

(1) all industries are profitable at some w, and

(2) for all w, one industry uses one factor more intensely than the other.

These two assumptions are needed. If (2) does not hold, the w for which all industries are profitable may not be one satisfying the factory intensity assumption so that $X(\mathbf{w})$ is singular. If (1) does not hold, one industry may not be profitable for any w, as is illustrated in figure 1.

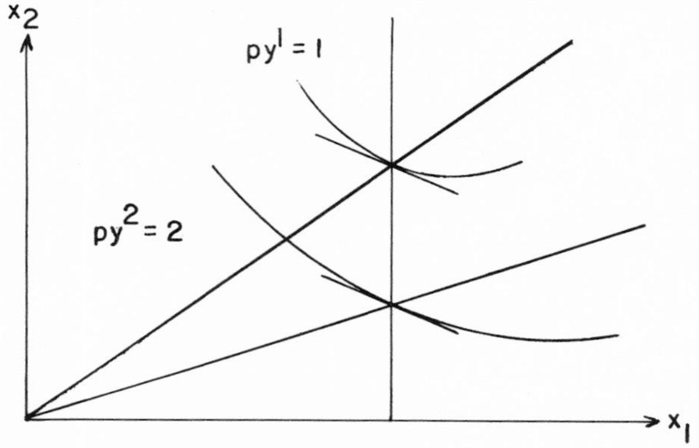

(figure 1)

In figure 1, iso-revenue curves, $py^i = 1$, $i = 1, 2$ are drawn. The curves are constructed to be vertically parallel. It can be seen that the ratio of x_2 to x_1 utilized in industry 1 always exceeds that utilized in industry 2. This is assumption (2). Nevertheless, there is not factor price equalization, since industry 1 is never profitable.

Questions arise to how Samuelson's basic results can be extended. First, does an increase in the number of industries increase or decrease the likelihood of factor price equalization. Second, is there factor price equalization when the number of factors exceeds two. In response to the second question, it must be noted that factor price equalization cannot be expected for $m > n$ since $x = X\xi$ does not map onto an m dimensional space of x's and hence the strictly positive orthant of ξ's cannot map onto an open set of x's. Therefore, we require $m \leq n$.

Beyond these generalizations, elimination of Samuelson's condition (1) leads to two versions of factor price equalization. First, given w, there exists p such that for some x there is factor price equalization. Second, given p, there exists w such that for some x there is factor price equalization. Each of these theorems is itself divided into two parts, first, that m industries operate, and second, that they have independent x^i.

Theorem 12. If w is strictly positive in every component and if technology is Leontief, then there is a price system p at which every industry is profitable. If the x^i are also linearly independent then there is factor price equalization.

The theorem is that of McKenzie [8] and is the generalization of Samuelson's result vis a vis the number of industries and factors.

Proof: For given w, solve

$$pY = wX,$$

or

$$p = wXY^{-1}. \qquad \text{QED.}$$

The more difficult theorem is that given p, there is a w which allows factor price equalization. If we consider p(w), we see that an m dimensional space is mapped into an n-dimensional space, $n > m$. In general, we would not expect p(w) to lead to the profitability of all industries. However, for factor price equalization all that is required is that m industries be operable. Nevertheless, the excess of number of industries over the number of factors complicates matters in-so-far as zero profitability in n industries does not insure non-positive profitability in the remaining industries.

Theorem 13. Let there be a Leontief technology and let f^i be continuously differentiable and satisfy a strict concavity property. If, given p, there are exactly m profitable industries and, also, there is factor price equalization for some w, then for all nearby p, there is factor price equalization.

Proof:

1. There is factor price equalization at (p, w) if and only if there are m profitable industries with linearly independent x^i. This follows since no change in w implies no change in the function $x^i(w)$. Therefore, absorption of an open set of factor endowments requires linearly independent factor utilization vectors, x^i.

2. For nearby p, no industries formerly unprofitable become profitable, since small changes in p lead to small changes in w and therefore lead to small changes in profits.

3. If we restrict attention to m industries with linearly independent x^i,

$$pY = wX,$$

or

$$\frac{\partial w}{\partial p} = YX^{-1}$$

since

$$w \frac{\partial X}{\partial w_i} = 0$$

by cost minimization. The differential equation may be solved for small changes in p, since X is continuous in w.

4. Since X(w) is continuous, for small changes in w, X(w) has the same m linearly independent columns. Applying 1 gives the theorem. QED.

We turn to results more general in terms of the goods price space. First we consider the two factor case, where a quite general theorem can be obtained. We can give a definite answer to question 1 in the two factor case. We also generalize Samuelson's condition (1).

Theorem 15. Suppose

(i) k industries are separately profitable at factor prices w^i, i=1,...,k,

(ii) there are two factors,

(iii) $k \geq 2$,

(iv) f^i is continuous and satisfies constant returns to scale. Then for each industry, i, there is another industry j such that both i and j are operated simultaneously. Therefore, if there is any industry i which has x^i linearly independent of all other j, there is factor price equalization.

The fact that x^i is independent of x^j and x^k does not preclude the possibility that x^k and x^j are linearly dependent. In effect, i can be chosen as one of the (somewhere) profitable industries, and it need not be the case that all x^i and x^j are linearly independent as in the Samuelson theorem. Therefore, an increase in the number of industries is seen to make factor price equalization more likely. The view of Samuelson [11] is confirmed.

Proof: Let S_i be the set of strictly positive factor endowments which lead to w for which industry i is profitable. S_i is closed, since

$$pf^i(x^i(w)) - w(x, p)\, x^i(w)$$

is zero in the limit, as

$$w \to w(x, p).$$

Therefore,

$$\bigcup_{j \neq i} S_i$$

is closed relative to the positive x. Also

$$\bigcup_{i} S_i$$

equals the set of strictly positive factor endowments, a connected set. A connected set cannot be disjointed into two closed sets, whereupon for each i

$$S_i \cap \left(\bigcup_{j \neq i} S_j \right)$$

is non-empty, i.e., there exists an x leading to w for which i is profitable and $\overline{w}$ for which j is profitable. We simply observe that whenever i is profitable for w in $\eta_1(x, p)$, j for $\overline{w}$ in $\eta_1(x, p)$, both i and j are profitable for w (theorem 5).

If x^i and x^j are independent there is factor price equalization at

$$x = \xi_i x^i + \xi_j x^j,$$

$$\xi_i > 0,$$

$\xi_j > 0$. QED.

We turn to the m factor case. Chipman [1] has generalized a result of Kuhn [7] which gives conditions insuring factor price equalization. In two dimensions, it appears that Kuhn's conditions require that factor inputs be used in fixed proportions except for a bounded set of factor utilizations. For Mrs. Robinson [10] and Kaldor [3], this may be well enough, but economists are usually interested in a larger variety of production functions. Hence, we proceed to analyze other conditions on production. It will be seen that the domain of p satisfying factor price equalization can be specified. In the two dimensional case, factor price equalization holds up to the point where Samuelson's factor intensity assumption fails.

<u>Theorem 14.</u> Suppose

(i) there is a Leontief technology

(ii) f^i is continuously differentiable and satisfies a strict concavity property, $i = 1,\ldots,n$,

(iii) for each factor i, either

(a) there is some good for which a minimum quantity of i is needed in order to produce a minimum quantity of the good, or

(b) $x^i \to 0$ implies F_i is bounded,

(iv) (a) either an infinite amount of one factor, i, combined with a non-zero amount of the other factors leads to an infinite output in some industry, or

(b) $x^i(w)$ is bounded for all i,

(v) $m = n$, and

(vi) all $x^i(w)$ are linearly independent so long as all industries are profitable, for $tp + (1-t)\overline{p}$, $\overline{p}$ allows factor price equalization, $0 \leq t \leq 1$.

Then for all p allowing positive revenues in each industry, there is factor price equalization.

Supposition (iii)a amounts to saying that for each factor, i, there is at least one industry, j, such that the production isoquant for other factors is asymptotic to hyperplanes x_i^j = constant. (iii)a and (iv)a together must refer to the same pairing of factors and industries insofar as an industry, j, for which (iii)a holds <u>vis a vis</u> factor i automatically does not satisfy (iv)a for the other factors. Therefore, in order for there to be enough industries to satisfy by (iii)a and (iv)a, i and j are uniquely associated.

A counter example appears in figure 1, where minimum inputs of a given factor are not needed for any goods, and in figure 2a, where both industries operate but the x^1 are not linearly independent, contradicting (vi).

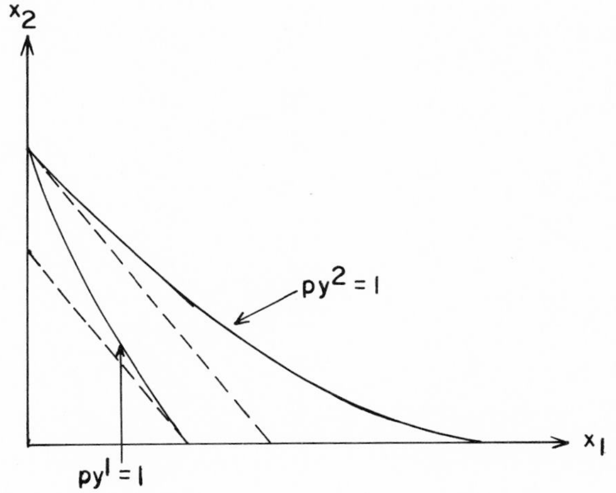

(figure 2a)

Supposition (iii)b covers the case where iso-product curves intersect the i axis(es), whereupon the marginal rate of transformation of i for i is bounded. A counter example appears in figure 2b, which is figure 2a when revenues in industry 2 are decreased. For revenues in industry 2 higher than is the case in figure 2, there is factor price equalization (figure 2b) where

$$w_1 = \frac{1}{\bar{x}_1},$$

$$w_2 = \frac{1}{\bar{x}_2}.$$

For smaller revenues in industry 2, in figure 2a, both industries may operate but there is not factor price equalization. Thereafter, only one industry is operated.

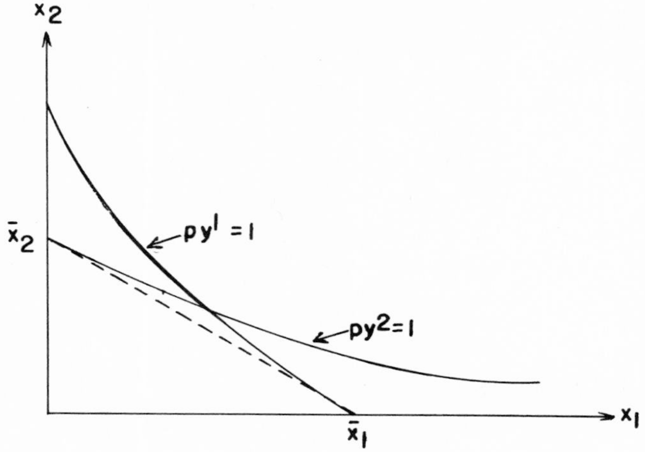

(figure 2b)

Supposition (iv)b is a quasi-Leontief assumption in that substitution is limited. It appears that (iii)a and (iv)b are the assumptions used by Kuhn [7] and Chipman [1].

Supposition (vi) is a generalization of Samuelson's two dimensional assumption of no factor reversal. In two dimensions, the x^i are independent for all w if and only if the factor ratios remain different for all w. Since these factor ratios are continuous in w, they cannot be reversed.

Proof: Apply theorem 11 to obtain $\overline{p}$, for which w is strictly positive and therefore $\overline{p}Y$ is non-negative and for which there is factor price equalization. As we change p, we simply solve for w as

$$\frac{\partial w}{\partial p} = YX^{-1}$$

which is solved so long as X is bounded.

So long as w is bounded, both from infinity and from zero, $x^{-1}(w)$ is continuous in w and bounded. Therefore

$$w(p) = \int_L \frac{\partial w}{\partial p} \, dp$$

$$L = [p, \overline{p}]$$

gives a solution of w for p which makes all m industries zero profitable.

Now consider a fixed ξ so that

$$Y = Y\xi$$

is fixed. Then .

$$wX = pY$$

is fixed, so that

$$w_i \to \infty,$$

implies

$$x_i \to 0.$$

In case (iii)a, this is impossible if one is to produce y. In case (iii)b,

$$x_i \to 0$$

implies F_i bounded so that eventually

$$w_i > pF_i$$

and x_i is identically zero. This contradicts the linear independence of the x^j.

On the other hand, if

$$w_i \to 0,$$

(iv)a applies so that industry j can use x_j^i intensely to obtain a virtually zero cost and therefore a positive profit (for pY strictly positive). Therefore we cannot have

$$w_i \to 0.$$

In the absence of (iv)a, (iv)b insures that X is continuous as

$$w_i \to 0.$$

It remains to verify that zero profitable industries at X(w) necessarily have non-positive profits for other factor combinations. This follows from the weak concavity of pf_i, for

$$p > 0,$$

whereby

$$py^i - py^i = pf^i(x^i) - pf^i(x^i)$$

$$pF^i(x^i - x^i) = wx^i - wx^i.$$

(Saaty and Bram [11, p. 101]). Therefore, other factor utilizations producing y^i are no more profitable. QED.

6. State Policies

Presuming full employment of factors, three instruments of state policy come to mind: Taxes on factor income, taxes on goods, and taxes on imports. Of course each of these policies has a negative side, namely a subsidy. The theory is the same, whether the tax is negative or positive.

Following Kreuger and Sonnenschein [6], we say that a policy leads to no potential loss if the government obtains revenues which can be used in the foreign market to purchase goods which in turn can be granted in subsidy so as to restore all individuals to a position at least as good as the one before the policy. Otherwise, there is a potential loss. This is the Hicks-Kaldor criterion. Only if the no policy situation also leads to no potential loss vis à vis the policy can it be said that the notion of potential loss has welfare content. Otherwise, the policy would lead to a loss vis à vis the initial position of consumers but the new situation would be better than anything without the policy which is comparable with regard to the distribution of benefits among consumers.

Theorem 16. Taxes on factor wages involve no potential loss. This proposition is a version of the theorem of Hotelling [2].

Proof: Taxes on factor income must not affect the wages firms pay, for only at those wages can the factor market be equilibrated, given the factor supplies (theorem 6). Therefore, the only effect of the taxes is to reduce the income of factors and their demands for goods. Presuming that all industries are subject to international competition, either because they export to the international market or because they import some quantity of foreign goods, there is no change in prices of goods. All the loss in factor income accrues to the state and the state may use the proceeds to restore individuals to the position at which they would have been, simply by buying and distributing among individuals goods equal to the goods bought without tax minus goods bought after the tax. QED. Theorem 16 applies equally well to negative as to positive taxes. Therefore, reversing taxes on factors leads to no potential loss if and only if government revenues are sufficient to purchase at the international price system, the goods purchased by consumers before the policy.

Remark 6. A tax tariff policy leads to a potential loss if and only if government revenues are insufficient to purchase at the international price system, the goods purchased by consumers before the policy.

Proof: The government can always buy effectively at the

international price system since anything in excess of it is collected by the government as a tax and therefore the extra charge is illusory. Whatever the government purchases can be parcelled out to consumers via subsidies on factor wages. QED. In particular, Remark 6 applies to show that the reversal of a tax-subsidy scheme leading to a potential loss leads to a gain. Therefore, the notion of potential loss is not dependent upon the socially preferred distribution of benefits.

Theorem 17. Taxes on goods do not change output decisions and no potential loss occurs.

The rationale for the theorem is that the equilibrium of the factor market and the preservation of factor wages normally require that producers obtain a particular profit which must be invariant to prices.

Taxes on goods force consumers to pay higher prices but do not affect the effective price of goods to produce since this is determined by the international market, subject to whatever tariff restrictions are in effect. Normally, increases in the price of goods, p to $\bar{p}$, will influence consumers to decrease their purchases of the taxed goods so that the state will obtain revenues less than the amount which the consumers' originally bought. That is to say

$$(\bar{p} - p)(\bar{d} - d) \leq 0$$

where d is the consumers' purchases under p and $\bar{d}$ is the consumers' purchases under $\bar{p}$. Nevertheless, the state will be able to make purchases sufficient to restore consumers to their old position.

Proof: The value of the consumers' old purchases, possibly after some income transfers, will be

$$pd = wx,$$

but for the new purchases with the new price system, $\bar{p}$, it will also be

$$\overline{pd} = wx.$$

In order to return the consumers to their old position, d, the state must purchase internationally the amount, $d - \bar{d}$, at a cost of $p(d - \bar{d})$.

The state's new revenues are $(\bar{p} - p)\bar{d}$. The state can buy goods on the international market at price p. Since

$$p(d - \bar{d}) - (\bar{p} - p)\bar{d} = pd - \overline{pd} = 0,$$

it is possible to restore the economy to $\bar{d}$. Therefore, there is neither a potential loss nor a potential gain. QED.

We present a generalization of a theorem of Samuelson [13] (See also Kemp [4]).

Theorem 18. If the tariff leads to a less profitable production, there is a potential loss from a tax subsidy scheme, and it is an inferior method of raising factor income. Otherwise, the tariff involves no potential gain over the tax-subsidy scheme.

Proof: The imposition of a tariff has two effects. First, there are changes in factor wages in order to preserve zero profitability of industries. Second, the state obtains revenues from imported goods. We presume that $\overline{p}_i > p_i$ only for import industries since there is no point in placing a tariff on an exported good. Also, wages change to $\overline{w}$. If $\overline{d}$ is the new demand for goods and $\overline{y}$ is the new home supply, then the state receives the tariff weighted by imports equal to

$$0 \leq (\overline{p} - p)(\overline{d} - \overline{y}) = \overline{p}(\overline{d} - \overline{y}) - p(\overline{d} - \overline{y})$$

$$= -p(\overline{d} - \overline{y})$$

Factor income changes from wx to $\overline{wx}$, where

$$\overline{pd} = \overline{py} = \overline{wx}.$$

An alternative state policy is to tax by the amount $(\overline{p} - p)$, yielding revenues $(\overline{p} - p)\overline{d}$ and to subsidize so as to obtain the same factor income as under the tariff which sum to $\overline{wx}$. The subsidy would be equal to

$$\overline{wx} - wx = \overline{pd} - pd.$$

The remaining revenues would be equal to

$$(\overline{p} - p)\overline{d} - \overline{pd} + pd = pd - \overline{pd} = p(d - \overline{d}) = p(y - \overline{d}).$$

Factor income would be as high as under the tariff and the revenues would be higher by the amount

$$p(y - \overline{d}) + p(\overline{d} - \overline{y}) = p(y - \overline{y}) > 0. \quad \text{QED.}$$

A tariff proposed is one of divergence if the new tariff, $p - \overline{p}$, is proportional to the old, δ^2.

Theorem 19. If profits are reduced by a divergence tariff, then in fact they yield less consumer welfare than a tax-subsidy scheme supplementing the old tariff and tax system. This is a version of the so-called price divergence theorem (Kreuger and Sonnenschein [5]). The farther the prices diverge from free trade, the greater the potential loss.

Proof: In the general case, where there already exists taxes and tariffs, the increases in state revenues due to a tariff is given by

$$(\overline{p} - p)(\overline{d} - \overline{y}) + \delta^1(\overline{d} - d)$$

$$+ \delta^2((\overline{d} - d) - (\overline{y} - y) + \delta^3(\overline{w} - w)$$

where δ^1 is the prevailing tax on goods, δ^2 is the former level of tariffs, and δ^3 is the level of taxes on factor income. It is conceivable that the increase in revenues is sufficiently large and positive to give the tariff a potential gain. However, a tax-subsidy combination can always accomplish the same thing or do better, even with the given tariff. This can be accomplished by taxing goods by $(\overline{p} - p)$ and subsidizing the factors of production which increases state revenues by

$$((\overline{p} - p)\overline{d} - \overline{pd} + pd) + \delta^1(\overline{d} - d) + \delta^2(d - \overline{d}).$$

These revenues are greater than those due to the tariff provided that $\delta^2(\overline{d} - d)$ is not less than

$$\delta^2((\overline{d} - d) - (\overline{y} - y)),$$

or provided

$$\delta^2(\overline{y} - y) \geq 0.$$

If

$$t\delta^2 = (\overline{p} - p)$$

then

$$(\overline{p} - p)\ (\overline{y} - y) \geq 0. \quad \text{QED.}$$

7. An Application: Factor Accumulation in Developing Country

Consider the case where a particular factor, x_j, is increasing in quantity. So long as there are not m independent x^i, there will be changes in the factor wages and in fact the wages will fall (theorem 9). Also, eventually the w's will pass through regions in which there are not m independent x^i (theorems 12 and 13).

Whether total factor income will decrease or increase is a complex story depending upon the extent to which other factor prices change, upon the response of the share of the factor in the industries' outputs, which is determined by the elasticity of substitution in each industry to changes in factor endowments. In any case, the income of the changing factor can be improved by a government subsidy or by an appropriate tariff which allows the new factor endowment to be employed in a new industry, after a transfer of resources from other industries.

What is required is that there be an industry available to absorb the new factor supply and that it be possible to make this industry profitable without changing the factor prices. It would then follow that the price of the growing factor would not fall. All this will occur if

(i) there are exactly n industries with linearly independent y^i

(ii) of which m have linearly independent $x^i(w)$, and

(iii)

$$x = \sum_i \xi_i x^i,$$

$$\xi_i > 0.$$

In this case, for a time, increases in x_j can be absorbed simply by insuring that all industries are profitable which can be accomplished by an appropriate tariff system (theorem 11). (The restriction to n industries prevents the situation where one industry must have positive profits in order for another to be profitable.)

For example, suppose a country has a sufficiently low capital/labor ratio to be below the range where factor price equalization occurs. To absorb the large labor force, it is necessary that the labor intensive industry be the only operating industry due to a high price of capital and a low price of labor. As capital accumulates, a tariff may be imposed to make the capital intensive industry profitable (theorem 12). The new capital can then be absorbed without affecting factor prices. As capital continues to accumulate, the capital intensive industry eventually exhausts the labor force. Thereafter, the price of capital must fall to absorb great quantities of capital.

We can also consider that if such a policy is followed, a particular factor increases its income only in response to an increase in its quantity. That is to say, there is a tariff policy by which an increase in one factor, say capital, gives no benefit to the other factors, say labor.

For example, consider a foreign investment in a new industry, with a protective tariff. If the profitability of other industries is not disturbed, there will be no benefits for the home country since the investment will not increase the income of any other factors. In addition the home country's consumers must pay the higher price so that there is a potential loss. The tariff cannot raise enough revenues to subsidize the home producers by an amount equal to the added cost since tariff revenues, $(\overline{p} - p)\overline{y}$, do not equal consumer costs, $(\overline{p} - p)\overline{d}$. Therefore, consumers cannot be returned to their former position. There is a potential loss.

As a second example, capital accumulation leads to a decrease in the rate of return on capital. Outside the set of factor endowments where there is factor price equalization, the return to capital will fall. Assuming the accumulation of capital to depend positively upon its price, this will lead to a slower accumulation of capital. The likelihood is that very low income countries, specializing in labor intensive goods, and very high income countries, specializing in capital intensive goods, will experience this effect. There may be some tendency to increase growth rates by raising tariffs. Of course, the tariff leads to an effect in reducing the real return to capital due to the higher price of consumer goods purchased with capital income. In general, the tariff will be inferior to direct tax-subsidy in this regard, but for an underdeveloped country, the impossibility of an effective tax-subsidy system may make a tariff the best available stimulus for growth.

FOOTNOTES

1. z is an internal point of Z if for any vector w in E^{n+1}, $z + tw \varepsilon Z$ for t sufficiently small.

2. $$Z = \sum_{i=1}^{k} Z_i$$

is equivalent to

$$Z = \{z | z = \sum_{i=1}^{k} z^i, z^i \varepsilon Z_i\}.$$

3. $y >> z$ whenever y is greater than z in every component.

4. The uniqueness of w can be proved without using continuous differentiability of f^i, provided that there are m linearly independent x^i (McKenzie [8]). Using the notation developed for the Leontief technology for these industries and recalling from the proof of theorem 3 that given that (x^i, y^i) is profitable under one (w, p) it is profitable under another,

$$w = pY(X)^{-1}$$

$$x = X\xi.$$

(Of course, Y is not necessarily invertible nor even square). Therefore, for any p, η_1 is determined to be w computed above.

5. $$\Delta v = \overline{v} - v$$

represents a change in a quantity.

REFERENCES

1. Chipman, J., "A Survey of the Theory of International Trade, III," Econometrica, 1966.

2. Hotelling, H., "The General Welfare in Relation to Problems of Taxation and Railway and Utility Rates," Econometrica, 6, (1938).

3. Kaldor, N., "A Model of Economic Growth," Economic Journal, 1957.

4. Kemp, M., "The Gain from International Trade," Economic Journal, 72 (1962), pp. 803-819.

5. Koopmans, T.C., Three Essays on the State of the Economic Science, 1959.

6. Kreuger, A., and Sonnenschein, H., "The Terms of Trade, the Gains from Trade and Price Divergence." International Economic Review, 8 (1967), pp. 121-127.

7. Kuhn, "Factor Endowments and Factor Prices: Mathematical Appendix," Economica, N.S., 26 (May 1959), pp. 142-144.

8. McKenzie, L., "Equality or Factor Price in World Trade," Econometrica, 23, pp. 239-257 (1955).

9. McKenzie, L., "Matrices with Dominant Diagonals and Economic Theory," Mathematical Methods in the Social Sciences, Stanford, 1960.

10. Robinson, J., The Accumulation of Capital, Irwin, 1956.

11. Saaty and Bram, Non-linear Mathematics, McGraw-Hill, 1964.

12. Samuelson, P.A., "International Factor Price Equalization Once Again," Economic Journal, 59 (1949).

13. Samuelson, P.A., "The Gain from International Trade," Canadian Journal of Economics and Political Science, 1938 (reprinted in Readings in the Theory of International Trade, London, Allen and Unwin 1950.

14. Stolper, W., and Samuelson, P.A., "Protection and Real Wages," Review of Economic Studies, 9,(1941),pp. 58-73.

POLICIES TO ATTAIN EXTERNAL AND INTERNAL BALANCE: A REAPPRAISAL*

by

James P. Quirk and Arvid M. Zarley
University of Kansas

1. Introduction

This paper is concerned with the reexamination of the problems of external and internal balance within the context of a macroeconomic model in which the interrelationships among the labor market, the money market and the goods market are treated explicitly, under the Keynesian assumption of lack of flexibility of money wages. Attention is centered upon the effectiveness of combined monetary and fiscal measures undertaken to attain a state of joint balance. Joint balance is defined in the usual manner: a state where domestic production is at the full employment rate and any deficit (surplus) in the merchandise account is exactly compensated for by capital inflows (outflows), gold flows being zero over the time period under consideration.

Sections 2 and 3 of the paper take up the static aspects of the problem, including the important issue of the existence and uniqueness of policy choices to attain joint balance. The remainder of the paper is concerned with the issue of convergence to a position of joint balance, given certain policy measures adopted by the fiscal and monetary authorities. The discussion of the convergence problem is essentially a summary of the work of Mundell [5, 6, 7], who first discussed the convergence problems in terms of a formal dynamic framework, with Mundell's approach being reformulated in terms of several alternative dynamic presuppositions.

The basic points that are developed in the paper may be summarized as follows. (1) In a Keynesian type economy which lacks perfect flexibility of money wages (and in which a liquidity trap may exist), there is no guarantee that there is any range of fiscal and monetary choices that is consistent with a position of joint external and internal balance. As Mundell has pointed out in a different context, the interest sensitivity of international capital flows becomes crucial; if such flows are either too sensitive or too insensitive to interest rate differentials, no balance positions need exist. (2) In general, if there exists some combination of monetary and fiscal policy consistent with a position of joint balance, then there will exist a multiplicity of such policy mixes (various combinations of real government expenditure and money supply levels), none of which are unique with respect to the policy choices made, i.e. within the context of the model it is not always true that monetary policy is the unique choice to achieve external balance and fiscal policy the unique choice for achieving internal balance. It thus becomes necessary not only to examine the convergence properties of various policy prescriptions, but, in addition, the need now also arises for some choice criterion to distinguish among alternative positions of external and internal balance. (3) the local convergence properties of several approaches to the joint balance problem are studied, with results similar to those obtained by Mundell; it is shown in addition that these results are quite sensitive to the assumptions made concerning disequilibrium states of the system. In particular, the conclusion that fiscal policy should be directed towards internal balance and monetary policy should be directed towards external balance does not necessarily hold if the price level is assumed to be determined endogenously, under the assumption that the money market is always in equilibrium; (4) for certain special cases, global convergence results are presented.

2. The Static Aspects of Joint Balance

The macroeconomic model we will use is a model formulated in real terms and appropriate to the "small country" case in international trade theory. That is, we assume that the changes induced in the domestic economy by monetary and fiscal actions will not produce retaliatory actions by other countries. Further, we ignore the induced impact of these changes on such variables as the levels of prices and outputs in other countries. To the extent that retaliation occurs and to the extent that the worldwide general equilibrium nature of the problem becomes crucial, the results stated here would require modification, perhaps in some cases drastically. Finally, we deal here only with the case of fixed exchange rates.

The static macroeconomic model employed is that developed by Marschak [4] and Brownlee [2], here specialized to the "Keynesian" case, with assumptions as follows:

A. Labor Market

Let N_D = number of labor units demanded

N_S = number of labor units supplied

N = number of labor units hired

w = money wage rate per labor unit

P = price level

$w^* \equiv w/p$ = real wage rate per labor unit

Y = money value of output (Net National Product)

$X \equiv Y/P$ = real value of output

A.1 $X = X(N)$ where $X'(N) > 0$, $X''(N) < 0$ (Short run assumption that the stock of capital is fixed and fully employed).

A.2 $N_D = N_D(w^*)$ where $N_D'(w^*) < 0$

A.3 $N_S \leqq N_F(w)$ where $N_F'(w) > 0$. (The supply of labor is a function of the money wage; at any given money wage rate w, the supply is perfectly elastic up to the "full employment" level of labor hiring, $N_F(w)$).

A.4 $w = w_o$ (Union determined money wage rate.)

A.5 $N = \min \; (N_D(w^*), N_F(w))$

Given the perfect inflexibility of money wage rates and the money illusion assumptions incorporated into A.1 - A.5, Figure 1 below shows a graphical derivation of the "aggregate supply function," $X_S(P)$ for the economy:

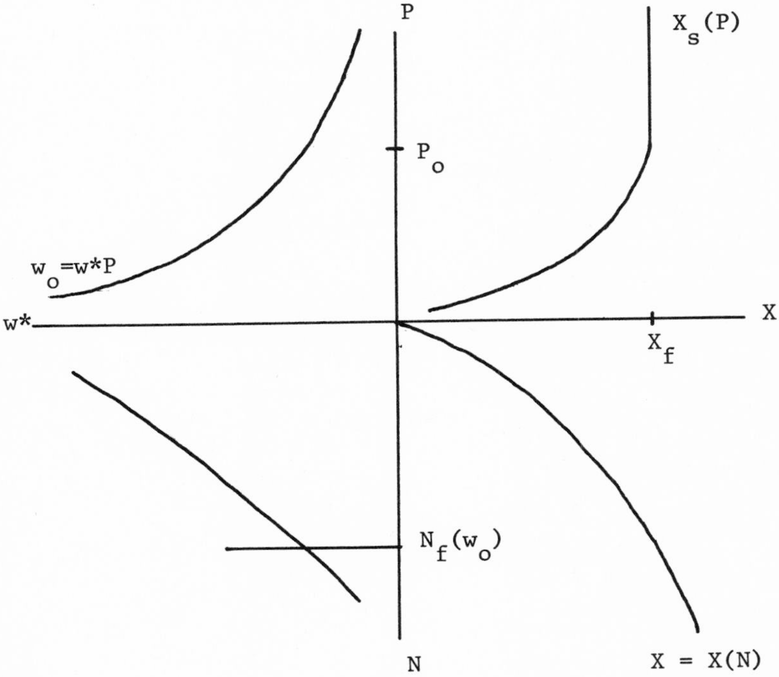

Figure 1

In Figure 1, X_F denotes the full employment level of output for the economy. We define internal balance as a situation in which every worker that wants a job at the going money wage rate is hired; thus when internal balance occurs, $N = N_F$ and $X = X_F$.[1] Both of these magnitudes are increasing functions of w. When w is fixed at w_o, the diagram shows that internal balance occurs only if $P \geq P_o$.

An alternative formulation of the Keynesian labor market assumptions is to postulate downward rigidity of the money wage rate but perfect flexibility in an upwards direction. Strictly speaking, questions of flexibility of money wages are dynamic questions and to handle them within the context of a static model raises some difficulties. However, given once and for all changes in parameter values, a formulation of the "rigid downwards, flexible upwards" assumption is as below:

Replace A.3 - A.5 by:

A.3' $N_S = N_S(w^*)$ where $N_S'(w^*) > 0$

A.4' Let w_o, P_o denote the "current" money wage rate and the price level at which full employment occurs. Then

$$w = w_o \quad \text{for} \quad P \leq P_o$$

$$w = w_o \frac{P}{P_o} \quad \text{for} \quad P \geq P_o$$

A.5' $N = \min(N_D(w^*), N_S(w^*))$

Figure 2 exhibits the properties of the $X_S(P)$ function under A.1, A.2, A.3', A.4', A.5'.

Figure 2 shows that the general properties of the $X_S(P)$ function remain unaltered; however N_F and X_F are now fixed numbers, independent of w. Further, the "rachet" effect of successive changes in prices is not shown on the diagram; in effect, successive increases in prices lead to successively higher values of the price level at which the $X_S(P)$ function becomes inelastic as shown in Figure 3.

B. Money Market

Let M_S = money value of the money supply

M_1 = money value of the transactions demand for money

M_2 = money value of the liquidity demand for money

r = interest rate

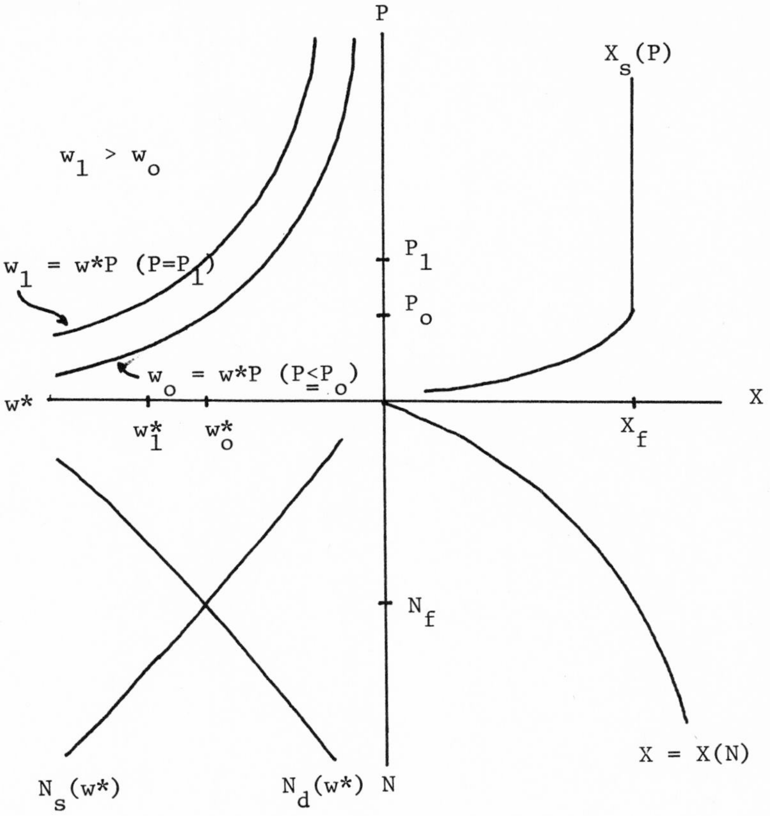

Figure 2

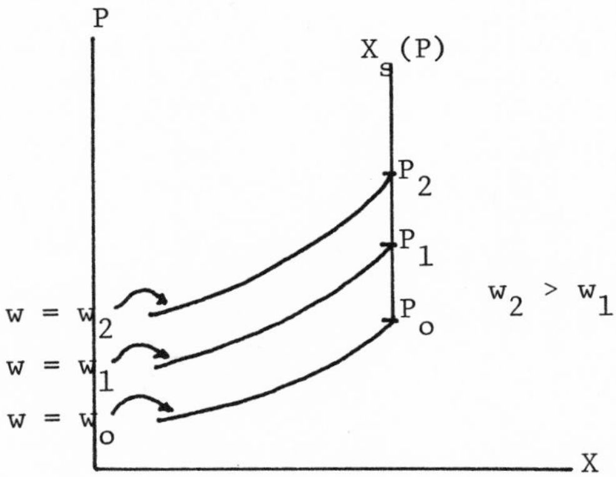

Figure 3

M_D = money value of the total demand for money

$M_S^* \equiv M_S/P$
$M_1^* \equiv M_1/P$
$M_2^* \equiv M_2/P$
$M_D^* \equiv M_D/P$

} all refer to real magnitudes

B.1 $M_1^* = kX$ where $k > 0$

B.2 $M_2^* = L(r)$ where $L'(r) < 0$ and $L'(r) \to -\infty$ as $r \to r_o$

B.3 $M_S = M_{S_o}$ (exogenous control of the money supply)[2]

B.4 $M_D^* \equiv M_1^* + M_2^* = M_S^*$

In Figure 4 below we derive, for selected values of M_S, those combinations of values of P and r that are jointly consistent with equilibrium in the money market and the assumption that $X = X_F$. The resulting LM schedules thus describe the relationship between monetary equilibrium and internal balance.

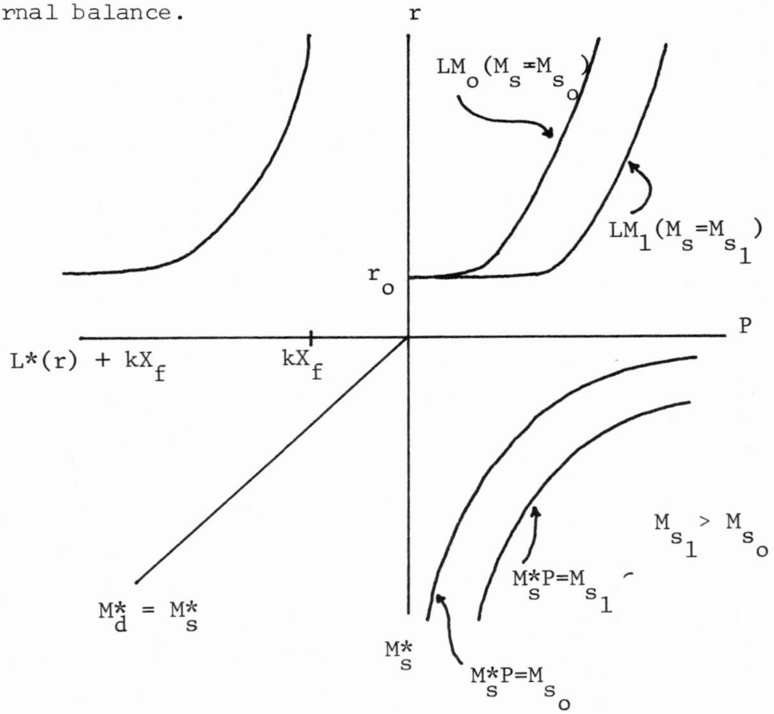

Figure 4

C. Goods Market

Let C = money value of domestic consumption expenditures

I_D = money value of domestic investment expenditures

x = money value of exports

m = money value of imports

$E \equiv x - m$ = money value of net exports

G = money value of net government expenditures

$C^* \equiv C/P$

$I_D^* \equiv I_D/P$

$x^* \equiv x/P$

$m^* \equiv m/P$

$E^* \equiv E/P$

(all refer to real values)

$G^* \equiv G/P$

C.1 $C^* = C^*(X)$ where $0 < \frac{\partial C^*}{\partial X} < 1$

C.2 $I_D^* = I_D^*(r)$ where $\frac{\partial I^*}{\partial r} < 0$

C.3 $x^* = x^*(P)$ where $\frac{\partial x^*}{\partial P} < 0$

C.4 $m^* = m^*(P,X)$ where $\frac{\partial m^*}{\partial P} > 0$, $\frac{\partial m^*}{\partial X} > 0$

C.5 $G^* = G_o^*$ (real government expenditures are determined exogenously)

C.6 $X = C^* + I_D^* + (x^* - m^*) + G^* \equiv C^* + I_D^* + E^* + G^*$

It will be noted that the real balance effect has not been incorporated into this model and further no link has been given between the money supply and the level of government expenditures.[3]

Figure 5 below shows the derivation of combinations of values of r and P for a given value of G^* that are jointly consistent with equilibrium in the goods market and $X = X_F$ (internal balance) as summarized in the IS functions.

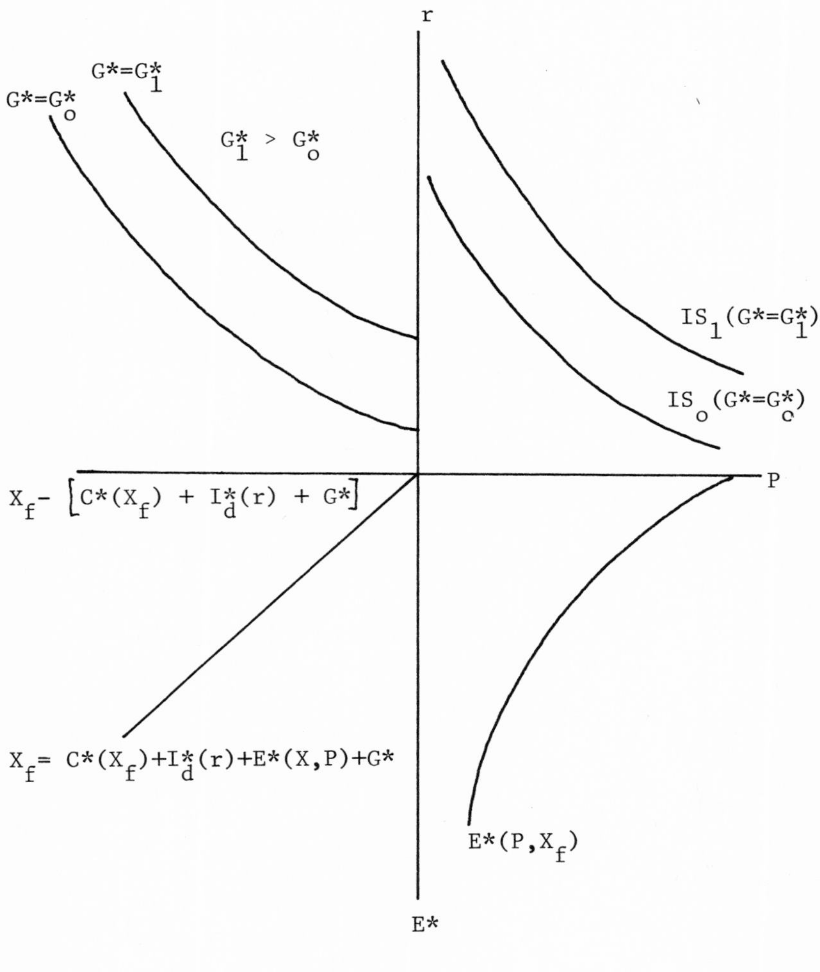

Figure 5

D. External Market

Let g = money value of gold inflow

K = net capital outflows in money terms

D.1 $K = K(r)$ where $\frac{\partial K}{\partial r} < 0$

D.2 $E(X,P) = g + K(r)$ where $\frac{\partial E}{\partial P} < 0$; $\frac{\partial E}{\partial X} < 0$

External balance is defined as a situation in which gold flows are zero. Figure 6 below shows the derivation of the EB curve, representing those combinations of P and r that are consistent with $g = 0$ and $X = X_F$ (joint external and internal balance):

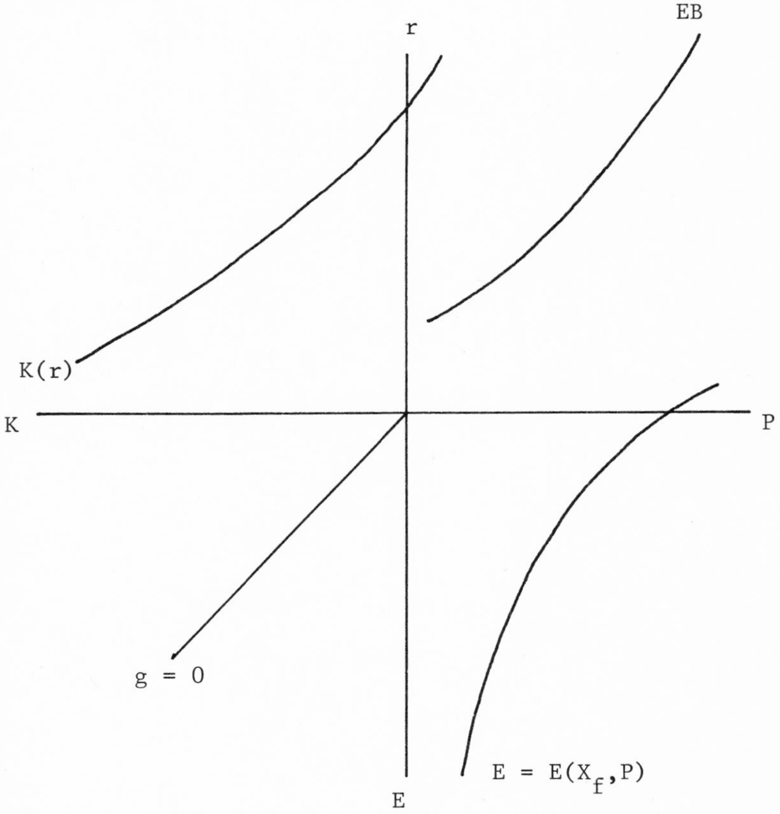

Figure 6

In Figure 7, the functional relationships indicating equilibrium in the labor, goods, money and external markets together with external and internal balance are plotted. Given the assumption of money wage rigidity and given that $w = w_o$, equilibrium in the labor market at a position of internal balance requires that $P \geq P_o$; equilibrium in the money market for $M_S = M_{S_o}$ occurs at $X = X_F$ along the LM ($M_S = M_{S_o}$)

schedule; equilibrium in the goods market when $G^* = G^*_o$ occurs at $X = X_F$ along the IS ($G^* = G^*_o$) schedule. Finally, $g = 0$ for $X = X_F$ along the EB curve:

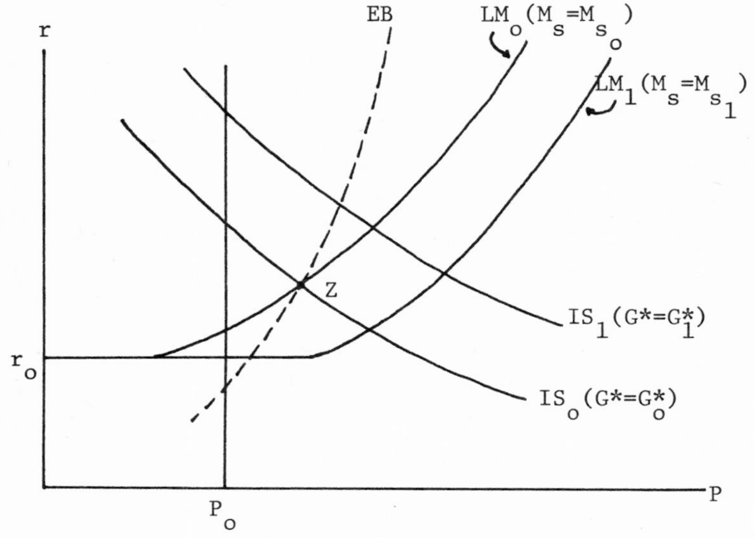

Figure 7

In the rigid wage case pictured in Figure 7, joint external-internal balance occurs at any point on or to the right of the $P = P_o$ line if such a point represents the intersection of the EB curve with an IS and an LM curve, such as, e.g., the point labelled Z. Points to the left of the $P = P_o$ line are inconsistent with the complete set of assumptions made concerning the various markets. To the right of the EB curve, $g < 0$ (gold outflows occur) because P is too high and r too low to permit external balance; to the left of the EB curve, $g > 0$ (gold inflows occur).

With the curves as drawn in Figure 7, infinitely many intersections of the IS and LM curves occur on or to the right of the $P = P_o$ curve (i.e., internal balance is feasible for a wide range of choices of monetary and fiscal policies). In fact, there exist [G^*, M_S] combinations consistent with labor, money and goods market equilibrium and internal balance, at every pair (P, r) such that $P \geq P_o$, $r \geq r_o$. Thus the existence of joint internal-external balance under appropriate monetary and fiscal policy choices occurs except in those cases where the EB curve lies always to the left of the $P = P_o$ line or always below the $r = r_o$ line.

Consider Figure 6 again. If real capital flows are perfectly inelastic with respect to the interest rate, then the EB function becomes parallel to the r axis at the value of P at which E = K. Clearly if this value of P is less than P_o, joint internal and external balance is impossible without introducing wage flexibility in a downwards direction. In the absence of such wage flexibility, the economy can remain in internal balance only at the expense of continuing gold outflows. Similarly, if real capital flows are so sensitive to the interest rate that they become perfectly elastic (or approach perfect elasticity asymptotically) at an interest rate less than r_o, the downward rigidity of the interest rate precludes joint external-internal balance and the economy experiences a continual gold inflow. Figure 8 below indicates these extreme cases:

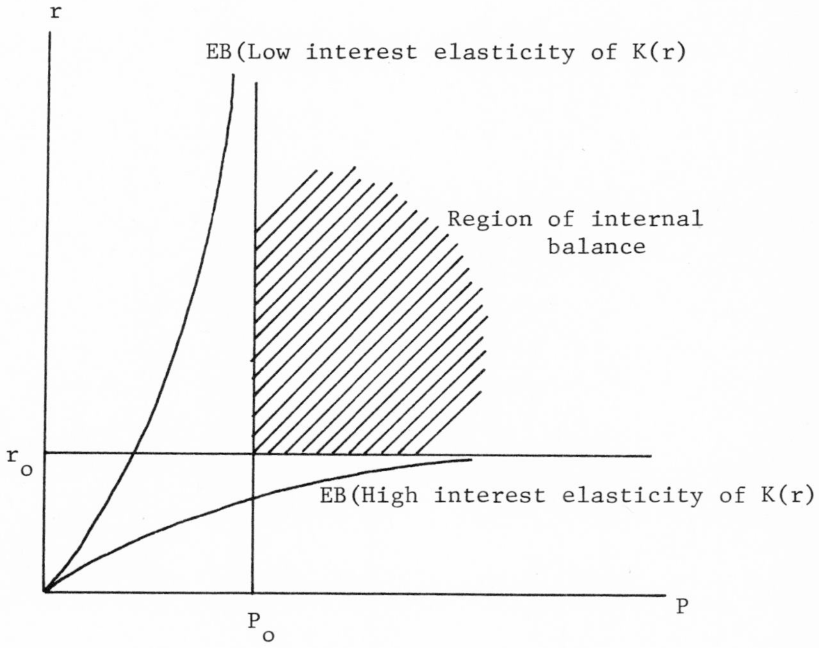

Figure 8

Other extreme cases deserve consideration. In the "crude Keynesian" case where investment and savings are perfectly inelastic with respect to the interest rate, if the IS curve associated with the given level of G* lies to the left of the $P = P_o$ line, then monetary policy alone is incapable of achieving joint balance; some increase in government expenditures is required. Similarly, in the "crude classical" case where the demand for real money balances is insensitive to the interest rate, the attainment of joint balance requires an expansion of the money supply if the LM curve associated with the given level of M_S lies to the left of the $P = P_o$ line. Less extreme cases also call for specific monetary or fiscal policy, as the curves shown in Figure 9 indicate. In Figure 9a, fiscal measures are required to attain joint balance and in Figure 9b monetary measures are required.

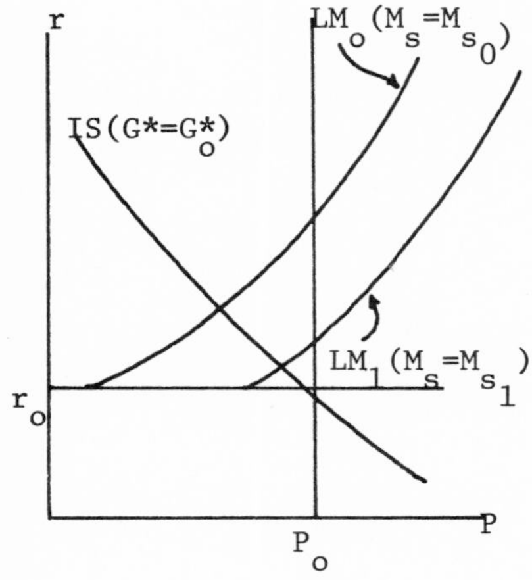

Figure 9a

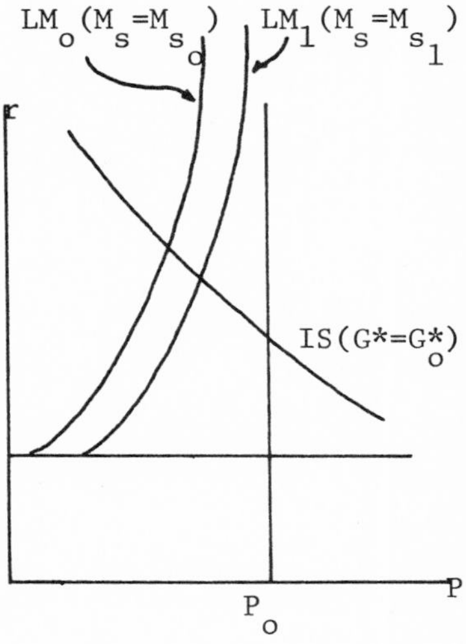

Figure 9b

In addition to the existence problems discussed above, questions concerning uniqueness arise in the discussion of any economic model. In Figure 8, note that the region defined as the region of internal balance is dense with points of internal balance, i.e., there are infinitely many intersections of IS and LM curves in this space. Joint external-internal balance can, however, be achieved by choosing any mix of monetary and fiscal measures which will allow the intersection of IS and LM curves along the EB curve as well, i.e., any point on the EB curve is a point of joint external-internal balance so long as the appropriate fiscal and monetary measures have been chosen in such a way that internal-external balance occurs.

The problem can be partially solved by the consideration of a model in which the nominal supply of money is determined endogenously as a function of the rate of interest. This behavioral relationship might be conceived as follows: when the rate of production is in the neighborhood of full employment, it might be expected that banks hold little or no excess reserves. In this case, the nominal money supply is determined by the availability of excess reserves. Assume, then, Federal reserve action in the form of an open market purchase which will be accompanied by a decline in the rate of interest and will add to the amount of excess reserves and hence will increase the supply of money. Then assumption B.3 above can be altered to include this behavioral assumption, i.e.,

$$\text{B.3}' \quad M_s = M_s(r) \text{ where } \frac{\partial M_s}{\partial r} < 0$$

Figures 10a and 10b exhibit the properties of the LM function under B.1, B.2, B.3', and B.4. The result is a single LM function in the [r, P] space. The LM curve so derived introduces the possibility that it might be negatively sloped, however. This becomes clear upon evaluation of the expression

$$\frac{dr}{dP} = \frac{\dfrac{-M_s}{P}}{P\dfrac{\partial L^*}{\partial r} - \dfrac{\partial M_s}{\partial r}}$$

which indicates that if the money supply is highly responsive to changes in the rate of interest relative to the interest responsiveness of the demand for real balances, the LM curve will be negatively sloped. If the opposite is true, the LM curve will have a positive slope.

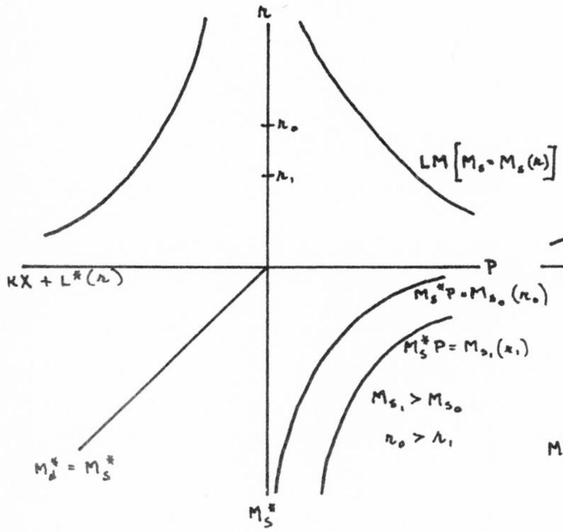

Figure 10a

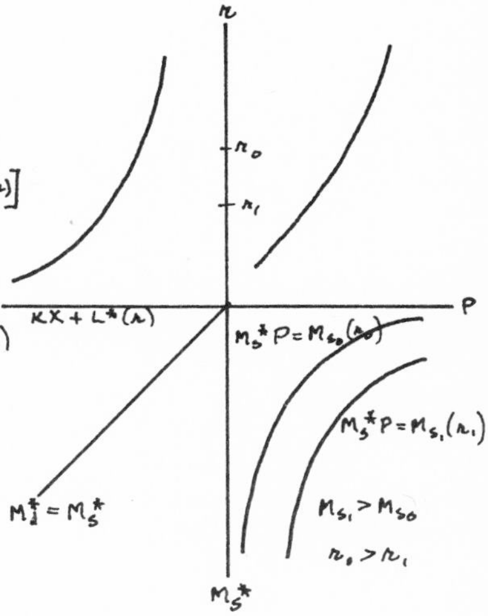

Figure 10b

Figure 11 plots the unique LM curve with the EB curve and the family of IS curves (with G* as an exogenous variable in the region of internal balance.)

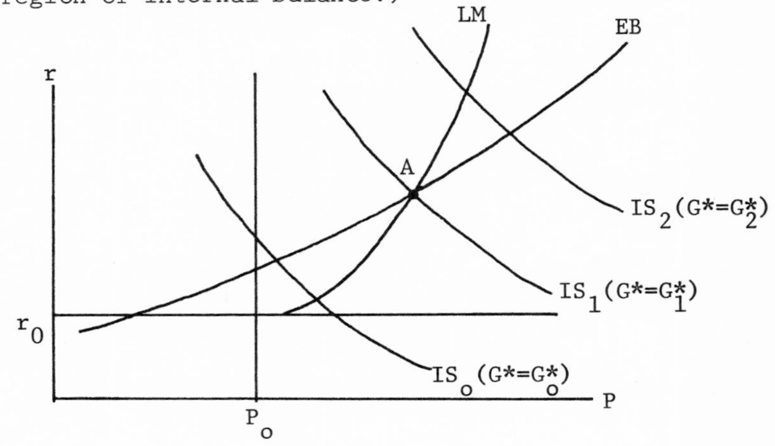

Figure 11

In the case shown, uniqueness is satisfied at the point A, which can be achieved by choosing $G^* = G^*_1$. Uniqueness in general, however, is not guaranteed, since conditions might prevail which would yield an LM curve which would be coincident with the EB curve.

In summary, downwards rigidity of the money wage rate and the existence of a liquidity trap might preclude the possibility of attaining joint balance through a mix of fiscal and monetary policies, unless international capital flows are neither too insensitive nor too sensitive to interest rate differentials. When joint balance positions are attainable through a mix of monetary and fiscal policy measures, then if the money supply is treated as being exogenously controlled by the monetary authorities, there is no unique combination of policy measures which will achieve the joint balance position. Even in the case in which the money supply is endogenously determined through interest rate manipulations, uniqueness of policy prescriptions to attain joint balance position is not necessarily guaranteed.

3. Policy Implications of the Static Model

The model formulated in the previous section raises some interesting problems for the fiscal and monetary authorities in their attempts to achieve joint internal and external balance. Certain of these problems relate to the convergence properties of rules of conduct adopted in the implementation of policy choices. Section 4 below considers some of these problems. Here we center attention upon the choice problems that arise because of the non-uniqueness of policy choices to attain joint balance. Figure 12 illustrates those choice problems:

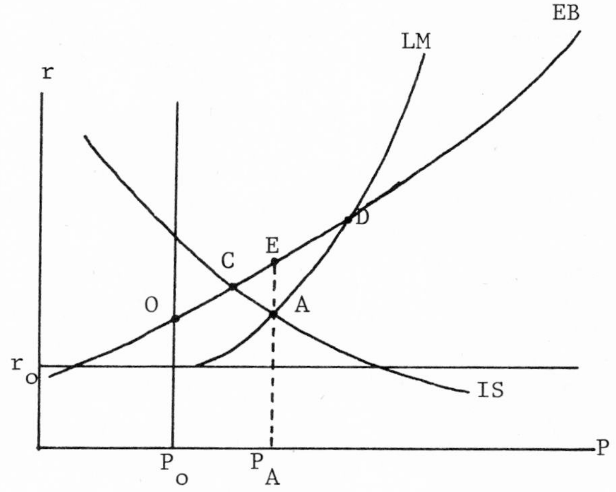

Figure 12

Assume the economy is in a position of internal balance (with gold outflows) at the point A. Then, under the wage rigidity assumption, any of the points on the EB curve to the right of the point 0 are admissible alternatives so far as joint internal and external balance is concerned. Thus a policy of reducing the money supply, with a fixed level of government expenditures, might be aimed at achieving the point of joint balance C, or alternatively, a policy of expanding the level of government expenditures, holding the money supply fixed, might be aimed at achieving the point D, and combinations of monetary and fiscal actions could be undertaken to attempt to achieve any of the other admissible joint balance positions. It should be pointed out, however, that if wages are flexible upwards and rigid downwards, then, given that the economy is presently at the point A, the only price levels consistent with internal balance are those at least as large as P_A; this effectively precludes any attempt to achieve joint balance by monetary measures alone. The money supply in this case may be reduced, but by no greater amount than that which would shift the LM curve to intersect the EB curve at the point E in Figure 12. But, if point E is the target, some increase in G* is necessary to achieve that point of joint equilibrium. The implication is that, in response to a gold outflow, to achieve joint balance in a world in which money wages are rigid downwards and flexible upwards, net government expenditures must be increased, whatever is the action taken by the monetary authorities.

The case in which the money wage rate is assumed to be

rigid in both directions affords a wider range of choices of joint balance positions for the fiscal and monetary authorities, but in either the perfectly rigid or rigid downwards-flexible upwards case fundamental welfare problems arise in connection with the choice made of a joint balance position. Consider, for example, choosing between the points D and E on the EB curve. Since both points satisfy internal (full employment) equilibrium it follows that the economy is on its production possibilities frontier. Since D involves a higher interest rate and price level than does E, the mix between public and private goods will generally be different at the two points, a choice of D favoring the public sector relative to the private sector as compared with E. (This assumes G* is increased by increasing government expenditures rather than through lowering taxes). Moreover, a higher rate of interest favors lenders vis à vis borrowers and thus involves a shift in the distribution of income in favor of the former. To some extent this is offset by the higher level of prices at the point D, which reduces the real burden of debts contracted in money terms. Further, if money wages are perfectly rigid, the real wage rate is lower at D than at E, involving a redistribution of income from labor to property owners and entrepreneurs.

Finally, the choice of D over E, with associated higher price level and interest rate, has implications for the level and composition of international trade. The choice of a higher price level and interest rate implies the choice to balance the external market with a smaller level of net exports and a higher rate of borrowing from foreigners, with attendant consequences for the development of the economy over time.

Beyond the welfare problems associated with the choice from among alternative joint balance points, difficulties arise in the attempt to implement such choices through fiscal and monetary policies because of the dynamic behavior of the economy. Thus, given differential lags in monetary versus fiscal policy measures, the choices from among alternative joint balance points might be partially governed by the time required to achieve joint balance, that mix of fiscal and monetary policy measures that yields joint balance in the quickest time being chosen over other mixes. We have made no attempt to investigate this problem, but the next section does summarize certain aspects of the problem of convergence to a given point of joint balance under alternative fiscal and monetary policies.

4. Dynamic Aspects of Joint Balance

Sections 2 and 3 have been concerned with the issues of the existence and uniqueness of positions of joint internal-external balance. Here we attempt to examine some of the dynamic features of the problem. Before discussing a class of dynamic models associated with the joint balance problem, some fundamental theorems concerning dynamic stability are noted.

Assume a dynamic system of the form

$$(4.1)\quad \dot{x}_1 = f_1(x_1,x_2)$$
$$\dot{x}_2 = f_2(x_1,x_2)$$

where the dot denotes differentiation with respect to time and f_1 and f_2 are assumed to be differentiable functions. Let $(\bar{x}_1, \bar{x}_2)$ denote an equilibrium point, that is, $f_1(\bar{x}_1, \bar{x}_2) = 0$, $f_2(\bar{x}_1, \bar{x}_2) = 0$. The equilibrium point $(\bar{x}_1, \bar{x}_2)$ is said to be <u>locally stable</u> if given any initial point (x_1^o, x_2^o) in a sufficiently small neighborhood of $(\bar{x}_1, \bar{x}_2)$, the system (4.1) generates time paths $x_1(t)$, $x_2(t)$ with the property that $\lim_{t\to\infty} x_1(t) = \bar{x}_1$, $\lim_{t\to\infty} x_2(t) = \bar{x}_2$. If $\lim_{t\to\infty} x_1(t) = \bar{x}_1$, $\lim_{t\to\infty} x_2(t) = \bar{x}_2$ for <u>any</u> initial point (x_1^o, x_2^o), then $(\bar{x}_1, \bar{x}_2)$ is said to be <u>globally stable</u>.

Necessary and sufficient conditions for local stability[4] are given by the Routh-Hurwitz criterion [3]:

$$(1)\quad \frac{\partial f_1}{\partial x_1} + \frac{\partial f_2}{\partial x_2} < 0; \qquad (2)\quad \frac{\partial f_1}{\partial x_1}\frac{\partial f_2}{\partial x_2} - \frac{\partial f_1}{\partial x_2}\frac{\partial f_2}{\partial x_1} > 0$$

(partial derivatives evaluated at $(\bar{x}_1, \bar{x}_2)$).

Sufficient conditions for global stability were derived by Olech [6].[5] Assume f_1 and f_2 have continuous derivatives everywhere. Then $(\bar{x}_1, \bar{x}_2)$ is globally stable if

$$(1)\quad \frac{\partial f_1}{\partial x_1}\ \frac{\partial f_2}{\partial x_2} < 0 \text{ everywhere}$$

$$(2)\quad \frac{\partial f_1}{\partial x_1}\frac{\partial f_2}{\partial x_2} - \frac{\partial f_1}{\partial x_2}\frac{\partial f_2}{\partial x_1} > 0 \text{ everywhere}$$

$$(3)\quad \text{either } \frac{\partial f_1}{\partial x_1}\frac{\partial f_2}{\partial x_2} \neq 0 \text{ everywhere or } \frac{\partial f_1}{\partial x_2}\frac{\partial f_2}{\partial x_1} \neq 0$$

everywhere.

For the system of three simultaneous equations

$$
\begin{aligned}
\dot{x}_1 &= f_1(x_1,x_2,x_3) \\
\dot{x}_2 &= f_2(x_1,x_2,x_3) \qquad (4.2) \\
\dot{x}_3 &= f_3(x_1,x_2,x_3)
\end{aligned}
$$

The Routh-Hurwitz conditions necessary and sufficient for local stability can be stated in terms of principal minors of the Jacobian matrix $J = \left[\frac{\partial f_i}{\partial x_j}\right]$ (evaluated at $(\bar{x}_1,\bar{x}_2,\bar{x}_3)$):

Let $k_i = (-1)^i$ x sum of the $i^{\underline{th}}$ order principal minors of J ($i = 1,2,3$) Then an equilibrium point $(\bar{x}_1,\bar{x}_2,\bar{x}_3)$ is locally stable if and only if

(1) $k_1 > 0$, $k_2 > 0$, $k_3 > 0$.

(2) $k_1 k_2 - k_3 > 0$.

Global stability conditions corresponding to those of Olech's theorem are not known for the case of three simultaneous differential equations.

To assist in the application of dynamic stability analysis to the static models formulated in the preceding section, we reproduce the graphs of the goods, money and labor markets for fixed values of G*, M_s and w. (It will be noted that the assumption that internal balance must hold, i.e., $X \equiv X_F$, is dropped in Figures 13a-c).

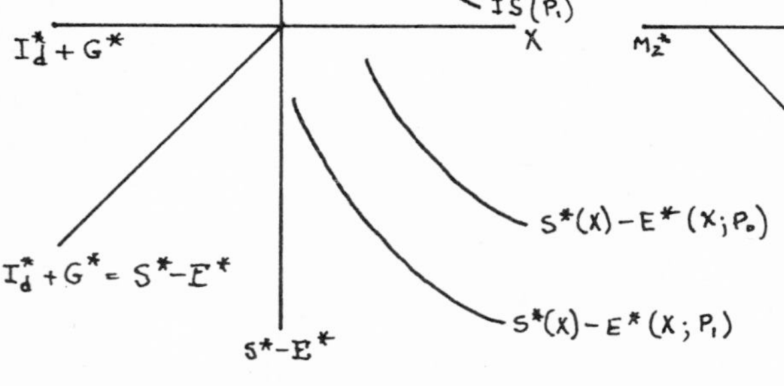

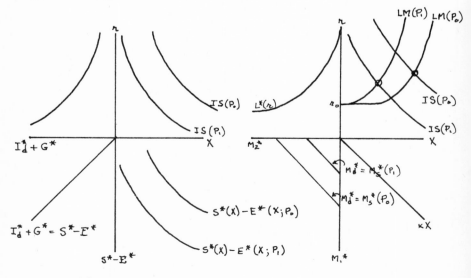

Figure 13a

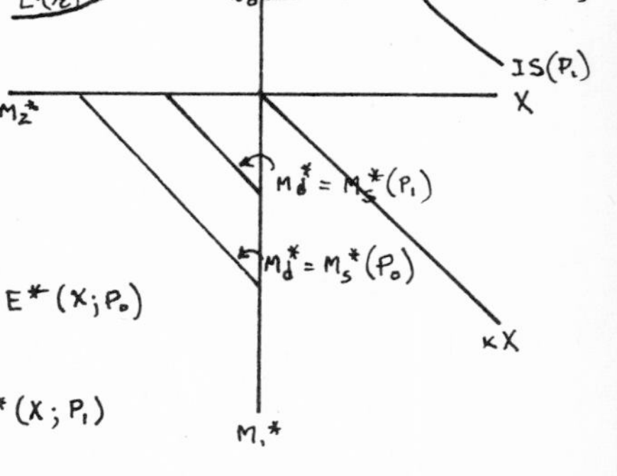

Figure 13b

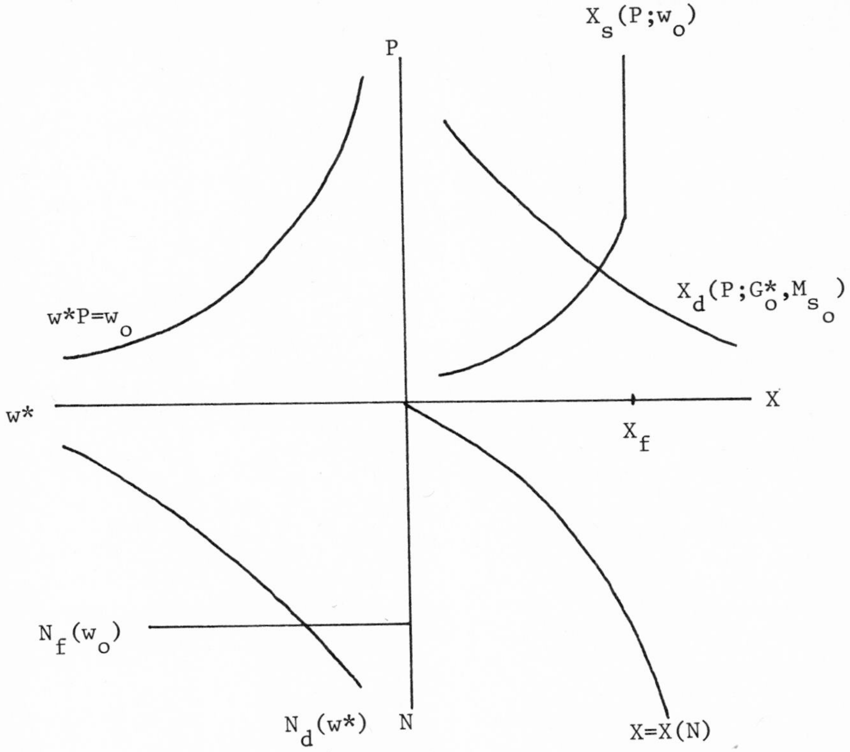

Figure 13c

We define excess demand in each of the three markets as follows:

$$D_X \equiv X_D - X_S = C^*(X) + I^*_D(r) + E^*(X,P) + G^* - X(N)$$

$$D_{M^*} \equiv M^*_D - M^*_S = kX + L^*(r) - \frac{M_S}{P}$$

$$D_N \equiv N_D - N_S = N_D(w^*) - N_S(w)$$

An equilibrium position of the static model, under conditions of inflexibility of money wages, is defined by the following conditions:

$$D_X = 0$$

$$D_{M^*} = 0$$

$$D_N \leqq 0.$$

Equilibrium at full employment implies $D_N = 0$.

In the absence of fiscal or monetary controls, a possible formulation of the "automatic" dynamic adjustment mechanism governing the behavior of this model, in the spirit of the Walrasian tâtonnement process, is given by the system

$$\dot{P} = a_1 D_X$$
(4.3)
$$\dot{r} = a_2 D_{M*}$$

where a_1 and a_2 are positive constants, to be interpreted as the "speeds of adjustment" of the price level and the interest rate respectively. Thus positive excess demand for output leads to a rise in the price level and positive excess demand for real money balances leads to a rise in the interest rate. We further assume that $X = X(N)$ with $N = N_D$. It will be noted that the possibility of a more than full employment output is admitted.

Let $(\overline{P}, \overline{r})$ denote equilibrium values of P and r for the system (4.3) for fixed values of G*, M_S and w, so that $D_X(\overline{P}, \overline{r}) = 0$, $D_{M*}(\overline{P}, \overline{r}) = 0$ (and $D_N(\overline{P}, \overline{r}) \leqq 0$). Then the Jacobian matrix of the system (4.3) is given by

$$J = \begin{bmatrix} a_1 \frac{\partial D_X}{\partial P} & a_1 \frac{\partial D_X}{\partial r} \\ a_2 \frac{\partial D_{M*}}{\partial P} & a_2 \frac{\partial D_{M*}}{\partial r} \end{bmatrix}$$

Assume that $0 < \frac{\partial C^*}{\partial X} + \frac{\partial E^*}{\partial X} < 1$. Then under the assumptions made in section 2 concerning the signs of partial derivatives, the sign pattern of J is

$$\text{sgn } J = \begin{bmatrix} - & - \\ + & - \end{bmatrix}$$

The matrix J is "sign stable" (see [9]); that is, the Routh-Hurwitz conditions for local stability are satisfied for any values of the entries in J that preserve the sign pattern of J. Consequently, the equilibrium point $(\overline{P}, \overline{r})$ is locally stable for any positive speeds of adjustment a_1 and a_2. Further, if these sign conditions are satisfied everywhere, the Olech theorem guarantees global stability of equilibrium.[6] The stable phase diagram associated with this system is shown in Figure 14:

Below the $D_{M*} = 0$ curve, excess demand for real money balances is negative, while above $D_{M*} = 0$, such excess demand is positive; similarly, to the right of the $D_X = 0$ curve,

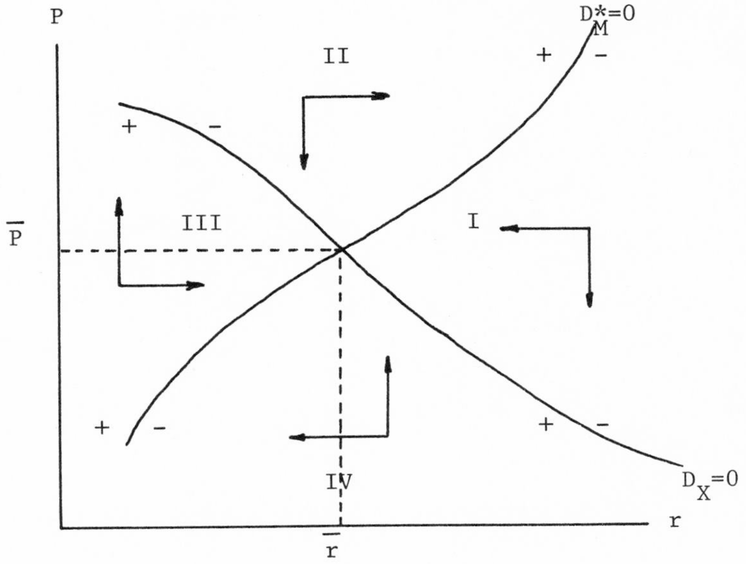

Figure 14

excess demand for output is negative, while to the left excess demand is positive. Given any point (P, r) lying in quadrant I, $D_{M*} < 0$, $D_X < 0$, hence, according to the system (4.3), P falls and r falls, as indicated by the arrows, with a similar interpretation being given to points in the other quadrants. In the phase diagram of Figure 14, any disturbance to equilibrium results in a movement over time of P and r back to the equilibrium point $(\overline{P}, \overline{r})$. It might be noted parenthetically that this is true whether or not the equilibrium position is one of full employment.

We consider next the application of these concepts to the problem of converging to a point of joint internal-external balance under monetary and/or fiscal policies. Mundell has already examined a number of cases which are summarized here, formulated in terms of the framework adopted in section 2.

In his discussion [5] of the relative merits of fixed versus flexible exchange rates, Mundell considers two basic dynamic models. In the fixed exchange rate case, the monetary authorities adjust the interest rate to correct for external imbalance, while the price level adjusts automatically to correct for internal imbalance. In the case of flexible exchange rates, monetary policy takes the form of price level adjustments through open market operations in the foreign exchange market, while the interest rate automatically adjusts for internal imbalance. In both cases the money supply and the level of real government expenditures are taken to be fixed.

For the fixed exchange rate case a dynamic adjustment mechanism representing the above is given by:

$$(4.4)\qquad \begin{aligned} \dot{P} &= a_1 D_X \\ \dot{r} &= -a_2 g \qquad (a_1 > 0,\ a_2 > 0) \end{aligned}$$

Assume that G* and M_S have been chosen so that $D_X = 0$ at $X = X_F$ and that for those choices, $g = 0$. (As section 2 has already made clear, for a Keynesian economy, this already imposes some restrictions on the IS, LM and K(r) functions.) In this case, the expression for the Jacobian matrix is

$$J = \begin{bmatrix} a_1 \dfrac{\partial D_X}{\partial P} & a_1 \dfrac{\partial D_X}{\partial r} \\ -a_2 \dfrac{\partial g}{\partial P} & -a_2 \dfrac{\partial g}{\partial r} \end{bmatrix} =$$

$$\begin{bmatrix} a_1 \left\{\left(\dfrac{\partial C^*}{\partial X} + \dfrac{\partial E^*}{\partial X} - 1\right) \dfrac{\partial X}{\partial N} \dfrac{\partial N_D}{\partial P} + \dfrac{\partial E^*}{\partial P}\right\} & a_1 \dfrac{\partial I_D^*}{\partial r} \\ -a_2 \left(\dfrac{\partial E}{\partial P} + \dfrac{\partial E}{\partial X} \dfrac{\partial X}{\partial N} \dfrac{\partial N_D}{\partial P}\right) & a_2 \dfrac{\partial K}{\partial r} \end{bmatrix}$$

Assume that $0 < \dfrac{\partial C^*}{\partial X} + \dfrac{\partial E^*}{\partial X} < 1$. Using the assumptions of section 2 concerning signs of partial derivatives, we have

$$\text{sgn } J = \begin{bmatrix} - & - \\ + & - \end{bmatrix}$$

so that comments concerning stability of this system are the same as those made concerning (4.3) above.

For the flexible exchange rate case, the dynamic process is

$$(4.5)\qquad \begin{aligned} \dot{r} &= a_1 D_X \\ \dot{P} &= a_2 g \qquad (a_1 > 0,\ a_2 > 0) \end{aligned}$$

with $\text{sgn } J = \begin{bmatrix} - & - \\ + & - \end{bmatrix}$

Thus, global stability can be proved for either of the policy measures suggested by Mundell. (Mundell proves local stability in both cases).[7]

Relative to the discussion of existence and uniqueness of policy measures to attain joint balance given in section 2, it might be noted that since G^* and M_S are fixed, if a position of joint balance exists, then such a position is unique. Further, Mundell restricted his attention in the paper cited to the "classical" case in which all internal prices (including the wage rate) are flexible, so that existence of a joint balance point is guaranteed. In particular, a world of flexible prices has the property that $D_X = 0$ only at $X = X_F$ for any choice of G^* and M_S. In the Keynesian model we are concerned with, equilibrium might well occur at less than full employment positions, as is illustrated in Figure 13 above. It is obvious that limiting policy prescriptions to monetary actions alone has serious drawbacks in such a world. Because of the stability analysis above, convergence is guaranteed; the difficulty is that the system converges to the point where $D_X = 0$ and $g = 0$, which need not be a point of internal balance unless G^* (and M_S) have been properly chosen. As Mundell has pointed out, in classical worlds, the issue is essentially that of attaining a <u>single</u> goal - external balance; the only internal equilibrium positions are full employment positions. In contrast, in a Keynesian world, both internal and external balance become goals towards which policy needs to be directed.

In the context of this problem, Mundell [6] has examined the role of monetary versus fiscal policy and has argued that monetary policy should be directed towards external balance with fiscal policy concerned with attaining full employment. We wish to examine in detail the assumptions under which this conclusion holds.

A model appropriate to this direction of fiscal versus monetary policy is (4.6):

$$
(4.6)\qquad \begin{aligned} \dot{G}^* &= -a_1(X_D - X_F) \\ \dot{r} &= -a_2 g \\ \dot{P} &= a_3 D_X \qquad\qquad (a_1 > 0,\ a_2 > 0,\ a_3 > 0) \end{aligned}
$$

with the money supply assumed to be fixed and with X_F a fixed number.

Within the context of this three equation system, it can be shown that convergence occurs when international capital flows are sensitive to the interest rate. The Jacobian matrix J is as follows:

$$J = \begin{bmatrix} -a_1 \dfrac{\partial X_D}{\partial G^*} & -a_1 \dfrac{\partial X_D}{\partial r} & -a_1 \dfrac{\partial X_D}{\partial P} \\ -a_2 \dfrac{\partial g}{\partial G^*} & -a_2 \dfrac{\partial g}{\partial r} & -a_2 \dfrac{\partial g}{\partial P} \\ aa_3 \dfrac{\partial D_X}{\partial G^*} & a_3 \dfrac{\partial D_X}{\partial r} & a_3 \dfrac{\partial D_X}{\partial P} \end{bmatrix} =$$

$$\begin{bmatrix} -a_1 & -a_1 \dfrac{\partial I_D^*}{\partial r} & -a_1 \left\{ \dfrac{\partial E^*}{\partial P} + \left(\dfrac{\partial C^*}{\partial X} + \dfrac{\partial E^*}{\partial X} \right) \dfrac{\partial X}{\partial N} \dfrac{\partial N_D}{\partial P} \right\} \\ 0 & a_2 \dfrac{\partial K}{\partial r} & -a_2 \left(\dfrac{\partial E}{\partial P} + \dfrac{\partial E}{\partial X} \dfrac{\partial X}{\partial N} \dfrac{\partial N_D}{\partial P} \right) \\ a_3 & a_3 \dfrac{\partial I_D^*}{\partial r} & a_3 \left\{ \dfrac{\partial E^*}{\partial P} + \left(\dfrac{\partial C^*}{\partial X} + \dfrac{\partial E^*}{\partial X} - 1 \right) \dfrac{\partial X}{\partial N} \dfrac{\partial N_D}{\partial P} \right\} \end{bmatrix}$$

Let $k_1 = -$ (sum of the diagonal elements of J), k_2 = sum of the 2 x 2 principal minors of J, $k_3 = -|J|$. The Routh-Hurwitz conditions for local stability require that $k_1 > 0$, $k_2 > 0$, $k_3 > 0$ and $k_1 k_2 - k_3 > 0$. Then it can be verified by some simple computations that if $\frac{\partial C^*}{\partial X} + \frac{\partial E^*}{\partial X} < 1$, and under the assumptions made above concerning the signs of the partial derivatives, $k_1 > 0$, $k_2 > 0$, while $|J| = a_1 a_2 a_3 \frac{\partial K}{\partial r} \frac{\partial X}{\partial N} \frac{\partial N_D}{\partial P}$ is negative if capital flows are responsive to the interest rate so that $k_3 > 0$. It is also straightforward to show that $k_1 k_2 - k_3 > 0$. As was mentioned earlier, global stability properties of this three equation model are not known.

When fiscal policy is directed towards external balance and monetary policy towards internal balance, (4.7) expresses the system:

$$\begin{aligned} \dot{r} &= a_1(X_D - X_F) \\ \dot{G}^* &= -a_2 g \qquad\qquad (4.7) \\ \dot{P} &= a_3 D_X \qquad\qquad (a_1 > 0,\ a_2 > 0,\ a_3 > 0) \end{aligned}$$

It can be verified for this system that $\frac{\partial K}{\partial r} < 0$ implies the system is locally unstable, hence Mundell's conclusion follows.

It might be thought that these conclusions concerning local stability conflict with the analysis of uniqueness of points of joint balance given in section 2. It should be noted, however, that the diagrams presented there show unique joint balance positions ($\overline{P}$, $\overline{r}$, $\overline{G^*}$); lack of uniqueness arises when M_S and G^* are the choice variables and P and/or r are dependent. Further, given any $P \neq \overline{P}$, $X \neq X_F$, since X is treated as a strictly increasing function of P. In particular if, in models (4.6) and (4.7), the price level is treated as a dependent variable, say by assuming the money market is always in equilibrium ($kX + L^*(r) = M_S/P$ for every X, r), then policy choices to achieve joint balance are not necessarily unique; if the LM and EB schedules coincide with one another, then multiple joint balance positions characterized by values of $\overline{r}$ and $\overline{G^*}$ can occur, as indicated in Figure 15:

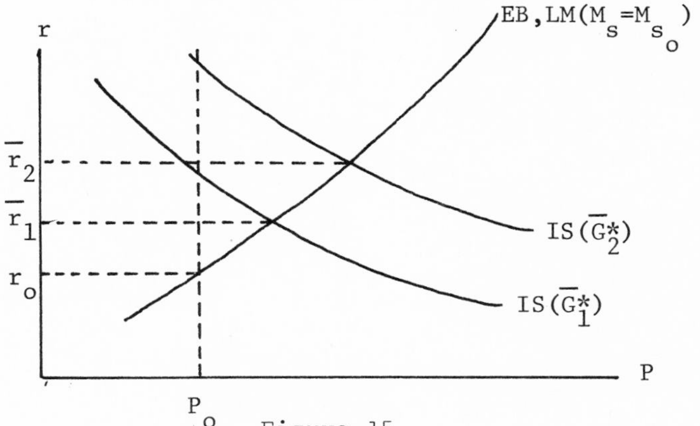

Figure 15

(In Figure 15, joint balance occurs at both ($\overline{G}^*_1$, $\overline{r}_1$) and ($\overline{G}^*_2$, $\overline{r}_2$), among other such joint balance points.)

Using the assumption that the money market is always in equilibrium together with the system

$$\text{(4.8)} \quad \begin{aligned} \dot{G}^* &= -a_1(X_D - X_F) \\ \dot{r} &= -a_2 g \qquad (a_1 > 0,\ a_2 > 0) \end{aligned}$$

J has the form

$$J = \begin{bmatrix} -a_1 \dfrac{\partial X_D}{\partial G^*} & -a_1 \dfrac{\partial X_D}{\partial r} \\ -a_2 \dfrac{\partial g}{\partial G^*} & -a_2 \dfrac{\partial g}{\partial r} \end{bmatrix} =$$

$$\begin{bmatrix} -a_1 & -a_1 \left\{ \dfrac{\partial I_D^*}{\partial r} + \left(\dfrac{\partial C^*}{\partial X} + \dfrac{\partial E^*}{\partial X} - 1 \right) \dfrac{\partial X}{\partial N} \dfrac{\partial N_D}{\partial P} \dfrac{\partial P}{\partial r} + \dfrac{\partial E^*}{\partial P} \dfrac{\partial P}{\partial r} \right\} \\ 0 & -a_2 \left\{ \left(\dfrac{\partial E}{\partial X} \dfrac{\partial X}{\partial N} \dfrac{\partial N_D}{\partial P} + \dfrac{\partial E}{\partial P} \right) \dfrac{\partial P}{\partial r} - \dfrac{\partial K}{\partial r} \right\} \end{bmatrix}$$

where $\dfrac{\partial P}{\partial r} = \dfrac{-\dfrac{\partial L^*}{\partial r}}{k\dfrac{\partial X}{\partial N}\dfrac{\partial N_D}{\partial P} + \dfrac{\partial M_S}{\partial P^2}} > 0$ from the liquidity preference relation. Because J_S is decomposable, the Routh-Hurwitz conditions are satisfied if and only if $\dfrac{\partial E}{\partial X}\dfrac{\partial X}{\partial N}\dfrac{\partial N_D}{\partial P} + \dfrac{\partial E}{\partial P}\dfrac{\partial P}{\partial r} - \dfrac{\partial K}{\partial r} > 0$

i.e., $\left| \left(\dfrac{\partial E}{\partial X} \dfrac{\partial X}{\partial N} \dfrac{\partial N_D}{\partial P} + \dfrac{\partial E}{\partial P} \right) \dfrac{\partial P}{\partial r} \right| < \left| \dfrac{K}{r} \right|$.

When the right hand term is smaller than the left, the joint balance point is unique but unstable; when the right hand term is larger than the left, the joint balance term is unique but stable; when the two terms are equal, the EB and LM curves are coincident. It is easy to show that when uniqueness is absent, "system stability" in the sense of Arrow and Hurwitz [1] characterizes the model, that is, given any initial values for G* and r, convergence occurs to some joint balance point. The phase diagram is of the form shown in Figure 16:

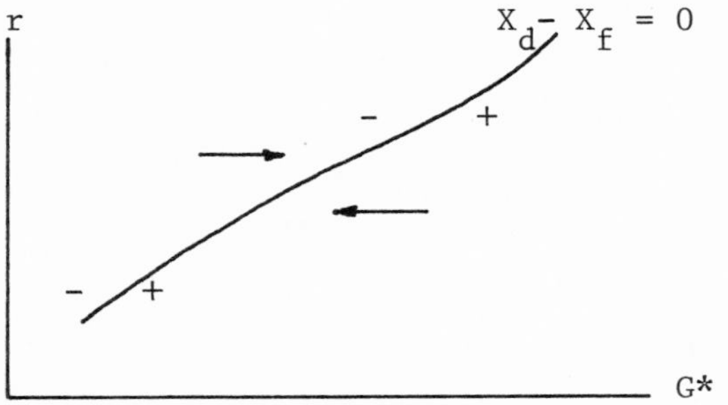

Figure 16

Further if the roles of fiscal policy and monetary policy are reversed in the system just considered, i.e.,

$$(4.9)\qquad \begin{aligned} \dot{r} &= a_1(X_D - X_F) \\ \dot{G}^* &= -a_2 g \qquad\qquad (a_1 > 0,\ a_2 > 0) \end{aligned}$$

with the money market always in equilibrium, the Jacobian J has the form

$$J = \begin{bmatrix} a_1 \left\{ \dfrac{\partial I_D^*}{\partial r} + \left(\dfrac{\partial C^*}{\partial X} + \dfrac{\partial E^*}{\partial X} - 1 \right) \dfrac{\partial X}{\partial N} \dfrac{\partial N_D}{\partial P} \dfrac{\partial P}{\partial r} + \dfrac{\partial E^*}{\partial P} \dfrac{\partial P}{\partial r} \right\} & a_1 \\ -a_2 \left\{ \left(\dfrac{\partial E}{\partial X} \dfrac{\partial X}{\partial N} \dfrac{\partial N_D}{\partial P} + \dfrac{\partial E}{\partial P} \right) \dfrac{\partial P}{\partial r} - \dfrac{\partial K}{\partial r} \right\} & 0 \end{bmatrix}$$

Here local stability or system stability occurs under precisely the same conditions that characterize the model considered above. Thus if monetary equilibrium is assumed to hold for all values of G* and r, Mundell's conclusion concerning the proper roles for monetary versus fiscal policy in the attainment of joint balance positions does not hold.

Finally, we consider a model in which both the money supply (rather than the interest rate) and the level of real government expenditures are control variables. The price level adjusts to correct excess demand for output and again the money market is assumed always to be in equilibrium, so that the interest rate is determined endogenously. (4.10) expresses these assumptions in the case where fiscal policy is used to attain internal balance and monetary policy is used to attain external balance:

$$(4.10)\qquad \begin{aligned} \dot{G}^* &= -a_1(X_D - X_F) \\ \dot{M} &= a_2 g \\ \dot{P} &= a_3 D_X \qquad\qquad (a_1 > 0,\ a_2 > 0,\ a_3 > 0)\,. \end{aligned}$$

Assuming that $kX + L^*(r) = M_S/P$ for any M_S, P, we have J given by

$$J = \begin{bmatrix} -a_1 & -a_1\left(\dfrac{\partial I_D^*}{\partial r} \dfrac{\partial r}{\partial M_S} \right) & -a_1 \left\{ \dfrac{\partial E^*}{\partial P} + \left(\dfrac{\partial C^*}{\partial X} + \dfrac{\partial E^*}{\partial X} \right) \dfrac{\partial X}{\partial N} \right\} \dfrac{\partial N_D}{\partial P} \\ 0 & -a_2 \left(\dfrac{\partial K}{\partial r} \dfrac{\partial r}{\partial M_S} \right) & a_2 \left(\dfrac{\partial E}{\partial P} + \dfrac{\partial E}{\partial X} \dfrac{\partial X}{\partial N} \dfrac{\partial N_D}{\partial P} \right) \\ a_3 & a_3 \left(\dfrac{\partial I_D^*}{\partial r} \dfrac{\partial r}{\partial M_S} \right) & a_3 \left\{ \dfrac{\partial E^*}{\partial P} + \left(\dfrac{\partial C^*}{\partial X} + \dfrac{\partial E^*}{\partial X} - 1 \right) \dfrac{\partial X}{\partial N} \dfrac{\partial N_D}{\partial P} \right\} \end{bmatrix}$$

where $\frac{\partial r}{\partial M_S} = \frac{1}{P\frac{\partial L^*}{\partial r}} < 0$. It is straightforward to verify that

in this system local stability occurs when $\frac{\partial K}{\partial r} < 0$, just as in system (4.6). If the roles of fiscal and monetary policy

are reversed, then $\frac{\partial K}{\partial r} < 0$ implies an unstable system.

5. Conclusions

The convergence properties of several approaches to the problem of attaining joint balance have been explored in section 4, under supply oriented assumptions concerning the level of output (= real income) in disequilibrium states. Mundell's conclusions concerning the stability properties of monetary policy aimed at external balance in a fixed or flexible exchange rate world are obtained; these are particularly appropriate to a world of flexible internal prices (including flexible wages), since in a Keynesian world, in general fiscal policies are required to insure that internal balance will hold.

Mundell's conclusion that fiscal policy should be directed towards internal balance while monetary policy is used to correct external imbalance follows if it is assumed that the price level is an independent variable of the macrosystem; on the other hand, if it is assumed that the money market is always in equilibrium, then the conditions for convergence of the economy to a point of joint balance are the same under an externally directed monetary-internally directed fiscal policy as under an externally directed fiscal policy combined with an internally directed monetary policy. Finally, it is shown that when price is an independent variable, Mundell's conclusions follow when the supply of money rather than the interest rate is the control variable of the monetary authorities, under the assumption that the money market is always in equilibrium.

Our analysis certainly does not exhaust the possibilities of fiscal-monetary policy mixes aimed at solving the joint balance problem, nor the possible dynamic models that might be used to analyze these. Beyond the conclusions concerning the dynamic behavior of the system, there remains the basic point that policy choices to attain joint balance positions are, in general, non-unique, so that choices must be made by the appropriate authorities as among the joint balance points. In this choice problem, the convergence properties of the system represent only one of many considerations to take into account.

FOOTNOTES

* This paper was presented at the meeting of the Midwest Economics Association, April 22, 1967. The work was supported in part under grants from the National Science Foundation and the University of Kansas Research Fund and International Studies Program.

1. This is less restrictive than the notion of internal balance sometimes employed in the literature which involves both full employment and stable prices. In the present treatment, in general the price level will be permitted to vary.

2. Alternatively, the money supply might be an endogenously determined variable dependent upon the interest rate. The implications of this behavioral assumption are explored below.

3. For simplicity, we have ignored taxes and transfer payments in this model. The basic results are unaffected by this omission at least for the usual case in which the marginal real tax rate lies between 0 and 1 and the marginal real transfer rate lies between 0 and -1.

4. In what follows, we will consider only situations in which the Jacobian of the dynamic system is non-singular. Hence, "local stability" always refers to "linear approximation stability".

5. See [10] for a discussion of the application of the Olech theorem to certain economic problems.

6. To insure the existence of derivatives, it can be assumed that $L^*(r)$ approaches r^o asymptotically.

7. While Mundell's analysis is concerned only with the case in which monetary policy takes the form of interest rate or price level manipulations, the money supply being held fixed, it is straightforward to verify that the same conclusions concerning stability hold if the money supply is the control variable, it being assumed that the money market is always in equilibrium.

REFERENCES

[1] Arrow, K. and L. Hurwitz, "On the Stability of the Competitive Equilibrium," Part I, Econometrica, Vol. XXVI (October, 1958), pp. 522-52.

[2] Brownlee, Oswald H., "The Theory of Employment and Stabilization Policy," Journal of Political Economy, Vol. LVIII (October, 1950), pp. 412-24.

[3] Gantmacher, F. R., The Theory of Matrices, Vols. I and II, New York, Chelsea Publishing Co., 1960.

[4] Marschak, Jacob, Income, Employment and the Price Level, New York, Augustus M. Kelley, Inc., 1951.

[5] Mundell, R. A., "The Monetary Dynamics of International Adjustment Under Fixed and Flexible Exchange Rates," Quarterly Journal of Economics, Vol. LXXIV (1960), pp. 227-57.

[6] Mundell, R. A., "The Appropriate Use of Monetary and Fiscal Policy for Internal and External Stability," International Monetary Fund Staff Papers, Vol. IX (March, 1962), pp. 70-79.

[7] Mundell, R. A., "Capital Mobility and Stabilization Policy Under Fixed and Flexible Exchange Rates," Canadian Journal of Economics and Political Science, Vol. 29 (November, 1963), pp. 475-85.

[8] Olech, "On the Global Stability of an Autonomous System on the Plane," in Contributions to Differential Equations, Vol. I (1963).

[9] Quirk, J. and R. Ruppert, "Qualitative Economics and the Stability of Equilibrium," Review of Economic Studies, Vol. 32 (1965), pp. 311-26.

[10] Quirk, J. and R. Ruppert, "Phase Diagrams and Global Stability," Research Papers in Theoretical and Applied Economics, University of Kansas, Paper no. 11, 1967.

IV.

THEORY OF THE FIRM

THE EFFECTS OF MONOPOLY POWER IN THE INITIATION AND PROPAGATION OF PRICE LEVEL CHANGES

by

Charles G. Stalon
Southern Illinois University

I. The purpose of this paper is to demonstrate how the existence of widespread monopoly power propagates and amplifies any upward pressure on any aggregate index of the price level. As a second level consideration it also argues that the existence of widespread monopoly power may be sufficient, in itself, to explain a slowly rising price level if money wages are downwardly rigid.

The argument is not meant to explain rapid price level changes, and it neither contradicts nor supports, but complements, the more orthodox theories of money induced, expenditure induced, or cost induced price level changes. The only contact with monetary theories of price level changes is the assumption that these theories do not determine "exactly" the price level and its movements but merely establish a band in which the price level can exist. The movements discussed herein are assumed to be within that band.

An argument contrary to the one to be presented is common. Professor Stigler, for example, has said:

> Traditional economic theory argues that oligopoly and monopoly prices have no special relevance to inflation. A monopolist (to take the simpler case) sets a profit-maximizing price for given demand-and-cost conditions. If inflation leads to a rise in either demand or costs, a new and usually higher price will be set. The price will usually be above the competitive level at any given time, but its pattern will not be other than passively responsive to monetary conditions.[1]

Henry W. Briefs recently stated the same argument:

> Orthodox price theory provides no basis whatever for believing that market power leads to inflation. True, prices will tend to be 'too high' as profit opportunities are exploited by monopolists and oligopolists, but without convincing evidence of an extraordinary sudden and widespread accretion of market power, it is difficult to see how rising prices in an inflation can be explained by reference to the aggressive use of power . . . Why should monopolists whose prices are, by and large, in line

with long-run maximum profits, increase their prices further?[2]

Both Stigler and Briefs agree that an increase in monopoly power might be responsible for causing the price level to rise, but not the existence of monopoly power per se. Gottfried Haberler summarized the orthodox position effectively by saying,

> I admit, of course, that business monopolies (to the extent that they are not effectively regulated) keep prices higher than they would be under competition; but there is no reason to assume that such monopoly prices would be pushed higher and higher. To put it differently, the introduction of numerous monopolies where there was competition before, would lead to higher prices and would be called inflationary. But the existence of monopolies does not lead to continuing pressure on prices.[3]

The argument to be presented has three parts. In Section II, the methodological approach and some necessary assumptions are stated and defended. In Section III an analysis of the effects of monopoly power on the propagation of price level changes is given. In Section IV the tendency of monopoly power to initiate price level change is examined.

II. To "explain" a variable in the methodology of static and comparative static economics, an economist must show the relationship of the endogenous variable to the exogenous variables and parameters, i.e., to those variables and parameters which the economist is willing to leave unexplained or only partially explained. To "explain," thereby, a variable which is obviously under the willful control of an economic decision unit, such as a monopolist's price, it is necessary to show that the decision unit wills a value for the variable which is exactly determined by the values of the exogenous variables and parameters. The fact that some of the exogenous variables might be under the willful control of the decision unit being analyzed does not necessarily invalidate the procedure.

The economist relegates to the exogenous category two types of variables: (1) those whose values he accepts as being determined outside the boundaries of economics, and (2) those whose values he accepts as being determined within the boundaries of economics but for reasons of ignorance or expository convenience he prefers not to "explain." But it is variables and not decision units which are neatly categorized; it is variables and not decision units which are reduced to passivity.

In the special case in which all the decision unit's willful variables are endogenous, or the exogenous ones under its control can be assumed to be fixed, then it is an obvious contradiction to claim both that one has "explained" the actions of the decision unit (i.e., the level at which it sets the endogenous variables under its control), and that the decision unit can be the source of any change in any endogenous variable. It is this special case which Stigler, Briefs and Haberler seem to think relevant in interpreting the role of the firm with monopoly power in price level changes.

Such a special case ignores the importance of a second variable under the control of a firm with monopoly power: selling costs. In Section IV it is argued that categorization of selling costs as an exogenous variable controllable by the monopolist is a useful approach. With such a categorization system the conclusion that a monopolist will adjust selling costs in such a way that it will initiate price level increases is easily made plausible.

A more complete theory might reclassify some of the variables which I have called exogenous into the endogenous category, thereby reducing the monopolist to the passive state described by Stigler _et al_; still the categorization system used here is justified by the way in which the exogenous variables are likely to be changed by large firms in a world of uncertainty.

Before examining the selling behavior of a monopolist, it is useful to examine the role of the monopolist as a passive adjuster to exogenous forces, i.e., _sans_ selling costs. This is done in Section III.

III. A. _The Markup Hypothesis_

The hypothesis used and defended in this paper is that the "markup" (i.e., price minus marginal cost) of a monopolist is proportional to the monopolist's price, i.e.,

(1) $\pi_i = p_i P_i$ for all firms,

and π_i = markup per unit of output

P_i = price per unit of output

p_i = a variable obviously under the willful control of the monopolist but treated as an exogenous variable. In this section p_i is a parameter.

The markup hypothesis can be considered as equivalent to the assumption that monopolists equate marginal costs and marginal revenue as in orthodox Marshallian partial equilibrium analysis, and price elasticities do not change as demand curves shift.

There are, however, other more plausible reasons for accepting hypothesis (1) as being useful in aggregate models. The burden which the orthodox price theorist assigns to the firm with monopoly power which desires to maximize its profits is not a light one. It requires that the monopolist know not only the position of its demand curve but its slope as well. If it recognizes, as it must, that the elasticity of demand is a function of time, then the monopolist must recognize that it faces a different demand curve for every planning horizon.

These characteristics of a monopolist's demand are not easily discovered, because experimentation and testing to discover their nature is practically impossible for a monopolist.

Moreover, as J. R. Hicks and others have argued,

> . . . the variation in monopoly profit for some way on either side of the highest profit output may often be small . . . and if this is so, the subjective costs involved in securing a close adaptation to the most profitable output may well outweigh the meager gains offered.[4]

In summary, in a world of uncertainty, a world in which time and transition periods are important, a world in which experimentation and testing is difficult, a world of ever-present change, we should not expect a monopolist to be capable of, or strongly concerned with, the problem of computing and recomputing demand curves and the slopes of demand curves. In such a world, hypothesis (1) can be highly descriptive.

The above argument is not meant to imply that a monopolist is not at all concerned with the elasticity of his demand curve. A firm may revise its markup policy as it changes its estimates of the relevant market elasticities. Such a change, however, can best be viewed as a major policy change and not a change to be made frequently. In such a case, it is methodologically preferable to treat p as an exogenous variable.

B. A Numerical Example

The argument to be presented about the influence of monopoly power on the propagation of price level changes can be illustrated with a simple numerical example. Case I of Table I describes a simple unidirectional circular flow economy. Firm I sells to firm II which sells to firm III, etc. Each firm sells one unit of output and sets prices according to hypothesis (1). For convenience it is assumed that all firms use a ten percent markup.

Case II of Table I differs in that labor costs increased to firm I. As a consequence of this exogenous change, the price policy of hypothesis (1), and the assumption that each firm still sells one unit of output (i.e., real output did not change), a comparison of the two cases in Table I permits the following conclusions:

1) final goods prices increased by 29.08%,

2) the money income of labor increased by 25%,
3) the labor share of money (and real) income fell from 76.31%, (40.00/52.413)•100, to 73.90%, i.e. (50.00/67.656)•100,
4) the profit share of money (and real) income rose from 23.69% to 26.10%.

Table I illustrates the possibility that a wage push in a basic sector or sectors will cause, when combined with a markup pricing policy, a change in the distribution of income against labor. It also invites speculations that during the interequilibrium adjustment process, firms would be continuously complaining about the "profit squeeze" and the inability to maintain "traditional" profit margins even as the distribution of income turns relatively towards profits.

Table I

A Comparison of Two Cost Structures

Case I

	(1) Materials Cost $	(2) Labor Cost $	(3) Total Input Cost $	(4) Markup (10% of Price) $	(5) Output Price $
Firm I	0	10.00	10.00	1.11	11.11
Firm II	11.11	10.00	21.11	2.345	23.455
Firm III	23.455	10.00	33.455	3.717	37.172
Firm IV	37.172	10.00	47.172	5.241	52.413
Totals	——	40.00	——	12.413	——

Case II

	(6) Materials Cost $	(7) Labor Cost $	(8) Total Input Cost $	(9) Markup (10% of Price) $	(10) Output Price $
Firm I	0	20.00	20.00	2.222	22.222
Firm II	22.222	10.00	32.222	3.580	35.802
Firm III	35.802	10.00	45.802	5.089	50.891
Firm IV	50.891	10.00	60.891	6.765	67.656
Totals	——	50.00	——	17.656	——

C. Price Level Propagation Effects of Markup Pricing

In order to examine the effects of markup pricing in a more realistic setting it is necessary to construct a general equilibrium model which permits each sector to buy from and sell to all other sectors.

The simplest model which meets these needs and which offers the possibility of measuring the relevant parameters is the Leontief input-output model.[5] Leontief has shown how this input-output model can be "opened" to the household sector (and/or any sector which the analyst wants to consider as a source of exogenous change) and used as a comparative static model to analyze the consequences on prices and price levels of exogenous cost changes.[6]

The necessary assumptions for such a model are:

1. the production function of each sector shows constant returns to scale,
2. each sector (except the household sector) uses all inputs in fixed proportions (in Section IV the quantity of labor used per unit of output will be permitted to vary),
3. there exist technological parameters a_{ij} which are measures of the physical amount of output of sector i used to produce one unit of output in sector j,
4. there are n sectors in the economy.

Two further assumptions simplify the argument substantially and so will be used:

5. all production occurs in the business sector,
6. the economic system is closed, i.e., there is no foreign trade.

The following notation is used in the argument:

L_w a Laspeyres wholesale price index

L_y a Laspeyres final goods price index

P_i the price of output of sector i

Y_i value of final output of sector i

X_i total value of output (both intermediate and final) of sector i

w_i direct weight of sector i in a wholesale type price index

v_i direct weight of sector i in a final goods price index

λ_i labor cost per unit of output of sector i

π_i profit per unit of output of sector i

$R_i = \lambda_i + \pi_i$ = value added per unit of output of sector i

p_i = ratio of markup to price in sector i

$u_i = w_i - v_i$

x_{ij} the value of output of sector i used in sector j during the base period

a_{ij} the physical amount of output of sector i used directly to produce one unit of output in sector j

A_{ij} an element in the inverse of the Leontief matrix which measures the physical amount of output of sector i used both directly and indirectly to produce one unit of final output in sector j

Vectors and matrices:

a a technological matrix of the input coefficient a_{ij}'s

I an n x n unit matrix

(I-a) the Leontief matrix

$A = (I-a)^{-1}$

A_i a column vector consisting of the ith row of matrix A

h an n dimensional column vector having $h_i = 1$ for $i = 1, \ldots, n$

P a column vector of sector prices

Y a column vector of the value of final output of sectors

X a column vector of the value of total output of sectors

λ a column vector of labor cost per unit

π a column vector of profit per unit

$R = \lambda + \pi$

p = a column vector of markup parameters

m = a diagonal matrix with p_i in the ith diagonal position

$B = (I-a-m)^{-1}$

B_i = a column vector consisting of the ith row of matrix B.

Three accounting definitions follow directly from the assumptions. They are:

(2) $P_j = P_1 a_{1j} + \ldots + P_n a_{nj} + R_j, \quad j = 1, \ldots, n.$

(3) $X_i = x_{i1} + \ldots x_{in} + Y_i, \quad i = 1, \ldots, n.$

(4) $x_{ij} = a_{ij} X_j, \quad i = 1, \ldots, n; \quad j = 1, \ldots, n.$

Equation (2) expresses the accounting definition that the price of j is equal to the sum of all the costs of producing a unit of j when $P_j a_{jj}$ and R_j are considered a part of the cost of production. Equation (3) recognizes that all the output of sector i is used to produce output in sector i, to produce output in other sectors, or is sold to final purchasers. Equation (4) follows from the assumption that all inputs are used in fixed proportion in all sectors. It asserts that the value of output of sector i used to produce output in sector j during the base period is equal to the amount of i needed to produce one unit of j (i.e., a_{ij}) times the total value of j produced during that period.

Using this model, hypothesis (1), the assumption that the price of labor to sector i is exogenous, and the assumption that the price of labor to sector i can change without affecting the price of labor in other sectors, five theorems can be proven.

<u>Theorem one</u>: If R_i increases in any sector and real output does not change, the percentage increase in a Laspeyres Final Goods Price Index (FGPI) equals the percentage increase in the money earnings of the factors of production, i.e., wages plus profits.

<u>Proof</u>: Transposing (3) gives

(5) $Y_i = X_i - x_{i1} - \quad \ldots \quad - x_{in}, \quad i = 1, \ldots, n.$

Substituting (4) into (5) gives:

(6) $Y_i = X_i - a_{i1}X_1 - \quad \ldots \quad - a_{in}X_n, \quad i = 1, \ldots, n.$

In matrix form,

(7) $Y = (I-a)X.$

The set of equations given in (2) can also be stated in matrix notation. They become

(8) $R = (I-a)'P.$

Since there are no "natural" units in which the a_{ij}'s must be measured, a unit can be chosen to suit the analysis. Let quantity units, therefore, be defined to be "one dollar's worth" in base period prices. All prices in the base period are then equal to one. Equation (8) then becomes, in the base period,

(9) $R = (I-a)'h$

and the a_{ij}'s represent the physical amount of i needed to produce one dollar's worth of j in base period prices. The assumption that all prices equal one in the base period also permits the interpretation of x_{ij}, X_j, and Y_j as quantity as well as value units during the base period, and as quantity units during later periods.

Equation (8) can be solved explicitly for P as a function of value added.[7] Since $A = (I-a)^{-1}$,

(10) $P = A'R$

The relationships between price indexes and the input-output model are straightforward.[8] By definition of a Laspeyres Final Goods Price Index

(11) $L_y = v_1P_1 + v_2P_2 + \quad \ldots \quad + v_nP_n.$

Where the weights for such an index are defined as follows:

(12) $v_i = \dfrac{Y_i}{\Sigma Y_i}, \; i = 1, \ldots, n.$

The index number can be written concisely in matrix notation: i.e.,

(13) $L_y = \dfrac{Y'P}{Y'h},$

where Y is a vector of quantities (or weights) from the base period.

In the base period money GNP equals Y'h, and in later periods money GNP equals (assuming quantities do not change) Y'P. Assume that value added per unit of output of sector i increases. The percentage change in the final goods index and in money GNP can be computed as follows: from equation (7) it follows that:

(14) $Y' = X'(I-a)'.$

The product Y'P is given by (14) and (10), i.e.,

(15) $Y'P = X'(I-a)'A'R$

(16) $Y'P = X'R$

The change in money GNP induced by the change in per unit value added in sector i is found by differentiating (16) with respect to R_i, i.e.,

(17) $\dfrac{d[Y'P]}{dR_i} = X' \left(\dfrac{dR}{dR_i} \right)$

and

(18) $dY'P = X'dR,$

which is the change in money GNP.

The percentage change in money GNP is

(19) $\dfrac{dY'P}{Y'h} = \dfrac{X'dR}{Y'h}.$

That this is also the percentage change in L_y can be shown by differentiating (13) with respect to a change in per unit value added, i.e.,

(13) $L_y = \frac{Y'P}{Y'h} = \frac{X'R}{Y'h}$,

(20) $\frac{dL_y}{dR_i} = \frac{X'\left(\frac{dR}{dR_i}\right)}{Y'h}$,

and

(21) $dL_y = \frac{X'dR}{Y'h}$.

Therefore, from (19) and (21)

(22) $\frac{dL_y}{L_y} = \frac{dY'P}{Y'h} = \frac{dY'P}{Y'P} = \frac{X'dR}{X'R}$.

Theorem two: (i) if λ_i increases in any sector, (ii) if firms price according to hypothesis (1), (iii) if all firms have the same p, and (iv) real output does not change, the percentage increase in profits equals the percentage increase in a Laspeyres Wholesale Type Price Index (WPI).

Proof: By definition of a Laspeyres Wholesale Type Price Index,

(23) $L_w = w_1P_1 + w_2P_2 + \ldots + w_nP_n$

where

$$w_i = \frac{X_i}{\Sigma X_i}, \quad i = 1, \ldots, n.$$

In matrix notation,

(24) $L_w = \frac{X'P}{X'h}$.

Differentiating (24) with respect to λ_i gives

(25) $\frac{dL_w}{d\lambda_i} = \frac{X'\left(\frac{dP}{d\lambda_i}\right)}{X'h}$

and

(26) $dL_w = \frac{X'dP}{X'h}$.

Since all prices were assumed to equal one in the base period, (26) is the percentage increase in the WPI.

Since π_iX_i is total profits in sector i, and

(27) $\pi_iX_i = p_iP_iX_i$

$$(28)\quad \frac{d\pi_i X_i}{d\lambda_j} = p_i X_i \frac{dP_i}{d\lambda_j}$$

and

$$(29)\quad d\pi_i X_i = p_i X_i dP_i \ .$$

The total increase in profits equals

$$(30)\quad \Sigma d\pi_i X_i = \Sigma p_i X_i dP_i \ .$$

Profits in the base period equal $\Sigma\pi_i X_i$, so the percentage increase in profits is

$$(31)\quad \frac{\Sigma d\pi_i X_i}{\Sigma\pi_i X_i} = \frac{\Sigma p_i X_i dP_i}{\Sigma p_i X_i} \ ,$$

Since all p_i are equal the right hand side of (31) becomes

$$(32)\quad \frac{\Sigma d\pi X_i}{\Sigma\pi_i X_i} = \frac{X'dP}{X'h} \ .$$

From (26) and (32)

$$(33)\quad \frac{dL_w}{L_w} = \frac{\Sigma d\pi_i X_i}{\Sigma\pi_i X_i} \ .$$

<u>Theorem three</u>: If (i) real output does not change, (ii) if λ_i increases in a sector which causes a Laspayres WPI to rise by a larger percentage than does a Laspeyres FGPI, and (iii) if p_i is constant over i, the labor share of income will fall.

The proof follows directly from theorems one and two, since together they imply that the change in λ_i produced a percentage increase in profits greater than the percentage increase in income. Labor's share then must fall.

<u>Theorem four</u>: The greater p_i for any i the greater the increase in both a Laspeyres WPI and FGPI induced by a given change in at least one λ_j.

<u>Proof</u>: An alternative statement for equation (2) is (34)

$$(34)\quad P_j = P_1 a_{1j} + \ldots + P_n a_{nj} + \lambda_j + \pi_j, \quad j = 1, \ldots, n$$

or

$$(35)\quad P = a'P + \lambda + \pi.$$

Let m be a diagonal matrix with the markup parameter p_i in the ith diagonal position, then

$$P = a'P + \lambda + mP$$

$$P - a'P - mP = \lambda$$

$$(I-a-m)'P = \lambda.$$

Let $B = (I-a-m)^{-1}$, then

$$(36) \quad P = B'\lambda.$$

From the theorem that[9]

$$(37) \quad A = I + a + a^2 + a^3 + \ldots$$

it can be asserted by analogy that[10]

$$(38) \quad B = I + (a+m) + (a+m)^2 + (a+m)^3 + \ldots$$

Since all diagonal elements of $(a+m)$ are greater than the diagonal elements of a, by observation it is obvious that

$$(39) \quad B_{ij} \geq A_{ij} \text{ for all } i \text{ and } j$$

and

(40) $B_{ij} > A_{ij}$ for at least one i and j in each row and column; i.e., the diagonal elements.

By observation it is also obvious that any increase in p_j will increase at least one element of B; i.e., B_{jj}.

Substituting (36) into (13) and (24) gives

$$(41) \quad L_y = \frac{Y'B'\lambda}{Y'h}$$

and

$$(42) \quad L_w = \frac{X'B'\lambda}{X'h} .$$

Differentiating with respect to λ_j gives

$$(41a) \quad \frac{dL_y}{d\lambda_j} = \frac{Y'B_j}{Y'h}$$

and

$$(42a) \quad \frac{dL_w}{d\lambda_j} = \frac{X'B_j}{X'h} .$$

From (41a) and (42a) we can deduce that an increase in p_j will increase the price indexes increase in response to a change in λ_j. That proves the theorem.

We are free to speculate, moreover, that unless the matrix a contains a large number of judiciously placed zeros, B_{ij} will be greater than A_{ij} for all i and j, and an increase in __any__ p_j will increase __all__ elements of B. Our knowledge of A, derived from input-output studies supports the speculation.

__Theorem five__: An increase in λ_i for some i will increase a Laspeyres WPI more than it will increase a Laspeyres FGPI.

__Proof__: Substituting (10) into (13) and (24) gives

$$(43) \quad L_y = \frac{Y'A'R}{Y'h}$$

$$(44) \quad L_w = \frac{X'A'R}{X'h} \ .$$

Differentiating (43) and (44) with respect to λ_i gives

$$(45) \quad \frac{dL_y}{d\lambda_i} = \frac{Y'A'dR/d\lambda_i}{Y'h}$$

$$(46) \quad \frac{dL_w}{d\lambda_i} = \frac{X'A'dR/d\lambda_i}{X'h} \ .$$

Multiplying both sides of (45) and (46) by $d\lambda_i$ and subtracting (45) from (46) gives

$$(47) \quad dL_w - dL_y = \frac{X'A'dR}{X'h} - \frac{Y'A'dR}{Y'h} \ .$$

Expanding (47) gives

$$(48) \quad dL_w - dL_y = u_1(\Sigma_i A_{i1} dR_i) + \ldots + u_n(\Sigma_i A_{in} dR_i).$$

The sums in the parentheses represent the percentage change in prices of each sector which is induced by the change in the value added vector. For ease of writing, let $c_j = \Sigma_i A_{ij} dR_i$. Then (48) becomes

$$(49) \quad dL_w - dL_y = \Sigma_j c_j u_j .$$

It is possible to determine the conditions under which the wholesale price index will differ from the final goods price index, as follows.[11]

Let $\bar{c} = \frac{1}{n} \Sigma_j c_j$.

Then (49) becomes

$$(50) \quad dL_w - dL_y = \Sigma_j \{\bar{c} + (c_j - \bar{c})\} \ u_j$$

$$(51) \quad = \Sigma (c_j - \bar{c}) \ u_j$$

since $\Sigma \bar{c} u_j = \bar{c} \Sigma u_j = 0$.

The sample covariance (σ_{cu}) is defined as

$$\sigma_{cu} = \frac{\Sigma(c_j - \bar{c})(u_j - \bar{u})}{n}$$

therefore, (since $\bar{u} = 0$)

$$(52) \quad dL_w - dL_y = n\,\sigma_{cu}.$$

The linear correlation coefficient (r) between c and u is defined as follows:

$$(53) \quad r = \frac{\sigma_{cu}}{\sigma_c \, \sigma_u}$$

where σ_c and σ_u are defined as the standard deviation of the distribution of the c's and u's respectively.

Substituting (53) into (52) gives[12]

$$(54) \quad dL_w - dL_y = rn\,\sigma_c\,\sigma_u.$$

The interpretation of this expression is straightforward. The term σ_u could be zero if $w_i = v_i$ for all i. This would occur only if every sector carried the same weight in both the FGPI and WPI. This however, cannot occur. There are many products in the WPI, such as crude oil, iron ore, wheat, etc., which are of substantial importance as intermediate products, but if sold at all as final goods, are sold only in infinitesimal amounts. Therefore $\sigma_u > 0$.

The term σ_c will be zero only if the price level change is perfectly homogeneous, that is, if all prices change by exactly the same percentage. The more heterogeneous the price changes, the larger will be σ_c. In a heterogeneous price level change, $\sigma_c > 0$, $\sigma_u > 0$ and, of course, $n > 0$, so the wholesale price index change will be less than, equal to, or greater than the change in the final goods price index as r is negative, zero, or positive.

If the above average price increases generally occur in those sectors in which u_j is positive; i.e., when $w_j > v_j$, then r will be positive and the change in the WPI will be greater than the change in the FGPI.

D. Summary of Section III

The conclusion illustrated by Table I can be restated for a more complex economic system. The existence of widespread monopoly power exercised through markup pricing will tend to convert a strong wage push in the basic sectors into greater absolute and relative profits.

More important for price level analysis, however, are some less rigorous generalizations which theorems one through five support. Two generalizations are important for the analysis of the next section. First, from the markup hypothesis and theorems one, two, three, and five, it seems plausible to assert that profits are likely to be more highly correlated with total sales than with final sales. Secondly, from the markup hypothesis and theorem four, it seems plausible to assert that the greater the monopoly power in existence, the greater the increase in total sales and profits that will result from any exogenous increase in hired factor costs.

The principal argument of the next section is an attempt to show that selling effort by firms with monopoly power almost certainly increases total sales (in money terms), and likely increases the total sales (in percentage terms) more than final sales (in percentage terms).

IV. In this section a brief analysis of monopoly power as the initiator of changes which affect the price level is given. No attempt is made to argue that widespread monopoly power <u>necessarily</u> produces increases in price level measures. That task is reserved for another paper. The mere recognition of this possibility adds meaning and importance to the arguments of Section III, and serves the purpose of the paper.

This section argues that some of the determinants of price commonly "left out" of price analysis are important enough to significantly influence prices and therefore the price level. The effect of the simplifying assumptions of orthodox price analysis is to ignore some elements of monopoly behavior which are important in price level analysis.

The costs of a monopolist can be divided conceptually into two types. First are the costs involved in changing the physical form, structure, or location of material within a producing establishement. These costs can loosely be called production costs. When the theory of price is examined in textbooks, it is these costs which are always recognized. Secondly, are the costs involved in buyers finding and informing sellers, sellers finding and informing buyers, the striking of agreements between buyers and sellers, and the transfer of products or materials, or services from seller to buyer. These costs can loosely be called organizational costs. When the theory of price is examined in textbooks, it is these costs which are usually abstracted out of the discussion and by implication assumed to be of minor importance. Abstracting from such elements of total costs tendsto be misleading in an age in which "the single largest cost for packaged-goods manufacturers ... is advertising."[13]

It is always necessary that someone or some institution bear the cost of bringing together interested or potentially interested buyers and sellers; of discovering and disseminating knowledge about the uses and potential uses of products and services; of discovering or compiling knowledge of prices and standards of quality; of creating and promulgating standards of terminology for buying and selling.

These tasks can be expensive in an economic system undergoing rapid change. While some of them are considered to be the tasks of government, in an economic system where "free enterprise" is interpreted to mean not only the right to compete in a "market" but also the right to compete in the "organization" of the market, and where the ideological atmosphere severely limits the role of government in market organization, many or all of these tasks are undertaken privately. In fact, rivalry in these areas has become almost synonymous with the concept of competition. Wesley C. Mitchell described the purpose and nature of this activity when he said, "This task of stimulating demand is never done ..."[14]

The monopolist has an incentive to engage in selling and organizational effort. Since it operates with marginal cost below price, each additional unit it can sell, at a given price, will expand its profits. In an uncertain world, the profit seeking oligopolist and monopolist can be expected to experiment by incurring increments to its total costs in an attempt to shift the demand curve it faces. Such demand increasing activity commonly takes the form of sellers absorbing various costs which the buyers would otherwise have to bear. Buyers will accept such services from sellers as the equivalent of a price reduction even though the buyer might be able to provide himself with the same service at a lower absolute cost than that incurred by the monopolist. The perceived incremental cost to the buyer of accepting the supplementary service is frequently zero if he purchases the monopolist's product. Under such circumstance it should be expected that monopolists will repeatedly provide services which raise their costs more than it lowers their customers' costs--and in order to cover their increased cost, the monopolist may raise his price.

The argument of this section can again be illustrated with a simple numerical example. In Table II note that Case I differs from Case II in that firm III's labor cost has risen by ten dollars and firm IV's labor cost has declined by ten dollars. This could arise as firm III attempted to stimulate its sales by providing a supplementary service for firm IV.

If it is assumed, however, that total real output does not change and that the firms set price according to hypothesis (1), a comparison of the two cases permit the following conclusions:

1) final goods prices increased by 1.92%; i.e.,
2) the money income of labor did not change,
3) the laborer's share of money (and real) income fell from 78.71% to 77.21%,

4) the proportion of income accruing to profits increases from 21.29% to 22.79%.

Table II illustrates the possibility that a mere shift "backward" in the source of the cost of labor can both bid up the price level and bid down the labor share of income. Table II, like Table I, also invites speculation that during the interequilibrium adjustment process firms would be complaining about "profit squeeze."

Table II

An Analysis of Cost Shifting

Case I

	(1) Materials Cost $	(2) Labor Cost $	(3) Total Input Cost $	(4) Markup (10% of Price) $	(5) Output Price $
Firm I	0	10.00	10.00	1.11	11.11
Firm II	11.11	10.00	21.00	2.345	23.455
Firm III	23.455	10.00	33.455	3.717	37.172
Firm IV	37.172	20.00	57.172	6.352	63.524
Totals	——	50.00	——	13.524	——

Case II

	(6) Materials Cost $	(7) Labor Cost $	(8) Total Input Cost $	(9) Markup (10% of Price) $	(10) Output Price $
Firm I	0	10.00	10.00	1.11	11.11
Firm II	11.11	10.00	21.11	2.345	23.455
Firm III	23.455	20.00	43.455	4.828	48.283
Firm IV	48.283	10.00	58.283	6.475	64.758
Totals	——	50.00	——	14.758	——

The concept of "basic" sectors and the degree of "basicness" of a sector is one that is difficult to make exact in a general equilibrium model, but it appears reasonable to assume that generally, for any transaction, the seller is "further back" than the buyer.[15]

From such an assumption, the phenomenon of selling and organizational rivalry which takes the form of sellers providing an ever increasing volume of services to buyers can be expected to bid up a price level. If this trade rivalry merely shifts labor costs (or other transferable costs) backward, the consequence is to turn the distribution of income against labor. This conclusion follows from the generalizations made in the summary of section III. If this trade rivalry not merely shifts costs, but also increases them in the process, then the price level rises even more than the preceding analysis implies, but the change in the distribution of income is indeterminate.

In the case in which firms are shifting costs from the final buyers back into the production system, it is obvious that prices will be bid up. It is not obvious what happens to the distribution of income.

In summary, if firms with monopoly power shift costs backwards efficiently, they increase the price level and turn the distribution of income against labor. If firms with monopoly power shift costs backwards inefficiently, they increase the price level even more, but they might shift the distribution of income against themselves.

If the markup hypothesis is correct, we cannot assume that selling and organizational rivalry are

> ... frictions which may simply retard or slightly modify the effects of the active forces of competition but which the latter ultimately succeeded in substantially overcoming. Many of the obstacles which break up the unity of the market which is the essential condition of competition are not of the nature of "frictions" but are themselves active forces which produce permanent and even cumulative effects.[16]

If monopoly power is widespread and monopolists do price according to hypothesis (1), a rising price level and rising costs do not narrow profit margin and dampen selling effort. In fact, absolute margins widen and perhaps stimulate more vigorous efforts in this direction.

This conclusion, together with the propagation effects of monopoly power, justifies close attention to the exercise of monopoly power in a society facing the Phillips Curve dilemma.

FOOTNOTES

[1]George J. Stigler, "Administered Prices and Oligopolistic Inflation," Journal of Business, January 1962, p. 8.

[2]Henry W. Briefs, "Pricing Power and Administrative Inflation," American Enterprise Institute for Public Policy Research, Washington, D. C., 1962, p. 36.

[3]"Internal Factors Causing and Propagating Inflation," Inflation, ed. D. C. Hague (London, MacMillan and Co., 1962), p. 28. (The italics are in the original.)

[4]"Annual Survey of Economic Theory: The Theory of Monopoly," Econometrica, vol. III (1935), Reprinted in Readings in Price Theory, American Economics Assoc., Richard D. Irwin, 1952, p. 369.

[5]Wassily W. Leontief, The Structure of American Economy, 2nd ed. (New York, Oxford University Press, 1951).

[6]Ibid., Part IV. C.

[7]The assumption that (I-a) has an inverse is a necessary but not sufficient condition for (10) to be a meaningful economic statement. It is also necessary that matrix A transform every nonnegative vector R into a nonnegative vector P. A necessary and sufficient condition for this to occur is that every element in A be nonnegative. That every element in A is nonnegative when $0 \leq a_{ij} < 1$ and $\Sigma a_{ij} < 1$ (summed over i) is proved in G. Hadley, Linear Algebra (Reading Massachusetts, Addison-Wesley Publishing Company, Inc., 1961), pp. 116-119. The assumptions (1) that all prices equal one, and (2) that the system is viable; i.e., that R_j is positive for all j, provides the assumptions necessary to show that $0 \leq a_{ij} < 1$ and $\Sigma a_{ij} < 1$ (summed over i). Equation (2), when $P_j = 1$ for all j, states that $1 = \Sigma a_{ij} + R_j$ (summed over i). Since $R_j > 0$, $\Sigma a_{ij} < 1$. Since inputs are by definition nonnegative, $a_{ij} \geq 0$. Since $\Sigma a_{ij} < 1$ (summed over i), and $0 \leq a_{ij} < 1$, Equation (10) is a meaningful economic statement.

[8]See Richard Stone, Quantity and Price Indexes in National Accounts (Paris, Organization for European Economic Cooperation, 1956), Chap. 3.

[9] Hadley, *op. cit.*, p. 116.

[10] Sufficient conditions for B to exist and have non-negative elements are given in footnote 7. If it is further assumed that a is a semipositive indecomposable matrix, then (a + m) is also semipositive and indecomposable. Matrices A and B are then strictly positive, and $B_{ij} > A_{ij}$ for all i and j. Under this stronger assumption the inequality of (39) holds and statement (40) is unnecessary. See R. Dorfman, P. A. Samuelson, and R. Solow, *Linear Programming and Economic Analysis*, McGraw-Hill Book Co., New York, 1958, p. 255.

[11] The term $\bar{c}$ and the other sample statistics computed below should not be interpreted as random variables. The collection of A_{ij}'s from which $\bar{c}$ is computed is a sample, but not in any sense useful in this paper could it be called a random sample. The sample statistics are not to be considered parametric estimates, but should be considered only as useful means of summarizing mass data.

[12] The following method of comparing price indexes is given by Robin Marris, *Economic Arithmetic* (London, MacMillan and Company Ltd., 1958), pp. 205ff.

[13] "Can Advertising Be Measured," *Duns Review*, September, 1964, p. 43.

[14] *Business Cycles: The Problem and Its Setting* (New York, National Bureau of Economic Research, 1927), p. 166.

[15] Theorem Five does provide one method for determining the relative "basicness" of a sector. Using the standard that the higher the ratio (dL_w/dL_y) for a given absolute total labor cost change, in a sector, the more basic is the industry, the degree of "basicness" of the 44 sectors of the 1947 input-output study was determined. Although the assumptions made were restrictive, the results corresponded roughly to what one would expect. Some of the more "basic" industries listed in order of increasing "basicness" were Stone, Clay and Glass; Iron and Steel; Lumber and Wood Products; Non Ferrous Metals; Fabricated Structural Metal Products; and (most basic of all) Scrap.

[16] Piero Sraffa, "The Laws of Returns Under Competitive Conditions," *Economic Journal*, December 1962, p. 542.

OPTIMAL PRODUCTION, INVESTMENT AND OUTPUT INVENTORY CONTROLS FOR THE COMPETITIVE FIRM

by

Russell G. Thompson, Melvin D. George and Michael S. Proctor

(Texas A & M University, University of Missouri, Texas A & M University)

1. Introduction

In an earlier paper, Thompson and George [6] derived the optimal production and investment controls for a competitive firm basically linear in structure. Those controls were found to be readily computable; and to illustrate this, solutions for four example problems were calculated.

In this paper, our objective is to extend that model to include output inventories. This model will again be basically linear in structure and account for the costs of borrowed money as well as the returns from savings. As before, the methods of control theory will be used to derive the optimal controls.

Since comprehensive discussions of the inventory problem and previous works are given by Arrow, Karlin and Scarf [1] and more recently by Scarf, Gilford and Shelly [5], we will limit further introductory remarks to a methodological comment. It was recognized by Arrow, Karlin and Scarf [1, p. 39] in 1958 that the problem is one of the calculus of variations; but that the classical methods are not applicable because of inequality constraints. Thus they had to solve the problem in unconventional ways.

Since then, the problem has been largely resolved with developments in control theory. These methods, which Berkovitz [2] has shown can be derived using the calculus of variations, do allow for inequality constraints. As mentioned above, we propose to use those methods to study the production, investment and output inventory problem of the competitive firm.

2. General Description of the Model

The objective of the firm is to maximize the discounted value of revenues from sales less the costs of production, interest, new capacity and storage over a finite interval plus the discounted value of capacity and inventory at the end of the period. This maximization is constrained by three differential equations describing the change in capacity, debt and inventory, as well as several inequality constraints.

Capacity, debt and inventory are state variables; while

the scale of operation, rate of purchase of new capacity and rate of change of output inventory are controls. Capacity, debt and output inventory at the end of the period are control parameters.

The firm is assumed to have a positive amount of capacity at the beginning of the period. Attrition of this capacity as well as attrition of additions to it are allowed for. Purchases of new capacity cannot exceed a specific upper bound that is a function of time. This upper bound might be regarded as the maximum rate that the firm can efficiently employ new capacity.

Investments in new capacity are paid for out of earnings, or from borrowed funds, or out of savings. Neither the rate of borrowing nor the amount of borrowing is restricted. Savings, when they occur, cannot exceed the rate of net profits from sales minus interest charges, storage costs and investments in capacity.

Inventories can be either built-up or depleted over the decision-making interval. In a period of build-up they cannot be increased faster than the rate of production; while in a period of depletion they cannot be depleted faster than the (current) level of inventory.

Initial and terminal times are fixed as well as initial capacity, debt and inventory. Terminal capacity, debt and inventory can vary, however, along a terminal manifold.

3. Definitions of Variables and Functions

$\pi_1(t)$ is the revenue per unit of output; $g_1(t)$ is the output of a unit of capacity in a unit of time; $c(t)$ is the price of a unit of capacity; $i(t)$ is the money rate of interest; $r(t)$ is the per unit cost of storage for a unit of time; $\pi_2(t)$ is the cost per unit of the factor input; $g_2(t)$ is the amount of the factor used by a unit of capacity in a unit of time; $\gamma(t^2)$ and $\theta(t^2)$ are the (non-negative) amounts by which the prices of inventory and capacity must be decreased, respectively, at t^2 in order to sell them; $\alpha(t)$ is the rate of attrition of capacity; and $M(t)$ is the upper bound on the rate of purchase of new capacity. These functions are known over the decision-making interval.

$u(t)$ is the scale level in units of capacity; $v(t)$ is the rate of purchase of units of new capacity; and $\eta(t)$ is the rate of change of inventory. These are the control functions. $x(t)$ is the capacity of the firm; $D(t)$ is the <u>net</u> debt of the firm; and $\xi(t)$ is the amount of inventory. These are the state functions.

b_1, b_2, b_3 are the control parameters. $b \equiv (b_1, b_2, b_3)$.

$\Phi(t) = \exp - \int_{t^1}^{t} \delta(s)ds$ where δ is the rate of time preference. $\dot{x}(t) = d\,x(t)/dt$, $\dot{D}(t) = d\,D(t)/dt$, and $\dot{\xi}(t) = d\,\xi(t)/dt$. $[t^1, t^2]$ is the fixed decision making interval.

4. The Problem[1,2]

Maximize $I = (c(t^2) - \Theta(t^2))\,\Phi(t^2)b_1 + (\pi_1(t^2) - \gamma(t^2))\,\Phi(t^2)b_3$

$$+ \int_{t^1}^{t^2} \{\pi_1(t)g_1(t)u(t) - \pi_1(t)\,\eta(t) - \pi_2(t)g_2(t)u(t) - c(t)\,v(t) - i(t)D(t) - r(t)\,\xi(t)\}\;\Phi(t)dt$$

in the class of arcs $(x(t), D(t), \xi(t), u(t), v(t), \eta(t), b_1, b_2, b_3)$ satisfying the differential equations

(1) $\dot{x}(t) = v(t) - \alpha(t)x(t))$

(2) $\dot{D}(t) = c(t)v(t) + i(t)D(t) + r(t)\,\xi(t) + \pi_1(t)\,\eta(t) + \pi_2(t)g_2(t)u(t) - \pi_1(t)g_1(t)u(t)$

(3) $\dot{\xi}(t) = \eta(t)$ with $x(t^1) = x_1$, $D(t^1) = D_1$, $\xi(t^1) = \xi_1$ given, $x(t^2) = b_1$, $D(t^2) = b_2$, $\xi(t^2) = b_3$, and the con- constraints

(4) $0 \leq u(t) \leq x(t)$, i.e. $u(t) - x(t) \leq 0$, $-u(t) \leq 0$,

(5) $0 \leq v(t) \leq M(t)$, i.e. $v(t) - M(t) \leq 0$, $-v(t) \leq 0$,

(6) $-\xi(t) \leq \eta(t) \leq g_1(t)u(t)$ i.e. $\eta(t) - g_1(t)u(t) \leq 0$, $-\xi(t) - \eta(t) \leq 0$

Following the terminology of Hestenes [3], an arc $(x(t), D(t), \xi(t), u(t), v(t), \eta(t), b)$ is a system of state functions $x(t)$, $D(t)$, $\xi(t)$ that are continuous on $[t^1, t^2]$, control functions $u(t)$, $v(t)$, $\eta(t)$ that are piecewise continuous on $[t^1, t^2]$, and control parameters $b = (b_1, b_2, b_3)$.

The maximand function is constrained by the three differential equations (1), (2) and (3) and by the three sets of inequalities (4), (5) and (6). Equation (1) describes the rate of change of capacity; equation (2) describes the rate of change of net debt; and equation (3) describes the rate of change of inventory. The first and third equations are self-explanatory; and the second one describes how the firm is financed. The firm has one financial account from which it can borrow or into which it can save: $D(t)$ can be either positive or negative.

We assume the following: x_1 and ξ_1, the initial capacity and inventory respectively, are positive; the functions $M(t)$, $\alpha(t)$, $c(t)$, $\pi_1(t)$, $\pi_2(t)$, $i(t)$, $g_1(t)$, $g_2(t)$, $r(t)$ are continuously differentiable and positive on $[t^1, t^2]$; $0 < \theta(t^2) \leqq c(t^2)$; $0 < \gamma(t^2) \leqq \pi_1(t^2)$; and $x_Q \equiv (x_0(t), D_0(t), \xi_0(t), u_0(t), v_0(t)\ \eta_0(t), b_0)$ maximizes I in the class of arcs described above.

We now wish to determine the characteristics of the extremal arc using a theorem of Hestenes [3, Thm. 3.1, pp. 26-27]. In order to do so, we must verify that Hestenes' constraint condition [3, p. 26] is satisfied. The matrix involved is:

$$Q \equiv \begin{bmatrix} 1 & 0 & 0 & u-x_0(t) & 0 & 0 & 0 & 0 & 0 \\ -1 & 0 & 0 & 0 & -u & 0 & 0 & 0 & 0 \\ 0 & 1 & 0 & 0 & 0 & v-M & 0 & 0 & 0 \\ 0 & -1 & 0 & 0 & 0 & 0 & -v & 0 & 0 \\ 0 & 0 & 1 & 0 & 0 & 0 & 0 & \eta-g_1u & 0 \\ 0 & 0 & -1 & 0 & 0 & 0 & 0 & 0 & -\xi_0(t)-\eta \end{bmatrix}$$

That Q has rank 6 whenever $0 \leqq u \leqq x_o(t)$, $0 \leqq v \leqq M$, $-\xi_o(t) \leqq \eta \leqq g_1 u$ and t is in $[t^1, t^2]$ follows immediately by the following lemmas.

<u>Lemma 1</u>. $x_o(t) > 0$ on $[t^1, t^2]$.

<u>Proof</u>: Since $\dot{x}_0(t) = v_0(t) - \alpha(t)\, x_0(t)$ on $[t^1, t^2]$ and $x(t^1) = x_1$, we have

$$x_0(t) = (\exp - \int_{t^1}^{t} \alpha(s)ds)\ \{x_1 + \int_{t^1}^{t} v_0(s) \text{ times}$$

$$(\exp \int_{t^1}^{s} \alpha(w)dw)ds$$

Since $x_1 > 0$ and $v_0(t) \geq 0$, $x_0(t) > 0$ for all t.

QED.

<u>Lemma 2</u>. $\xi_o(t) > 0$ on $[t^1, t^2]$.

<u>Proof</u>: Since $\dot{\xi}(t) = \eta(t)$ and $\eta(t) = -\xi(t)$ is the maximum rate at which inventories can be depleted, we have $\xi_*(t) = \xi_1 \exp(t^1 - t) = \min \{\xi(t)\ |\dot{\xi}(t) = \eta$ and $-\xi(t) \leqq \eta \leqq g_1 u$

and $\xi(t^1) = \xi_1\}$. It is assumed $\xi_1 > 0$ · $\xi_0(t)$ cannot be less than $\xi*(t)$. Hence, $\xi_o(t) \geq \xi*(t) > 0$ on $[t^1, t^2]$. QED.

Hence, the existence of the multipliers λ_0, $p_1(t)$, $p_2(t)$, $p_3(t)$, $\mu_1(t)$, $\mu_2(t)$, $\mu_3(t)$, $\mu_4(t)$, $\mu_5(t)$, $\mu_6(t)$ and the associated functions H and G, as described in Hestenes Thm. 3.1, is guaranteed.

5. Preliminary Results

$$H = \lambda_o\{\pi_1 g_1 u - \pi_1 \eta - \pi_2 g_2 u - cv - iD - r\xi\}\,\Phi + p_1(v - \alpha x)$$
$$+ p_2(cv + iD + r\xi + \pi_1\eta + \pi_2 g_2 u - \pi_1 g_1 u) + p_3\eta$$
$$- \mu_1(u - x) + \mu_2 u - \mu_3(v - M) + \mu_4 v$$
$$- \mu_5(\eta - g_1 u) + \mu_6(\xi + \eta).$$

$$G = -\lambda_o[(c(t^2) - \theta(t^2))b_1\Phi(t^2) + (\pi_1(t^2) - \gamma(t^2))b_3\ \Phi(t^2)].$$

The Euler-Lagrange equations are

(i) $0 = H_u = \lambda_0(\pi_1 g_1 - \pi_2 g_2)\Phi + p_2(\pi_2 g_2 - \pi_1 g_1) - \mu_1 + \mu_2 + \mu_5 g_1$

(ii) $0 = H_v = -\lambda_0 c\Phi + p_1 + p_2 c - \mu_3 + \mu_4$

(iii) $0 = H_\eta = -\lambda_0\pi_1\Phi + p_2\pi_1 + p_3 - \mu_5 + \mu_6$

(iv) $p_1(t) = -\int_{t^1}^{t} (-p_1(s)\alpha(s) + \mu_1(s))ds + c_1$

(v) $p_2(t) = -\int_{t^1}^{t} (-\lambda_0 i(s)\Phi(s) + p_2(s)i(s))ds + c_2$

(vi) $p_3(t) = -\int_{t^1}^{t} (-\lambda_0 r(s)\Phi(s) + p_2(s)r(s) + \mu_6(s))ds + c_3$

Proposition 1. $p_1(t^2) = \lambda_0(c(t^2) - \theta(t^2))\Phi(t^2)$, $p_2(t^2) = 0$. $p_3(t^2) = \lambda_0(\pi_1(t^2) - \gamma(t^2))\Phi(t^2)$

Proof: Immediate from the transversality condition.

Proposition 2. $\lambda_0 > 0$.

Proof: Suppose $\lambda_0 = 0$. Then $(\lambda_0, p_1(t^2), p_2(t^2), p_3(t^2)) = (0,0,0,0)$. Hence, by Berkovitz [2, p. 156] all of the multipliers vanish at t^2; this is impossible. Thus, the proposition is proved since $\lambda_0 \geq 0$.

Multiplying the set of multipliers by $1/\lambda_0$, we may

assume that $\lambda_0 = 1$.

Proposition 3.

$$p_2(t) = -[\exp - \int_{t^1}^{t} i(s)ds] \int_{t}^{t^2} i(s)\Phi(s) [\exp \int_{t^1}^{s} i(w) dw]ds$$

Proof: Since $-i\Phi + p_2 i$ is continuous on $[t^1, t^2]$ we may differentiate equation (v) to obtain

$\dot{p}_2(t) = i(t)\Phi(t) - i(t)p_2(t)$ on $[t^1, t^2]$. By Prop. 1,

$p_2(t^2) = 0$. Thus, solution of this final value problem gives the result. QED.

Proposition 4. $\mu_1 - \mu_2 = (\pi_1 g_1 - \pi_2 g_2)(\Phi - p_2) + \mu_5 g_1$ and $\mu_5 - \mu_6 = (p_2 - \Phi)\pi_1 + p_3$

Proof: Immediate from 5(i) and (iii), respectively. QED.

Lemma 3. $\dot{p}_3 = f(t,p_3) = r(\Phi - p_2) - \mu_6$ satisfies the Lipschitz condition on $[t^1, t^2]$ and hence has a unique solution on $[t^1, t^2]$.

Proof:

(i) First it must be verified that $\dot{p}_3 = f(t,p_3)$ exists on $[t^1, t^2]$. From equation (vi), $\dot{p}_3 = r(\Phi - p_2) - \mu_6$ if $r(\Phi - p_2) - \mu_6$ is continuous. Since r, Φ, and p_2 are known continuous functions, we need to show only that $\mu_6(t)$ is continuous. From Proposition 4, $\mu_5 - \mu_6 = \pi_1(p_2 - \Phi) + p_3$, where at most one of the multipliers μ_5, μ_6 is positive. We find that $\pi_1(\Phi - p_2) - p_3 \leq 0$ implies $\mu_6 = 0$ and $\pi_1(\Phi - p_2) - p_3 > 0$ implies $\mu_5 = 0$. Thus we may write $\mu_6 = \max\{0, \pi_1(\Phi - p_2) - p_3\}$. Since Φ, p_2, π_1, and p_3 are continuous, μ_6 is continuous and $\dot{p}_3 = r(\Phi - p_2) - \mu_6$.

(ii) The Lipschitz condition requires

$$|f(t,p_3') - f(t,p_3'')| \leqq K\,|p_3' - p_3''|$$

Since $f(t,p_3)$ is either $(r-\pi_1)(\Phi - p_2) + p_3$ or $r(\Phi - p_2)$, there are four possible cases:

(1) $|(r-\pi_1)(\Phi - p_2) + p_3' - (r-\pi_1)(\Phi - p_2) - p_3''| = |p_3' - p_3''|$

(2) $|r(\Phi - p_2) - r(\Phi - p_2)| = 0$

(3) $\quad |(r-\pi_1)(\Phi-p_2) + p_3' - r(\Phi-p_2)| = |p_3'-\pi_1(\Phi-p_2)|$

(4) $\quad |r(\Phi-p_2) - (r-\pi_1)(\Phi-p_2) - p_3''| = |\pi_1(\Phi-p_2) - p_3''|$

Obviously (1) and (2) satisfy the Lipschitz condition (L.C.) for K = 1. To show that (3) and (4) satisfy the L.C. notice that $\partial f/\partial p_3$ is either 1 or 0. Thus picking K = 1, $\partial f/\partial p_3 \leq$ K = 1.

Also $|f(t,p_3') - f(t,p_3'')| = \left| \sum\limits_{i=1}^{n-1} \int\limits_{p_3^i}^{p_3^{i+1}} \partial f/\partial p_3 \, d \, p_3 \right|$

where $p_3^1 = p_3'$, $p_3^n = p_3''$, and p_3^i for i = 2,...,n-1 are values of p_3 where f switches from $(r-\pi_1)(\Phi-p_2) + p_3$ to $r(\Phi-p_2)$ or vice versa. Thus

$$|f(t,p_3') - f(t,p_3'')| = \left| \sum\limits_{i=1}^{n-1} \int\limits_{p_3^i}^{p_3^{i+1}} \partial f/\partial p_3 \, dp_3 \right|$$

$$\leq \left| \sum\limits_{i=1}^{n-1} \int\limits_{p_3^i}^{p_3^{i+1}} d \, p_3 \right|$$

$$= \left| \sum\limits_{i=1}^{n-1} (p_3^{i+1} - p_3^i) \right|$$

$$= | p_3^n - p_3^1 | = K|p_3' - p_3''|$$

Thus $f(t,p_3)$ satisfies the L.C. on $[t^1, t^2]$ and by a well-known theorem from differential equations [2, p. 223], $p_3(t)$ has a unique solution on t^1, t^2. QED.

Proposition 5.

(a) $p_3(t) = [\pi_1(t^2) - \gamma(t^2)] \Phi(t^2) \exp(t-t^2) - \exp(t-t^2)$ times

$\int_t^{t^2} \{\exp(t^2-s)[r(s)-\pi_1(s)][\Phi(s)-p_2(s)]\}$ ds

for all t in $(\Gamma^n,t^2]$ where Γ^n represents the largest value of t such that $p_3(t) - \pi_1(t) [\Phi(t) - p_2(t)] = 0$.

(b) $p_3(t) = p_3(\Gamma^i) \exp(t-\Gamma^i) - \exp(t-\Gamma^i) \int_t^{\Gamma^i} \exp(\Gamma^i-s)$ times

$[r(s) - \pi_1(s)] [\Phi(s) - p_2(s)]$ ds

for all t in $[t^1, t^2]$ such that $p_3(t) - \pi_1(t)[\Phi(t)-p_2(t)] \leq 0$,

(c) $p_3(t) = p_3(\Gamma^i) - \int_t^{\Gamma^i} r(s)[\phi(s) - p_2(s)]ds$ for all t in $[t^1, t^2]$ such that $p_3(t) - \pi_1(t)\ \phi(t) - p_2(t) \geq 0$, where $\Gamma^{n+1} = t^2$ and Γ^i, $i=1,\ldots,n$, are the values of t in $[t^1, t^2]$ such that $p_3(t) - \pi_1(t)\ [\phi(t) - p_2(t)] = 0$.

Proof: It follows from Lemma 3 that $\dot{p}_3 = r(t)\ [\Phi(t) - p_2(t)] - \mu_6(t)$, where $\mu_6 = \max\{0, (\phi-p_2)\pi_1 - p_3\}$ is continuous. Since $\pi_1(t^2)[p_2(t^2) - \phi(t^2)] + p_3(t^2) = -\gamma(t^2)\phi(t^2) < 0$, there exists a $\delta > 0$ such that $\pi_1(t)[p_2(t) - \Phi(t)] + p_3(t) < 0$ for all t in $[t^2 - \delta, t^2]$. Let $\Gamma^n = t^2 - \delta$. Hence, by continuity $\dot{p}_3 = (r-\pi_1)\ (\phi-p_2) + p_3$ on $[\Gamma^n, t^2]$. Since $p_3(t^2) = [\pi_1(t^2) - \gamma(t^2)]\Phi(t^2)$, solution of this final-value problem gives the result desired on $[\Gamma^n, t^2]$. By Hestenes' Theorem 3.1, $p_3(t)$ is continuous on $[t^1, t^2]$; and by Lemma 3, $p_3(t)$ is unique on $[t^1, t^2]$. Thus $p_3(\Gamma^n)$ is known and provides the terminal condition for (b) or (c) above. It may be that $\pi_1(p_2-\Phi) + p_3$ does not alternate between being positive and negative; for example, it could be positive, zero, and then positive. In such a case Lemma 3 guarantees uniqueness and p_3 is computed as if $\pi_1(p_2-\Phi) + p_3$ alternates. If the rule does not alternate, then the computation of p_3 would be incorrect. Such a discrepancy would show up in comparing the value used for $\dot{p}_3$ with the sign of the rule, $\pi_1(p_2-\Phi) + p_3$. This completes the derivation of the solution for $p_3(t)$ on $[t^1, t^2]$. QED.

Proposition 6. $p_1(t) = [\exp - \int_t^{t^2} \alpha(s)ds]\{(c(t^2)-\theta(t^2))$ times $\Phi(t^2)$

$$+\int_t^{t^2} [\exp\int_s^{t^2} \alpha(w)dw]\ h(s)ds\}$$ where

$$h = \max\ \{0, (\pi_1 g_1 - \pi_2 g_2)(\Phi-p_2) + \mu_5 g_1\}$$ and

$$\mu_5 = \max\ \{0, (p_2-\Phi)\pi_1 + p_3\}$$

Proof: By Prop. 5, $\mu_5 - \mu_6 = (p_2-\Phi)\pi_1 + p_3$ where p_2 and

p_3 are known continuous functions; moreover, at least one of the multipliers μ_5, μ_6 must be zero. It follows that $(p_2-\Phi)\pi_1 + p_3 \leq 0$ implies $\mu_5 = 0$ and $(p_2-\Phi)\pi_1 + p_3 > 0$ implies $\mu_6 \doteq 0$. Hence, $\mu_5 = \max\{0, (p_2-\Phi)\pi_1 + p_3\}$, which is a known continuous function. By Prop. 5, $\mu_1 - \mu_2 = (\pi_1 g_1 - \pi_2 g_2)(\Phi-p_2) + \mu_5 g_1$; and again at least one of the multipliers μ_1, μ_2 must be zero. We find that $(\pi_1 g_1 - \pi_2 g_2)(\Phi-p_2) + \mu_5 g_1 \leqq 0$ implies $\mu_1 = 0$, and $(\pi_1 g_1-\pi_2 g_2)(\Phi-p_2) + \mu_5 g_1 > 0$ implies $\mu_2 = 0$. Hence, $\mu_1 = \max\{0, (\pi_1 g_1-\pi_2 g_2)(\Phi-p_2) + \mu_5 g_1\}$, which is a known continuous function. Hence, equation (iv) may be differentiated to obtain $\dot{p}_1 = \alpha p_1 - \mu_1$. We know by Prop. 1 that $p_1(t^2) = (c(t^2) - \theta(t^2))\Phi(t^2)$. Therefore, the solution of this final-value problem gives the solution desired. QED.

6. Description of the Extremal Arc[3]

Theorem.

(a) $$v_o(t) = \begin{cases} 0 \text{ if } p_1(t) - c(t)(\Phi(t) - p_2(t)) < 0 \\ M(t) \text{ if } p_1(t) - c(t)(\Phi(t) - p_2(t)) > 0 \end{cases}$$

The values of $v_o(t)$ when $p_1(t) - c(t)(\Phi(t) - p_2(t)) = 0$ are immaterial in that they do not affect the value of I.

(b) (1) $u_o(t) = 0$ and $\eta_o(t) = -\xi_o(t)$ if $A(t) < 0$ and $B(t) < 0$;

(2) $u_o(t) = x_o(t)$ and $\eta_o(t) = g_1(t)u_o(t)$ if $A(t) > 0$ and $B(t) > 0$;

(3) $\eta_o(t) = g_1(t)u_o(t)$ if $A(t) < 0$ and $B(t) > 0$; moreover, $u_o(t) = 0$ if $A(t) + B(t)g_1(t) < 0$, and $u_o(t) = x_o(t)$ if $A(t) + B(t)g_1(t) > 0$

(4) $u_o(t) = x_o(t)$ and $\eta_o(t) = -\xi_o(t)$ if $A(t) > 0$ and $B(t) < 0$.

where $A(t) \equiv (\pi_1(t)g_1(t)-\pi_2(t)g_2(t)(\phi(t)-p_2(t))$

and $B(t) \equiv p_3(t) - \pi_1(t)(\Phi(t) - p_2(t))$.

The values of $u_o(t)$ and $\eta_o(t)$ when $A(t) = 0$ and $B(t) = 0$, respectively, are immaterial in that they do not affect the value of I.

Proof:

Part (a). We apply the Maximum Principle with $u = u_0$ and $\eta = \eta_0$. Then $-cv\Phi + p_1 v + p_2 cv \leq cv_0\Phi + p_1 v_0 + p_2 cv_0$ for all $0 \leq v \leq M$, t in $[t^1, t^2]$. Hence, $v_0 = 0$ or M depending upon the sign of $p_1 + p_2 c - c\Phi$ as claimed. To complete the proof of this part of the theorem, we need to show that I has the same value on any two admissible arcs $[x_0^1, D_0^1, \xi_0^1, u_0^1, v^1, \eta_0^1, b_0^1)$ and $(x_0^2, D_0^2, \xi_0^2, u_0^2, v^2, \eta_0^2, b_0^2)$ where $u_0^1 = u_0^2$, $\eta_0^1 = \eta_0^2$ and $v^1 = v^2$ except possibly when $p_1 + p_2 c - c\Phi = 0$. The proof is straightforward, but lengthy and is omitted here.

Part (b). We apply the Maximum Principle with $v = v_0$. Then $(\pi_1 g_1 - \pi_2 g_2)(\Phi - p_2)u + (p_3 - \pi_1)(\Phi - p_2))\eta \leqq (\pi_1 g_1 - \pi_2 g_2)$ times $(\Phi - p_2)u_0 + (p_3 - \pi_1(\Phi - p_2))\eta_0$ for all $0 \leqq u \leqq x_0(t)$, $-\xi_0 \leqq \eta \leqq g_1 u$, t in $[t^1, t^2]$.

Case (1). $\pi_1 g_1 - \pi_2 g_2 < 0$ and $p_3 - \pi_1(\Phi - p_2) < 0$. Then clearly $u_0 = 0$ and $\eta_0 = -\xi_0$.

Case (2). $\pi_1 g_1 - \pi_2 g_2 > 0$ and $p_3 - \pi_1(\Phi - p_2) > 0$. Then $u_0(t) = x_0(t)$ and $\eta_0 = g_1 u_0$.

Case (3). $\pi_1 g_1 - \pi_2 g_2 < 0$ and $p_3 - \pi_1(\Phi - p_2) > 0$. Then it is immediate that $\eta_0 = g_1 u_0$. Hence, $u_0 = 0$ or $x_0(t)$ depending upon the sign of $(\pi_1 g_1 - \pi_2 g_2)(\Phi - p_2) + [p_3 - \pi_1(\Phi - p_2)]g_1$.

Case (4). $\pi_1 g_1 - \pi_2 g_2 > 0$ and $p_3 - \pi_1(\Phi - p_2) < 0$. Then $u_0(t) = x_0(t)$ and $\eta_0 = -\xi_0$.

Again to complete the proof of this part of the theorem, we need to show that I has the same value on any two admissible arcs $(x_0^1, D_0^1, \xi_0^1, u^1, v_0^1, \eta^1, b_0^1)$ and $(x_0^2, D_0^2, \xi_0^2, u^2, v_0^2, \eta^2, b_0^2)$ where $u^1 = u^2$, $v_0^1 = v_0^2$ and $\eta^1 = \eta^2$ except possibly when $\pi_1 g_1 - \pi_2 g_2 = 0$ and $p_3 - \pi_1(\Phi - p_2) = 0$. The proof is again straightforward, but lengthy and omitted here.

The state variables $\xi_0(t)$ and $x_0(t)$ can be computed directly from 4(3) and 4(1) and the respective initial conditions

ξ_1 and x_1 as soon as the controls η_o and u_o are determined. Then given these results, the state variable $D_o(t)$ can be computed directly from 4(2) and the initial condition D_1. This completes the derivation of the controls and the states; they completely describes the extremal arc.

It should be noted that a computational procedure is immediate. The multipliers $p_1(t)$, $p_2(t)$, $p_3(t)$ are expressed in terms of given functions. Thus, to compute the controls $u_o(t)$, $v_o(t)$, and $\eta_o(t)$, one first determines the zeros of $p_1(t) - c(t)(\Phi(t) - p_2(t))$, $B(t)$, $A(t)$, and $A(t) + B(t)g_1(t)$ and then the signs of each of these entities between zeros.

7. Interpretation of the Results

Using Berkovitz's Value Equation and its properties [2, p. 164, Thm. 4], economic interpretations can be made of the multipliers $p_1(t)$, $p_2(t)$ and $p_3(t)$ which are, respectively, the partial derivatives of the Value Equation with respect to capacity, net debt, and product inventory. Since the Value Equation represents the discounted value of capacity and inventory at the end of the period plus the discounted value of savings over the period (where the controls and states are optimally determined), $p_1(t)$, $p_2(t)$ and $p_3(t)$ are the marginal discounted contributions to net worth of an additional unit of capacity, net debt and inventory. Letting $S(t)$ represent net savings and $S(t) = -D(t)$, $-p_2(t)$ (which is positive on $[t^1, t^2]$) is the present marginal value in terms of net worth of a unit increase in savings, which is either invested in the firm or a like firm in the industry. $\Phi(t)$ is the discount function, and thus represents the adjustment necessary in a unit of money to account for temporal time preference of the entrepreneur for money. Therefore, $\Phi(t) - p_2(t)$ represents the total adjustment needed in the value of a unit of money either received in profits from production or committed to the buildup of the asset structure. This adjustment discounts both profits and durable good costs from t to t^1, and in addition accounts for the present value of the returns (costs) from (of) a unit of money between t and t^2. This implies $c(t)(\Phi(t) - p_2(t))$ is the (effective) present marginal value of an investment in a unit of new capacity. Therefore, as far as investment is concerned, the firm will invest whenever the present (effective) marginal value of a unit of new capacity is greater than the present (effective) marginal value of the costs of that unit, and the firm will not invest whenever the opposite is the case.

With respect to production and inventory the firm will follow the following policies: (1) the firm will operate at full capacity whenever the present (effective) value of the profit stream, A(t), is positive, and will build up its inventory at the maximum possible rate whenever the present (effective) net marginal value of inventory, B(t), is positive, and will deplete its inventory at the maximum possible rate whenever this net marginal value is negative. (2) If the present (effective) value of the profit stream is negative and if the present (effective) net marginal value of inventory is negative, the firm will stand idle and will deplete its inventory at the maximum rate; however, if the present (effective) net marginal value of inventory is positive, the firm may operate at full capacity even though the present (effective) value of the profit stream is negative. In this case, the firm will build up its inventory at the maximum rate; and it will either produce at full capacity or not at all depending upon the sign of $A(t) + B(t)g_1(t)$. If this sum is positive, the firm will operate at full capacity while if this sum is negative, the firm will not operate at all.

8. Solutions for Three Special Cases

Using the decision rules for the production, investment and inventory controls and solutions of the initial-value problems $\dot{x} = v - \alpha x$, $x(t^1) = x_1$, $\dot{D} = cv+iD+r\xi+\pi_1\eta_1+\pi_2 g_2 u-\pi_1 g_1 u$, $D(t^1) = D_1$ and $\xi = \eta$, $\xi(t^1) = \xi_1$, solutions were calculated for the three cases given in Table 1. Three different profit margins were allowed for. In Case 1, the profit margin varies seasonally around 15 cents per unit of output, while in Cases 2 and 3 this margin increases and decreases 3 percent per year, respectively. All of the other temporal parameters as well as the initial values of the states variables are the same for all three cases.

In all three cases, the initial investment policy of the firm is one of growth, see Figures 1, 2, and 3. This policy is followed for a maximum of 1004 weeks in Case 2 and for a minimum of 770 weeks in Case 3. In these initial periods, capacity increases continuously. It attains absolute maxima of 1200, 1275 and 1170 units of capacity after 850, 1003 and 769 weeks in Cases 1, 2, and 3, respectively. Then capacity decreases continuously to terminal values of 830 and 710 units in Cases 1 and 3. The pattern is different for Case 2. There the firm lets its capacity run down from the 1004th to 1038th week and then, curious as it might seem, purchases new capacity at the maximum rate in the last 2 weeks.

With regard to inventories, there are clearly many more switch points than in the case of investment. The firm tends to build up its inventories in periods of unfavorable seasonal prices and deplete them in periods of favorable seasonal prices. This seasonal pattern is influenced to a limited degree by the cyclical pattern of prices. If prices are

Table 1. Values of the Temporal Parameters and Functions and Initial Values of the State Variables for Three Different Profit Situations

*t is measured in weeks
**the period is 52 weeks

Temporal Parameters and Functions	Case 1	Case 2	Case 3
$i(t)$	.08/52	.08/52	.08/52
$\alpha(t)$	.10/52	.10/52	.10/52
$\delta(t)$	.05/52	.05/52	.05/52
$\pi_1(t)g_1(t)-\pi_2(t)g_2(t)$**	.15+.10 sin.121t	.15 exp.03t/52 +.10 sin.121t	.15 exp-.03t/52 +.10 sin. 121t
$c(t)$	1000 exp. 06t/52	1000 exp.06t/52	1000 exp.06t/52
$r(t)$	.06/52	.06/52	.06/52
$\gamma(t^2)$	.05	.05	.05
$M(t)$	2.8	2.8	2.8
$x(t^1)$	160	160	160
$D(t^1)$	$120,000	$120,000	$120,000
$\xi(t^1)$	60,000	60,000	60,000

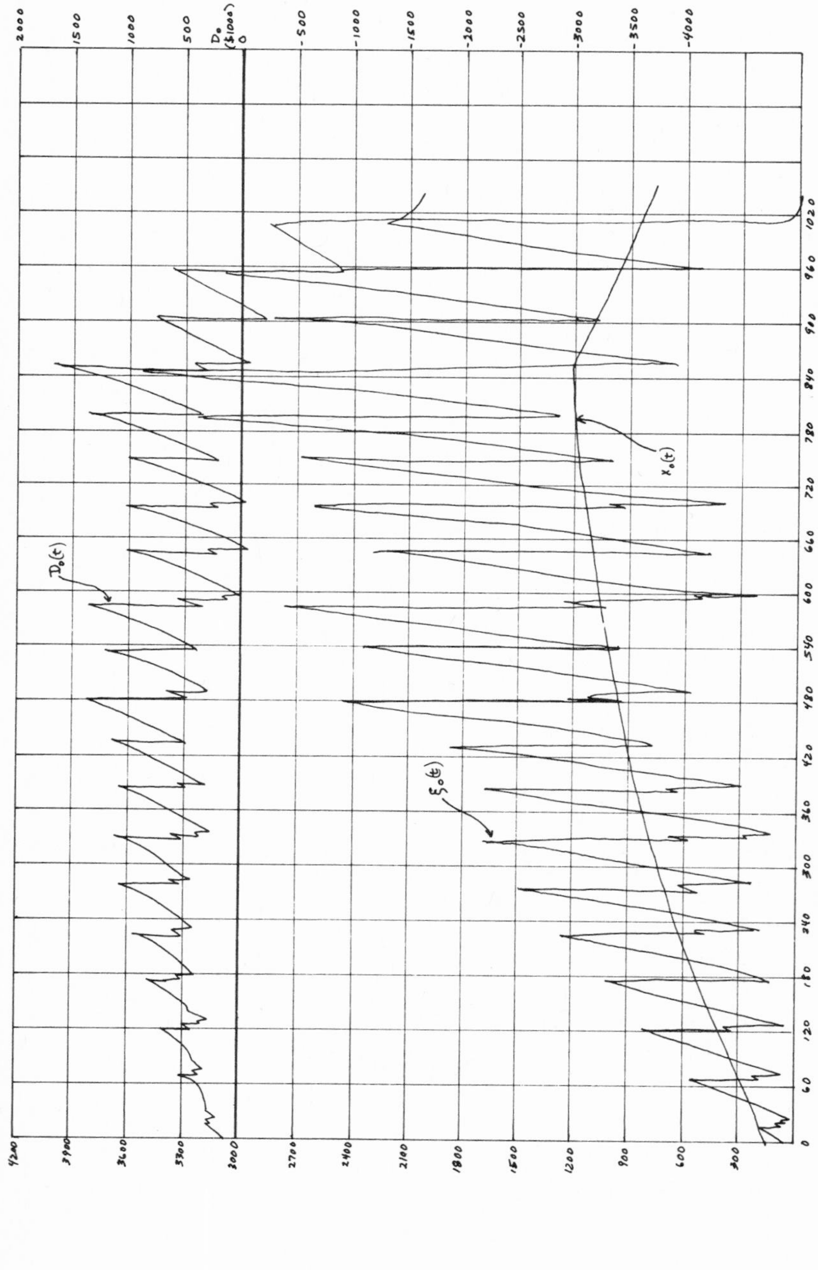

Time in Weeks

Figure 1: Optimal Capacity, Inventory and Debt of the Firm for Case 1 in Table 1.

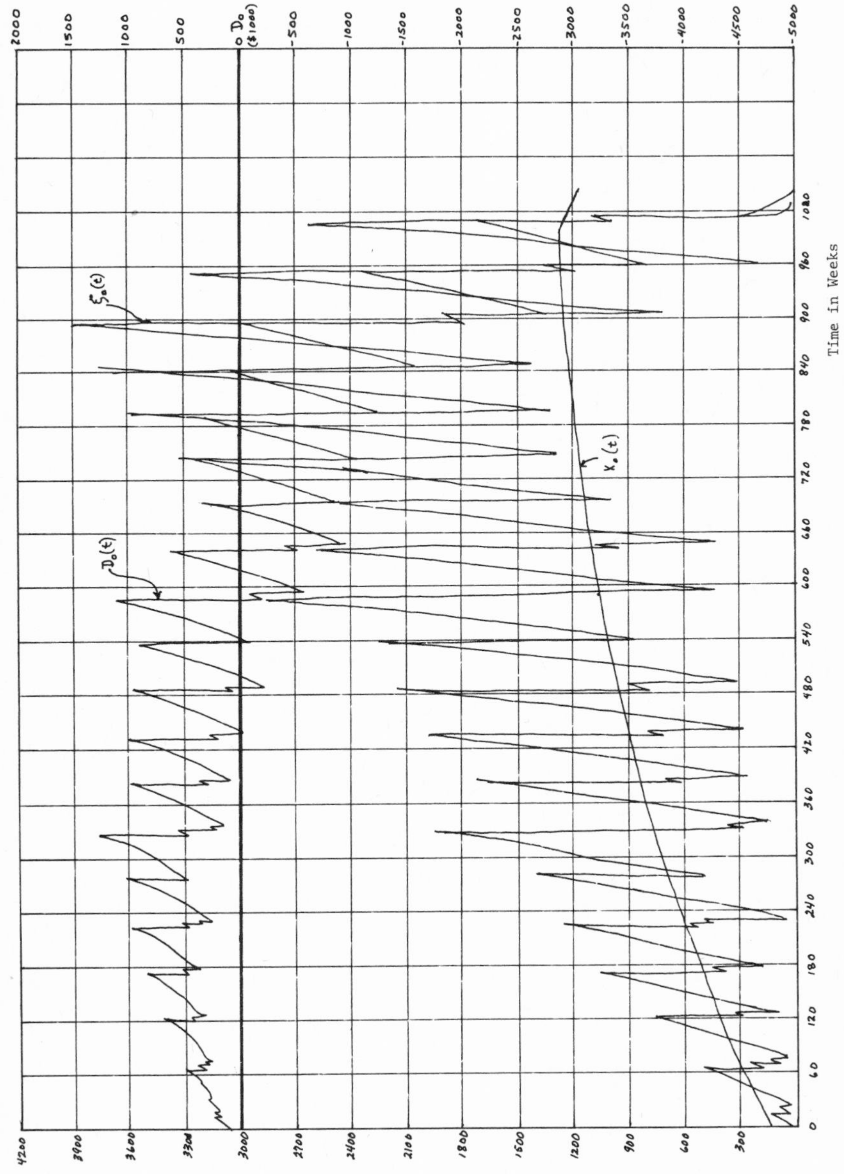

Figure 2: Optimal Capacity, Inventory and Debt of the Firm for Case 2 in Table 1.

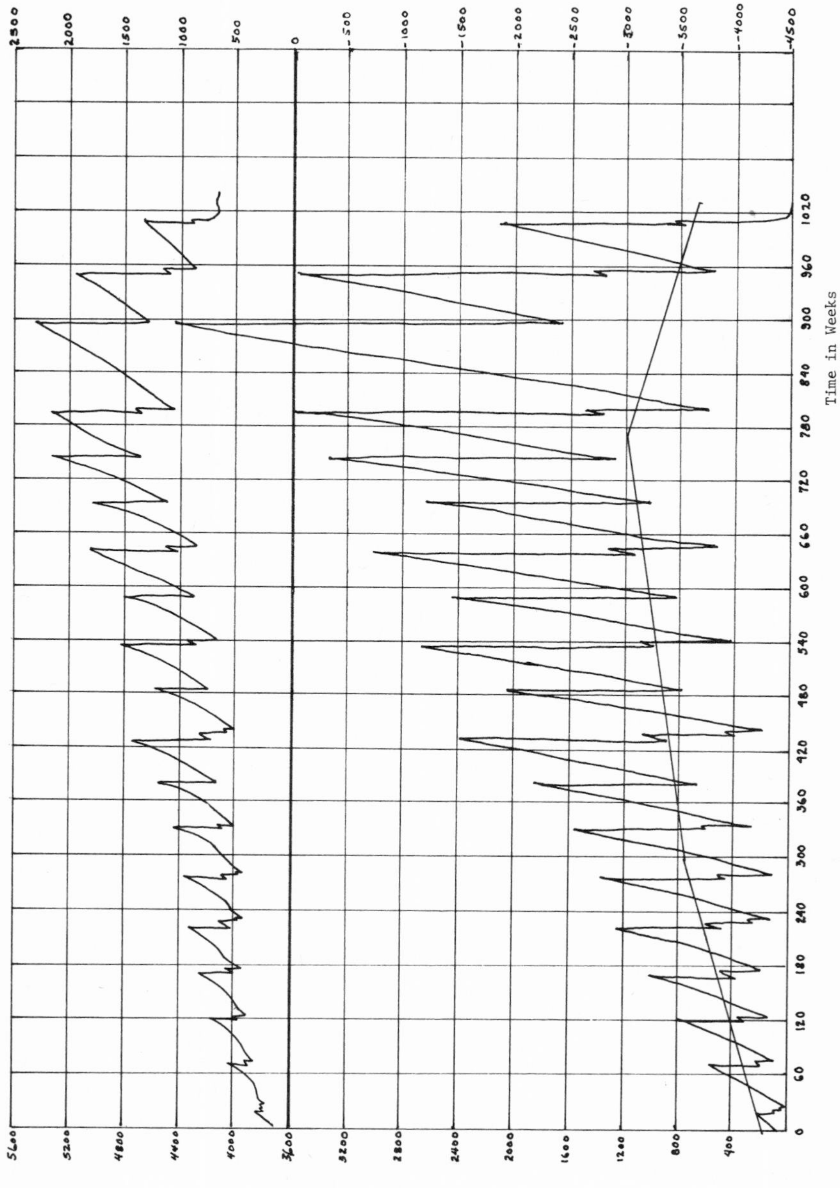

Figure 3: Optimal Capacity, Inventory and Debt of the Firm for Case 3 in Table 1.

rising cyclically, then the number of switch points in inventory policy is slightly less than when prices are not rising or falling cyclically. It is impossible to tell from this limited analysis what relationship might characterize these differences.

We can observe, however, a definite relationship between inventory management and firm growth when the earlier results of Thompson and George [6] are compared with those of this study. They used the same values for the temporal parameters in Case 1 of that study as we used in Case 1 of this study. Inventory possibilities represent the fundamental difference between the two studies. In the earlier study the firm grew continuously for only the first 477 weeks where it reached its maximum size of 938 units, while in this study the firm grows continuously for the first 850 weeks where it reaches its maximum size of 1200 units. This result would be expected since the firm has more decision making opportunities by which to make money. It can now make profits from holding inventories as well as from production. Those profits provide a further incentive to expand the size of the firm and in turn manage inventories so that larger profits can be made.

APPENDIX
Special Case of Hestenes Theorem 3.1

An arc is represented by the system $x^i(t)$, $u^k(t)$, b_j, $t^1 \leqq t \leqq t^2$; i=1,...,n; k=1,...,q; j=1,...,r, of n continuous functions $x^i(t)$, called state functions, q piecewise continuous functions $u^k(t)$, called control functions, and r constants bj, called control parameters.

The problem to be considered is that of minimizing a function

$$Io(x) = go(b) + \int_{t^i}^{t^2} L_o(t,x(t), u(t))dt$$

in a class of arcs

$$x: \ x(t), u(t), b, \qquad t^1 \leqq t \leqq t^2,$$

satisfying a system of differential equations

$$(1) \qquad \dot{x}^i(t) = f^i(t,x(t), u(t)$$

$$(2) \qquad \phi_\alpha(t, x(t), u(t)) \leqq 0 \qquad 1 \leqq \alpha \leqq m'$$

$$\phi_\alpha(t, x(t), u(t)) = 0 \qquad m' < \alpha \leqq m$$

and a set of initial and terminal conditions

$$(3) \qquad x^i(t^1) = x_1^{\ i} \quad , \quad x^i(t^2) = b_i.$$

(We are giving here a special case where n=r).

It will be assumed that all functions used are of class C' on a region R in (t,x,u,b) - space. The class of all elements (t,x,u,b) in R satisfying the conditions

$$(4) \qquad \phi_\alpha(t,x,u,b) \leqq 0 \qquad 1 \leqq \alpha \leqq m',$$

$$(5) \qquad \phi_\alpha(t,x,u,b) = 0 \qquad m' < \alpha \leqq m$$

will be denoted by Ro and will be called the class of admissible elements.

An arc

$$x: \ x(t), u(t), b, \qquad t^1 \leqq t \leqq t^2$$

will be called admissible if its elements (t,x(t), u(t), b) are in Ro. The class of admissible arcs will be denoted by A. The class of admissible arcs satisfying the conditions (1) and (3) will be denoted by B. We assume that we have been given an admissible arc

$$x_o: \ x_o(t), u_o(t), b_o, \qquad t^1 \leqq t \leqq t^2$$

in B that minimizes Io(x) on B. In addition, we assume the matrix

$$(6)\quad \left(\frac{\partial\phi\alpha}{\partial u^k}\ ,\quad \delta_{\alpha\beta}\ \phi_\beta\right),\ \alpha,\beta=1,\ \ldots,\ m;\ \beta \text{ not summed; } k=1,\ldots,q;\ \delta_{\alpha\alpha}=1,\ \delta_{\alpha\beta}=0(\alpha\neq\beta);$$

has rank m at each element $(t,\ x_o(t),\ u,\ b_o)$ in Ro. Here α denotes the row index and k,β are column indices.

FIRST ORDER NECESSARY CONDITIONS AND A MAXIMUM PRINCIPLE.

Suppose that the arc

$$x_o(t),\ u_o(t),\ b_o, \qquad t^1 \leqq t \leqq t^2$$

described above affords a minimum to Io on B. Then there exist multipliers

$$\lambda o \geqq 0,\ p_i(t),\ \mu_\alpha(t),\ i=1,\ldots,n;\ \ =1,\ldots,m;$$

not vanishing simultaneously on $t^1 \leqq t \leqq t^2$, and functions

$$H(t,x,u,p,\mu) = p_i\ f^i - \lambda oLo - \mu_\alpha\phi_\alpha,\ G(b) = \lambda ogo$$

such that the following relations hold.

(i) The multipliers $\mu_\alpha(t)$ are piecewise continuous and are continuous at each point of continuity of $u_o(t)$. Moreover, for each $\alpha \leqq m'$, the relation $\mu_\alpha(t) \geqq 0$ holds and the equation

(7) $\mu_\alpha(t)\ \phi\alpha(t,\ x_o(t),\ u_o(t)) = 0$, α not summed, holds on $t^1 \leqq t \leqq t^2$.

(ii) The multipliers $p_i(t)$ are continuous and have piecewise continuous derivatives. In fact there are constants c_i, c such that the relations

$$(8)\quad p_i = - \int_{t^i}^{t} H_{x^i}\ ds + c_i, \qquad H = \int_{t^1}^{t} H_t\ ds + c,$$

$$(9)\quad H_u k = 0$$

hold along x_o, with $p_i = p_i(t)$, $\mu_\alpha = \mu_\alpha(t)$.

(iii) The transversality condition

$$(10)\quad dG + p_i(t^2)\ dX^{i2} = 0$$

is an identity in db_i on x_o.

(iv) The inequality

(11) $H(t,\ x_o(t),\ u,\ p(t),\ 0) \leqq H(t,x_o(t),\ u_o(t),\ p(t)$

holds whenever $(t,x_o(t),\ u,\ b_o)$ is in Ro.

FOOTNOTES

1. This analysis subsumes the production function of the firm and assumes that the firm operates along the optimal expansion path. Since the rate of total production is assumed to be linear in u, i.e. $g(t)u(t)$, this assumes that the expansion path of the firm is linear and hence the underlying production function is linear-homogenous.

2. The lower bound constraint on $\eta(t)$ which is $-\xi(t)$ is indicative of a general class of such restrictions. For example, this restriction could be replaced by $-M(t)\ \xi(t)$ where $M(t)$ is any positive bounded, continuously differentiable function defined on $[t^1, t^2]$.

3. The same decision making rules for the optimal controls are obtained if increasing marginal production costs are allowed for: $-g_2$ is strictly concave in u. Computing is the basic difference between such an analysis and this one.

REFERENCES

[1] Arrow, Kenneth J., Samuel Karlin, and Herbert E. Scarf, Studies in the Mathematical Theory of Inventory and Production. Stanford University Press, 1958.

[2] Berkovitz, Leonard D., "Variational Methods in Problems of Control and Programming," J. Math. Anal. Appl., 3 (1961), pp. 145-169.

[3] Coddington, Earl A., Ordinary Differential Equations. Prentice-Hall, Inc., 1961.

[4] Hestenes, Magnus R., "On Variational Theory and Optimal Control Theory," J. SIAM Control, Ser. A, Vol. 3, No. 1 (1966) pp. 23-48.

[5] Hicks, John R., Value and Capital, 2nd ed., Oxford University Press, London, 1946.

[6] Scarf, Herbert E., Dorothy M. Gilford, and Maynard W. Skelly, Multistage Inventory Models and Techniques, Stanford University Press, 1963.

[7] Thompson, Russell G., and Melvin D. George, "Optimal Production and Investment Controls for the Firm," presented before the 1967 Summer Meetings of the Econometrics Society held jointly with The American Mathematics Society and the Mathematics Association of America, Toronto, Ontario, Canada and to appear in Mgt. Sc. A.

MONOPOLY EQUILIBRIUM UNDER DYNAMIC CERTAINTY[1]

by

S. Y. Wu
University of Iowa

and

James C. Moore
University of Missouri

This paper will examine how, under conditions of certainty a monopolist facing a multi-period decision horizon will select his inventory, sales, and production policies. While this problem received some attention in the literature during the late 1930's and early 1940's including contributions by G. C. Evans [3], Arthur Smithies [7], E. S. Shaw [6], Gerhard Tintner [8], and Moses Abramowitz [1], these earlier works did not include provisions for sales contracted in one period but delivered in later periods of the planning horizon and did not give attention to the nonnegative constraints of the decision variables. The present paper attempts to remedy these shortcomings.

The basic assumptions of the model to be presented are as follows:

1. The time unit adopted is a marketing period, that is, an interval of sufficient length for sales transactions to take place. We assume that there is only one actual functional relationship between the various possible quantities demanded and the various price levels within this marketing time period and that this relationship constitutes the monopolist's demand function.

2. We assume that only the market demand function for the product fluctuates over time. Production technology and factor prices are assumed to be constant.

3. The monopolist's revenue function is assumed to be concave; while his production cost, inventory cost, and backlogged order penalty cost functions are all assumed to be convex. Moreover, it is assumed that all these functions are differentiable.

The Model.

If the monopolist knows with certainty his demand function within the planning horizon and if the demand function is expected to fluctuate, the monopolist, in order to maximize profits over the entire planning horizon, may set his level of sales different from his rate of production in each period. Inventory will be accumulated when current production plus inventory on hand at the beginning of the period exceeds current deliveries. The sales in period t are defined as the sum of sales contracted and delivered in period t and the sales contracted in period t but delivered in period k, where $t < k \leq n$.

Let the monopolist's demand function in period t be

$$(1) \quad P_t = f_t\left(\sum_{k=t}^{n} S_{t,k}\right)$$

P_t = price of the product in period t

$S_{t,k}$ = sales contracted in period t to be delivered in period k.

The present value of the revenue expected by the monopolist for sales made in period t is

$$(2) \quad R_t = \sum_{k=t}^{n} a^{k-t} R_{t,k} = \sum_{k=t}^{n} a^{k-t} f_t\left(\sum_{k=t}^{n} S_{t,k}\right)\cdot S_{t,k}$$

where a denotes the appropriate discount factor.

When the monopolist cannot meet his current demand immediately, i.e., if $S_{t,k} > 0$, for $t < k \leq n$, he may deliver the balance in the future with a certain penalty. This penalty includes, for example, a penalty price reduction and a loss in good will. Let this penalty function be denoted by

$$(3) \quad \psi_{k-t} = \psi_{k-t}(S_{t,k}),\ t \leq k \leq n, \text{ where } \psi_o(S_{t,t}) \equiv 0.$$

Assuming that the monopolist's planning horizon is n periods, then the present value of the total profits expected by the monopolist for the entire planning horizon under certainty is

$$(4) \quad \pi = \sum_{t=1}^{n} \sum_{k=t}^{n} a^k f_t\left(\sum_{t=k}^{n} S_{t,k}\right)\cdot S_{t,k} - \sum_{t=1}^{n} \sum_{k=t}^{n} a^t \psi_{k-t}(S_{t,k})$$

$$- \sum_{t=1}^{n} a^t C(q_t) - \sum_{t=1}^{n} a^t \phi(I_t) - \sum_{t=1}^{n} a^t \left(\frac{\gamma}{2}\right) (q_t - q_{t-1})^2$$

where

$C(q_t)$ = the cost of producing q_t units

$\phi(I_t)$ = the cost associated with I_t units of inventory

$\frac{\gamma}{2}$ = the cost associated with changing the rate of production.

We shall assume that R_t is concave, that $\psi_{k-t}(S_{t,k})$, $C(q_t)$, and $\phi(I_t)$ are convex; and that all these functions are differentiable. We shall also assume that $S_{o,k}$ is given for k = 0, 1, ..., n, and that I_o and I_n are given. The monopolist's decision problem can now be expressed as the concave programming problem:

$$\text{Maximize } \pi = \sum_{t=1}^{n} \sum_{k=t}^{n} a^k f_t\left(\sum_{t=k}^{n} S_{t,k}\right) \cdot S_{t,k}$$

$$- \sum_{t=1}^{n} \sum_{k=t}^{n} a^t \psi_{k-t}(S_{t,k}) - \sum_{t=1}^{n} a^t C(q_t)$$

$$- \sum_{t=1}^{n} a^t \phi(I_t) - \sum_{t=1}^{n} a^t \frac{\gamma}{2} (q_t - q_{t-1})^2,$$

(5) subject to: $S_{t,k} \geqq 0$, $t = 1, \ldots, n$, $t \leqq k \leqq n$,

$q_t \geqq 0$, $t = 1, \ldots, n$,

$I_t \geqq 0$, $t = 1, \ldots, n-1$,

$$q_t + I_{t-1} - I_t - \sum_{\ell=0}^{t} S_{\ell,t} = 0,\ t = 1, \ldots, n.$$

The Equilibrium Conditions.

Our assumptions imply the profit function π is concave and differentiable; and, moreover, the constraint functions

$$q_t + I_{t-1} - I_t - \sum_{\ell=0}^{t} S_{\ell,t} \quad t = 1, \ldots, n,$$

are linear, and therefore concave and differentiable. Hence the necessary and sufficient conditions for the profit-maximizing problem represented by equation (5) can be obtained by applying the Kuhn-Tucker theorem[2] and finding the saddle point of the Lagrangean function associated with (5). The

Lagrangean function associated with (5) is given by:

$$(6)\quad L(\underset{\sim}{S}, \underset{\sim}{q}, \underset{\sim}{I}, \underset{\sim}{\lambda}) = \pi + \sum_{t=1}^{n} \lambda_t (q_t + I_{t-1} - I_t - \sum_{\ell=0}^{t} S_{\ell,t}),$$

where $\lambda_1, \ldots, \lambda_n$ are the Lagrangean multipliers.

According to the Kuhn-Tucker theorem, the saddle point $(\underset{\sim}{S}^o, \underset{\sim}{q}^o, \underset{\sim}{I}^o, \underset{\sim}{\lambda}^o)$ of the above Lagrangean function satisfies the conditions:

$$(7.1)\quad a^k R'_{t,k} - a^t \psi'_{k-t}(S^o_{t,k}) - \lambda_k \leqq 0,\ t = 1, \ldots, n,$$

$$t \leqq k \leqq n,$$

where

$$R'_{t,k} \equiv f_t(\sum_{k=t}^{n} S^o_{t,k}) + f'_t(\sum_{k=t}^{n} S^o_{t,k})\, S^o_{t,k},$$

$$(7.2)\quad -a^t C'(q^o_t) - a^t \gamma(q^o_t - q^o_{t-1}) + a^{t+1}\gamma(q^o_{t+1} - q^o_t) + \lambda_t \leqq 0$$

$$t = 1, \ldots, n,$$

$$(7.3)\quad -a^t \phi'(I^o_t) + \lambda_{t+1} - \lambda_t \leqq 0 \qquad t = 1, \ldots, n-1,$$

$$(8)\quad \sum_{t=1}^{n} \sum_{k=t}^{n} [a^k R'_{t,k} - a^t \psi_{k-t}(S^o_{t,k}) - \lambda_k] S^o_{t,k}$$

$$+ \sum_{t=1}^{n} [\lambda_t + a^{t+1}\gamma(q^o_{t+1} - q^o_t) - a^t \gamma(q^o_t - q^o_{t-1}) - a^t C'(q^o_t)] q^o_t$$

$$+ \sum_{t=1}^{n} [\lambda_{t+1} - \lambda_t - a^t \phi'(I^o_t)] = 0$$

$$(9)\quad q^o_t + I^o_{t-1} - I^o_t - \sum_{\ell=0}^{t} S^o_{\ell,t} = 0 \qquad t = 1, \ldots, n$$

$$(10)\quad S^o_{t,k} \geqq 0 \qquad t = 1, \ldots, n \quad t \leqq k \leqq n,$$

$$(11)\quad q^o_t \geqq 0 \qquad t = 1, \ldots, n,$$

$$(12)\quad I^o_t \geqq 0 \qquad t = 1, \ldots, n-1.$$

The conditions (7.1) through (8) state that if $S^o_{t,k} > 0$, $t \leqq k \leqq n$, $t = 0, 1, \ldots, n$, it will be the strict equality which will hold for (7.1); and, conversely, if the strict inequality holds in (7.1), $S^o_{t,k} = 0$. Similarly, if $q^o_t > 0$, equality holds for (7.2); while if the strict inequality holds in (7.2), $q^o_t = 0$, and so on. The conditions (9) through (12) restate the constraints imposed upon the monopolist.

Economic Interpretation of the Equilibrium Conditions.

In order that the monopolist's sales policy be profit-maximizing, conditions (7.1), (8), and (10) must be satisfied. These conditions can be restated as:

(13.1) if $S^o_{t,t} > 0$, then

(i) $R'_{t,t} = a^{-t}\lambda_t$ for $t = 1, \ldots, n$;

if $S^o_{t,k} > 0$, then

(ii) $R'_{t,k} - a^{-(k-t)}\psi'_{k-t}(S^o_{t,k}) = a^{-k}\lambda_k$ for

$t = 1, \ldots, n, \quad t \leqq k \leqq n$;

(13.2) if $S^o_{t,t} = 0$, then

(i) $R'_{t,t} \leqq a^{-t}\lambda_t$ for $t = 1, \ldots, n$;

if $S^o_{t,k} = 0$, then

(ii) $R'_{t,k} - a^{-(k-t)}\psi'_{k-t}(S^o_{t,k}) \leqq a^{-k}\lambda_k$ for

$t = 1, \ldots, n, \quad t \leqq k \leqq n$

Similarly, (7.2), (8), and (11) can be restated as:

(14.1) if $q^o_t > 0$, then

$$C'(q^o_t) + \gamma(q^o_t - q^o_{t-1}) - a\gamma(q^o_{t+1} - q^o_t) = a^{-t}\lambda_t,$$

for $t = 1, \ldots, n$;

(14.2) if $q^o_t = 0$, then

$$C'(q^o_t) + \gamma(q^o_t - q^o_{t-1}) - a\gamma(q^o_{t+1} - q^o_t) \geqq a^{-t}\lambda_t,$$

for $t = 1, \ldots, n$.

Combining (13.1) (i) and (14.1), we see that:

(15) if $S^o_{t,t} > 0$, $q^o_t > 0$, then

$$R'_{t,t} = C'(q^o_t) + \gamma(q^o_t - q^o_{t-1}) - a\gamma(q^o_{t+1} - q^o_t),$$

$$\text{for } t = 1, \ldots, n, \quad t \leqq k \leqq n.$$

Similarly, from (13.1) (i) and (ii), we have:

(16) if $S^o_{t,k} > 0$, $S^o_{k,k} > 0$,

$$a^{k-t}(R'_{t,k} - R'_{k,k}) = \psi'_{k-t}(S^o_{t,k})$$

$$\text{for } t = 1, \ldots, n, \quad t \leqq k \leqq n.$$

while from (15) and (16):

(17) if $S^o_{t,k} > 0$, $S^o_{k,k} > 0$, $q^o_k > 0$, we have:

$$a^{k-t}[R'_{t,k} - C'(q^o_k) - \gamma(q^o_k - q^o_{k-1}) + a\gamma(q^o_{k+1} - q^o_k)]$$

$$= \psi'_{k-t}(S^o_{t,k}) \quad \text{for } t = 1, \ldots, n, \quad t \leqq k \leqq n.$$

Equation (15) states that if the optimal quantity of sales made and delivered in period t is positive and the optimal production in period t is positive, then the marginal revenue derived from these sales must be equal to the sum of the marginal cost of production incurred in period t, and the net changes in the discounted marginal costs associated with changing the rate of production for the periods (t-1, t) and the periods (t+1, t). Equation (16) states that if the quantity of sales to be made in period t and delivered in period k is positive, $t < k \leqq n$, and $S^o_{k,k} > 0$, then the discounted marginal revenue derived from the sales contracted in period t and delivered in period k minus the discounted marginal revenue derived from sales contracted in period k for delivery in period k must be equal to the marginal penalty cost incurred for backlogged orders received in period t and honored in period k. A similar interpretation is derived from (17).

On the other hand, if the optimal quantity of sales to be made and delivered in period t is zero, the inequalities (13.2) (i) and (14) together state that the marginal revenue derived from sales contracted in period t and delivered in period t must be no greater than the sum of the marginal cost of production in period t and the net changes in the discounted marginal costs associated with changing the rate of production for the periods (t-1, t) and the periods (t +1, t). If the optimal quantity of sales to be made in period t and delivered in period k is zero, the inequalities (13.2)(ii) and (14) together state that the discounted marginal revenue derived from sales to be contracted in period t and to be delivered in period k minus the discounted marginal cost of production in period k and the discounted net changes in the marginal costs associated with changing the rate of production for the periods (t-1, t) and the periods (t+1, t) is no greater than the marginal penalty cost incurred for backlogged orders received in period t and honored in period k.

Conditions (7.3), (8) and (12) must be satisfied if the monopolist's inventory policy is to be optimal. The monopolist, in order to sell an extra unit of output in period (t+1), has two alternatives: (i) to produce the extra unit in period (t+1), or (ii) to produce the extra unit in period t, store it in period t and sell it in period (t+1). The opportunity cost of alternative (i) is the discounted marginal cost of production in period (t+1) plus the discounted net changes in marginal cost associated with changing the rate of production for the periods (t+2, t+1) and (t+1 , t); on the other hand, the opportunity cost of alternative (ii) is the marginal cost of carrying the extra output as inventory to be sold in period (t+1) plus the lost revenue from not selling the unit in period t. Conditions (7.3), (8) and (12) can be restated as:

(18.1) if $I_t^o > 0$, then

$$\phi'(I_t^o) + a^{-t}\lambda_t = a^{-t}\lambda_{t+1} \quad \text{for } t = 1, \ldots, n-1;$$

(18.2) if $I^o = 0$, then

$$\phi'(I_t^o) + a^{-t}\lambda_t \leqq a^{-t}\lambda_{t+1} \quad \text{for } t = 1, \ldots, n-1.$$

Combining (13.1)(i), (14.1), and (18.1), we have:

(19) if $I_t^o > 0$, $S_{t,t}^o > 0$, $q_{t+1}^o > 0$, then,

$$\phi'(I_t^o) + R'_{t,t} = a[C'(q_{t+1}^o) + \gamma(q_{t+1}^o - q_t^o) - a\gamma(q_{t+2}^o - q_{t+1}^o)] \quad \text{for } t = 1, \ldots, n-1;$$

while from (13.1)(i) with (18.1) we obtain:

(20) if $I_t^o > 0$, $S_{t,t}^o > 0$, $S_{t+1,\, t+1}^o > 0$, then

$$\phi'(I_t^o) = aR'_{t+1,\ t+1} - R'_{t,t} \quad \text{for } t = 1, \ldots, n-1.$$

Similarly from (14.1) and (18.1):

(21) if $I_t^o > 0$, $q_t^o > 0$, $q_{t+1}^o > 0$, then

$$\phi'(I_t^o) + C'(q_t^o) + \gamma(q_t^o - q_{t-1}^o) - a\gamma(q_{t+1}^o - q_t^o)$$

$$= a[C'(q_{t+1}^o) + \gamma(q_{t+1}^o - q_t^o) - a\gamma(q_{t+2}^o - q_{t+1}^o)]$$

for $t = 1, \ldots, n-1$.

Equation (19) states that if the quantity of inventory kept at the end of period t is positive and $S_{t,t}^o > 0$, $q_{t+1}^o > 0$, the optimal quantity of inventory must be such that the opportunity cost of alternative (i) is equal to the opportunity cost of (ii). Similarly, from (20), we see that if the quantity of inventory kept at the end of period t is positive, and $S_{t,t}^o > 0$, $S_{t+1,\ t+1}^o > 0$, the optimal quantity of inventory must be such that the marginal cost of carrying the inventory is equal to the difference between the discounted marginal revenue of sales contracted for and delivered in period t+1 and the marginal revenue of sales contracted for and delivered in period t. Finally, from (21), we see that if $I_t^o > 0$, and production is positive in both period t and period t+1, the marginal cost of carrying additional inventory plus the marginal cost of changing output in period t is equal to the discounted marginal cost of changing output in period t+1.

Assuming that $S_{o,k}^o$, $k = 0, \ldots, n$ and I_o^o and I_n^o are given, (7.1) through (12) determine the optimal quantity of sales to be made and delivered in period t, $S_{t,t}^o$, $t = 1, \ldots, n$, the optimal quantity of sales to be made in period t and to be delivered in period k, $S_{t,k}^o$, $k = t+1, \ldots, n$, the optimal production in period t, q_t^o, $t = 1, \ldots, n$, the optimal quantity of inventory at the end of period t, I_t^o, $t = 1, \ldots, n-1$ and the values of λ_t^o, $t = 0, \ldots, n$. With these variables determined, the equilibrium market price, P_t^o, is determined by the demand function in period t

(15) $P_t^o = f_t(\sum_{k=t}^{n} S_{t,k}^o)$ $t = 0, 1, \ldots, n.$

Conclusion.

We have presented a model which describes how the monopolist acting with certainty selects his inventory, sales, and production policies when facing a multi-period decision horizon. The model included provisions for sales contracted in one period but delivered in a later period and included the constraints that inventory, production, and sales were nonnegative.

FOOTNOTES

1. This research was supported by the National Science Foundation grant NSF GS-1491.

2. The Kuhn-Tucker Theorem [5]: Let the functions $f(y)$, $g_1(y), \ldots, g_m(y)$ be <u>concave</u> as well as differentiable for $y \geq 0$, where y is an n-dimensional vector. Then y^o is a solution of the maximization problem if and only if y^o and some λ^o, an m-dimensional vector, give a solution of the saddle value problem for the Lagrangean function

$$\phi(y, \lambda) = f(y) + \sum_{j=1}^{m} \lambda_j g_j(y),$$

provided that there exists no singularity on the boundary of the constraint set. A point (y^o, λ^o) is a saddle point of ϕ if

$$\text{(i)} \quad \phi_y^o \leq 0, \; \phi_y^{o\prime} y^o = 0, \; y^o \geq 0$$

$$\text{(ii)} \quad \phi_\lambda^o \geq 0, \; \lambda^{o\prime} \phi_\lambda^o = 0, \; \lambda^o \geq 0,$$

where ϕ_y^o is a (nx1) column vector

$$\phi_y^o = \begin{bmatrix} \dfrac{\partial\phi\ (y, \lambda)}{\partial y_1} \\ \cdot \\ \cdot \\ \cdot \\ \dfrac{\partial (y, \lambda)}{\partial y_n} \end{bmatrix}_{(y^o, \lambda^o)},$$

and ϕ_λ^o is a (mx1) column vector

$$\phi_\lambda^o = \begin{bmatrix} \dfrac{\partial\phi(y, \lambda)}{\partial \lambda_1} \\ \cdot \\ \cdot \\ \cdot \\ \dfrac{\partial (y, \lambda)}{\partial \lambda_m} \end{bmatrix}_{(y^o, \lambda^o)}.$$

If the constraints are equalities, that is

$$g_j(y_1, y_2, \ldots, y_n) = 0, \; j=1, \ldots, n$$

then, condition (ii) becomes

$$\phi_\lambda^o = 0.$$

REFERENCES

[1] Moses Abramowitz, An Approach to a Price Theory for a Changing Economy (New York: Columbia University Press, 1939), pp. 94-110.

[2] Kenneth Arrow, Samuel Karlin, and Herbert Scarf, Studies in the Mathematical Theory of Inventory Production (Stanford: Stanford University Press, 1958), pp. 3-36.

[3] G. C. Evans, Mathematical Introduction to Economics (New York: McGraw-Hill, 1930), pp. 50-61.

[4] Charles Holt, Franco Modigliani, John Muth and Herbert Simon, Planning Production Inventory and Work Force (Englewood Cliffs: Prentice-Hall, 1960).

[5] H. W. Kuhn, and A. W. Tucker, "Nonlinear Programming," Second Berkeley Symposium on Mathematical Statistics and Probability, ed. J. Neyman (Berkeley: University of California Press, 1951), pp. 481-492.

[6] E.S. Shaw, "Elements of a Theory of Inventory," Journal of Political Economy, XLVIII (August, 1940), pp. 465-485.

[7] Arthur Smithies, "The Maximization of Profits Over Time with Changing Cost and Demand Functions," Econometrica, VII (October, 1939), pp. 312-318.

[8] Gerhard Tintner, "Monopoly Over Time," Econometrica, V, No. 2 (April, 1937), pp. 160-170.

V.

DECISION THEORY

RISK AVERSION AND BIDDING THEORY

by

D. L. Hanson[1] and C. F. Menezes[2]
University of Missouri

1. Introduction and Summary

This paper provides a theory of individual bidding behavior in competitive sealed tender markets. The objective is to formulate a bidding model in terms of modern utility theory and to derive its basic properties. The model presented in this paper differs in important ways from the expected utility maximization bidding models independently formulated by Greismer, Levitan, and Shubik [4], and by Vernon Smith [7]. For one thing, both Greismer, et al, and Smith assume that the bidder maximizes expected utility of income. We assume that the bidder maximizes expected utility of wealth, the improvement being that utility is made to depend on both the size of the payoff and the level of initial wealth.

A second difference relates to the form of the utility function. Greismer, et al, implicitly assume that utility is a homogeneous linear function of income. It is well known that linear utility functions, whether or not homogeneous, imply "neutrality" to risk; i.e., the individual will be indifferent between engaging in any arbitrary bet and receiving the sure option equal to the actuarial value of the bet. This type of implied behavior seems hardly consistent with intuitive evidence or observation. On the other hand, Smith assumes in places that utility is quadratic in income. This form of utility function is very prevalent in the literature on decision making under uncertainty and has been the basis for the mean-variance approach to the theory of portfolio selection. However, the quadratic utility function implies implausible behavior. As K. J. Arrow [2] has noted, it violates the principle of decreasing absolute risk aversion. It also implies that eventually wealth has negative marginal utility, so that it would be better to throw some away. Because of the implausible behavioral implications of linear and quadratic utility functions, we assume that utility is a concave function of wealth, this being the most general form of utility function which characterizes risk averse behavior.

Finally, the emphasis in this paper on deriving the formal properties of the model and giving their economic interpretation is also quite unique and turns out to be rewarding. A natural relationship emerges between the principal properties of the model and certain tools and concepts which have been developed in some branches of mathematical statistics on the one hand, and in the theory of risk aversion on the other. Specifically, an investigation of the solution properties of the model reveals the important role of the "hazard rate" or "failure rate" function, a basic concept in the mathematical theory of reliability [3]. At the same time, we find that some of the more important comparative statics properties of the model depend on the behavior of two functions one of which has been independently established as a measure of risk aversion by K. J. Arrow [1], [2], and by J. W. Pratt [6]. As far as we know, the other function has not been interpreted as a measure of risk aversion in the literature prior to this. We establish it as such and relate it to the work of Arrow and to that of Pratt.

In Section 2 we formulate the bidding model and give conditions under which the model has a unique solution. The hazard rate function is interpreted and the expression determining the optimal bid is shown to have a straightforward behavioral meaning. Section 3 contains a summary of the work of Arrow and Pratt and some new results in the theory of risk aversion. Section 4 contains an investigation of the comparative statics properties of the model and their relation to the existence of risk aversion and the behavior of two measures of risk aversion. In contrast to the usual treatment of comparative statics in economic theory, both the direction of change in the optimal bid price and bounds on its magnitude are considered. The analysis is somewhat revealing of the nature of the substitutions between "safety" (as measured by the probability of success) and potential profits that underlie the bidder's response to a change in a specified parameter. In Section 5 we briefly outline possible directions in which the model can be extended.

2. An Expected Utility Maximization Bidding Model

This section deals with the structure and basic properties of an expected utility maximization bidding model for the sealed tender selling market. The institutional features of this market are outlined as follows: the market consists of a number of sellers competing for a single contract; each seller submits a single sealed bid; and the contract is awarded to the lowest bidder. Each seller's decision variable is his bid price. Every seller realizes that the higher his bid price the smaller the probability of getting the contract, but the larger the profits should he get it. Thus, each submitted bid reflects an attempt to balance probability and profit considerations.

To introduce the model we focus on a typical seller and denote his average cost by c. Because n, the size of the contract, is fixed in the type of market under consideration, $c = c(n)$ is a constant for any given bidding decision. Regarding the seller's beliefs about the bidding behavior of his opponents, we assume that the seller attaches a probability distribution $F(b)$ to the minimum of his competitor's bid prices b. We let p denote the bid submitted by the seller. He will get the contract if he submits a bid that is below all of the bids submitted by his competitors, that is, if $p < b$. The probability that his bid will be successful is

$$(2.1) \qquad \Pr\{p < b\} = 1 - F(p).$$

We assume that F is continuous, so that the probability of a "tie" between bids is zero; because F is continuous, what happens in case of a tie does not affect the seller's probability of getting the contract.

The bidding situation facing the seller is equivalent to choosing p in a lottery which offers a prize of $n(p - c)$ with probability $1 - F(p)$ and a prize of zero with probability $F(p)$. Note that the prize zero corresponds to an unsuccessful bid. The utility of a prize depends on its size and on the seller's initial wealth w. In particular, the utility of the prize zero is $u(w)$. The seller, being a von Neumann-Morgenstern expected utility maximizer, chooses p so as to maximize his expected utility $E(p;c,w,n)$, where

$$(2.2) \qquad E(p;c,w,n) \equiv [1 - F(p)]u[n(p - c) + w] + F(p)u(w).$$

A rearrangement of terms reduces this to the more convenient form

$$(2.3) \qquad E(p;c,w,n) \equiv [1 - F(p)]\,[u\{n(p - c) + w\} - u(w)] + u(w).$$

Any p which maximizes $E(p;c,w,n) \equiv E(p)$ for fixed values of the parameters c,w, and n will be called a solution of the model or an optimal bid.

Our immediate concern is whether the model has a solution, and if so, whether the solution is unique. The two theorems presented below give conditions under which there exists an optimal bid and conditions under which that optimal bid is unique. To state the theorems we need to define the number

$$(2.4) \qquad \lambda = \min\{p : F(p) = 1\}.$$

From the definition of λ it follows that if the seller submits a bid greater than or equal to λ then one of his opponents will get the contract, so $E(p) = u(w)$ for all $p \geq \lambda$. If, on the other hand, the seller's bid p is less than or equal to his unit cost c, then he has nothing to gain even if he wins the contract since $E(p) \leq u(w)$ for all $p \leq c$. Thus, for a bid p to be "reasonable," it must satisfy $c < p$

and $p < \lambda$. In order that a "reasonable" bid be available to the seller we require that $c < \lambda$. We note from (2.3) that every bid in the interval (c, λ) gives a higher expected utility $E(p)$ than $u(w)$. We are now in a position to state our two theorems on the existence and uniqueness of an optimal bid.

Theorem 1[3]: (Existence Theorem) If

(A1) $c < \lambda < \infty$,
(A2) u is continuous and strictly increasing, and
(A3) F is continuous (with or without a density),

then there exists an optimal bid (not necessarily unique) in the interval (c, λ).

Proof: Under assumptions (A1), (A2), and (A3) we see that $E(p) = [1-F(p)]\,[u\{n(p-c) + w\} - u(w)] + u(w)$ is a continuous function of p on the compact set $[c, \lambda]$, that $E(p) > u(w)$ for all p in (c, λ), and that $E(c) = E(\lambda) = u(w)$. Thus there exists a number p_o (not necessarily unique) in $[c, \lambda]$ such that $E(p_o) = \max\{E(p) \mid c \le p \le \lambda\}$, and since $E(p) > u(w) = E(c) = E(\lambda)$ for all p in (c, λ), it follows that $p_o \neq c$ and $p_o \neq \lambda$.

Having given conditions under which there exists an optimal bid, we now show that under suitable assumptions this optimal bid is unique. Note that in the following theorem assumptions (A2a) and (A3a) imply (A2) and (A3) of Theorem 1 respectively.

Theorem 2: (Uniqueness theorem) Suppose:

(A1) $c < \lambda < \infty$;
(A2a) u is continuous, strictly increasing, and concave;
(A3a) F is absolutely continuous with density f, and the hazard rate function $f(p)/[1-F(p)]$ is a nondecreasing function of p.

Then there is a unique optimal bid p_o in the interval (c, λ), and for p in (c, λ), the expression

$$(2.5) \qquad \frac{nu'[n(p - c) + w]}{u[n(p - c) + w] - u(w)} - \frac{f(p)}{1-F(p)}$$

is positive for $p < p_o$ and negative for $p > p_o$. In (2.5), the marginal utility function u' can be taken to be the right derivative of u, that is

$$u'(t) = \lim_{h \downarrow 0} \frac{u(t + h) - u(t)}{h}$$

If $f(p)$ and $u'[n(p - c) + w]$ are continuous for p in (c, λ), then p_o is the unique zero in (c, λ) of expression

(2.5).

Proof:

Because of the assumptions made about u and f,

$$E(p) + [1 - F(p)][u\{n(p - c) + w\} - u(w)] + u(w)$$

has a right derivative $D^+(E(p))$ almost everywhere and is the integral of this right derivative. (We can consider f to be the right derivative of F.)

We have
$$D^+(E(p)) = -f(p)\,[u\{n(p-c)+w\} - u(w)] + [1-F(p)]\,nu'[n(p-c)+w] \equiv (a) \cdot (b)$$

where

$$a \equiv [1-F(p)][u\{n(p-c) + w\} - u(w)]$$

and

$$b \equiv \frac{nu'[n(p-c) + w]}{u[n(p-c) + w] - u(w)} - \frac{f(p)}{1-F(p)}$$

and $u'(t) = D^+(u(t))$ is the marginal utility. From the definition of λ we see that $[1-F(p)] > 0$ for all $p < \lambda$, and since u is strictly increasing, $u\{n(p-c) + w\} - u(w) > 0$ for $p > c$. Thus the expression (a) is positive for $c < p < \lambda$.

We will show that there exists a unique p_o in the interval (c, λ) such that the expression (b) is positive for $p < p_o$ and negative for $p > p_o$. Then, for p in (c, λ), this would make $D^+(E(p))$ positive for $p < p_o$ and negative for $p > p_o$ so that $E(p)$ is strictly increasing for $p < p_o$ and strictly decreasing for $p > p_o$, and thus $E(p)$ has a unique maximum at $p = p_o$.

We note that:

(1) $u'[n(p-c) + w]$ is positive and non-increasing in p since u is concave and strictly increasing;

(2) $\lim_{p\to c} u[n(p-c) + w] - u(w) = 0$;

(3) $u[n(p-c) + w] - u(w)$ is strictly increasing in p;

so that

(4) $\dfrac{u'[n(p-c) + w]}{u[n(p-c) + w] - u(w)}$ is strictly decreasing in p for $c < p$;

and

(5) $$\lim_{p\downarrow c} \frac{u'[n(p-c) + w]}{u[n(p-c) + w] - u(w)} = \infty.$$

By assumption, $\dfrac{f(p)}{1-F(p)}$ is non-decreasing, so expression (b) is strictly decreasing in p. If $\lim_{p\downarrow c} (b) > 0$ and $\lim_{p\uparrow\lambda} (b) < 0$, then the desired p_o exists. But $\lim_{p \downarrow c} \frac{f(p)}{1-F(p)}$ is non-negative and finite, so it follows from (5) that $\lim_{p \downarrow c}(b) = +\infty > 0$. "Obviously" $\lim_{p \uparrow \lambda} \frac{f(p)}{1-F(p)} > 0$.

Since $\lambda < \infty$,

$$0 = \frac{1-F(\lambda)}{1-F(0)} = e^{\log (1-F(\lambda)) - \log (1-F(0))}$$

$$= \exp \int_0^\lambda \frac{d}{dt} \log (1-F(t))dt$$

$$= \exp \left[-\int_0^\lambda \frac{f(t)}{1-F(t)} dt \right]$$

so that $\int_0^\lambda \frac{f(t)}{1-F(t)} dt = \infty$. Since $\lambda < \infty$ and $\frac{f(t)}{1-F(t)}$ is non-decreasing we must have $\lim_{t \uparrow \lambda} \frac{f(t)}{1-F(t)} = \infty$. Thus we see that $\lim_{p \uparrow \lambda}(b) = -\infty < 0$. Hence conditions for the desired p_o to exist are satisfied.

If $u'(n(p-c) + w)$ and $f(p)$ are continuous for p in (c, λ), then expression (b) is continuous for p in (c, λ) and must assume the value zero somewhere in the interval by the mean value theorem. Since (b) is either positive or negative for each $p \neq p_o$ in (c, λ), it follows that p_o is the unique zero of expression (b) in (c, λ).

In the remainder of this section we demonstrate that the expression (2.5) determining the optimal bid has a meaningful economic interpretation. To show this we define

$$H(p) \equiv \frac{f(p)}{1-F(p)} \quad \text{and} \quad G(p) \equiv \frac{nu'[n(p-c) + w]}{u[n(p-c) + w] - u(w)} .$$

G(p) can be thought of as the rate of proportionate change in utility of profits as a function of the bid price p. Note that because of the assumptions about u, G(p) is a strictly decreasing function of p. The function H plays an important role in many disciplines, particularly actuarial science and the mathematical theory of reliability, and is usually called the "hazard rate" or the "failure rate." In the context of our model, H(p)dp approximately represents the probability that a bid of size p + dp would be unsuccessful given that a bid of size p would have been successful. Thus H(p) is the rate of proportionate increase in the probability of <u>losing</u> the contract as a function of p. It seems natural to assume that H(p) is a non-decreasing function of p. This is equivalent to assuming that the conditional probability that the minimum of the opponents' bids is at least p + dp given that it is at least p is a non-increasing function of p. (Intuitively, one might think of this, when applied to an individual, as saying that if a person is contemplating making a bid of p, then he is more likely to raise it an amount dp if p is a low bid than if p is a high bid.)

The above definitions enable us to rewrite expression (2.5) as G(p) - H(p). From Theorem 2 we know there exists a unique optimal bid p_o in the interval (c, λ) such that $G(p) \gtrless H(p)$ when $p \lessgtr p_o$. Thus for bids less (greater) than p_o the rate of proportionate increase in the utility of profits exceeds (falls short of) the rate of proportionate increase in the probability of losing the contract, and expected utility can be increased by raising (lowering) the bid. Theorem 2 further states that if the marginal utility $u'[n(p-c) + w]$ and the probability density f(p) are continuous functions of p in the interval (c, λ), then the optimal bid p_o is the unique solution of the equation G(p) = H(p). That is, $G(p_o) = H(p_o)$ and $G(p) \gtrless H(p)$ when $p \lessgtr p_o$ Thus when marginal utility and the probability denisty are continuous functions of p, expected utility is maximized and the optimal bid is determined by equating the rate of proportionate increase in the utility of profits to the rate of proportionate increase in the probability of losing the contract. This is an intuitively meaningful result and is not immediately obvious from an examination of the structure of the model. Figure 1 presents a graphic illustration of the solution of the equation G(p) = H(p). Figure 2 indicates what can happen when the hazard rate function is discontinuous. The same sort of thing can happen when G(p) instead of H(p) is discontinuous. For these cases p_o is the unique value of p for which the expression G(p) - H(p) changes sign.

3. Risk Aversion and its Measurement

Let u be a utility function for wealth with marginal utility strictly positive. The purpose of this section is to demonstrate that the functions $A(t) = -u''(t)/u'(t)$ and $P(t; w) = -tu''(t+w)/u'(t+w)$ for each fixed w can be interpreted as two measures of risk aversion. We set forth the economic meanings of A and P here because, as will be shown later, some important comparative statics properties of the bidding model can be determined from the behavior of these two functions.

We begin by defining risk aversion. An individual is a risk averter if for any arbitrary risk he prefers the

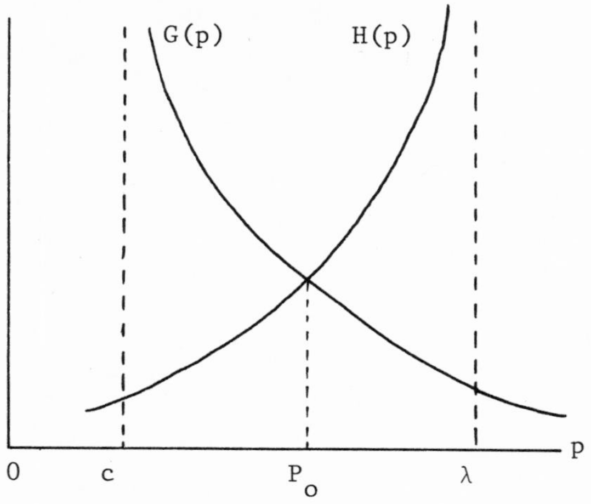

Figure 1

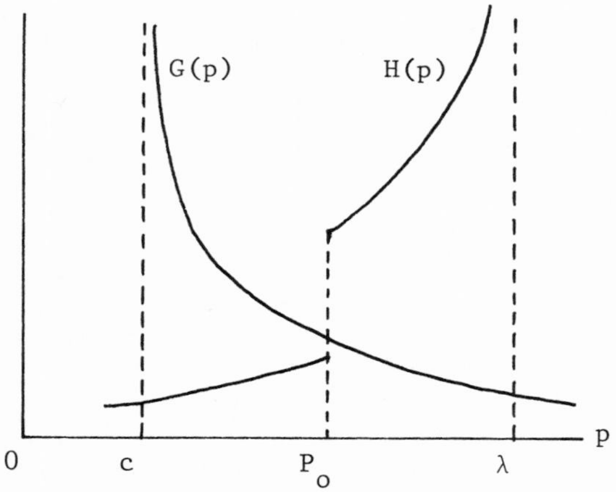

Figure 2

non-random amount equal to the actuarial value of the risk to the risk itself. Let w be his initial wealth and z, a random variable, be his income. He is risk averse if

(3.1) $$u[w + E(z)] > E[u(w+z)]$$

where E is the expectation operator. A necessary and sufficient condition for (3.1) to hold for all values of w and all risks z is that the utility of wealth function u be strictly concave, or equivalently that it be the integral of a strictly decreasing marginal utility of wealth function u'. (u' may be assumed to be either the right or the left derivative of u if such is convenient.) This guarantees

(3.2) $u''(t) \leq 0$ for all $t \geq 0$

and a little more.

While (3.2) indicates the existence of (a weak form of) risk aversion, the magnitude of $u''(t)$ has in itself no meaning. The reason is that if u is a von Neumann-Morgenstern utility function, then the preference ordering represented by $E(u)$ does not change when the utility function u is replaced by the utility function $cu + b$ if c is positive. However, such transformations change the magnitude of $u''(t)$, although they do not alter its sign. Thus the sign but not the magnitude of $u''(t)$ is significant.

The foregoing suggests that a measure of risk aversion should in some sense measure the concavity of u and should remain invariant under positive linear transformations of the utility function. The functions $A(t) = -u''(t)/u'(t)$ and $P(t;w) = -tu''(t+w)/u'(t+w)$ fulfill both requirements and hence qualify as measures of risk aversion. We will show that these measures have straightforward behavioral interpretations.

A as a Measure of Risk Aversion

A is called absolute risk aversion. Its role as a measure of risk aversion was discovered independently by Kenneth J. Arrow [1], [2], and by John W. Pratt [6]. Pratt interprets A in terms of the risk permium π defined by the equation

$$u[w + E(z) - \pi] = E[u(w+z)].$$

π can be regarded as the maximum amount, beyond the negative of the expected value of the risk itself, which an individual with wealth equal to w would pay to insure against the risk z. Pratt [5, page 125] indicates that under suitable regularity conditions

(3.3) $$\pi = (\sigma^2/2)A(w + E(z)) + o(\sigma^2)$$

where σ^2 is the variance of z. (We use $o(t)$ to denote any function which is of smaller order of magnitude than t near o. In particular, $o(\sigma^2)/\sigma^2 \to 0$ as $\sigma^2 \to 0$.) Thus, when σ^2 is small, $\pi \simeq (\sigma^2/2)A(w+E(z))$. It follows that $A(w)$ is about twice the risk premium per unit of variance for "small" actuarially neutral ($E(z) = 0$) risks. Note that in view of (3.2), the risk premium is non-negative.

Still another interpretation of A has been provided by Arrow [2, pages 33 and 34.] He considers a risk which involves winning or losing an amount h with probabilities p and $1 - p$, respectively. Given the amount of the bet h and the initial wealth w, consider the probability p' such that the individual is just indifferent between accepting and rejecting the bet. The value of p' is determined from the equation

$$u(w) = p'u(w+h) + (1-p')u(w-h)$$

using finite Taylor's series expansions of u(w+h) and u(w-h) about w. Under suitable regularity conditions on u

$$p' = \frac{1}{2} + \frac{h}{4}A(w) + o(h).$$

Thus for sufficiently small values of h,

$$p' \simeq \frac{1}{2} + \frac{h}{4}A(w). \tag{3.4}$$

In view of (3.2), $p' \geq \frac{1}{2}$. It follows that absolute risk aversion measures the individual's demand for more-than-fair odds.

A(w) may increase, decrease, or remain constant with increasing wealth. A may be non-monotone for some utility functions and may be bounded or unbounded. Decreasing (increasing) absolute risk aversion means that the individual will pay less (more) for insurance against a given risk as his wealth increases; alternatively, that the size of favorable odds required to stake a given amount diminishes (increases) with increasing wealth.

R as a Measure of Risk Aversion

$P(t; w) = -tu''(t+w)/u'(t+w)$ has so far as we know not appeared in the literature prior to this. However, it appears to be a variant of the measure $R(t) = -tu''(t)/u'(t)$, which is called relative risk aversion by Arrow and proportional risk aversion by Pratt. The comparative statics of the bidding model do not depend on the behavior of R, but since Arrow and Pratt have provided an interpretation for R, we look at this measure in order to obtain a clue as to how to interpret P.

The interpretation of R follows quite easily from that of A. Suppose the risk premium and the risk itself are measured not in absolute terms but as proportions of initial wealth. Let $\pi^o = \pi/w$ and $z^o = z/w$ denote the proportional risk premium and the proportional risk, respectively. Then, as Pratt shows, if z^o is actuarially neutral (i.e., if $E(z^o) = 0$),

$$\pi^o = (\sigma^2/2)R(w) + o(\sigma^2),$$

where σ^2 is now the variance of z^o. A similar interpretation is provided by Arrow. Let $h = h^o w$, so that h^o is the fraction of wealth at stake. Then, Arrow shows that

$$p' = \frac{1}{2} + \frac{h^o}{4}R(w) + o(h^o).$$

Relative risk aversion may increase, decrease, or remain constant with increasing wealth. Increasing (decreasing) relative risk aversion means that the proportion of wealth spent for insurance increases (decreases) when wealth and risk are increased in the same proportion; alternatively, that the size of favorable odds demanded increases (decreases) when wealth and bet size are increased in the same proportion.

P as a Measure of Risk Aversion

We are now in a position to interpret the function P as a measure of risk aversion. Suppose the individual's wealth w is increased by an arbitrary amount t. Now measure the risk premium and the risk itself as proportions of t. Let $\bar{\pi} = \pi/t$ and $\bar{z} = z/t$ denote the risk premium and the risk respectively, each measured as a proportion of the increase in wealth. Under suitable regularity conditions it can be shown that

$$\bar{\pi} = \frac{\sigma^2}{2(1+E(\bar{z}))} P[t(1+E(\bar{z}));w] + o(\sigma^2) \tag{3.5}$$

where σ^2 is the variance of $\bar{z}$. If $E(\bar{z}) = 0$ then $\bar{\pi} \simeq (\sigma^2/2)P(t;w)$.

The measure P can also be interpreted in terms of the more-than-fair odds concept. Let $h = \bar{h}t$, so that $\bar{h}$ is the fraction of additional wealth that is at stake. Then it is easy to show that

$$p' = \frac{1}{2} + \frac{\bar{h}}{4} P(t;w) + o(\bar{h}). \tag{3.6}$$

At a formal level the measures R and P appear to be quite similar. However, they are associated with two different types of betting situation. Relative risk aversion is relevant when the ratio of the bet size to wealth is being considered. The function P is important when the ratio of the bet size to additional wealth is under consideration. Note that if the ratio of the bet size to wealth remains constant then the ratio of the bet size to additional wealth decreases as wealth increases. Conversely, if the ratio of the bet size to additional wealth is kept constant then the ratio of the bet size to wealth must increase as wealth increases.

The following propositions and discussion are intended to provide some insight into the behavior of P. For the remainder of this section we assume that u is non-decreasing, that u is concave (but not necessarily strictly concave), that u has a continuous first derivative u', and that u' is the integral of some function u" (possibly the regular derivative, the right derivative, or the left derivative of u').

Proposition 1: Fix w. If P(t;w) is non-increasing in t for t in some interval $(0, t_o)$ with $t_o > 0$, then either $P(t;w) = 0$ (and consequently $u''(t+w) \stackrel{\circ}{=} 0$ for $0 < t < t_o$) or else $w = 0$.

Proof: $P(t;w)$ is non-negative. Assume it is non-increasing and not identically zero for $0 < t < t_o$. Then $\lim_{t \downarrow 0} P(t;w) > 0$.

Now u' is non-increasing and non-negative and can't be identically zero on $(0, t_o)$ if $P(t;w)$ is to make sense.

Thus we find $a > 0$, $b > 0$ such that for $0 < t \leq b$ we have $P(t,w) > a$ and $u'(t+w) > a$. Then for $0 < t \leq b$

$$u''(t+w) < -\frac{a}{t}u'(t+w) < -\frac{a^2}{t}$$

and integrating gives

$$u'(w+b) - u'(w) < \int_0^b (a^2/t)dt = -\infty$$

so that $u'(w) = +\infty$. Because u' is non-increasing this can happen only when $w = 0$ and then only for some utility functions.

Proposition 2: Fix $w > 0$ and suppose $t_o > 0$. If $P(t; w)$ is monotone (strictly monotone) in t for $0 < t < t_o$, then it is non-decreasing (strictly increasing) there.

Proof: Suppose $P(t;w)$ is non-increasing for $0 < t < t_o$. Then by Proposition 1 we have $P(t;w) = 0$ for $0 < t < t_o$. Thus $P(t;w)$ can't be strictly decreasing for $0 < t < t_o$, and if it is non-increasing it is in fact also non-decreasing since it is a constant.

These two propositions indicate that if $w > 0$ and we for some reason believe $P(w;t)$ to be monotone in t, then we must believe either that $P(w;t)$ is strictly increasing in t or that $u(t)$ is linear. If we require strict concavity of u, then we can rule out the latter. Unfortunately, fluctuations are possible. It is possible to construct a bounded or unbounded utility function with a continuous second derivative for which P is not monotone or for which R is not monotone. It would thus seem that any assumptions about the monotonicity of P must be made on the basis of either intuitive of empirical considerations.

We conclude this section with the following observation:

Proposition 3: If either $A(t)$ or $R(t)$ is non-decreasing then either $u''(t) \equiv 0$ (so that u is linear), or else $P(t;w)$ is a strictly increasing function of t for each fixed w.

4. Comparative Statics of the Bidding Model

Recall that in Section 2 an optimal bid price was defined as any value of p which maximizes expected utility $E(p;c,w,n)$ for given values of the parameters c, w, and n. It was demonstrated that under economically meaningful conditions there exists a unique optimal bid price p_o. The purpose of this section is the investigation of the change in the optimal bid price p_o caused by independent variations in the three parameters c, w, and n. Both the direction of change of p_o and bounds on its magnitude are of interest.

Throughout this section we will assume, unless specifically stated otherwise, that changes in the parameters c, w, and n will not cause the seller to revise his estimate of the bidding behavior of his competitors. Thus the probability distribution F(p), and hence the hazard rate function H(p), are assumed fixed under changes in c, w, and n. This is, of course, a reasonable assumption for changes in w, and also for changes in c that are internal to the firm. The assumption might be somewhat unrealistic for a change in n since such a change directly affects all firms competing for the contract. Later in this section we will comment on how our analysis must be extended in order to take into account revisions in the seller's estimate of the bidding behavior of his competitors.

The Effect on the Optimal Bid Price of a Change in Average Cost

The results of this subsection are summarized in the following theorem.

Theorem 3: Suppose conditions (A1), (A2a), and (A3a) are satisfied and that u' and f are the right derivatives of u and F respectively. If the average cost c is raised (lowered) by an amount Δc, then the new optimal bid price p_1 satisfies the inequalities

(4.1) $p_o \le p_1 \le p_o + \Delta c \qquad (p_o \ge p_1 \ge p_o - \Delta c)$

where p_o is the original optimal bid. If u' and f are continuous, then

(4.2) $p_o < p_1 \qquad (p_o > p_1)$.

If, in addition, the hazard rate function is strictly increasing then

(4.3) $p_1 < p_o + \Delta c \qquad (p_1 > p_o - \Delta c)$.

Proof:

Note that the basic assumptions used in this theorem are the same ones that were used in Theorem 2. We are thus guaranteed the existence and uniqueness of optimal bids for the various values of c under consideration provided only that they are all less than λ (see (2.4)).

Earlier we defined and interpreted the functions

$G(p) = \dfrac{nu'[n(p-c) + w]}{u[n(p-c) + w] - u(w)}$ and $H(p) = \dfrac{f(p)}{1-F(p)}$. From

Theorems 1 and 2 we know that, for fixed c, w, and n, the expected utility $E(p;c, w, n)$ has its unique maximum at p_o, the point where the expression $G(p) - H(p)$ changes sign. Equivalently, p_o is the "crossover point" of the graphs of $G(p)$ and $H(p)$ (see Figures 1 and 2). One might therefore expect to obtain some information about the direction of change in p_o from the shifts in the graphs of $G(p)$ and $H(p)$ due to a change in the parameter c.

By assumption the graph of $H(p)$ does not change when c changes. However, for fixed p and $c < p$, we see that $u'[n(p-c) + w]$ is non-decreasing in c and $u[n(p-c) + w]$ is strictly decreasing in c, so that $G(p) = \dfrac{nu'[n(p-c)+w]}{u[n(p-c)+w]-u(w)}$ is a strictly increasing function of c. This argument shows that the whole graph of $G(p)$ is raised when c increases and lowered when c decreases. (Refer back to Figures 1 and 2 to visualize this.) Thus p_o is a non-decreasing function of c. p_o is a strictly increasing function of c if both f and u' are continuous so that G and H are continuous. The various cases provide the proper inequalities between p_o and p_1.

Now let $t = p - c$ so that $G(t+c) = \dfrac{nu'(nt+w)}{u(nt+w) - u(w)}$ and $H(t+c) = \dfrac{f(t+c)}{1-F(t+c)}$. For fixed c, the "crossover point" t_o of the graphs of $G(t+c)$ and $H(t+c)$ is just $t_o = p_o - c$. The function $G(t+c)$ (and therefore its graph) does not depend on c, while $H(t+c)$ is non-decreasing in c for each fixed t. It follows (see Figure 3) that t_o is a non-increasing function of c. (t_o is a strictly decreasing function of c if H is strictly increasing and if both u' and f are continuous - - so that G and H are continuous.) In particular, if t_1 and p_1 are the "crossover points" corresponding to an average cost of $c + \Delta c$, then $p_1 - (c + \Delta c) = t_1 \leq t_o = p_o - c$ if $\Delta c > 0$, or equivalently, $p_1 \leq p_o + \Delta c$. (We get strict inequality if t_o is a strictly decreasing function of c.) The other inequalities follow by considering a decrease in c by an amount Δc.

The conclusions of this theorem are intuitively quite appealing. Suppose average cost is increased by an amount Δc. If the bid price is left unchanged, potential average profit will decline from $(p_o - c)$ to $(p_o - c - \Delta c)$. Note that the probability of getting this smaller profit is still $1 - F(p_o)$. A smaller profit is now associated with the former probability of success, and the theorem tells us that the bidder "trades off" some of his probability of success for an increase in his potential profit. He therefore raises his bid price. However, since the bidder is risk averse, his willingness to "trade off" probability

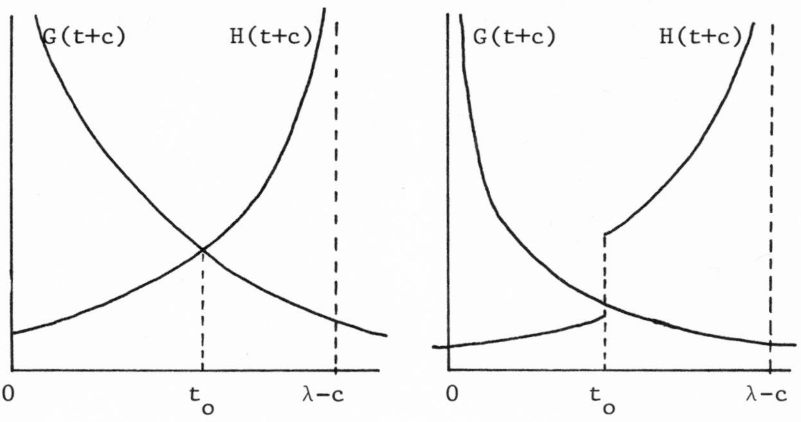

Figure 3

of success for potential profit declines as potential profit increases and probability of success decreases. In particular, the theorem tells us that he is totally unwilling to continue this type of "trade off" once he has obtained his old level of potential average profit.

The Effect on the Optimal Bid Price of a Change in Initial Wealth

The result of this subsection depends on an assumed monotonicity of the absolute risk aversion function A. Our result gives the direction of change in the bid price due to a change in initial wealth, but gives no bound on this change.

Theorem 4: Suppose conditions (A1), (A3a),

(A2b) u is strictly increasing, concave, and continuously differentiable,

(A4) u' is right differentiable and is the integral of its right derivative u",

are satisfied, and that c and n are fixed. If the bidder's initial wealth is raised (lowered), and if the function A is non-increasing, then the new optimal bid price p_1 satisfies the inequality

(4.4) $$p_o \leq p_1 \qquad (p_o \geq p_1).$$

If, in addition, f is continuous and A is strictly decreasing, then the inequalities above are strict. If A is non-decreasing (strictly increasing) instead of non-increasing (strictly decreasing), then the inequalities are reversed.

Proof:

We begin by finding an equivalent expression for G(p). Setting $\theta = n(p - c)$, we have

$$G(p) = \frac{1}{p - c} \cdot \frac{\theta u'(\theta+w)}{u(\theta+w) - u(w)} = \frac{1}{p - c} \cdot \frac{\theta u'(\theta+w)}{\int_0^\theta u'(t+w)\,dt}$$

$$= \{(p-c) \int_0^1 [u'(\theta\tau+w)/u'(\theta+w)]d\tau\}^{-1}$$

where we have made the change of variables $t = \theta\tau$. Using the fact that $a/b = \exp(\log a - \log b)$ when a and b are positive, we obtain

$$G(p) = [(p-c) \int_0^1 \exp(\log u'(\theta\tau+w) - \log u'(\theta+w))d\tau]^{-1}$$

$$= [(p-c) \int_0^1 \exp(\int_\theta^{\theta\tau} \frac{d}{dx}\log u'(x+w)dx)d\tau]^{-1}$$

$$= [(p-c) \int_0^1 \exp(\int_\theta^{\theta\tau} -A(x+w)dx)d\tau]^{-1}$$

$$= [(p-c) \int_0^1 \exp(\theta\int_\tau^1 A(\theta y+w)dy)d\tau]^{-1}$$

where we have made the change of variables $x = \theta y$, and have noted that the reversal of the limits of integration changes the sign of the integral. Our final expression for G(p) is

$$(4.5) \qquad G(p) = [(p-c) \int_0^1 \exp[n(p-c) \int_\tau^1 A(ny(p-c)+w)dy]d\tau]^{-1}$$

By hypothesis, H is not affected by changes in w. However, from (4.5) we see that if A is non-increasing (strictly decreasing, non-decreasing, strictly increasing), then G(p) is a non-decreasing (strictly increasing, non-increasing, strictly decreasing) function of w for each fixed p.

The remainder of the proof uses the arguments of Theorem 3 and will be omitted.

Theorem 4 indicates the relationship between the behavior of the absolute risk aversion function A and the direction of change in the bid price due to a change in initial wealth. It might be helpful to look at this result in intuitive terms. Suppose that A decreases with wealth, i.e., an individual's willingness to engage in a bet, as measured either by the risk premium or by the favorable odds demanded, increases with wealth. This means that as his wealth increases, the bidder raises his bid price (consequently reducing 1 - F(p), his probability of getting the contract) in order to increase potential (and, incidentally, also expected) profit. The opposite type of argument can be used to explain the claim of Theorem 4 that the bid price decreases if A increases with wealth.

Whether A increases or decreases with wealth would seem to be an empirical rather than a theoretical issue. On the basis of intuitive evidence and casual observation we are inclined to accept Arrow's [2, page 35] hypothesis that absolute risk aversion decreases with wealth.

The Effect on the Optimal Bid Price of a Change in Contract Size

The first theorem of this subsection gives the direction of change of the optimal bid price. It depends on an assumed monotonicity of the function $P(t; w)$ introduced at the beginning of section 3. (Recall that proposition 2 of that section states that if $P(t; w)$ is monotone in t, then it must be non-decreasing.) Our other theorem provides a bound on this change.

Theorem 5: Suppose conditions (A1), (A2b), (A3a), and (A4) are satisfied and that c and w are fixed. If the contract size is increased (decreased), and if the function $P(t; w)$ is non-decreasing in t, then the new optimal bid price p_1 satisfies the inequality

$$(4.6) \qquad p_o \geq p_1 \qquad\qquad (p_o \leq p_1).$$

If, in addition, f is continuous and $P(t; w)$ is a strictly increasing function of t, then the inequalities above are strict.

Proof:

From (4.5) and the definitions of A and P we see that

$$(4.7) \qquad G(p) = [(p-c) \int_0^1 \exp[\int_\tau^1 (1/y)P(n(p-c)y;w)dy]d\tau]^{-1}$$

The proof of this theorm is essentially a repetition of the proof of theorem 4 using (4.7), P, and n instead of (4.5), A, and w. We omit it.

Under the assumption that $P(t; w)$ is a non-decreasing function of t, one's intuition agrees with the theorem's description of the bidder's behavior. If the contract size is increased from n to $n + \Delta n$, then both the bidder's potential profit and his expected profit are multiplied by a factor of $(n + \Delta n)/n$ if he maintains his old bid price p_o (and if his opponents' bidding behavior is unchanged). It is intuitively reasonable that he should "trade off" some of his additional potential profit (and expected profit) for some extra probability of success (extra safety). Thus he should lower his bid price.

Note that Theorem 5 does not indicate how much of his additional potential profit the bidder will "trade off" for an increase in his probability of success. The following theorem bounds this "trade off."

Theorem 6: Suppose conditions (A1), (A2a), and (A3a) are satisfied, that c and w are fixed, and that u' and f are the right derivatives of u and F respectively. Then potential profit is a non-decreasing function of n. In particular, if the contract size n is raised (lowered) by an amount Δn, then the new optimal bid price p_1 satisfies the inequality

$$(4.8) \quad p_1 \geq p_o - \frac{\Delta n}{n+\Delta n}(p_o - c) \qquad \left(p_1 \leq p_o + \frac{\Delta n}{n+\Delta n}(p_o - c)\right).$$

If, in addition, u' and f are continuous, then the inequalities above are strict.

Proof:

The proof of this theorem is quite similar to the proof of the second part of Theorem 3. We let $s = n(p-c)$ so that

$$G\left(\frac{s}{n} + c\right) = \frac{nu'(s+w)}{u(s+w)-u(w)} \quad \text{and} \quad H\left(\frac{s}{n} + c\right) = \frac{f\left(\frac{s}{n} + c\right)}{1-F\left(\frac{s}{n} + c\right)}.$$

For fixed c and n, the "crossover point" s_o of the graphs of $G(\frac{s}{n} + c)$ and $H(\frac{s}{n} + c)$ as functions of s is just $n(p_o - c)$.

For each fixed s we see that $G(\frac{s}{n} + c)$ is a strictly increasing function of n, and $H(\frac{s}{n} + c)$ is a non-increasing function of n since H(t) is non-increasing in t. Thus s_o is a non-decreasing function of n (and is strictly increasing if both u' and f are continuous). The inequalities are an immediate consequence of this.

Again, the results of this theorem are quite reasonable. One would expect at least as large a total potential profit on a large order as on a small order even if the profit per unit were smaller.

Theorems 5 and 6 together indicate that if the contract size n is raised by an amount Δn, then the new optimal bid price p_1 satisfies the inequalities

$$(4.9) \qquad p_o - \frac{\Delta n}{n+\Delta n}(p_o - c) \leq p_1 \leq p_o.$$

The inequalities are reversed if the contract size is lowered by an amount Δn.

The preceding analysis has been based on the assumption that average cost is constant. We now consider briefly how p_o varies with n when average cost c depends on the level of output. The analysis for decreasing average cost is straightforward. Suppose an increase in contract size from n to $n + \Delta n$ decreases average cost from c to $c - \Delta c$. The effect of such a change on the optimal bid price can be decomposed into two parts. First, we have seen that an increase in contract size of Δn with cost remaining constant at c will reduce the bid price. Similarly, a net decrease in average cost of Δc with contract size constant at $n + \Delta n$ will decrease the bid price even further. These two effects together lower the bid price more than either one does by itself. For cost as an increasing function of contract size, the two effects work in opposite directions. Whether the optimal bid price will increase or decrease depends on the size of the increases in contract size and cost, and on the specific utility function of the bidder.

Remarks about the Effect on the Optimal Bid Price of a Change in the Probability Distribution F.

Changes in F represent revisions in the bidder's beliefs about the bidding behavior of his competitors. Such changes can be dealt with if they can be expressed as appropriate changes in the hazard rate function H. Suppose, for example, that the bidder believes that the minimum of his competitors' bid prices is increased by the amount Δc (due, perhaps, to an increase of Δc in the costs of each of his competitors). One way of expressing this revision in his beliefs is by setting $F^*(p) = F(p - \Delta c)$, where F^* and F are the distribution functions expressing his new and old beliefs about the minimum of his competitors' bid prices. If H^* and H are the corresponding hazard rate functions, then $H^*(p) = H(p - \Delta c)$, and if H is non-decreasing, then using H^* instead of H amounts to lowering the whole H curve (or at least to not raising it anywhere). Thus, the intersection of the curves of H^* and G will be to the right of the intersection of the curves of H and G and will therefore result in a higher bid price. Notice that this type of argument can still be used even if the relation between F^* and F is not clearly defined so long as the bidder is willing to assume that H^* is non-decreasing and that $H^*(p) \leq H(p)$ for all p. In many cases this would be a reasonable assumption. It merely amounts to assuming that if the minimum of his competitors' bid prices is at least p, then it is at least as likely to be close to p under the old distribution F as under the new distribution F^*.

5. Possible Extensions of the Model

The model developed in this paper is formulated for competitive sealed tender selling markets. With minor modifications, the model is applicable to individual bidding behavior in sealed tender buying markets and Dutch auctions.

A promising application of the model is in the study of investment decisions associated with the submission of proposals for the acquisition of Research and Development (R & D) contracts. We briefly describe the mechanics of one kind of R & D contract market.[4] The market consists of a group of firms competing for a single contract to produce a specified quantity of a new product. The product is defined in terms of certain "standards of performance" and cannot be produced with existing technology. Each participating firm is required to submit a proposal on or before a given future date. The proposal consists of (1) a detailed statement of the production process the firm will use if awarded the contract and (2) a bid price. The contract is awarded to the lowest bidder from among the proposals that meet the required standards of performance.

Initially each firm must decide whether to begin the R & D work necessary for submission of a proposal. R & D costs, production costs, and the payoff are all unknown at this time. A first step toward a model explaining R & D proposal submission decisions might be the extension of the model developed in this paper to the case where production costs c are assumed to be random. Such a model would, of course, be useful in itself.

FOOTNOTES

[1]Research partially sponsored by the Air Force Office of Scientific Research, Office of Aerospace Research, United States Air Force, under AFOSR Grant NO. AF-AFOSR-746-65 and partially sponsored by the National Space Administration under Contract NGR-26-004-012.

[2]Research sponsored by the National Space Administration under Contract NGR-26-004-012.

[3]The assumption $\lambda < \infty$ is not necessary in this work. In this proof we use $[1-F(p)]u\{n(p-c)+w\} \to 0$ as $p \to \lambda$. This is true if u is bounded, or if $\lambda < \infty$, or if $\int p dF(p)$ is finite and u is concave. We use $\lambda < \infty$ not only because the assumption simplifies the proof of this theorem, but also because it is difficult (if not impossible) to conceive of a situation in which $\lambda = \infty$.

[4]We are indebted to Walter L. Johnson for information about the institutional features of this market.

REFERENCES

[1] Arrow, K.J.: "'Comment' on James S. Dusenberry, 'The Portfolio Approach to the Demand for Money and Other Assets,'" Review of Economics and Statistics, XLV, (Supplement. February 1963).

[2] __________: Aspects of the Theory of Risk Bearing, The Academic Book Store, Helsinki, Finland. 1965.

[3] Barlow, R.E., and Proschan,F.: Mathematical Theory of Reliability, John Wiley and Sons, Inc., New York, 1965.

[4] Greismer, J. H., Levitan, R. E., and Shubik, M.: "Toward a Study of Bidding Processes, Part IV: Unknown Competitive Costs," IBM Research Paper, 1966.

[5] Hernstein, I. N., and Milnor, J.: "An Axiomatic Approach to Measurable Utility," Econometrica, 21, April 1953.

[6] Pratt, J. W.: "Risk Aversion in the Small and in the Large," Econometrica, 32, 1964.

[7] Smith, V. L.: "Bidding Theory and the Treasury Bill Auction: Does Price Discrimination Increase Bill Prices?", Review of Economics and Statistics, XLVIII, No. 2, 1966.

A COMPUTABLE APPROACH TO RISK PROGRAMMING IN LINEAR MODELS*

by

J. K. Sengupta
Iowa State University

1. Introduction

The introduction of risk in linear programming models is motivated by several factors of which the following are specially important: (a) the sensitivity of optimal solution with changes in parameters S = (A,b,c) in static and dynamic situations (b) the effects of specific assumptions about the probability distribution of the elements of the set S in setting confidence interval for the optimal solution and (c) the need for providing appropriate safety margins when partial violation of the constraints is allowed for. There are several methods [1 - 5] of probabilistic programming available now, which can be considered for obtaining partial solutions to the above problems; however these methods have two basic limitations when viewed in the context of economic models, where most of the elements of the set S have to be nonnegative and the sample size is invariably very small, e.g.,

(a) the assumption of normality of the distribution of random elements at one stage or another, so that the results are not distribution-free

(b) and the neglect of differing implications of alternative sample estimates of the parameters (A,b,c) for the optimal solution vector.

The object of this paper is to present some computable methods for relaxing the above limitational assumptions; these methods are operational and in principle computable, hence applicable to several types of linear economic models both static and dynamic.

2. The Problems of Distribution

Consider an ordinary linear programming (LP) problem: $\max z = c'x$, $Ax \leq b$, $x \geq 0$ which we denote by $\max z = z(x \in X, S)$ where $S = (A,b,c)$ and X is the feasible set satisfying $Ax \leqq b$, $x \geqq 0$. When the elements of the set S vary with known or unknown probabilities, we denote by $S_k = (A_k, b_k, c_k)$ with $k = 1,2,\ldots,K$ a specific selection of the triple (A,b,c) where certain regularity conditions are imposed on the domain of variability of the elements. For any fixed S_k assume that the LP problem has finite optimal solutions denoted by $(z_k, x_k; k=1, \ldots, K)$ where x_k is a vector and z_k is a scalar. For any fixed k, the set of basic feasible solutions are denoted by R_k and the following ordering is introduced in the set R_k:

$$
\begin{aligned}
z_{1k} &= (\max z = c'x,\ x \in R_k;\ k \text{ fixed}) \\
z_{2k} &= (\max z = c'x,\ x \in R_k;\ z < z_{1k};\ k \text{ fixed}) \\
z_{3k} &= (\max z = c'x,\ x \in R_k;\ z < z_{2k};\ k \text{ fixed})
\end{aligned}
\tag{1}
$$

where $R_k = \{x | x \geqq 0,\ Ax \leqq b \text{ with given } S_k\}$. These three maximum values may be called respectively the first best, the second best and the third best maximand and the associated basic feasible solution vectors denoted by (x_{1k}, x_{2k}, x_{3k}) may be termed the three best solutions or policies of the decision maker. Naturally this ordering may be extended beyond the third order to define e.g.

$$z_{1k} > z_{2k} > z_{3k} > z_{4k} > \ldots > z_{tk}. \quad (k=1,\ldots K)$$

and the associated basic vectors denoted correspondingly by $(x_{1k},\ldots,x_{tk};\ k=1,\ldots,K)$.

Our main interest will be to analyze the implications of the two extreme solutions $(x_{1k}, z_{1k}; x_{tk}, z_{tk})$ and any other extreme solution which may be interpreted in some sense as an average (e.g. median). Now so long as k is fixed, there would be no interest in the solutions other than the first best. But whenever k varies over the index set either with known or unknown probabilities, it is important to analyze not only the first best strategy but the second best, the third best and other strategies also.

Now three types of distribution problems may be proposed. First, the set S may be viewed as a set of parameters with some information on the probability distribution of the elements (i.e., population distribution problem). Second, the set S may be approximated by a sample estimate denoted by $S = (\hat{A}, \hat{b}, \hat{c})$ and the problem is to define in some sense the best procedure of sampling approximation under conditions when the parameter set S may be known either precisely or very imprecisely in the distribution sense. This may be termed the sample distribution problem, which is also termed the problem of deterministic equivalents. Third, there is the problem of characterizing the distribution of the three best solutions defined in (1) in order that appropriate solutions may be selected as an optimal strategy in the decision space.

Before we mention the specific distribution problems, it is necessary to point out two explicit assumptions required for the whole discussion. First, the set of feasibility X out of which the decision maker has to select x is assumed to be convex. Second, the preference scheme f(g) induced by a real valued function g = g(x) on X is assumed to satisfy the ordering conditions of a natural preference function. Now for the population distribution problem we analyze two different types of distribution problems, according as the random variations are specially structured around the expected optimal basis or not; and as a typical nonnormal and nonnegative distribution we select chi-square distribution, since other continuous distributions like gamma and exponential can be easily derived therefrom.

First, we consider the methods of stochastic linear programming [6] and make the following assumptions:

<u>Assumption 1</u>: The elements of the set S = (A,b,c) are mutually independently distributed like a central chi-square variate.

<u>Assumption 2</u>: If $\bar{S} = (\bar{A}, \bar{b}, \bar{c})$ denote the expected values of (A,b,c) then the following LP problem: $\max z = (\bar{c} + \gamma)'x$, (2) $(\bar{A} + \alpha)x \leq \bar{b} + \beta$; $x \geq 0$

has the unique optimal basis $\bar{A}_o$ and the associated optimal vector x_o for $\gamma = 0 = \alpha = \beta$ such that the subscripts of the optimal basis are preserved by every admissible random variable in $(A = \bar{A} + \alpha,$

$b = \bar{b} + \beta$, $c = \bar{c} + \gamma$) and further, as (A,b,c) tends to $(\bar{A},\bar{b},\bar{c})$, the optimal basis with (A,b,c) tends with probability one to the optimal basis $\bar{A}_o$ with $(\bar{A},\bar{b},\bar{c})$. This assumption is not so restrictive as it appears and it has been made by a number of recent studies on stochastic linear programming [7].

Now we write the optimal basis equations from (2) as

(3) $(\bar{A}_o + \alpha)x_o = \bar{b}_o + \beta$; $x_o \geqq 0$

and then consider the statistical distributions of x_o and $z_o = (\bar{c}_o + \gamma)'x_o$. Now denoting the i-th constraint of (3) as

(3a) $Y_i = b_i$, where b_i is the i-th element of $(\bar{b}_o + \beta)$; and following the method of mixtures developed by Robbins and Pitman and others [8], we could write the cumulative distribution function $G_i(t_i) = \text{Prob}\,(Y_i \leq t_i)$ as

$$\text{(3b)}\quad G_i(t_i) = \frac{(t_i)^{M_i/2}}{2^{M_i/2}\cdot\left(\prod_{j=1}^{m}(x_j)^{m_{ij}}\right)}$$

$$\sum_{k=0}^{\infty} \frac{(-t_i)^k}{k!}\cdot\frac{E(Y_i^{\,o})^k}{\Gamma(\frac{M_i}{2}+k+1)}$$

where $M_i = \sum_{j=1}^{m} m_{ij}$, $m_{ij} = E(a_{ij})$, E = expectation

and $Y_i^{\,o} = \sum_{j=1}^{m} (a_{ij}/4x_j)$; $x_j \in x_o$

Note that our distribution function is valid only at nondegenerate optimal solution vector with all x_j in x_o positive; (otherwise slight modifications are required). The expression (3b) can also be expressed as a weighted sum of cdf of central chi-square variates

(3c) $G_i(t_i) = \sum_{j=1}^{m} h_j F_{M_i + 2j}(t_i)$;

where $F_{M_i+2j}(t_i)$ is the cdf of a central chi-square variate with mean $(M_i + 2j)$. This weighted sum of chi-square variates may be very closely approximated by a single non-central chi-square with a noncentrality parameter L. Other approximations are also available [9]. Again, since by assumption 1, the i-th element b_i of the vector $(\bar{b}_o + \beta)$ is distributed like a central chi-square variate with mean $\bar{b}_i$, one notes that the following ratio K_i

(3d) $K_i = b_i/a_i'x$, where $a_i'x$ = i-th element of $(\bar{A}_o + \alpha)x_o$

is distributed approximately like the ratio of two independent chi-square variates and hence it has the distribution of a non-central F-distribution, which is well tabulated [10]. This explicit distribution may now be utilized in two ways, i.e.,

(a) to set up confidence limits for the optimal solutions e.g. Prob $(k_1 \leq x_o \leq k_2) = 0.95$ where k_1, k_2 are to be determined

(b) to consider the sensitivity of the maximand (e.g. variance) in terms of the variances contributed by each optimal activity.

Note that when only assumption 1 holds but not assumption 2, then the above results can be utilized in another interesting way. For instance, the distribution of the ratio $Q_i = Y_i/b_i$ closely approximates the quantity $r \cdot F(M_1, M_2)$, where $F(M_1, M_2)$ is the standard F-distribution with degrees of freedom M_1, M_2 defined as

$$r = \left(\sum_{j=1}^{n} m_{ij} x_j^2\right)\left(\sum_{j=1}^{n} m_{ij}\right)/\bar{b}_i \left(\sum_{j=1}^{n} m_{ij} x_j\right)$$

$$M_1 = \sum_{j=1}^{n} m_{ij}; \quad M_2 = \bar{b}_i = E\, b_i$$

(For more precision, non-central F has to replace central F variate here). Now the chance-constrained type approach may be formulated, where the tolerance level u_i $(0 < u_i < 1)$ is preassigned i.e.,

$$\text{Prob}(F(M_1, M_2) \leqq 1/r) \geqq u_i$$

and then we solve for optimal x satisfying these chance-constraints and maximizing a suitable deterministic objective function [11,12]. One such possible formulation of the reduced form model is:

$$\text{maximize } z = c'x$$

under the restrictions

$$(4)\quad b_i\left(\sum_{j=1}^{n} \bar{a}_{ij} x_j\right) - k_i \cdot \left(\sum_{j=1}^{n} \bar{a}_{ij} x_j^2\right)\left(\sum_{j=1}^{n} \bar{a}_{ij}\right) \geqq 0$$

$$x_i \geqq 0;\ i = 1,\ldots,m$$

where $1/r = [\bar{b}_i \cdot (\sum_{j=1}^{n} \bar{a}_{ij} x_j)/(\sum_j \bar{a}_{ij} x_j^2)(\sum_j \bar{a}_{ij})] \geq k_i > 0.$

Likewise if the net prices c_j are mutually independently distributed as a chi-square variate with mean $\bar{c}_j$ and denoted as $\chi_j^2(\bar{c}_j)$, then the distribution of the quantity $R = \sum_{j=1}^{n} x_j \chi_j^2(\bar{c}_j)$ can be closely approximated by

$$R \simeq k\ \chi^2(h) \text{ where } k = \frac{\sum_j \bar{c}_j\ x_j^2}{\sum_j \bar{c}_j\ x_j};\quad h = \sum_{j=1}^{n} \bar{c}_j$$

A comparison of the accuracy of this type of approximation of a weighted sum of chi-square series through a single noncentral and then a central chi-square is discussed in Box and Satterthwaite [13]. Now the chance-constrained relation

$$\text{Prob } (z \geq z_o) = u_o;\ 0 < u_o < 1$$

may be written as

$$\text{maximize } z_o = w_o \sum_{j=1}^{n} \bar{c}_j\ x_j^2 \Big/ \sum_j \bar{c}_j\ x_j$$

with restrictions as in (4),

where $w_o = F^{-1}(1 - u_o)$, a positive constant

$F(v)$ = cdf of a central chi-square variate with mean v.

This is a problem which could be solved by the methods of nonlinear fractional functional programming [14] or other methods of concave programming.

A second type of population distribution problem is to define deterministic transformations of stochastic linear programs by methods which are relatively distribution-free or non-parametric. As an illustration consider a linear stochastic program with only the vector c random, where its elements c_j are known to be distributed with finite means and variances. Then by Tchebycheff inequality,

$$\text{Prob }(z \leq z_o) \leq \text{var } z/(Ez - z_o)^2$$

where $Ez = (ec)'\underline{x}$; $\text{Var } z = x'Vx$;

$V = E(c - \bar{c})' (c - \bar{c})$

z_o = disaster level of profits the chance of which is to be minimized.

Here we can apply the safety first principle [15] which assert that it is reasonable for an individual to seek to reduce as far as possible the chance of a disaster, when the outcome is probabilistic. If we adopt this principle and be concerned that total profits z should not be less than z_o, then in default of minimizing the chance $P(z \leqq z_o)$, we minimize its upper bound; the final reduced form of the model then becomes:

$$\underset{x \in X}{\text{maximize}}\ (z_o - Ec'x)^2/x'Vx;\ x \in X$$

This problem could be solved either by methods of nonlinear fractional functional programming or by solving the following saddle-point problem: find vectors x, $x_o \in X$ and scalars λ, $\lambda_o \in L$ where L is a closed bounded set, such that

$$F(x, \lambda_o) \leq F(x_o, \lambda_o) \leq F(x_o, \lambda)$$

where

$$F(x, \lambda) = (z_o - Ec'x)^2 - \lambda(x'Vx)$$

and $N(x) = (z_o - Ec'x)^2$ and $D(x) = x'Vx$ are assumed to be continuous functions on X. Since $F(x_o, \lambda)$ can be shown to be convex and monotonically decreasing function of $\lambda \in L$ with fixed $x_o \in X$, where X is assumed to be closed, bounded, connected and D(x) is assumed to be positive for all feasible

$x \in X$, therefore the convergence of $F(x_o, \lambda)$ to $F(x_o, \lambda_o)$ can be established by the sequence $\lambda_{k+1} = N(x_k)/D(x_k)$ where x_k is the optimal solution of the concave program

$$\text{maximize } N(x) - \lambda_k D(x) \text{ with } x \in X,\ \lambda_k \in L$$

and as $\lambda_k \to \lambda_o$, $x_k \to x_o$.

Two comments are in order. First, the use of Tchebycheff-type inequalities can be extended to the constraints $Ax \leqq b$ also. Second, other probabilistic inequalities more general than the Tchebycheff inequalities can be utilized. These aspects have been treated elsewhere [16].

2.1 Sample Distribution Problems

It is extremely interesting to view the sample distribution problem in the very simple case of a chance-constrained linear programming problem:

$$\text{maximize } z = c'x$$

$$\text{subject to } x \geqq 0;\ \text{Prob } (b_i \geqq a_i'x;\ i=1,\ldots,m) = u_i \text{ with } 0 < u_i < 1$$

assuming the resource vector b only random, with each element b_i assumed to have independent normal distribution $N(\mu_i, \sigma_i)$ with population means μ_i and variances σ_i^2 $(i=1,\ldots,m)$. However in almost all practical cases these population parameters are unknown, for nonexperimental data and all we would have is a sample of T observations b_{it} $(t=1,\ldots,T)$ for each $i=1,2,\ldots,m$ out of which we have to determine two limits B_{i1}, B_{i2} $(B_{i1} < B_{i2})$ such that the sample interval (B_{i1}, B_{i2}) can be asserted to satisfy the chance-constraint with 100 v_i percent probability. Assuming that we are seeking central confidence interval in the sense

$$\text{Prob } (B_{i1} \geqq a_i'x) = \text{Prob } (B_{i2} \leqq a_{ix}') = (1 - v_i)/2 \quad (0 < v_i < 1)$$

and that we have sample means $\bar{b}_i$ and variances s_i^2 for each b_i, it is natural to consider the sample functions $B_{ij} = m_i + k_{ij} s_i$ $(j=1,2;\ i=1,\ldots,m)$ in relation to the population range $a_i'x = \mu_i + K_{u_i}\sigma_i$ as

$$P(m_i + k_{ij}\mathcal{S}_i \geqq \mu_i + K_{u_i}\sigma_i) = \bar{v}_i, \text{ where } \bar{v}_i =$$

$(1 - v_i)/2$ from which it follows that

$$P(t_i \geqq -k_{i1}\, T^{1/2}) = \bar{v}_i;\ (i=1,\ldots,m)$$

where

$$t_i = [\{\sqrt{T}\,(m_i - \mu_i)/\sigma_i - K_{u_i}\sqrt{T}\}/(\mathcal{S}_i/\sigma_i)]$$

has a non-central t-distribution, for which tables are available [17] to compute exactly the quantities k_{ij} for example

$$k_{i1} = T^{-1/2}\, F^{-1}(1 - \bar{v}_i),$$

where $F(y) = P(t_i \leqq y)$. Numerically, if $T = 10$, $u_i = 0.10$, $v_i = 0.90$ then $k_{i1} = 0.71$ and $k_{i2} = 2.35$. Once k_{ij}'s are determined, B_{ij} $(j=1,2;\ i=1,\ldots,m)$ can be computed and it can be asserted that with $100\ v_i$ percent probability that the sample interval (B_{i1}, B_{i2}) contains $a_i'x$ for each restriction $i=1,\ldots,m$.

Two remarks may be made at this stage. First, the implications of non-normality through non-centrality parameters even when the population is normal are now clearly evident. Second, the above results could obviously be generalized in several directions. Two of these generalizations may be mentioned very briefly.

First, consider the above problem where each b_i is assumed to have unknown (but continuous) distributions with cdf $F(b_i)$ and let $F_T(b_i)$ be the sample cdf for each b_i $(i=1,\ldots,m)$ defined as 0 for $b_i < b_{i1}$, 1 for $b_i \geqq b_{iT}$ while increasing by T^{-1} at each of the values b_{it} $(t=1,\ldots,T)$; in other words $TF_T(b_i)$ denotes the number of observations less than or equal to b_i. Now since $F_T(b_i)$ converges stochastically to $F(b_i)$ as T becomes infinitely large, one could suggest the following method for constructing the lower $B_{i1} = B_{i1}(b_{i1},\ldots, b_{iT})$ and upper $B_{i2} = B_{i2}(b_{i1},\ldots,b_{iT})$ limits of a confidence band for the unknown cdf $F(b_i)$

$$B_{i1} = \begin{cases} F_T(b_i) - k_i, & \text{if } F_T(b_i) - k_i > 0 \\ 0, & \text{otherwise} \end{cases}$$

$$B_{i2} = \begin{cases} F_T(b_i) + k_i, & \text{if } F_T(b_i) + k_i < 1 \\ 1, & \text{otherwise} \end{cases}$$

where k_i is a constant determined such that

$$P(B_{i1} \leqq F(b_i) \leqq B_{i2}) = v_i;\ 0 < v_i < 1.$$

Define $\lambda_i = k_i T^{1/2}$

then the result due to Kolmogorov and Smirnov [18] may be utilized to define the following convergent series

$$\lim_{T\to\infty} v_i = 1 - 2 \sum_{j=1}^{\infty} (-1)^{j-1} \exp(-2j^2 \lambda_i^2) = (2\pi)^{1/2} \lambda_i^{-1} \sum_{j=1}^{\infty} \exp\left(\frac{-\pi^2 (2j-1)^2}{8\lambda_i^2}\right)$$

Given any confidence coefficient v_i the numerical tables on this convergent series may be readily used to find the value of λ_i, from which the appropriate value of $k_i = \lambda_i T^{-1/2}$ can be computed. Also, given v_i and k_i the required sample size T can be computed. Now we can use the computed values of B_{i1} and B_{i2} for each i=1,...,m (the constraints i and j are assumed independent) to set up a pair of linear programs e.g.,

$$\text{(I)} \quad \max z = c'x,\ B_{i1} \geqq a_i'x,\ x \geqq 0;\ i=1,\ldots,m$$

$$\text{(II)} \quad \max z = c'x,\ B_{i2} \geqq a_i'x,\ x \geqq 0;\ i=1,\ldots,m.$$

If both problems have optimal feasible solutions denoted by vectors x_I and x_{II} then the corresponding maximands z_I and z_{II} provide the confidence interval with probability $v = \prod_{i=1}^{m} v_i$.

In case one-sided confidence limits are used e.g.,

$$P(F(b_i) \leqq B_{i2}) = \bar{v}_i, \text{ or } P(F(b_i) \geqq B_{i1}) = \bar{v}_i$$

then the Kolmogorov-Smirnov limit theorem becomes

$$\lim_{T\to\infty} \bar{v}_i = 1 - \exp(-2\lambda_i^2); \ \lambda_i = k_i T^{1/2}$$

where it is much simpler to derive the optimal feasible solution. In the general case when T observations are available for the set (A,b,c) as $(a_{ijt}, b_{it}, c_{jt}; t=1,\ldots,T)$ and $F_T(z)$ denotes the sample cdf of the maximand z, we may define

$$D_T = \text{Sup}\,[F_T(z) - F(z)]$$

where F(z) is the unknown population cdf assumed continuous. The limiting distribution of D_T as $T \to \infty$ takes the following simple form

$$P(D_T \leqq r) \to 1 - \exp(-2T\, r^2), \ r > 0$$

Here several choices of r implying several types of decision rules are available.

Second, another type of distribution problem is raised when we consider the i-th constraint

$$y_i = b_i - a_i'x \qquad (i=1,\ldots,m)$$

under the assumption that each b_i and a_{ij} are normally and independently distributed with one additional condition that each y_i has to be non-negative for feasibility. In other words the probability density function of the normal variate y_i with mean $\bar{y}_i$ and standard deviation h_i is truncated on the left at a fixed terminus $y_{io} = 0$ and its density may be written as

$$f(y_i) = (I_{1i} h_i/\sqrt{2\pi})^{-1} \exp(-(y_i-\bar{y}_i)^2/2h_i^2);$$

$0 \leq y_i \leq \infty$ where $I_{1i} = I\left(\frac{y_{io} - \bar{y}_i}{h_i}\right)$ denotes the percentage of complete distribution retained after truncation, i.e.,

$$I_{1i} = \int_{g_1}^{\infty} N(t)\, dt; \; N(t) = (2\pi)^{-1/2} \exp(-t^2/2)$$

$$g_1 = (y_{io} - \bar{y}_i)/h_i = - \bar{y}_i/h_i$$

Now if the population distribution is known to be truncated normal as above and the sample observations a_{ijt}, b_{it} are used to define a deterministic approximation to the stochastic programming problem, then the question is how to evaluate different deterministic approximations (e.g. the elements $\max_t (0, a_{ijt})$ and $\min_t (-\infty, b_{it})$, $t=1,\ldots,T$) leading to a least possible value of the maximand z assuming the vector c to be fixed, may be compared with other solutions. This question is partly one of defining a best sampling method in some sense and partly one of evaluating the penalties for approximating the population distribution of m truncated normal distributions with different truncation points y_{io} $(i=1,\ldots,m)$.

3. Extreme Value Problems

It has to be emphasized at this stage that most of the transformations of stochastic linear programs into deterministic nonlinear programming problems, based on the first two moments namely the mean and the variance (e.g., the portfolio analysis model of Markowitz and others [19], the chance-constrained approach [2], the risk programming model of Freund [20]), are essentially dependent on the assumption of normality directly or indirectly. However when the extremes of sample values $(a_{ijt}, b_{it}, c_{jt})$ are considered, the resulting distribution of optimal solution and the maximand tends to have high degrees of skewness which may not be reduced by increasing the sample size. In these cases the normal approximations for non-normal distributions may be very imprecise, if not erroneous, to say the least.

To fix ideas on these two-point extreme value problems, extremes in the sample space (A,b,c) and also in the decision space (i.e., optimal $x \in X$), consider the very simple case where the net prices c_j only are assumed random satisfying.

Assumption 3: The set (c_{jt}, t=1,...,T) specifies samples of size T drawn independently at random from a unit normal population such that each extreme vector $c^* = (c_j^*) = (\max_t c_{jt})$ with mutually independent components c_j^* defines a non-degenerate and unique optimal solution vector x^* for a standard linear program ($x^* \in X$, where X is the constraint set).

Under the above assumption the following result may be stated:

Theorem 1.

The statistical distribution of the maximand z* defined as

$$z^* = \max_x \sum_j (\max_t c_{jt})\, x_j$$

$$\text{with } x \in X: \{x \,|\, Ax \leqq b,\ x \geqq 0\}$$

tend to have a limiting distribution under assumption 3 such that it is far from normal in the sense that its skewness and kurtosis coefficients do not tend to zero as the sample size T increases, unless z* has a degenerate distribution.

Proof: If z* has a non-degenerate distribution, then at least for one index i in the optimal basis, $c_i^* x_i^*$ is a random variable with a non-degenerate distribution with $x_i^* > 0$. Since by assumption 3, each c_i^* comes from a unit normal distribution, therefore the probability density function $p(u_i^*)$ of $u_i^* = c_i^* x_i^*$ ($x_i^* > 0$, c_i^* non-degenerate) can be computed by using the statistical theory of extreme values as:

$$p(u_i^*) = (k_i\, T^2/x_i^*) \exp\,[-k_i\, u_i^*/x_i^* - T^2 \exp (-k_i\, u_i^*/x_i^*)]$$

$$\text{where } k_i = (2 \log_e T)^{1/2} \qquad -\infty \leqq u_i^* \leqq \infty$$

It can be shown that the first four moments (i.e., mean and the second, third and fourth moments about the mean) of this distribution of u_i^* are given by

$$\mu_{1i} = \text{mean} = (0.5772 + 2 \log T)/(\sqrt{2} \log T/x_i^*)$$

$$\mu_{2i} = \text{variance} = (\pi^2/6)\,(x_i^*)^2/(2 \log T)$$

$$\mu_{3i} = \text{third moment} = 2.404\,(x_i^*)^3/(2 \log T)^{3/2}$$

$$\mu_{4i} = \text{fourth moment} = (3\pi^4/20)(x_i^*)^4/(2 \log T)^2$$

$$\beta_{1i} = \text{skewness} = \mu^2_{3i}/\mu^3_{2i} = 1.299$$

$$\beta_{2i} = \text{kurtosis} = \mu_{4i}/\mu^2_{2i} = 5.40$$

Since the skewness and kurtosis coefficients for the distribution of $u_i^* = c_i^*\, x_i^*$ are independent of sample size, the distribution of u_i^* does not tend to normal in the limit. Again since $z^* = \sum_i u_i^*$ defines a mixture of the sequence u_i^*, where each u_i^* has a distribution with probability density function $p(u_i^*)$, therefore z^* has the pdf $\sum_i p(u_i^*)$. But since by assumption 3, c_j^* and c_i^* are mutually independent for $i \neq j$ and the vector x^* is non-degenerate and unique, therefore the distribution of z^* does not tend to normality in the limit in the sense that its skewness and kurtosis coefficients do not tend to zero as the sample size T gets infinitely large.

We should note that several generalizations of the above theorem are possible but since most of them are mentioned elsewhere [21], two implications which are of considerable importance for economic models may be briefly noted. First, there is the need for analyzing situations which are far from normal and hence for emphasizing the role of third and fourth moments (particularly because economic models operate under typically small sample conditions) in the specification of an optimal decision rule. In this connection the following remark by Geary [22] is worth quoting: "Normality is a myth; there never was and never will be a normal distribution. This is an over-statement from the practical point of view but it represents a safer initial mental attitude than any in fashion during the past two decades". A similar attitude is expressed by Tukey [23] in his recommending careful judgment and "appropriate trimming" of samples in the presence of wild points or outliers, before decision rules based on normality of the parent universe could be applied. Second, the economists have not paid much attention in developing decision rules applicable to extreme rather than an average behavior. A gambler shows an extreme behavior in the sense of basing himself on the criterion of $\max_x \sum_j (\max_t c_{jt}) x_j$, which is as much rational as a safety-first minded behavior which is based on $\max_x \sum_j (\min_t c_{jt}) x_j$ and both may be combined to represent an average behavior based on $\max_x \sum_j d_j x_j$ where $d_j = w_j \max_t c_{jt} + (1 - w_j) \min_t c_{jt}$ with $0 \leqq w_j \leqq 1$. As a matter of fact there are several cases where the extreme behavior is better than an average behavior, if we restrict to the first two moments only and the smallness of sample size. The closest reference to the importance of analyzing such extreme behavior for economic models may be found in Shackle's theory of expectation based on focus-gain and focus-loss [24], Simon's concept of satisficing behavior [25] and the analysis of game-theoretic decision models in terms of minimax criteria of various sorts [26].

3.1 Use of Second-best Strategies

There is another type of extreme value problem based on the second-best and third best extreme-point solution vectors defined in (1) before. In a deterministic linear program the local maximum whenever it exists is also a global maximum and hence there is not much point in using sub-optimal or second best solution as a possible strategy in the decision space, unless the first best solution is not computationally feasible; however in a general nonlinear program (e.g. dynamic programming algorithm applied to a general nonlinear program) much attention is paid to the sub-optimal solutions which are in some sense locally optimal, without necessarily being globally optimal. But in linear programs where the parameter set S = (A,b,c) has a certain type of probabilistic variation, the three maximands z_{1k}, z_{2k} and z_{3k} defined in (1) before may have unequal distribution characteristics e.g. the second best maximand z_{2k} may have significantly smaller coefficient of variation than the first best maximand z_{1k}, so that the second best solution may be a less risk strategy compared to the first best, if only the first two moments are considered. Some distributional results on the three best maximands are known [27] but these are dependent on the condition that sample observations are available to observe the sequence of outcomes. In case the observations are very few, the following construction of ordered linear programs may be helpful in ranging the optimal profit solution. To fix ideas, assume the set $S = (a_{ijt}, b_{it}, c_{jt}; t=1,\ldots,T)$ to be nonnegative for all t such that the elements are ordered as follows.

$$a_{ij1} \geqq a_{ij2} \geqq \cdots \geqq a_{ijT}$$

$$b_{i1} \leqq b_{i2} \leqq \cdots \leqq b_{iT}$$

$$c_{j1} \leqq c_{j2} \leqq \cdots \leqq c_{jT}; \text{ all } i=1,\ldots,m; \text{ all } j=1,\ldots,n.$$

Define the sets

$$S_k = (a_{ijk}, b_{ik}, c_{jk}); k=1,2,\ldots,T$$

sequentially and assume that for all k the linear programs based on those parameters have optimal basic feasible solutions attained in the constrained set R_k. The maximand z_k for any fixed $k=1,\ldots,T$ is denoted by z_{1k}, while the second best and third best maximands are z_{2k} and z_{3k} by the notation used in (1). Note that by construction of the ordered sets S_k, the maximand $z_k = z_{1k}$ is ordered as follows:

$$z_{11} \leqq z_{12} \leqq z_{13} \leqq \cdots \leqq z_{1T}$$

Also by construction

$$z_{1k} > z_{2k} > z_{3k}, \text{ all } k=1,\ldots,T$$

Again, to fix ideas consider the state of nature in terms of three values of the set S_k with $k=1,T$ and the median value (S_1, S_m, S_T) and consider the strategy set in terms of the three best solution vectors (x_{1k}, x_{2k}, x_{3k}) associated with the three best maximands (z_{1k}, z_{2k}, z_{3k}). Let the utility function be defined by the nonegative pay-off matrix (u_{ij}) with finite elements where $i=1,2,3$ for the three best strategies and $j=1$, $m=2$, T for the three best strategies and j=1, m=2, T for the three states of nature. We assume that this real-valued utility function satisfies the ordinary ordering conditions of a natural preference function.

Now since the elements of the pay-off matrix are explicitly computable by solving the different linear programs and since the explicit probability distribution of the random elements is assumed either unknown or very imprecisely known, use could be made of the various game-theoretic criteria under uncertainty e.g.

Wald: minimax: $\max_i \min_j u_{ij}$

Laplace: equal probability: $\max_i \text{average}_j u_{ij}$

Hurwicz: optimum-pessimism index:

$$\max_i (\alpha \max_j u_{ij} + (1 - \alpha) \min_j u_{ij}) \text{ with } 0 < \alpha < 1$$

Savage: minimax regret: $\max_i \min_j r_{ij}$, where

$$r_{ij} = (u_{ij} - \max_i u_{ij})$$

to define a best strategy. However since our set S_k is ordered in a specific way, the following result holds

Theorem 2.

If the pay-off matrix elements u_{ij} are each monotonically increasing functions of the maximands z_{ij} (i=1,2,3 and j=1,m,T) such that for all i it holds that $z_{i1} < z_{im} < z_{iT}$, then all the three criteria, Wald, Laplace and Savage prescribe the first best as the optimal strategy. On the other hand if u_{ij} are each monotonically decreasing functions of the maximands z_{ij} such that for all i it holds that $u_{i1} > u_{im} > u_{iT}$, then all the three criteria, Wald, Laplace, and Savage prescribe the third best as the optimal strategy.

Proof: For the first part, since $z_{iT} > z_{im} > z_{i1}$ therefore by hypothesis u_{i1} is the minimum for a given i, but since $z_{11} > z_{21} > z_{31}$, therefore max (u_{11}, u_{21}, u_{31}) defines the first best solution as the best strategy by Wald's criterion. Similar arguments for Laplace and Savage criteria. For the second part, since $z_{iT} > z_{im} > z_{i1}$ implies by hypothesis that $u_{iT} < u_{im} < u_{i1}$ for all i, therefore u_{iT} is the minimum for a given i; Again since $z_{1T} > z_{2T} > z_{3T}$, therefore $u_{1T} < u_{2T} < u_{3T}$ by hypothesis; hence max (u_{1T}, u_{2T}, u_{3T}) prescribes the third best as the optimal strategy by Wald's minimax rule; similar arguments hold for Laplace and Savage criteria.

Two implications of the above result may be emphasized. First, the need for analyzing two-point extreme value problems in terms of the neighboring extreme points of the first best solutions is all the greater in cases where there is little or no information on the probability generating mechanism. Second, since u_{ij} can be viewed as a utility function, it is still an open question how the sample information on the variability of z_{ij} can be fed into the utility function as possible arguments. Since the variability of z_{ij} is not likely to be normal in ordinary cases, there is some reason to believe that more than the first two moments of the observed distribution of z_{ij} would be required to characterize the variability of z_{ij} and feed into the utility functions $u_{ij} = u_{ij}(z_{ij})$.

4. Concluding Remarks

From an economic viewpoint the characterization of risk in linear probabilistic programming models is incomplete in two respects. First, non-normal situations are usually neglected. Second, the extreme behavior which is usually based on very small samples, a feature of most common occurrence in economic models is generally left out in preference for an average behavior. We have attempted to show how far these aspects could be built into our probabilistic linear programming framework in a very limited sense. Two basic points remain unexplored in our presentation. First, the sequential aspect of revising optimal strategies over time specially in dynamic models. Second, the interaction between prior and posterior probabilities with what has been called empirical Bayes estimator [28].

FOOTNOTES

* Work done under the NSF Project GS 1810/420-21-17 at the Department of Economics, Iowa State University.

REFERENCES

[1] Tintner, G. and J.K. Sengupta, "Stochastic Linear Programming and its Application to Economic Planning", _In Essays in Honor of Oscar Lange: On Political Economy and Econometrics_. Warsaw, 1964.

Sengupta, J.K., Tintner, G. and B. Morrison, "Stochastic Linear Programming with Applications to Economic Models", _Economica_, Vol. 30, 1963.

Babbar, M.M., "Distribution of Solutions of a Set of Linear Equations with Applications to Linear Programming", _Journal of American Statistical Association_, Vol. 50, 1955.

[2] Charnes, A. and W.W. Cooper, "Deterministic Equivalents for Optimizing and Satisficing Under Chance Constraints", _Operations Research_ Vol. 11, 1963.

[3] Madansky, A., "Methods of Solution of Linear Programs Under Uncertainty", _Operations Research_, Vol. 10, 1962.

[4] Prekopa, A., "On the Probability Distribution of the Optimum of a Random Linear Program", _SIAM J. on Control_, Vol. 4, 1966.

Bereanu, B., "On Stochastic Linear Programming" _Journal of Math. Analysis and Applications_, Vol. 15, 1966.

[5] Sengupta, J.K., "Econometric Models of Risk Programming". (To be published in Annual Econometric Number, Indian Economic Journal, 1967-68)

_______. "Safety first Rules Under Chance-Constrained Programming".

[6] Sengupta, J.K. and G. Tintner, "The Approach of Stochastic Linear Programming: A Critical Appraisal".

________. "Distribution Problems in Stochastic and Chance-Constrained Programming". (To be published in Essays in honor of Gerhard Tintner)

[7] Prekopa, A. op. cit.

[8] Robbins, H. and E.J.G. Pitman, "Application of the Method of Mixtures to Quadratic Forms in Normal Variates", Annals of Mathematical Statistics, Vol. 20, 1949.

[9] Sengupta, J.K., "Chance-Constrained Programming with Chi-square Type Deviates".

[10] Owen, D.B. Handbook of Industrial Statistics, London, 1962.

[11] Sengupta, J.K., "A Generalization of Chance-Constrained Programming with Applications".

[12] Sengupta, J.K., "Stochastic Linear Programming with Chance-Constraints". Forthcoming in International Economic Review)

[13] Box, G.E.P., "Some Theorems on Quadratic Forms Applied in the Study of Analysis of Variance Problems". Annals of Mathematical Statistics, Vol. 25, June 1954.

Satterthwaite, F.E., "Synthesis of Variance", Psychometrica, Vol. 6, 1941.

[14] Dinkelbach, W., "On Nonlinear Fractional Programming", Management Science, Vol. 13, No. 7, 1967.

[15] Roy, A.D., "Safety First and the Holding of Assets", Econometrica, Vol. 20, 1952.

[16] Sengupta, J.K., "Safety First Rules Under Chance-Constrained Programming".

[17] Owen, D.B. op. cit.

[18] Feller, W., "On the Kolmogorov-Smirnov Limit Theorems for Empirical Distributions", Annals

of Mathematical Statistics, Vol. 19, 1948.

Birnbaum, Z.W., "Numerical Tabulation of the Distribution of Kolmogorov's Statistic for Finite Sample Size", Journal of American Statistical Association, Vol. 47, 1952.

[19] Markowitz, H. Portfolio Selection: Efficient Diversification of Investments, New York, 1959.

Farrar, D.E. The Investment Decision Under Uncertainty, Englewood Cliffs, New Jersey, 1962.

[20] Freund, R.J., "The Introduction of Risk Into a Programming Model", Econometrica, July, 1956.

[21] Sengupta, J.K., "The Extreme of Extreme Value Solutions Under Risk Programming".

[22] Geary, R.C., "Testing for Normality", Biometrika, Vol. 34, 1947, pp. 209-242.

[23] Tukey, J.W., "The Future of Data Analysis", Annals of Mathematical Statistics, Vol. 33, 1962, pp. 1-67.

[24] Shackle, G.L.S., "Expectation in Economics", in Carter, C., Meredith, Ġ. and G. Shackle (ed.), Uncertainty and Business Decision: A Symposium, Liverpool, 1954.

[25] Simon, H.A. Models of Man, New York, 1957.

[26] Luce, R.D. and H. Raiffa. Games and Decisions, New York, 1957.

[27] Sengupta, J.K., "The Stability of Truncated Solutions of Stochastic Linear Programming", Econometrica, Vol. 34, January 1966.

________, "On the Sensitivity of Optimal Solutions Under Investment Planning and Programming", Arthaniti, January, 1965.

[28] Robbins, H., "An Empirical Bayes Approach to Statistics", Proceedings of Third Berkeley

Symposium on Statistics and Probability, Vol. 1, 1955, pp. 157-164, Berkeley, 1956.

A DYNAMIC DECISION MODEL FOR ARMS PROCUREMENT

by

Major Herman L. Gilster
U. S. Air Force Academy

1. Introduction

Most arms models have concentrated on the reaction processes that lead to a condition of equilibrium between hostile nations. As such, they have been primarily static in nature or have assumed the form of long-run growth models. In either case primary concern has been placed on the end result in these analyses. Little attention has been directed to the short-run period-to-period decision process in which a nation might find itself. The future affects the decision to be made today, but how far into the future we can foresee is a questionable matter. There should be some limited horizon, however, for which we can adequately predict the future values of inputs to a dynamic decision model. If so, optimal decisions can be formulated and subjected to rigid quantitative analysis.

The present study is an attempt to postulate such a model. The traditional theory of the consumer, utilizing a quadratic preference function and linear constraints, has been reformulated in a dynamic context. The resulting linear decision rules then provide a simple and elegant guide for decision making, for the evaluation of the decision-making process, and for the efficient allocation of limited resources.

Before specifying an arms model, it is necessary to fully understand what a nation's national security objectives might be. Obviously a model incorporating all objectives would be too cumbersome; therefore an attempt is made to eliminate all but the most important. Professor Huntington has concluded that past arms races have concentrated on one weapons system--that system which could hurt the enemy the most.(1) The arms race today seems to be characteristic of this description with attention being primarily focused on the intercontinental ballistic missile. The model presented in this paper will therefore be confined to the procurement decisions affecting this particular weapons system.

Our national objectives that can be satisfied with this system are severalfold, and often they are conflicting. First there is the question of a credible second-strike capability. We are interested in deterring a future war, but if deterrence should fail we are equally interested in limiting the resulting damage and winning the war. Our alliances impose still another objective upon us, especially if we are to defend a third area. To fulfill this objective some first-strike capability must be realized. But too credible a first-strike capability may precipitate the war we are trying to avoid.

How then do our procurement decisions influence these objectives? Take first the requirements for a credible second-strike capability. Here we are interested in the number of operational missiles that survive an enemy's first strike at our missile force. If we assume the enemy will distribute his missiles evenly over each of our sites and each of his missiles has an independent probability of kill, this relationship can be expressed in a simple, rather direct formula:

$$R_x = XP^{\frac{M}{Y}}$$

where: R_x = residual missiles surviving a single-salvo attack

X = number of own missiles

P = single-shot survival probability of a site complex with its missiles (assumed constant for the duration of the problem)

M = number of enemy missiles

Y = number of own site complexes

For a given site survival probability, P, and enemy missile force, M, R_x is a function of X and Y.

Now consider the other objective, a credible first-strike capability. Here we are interested in the number of missiles the enemy will have after we deliver the first strike. In addition, however, we must concern ourselves with a reserve missile force--missiles not committed to our first strike--that can be used in the further prosecution of the war.

Two situations may develop as a result of our strike. First, the enemy may decide to negotiate at that time using his remaining missile force as leverage. In this case our reserve missile force becomes critically important to our bargaining power. Second, the enemy may retaliate immediately. We would then be interested in the number of our missiles surviving this first exchange--R'_x.

Now the missile-to-site ratio that optimizes R_x will not necessarily optimize R'_x. For a given budget and prices our missile reaction curve takes the following general form:

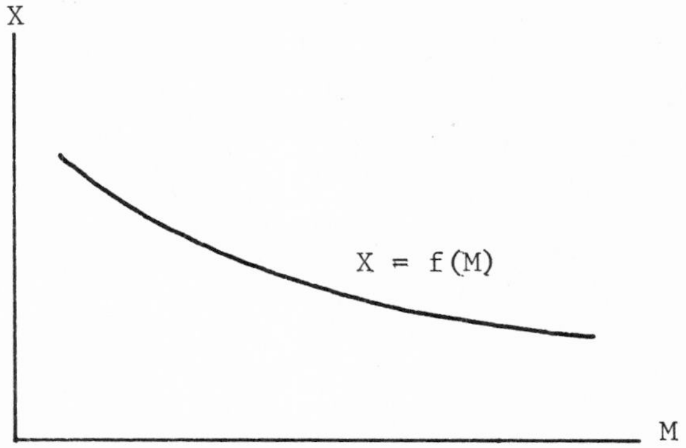

The fewer missiles the enemy possesses the higher should be our missile-to-site ratio. Surely the enemy's retaliatory force will contain fewer missiles than his first-strike force.

So we see that for a second-strike capability, our primary criterion, R_x, is a function of both missiles and sites. For a first-strike capability, however, missiles assume added importance. Only with missiles can we destroy the enemy's retaliatory force. If he does not retaliate immediately our reserve missile force will prove critical in the bargaining situation. If he does retaliate immediately, an optimal R'_x will call for a higher missile-to-site ratio than the optimal R_x predicated on the initial enemy force.

With these thoughts in mind, we now turn to the formulation of the model that will be the subject of this study. In Section II the objective function and constraints will be discussed. In Section III the solution to the model will be derived and evaluated. Section IV will be devoted to a discussion of optimal budget allocations. In Section V losses due to sub-optimal decisions and improper forecasts will be examined. Finally, in Section VI the model is reformulated as a long-term growth model and several possible missile time paths are investigated.

The Arms Model

The General Objective Function. The general objective function should incorporate the primary objectives discussed in the previous section. These objectives, as we have already noted, may be conflicting in nature. The maximization process, however, takes these conflicts into account and gives optimal solutions that, if followed, will provide the highest level of utility consistent with the constraints under which a nation must operate.

A missile objective function is surely the first candidate for consideration. Such a function could take the following form:

$$c_1[(x_0 + \sum_{t=1}^{n} x_t) - c_2(m_0 + \sum_{t=1}^{n} m_t) + c_3]^2$$

where: c_1 = social cost of not satisfying this objective

x_0 = initial endowment of own missiles

x_t = own missile procurement for period t

c_2 = ratio of our missiles to enemy missiles that we prefer

m_0 = initial endowment of enemy missiles

m_t = enemy missile procurement for period t

c_3 = constant reflecting asymmetry in preferences

What is being reflected here is that at any time period we desire our total missile force be some proportion of the enemy's total force. The constant, c_2, denotes this proportion. The function is squared to reflect that there is an increasing social cost of either over or underfulfilling our objective. If we do not meet the objective our security may be jeopardized. Conversely, if we more than meet it we may precipitate an enemy attack. The budget could be better spent on some other national objective. The constant, c_3, is included to account for possible asymmetry in our preferences. (Note that c_2 is not the "preferred ratio" if $c_3 \neq 0$; however, for c_3 small, the loss in accuracy is slight.)

We also know from the R_x formula that the dispersal of our force (more y) is important in meeting our objectives. A site objective function, therefore, must be included:

$$c_4[(x_0 + \sum_{t=1}^{n} x_t) - c_5(y_0 + \sum_{t=1}^{n} y_t) + c_6]^2$$

where: c_4 = social cost of not satisfying this objective

x_0 = initial endowment of own missiles

x_t = own missile procurement for period t

c_5 = ratio of sites-to-missiles we prefer

y_0 = initial endowment of own sites

y_t = own site procurement for period t

c_6 = constant reflecting asymmetry in preferences

The structure of this function is essentially the same as that above. There is an increasing social cost of either under or overfulfilling the objective. There are economies of scale in command and control to assigning more missiles to each site complex, but the more sites we have the greater will be the number of surviving missiles. The constant, c_5, denotes the compromise ratio. Again, the constant, c_6, reflects the possibility of asymmetry in preferences.

The general objective function to be utilized in the model will incorporate the two individual objective functions described above. We now turn to the budget constraints under which the nation must operate.

Budget Constraints. The periodic budget constraints, k_t, are partitioned into two general cost categories. First we have periodic procurement costs:

c_7x_t missile cost $\qquad$ c_8y_t site cost

Here we assume that procurement costs are not a function of the number of missiles and sites purchased and do not increase over time. This last assumption could be dropped by specifying a cost vector depicting different cost coefficients for different time periods. In fact, all scalars in the model could be treated in this manner. For the subsequent analysis, however, all costs will be considered as constant over time.

In addition to procurement costs we also have operations and maintenance costs on the force-in-being:

$$c_9(x_0 + \sum_{t=2}^{n} x_{t-1}) \qquad c_{10}(y_0 + \sum_{t=2}^{n} y_{t-1})$$

Here we state that out of each period's budget not only must we provide for the procurement of additional missiles and sites, but must also pay the expenses of operating and maintaining the force-in-being for that period. The expressions above might also serve as proxies for obsolescent rates on missiles and sites. This would be equivalent to assuming that in each time period a certain proportion of the force must be replaced.

The Combined Function. Now that the various parts of the model have been described we draw them together into a general objective function to be minimized subject to a periodic budget constraint:

$$\text{Minimize:} \quad \sum_{t=1}^{n} \{c_1[(x_0 + \sum_{t=1}^{n} x_t) - c_2(m_0 + \sum_{t=1}^{n} m_t) + c_3]^2$$

$$+ c_4[(x_0 + \sum_{t=1}^{n} x_t) - c_5(y_0 + \sum_{t=1}^{n} y_t)$$

$$+ c_6]^2\}$$

Subject to: $$k_t = c_7x_t + c_8y_t + c_9(x_0 + \sum_{t=2}^{n} x_{t-1}) + c_{10}(y_0 + \sum_{t=2}^{n} y_{t-1})$$

The expression between the brackets {} gives the social cost of not satisfying our objective function in each time period. The summation sign preceding the brackets calls for summing the individual period costs to obtain a total social cost covering the time horizon from t=1 to t=n. As can readily be seen, we require to minimize the total sum of squares subject to a periodic budget constraint.

The Solution of a Three-Period Horizon Model

A solution will now be provided for a three-period horizon model. For the purposes of this analysis a period will be defined to coincide with the production lag we face. Orders are placed at the first of each period and delivery is made at the end. In the three-period model we are assuming that three periods are as far as we can accurately forecast future inputs and parameters of the model.

First we specify the values of the parameters of the model. Let us assume these parameters take the following values:

$c_1 = 1$	$c_4 = 1$	$c_7 = 5$	$c_9 = 1$
$c_2 = 1.5$	$c_5 = 3$	$c_8 = 10$	$c_{10} = 2$
$c_3 = 0$	$c_6 = 0$		

In general we are saying that equal weights are being placed on our missile and site objective functions (c_1, c_4). We desire 50% more missiles than the enemy (c_2) and the desired missile-to-site ratio is 3(c_5). For convenience, it is assumed that the costs of not satisfying the two objective functions are symmetrical (c_3, c_6). The price of sites is twice that of missiles (c_7, c_8) and they are twice as costly to operate and maintain (c_9, c_{10}). Although the choice of values is somewhat arbitrary, it does serve the purpose at hand. In any case, tests can be made later to determine the sensitivity of the solution to the assumed values.

The solution to the model can be expedited by converting it into matrix notation and comparing it with the general quadratic form:

Maximize: $a'x + b'y + 1/2(x'Ax + y'By + x'Cy + y'C'x)$

Subject to: $y = Rx + s$

where the small letters denote vectors and the large letters, matrices.

The missile model, written again to include the assumed parameters, is:

$$\text{Minimize:} \quad \sum_{t=1}^{3} \{[(x_0 + \sum_{t=1}^{3} x_t) - 1.5(m_0 + \sum_{t=1}^{3} m_t)]^2 + [(x_0 + \sum_{t=1}^{3} x_t) - 3(y_0 + \sum_{t=1}^{3} y_t)]^2\}$$

$$\text{Subject to:} \quad k_t = 5x_t + 10y_t + (x_0 + \sum_{t=2}^{3} x_{t-1}) + 2(y_0 + \sum_{t=2}^{3} y_{t-1})$$

Multiplying through the general objective function by -1 and then maximizing is equivalent to minimizing the original function. Summing over time, gathering terms, and comparing with the general quadratic function we find: (See Appendix A)

$$a = \begin{bmatrix} -12x_0 + 18y_0 + 9m_0 + 9m_1 + 6m_2 + 3m_3 \\ -8x_0 + 12y_0 + 6m_0 + 6m_1 + 6m_2 + 3m_3 \\ -4x_0 + 6y_0 + 3m_0 + 3m_1 + 3m_2 + 3m_3 \end{bmatrix}$$

$$b = \begin{bmatrix} 18x_0 + 15y_0 \\ 12x_0 - 36y_0 \\ 6x_0 - 18y_0 \end{bmatrix}$$

$$A = -4T \qquad B = -18T \qquad C = 6T \qquad \text{where: } T = \begin{bmatrix} 3 & 2 & 1 \\ 2 & 2 & 1 \\ 1 & 1 & 1 \end{bmatrix}$$

It should be noted that both a and b are column vectors and not matrices. The elements of these vectors are the sums of the terms across each row.

Now for the budget constraints. Solving these constraints for y and comparing with the general constraint, $y = Rx + s$, we find that:

$$R = -.5I$$

$$s = \begin{bmatrix} -\ .100x_0 - .200y_0 + .100k_1 \\ -\ .080x_0 - .160y_0 - .020k_1 + .100k_2 \\ -\ .064x_0 - .128y_0 - .160k_1 - .020k_2 + .100k_3 \end{bmatrix}$$

I is the identity matrix and s is a column vector of additive terms.

To further simplify notation, we now substitute the constraint into the objective function and regroup terms. The function to be maximized then becomes:

$$U(x,\ Rx + s) = p_0 + p'x + 1/2x'Px$$

where:

$$p_0 = b'x + 1/2s'Bs$$

$$p = a + R'b + (C + R'B)s$$

$$P = A + R'BR + CR + R'C'$$

Equating the first derivative of the above function to zero, the optimal missile procurement decisions become:

$$\hat{x} = -\ P^{-1}p,$$

as long as P is nonsingular and negative definite. It naturally follows that the optimal site procurement decisions and the shadow prices on the budget constraints will be:

$$\hat{y} = R\hat{x} + s$$

and:

$$\hat{\lambda} = b + C\hat{x} + B\hat{y}$$

The P matrix and its inverse take the values:

$$P = -\begin{bmatrix} 43.5 & 29 & 14.5 \\ 29 & 29 & 14.5 \\ 14.5 & 14.5 & 14.5 \end{bmatrix}$$

$$P^{-1} = \frac{-1}{14.5}\begin{bmatrix} 1 & -1 & 0 \\ -1 & 2 & -1 \\ 0 & -1 & 2 \end{bmatrix}$$

The P matrix is nonsingular and negative definite, so a stable maximum can be obtained. Reference to these matrices will be made later in the paper as they both become important in evaluating losses due to bad forecasts and misspecification of the model.

The solution to the problem in the form of a decision matrix appears in Table I.

Directing our attention first to the missile procurement decisions (x_1, x_2, and x_3), we see that the influence of initial endowments (x_0, y_0, and m_0) decreases through time. If for some reason the ratios of the initial endowments do not

TABLE I

DECISION MATRIX

	x_0	y_0	m_0	m_1	m_2	m_3	k_1	k_2	k_3
x_1	- .586	.828	.207	.207			.103		
x_2	- .083	- .166			.207		- .021	.103	
x_3	- .066	- .135				.207	- .017	- .021	.103
y_1	.193	- .614	- .103	- .103			.048		
y_2	- .039	- .077			- .103		- .010	.048	
y_3	- .031	- .061				- .103	- .008	- .010	+ .048
λ_1	- 2.433	-4.981	9.315	9.315	6.210	3.105	- .642	- .465	- .255
λ_2	- 1.413	-2.901	6.210	6.210	6.210	3.105	- .357	- .465	- .255
λ_3	- .633	-1.311	3.105	3.105	3.105	3.105	- .177	- .210	- .255

conform to our preferences, a majority of the adjustment is made during the first period. Looking next at the enemy's expected procurements (m_1, m_2, and m_3) we see that our periodic decisions are affected only by the enemy's procurements in the current period. If our missile-to-site operating and procurement costs were not in the same ratio, the decisions would also be influenced by the enemy's off-period procurements. However, the influence would be small unless our operating costs were large compared to procurement costs--a relationship that does not appear to hold in reality. Finally, we see that procurement decisions are influenced by the current and all preceding budgets. This is so because what we purchased in period t-1 must be operated and maintained during period t.

Site procurement decisions (y_1, y_2, and y_3) follow the same pattern. Since site procurement is a by-product of missile procurement, this could be expected.

Now if we are interested in possible reallocation of our budgets over time, the shadow prices (λ_1, λ_2, and λ_3) become important. The shadow prices reveal how much an additional increment to each budget would be worth to us. It is obvious that, if possible, we would prefer to reallocate the budgets in a manner that would minimize the shadow prices.

The shadow prices are influenced by all inputs to the model, but the inputs have a decreasing influence over time. Directing attention to the coefficients of m_1, m_2, and m_3, it appears that the influence of previous and current expected m's for each λ remain constant, but that future m's have a decreasing influence. For the budgets (k_1, k_2, and k_3), we find a somewhat different phenomena. The current budget for each period exerts the greatest influence and the influence of preceding and succeeding budgets diminishes as we move further away in time.

This all suggests that there may be some practical limit to the length of the horizon we would want to consider. After some number of periods the influence of future inputs becomes negligible. It should also be noted that the model is predicated on the assumption that the expected values of the m's are independent of our procurement decisions. In other words, the distribution of m_{t+1} must not be influenced by x_t. Although this assumption may be realistic for a limited period of time, it probably will not hold indefinitely.

Optimal Budget Allocations

In this section several examples will be given to demonstrate how the model described in the previous section may be utilized to more efficiently allocate the missile and site budgets over time. As a first example let us take the case of constant periodic budgets and the expectation that enemy missile procurement will remain constant over the three periods in which we are concerned.

Case I: Constant k_t and m_t

Let:

$$x_0 = 10 \qquad k_1 = 100 \qquad m_1 = 10$$
$$y_0 = 5 \qquad k_2 = 100 \qquad m_2 = 10$$
$$m_0 = 10 \qquad k_3 = 100 \qquad m_3 = 10$$

The shadow prices then become:

$$\lambda_1 = 94.01$$
$$\lambda_2 = 81.31$$
$$\lambda_3 = 47.11$$

The shadow prices on the budgets for the first two periods are much higher than for the third period. This means that if we had a gross budget of 300 we could derive greater satisfaction from allocating a major portion of it to earlier period procurements. It also implies that if we are constrained by constant yearly budgets we would find it beneficial to borrow ahead, if possible, in order to increase our earlier procurements. Of course, the rate of interest must then be included as an additional cost.

Our goal could be to minimize the sum of the absolute values of the three shadow prices subject to a total budget constraint. I say absolute values because if we note the signs in the following equations:

$$\lambda_1 = 230.21 \quad -.642k_1 \quad -.465k_2 \quad -.255k_3$$
$$\lambda_2 = 188.71 \quad -.357k_1 \quad -.465k_2 \quad -.255k_3$$
$$\lambda_3 = 111.31 \quad -.177k_1 \quad -.210k_2 \quad -.255k_3,$$

it is apparent that if the budget is sufficiently large and we are required to use it, the shadow prices become negative. This means that we are overfulfilling our objective and experiencing increasing disutility with every additional dollar spent in the missile field. One way out of this dilemma would be to formulate the problem in the following linear programing format:

$$\text{Minimize:} \quad \sum_{t=1}^{n} |\lambda_t|$$

$$\text{Subject to:} \quad K_{total} \geq \sum_{t=1}^{n} k_t$$

and: $k_t \geq$ operations and maintenance costs in period t

The value of this program is that we do not require the total budget to be spent. The individual shadow prices will always be nonnegative. An important by-product of this formulation is that if the equality in the overall budget constraint is satisfied, a new shadow price, λ_k, on this constraint is obtained. λ_k can then be compared with the shadow prices of funds spent on other national objectives over the same time horizon. This comparison could serve as a guide for a more efficient distribution of the total national budget.

The one drawback in the above formulation is that we do not know what the operations and maintenance costs will be for each period until we have determined the k_t's. A priori specifications and several iterations will be required to obtain the optimal allocation. With a little insight, however, the process should converge rather rapidly.

As an example of how reallocation can improve our satisfaction, if we shift 50 from the third period budget to the first period budget in the above case, the shadow prices become:

$$\lambda_1 = 74.66$$
$$\lambda_2 = 75.95$$
$$\lambda_3 = 51.01$$

We have decreased the value of the first and second period shadow prices at the expense of only a small increase in the third period shadow price.

Case II: Constant k_t, Increasing m_t

Let:	$x_0 = 10$	$k_1 = 100$	$m_1 = 4$
	$y_0 = 5$	$k_2 = 100$	$m_2 = 8$
	$m_0 = 10$	$k_3 = 100$	$m_3 = 16$

Then:
$$\lambda_1 = 44.33$$
$$\lambda_2 = 50.31$$
$$\lambda_3 = 40.88$$

In this case the enemy's procurement has started out at a low level but has doubled each period. Notice now that the shadow price for the second period is the highest. This would call for reallocating a portion of the third budget to the second period.

One may wonder at the seemingly peculiar behavior of the shadow prices. For instance, in the first case we have constant budgets out of which we must pay the operations and maintenance costs of the force-in-being. This means that the periodic increments to our force are decreasing over time. The enemy's procurement, however, remains constant. It would seem that we should shift a portion of the first budget to later periods so that we might more adequately match his procurement path. But, the model tells us otherwise. Why is this so?

If we backtrack a moment to reconsider the general objective function the reason will become apparent:

$$\sum_{t=1}^{3} \{[(x_0 + \sum_{t=1}^{3} x_t) - 1.5(m_0 + \sum_{t=1}^{3} m_t)]^2 + [(x_0 + \sum_{t=1}^{3} x_t) - 3(y_0 + \sum_{t=1}^{3} y_t)]^2\}$$

The term inside the brackets {} gives the costs of not satisfying our objectives for each period. Notice that the first period procurements are included in the cost determination for each of the three periods, whereas period three's procurement only enters the third period function. We are interested in the total cost over time, so when we sum the costs for all three periods, the earlier procurements are more heavily weighted than the later ones. Inherent in the model is an automatic "quasi-discounting" mechanism.

The mention of discounting brings up another feature that the model can easily handle. If the likelihood of war is eminent we may desire to further discount the expected values of future budgets and enemy missiles. These discounted values would then be used as the entering arguments to the decision matrix of Table I.

Losses Due to Suboptimal Decisions and Improper Forecasts

It was mentioned earlier in the paper that one advantage of this model is its adaptability to sensitivity tests for imperfect specification of the objective function and constraints. This section will be devoted to a brief discussion of these tests.

The general formula for the loss due to a suboptimal decision follows:

$$L = -1/2(x - \hat{x})' P(x - \hat{x})$$

where: x = actual decision made

$\hat{x}$ = optimal decision

P = the matrix described in Section III

Inserting the appropriate P matrix we have:

$$L = \begin{bmatrix} 21.75 & 14.50 & 7.25 \\ 14.50 & 14.50 & 7.25 \\ 7.25 & 7.25 & 7.25 \end{bmatrix} (dx)^2$$

The social cost of a unit deviation from the optimal decision for any period can be obtained from the appropriate diagonal element in the above matrix.

Cost of a first period unit error = 21.75
Cost of a second period unit error = 14.50
Cost of a third period unit error = 7.25

Positive off-diagonal elements imply that the errors between periods must be added. In other words, the cost of making a positive unit error in both period one and period two is not:

$$21.75 + 14.5 = 36.25$$

but:

$$21.75 + 14.5 + 2(14.5) = 62.25$$

The cross products must be included to derive the total cost.

Two costs in which we might be particularly interested are those resulting from improper forecasts of future budgets and enemy missiles. Our forecasts for future budgets are contained in the s vector:

$$s = \begin{bmatrix} -.100x_0 - .200y_0 + .100k_1 \\ -.080x_0 - .160y_0 - .020k_1 + .100k_2 \\ -.064x_0 - .128y_0 - .016k_1 - .020k_2 + .100k_3 \end{bmatrix}$$

The change in x given by a change in S is:

$$dx = - P^{-1}(C + R'B)ds$$

Inserting this into the loss formula above we have:

$$L = \begin{bmatrix} 23.28 & 15.52 & 7.76 \\ 15.52 & 15.52 & 7.76 \\ 7.76 & 7.76 & 7.76 \end{bmatrix} (ds)^2$$

It would take an error of 10 in k_1 to effect a unit change in the first element of the s vector. This means that if the first budget was misspecified by this amount, the cost would equal 23.28. Again we note that the off-diagonal elements are positive.

The enemy missile forecasts are contained in the a vector:

$$a = \begin{bmatrix} -12x_0 + 18y_0 + 9m_0 + 9m_1 + 6m_2 + 3m_3 \\ -8x_0 + 12y_0 + 6m_0 + 6m_1 + 6m_2 + 3m_3 \\ -4x_0 + 6y_0 + 3m_0 + 3m_1 + 3m_2 + 3m_3 \end{bmatrix}$$

The change in x given by a change in a is:

$$dx = - P^{-1} da$$

Inserting this in the loss formula:

$$L = \begin{bmatrix} .0345 & -.0345 & .0000 \\ -.0345 & .0690 & -.0345 \\ .0000 & -.0345 & .0690 \end{bmatrix} (da)^2$$

If we miss our forecast of m_1 by 1, the change in the first element of the a vector is 9. The first period cost will then be:

$$.0345(9)^2 = 2.79$$

Converse to the examples given above, the off-diagonal elements are negative between adjacent periods and zero between others.

In general, we can derive the loss due to misspecification of any of the coefficients of the objective function or constraints with the following formula:

$$dx \simeq - P^{-1}(C + R'B)[(dR)\hat{x} + ds] - P^{-1}[(dR)'\hat{\lambda} + dw]$$

where: $dw = da + (dA)\hat{x} + (dC)\hat{y} + R'[db + (dC)'\hat{x} + (dB)\hat{y}]$

The symbol $\simeq$ is utilized because the effects of specification errors in the matrices A, B, C, and R are nonlinear. However, if the errors in these matrices are small, a satisfactory approximation to the decision error is obtained if we replace the curvilinear reaction functions by their tangent planes in the optimal decision. This means that terms of the second order of smallness are neglected.(5)

A Long-Term Growth Model

With a few simple modifications the limited horizon model can be converted into a long-term growth model. If we assume the missile-site preference is always fulfilled, the entire relationship can be expressed in terms of missiles and the budget. The model is then a function of the assumption we make about the growth of the budget. If we assume that constant increments will be added to the budget each period, the relationship can be expressed in the following manner:

$$\dot{x} = \beta(K + nt - \delta x)$$

where: $\dot{x}$ = time derivative of x
β = proportion of the budget going to x/price of x
K = initial budget
n = periodic increments to K

δ = operations and maintenance costs in terms of x
x = current inventory of missiles

The resulting time path will be: (See Appendix B)

$$x = \frac{\beta K}{\alpha}(1 - e^{-\alpha t}) - \frac{\beta n}{\alpha^2}(1 - e^{-\alpha t}) + x_0 e^{-\alpha t} + \frac{\beta n t}{\alpha}$$

where: $\alpha = \beta\delta$
x_0 = initial endowment of missiles

As t approaches infinity, the first term on the right converges to $\beta K/\alpha$, the second term to $-\beta n/\alpha^2$, and the third term to 0. The fourth term, however, does not converge. The whole expression then converges to a straight line with the slope, $\beta n/\alpha$.

Three possible time paths are depicted in Figure I. If n just covers the operations and maintenance costs of last period's procurement we have a straight line expansion path (b). If it more than covers these costs, periodic increments will increase over time, finally converging to a constant incremental increase (a). If it does not cover these costs, we experience path c.

Only if n = 0, does the function converge:

$$x = \frac{\beta K}{\alpha}(1 - e^{-\alpha t}) + x_0 e^{-\alpha t}$$

For example,

If: $x = 3y$ $\quad C_7 = 5 \quad C_9 = 1$

$C_8 = 10 \quad C_{10} = 2$

then: $$\beta = \frac{5x}{5[5x + 10(1/3)x]} = 3/25$$

$$\delta = 1 + 2(1/3) = 5/3$$

$$\alpha = (3/25)(5/3) = 1/5$$

and: $x = .6K$ for large t

If the initial budget is 100, the missile inventory converges to 60.

If the budget is compounded each period we obtain the following relationship:

$$\dot{x} = \beta[K(1 + r)^t - \delta x]$$

where: r = rate of growth of the budget

The resulting time path will be:

$$x = \frac{\beta K e^{t \log(1 + r)}}{\log(1 + r) + \alpha} + \left(x_0 - \frac{\beta K}{\log(1 + r) + \alpha}\right)e^{-\alpha t}$$

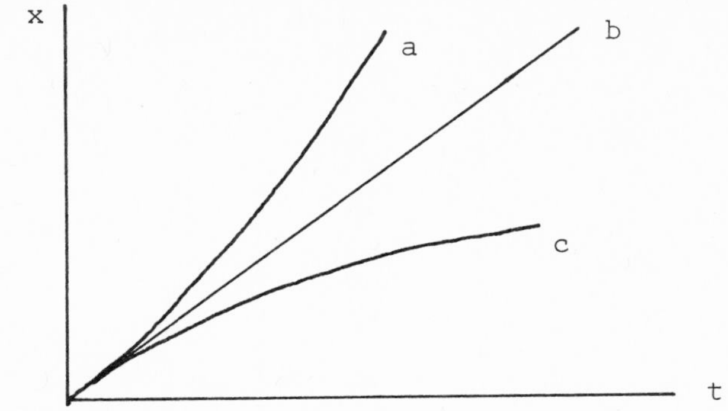

FIGURE I

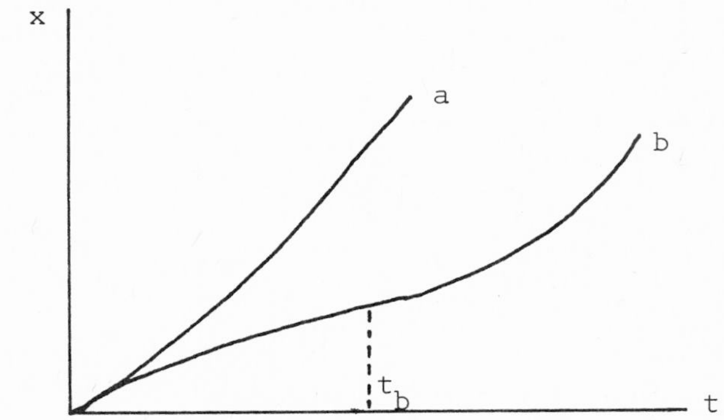

FIGURE II

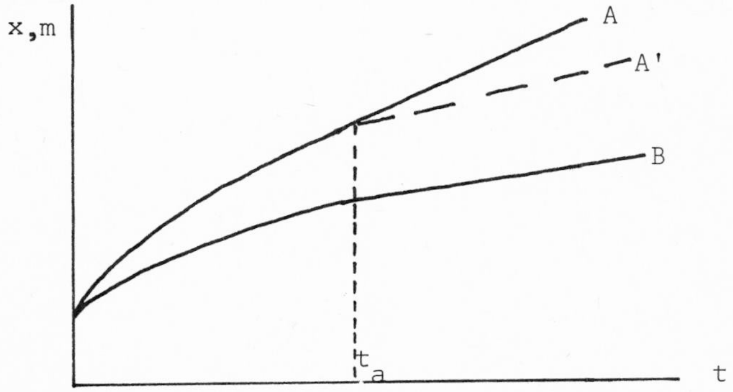

FIGURE III

Again the function does not converge unless $r = 0$. We are faced with an exponential growth path. Two possible paths are plotted in Figure II. If $K \cdot r$ covers the operations and maintenance costs of last period's procurement, periodic increments increase in an exponential manner (a). If $K \cdot r$ does not initially cover the costs, we experience decreasing increments followed by increasing increments over time (b).

It is obvious that as long as r is positive and there is no increasing disutility of arms expenditures over time, the arms race will be explosive. The employment of a disutility index has been analyzed by other authors, so no attempt to expand the study in this direction has been made.(2)

Time paths that are predicated primarily on economic potential do, however, pose some interesting questions.(3) For instance, suppose we are faced with the situation depicted in Figure III. Nation A is economically stronger than B and demands a superiority in missile strength. Nation B is reluctant to assume a position of "second best" and demands parity. At some time, t_a, A will achieve its objective and alter its path so that this objective is continually satisfied. How then is this deleterious race ever halted? Can A ever enforce his preferences on B? If so, he must establish the credibility of both his preferences and economic potential. This may take some time.

Another avenue of approach is through bargaining.(4) A may threaten to increase the missile gap if B does not halt the race. Or A may promise to decrease the gap if B halts. A combination of the two might be considered. A could threaten to increase the gap if B does not halt, but promise to decrease it if B does. The particular tactic employed might well depend on the asymmetry of costs in A's objective function.

The above tactics are also open to B. Although he cannot close the missile gap, he can surely threaten to continue the arms race.

There would seem to be an added incentive for halting the race if the participants are faced with the exponential paths depicted in Figure II. The point of inflection (t_b) in curve b could provide a time focal point--a time before which negotiations should be completed.

Summary

"Whenever a real-world situation can be approximated by means of quadratic preference functions and linear constraints . . .linear decision rules provide a powerful tool for handling dynamic problems in the face of uncertainty."(5) This declaration by H. Theil provides the rationale upon which the preceding analysis was based. A three-period arms model was formulated incorporating a quadratic objective function and linear budget constraints. The solution to the model provided a simple guide for the evaluation of the decision-making process. Optimal procurement decisions were derived and analyzed. It was demonstrated how the by-products of these decisions, the shadow prices, could be utilized to determine a more efficient allocation of the budget. Losses due to suboptimal decisions and improper forecasts were then analyzed. Finally it was shown how, with minor modifications, the discrete model could be converted into a long-term growth model.

One further observation is necessary. The fact that we have solved the problem for a three-period time horizon in order to investigate the budget allocations in no way precludes resolving the problem at each time interval. In fact, this is what should be done. Preferences and costs change over time and theoretically the enemy's first procurement decision, m_1, becomes a known value at the end of the first period. This additional information might well change the optimal procurement decision for the second period. Feedback is an important ingredient to any efficient decision process and the dynamic model described in this paper can make use of this valuable input.

APPENDIX A

CONVERSION OF THE ARMS MODEL INTO MATRIX FORM

I. The General Objective Function

$$\text{Maximize:} \quad -\sum_{t=1}^{3} \{[(x_0 + \sum_{t=1}^{3} x_t) - 1.5(m_0 + \sum_{t=1}^{3} m_t)]^2 + [(x_0 + \sum_{t=1}^{3} x_t) - 3(y_0 + \sum_{t=1}^{3} x_t)]^2\}$$

The individual objective functions are additive so each function can be treated separately. The missile objective function, upon being squared, takes the following general form:

$$-\sum_{1}^{3} (x^2 - 2(1.5)xm + m^2)$$

This expression is additive so each term can be treated individually and summed over time. The third term is not a function of either policy variable, x or y, and will disappear upon differentiation. (This is true of all constants.) Therefore it need not be considered further. The first term, summed over the three periods, is:

$$- (x_0 + x_1)^2$$

$$- (x_0 + x_1 + x_2)^2$$

$$- (x_0 + x_1 + x_2 + x_3)^2$$

$$- (3x_0^2) - (6x_0x_1 + 4x_0x_2 + 2x_0x_3) - (3x_1^2 + 4x_1x_2 + 2x_1x_3 + 2x_2^2 + 2x_2x_3 + x_3^2)$$

Dropping the constant $(-3x_0^2)$, the first term in matrix form is:

$$(1) \quad - [6x_0 \quad 4x_0 \quad 2x_0]x - x' \begin{bmatrix} 3 & 2 & 1 \\ 2 & 2 & 1 \\ 1 & 1 & 1 \end{bmatrix} x \quad \text{where:} \quad x = \begin{bmatrix} x_1 \\ x_2 \\ x_3 \end{bmatrix}$$

The second term, summed over time, is:

$$3(x_0 + x_1)(m_0 + m_1)$$

$$+ 3(x_0 + x_1 + x_2)(m_0 + m_1 + m_2)$$

$$+ 3(x_0 + x_1 + x_2 + x_3)(m_0 + m_1 + m_2 + m_3)$$

$$(9x_0m_0 + 9x_0m_1 + 6x_0m_2 + 3x_0m_3) + 9m_0x_1 + 9m_1x_1 + 6m_2x_1$$

$$+ 3m_3x_1 + 6m_0x_2 + 6m_1x_2 + 6m_2x_2 + 3m_3x_2 + 3m_0x_3$$

$$+ 3m_1x_3 + 3m_2x_3 + 3m_3x_3$$

Dropping the constants (in parentheses), the second term in matrix form is:

$$(2)\ [9m_0 + 9m_1 + 6m_2 + 3m_3,\ 6m_0 + 6m_1 + 6m_2 + 3m_3,\ 3m_0 + 3m_1 + 3m_2 + 3m_3]x$$

The site objective function contains two policy variables. Upon being squared it will take the general form:

$$-\sum_{1}^{3} (x^2 - 3xy - 3yx + 9y^2)$$

The first term is identical to the first term of the missile objective function:

$$(3)\ -[6x_0\ \ 4x_0\ \ 2x_0]x - x' \begin{bmatrix} 3 & 2 & 1 \\ 2 & 2 & 1 \\ 1 & 1 & 1 \end{bmatrix} x$$

The second term, summed over time, is:

$$3(x_0 + x_1)(y_0 + y_1)$$

$$+ 3(x_0 + x_1 + x_2)(y_0 + y_1 + y_2)$$

$$+ 3(x_0 + x_1 + x_2 + x_3)(y_0 + y_1 + y_2 + y_3)$$

$$(9y_0x_0) + (9y_0x_1 + 6y_0x_2 + 3y_0x_3) + (9x_0y_1 + 6x_0y_2 + 3x_0y_3)$$

$$+ (9x_1y_1 + 6x_1y_2 + 6y_1x_2 + 3x_1y_3 + 3y_3x_1 + 6x_2y_2$$

$$+ 3x_2y_3 + 3y_3x_2 + 3x_3y_3)$$

Dropping the constant $(9y_0x_0)$, the second term is:

$$(4)\ [9y_0\ \ 6y_0\ \ 3y_0]x + [9x_0\ \ 6x_0\ \ 3x_0]y + 3x' \begin{bmatrix} 3 & 2 & 1 \\ 2 & 2 & 1 \\ 1 & 1 & 1 \end{bmatrix} y$$

The third term is the transpose of the second term:

$$(5)\quad x' \begin{bmatrix} 9y_0 \\ 6y_0 \\ 3y_0 \end{bmatrix} + y' \begin{bmatrix} 9x_0 \\ 6x_0 \\ 3x_0 \end{bmatrix} + 3y' \begin{bmatrix} 3 & 2 & 1 \\ 2 & 2 & 1 \\ 1 & 1 & 1 \end{bmatrix} x$$

The last term in y^2 takes essentially the same form as the first term multiplied by the scalar 9:

$$(6)\quad - [54y_0 \quad 36y_0 \quad 18y_0]y - 9y' \begin{bmatrix} 3 & 2 & 1 \\ 2 & 2 & 1 \\ 1 & 1 & 1 \end{bmatrix} y$$

Terms (1), (2), (3), (4), (5), and (6) make up the general objective function. Summing the coefficient vectors and matrices of the variables x, y, x'x, y'y, x'y, and y'x and comparing with the general quadratic form:

$$a'x + b'y + 1/2(x'Ax + y'By + x'Cy + y'C'x),$$

the values of a, b, A, B, and C utilized in the text are obtained.

II. The Budget Constraints

$$k_t = 5x_t + 10y_t + x_0 + \sum_2^3 x_{t-1} + 2y_0 + 2\sum_2^3 y_{t-1}$$

The budget constraints for the three periods will be:

$$k_1 = 5x_1 + 10y_1 + x_0 + 2y_0$$

$$k_2 = 5x_2 + 10y_2 + x_0 + 2y_0 + x_1 + 2y_1$$

$$k_3 = 5x_3 + 10y_3 + x_0 + 2y_0 + x_1 + 2y_1 + x_2 + 2y_2$$

These equations can be expressed in the matrix form:

$$\begin{bmatrix} k_1 - x_0 - 2y_0 \\ k_2 - x_0 - 2y_0 \\ k_3 - x_0 - 2y_0 \end{bmatrix} = \begin{bmatrix} 5 & 0 & 0 \\ 1 & 5 & 0 \\ 1 & 1 & 5 \end{bmatrix} x + \begin{bmatrix} 10 & 0 & 0 \\ 2 & 10 & 0 \\ 2 & 2 & 10 \end{bmatrix} y$$

Solving for y and comparing with the general constraint:

$$y = Rx + s,$$

the values of R and s utilized in the text are obtained.

APPENDIX B

SOLUTIONS OF THE LONG-TERM GROWTH MODELS

I. Constant Increments to the Budget

$$\dot{x} = \beta(K + nt - \delta x)$$

$$\dot{x} = \beta(K + nt) - \alpha x \qquad \alpha = \beta\delta$$

$$\dot{x} + \alpha x = \beta(K + nt)$$

$$(\dot{x} + x)e^{\alpha t} = \beta(K + nt)e^{\alpha t} \qquad e^{\alpha t} = \text{factor of integration}$$

$$xe^{\alpha t} = \int \beta(K + nt)e^{\alpha t}dt$$

$$xe^{\alpha t} = \beta(K + nt)\frac{1}{\alpha}e^{\alpha t} - \int \beta n\frac{1}{\alpha}e^{\alpha t}dt + C \quad \text{(Integration by parts)}$$

$$xe^{\alpha t} = \frac{\beta}{\alpha}(K + nt)e^{\alpha t} - \frac{\beta n}{\alpha^2}e^{\alpha t} + C$$

$$C = x_0 - \frac{\beta K}{\alpha} + \frac{\beta n}{\alpha^2} \qquad \text{At } t = 0$$

$$xe^{\alpha t} = \frac{\beta}{\alpha}(K + nt)e^{\alpha t} - \frac{\beta n}{\alpha^2}e^{\alpha t} + x_0 - \frac{\beta K}{\alpha} + \frac{\beta n}{\alpha^2}$$

$$x = \frac{\beta}{\alpha}(K + nt) - \frac{\beta n}{\alpha^2} + \left(x_0 - \frac{\beta K}{\alpha} + \frac{\beta n}{\alpha^2}\right)e^{-\alpha t}$$

$$x = \frac{\beta K}{\alpha}(1 - e^{-\alpha t}) - \frac{\beta n}{\alpha^2}(1 - e^{-\alpha t}) + x_0 e^{-\alpha t} + \frac{\beta n t}{\alpha}$$

II. Budget Compounded Each Period

$$\dot{x} = \beta[K(1 + r)^t - \delta x]$$

$$\dot{x} = \beta K(1 + r)^t - \alpha x \qquad \alpha = \beta\delta$$

$$\dot{x} + \alpha x = \beta K(1 + r)^t$$

$$(\dot{x} + \alpha x)e^{\alpha t} = \beta K(1 + r)^t e^{\alpha t} \qquad e^{\alpha t} = \text{factor of integration}$$

$$xe^{\alpha t} = \int \beta K e^{\log(1 + r)t + \alpha t} \qquad (1 + r)^t = e^{\log(1+r)t}$$

$$xe^{\alpha t} = \frac{\beta K e^{\log(1 + r)t + \alpha t}}{\log(1 + r) + \alpha} + C$$

$$C = x_0 - \frac{\beta K}{\log(1 + r) + \alpha} \qquad \text{At } t = 0$$

$$xe^{\alpha t} = \frac{\beta K e^{\log(1 + r)t + \alpha t}}{\log(1 + r) + \alpha} + x_0 - \frac{\beta K}{\log(1 + r) + \alpha}$$

$$x = \frac{\beta K e^{\log(1 + r)t}}{\log(1 + r) + \alpha} + (x_0 - \frac{\beta K}{\log(1 + r) + \alpha} e^{-\alpha t}$$

REFERENCES

[1] Huntington, Samuel P. "Arms Races: Prerequisites and Results." Public Policy, Edited by Carl J. Friedrich and Seymour E. Harris. Cambridge: Graduate School of Public Administration, 1958. pp. 41-86.

[2] McGuire, Martin C. Secrecy and the Arms Race. Cambridge: Harvard University Press, 1965. pp. 33-46, 142-82.

[3] Schelling, Thomas C. "Managing the Arms Race." National Security: Political, Military, and Economic Strategies in the Decade Ahead. Edited by David M. Abshire and Richard V. Allen. New York: Praeger, 1963. pp. 601-16.

[4] __________. The Strategy of Conflict. New York: Oxford University Press, 1963. pp. 119-61.

[5] Theil, H. Optimal Decision Rules for Government and Industry. Chicago: Rand McNally, 1964. (General Reference for linear decision rules.)

VI.

ABSTRACTS OF OTHER PAPERS GIVEN AT SEMINAR MEETINGS

AN EMPIRICAL ANALYSIS OF DEMAND FOR AUTOMOBILES: A DISCRETE STOCK ADJUSTMENT MODEL

De-Min Wu
University of Kansas

The main hypotheses investigated in this paper are that an individual household has a probability of purchasing automobiles in a given time period; that the probability of purchase is proportional to the difference between desired and actual stock; that once purchase is made the desired stock is attained; and that desired stock is a linear function of expected income and taste of the individual household. The hypotheses are presented as an alternative to the conventional stock adjustment model where it is hypothesized that the amount of investment on stock is proportional to the difference between desired and actual stock. No attempt has been made to justify the hypotheses as a rational behavior.

The statistical model used is essentially that of classical linear regression model with problems of specification error; i.e., the existence of unobservable taste factor and errors in variables. Two estimation methods which yield consistent estimators are proposed: (1) grouping method and (2) the least squares method with adjustment to eliminate the asymptotic bias. The data used are the Surveys of Consumer Finances 1961-1962 (reinterview samples).

Implications of the hypotheses for behavior of aggregate investment on automobiles are explored. The main conclusion is that aggregate investment can be approximated by a stock adjustment model with a variable stock adjustment coefficient.

OLIGOPOLY PRICE, PRODUCTION, AND SALES EQUILIBRIUM UNDER UNCERTAINTY: WITH APPLICATION TO SELECTED OLIGOPOLISTIC INDUSTRIES

Shih-Yen Wu
University of Iowa

This paper developed an integrated, three part model for the determination of price, output, and sales equilibrium in an oligopolistic industry under conditions of uncertainty. While the literature contains a number of models that purport to explain the price-output behavior of oligopolists, these attempts have not been wholly successful. Their limitations stem from their failure to recognize that the oligopolists' decision process necessarily embraces all the following phases: (1) forecasting demand and cost; (2) determining price, output, and sales policies; and (3) evaluating the forecasts and the resulting policy decisions and revising these when necessary. The distinguishing feature of this paper is that it formulates and tests a model that integrates these three phases into the oligopolists' total decision process.

To forecast the demand functions for an oligopolist, multiple time series is used which includes price, sales of the product, an index of industrial production, and other relevant variables.

The forecasted demand functions, together with the stochastic policy decision model, is used to obtain optimal price and production policies. Regarding the stochastic policy decision model, (1) price and rate of production are treated as decision variables, while inventory and sales are determined as residuals; (2) fluctuations in market demand, uncertainty, and production lags are the conditions, and (3) maximization of profit over a finite planning horizon is the premise.

The conclusion of this paper is that when the entrepreneur is faced with uncertainty, he will prefer a constant price and a relative constant rate of production, and will allow sales to vary in accordance with the firm's demand function.

However, it is obvious that with secular changes in market conditions, a constant price and output cannot be maintained indefinitely. It is necessary for firms to develop criteria for distinguishing systematic and random changes in market demand and to revise price and output decisions when a systematic change has been perceived. Thus, in describing oligopolistic behavior, forecasting and policy decision models need to be supplemented with an evaluation model. It is suggested that relevant criterion for evaluating a price and output policy is whether forecasted sales under the selected policy lie within an appropriate confidence interval. If not, a revision of the forecast and the price and output policy is indicated.

A GENERAL THEORY OF DEPRECIATION AND VALUATION

Oscar R. Burt
University of Missouri

A theory of depreciation is developed that yields identical results whether depreciation is viewed as capital consumption or changes in imputed value of an asset. This reconciliation has been absent in earlier theories, and it is shown that several measures of depreciation appearing in the literature are special cases of the one developed here. As special cases, they imply certain tacit assumptions in order to be logically valid. A consistent depreciation theory is shown to require explicit recognition of value changes associated with mere passage of time as separate and distinct from value changes associated with aging of the asset.

QUALITATIVE ECONOMICS AND THE SCOPE OF THE CORRESPONDENCE PRINCIPLE

Lowell Bassett, University of Washington
John Maybee, University of Colorado
James Quirk, University of Kansas

This paper is concerned with the problem of determining the class of qualitatively specified systems for which the hypothesis of stability of the coefficient matrix of the system permits the derivation of comparative statics results. In addition, a solution is given to the problem posed by Gorman and Lancaster concerning "sign solvability" of a purely qualitative system. Among other results, necessary and sufficient conditions are derived for qualitatively specified indecomposable matrices (with diagonal elements negative) such that the sign pattern of the inverse matrix is known (a) in the purely qualitative case, and (b) in the case where it is assumed that the matrix is stable.

In essence, the conclusions reached in the paper are that Samuelson's correspondence principle is particularly important in the analysis of qualitatively specified systems when the coefficient matrix is of the Morishima class, but is of less importance when the Morishima conditions are violated.

THE "CORRESPONDENCE PRINCIPLE": AN EVALUATION

Lowell Bassett
University of Washington

In The Foundations of Economic Analysis Professor Samuelson is principally concerned with comparative statics analysis which he suggests is the method for deriving meaningful theorems in many different fields of economics. As sources of meaningful results he proposes two general hypotheses to restrict the possible outcomes of the comparative statics model:

(1) that the conditions of equilibrium are equivalent to the maximization (minimization) of some variable;
(2) that equilibrium positions are stable.

The maximization hypothesis has been thoroughly examined but the second hypothesis, the "correspondence principle," received only fragmentary treatment in the Foundations and has only been indirectly evaluated as a source of comparative statics theorems.

This paper examines the correspondence principle and shows its ability to restrict the model and thus provide meaningful results is extremely limited. The analysis is carried out by using the principal result from maximization (minimization), Samuelson's "conjugate pairs" theorem, as a standard by which the results of the stability hypothesis may be judged. The implications of stability are evaluated with the help of the Routh-Hurwitz criterion. We conclude that stability is much weaker than maximization as a restrictive hypothesis and that in fact comparative statics results have only been derived from the subset of stable matrices that are Hicksian.

A TRANSACTIONS CONCEPT OF SAVINGS

Leland J. Pritchard
University of Kansas

In the Keynesian system real savings equal real investment; $S = I$.

In the national income accounts savings are a residual, made equal by definition to expenditures on real investment plus government deficits (or minus government surpluses); $S = I + (G - T_n)$.

Using insofar as possible the national income symbols and definitions, a transactions concept of savings may be represented by the following equation:

$$S = (I-I_b) + [(G-G_b) - T_n] + (S_e-S_b) + S_f + D_s + S_c + S_t$$

where:

- S: the volume of monetary savings effected in a given period
- I: the gross private domestic real investment plus net foreign real investment effected in a given period
- I_b: that part of I financed through commercial and Reserve bank credit
- G: government expenditures on GNP items in a given period
- G_b: that part of G financed through commercial and Reserve bank credit
- T_n: government income from tax sources disposed of on GNP items
- S_e: the volume of monetary savings held by the nonbank public at the end of the given period
- S_b: the volume of monetary savings held by the nonbank public at the beginning of the given period
- S_f: the volume of monetary savings utilized in the financing of financial investment in a given period
- D_s: the volume of monetary savings carried over to a given period and spent by the saver on consumption items
- S_c: the volume of monetary savings provided and spent for consumption purposes in a given period
- S_t: the volume of monetary savings used to finance transfer payments in a given period

The volume of monetary savings existing at any given time (S_b or S_e) is equal to:

(1) the volume of demand deposit liabilities of commercial banks plus currency held by businesses and individuals for nonexpense or nonconsumption purposes. In other words, money that can be validly listed on the balance sheet in juxtaposition to the net worth.

(2) the volume of time deposit liabilities of commercial banks held by businesses and individuals.

A transactions concept of savings is a flow not a stock concept, although the inclusion of a stock concept (S_b and S_e) is a necessary adjunct to formulating a valid flow concept.

A transactions concept of savings emphasizes the fact that there are both uses and nonuses of monetary savings, and that not all uses contribute to financing GNP.

The uses of monetary savings may be appropriately classified into three categories:

(1) Those uses which make a direct contribution to GNP. In the above equation this includes the items: $(I-I_b)$, $(G-G_b)$, D_s, and S_c.

(2) Those uses which provide money incomes, but do not make any immediate direct contribution to GNP; represented above by the symbol S_t.

(3) Those uses of savings which finance the transfer of existing properties, goods or claims thereto, but make no direct contribution to either money incomes or the financing of final output S_f.

It will be noted in contrast to the national income concept of savings that the items I_b and G_b have been subtracted from the items I and G respectively. The utilization of bank credit to finance private real investment or government deficits does not constitute a utilization of monetary savings, since bank financing is accomplished through the creation of new money, money which obviously has not been saved by anybody. Never are commercial banks intermediaries in the savings-investment process.

The transactions approach to the analysis of savings provides many useful and important policy clues. Due to space limitations only one will be mentioned here. Higher levels of production and employment in the private sector could, for example, be promoted by minimizing the nonuses of savings as well as those uses which do not contribute to GNP.

To minimize the nonuses of savings involves, among other things, minimizing the holding of monetary savings. The problem here centers around the vast and rapid growth of time deposits in recent years.

The appropriate policy action in this instance is for the Board of Governors of the Federal Reserve System (and the Federal Deposit Insurance Corporation) to reduce the maximum interest ceilings commercial banks are allowed to pay on time deposits (including capital notes and debentures).

OPTIMAL OPERATIONS AND INVESTMENTS OF THE FIRM

Russell G. Thompson, Texas A & M University
Melvin D. George, University of Missouri

In this paper, a dynamic continuous time model of the firm, encompassing operations and investments, is formulated as an optimal control problem in an activity analysis context. In the model. the objective of the firm is to maximize, subject to various constraints, the discounted value of operating profits less the costs of new capacity and the interest on borrowed funds (or plus the interest on savings) over a fixed decision-making interval plus the discounted value of capacity at the end of the period. The state variables are capacity and debt, and the controls are scale of operation and rate of purchase of new capacity; the final capacity and debt are control parameters. There are several inequality constrints.

Using results in control theory, the optimal controls are determined for the case the rate of production is linear in the scale variable, the growth of capacity is linear in the rate of purchase of new capacity and the attrition of capacity is linear in the amount of capacity. Extensions of the model are made to include multiple processes.